galaxy

literary modes and genres

edited by **mark schorer**

University of California, Berkeley

Harcourt, Brace & World, Inc.

New York / Chicago / San Francisco / Atlanta

For Annette Kolodny

Gratitude and Affection

COVER PHOTO: Detail of "The Sun," a gold-wire mobile construction by Richard Lippold. Courtesy The Metropolitan Museum of Art, Fletcher Fund, 1956.

Library of Congress Catalog Card Number: 67-17507

Printed in the United States of America

ACKNOWLEDGMENTS

I am grateful to the following publishers and individuals for permission to reprint these works:

ATHENEUM HOUSE, INC. For "The Broken Home" from *Nights and Days* by James Merrill. Copyright © 1965, 1966 by James Merrill. This poem appeared first in *The New Yorker*.

CHATTO AND WINDUS LTD. For "Dulce et Decorum Est" and "Anthem for Doomed Youth" from *The Collected Poems of Wilfred Owen*.

COLLINS-KNOWLTON-WING, INC., NEW YORK, and A. P. WATT & SON, LONDON. For "Ulysses" and "Down, Wanton, Down!" Copyright © 1955 by International Authors N. V. From *Collected Poems 1955* by Robert Graves, Doubleday & Company, U.S.A., Cassell & Co. Ltd., England.

J. M. DENT & SONS LTD., and the LITERARY EXECUTORS OF THE DYLAN THOMAS ESTATE. For "Twenty-Four Years," "In My Craft or Sullen Art," "A Refusal to Mourn the Death, by Fire, of a Child in London," and "Do Not Go Gentle into That Good Night" from *Collected Poems of Dylan Thomas*.

DOUBLEDAY & COMPANY, INC. For "I Knew a Woman," copyright 1954 by Theodore Roethke, and "Reply to a Lady Editor," copyright © 1957 by Theodore Roethke, both from *Words for the Wind*.

foreword

A book such as this is by its nature a statement of personal prefer-
ences. One would hardly include anything that had not given one
great pleasure. Yet the personal principle as it operates in such a book
is not wayward, even if editorial taste might be: it is given direction
by the nature of the audience for which the book is presented.

I was thinking of a group of college students assembled in a course
that is to introduce them to literature. I asked myself what materials
I as a teacher in such a course would like to have available in a single,
manageable volume. Considerations of availability and space, of course,
affected my choices. For example, it was obviously impossible to
present a full-length novel. However, the stories by Unamuno and
Sartre are probably long enough to qualify for the fluid designation
novelette, and the stories by Hawthorne, James, Fitzgerald, and
Flannery O'Connor are close to that length. There are no epics and
no long narrative poems. It seemed preferable to offer many short
poems rather than to give their pages to a relatively few long ones.
Yet some quite long (and very different) poems will be found here:
Johnson's "London," Wordsworth's "Tintern Abbey," Yeats's "Vacillation," one of Eliot's *Four Quartets*. No work by the world's greatest
dramatist is in my group of plays; he must be purchased in a volume
of his own and carried around always by any student who happens to
want to be loved by me.

Granted, then, that not everything is here. I would suggest, nevertheless, that there is such an abundance as to engage students and
teachers in a course that might run for as long as a full academic year
and such a variety in that abundance as to prepare the enterprising
student to explore on his own if he is not to have further formal
instruction in literature.

Personal pleasure, abundance, variety—these were my criteria. The organization of my choices is simply chronological by the authors' dates of birth and, within a single poet's work, by dates of composition. Some books designed with the same purpose as this present a much more elaborate organization. Some group their selections according to "themes," some according to techniques, some even by "effect" on the reader. Again, I have exercised a personal preference: when I choose a textbook, I want the texts, not the other teacher; I am interested in his taste but not, for my teaching purposes, in his interpretations. Elaborately organized textbooks almost organize the course itself; I prefer the freedom of organizing my own course and changing my organization when the developing direction of the group and its interests or my pedagogical inclination suggests change.

Even without my intending them, interrelations within the selections, not really very mysteriously, established themselves. Teachers will have no difficulty discovering them and, when they wish, using them in their classes. I might point out a few here. The first selection in the book is Hawthorne's "My Kinsman, Major Molineux"; the last is Robert Lowell's adaptation of that story for the stage. Reading the two together should provide a basic exercise in discriminating between the conventions and techniques of narrative and dramatic art. Example within the example: Hawthorne's story has one boy; Lowell's adaptation has two. The reason for the alteration probably gives us the primary generic distinction.

The stories range from the most direct fable to the subtlest psychological drama: from Tolstoy to Mishima. The fables themselves range from the simplest, Tolstoy's "The Three Hermits," to the most elusive, Kafka's "A Hunger Artist." It is interesting to observe that stories told in the naturalistic convention, such as Verga's "The She-Wolf" and Lawrence's "You Touched Me," can yet take on a quality of fable. Probably every story has a fable at its heart.

There are, I see, four stories about frustrated parents and their children: those by Anderson, Joyce, Katherine Anne Porter, and Fitzgerald, each, except for the thematic connection, utterly different from the others. Two other stories deal with parents and their adult young: those by Hemingway and Sartre. War, not surprisingly, is a recurrent theme. And love, of course—throughout the book but perhaps especially in the section given to poems.

That section begins with a famous poem of anonymous yearning, and that yearning echoes through the centuries, quite literally, for example, in Tennyson's "O That 'Twere Possible" and perhaps later in Yeats's "Politics." Prayers, too, run through the ages and may be compared: Donne, Jonson, Taylor, Hopkins, Auden, and the irreverent

Amis. There is a series of poems about London: Johnson, Blake, Wordsworth, and Shelley's "England in 1819." Poets talk about other poets: the young Milton on Shakespeare, Keats on Chapman and Homer, Browning on Wordsworth and Shelley, Eliot on Yeats (and others), Crane on Emily Dickinson, Tate on Pope, Auden on Yeats and Eliot, MacNeice on his contemporaries, Spender on MacNeice. Sometimes they talk about their own art, like Marianne Moore on poetry, like Dylan Thomas, or like Theodore Roethke in his "Letter" poem. The choice of the two Roethke poems was, granted, quite calculated. So was the inclusion of Hopkins' "Yes. Whý Do We Áll, Seeing of a Soldier, Bless Him?" and Day Lewis' "Yes, Why Do We All, Seeing a Red, Feel Small?" which provide a fascinating contrast; but it should be said in fairness to Mr. Lewis that he eliminated this poem from the later versions of his volume *A Time to Dance*.

Poets address everything. There are three poems to fathers (Cummings, Thomas, and Sylvia Plath) and at least two about sons (Jonson and Josephine Miles). They address parts of their own bodies when these interest them: Williams and Graves. With sad gravity, like Keats in "La Belle Dame sans Merci," or with zestful malice, like Aiken in "A Wedding," they write of cruel women; or, like Shakespeare, Marvell, Meredith, Robinson, and others, of love as that whimsical or cruel assailant, not me, out there, that one. Sin and guilt, too, those ruptures in the heart, become outsiders in poetry, monsters stalking gardens, sitting down on one, as in the poems by Warren and Berryman. Women are pursued and loved by birds, no less, as in Yeats and Lawrence. It is a cruel time for the young, say Housman and Owen. It is a hard time for poets, too, says Hardy in "In Tenebris: II"; and Yeats in "The Leaders of the Crowd," Frost in "The Road Not Taken," and Pound in "The Rest" all seem to echo him. Yet, as Auden says, poets continue to sing and, in

> Negation and despair,
> Show an affirming flame.
> ["September 1, 1939"]

In other Auden words, poets

> With the farming of a verse
> Make a vineyard of the curse.
> ["In Memory of W. B. Yeats"]

So, in Howard Baker's poem, motivated by the same historical events that lie behind Auden's September poem, we are told that a barren tree will probably once more burst into leaf. One hopes!

Teacher and student can, of course, pursue technical as well as thematic comparisons and contrasts. The sonnet selections from Shakespeare, Donne, Milton, Wordsworth, Meredith, and Hopkins offer a small handbook to the history of that form. The innovations of Browning and Tennyson in the dramatic monologue can be set beside those later ones in Eliot's "Prufrock." And characters reappear: Tennyson's Ulysses can be examined beside Robert Graves's and the two put beside the Ulysses of Giraudoux's play.

Three of the four plays seem to be much concerned with the plight of women, and three of them with war. Euripides' *The Trojan Women* gives us the end of the famous conflict, and *Tiger at the Gates* gives us the beginning. All the important characters of the first reappear in the second, but the second presents, too, many who are only talked about in the first. The Greek play is a tragedy, with the classic dimensions; the modern French play is something else again, wicked and witty, but what shall we call it? In contrast to both, the Chekhov play tells us that women in peacetime have their problems no less than in wartime, and perhaps that peacetime in Russia is less interesting, more dogged, than wartime as Giraudoux interprets it in ancient Greece.

Because I wanted to cut across long distances both in time and in geography, this book contains many works in translation. However, I have excluded poems in translation on the assumption that in poetry, much more intensely than in fiction and more than in most drama, the original language and the imaginative conception are an identity. I have not hesitated, however, in the earlier poems, to change spelling and punctuation according to present usage when such alterations do not change the tone or rhythm of the original.

In the poetry section, finally, I have included more poems by poets now writing than is usual in books such as this. Edmund Spenser is sacrificed to James Dickey, "Sir Patrick Spence" to "The Broken Home," George Herbert's "The Pulley" or "The Collar" to Kingsley Amis's "New Approach Needed," and so forth. Ridiculous? Not quite, I think. I think that we do have a new generation of students. I also think that one learns about the old, the classic, that other idiom, through the new, the familiar idiom, just as one learns about the new through the old. It is all finally one infinitely various garden, and more than a garden.

The dedication of this book is meant to express my gratitude to that friend and graduate student at Berkeley who compiled much of the material for the "Notes on the Authors."

Mark Schorer

contents

poems

plays

stories

My Kinsman, Major Molineux

After the kings of Great Britain had assumed the right of appointing the colonial governors,[1] the measures of the latter seldom met with the ready and general approbation which had been paid to those of their predecessors, under the original charters. The people looked with most jealous scrutiny to the exercise of power which did not emanate from themselves, and they usually rewarded their rulers with slender gratitude for the compliances by which, in softening their instructions from beyond the sea, they had incurred the reprehension of those who gave them. The annals of Massachusetts Bay will inform us, that of six governors in the space of about forty years from the surrender of the old charter, under James II., two were imprisoned by a popular insurrection; a third, as Hutchinson inclines to believe, was driven from the province by the whizzing of a musket-ball; a fourth, in the opinion of the same historian, was hastened to his grave by continual bickerings with the House of Representatives; and the remaining two, as well as their successors, till the Revolution, were favored with few and brief intervals of peaceful sway. The inferior members of the court party, in times of high political excitement, led scarcely a more desirable life. These remarks may serve as a preface to the following adventures, which chanced upon a summer night, not far from a hundred years ago. The reader, in order to avoid a long and dry detail of colonial affairs, is requested to dispense with an account of the train of circumstances that had caused much temporary inflammation of the popular mind.

It was near nine o'clock of a moonlight evening, when a boat crossed the ferry with a single passenger, who had obtained his conveyance at that unusual hour by the promise of an extra fare. While he stood on the landing-place, searching in either pocket for the means of fulfilling his agreement, the ferryman lifted a lantern, by the aid of which,

[1] In 1684 the Crown abolished the charter of Massachusetts, which had given the people of the colony the power to appoint their own governors. With the new charter of 1691, that power went formally to the Crown. The source of Hawthorne's information is a book by Thomas Hutchinson (1764-1828), *The History of the Colony of Massachusetts Bay*.

and the newly risen moon, he took a very accurate survey of the stranger's figure. He was a youth of barely eighteen years, evidently country-bred, and now, as it should seem, upon his first visit to town. He was clad in a coarse gray coat, well worn, but in excellent repair; his under garments were durably constructed of leather, and fitted tight to a pair of serviceable and well-shaped limbs; his stockings of blue yarn were the incontrovertible work of a mother or a sister; and on his head was a three-cornered hat, which in its better days had perhaps sheltered the graver brow of the lad's father. Under his left arm was a heavy cudgel formed of an oak sapling, and retaining a part of the hardened root; and his equipment was completed by a wallet, not so abundantly stocked as to incommode the vigorous shoulders on which it hung. Brown, curly hair, well-shaped features, and bright, cheerful eyes were nature's gifts, and worth all that art could have done for his adornment.

The youth, one of whose names was Robin, finally drew from his pocket the half of a little province bill of five shillings, which, in the depreciation in that sort of currency, did but satisfy the ferryman's demand, with the surplus of a sexangular piece of parchment, valued at three pence. He then walked forward into the town, with as light a step as if his day's journey had not already exceeded thirty miles, and with as eager an eye as if he were entering London city, instead of the little metropolis of a New England colony. Before Robin had proceeded far, however, it occurred to him that he knew not whither to direct his steps; so he paused, and looked up and down the narrow street, scrutinizing the small and mean wooden buildings that were scattered on either side.

"This low hovel cannot be my kinsman's dwelling," thought he, "nor yonder old house, where the moonlight enters at the broken casement; and truly I see none hereabouts that might be worthy of him. It would have been wise to inquire my way of the ferryman, and doubtless he would have gone with me, and earned a shilling from the Major for his pains. But the next man I meet will do as well."

He resumed his walk, and was glad to perceive that the street now became wider, and the houses more respectable in their appearance. He soon discerned a figure moving on moderately in advance, and hastened his steps to overtake it. As Robin drew nigh, he saw that the passenger was a man in years, with a full periwig of gray hair, a wide-skirted coat of dark cloth, and silk stockings rolled above his knees. He carried a long and polished cane, which he struck down perpendicularly before him at every step; and at regular intervals he uttered two successive hems, of a peculiarly solemn and sepulchral intonation. Having made these observations, Robin laid hold of the skirt of the old man's coat, just when the light from the open door and windows of a barber's shop fell upon both their figures.

"Good evening to you, honored sir," said he, making a low bow, and still retaining his hold of the skirt. "I pray you tell me whereabouts is the dwelling of my kinsman, Major Molineux."

The youth's question was uttered very loudly; and one of the barbers, whose razor was descending on a well-soaped chin, and another who was dressing a Ramillies wig,[2] left their occupations, and came to the door. The citizen, in the mean time, turned a long-favored countenance upon Robin, and answered him in a tone of excessive anger and annoyance. His two sepulchral hems, however, broke into the very centre of his rebuke, with most singular effect, like a thought of the cold grave obtruding among wrathful passions.

"Let go my garment, fellow! I tell you, I know not the man you speak of. What! I have authority, I have—hem, hem—authority; and if this be the respect you show for your betters, your feet shall be brought acquainted with the stocks by daylight, tomorrow morning!"

Robin released the old man's skirt, and hastened away, pursued by an ill-mannered roar of laughter from the barber's shop. He was at first considerably surprised by the result of his question, but, being a shrewd youth, soon thought himself able to account for the mystery.

"This is some country representative," was his conclusion, "who has never seen the inside of my kinsman's door, and lacks the breeding to answer a stranger civilly. The man is old, or verily—I might be tempted to turn back and smite him on the nose. Ah, Robin, Robin! even the barber's boys laugh at you for choosing such a guide! You will be wiser in time, friend Robin."

He now became entangled in a succession of crooked and narrow streets, which crossed each other, and meandered at no great distance from the water-side. The smell of tar was obvious to his nostrils, the masts of vessels pierced the moonlight above the tops of the buildings, and the numerous signs, which Robin paused to read, informed him that he was near the centre of business. But the streets were empty, the shops were closed, and lights were visible only in the second stories of a few dwelling-houses. At length, on the corner of a narrow lane, through which he was passing, he beheld the broad countenance of a British hero swinging before the door of an inn, whence proceeded the voices of many guests. The casement of one of the lower windows was thrown back, and a very thin curtain permitted Robin to distinguish a party at supper, round a well-furnished table. The fragrance of the good cheer steamed forth into the outer air, and the youth could

[2] A plaited wig with bows from Ramillies, Belgium, a cloth-making town.

not fail to recollect that the last remnant of his travelling stock of provision had yielded to his morning appetite, and that noon had found and left him dinnerless.

"Oh, that a parchment three-penny might give me a right to sit down at yonder table!" said Robin, with a sigh. "But the Major will make me welcome to the best of his victuals; so I will even step boldly in, and inquire my way to his dwelling."

He entered the tavern, and was guided by the murmur of voices and the fumes of tobacco to the public-room. It was a long and low apartment, with oaken walls, grown dark in the continual smoke, and a floor which was thickly sanded, but of no immaculate purity. A number of persons—the larger part of whom appeared to be mariners, or in some way connected with the sea—occupied the wooden benches, or leather-bottomed chairs, conversing on various matters, and occasionally lending their attention to some topic of general interest. Three or four little groups were draining as many bowls of punch, which the West India trade had long since made a familiar drink in the colony. Others, who had the appearance of men who lived by regular and laborious handicraft, preferred the insulated bliss of an unshared potation, and became more taciturn under its influence. Nearly all, in short, evinced a predilection for the Good Creature[3] in some of its various shapes, for this is a vice to which, as Fast Day sermons[4] of a hundred years ago will testify, we have a long hereditary claim. The only guests to whom Robin's sympathies inclined him were two or three sheepish countrymen, who were using the inn somewhat after the fashion of a Turkish caravansary; they had gotten themselves into the darkest corner of the room, and heedless of the Nicotian[5] atmosphere, were supping on the bread of their own ovens, and the bacon cured in their own chimney-smoke. But though Robin felt a sort of brotherhood with these strangers, his eyes were attracted from them to a person who stood near the door, holding whispered conversation with a group of ill-dressed associates. His features were separately striking almost to grotesqueness, and the whole face left a deep impression on the memory. The forehead bulged out into a double prominence, with a vale between; the nose came boldly forth in an irregular curve, and its bridge was of more than a finger's breadth; the eyebrows were deep and shaggy, and the eyes glowed beneath them like fire in a cave.

While Robin deliberated of whom to inquire respecting his kinsman's dwelling, he was accosted by the innkeeper, a little man in a

[3] Alcohol.
[4] Sermons delivered on special days of public penance.
[5] From *nicotine;* hence, smoke-filled air.

stained white apron, who had come to pay his professional welcome to the stranger. Being in the second generation from a French Protestant, he seemed to have inherited the courtesy of his parent nation; but no variety of circumstances was ever known to change his voice from the one shrill note in which he now addressed Robin.

"From the country, I presume, sir?" said he, with a profound bow. "Beg leave to congratulate you on your arrival, and trust you intend a long stay with us. Fine town here, sir, beautiful buildings, and much that may interest a stranger. May I hope for the honor of your commands in respect to supper?"

"The man sees a family likeness! the rogue has guessed that I am related to the Major!" thought Robin, who had hitherto experienced little superfluous civility.

All eyes were now turned on the country lad, standing at the door, in his worn three-cornered hat, gray coat, leather breeches, and blue yarn stockings, leaning on an oaken cudgel, and bearing a wallet on his back.

Robin replied to the courteous innkeeper, with such an assumption of confidence as befitted the Major's relative. "My honest friend," he said, "I shall make it a point to patronize your house on some occasion, when"—here he could not help lowering his voice—"when I may have more than a parchment three-pence in my pocket. My present business," continued he, speaking with lofty confidence, "is merely to inquire my way to the dwelling of my kinsman, Major Molineux."

There was a sudden and general movement in the room, which Robin interpreted as expressing the eagerness of each individual to become his guide. But the innkeeper turned his eyes to a written paper on the wall, which he read, or seemed to read, with occasional recurrences to the young man's figure.

"What have we here?" said he, breaking his speech into little dry fragments. " 'Left the house of the subscriber, bounden servant,[6] Hezekiah Mudge,—had on, when he went away, gray coat, leather breeches, master's third-best hat. One pound currency reward to whosoever shall lodge him in any jail of the province.' Better trudge, boy; better trudge!"

Robin had begun to draw his hand towards the lighter end of the oak cudgel, but a strange hostility in every countenance induced him to relinquish his purpose of breaking the courteous innkeeper's head. As he turned to leave the room, he encountered a sneering glance from the bold-featured personage whom he had before noticed; and no sooner was he beyond the door, than he heard a general laugh,

[6] An apprentice bound by contract to his master.

in which the innkeeper's voice might be distinguished, like the dropping of small stones into a kettle.

"Now, is it not strange," thought Robin, with his usual shrewdness, —"is it not strange that the confession of an empty pocket should outweigh the name of my kinsman, Major Molineux? Oh, if I had one of those grinning rascals in the woods, where I and my oak sapling grew up together, I would teach him that my arm is heavy though my purse be light!"

On turning the corner of the narrow lane, Robin found himself in a spacious street, with an unbroken line of lofty houses on each side, and a steepled building at the upper end, whence the ringing of a bell announced the hour of nine. The light of the moon, and the lamps from the numerous shop-windows, discovered people promenading on the pavement, and amongst them Robin hoped to recognize his hitherto inscrutable relative. The result of his former inquiries made him unwilling to hazard another, in a scene of such publicity, and he determined to walk slowly and silently up the street, thrusting his face close to that of every elderly gentleman, in search of the Major's lineaments. In his progress, Robin encountered many gay and gallant figures. Embroidered garments of showy colors, enormous periwigs, gold-laced hats, and silver-hilted swords glided past him and dazzled his optics. Travelled youths, imitators of the European fine gentlemen of the period, trod jauntily along, half dancing to the fashionable tunes which they hummed, and making poor Robin ashamed of his quiet and natural gait. At length, after many pauses to examine the gorgeous display of goods in the shop-windows, and after suffering some rebukes for the impertinence of his scrutiny into people's faces, the Major's kinsman found himself near the steepled building, still unsuccessful in his search. As yet, however, he had seen only one side of the thronged street; so Robin crossed, and continued the same sort of inquisition down the opposite pavement, with stronger hopes than the philosopher seeking an honest man, but with no better fortune. He had arrived about midway towards the lower end, from which his course began, when he overheard the approach of some one who struck down a cane on the flag-stones at every step, uttering, at regular intervals, two sepulchral hems.

"Mercy on us!" quoth Robin, recognizing the sound.

Turning a corner, which chanced to be close at his right hand, he hastened to pursue his researches in some other part of the town. His patience now was wearing low, and he seemed to feel more fatigue from his rambles since he crossed the ferry, than from his journey of several days on the other side. Hunger also pleaded loudly within him, and Robin began to balance the propriety of demanding, violently, and with lifted cudgel, the necessary guidance from the first solitary passenger whom he should meet. While a resolution to this effect was gaining strength, he entered a street of mean appearance, on either side of which a row of ill-built houses was straggling towards the harbor. The moonlight fell upon no passenger along the whole extent, but in the third domicile which Robin passed there was a half-opened door, and his keen glance detected a woman's garment within.

"My luck may be better here," said he to himself.

Accordingly, he approached the door, and beheld it shut closer as he did so; yet an open space remained, sufficing for the fair occupant to observe the stranger, without a corresponding display on her part. All that Robin could discern was a strip of scarlet petticoat, and the occasional sparkle of an eye, as if the moonbeams were trembling on some bright thing.

"Pretty mistress," for I may call her so with a good conscience, thought the shrewd youth, since I know nothing to the contrary,— "my sweet pretty mistress, will you be kind enough to tell me whereabouts I must seek the dwelling of my kinsman, Major Molineux?"

Robin's voice was plaintive and winning, and the female, seeing nothing to be shunned in the handsome country youth, thrust open the door, and came forth into the moonlight. She was a dainty little figure, with a white neck, round arms, and a slender waist, at the extremity of which her scarlet petticoat jutted out over a hoop, as if she were standing in a balloon. Moreover, her face was oval and pretty, her hair dark beneath the little cap, and her bright eyes possessed a sly freedom, which triumphed over those of Robin.

"Major Molineux dwells here," said this fair woman.

Now, her voice was the sweetest Robin had heard that night, the airy counterpart of a stream of melted silver; yet he could not help doubting whether that sweet voice spoke Gospel truth. He looked up and down the mean street, and then surveyed the house before which they stood. It was a small, dark edifice of two stories, the second of which projected over the lower floor, and the front apartment had the aspect of a shop for petty commodities.

"Now, truly, I am in luck," replied Robin, cunningly, "and so indeed is my kinsman, the Major, in having so pretty a housekeeper. But I prithee trouble him to step to the door; I will deliver him a message from his friends in the country, and then go back to my lodgings at the inn."

"Nay, the Major has been abed this hour or more," said the lady of the scarlet petticoat; "and it would be to little purpose to disturb him to-night, seeing his evening draught was of the strongest. But he is a kind-hearted man, and it would be as much as my life's worth to let a kinsman of his turn away from the door. You are the good old gentleman's very picture, and I could swear that was his rainy-weather hat. Also he has garments very much resembling those leather small-clothes. But come in, I pray, for I bid you hearty welcome in his name."

So saying, the fair and hospitable dame took our hero by the hand; and the touch was light, and the force was gentleness, and though Robin read in her eyes what he did not hear in her words, yet the slender-waisted woman in the scarlet petticoat proved stronger than the athletic country youth. She had drawn his half-willing footsteps nearly to the threshold, when the opening of a door in the neighborhood startled the Major's housekeeper, and, leaving the Major's kinsman, she vanished speedily into her own domicile. A heavy yawn preceded the appearance of a man, who, like the Moonshine of Pyramus and Thisbe,[7] carried a lantern, needlessly aiding his sister luminary in the heavens. As he walked sleepily up the street, he turned his broad, dull face on Robin, and displayed a long staff, spiked at the end.

"Home, vagabond, home!" said the watchman, in accents that seemed to fall asleep as soon as they were uttered. "Home, or we'll set you in the stocks by peep of day!"

"This is the second hint of the kind," thought Robin. "I wish they would end my difficulties, by setting me there to-night."

Nevertheless, the youth felt an instinctive antipathy towards the guardian of midnight order, which at first prevented him from asking his usual question. But just when the man was about to vanish behind the corner, Robin resolved not to lose the opportunity, and shouted lustily after him,—

"I say, friend! will you guide me to the house of my kinsman, Major Molineux?"

The watchman made no reply, but turned the corner and was gone; yet Robin seemed to hear the sound of drowsy laughter stealing along the solitary street. At that moment, also, a pleasant titter saluted him from the open window above his head; he looked up, and caught the sparkle of a saucy eye; a round arm beckoned to him, and next he heard light footsteps descending the staircase within. But Robin, being of the household of a New England clergyman, was a good youth, as well as a shrewd one; so he resisted temptation, and fled away.

He now roamed desperately, and at random, through the town, almost ready to believe that a spell was on him, like that by which a wizard of his country had once kept three pursuers wandering, a

---

[7] In Shakespeare's *A Midsummer Night's Dream*, V.i.135-51.

"I doubt not you deserve it," replied his new friend, good-naturedly; "but pray proceed."

"Well, sir, being nearly eighteen years old, and well grown, as you see," continued Robin, drawing himself up to his full height, "I thought it high time to begin the world. So my mother and sister put me in handsome trim, and my father gave me half the remnant of his last year's salary, and five days ago I started for this place, to pay the Major a visit. But, would you believe it, sir! I crossed the ferry a little after dark, and have yet found nobody that would show me the way to his dwelling; only, an hour or two since, I was told to wait here, and Major Molineux would pass by."

"Can you describe the man who told you this?" inquired the gentleman.

"Oh, he was a very ill-favored fellow, sir," replied Robin, "with two great bumps on his forehead, a hook nose, fiery eyes; and, what struck me as the strangest, his face was of two different colors. Do you happen to know such a man, sir?"

"Not intimately," answered the stranger, "but I chanced to meet him a little time previous to your stopping me. I believe you may trust his word, and that the Major will very shortly pass through this street. In the mean time, as I have a singular curiosity to witness your meeting, I will sit down here upon the steps and bear you company."

He seated himself accordingly, and soon engaged his companion in animated discourse. It was but of brief continuance, however, for a noise of shouting, which had long been remotely audible, drew so much nearer that Robin inquired its cause.

"What may be the meaning of this uproar?" asked he. "Truly, if your town be always as noisy, I shall find little sleep while I am an inhabitant."

"Why, indeed, friend Robin, there do appear to be three or four riotous fellows abroad to-night," replied the gentleman. "You must not expect all the stillness of your native woods here in our streets. But the watch will shortly be at the heels of these lads and—"

"Ay, and set them in the stocks by peep of day," interrupted Robin, recollecting his own encounter with the drowsy lantern-bearer. "But, dear sir, if I may trust my ears, an army of watchmen would never make head against such a multitude of rioters. There were at least a thousand voices went up to make that one shout."

"May not a man have several voices, Robin, as well as two complexions?" said his friend.

"Perhaps a man may; but Heaven forbid that a woman should!" responded the shrewd youth, thinking of the seductive tones of the Major's housekeeper.

The sounds of a trumpet in some neighboring street now became so evident and continual, that Robin's curiosity was strongly excited. In addition to the shouts, he heard frequent bursts from many instruments of discord, and a wild and confused laughter filled up the intervals. Robin rose from the steps, and looked wistfully towards a point whither people seemed to be hastening.

"Surely some prodigious merry-making is going on," exclaimed he. "I have laughed very little since I left home, sir, and should be sorry to lose an opportunity. Shall we step round the corner by that darkish house, and take our share of the fun?"

"Sit down again, sit down, good Robin," replied the gentleman, laying his hand on the skirt of the gray coat. "You forget that we must wait here for your kinsman; and there is reason to believe that he will pass by, in the course of a very few moments."

The near approach of the uproar had now disturbed the neighborhood; windows flew open on all sides; and many heads, in the attire of the pillow, and confused by sleep suddenly broken, were protruded to the gaze of whoever had leisure to observe them. Eager voices hailed each other from house to house, all demanding the explanation, which not a soul could give. Half-dressed men hurried towards the unknown commotion, stumbling as they went over the stone steps that thrust themselves into the narrow foot-walk. The shouts, the laughter, and the tuneless bray, the antipodes of music, came onwards with increasing din, till scattered individuals, and then denser bodies, began to appear round a corner at the distance of a hundred yards.

"Will you recognize your kinsman, if he passes in this crowd?" inquired the gentleman.

"Indeed, I can't warrant it, sir; but I'll take my stand here, and keep a bright lookout," answered Robin, descending to the outer edge of the pavement.

A mighty stream of people now emptied into the street, and came rolling slowly towards the church. A single horseman wheeled the corner in the midst of them, and close behind him came a band of fearful wind-instruments, sending forth a fresher discord now that no intervening buildings kept it from the ear. Then a redder light disturbed the moonbeams, and a dense multitude of torches shone along the street, concealing, by their glare, whatever object they illuminated. The single horseman, clad in a military dress, and bearing a drawn sword, rode onward as the leader, and, by his fierce and variegated countenance, appeared like war personified; the red of one cheek was an emblem of fire and sword; the blackness of the other betokened the mourning that attends them. In his train were wild figures in the Indian dress, and many fantastic shapes without a model, giving the whole march a visionary air, as if a dream had broken forth from some feverish brain, and were sweeping visibly through the midnight streets. A mass of people, inactive, except as applauding spectators, hemmed the procession in; and several women ran along the sidewalk, piercing the confusion of heavier sounds with their shrill voices of mirth or terror.

"The double-faced fellow has his eye upon me," muttered Robin, with an indefinite but an uncomfortable idea that he was himself to bear a part in the pageantry.

The leader turned himself in the saddle, and fixed his glance full upon the country youth, as the steed went slowly by. When Robin had freed his eyes from those fiery ones, the musicians were passing before him, and the torches were close at hand; but the unsteady brightness of the latter formed a veil which he could not penetrate. The rattling of wheels over the stones sometimes found its way to his ear, and confused traces of a human form appeared at intervals, and then melted into the vivid light. A moment more, and the leader thundered a command to halt: the trumpets vomited a horrid breath, and then held their peace; the shouts and laughter of the people died away, and there remained only a universal hum, allied to silence. Right before Robin's eyes was an uncovered cart. There the torches blazed the brightest, there the moon shone out like day, and there, in tar-and-feathery dignity, sat his kinsman, Major Molineux!

He was an elderly man, of large and majestic person, and strong, square features, betokening a steady soul; but steady as it was, his enemies had found means to shake it. His face was pale as death, and far more ghastly; the broad forehead was contracted in his agony, so that his eyebrows formed one grizzled line; his eyes were red and wild, and the foam hung white upon his quivering lip. His whole frame was agitated by a quick and continual tremor, which his pride strove to quell, even in those circumstances of overwhelming humiliation. But perhaps the bitterest pang of all was when his eyes met those of Robin; for he evidently knew him on the instant, as the youth stood witnessing the foul disgrace of a head grown gray in honor. They stared at each other in silence, and Robin's knees shook, and his hair bristled, with a mixture of pity and terror. Soon, however, a bewildering excitement began to seize upon his mind; the preceding adventures of the night, the unexpected appearance of the crowd, the torches, the confused din and the hush that followed, the spectre of his kinsman reviled by that great multitude,—all this, and, more than all, a perception of tremendous ridicule in the whole scene, affected him with a sort of mental inebriety. At that moment a voice of sluggish merriment saluted Robin's ears; he turned instinctively, and just behind the corner of the church stood the lantern-bearer, rubbing his eyes, and drowsily enjoying the lad's amazement. Then he heard a peal of laughter like the ringing of silvery bells; a woman twitched his arm, a saucy eye met his, and he saw the lady of the scarlet petticoat. A sharp, dry cachinnation appealed to his memory, and, standing on tiptoe in the crowd, with his white apron over his head, he beheld the courteous little innkeeper. And lastly, there sailed over the heads of the multitude a great, broad laugh, broken in the midst by two sepulchral hems; thus, "Haw, haw, haw,—hem, hem,—haw, haw, haw, haw!"

The sound proceeded from the balcony of the opposite edifice, and thither Robin turned his eyes. In front of the Gothic window stood the old citizen, wrapped in a wide gown, his gray periwig exchanged for a nightcap, which was thrust back from his forehead, and his silk stockings hanging about his legs. He supported himself on his polished cane in a fit of convulsive merriment, which manifested itself on his solemn old features like a funny inscription on a tombstone. Then Robin seemed to hear the voices of the barbers, of the guests of the inn, and of all who had made sport of him that night. The contagion was spreading among the multitude, when all at once, it seized upon Robin, and he sent forth a shout of laughter that echoed through the street,—every man shook his sides, every man emptied his lungs, but Robin's shout was the loudest there. The cloud-spirits peeped from their silvery islands, as the congregated mirth went roaring up the sky! The Man in the Moon heard the far bellow. "Oho," quoth he, "the old earth is frolicsome to-night!"

When there was a momentary calm in that tempestuous sea of sound, the leader gave the sign, the procession resumed its march. On they went, like fiends that throng in mockery around some dead potentate, mighty no more, but majestic still in his agony. On they went, in counterfeited pomp, in senseless uproar, in frenzied merriment, trampling all on an old man's heart. On swept the tumult, and left a silent street behind.

. . .

"Well, Robin, are you dreaming?" inquired the gentleman, laying his hand on the youth's shoulder.

Robin started, and withdrew his arm from the stone post to which he had instinctively clung, as the living stream rolled by him. His cheek was somewhat pale, and his eye not quite as lively as in the earlier part of the evening.

"Will you be kind enough to show me the way to the ferry?" said he, after a moment's pause.

"You have, then, adopted a new subject of inquiry?" observed his companion, with a smile.

"Why, yes, sir," replied Robin, rather dryly. "Thanks to you, and to my other friends, I have at last met my kinsman, and he will scarce desire to see my face again. I begin to grow weary of a town life, sir. Will you show me the way to the ferry?"

"No, my good friend Robin,—not to-night, at least," said the gentleman. "Some few days hence, if you wish it, I will speed you on your journey. Or, if you prefer to remain with us, perhaps, as you are a shrewd youth, you may rise in the world without the help of your kinsman, Major Molineux."

Leo Tolstoy / 1828–1910

The Three Hermits

An Old Legend Current in the Vólga District

> *And in praying use not vain repetitions, as the Gentiles do: for they think that they shall be heard for their much speaking. Be not therefore like unto them: for your Father knoweth what things ye have need of, before ye ask Him.*
>
> Matthew 6:7-8

A bishop was sailing from Archangel to the Solovétsk Monastery, and on the same vessel were a number of pilgrims on their way to visit the shrines at that place. The voyage was a smooth one, the wind favourable and the weather fair. The pilgrims lay on deck, eating, or sat in groups talking to one another. The Bishop, too, came on deck, and as he was pacing up and down he noticed a group of men standing near the prow and listening to a fisherman, who was pointing to the sea and telling them something. The Bishop stopped, and looked in the direction in which the man was pointing. He could see nothing, however, but the sea glistening in the sunshine. He drew nearer to listen, but when the man saw him, he took off his cap and was silent. The rest of the people also took off their caps and bowed.

"Do not let me disturb you, friends," said the Bishop. "I came to hear what this good man was saying."

"The fisherman was telling us about the hermits," replied one, a tradesman, rather bolder than the rest.

"What hermits?" asked the Bishop, going to the side of the vessel and seating himself on a box. "Tell me about them. I should like to hear. What were you pointing at?"

"Why, that little island you can just see over there," answered the man, pointing to a spot ahead and a little to the right. "That is the island where the hermits live for the salvation of their souls."

"Where is the island?" asked the Bishop. "I see nothing."

"There, in the distance, if you will please look along my hand. Do you see that little cloud? Below it, and a bit to the left, there is just a faint streak. That is the island."

The Bishop looked carefully, but his unaccustomed eyes could make out nothing but the water shimmering in the sun.

"I cannot see it," he said. "But who are the hermits that live there?"

"They are holy men," answered the fisherman. "I had long heard tell of them, but never chanced to see them myself till the year before last."

And the fisherman related how once, when he was out fishing, he had been stranded at night upon that island, not knowing where he was. In the morning, as he wandered about the island, he came across an earth hut, and met an old man standing near it. Presently two others came out, and after having fed him and dried his things, they helped him mend his boat.

"And what are they like?" asked the Bishop.

"One is a small man and his back is bent. He wears a priest's cassock and is very old; he must be more than a hundred, I should say. He is so old that the white of his beard is taking a greenish tinge, but he is always smiling, and his face is as bright as an angel's from heaven. The second is taller, but he also is very old. He wears a tattered peasant coat. His beard is broad, and of a yellowish grey colour. He is a strong man. Before I had time to help him, he turned my boat over as if it were only a pail. He too is kindly and cheerful. The third is tall, and has a beard as white as snow and reaching to his knees. He is stern, with overhanging eyebrows; and he wears nothing but a piece of matting tied round his waist."

"And did they speak to you?" asked the Bishop.

"For the most part they did everything in silence, and spoke but little even to one another. One of them would just give a glance, and the others would understand him. I asked the tallest whether they had lived there long. He frowned, and muttered something as if he were angry; but the oldest one took his hand and smiled, and then the tall one was quiet. The oldest one only said: 'Have mercy upon us,' and smiled."

While the fisherman was talking, the ship had drawn nearer to the island.

"There, now you can see it plainly, if your Lordship will please to look," said the tradesman, pointing with his hand.

The Bishop looked, and now he really saw a dark streak—which was the island. Having looked at it a while, he left the prow of the vessel, and going to the stern, asked the helmsman:

"What island is that?"

"That one," replied the man, "has no name. There are many such in this sea."

"Is it true that there are hermits who live there for the salvation of their souls?"

"So it is said, your Lordship, but I don't know if it's true. Fishermen say they have seen them; but of course they may only be spinning yarns."

"I should like to land on the island and see these men," said the Bishop. "How could I manage it?"

"The ship cannot get close to the island," replied the helmsman, "but you might be rowed there in a boat. You had better speak to the captain."

The captain was sent for and came.

"I should like to see these hermits," said the Bishop. "Could I not be rowed ashore?"

The captain tried to dissuade him.

"Of course it could be done," said he, "but we should lose much time. And if I might venture to say so to your Lordship, the old men are not worth your pains. I have heard say that they are foolish old fellows, who understand nothing, and never speak a word, any more than the fish in the sea."

"I wish to see them," said the Bishop, "and I will pay you for your trouble and loss of time. Please let me have a boat."

There was no help for it; so the order was given. The sailors trimmed the sails, the steersman put up the helm, and the ship's course was set for the island. A chair was placed at the prow for the Bishop, and he sat there, looking ahead. The passengers all collected at the prow, and gazed at the island. Those who had the sharpest eyes could presently make out the rocks on it, and then a mud hut was seen. At last one man saw the hermits themselves. The captain brought a telescope and, after looking through it, handed it to the Bishop.

"It's right enough. There are three men standing on the shore. There, a little to the right of that big rock."

The Bishop took the telescope, got it into position, and he saw the three men: a tall one, a shorter one, and one very small and bent, standing on the shore and holding each other by the hand.

The captain turned to the Bishop.

"The vessel can get no nearer in than this, your Lordship. If you wish to go ashore, we must ask you to go in the boat, while we anchor here."

The cable was quickly let out; the anchor cast, and the sails furled. There was a jerk, and the vessel shook. Then, a boat having been lowered, the oarsmen jumped in, and the Bishop descended the ladder and took his seat. The men pulled at their oars and the boat moved rapidly towards the island. When they came within a stone's throw, they saw three old men: a tall one with only a piece of matting tied round his waist, a shorter one in a tattered peasant coat, and a very old one bent with age and wearing an old cassock—all three standing hand in hand.

The oarsmen pulled in to the shore, and held on with the boathook while the Bishop got out.

The old men bowed to him, and he gave them his blessing, at which they bowed still lower. Then the Bishop began to speak to them.

"I have heard," he said, "that you, godly men, live here saving your own souls and praying to our Lord Christ for your fellow men. I, an unworthy servant of Christ, am called, by God's mercy, to keep and teach His flock. I wished to see you, servants of God, and to do what I can to teach you, also."

The old men looked at each other, smiling, but remained silent.

"Tell me," said the Bishop, "what you are doing to save your souls, and how you serve God on this island."

The second hermit sighed, and looked at the oldest, the very ancient one. The latter smiled, and said:

"We do not know how to serve God. We only serve and support ourselves, servant of God."

"But how do you pray to God?" asked the Bishop.

"We pray in this way," replied the hermit. " 'Three are ye, three are we, have mercy upon us.' "

And when the old man said this, all three raised their eyes to heaven, and repeated:

"Three are ye, three are we, have mercy upon us!"

The Bishop smiled.

"You have evidently heard something about the Holy Trinity," said he. "But you do not pray aright. You have won my affection, godly men. I see you wish to please the Lord, but you do not know how to serve Him. That is not the way to pray; but listen to me, and I will teach you. I will teach you, not a way of my own, but the way in which God in the Holy Scriptures has commanded all men to pray to Him."

And the Bishop began explaining to the hermits how God had revealed Himself to men; telling them of God the Father, and God the Son, and God the Holy Ghost.

"God the Son came down on earth," said he, "to save men, and this is how He taught us all to pray. Listen, and repeat after me: 'Our Father.' "

And the first old man repeated after him, "Our Father," and the second said, "Our Father," and the third said, "Our Father."

"Which art in heaven," continued the Bishop.

The first hermit repeated, "Which art in heaven," but the second blundered over the words, and the tall hermit could not say them properly. His hair had grown over his mouth so that he could not speak plainly. The very old hermit, having no teeth, also mumbled indistinctly.

The Bishop repeated the words again, and the old men repeated them after him. The Bishop sat down on a stone, and the old men stood before him, watching his mouth, and repeating the words as he uttered them. And all day long the Bishop laboured, saying a word twenty, thirty, a hundred times over, and the old men repeated it after him. They blundered, and he corrected them, and made them begin again.

The Bishop did not leave off till he had taught them the whole of the Lord's Prayer so that they could not only repeat it after him, but could say it by themselves. The middle one was the first to know it, and to repeat the whole of it alone. The Bishop made him say it again and again, and at last the others could say it too.

It was getting dark and the moon was appearing over the water, before the Bishop rose to return to the vessel. When he took leave of the old men they all bowed down to the ground before him. He raised them, and kissed each of them, telling them to pray as he had taught them. Then he got into the boat and returned to the ship.

And as he sat in the boat and was rowed to the ship he could hear the three voices of the hermits loudly repeating the Lord's Prayer. As the boat drew near the vessel their voices could no longer be heard, but they could still be seen in the moonlight, standing as he had left them on the shore, the shortest in the middle, the tallest on the right, the middle one on the left. As soon as the Bishop had reached the vessel and got on board, the anchor was weighed and the sails unfurled. The wind filled them and the ship sailed away, and the Bishop took a seat in the stern and watched the island they had left. For a time he could still see the hermits, but presently they disappeared from sight, though the island was still visible. At last it too vanished, and only the sea was to be seen, rippling in the moonlight.

The pilgrims lay down to sleep, and all was quiet on deck. The Bishop did not wish to sleep, but sat alone at the stern, gazing at the sea where the island was no longer visible, and thinking of the good old men. He thought how pleased they had been to learn the Lord's Prayer; and he thanked God for having sent him to teach and help such godly men.

So the Bishop sat, thinking, and gazing at the sea where the island had disappeared. And the moonlight flickered before his eyes, sparkling, now here, now there, upon the waves. Suddenly he saw something white and shining, on the bright path which the moon cast across the sea. Was it a seagull, or the little gleaming sail of some small boat? The Bishop fixed his eyes on it, wondering.

"It must be a boat sailing after us," thought he, "but it is overtaking us very rapidly. It was far, far away a minute ago, but now it is much nearer. It cannot be a boat, for I can see no sail; but whatever it may be, it is following us and catching us up."

And he could not make out what it was. Not a boat, nor a bird, nor a fish! It was too large for a man, and besides a man could not be out there in the midst of the sea. The Bishop rose, and said to the helmsman:

"Look there, what is that, my friend? What is it?" the Bishop repeated, though he could now see plainly what it was—the three hermits running upon the water, all gleaming white, their grey beards shining, and approaching the ship as quickly as though it were not moving.

The steersman looked, and let go the helm in terror.

"Oh Lord! The hermits are running after us on the water as though it were dry land!"

The passengers, hearing him, jumped up and crowded to the stern. They saw the hermits coming along hand in hand, and the two outer ones beckoning the ship to stop. All three were gliding along upon the water without moving their feet. Before the ship could be stopped, the hermits had reached it, and raising their heads, all three as with one voice, began to say:

"We have forgotten your teaching, servant of God. As long as we kept repeating it we remembered, but when we stopped saying it for a time, a word dropped out, and now it has all gone to pieces. We can remember nothing of it. Teach us again."

The Bishop crossed himself, and leaning over the ship's side, said:

"Your own prayer will reach the Lord, men of God. It is not for me to teach you. Pray for us sinners."

And the Bishop bowed low before the old men; and they turned and went back across the sea. And a light shone until daybreak on the spot where they were lost to sight.

Translated by Louise and Aylmer Maude

Giovanni Verga / 1840–1922

The She-Wolf

She was tall, thin; she had the firm and vigorous breasts of the olive-skinned—and yet she was no longer young; she was pale, as if always plagued by malaria, and in that pallor, two enormous eyes, and fresh red lips which devoured you.

In the village they called her the She-wolf, because she never had enough—of anything. The women made the sign of the cross when they saw her pass, alone as a wild bitch, prowling about suspiciously like a famished wolf; with her red lips she sucked the blood of their sons and husbands in a flash, and pulled them behind her skirt with a single glance of those devilish eyes, even if they were before the altar of Saint Agrippina. Fortunately, the She-wolf never went to church, not at Easter, not at Christmas, not to hear Mass, not for confession.—Father Angiolino of Saint Mary of Jesus, a true servant of God, had lost his soul on account of her.

Maricchia, a good girl, poor thing, cried in secret because she was the She-wolf's daughter, and no one would marry her, though, like every other girl in the village, she had her fine linen in a chest and her good land under the sun.

One day the She-wolf fell in love with a handsome young man who had just returned from the service and was mowing hay with her in the fields of the notary; and she fell in love in the strongest sense of the word, feeling the flesh afire beneath her clothes; and staring him in the eyes, she suffered the thirst one has in the hot hours of June, deep in the plain. But he went on mowing undisturbed, his nose bent over the swaths.

"What's wrong, Pina?" he would ask.

In the immense fields, where you heard only the crackling flight of the grasshoppers, as the sun hammered down overhead, the She-wolf gathered bundle after bundle, and sheaf after sheaf, never tiring, never straightening up for an instant, never raising the flask to her lips, just to remain at the heels of Nanni, who mowed and mowed and asked from time to time:

"What is it you want, Pina?"

One evening she told him, while the men were dozing on the threshing floor, tired after the long day, and the dogs were howling in the vast, dark countryside.

"It's you I want. You who're beautiful as the sun and sweet as honey. I want you!"

"And I want your daughter, instead, who's a maid," answered Nanni laughing.

The She-wolf thrust her hands into her hair, scratching her temples, without saying a word, and walked away. And she did not appear at the threshing floor any more. But she saw Nanni again in October, when they were making olive oil, for he was working near her house, and the creaking of the press kept her awake all night.

"Get the sack of olives," she said to her daughter, "and come with me."

Nanni was pushing olives under the millstone with a shovel, shouting "Ohee" to the mule, to keep it from stopping.

"You want my daughter Maricchia?" Pina asked him.

"What'll you give your daughter Maricchia?" answered Nanni.

"She has all her father's things, and I'll give her my house too; as for me, all I need is a little corner in the kitchen, enough for a straw mattress."

"If that's the way it is, we can talk about it at Christmas," said Nanni.

Nanni was all greasy and filthy, spattered with oil and fermented olives, and Maricchia didn't want him at any price. But her mother grabbed her by the hair before the fireplace, muttering between her teeth:

"If you don't take him, I'll kill you!"

The She-wolf was almost sick, and the people were saying that when the devil gets old he becomes a hermit. She no longer roamed here and there, no longer lingered at the doorway, with those bewitched eyes. Whenever she fixed them on his face, those eyes of hers, her son-in-law began to laugh and pulled out the scapular of the Virgin to cross himself. Maricchia stayed at home nursing the babies, and her mother went into the fields to work with the men, and just like a man too, weeding, hoeing, feeding the animals, pruning the vines, despite the northeast and levantine winds of January or the August sirocco, when the mules' heads drooped and the men slept face down along the wall, on the north side. "In those hours between nones and vespers when no good woman goes roving around," [1] Pina was the only living soul to be seen wandering in the countryside, over the burning stones of the paths, through the scorched stubble of the immense fields that became lost in the suffocating heat, far, far away toward the foggy Etna, where the sky was heavy on the horizon.

"Wake up!" said the She-wolf to Nanni, who was sleeping in the ditch, along the dusty hedge, his head on his arms. "Wake up. I've brought you some wine to cool your throat."

Nanni opened his drowsy eyes wide, still half asleep, and finding her standing before him, pale, with her arrogant breasts and her coal-black eyes, he stretched out his hands gropingly.

"No! no good woman goes roving around in the hours between nones and vespers!" sobbed Nanni, throwing his head back into the dry grass of the ditch, deep, deep, his nails in his scalp. "Go away! go away! don't come to the threshing floor again!"

The She-wolf was going away, in fact, retying her superb tresses, her gaze bent fixedly before her as she moved through the hot stubble, her eyes as black as coal.

But she came to the threshing floor again, and more than once, and Nanni did not complain. On the contrary, when she was late, in the hours between nones and vespers, he would go and wait for her at the top of the white, deserted path, with his forehead bathed in sweat; and he would thrust his hands into his hair, and repeat every time:

"Go away! go away! don't come to the threshing floor again!"

Maricchia cried night and day, and glared at her mother, her eyes burning with tears and jealousy, like a young she-wolf herself, every time she saw her come, mute and pale, from the fields.

[1] An old Sicilian proverb, which refers to the hours of the early afternoon, when the Sicilian countryside lies motionless under a scorching sun and no person would dare walk on the roads. Those hours are traditionally believed to be under the spell of malignant spirits. TRANSLATOR'S NOTE.

"Vile, vile mother!" she said to her. "Vile mother!"

"Shut up!"

"Thief! Thief!"

"Shut up!"

"I'll go to the Sergeant, I will!"

"Go ahead!"

And she really did go, with her babies in her arms, fearing nothing, and without shedding a tear, like a madwoman, because now she too loved that husband who had been forced on her, greasy and filthy, spattered with oil and fermented olives.

The Sergeant sent for Nanni; he threatened him even with jail and the gallows. Nanni began to sob and tear his hair; he didn't deny anything, he didn't try to clear himself.

"It's the temptation!" he said. "It's the temptation of hell!"

He threw himself at the Sergeant's feet begging to be sent to jail.

"For God's sake, Sergeant, take me out of this hell! Have me killed, put me in jail; don't let me see her again, never! never!"

"No!" answered the She-wolf instead, to the Sergeant. "I kept a little corner in the kitchen to sleep in, when I gave him my house as dowry. It's my house. I don't intend to leave it."

Shortly afterward, Nanni was kicked in the chest by a mule and was at the point of death, but the priest refused to bring him the Sacrament if the She-wolf did not go out of the house. The She-wolf left, and then her son-in-law could also prepare to leave like a good Christian; he confessed and received communion with such signs of repentance and contrition that all the neighbors and the curious wept before the dying man's bed.—And it would have been better for him to die that day, before the devil came back to tempt him again and creep into his body and soul, when he got well.

"Leave me alone!" he told the She-wolf. "For God's sake, leave me in peace! I've seen death with my own eyes! Poor Maricchia is desperate. Now the whole town knows about it! If I don't see you it's better for both of us . . ."

And he would have liked to gouge his eyes out not to see those of the She-wolf, for whenever they peered into his, they made him lose his body and soul. He did not know what to do to free himself from the spell. He paid for Masses for the souls in purgatory and asked the priest and the Sergeant for help. At Easter he went to confession, and in penance he publicly licked more than four feet of pavement, crawling on the pebbles in front of the church—and then, as the She-wolf came to tempt him again:

"Listen!" he said to her. "Don't come to the threshing floor again; if you do, I swear to God, I'll kill you!"

"Kill me," answered the She-wolf. "I don't care; I can't stand it without you."

As he saw her from the distance, in the green wheat fields, Nanni stopped hoeing the vineyard, and went to pull the ax from the elm. The She-wolf saw him come, pale and wild-eyed, with the ax glistening in the sun, but she did not fall back a single step, did not lower her eyes; she continued toward him, her hands laden with red poppies, her black eyes devouring him.

"Ah! damn your soul!" stammered Nanni.

Translated by Giovanni Cecchetti

Henry James / 1843–1916

The Middle Years

The April day was soft and bright, and poor Dencombe, happy in the conceit of reasserted strength, stood in the garden of the hotel, com-paring, with a deliberation in which, however, there was still some-thing of languor, the attractions of easy strolls. He liked the feeling of the south, so far as you could have it in the north, he liked the sandy cliffs and the clustered pines, he liked even the colourless sea. "Bourne-mouth as a health-resort" had sounded like a mere advertisement, but now he was reconciled to the prosaic. The sociable country postman, passing through the garden, had just given him a small parcel, which he took out with him, leaving the hotel to the right and creeping to a convenient bench that he knew of, a safe recess in the cliff. It looked to the south, to the tinted walls of the Island, and was protected behind by the sloping shoulder of the down. He was tired enough when he reached it, and for a moment he was disappointed; he was better, of course, but better, after all, than what? He should never again, as at one or two great moments of the past, be better than himself. The infinite of life had gone, and what was left of the dose was a small glass engraved like a thermometer by the apothecary. He sat and stared at the sea, which appeared all surface and twinkle, far shallower than the spirit of man. It was the abyss of human illusion that was the real, the tideless deep. He held his packet, which had come by book-post, unopened on his knee, liking, in the lapse of so many joys (his illness had made him feel his age), to know that it was there, but taking for granted there could be no complete renewal of the pleasure, dear to young experience, of seeing one's self "just out." Dencombe, who had a reputation, had come out too often and knew too well in advance how he should look.

His postponement associated itself vaguely, after a little, with a group of three persons, two ladies and a young man, whom, beneath him, straggling and seemingly silent, he could see move slowly together along the sands. The gentleman had his head bent over a book and was occasionally brought to a stop by the charm of this volume, which, as Dencombe could perceive even at a distance, had a cover alluringly red. Then his companions, going a little further, waited for him to come up, poking their parasols into the beach, looking around them at the sea and sky and clearly sensible of the beauty of the day. To these things the young man with the book was still more clearly in-different; lingering, credulous, absorbed, he was an object of envy to an observer from whose connection with literature all such artlessness had faded. One of the ladies was large and mature; the other had the spareness of comparative youth and of a social situation possibly inferior. The large lady carried back Dencombe's imagination to the age of crinoline; she wore a hat of the shape of a mushroom, decorated with a blue veil, and had the air, in her aggressive amplitude, of clinging to a vanished fashion or even a lost cause. Presently her com-panion produced from under the folds of a mantle a limp, portable chair which she stiffened out and of which the large lady took pos-session. This act, and something in the movement of either party, instantly characterised the performers—they performed for Den-combe's recreation—as opulent matron and humble dependant. What, moreover, was the use of being an approved novelist if one couldn't establish a relation between such figures; the clever theory, for in-stance, that the young man was the son of the opulent matron, and that the humble dependant, the daughter of a clergyman or an officer, nourished a secret passion for him? Was that not visible from the way she stole behind her protectress to look back at him?—back to where he had let himself come to a full stop when his mother sat down to rest. His book was a novel; it had the catchpenny cover, and while the romance of life stood neglected at his side he lost himself in that of the circulating library. He moved mechanically to where the sand was softer, and ended by plumping down in it to finish his chapter at his ease. The humble dependant, discouraged by his remoteness, wandered, with a martyred droop of the head, in another direction, and the exorbitant lady, watching the waves, offered a confused resemblance to a flying-machine that had broken down.

When his drama began to fail Dencombe remembered that he had, after all, another pastime. Though such promptitude on the part of the publisher was rare, he was already able to draw from its wrapper his "latest," perhaps his last. The cover of "The Middle Years" was duly meretricious, the smell of the fresh pages the very odour of sanctity; but for the moment he went no further—he had become conscious of a strange alienation. He had forgotten what his book was about. Had the assault of his old ailment, which he had so fallaciously come to Bournemouth to ward off, interposed utter blankness as to what had preceded it? He had finished the revision of proof before quitting London, but his subsequent fortnight in bed had passed the sponge over colour. He couldn't have chanted to himself a single sentence, couldn't have turned with curiosity or confidence to any particular page. His subject had already gone from him, leaving scarcely a superstition behind. He uttered a low moan as he breathed the chill of this dark void, so desperately it seemed to represent the completion of a sinister process. The tears filled his mild eyes; something precious had passed away. This was the pang that had been sharpest during the last few years—the sense of ebbing time, of shrinking opportunity; and now he felt not so much that his last chance was going as that it was gone indeed. He had done all that he should ever do, and yet he had not done what he wanted. This was the laceration—that practically his career was over: it was as violent as a rough hand at his throat. He rose from his seat nervously, like a creature hunted by a dread; then he fell back in his weakness and nervously opened his book. It was a single volume; he preferred single volumes and aimed at a rare compression. He began to read, and little by little, in this occupation, he was pacified and reassured. Everything came back to him, but came back with a wonder, came back, above all, with a high and magnificent beauty. He read his own prose, he turned his own leaves, and had, as he sat there with the spring sunshine on the page, an emotion peculiar and intense. His career was over, no doubt, but it was over, after all, with *that*.

He had forgotten during his illness the work of the previous year; but what he had chiefly forgotten was that it was extraordinarily good. He dived once more into his story and was drawn down, as by a siren's hand, to where, in the dim underworld of fiction, the great glazed tank of art, strange silent subjects float. He recognised his motive and surrendered to his talent. Never, probably, had that talent, such as it was, been so fine. His difficulties were still there, but what was also there, to his perception, though probably, alas! to nobody's else, was the art that in most cases had surmounted them. In his surprised enjoyment of this ability he had a glimpse of a possible reprieve. Surely its force was not spent—there was life and service in it yet. It had not come to him easily, it had been backward and roundabout. It was the child of time, the nursling of delay; he had struggled and suffered for it, making sacrifices not to be counted, and now that it was really mature was it to cease to yield, to confess itself brutally beaten? There was an infinite charm for Dencombe in feeling as he had never felt before that diligence *vincit omnia*.[1] The result produced in his little book was somehow a result beyond his conscious intention: it was as if he had planted his genius, had trusted his method, and they had grown up and flowered with this sweetness. If the achievement had been real, however, the process had been painful enough. What he saw so intensely to-day, what he felt as a nail driven in, was that only now, at the very last, had he come into possession. His development had been abnormally slow, almost grotesquely gradual. He had been hindered and retarded by experience, and for long periods had only groped his way. It had taken too much of his life to produce too little of his art. The art had come, but it had come after everything else. At such a rate a first existence was too short—long enough only to collect material; so that to fructify, to use the material, one must have a second age, an extension. This extension was what poor Dencombe sighed for. As he turned the last leaves of his volume he murmured: "Ah for another go!—ah for a better chance!"

The three persons he had observed on the sands had vanished and then reappeared; they had now wandered up a path, an artificial and easy ascent, which led to the top of the cliff. Dencombe's bench was half-way down, on a sheltered ledge, and the large lady, a massive, heterogeneous person, with bold black eyes and kind red cheeks, now took a few moments to rest. She wore dirty gauntlets and immense diamond ear-rings; at first she looked vulgar, but she contradicted this announcement in an agreeable off-hand tone. While her companions stood waiting for her she spread her skirts on the end of Dencombe's seat. The young man had gold spectacles, through which, with his finger still in his red-covered book, he glanced at the volume, bound in the same shade of the same colour, lying on the lap of the original

---

[1] Conquers all.

occupant of the bench. After an instant, Dencombe understood that he was struck with a resemblance, had recognised the gilt stamp on the crimson cloth, was reading "The Middle Years," and now perceived that somebody else had kept pace with him. The stranger was startled, possibly even a little ruffled, to find that he was not the only person who had been favoured with an early copy. The eyes of the two proprietors met for a moment, and Dencombe borrowed amusement from the expression of those of his competitor, those, it might even be inferred, of his admirer. They confessed to some resentment—they seemed to say: "Hang it, has he got it *already?*—Of course he's a brute of a reviewer!" Dencombe shuffled his copy out of sight while the opulent matron, rising from her repose, broke out: "I feel already the good of this air!"

"I can't say I do," said the angular lady. "I find myself quite let down."

"I find myself horribly hungry. At what time did you order lunch?" her protectress pursued.

The young person put the question by. "Doctor Hugh always orders it."

"I ordered nothing to-day—I'm going to make you diet," said their comrade.

"Then I shall go home and sleep. *Qui dort dine!*" [2]

"Can I trust you to Miss Vernham?" asked Doctor Hugh of his elder companion.

"Don't I trust *you?*" she archly inquired.

"Not too much!" Miss Vernham, with her eyes on the ground, permitted herself to declare. "You must come with us at least to the house," she went on, while the personage on whom they appeared to be in attendance began to mount higher. She had got a little out of ear-shot; nevertheless Miss Vernham became, so far as Dencombe was concerned, less distinctly audible to murmur to the young man: "I don't think you realise all you owe the Countess!"

Absently, a moment, Doctor Hugh caused his gold-rimmed spectacles to shine at her.

"Is that the way I strike you? I see—I see!"

"She's awfully good to us," continued Miss Vernham, compelled by her interlocutor's immovability to stand there in spite of his discussion of private matters. Of what use would it have been that Dencombe should be sensitive to shades had he not detected in that immovability a strange influence from the quiet old convalescent in the great tweed cape? Miss Vernham appeared suddenly to become aware of some

---

[2] "Who sleeps, dines." Or, "Sleeping is as good as eating."

such connection, for she added in a moment: "If you want to sun yourself here you can come back after you've seen us home."

Doctor Hugh, at this, hesitated, and Dencombe, in spite of a desire to pass for unconscious, risked a covert glance at him. What his eyes met this time, as it happened, was on the part of the young lady a queer stare, naturally vitreous, which made her aspect remind him of some figure (he couldn't name it) in a play or a novel, some sinister governess or tragic old maid. She seemed to scrutinise him, to challenge him, to say, from general spite: "What have you got to do with us?" At the same instant the rich humour of the Countess reached them from above: "Come, come, my little lambs, you should follow your old *bergère!*" [3] Miss Vernham turned away at this, pursuing the ascent, and Doctor Hugh, after another mute appeal to Dencombe and a moment's evident demur, deposited his book on the bench, as if to keep his place or even as a sign that he would return, and bounded without difficulty up the rougher part of the cliff.

Equally innocent and infinite are the pleasures of observation and the resources engendered by the habit of analysing life. It amused poor Dencombe, as he dawdled in his tepid air-bath, to think that he was waiting for a revelation of something at the back of a fine young mind. He looked hard at the book on the end of the bench, but he wouldn't have touched it for the world. It served his purpose to have a theory which should not be exposed to refutation. He already felt better of his melancholy; he had, according to his old formula, put his head at the window. A passing Countess could draw off the fancy when, like the elder of the ladies who had just retreated, she was as obvious as the giantess of a caravan. It was indeed general views that were terrible; short ones, contrary to an opinion sometimes expressed, were the refuge, were the remedy. Doctor Hugh couldn't possibly be anything but a reviewer who had understandings for early copies with publishers or with newspapers. He reappeared in a quarter of an hour, with visible relief at finding Dencombe on the spot, and the gleam of white teeth in an embarrassed but generous smile. He was perceptibly disappointed at the eclipse of the other copy of the book; it was a pretext the less for speaking to the stranger. But he spoke notwithstanding; he held up his own copy and broke out pleadingly:

"*Do* say, if you have occasion to speak of it, that it's the best thing he has done yet!"

Dencombe responded with a laugh: "Done yet" was so amusing to him, made such a grand avenue of the future. Better still, the young man took *him* for a reviewer. He pulled out "The Middle Years" from

---

³ Shepherdess.

under his cape, but instinctively concealed any tell-tale look of father-hood. This was partly because a person was always a fool for calling attention to his work. "Is that what you're going to say yourself?" he inquired of his visitor.

"I'm not quite sure I shall write anything. I don't, as a regular thing —I enjoy in peace. But it's awfully fine."

Dencombe debated a moment. If his interlocutor had begun to abuse him he would have confessed on the spot to his identity, but there was no harm in drawing him on a little to praise. He drew him on with such success that in a few moments his new acquaintance, seated by his side, was confessing candidly that Dencombe's novels were the only ones he could read a second time. He had come the day before from London, where a friend of his, a journalist, had lent him his copy of the last—the copy sent to the office of the journal and already the subject of a "notice" which, as was pretended there (but one had to allow for "swagger"), it had taken a full quarter of an hour to prepare. He intimated that he was ashamed for his friend, and in the case of a work demanding and repaying study, of such inferior manners; and, with his fresh appreciation and inexplicable wish to express it, he speedily became for poor Dencombe a remark-able, a delightful apparition. Chance had brought the weary man of letters face to face with the greatest admirer in the new generation whom it was supposable he possessed. The admirer, in truth, was mys-tifying, so rare a case was it to find a bristling young doctor—he looked like a German physiologist—enamoured of literary form. It was an accident, but happier than most accidents, so that Dencombe, exhilarated as well as confounded, spent half an hour in making his visitor talk while he kept himself quiet. He explained his premature possession of "The Middle Years" by an allusion to the friendship of the publisher, who, knowing he was at Bournemouth for his health, had paid him this graceful attention. He admitted that he had been ill, for Doctor Hugh would infallibly have guessed it; he even went so far as to wonder whether he mightn't look for some hygienic "tip" from a personage combining so bright an enthusiasm with a presum-able knowledge of the remedies now in vogue. It would shake his faith a little perhaps to have to take a doctor seriously who could take *him* so seriously, but he enjoyed this gushing modern youth and he felt with an acute pang that there would still be work to do in a world in which such odd combinations were presented. It was not true, what he had tried for renunciation's sake to believe, that all the combina-tions were exhausted. They were not, they were not—they were in-finite: the exhaustion was in the miserable artist.

Doctor Hugh was an ardent physiologist, saturated with the spirit of the age—in other words he had just taken his degree; but he was independent and various, he talked like a man who would have preferred to love literature best. He would fain have made fine phrases, but nature had denied him the trick. Some of the finest in "The Middle Years" had struck him inordinately, and he took the liberty of reading them to Dencombe in support of his plea. He grew vivid, in the balmy air, to his companion, for whose deep refreshment he seemed to have been sent; and was particularly ingenuous in describing how recently he had become acquainted, and how instantly infatuated, with the only man who had put flesh between the ribs of an art that was starving on superstitions. He had not yet written to him—he was deterred by a sentiment of respect. Dencombe at this moment felicitated himself more than ever on having never answered the photographers. His visitor's attitude promised him a luxury of intercourse, but he surmised that a certain security in it, for Doctor Hugh, would depend not a little on the Countess. He learned without delay with what variety of Countess they were concerned, as well as the nature of the tie that united the curious trio. The large lady, an Englishwoman by birth and the daughter of a celebrated baritone, whose taste, without his talent, she had inherited, was the widow of a French nobleman and mistress of all that remained of the handsome fortune, the fruit of her father's earnings, that had constituted her dower. Miss Vernham, an odd creature but an accomplished pianist, was attached to her person at a salary. The Countess was generous, independent, eccentric; she travelled with her minstrel and her medical man. Ignorant and passionate, she had nevertheless moments in which she was almost irresistible. Dencombe saw her sit for her portrait in Doctor Hugh's free sketch, and felt the picture of his young friend's relation to her frame itself in his mind. This young friend, for a representative of the new psychology, was himself easily hypnotised, and if he became abnormally communicative it was only a sign of his real subjection. Dencombe did accordingly what he wanted with him, even without being known as Dencombe.

Taken ill on a journey in Switzerland the Countess had picked him up at an hotel, and the accident of his happening to please her had made her offer him, with her imperious liberality, terms that couldn't fail to dazzle a practitioner without patients and whose resources had been drained dry by his studies. It was not the way he would have elected to spend his time, but it was time that would pass quickly, and meanwhile she was wonderfully kind. She exacted perpetual attention, but it was impossible not to like her. He gave details about his queer patient, a "type" if there ever was one, who had in connection with her flushed obesity and in addition to the morbid strain of a violent and aimless will a grave organic disorder; but he came back to his loved novelist, whom he was so good as to pronounce more essentially a poet than many of those who went in for verse, with a zeal excited, as all his indiscretion had been excited, by the happy chance of Dencombe's sympathy and the coincidence of their occupation. Dencombe had confessed to a slight personal acquaintance with the author of "The Middle Years," but had not felt himself as ready as he could have wished when his companion, who had never yet encountered a being so privileged, began to be eager for particulars. He even thought that Doctor Hugh's eye at that moment emitted a glimmer of suspicion. But the young man was too inflamed to be shrewd and repeatedly caught up the book to exclaim: "Did you notice this?" or "Weren't you immensely struck with that?" "There's a beautiful passage toward the end," he broke out; and again he laid his hand upon the volume. As he turned the pages he came upon something else, while Dencombe saw him suddenly change colour. He had taken up, as it lay on the bench, Dencombe's copy instead of his own, and his neighbour immediately guessed the reason of his start. Doctor Hugh looked grave an instant; then he said: "I see you've been altering the text!" Dencombe was a passionate corrector, a fingerer of style; the last thing he ever arrived at was a form final for himself. His ideal would have been to publish secretly, and then, on the published text, treat himself to the terrified revise, sacrificing always a first edition and beginning for posterity and even for the collectors, poor dears, with a second. This morning, in "The Middle Years," his pencil had pricked a dozen lights. He was amused at the effect of the young man's reproach; for an instant it made him change colour. He stammered, at any rate, ambiguously; then, through a blur of ebbing consciousness, saw Doctor Hugh's mystified eyes. He only had time to feel he was about to be ill again—that emotion, excitement, fatigue, the heat of the sun, the solicitation of the air, had combined to play him a trick, before, stretching out a hand to his visitor with a plaintive cry, he lost his senses altogether.

Later he knew that he had fainted and that Doctor Hugh had got him home in a bath-chair, the conductor of which, prowling within hail for custom, had happened to remember seeing him in the garden of the hotel. He had recovered his perception in the transit, and had, in bed, that afternoon, a vague recollection of Doctor Hugh's young face, as they went together, bent over him in a comforting laugh and expressive of something more than a suspicion of his identity. That identity was ineffaceable now, and all the more that he was disappointed, disgusted. He had been rash, been stupid, had gone out too soon, stayed out too long. He oughtn't to have exposed himself to strangers, he ought to have taken his servant. He felt as if he had fallen into a hole too deep to descry any little patch of heaven. He was confused about the time that had elapsed—he pieced the fragments together. He had seen his doctor, the real one, the one who had treated him from the first and who had again been very kind. His servant was in and out on tiptoe, looking very wise after the fact. He said more than once something about the sharp young gentleman. The rest was vagueness, in so far as it wasn't despair. The vagueness, however, justified itself by dreams, dozing anxieties from which he finally emerged to the consciousness of a dark room and a shaded candle.

"You'll be all right again—I know all about you now," said a voice near him that he knew to be young. Then his meeting with Doctor Hugh came back. He was too discouraged to joke about it yet, but he was able to perceive, after a little, that the interest of it was intense for his visitor. "Of course I can't attend you professionally—you've got your own man, with whom I've talked and who's excellent," Doctor Hugh went on. "But you must let me come to see you as a good friend. I've just looked in before going to bed. You're doing beautifully, but it's a good job I was with you on the cliff. I shall come in early to-morrow. I want to do something for you. I want to do everything. You've done a tremendous lot for me." The young man held his hand, hanging over him, and poor Dencombe, weakly aware of this living pressure, simply lay there and accepted his devotion. He couldn't do anything less—he needed help too much.

The idea of the help he needed was very present to him that night, which he spent in a lucid stillness, an intensity of thought that constituted a reaction from his hours of stupor. He was lost, he was lost —he was lost if he couldn't be saved. He was not afraid of suffering, of death; he was not even in love with life; but he had had a deep demonstration of desire. It came over him in the long, quiet hours that only with "The Middle Years" had he taken his flight; only on that day, visited by soundless processions, had he recognised his kingdom. He had had a revelation of his range. What he dreaded was the idea that his reputation should stand on the unfinished. It was not with his past but with his future that it should properly be concerned. Illness and age rose before him like spectres with pitiless eyes: how was he to bribe such fates to give him the second chance? He had had the one chance that all men have—he had had the chance of life. He went to sleep again very late, and when he awoke Doctor Hugh was sitting by his head. There was already, by this time, something beautifully familiar in him.

"Don't think I've turned out your physician," he said; "I'm acting with his consent. He has been here and seen you. Somehow he seems to trust me. I told him how we happened to come together yesterday, and he recognises that I've a peculiar right."

Dencombe looked at him with a calculating earnestness. "How have you squared the Countess?"

The young man blushed a little, but he laughed. "Oh, never mind the Countess!"

"You told me she was very exacting."

Doctor Hugh was silent a moment. "So she is."

"And Miss Vernham's an *intrigante*."[4]

"How do you know that?"

"I know everything. One *has* to, to write decently!"

"I think she's mad," said limpid Doctor Hugh.

"Well, don't quarrel with the Countess—she's a present help to you."

"I don't quarrel," Doctor Hugh replied. "But I don't get on with silly women." Presently he added: "You seem very much alone."

"That often happens at my age. I've outlived, I've lost by the way."

Doctor Hugh hesitated; then surmounting a soft scruple: "Whom have you lost?"

"Every one."

"Ah, no," the young man murmured, laying a hand on his arm.

"I once had a wife—I once had a son. My wife died when my child was born, and my boy, at school, was carried off by typhoid."

"I wish I'd been there!" said Doctor Hugh simply.

"Well—if you're here!" Dencombe answered, with a smile that, in spite of dimness, showed how much he liked to be sure of his companion's whereabouts.

"You talk strangely of your age. You're not old."

"Hypocrite—so early!"

"I speak physiologically."

"That's the way I've been speaking for the last five years, and it's exactly what I've been saying to myself. It isn't till we *are* old that we begin to tell ourselves we're not!"

"Yet I know I myself am young," Doctor Hugh declared.

"Not so well as I!" laughed his patient, whose visitor indeed would have established the truth in question by the honesty with which he changed the point of view, remarking that it must be one of the charms of age—at any rate in the case of high distinction—to feel that one has laboured and achieved. Doctor Hugh employed the common phrase about earning one's rest, and it made poor Dencombe, for an instant, almost angry. He recovered himself, however, to explain, lucidly

4 Adventuress.

enough, that if he, ungraciously, knew nothing of such a balm, it was doubtless because he had wasted inestimable years. He had followed literature from the first, but he had taken a lifetime to get alongside of her. Only to-day, at last, had he begun to *see,* so that what he had hitherto done was a movement without a direction. He had ripened too late and was so clumsily constituted that he had had to teach himself by mistakes.

"I prefer your flowers, then, to other people's fruit, and your mistakes to other people's successes," said gallant Doctor Hugh. "It's for your mistakes I admire you."

"You're happy—you don't know," Dencombe answered.

Looking at his watch the young man had got up; he named the hour of the afternoon at which he would return. Dencombe warned him against committing himself too deeply, and expressed again all his dread of making him neglect the Countess—perhaps incur her displeasure.

"I want to be like you—I want to learn by mistakes!" Doctor Hugh laughed.

"Take care you don't make too grave a one! But do come back," Dencombe added, with the glimmer of a new idea.

"You should have had more vanity!" Doctor Hugh spoke as if he knew the exact amount required to make a man of letters normal.

"No, no—I only should have had more time. I want another go."

"Another go?"

"I want an extension."

"An extension?" Again Doctor Hugh repeated Dencombe's words, with which he seemed to have been struck.

"Don't you know?—I want to what they call 'live.' "

The young man, for good-bye, had taken his hand, which closed with a certain force. They looked at each other hard a moment. "You *will* live," said Doctor Hugh.

"Don't be superficial. It's too serious!"

"You *shall* live!" Dencombe's visitor declared, turning pale.

"Ah, that's better!" And as he retired the invalid, with a troubled laugh, sank gratefully back.

All that day and all the following night he wondered if it mightn't be arranged. His doctor came again, his servant was attentive, but it was to his confident young friend that he found himself mentally appealing. His collapse on the cliff was plausibly explained, and his liberation, on a better basis, promised for the morrow; meanwhile, however, the intensity of his meditations kept him tranquil and made him indifferent. The idea that occupied him was none the less absorbing because it was a morbid fancy. Here was a clever son of the age, ingenious and ardent, who happened to have set him up for connoisseurs to worship. This servant of his altar had all the new learning in science and all the old reverence in faith; wouldn't he therefore put his knowledge at the disposal of his sympathy, his craft at the disposal of his love? Couldn't he be trusted to invent a remedy for a poor artist to whose art he had paid a tribute? If he couldn't, the alternative was hard: Dencombe would have to surrender to silence, unvindicated and undivined. The rest of the day and all the next he toyed in secret with this sweet futility. Who would work the miracle for him but the young man who could combine such lucidity with such passion? He thought of the fairy-tales of science and charmed himself into forgetting that he looked for a magic that was not of this world. Doctor Hugh was an apparition, and that placed him above the law. He came and went while his patient, who sat up, followed him with supplicating eyes. The interest of knowing the great author had made the young man begin "The Middle Years" afresh, and would help him to find a deeper meaning in its pages. Dencombe had told him what he "tried for;" with all his intelligence, on a first perusal, Doctor Hugh had failed to guess it. The baffled celebrity wondered then who in the world *would* guess it: he was amused once more at the fine, full way with which an intention could be missed. Yet he wouldn't rail at the general mind to-day—consoling as that ever had been: the revelation of his own slowness had seemed to make all stupidity sacred.

Doctor Hugh, after a little, was visibly worried, confessing, on inquiry, to a source of embarrassment at home. "Stick to the Countess —don't mind me," Dencombe said, repeatedly; for his companion was frank enough about the large lady's attitude. She was so jealous that she had fallen ill—she resented such a breach of allegiance. She paid so much for his fidelity that she must have it all: she refused him the right to other sympathies, charged him with scheming to make her die alone, for it was needless to point out how little Miss Vernham was a resource in trouble. When Doctor Hugh mentioned that the Countess would already have left Bournemouth if he hadn't kept her in bed, poor Dencombe held his arm tighter and said with decision: "Take her straight away." They had gone out together, walking back to the sheltered nook in which, the other day, they had met. The young man, who had given his companion a personal support, declared with emphasis that his conscience was clear—he could ride two horses at once. Didn't he dream, for his future, of a time when he should have to ride five hundred? Longing equally for virtue, Dencombe replied that in that golden age no patient would pretend to have contracted with him for his whole attention. On the part of the Countess was not such an avidity lawful? Doctor Hugh denied it, said there was no contract but only a free understanding, and that a sordid servitude was impossible to a generous spirit; he liked moreover to talk about art, and that was the subject on which, this time, as they sat together on the sunny bench, he tried most to engage the author of "The Middle Years." Dencombe, soaring again a little on the weak wings of convalescence and still haunted by that happy notion of an organised rescue, found another strain of eloquence to plead the cause of a certain splendid "last manner," the very citadel, as it would prove, of his reputation, the stronghold into which his real treasure would be gathered. While his listener gave up the morning and the great still sea appeared to wait, he had a wonderful explanatory hour. Even for himself he was inspired as he told of what his treasure would consist—the precious metals he would dig from the mine, the jewels rare, strings of pearls, he would hang between the columns of his temple. He was wonderful for himself, so thick his convictions crowded; but he was still more wonderful for Doctor Hugh, who assured him, none the less, that the very pages he had just published were already encrusted with gems. The young man, however, panted for the combinations to come, and, before the face of the beautiful day, renewed to Dencombe his guarantee that his profession would hold itself responsible for such a life. Then he suddenly clapped his hand upon his watch-pocket and asked leave to absent himself for half an hour. Dencombe waited there for his return, but was at last recalled to the actual by the fall of a shadow across the ground. The shadow darkened into that of Miss Vernham, the young lady in attendance on the Countess; whom Dencombe, recognising her, perceived so clearly to have come to speak to him that he rose from his bench to acknowledge the civility. Miss Vernham indeed proved not particularly civil; she looked strangely agitated, and her type was now unmistakable.

"Excuse me if I inquire," she said, "whether it's too much to hope that you may be induced to leave Doctor Hugh alone." Then, before Dencombe, greatly disconcerted, could protest: "You ought to be informed that you stand in his light; that you may do him a terrible injury."

"Do you mean by causing the Countess to dispense with his services?"

"By causing her to disinherit him." Dencombe stared at this, and Miss Vernham pursued, in the gratification of seeing she could produce an impression: "It has depended on himself to come into something very handsome. He has had a magnificent prospect, but I think you've succeeded in spoiling it."

"Not intentionally, I assure you. Is there no hope the accident may be repaired?" Dencombe asked.

"She was ready to do anything for him. She takes great fancies, she lets herself go—it's her way. She has no relations, she's free to dispose of her money, and she's very ill."

"I'm very sorry to hear it," Dencombe stammered.

"Wouldn't it be possible for you to leave Bournemouth? That's what I've come to ask of you."

Poor Dencombe sank down on his bench. "I'm very ill myself, but I'll try!"

Miss Vernham still stood there with her colourless eyes and the brutality of her good conscience. "Before it's too late, please!" she said; and with this she turned her back, in order, quickly, as if it had been a business to which she could spare but a precious moment, to pass out of his sight.

Oh, yes, after this Dencombe was certainly very ill. Miss Vernham had upset him with her rough, fierce news; it was the sharpest shock to him to discover what was at stake for a penniless young man of fine parts. He sat trembling on his bench, staring at the waste of waters, feeling sick with the directness of the blow. He was indeed too weak, too unsteady, too alarmed; but he would make the effort to get away, for he couldn't accept the guilt of interference, and his honour was really involved. He would hobble home, at any rate, and then he would think what was to be done. He made his way back to the hotel and, as he went, had a characteristic vision of Miss Vernham's great motive. The Countess hated women, of course; Dencombe was lucid about that; so the hungry pianist had no personal hopes and could only console herself with the bold conception of helping Doctor Hugh in order either to marry him after he should get his money or to induce him to recognise her title to compensation and buy her off. If she had befriended him at a fruitful crisis he would really, as a man of delicacy, and she knew what to think of that point, have to reckon with her.

At the hotel Dencombe's servant insisted on his going back to bed. The invalid had talked about catching a train and had begun with orders to pack; after which his humming nerves had yielded to a sense of sickness. He consented to see his physician, who immediately was sent for, but he wished it to be understood that his door was irrevocably closed to Doctor Hugh. He had his plan, which was so fine that he rejoiced in it after getting back to bed. Doctor Hugh, suddenly finding himself snubbed without mercy, would, in natural disgust and to the joy of Miss Vernham, renew his allegiance to the Countess. When his physician arrived Dencombe learned that he was feverish and that this was very wrong: he was to cultivate calmness and try, if possible, not to think. For the rest of the day he wooed stupidity; but there was an ache that kept him sentient, the probable sacrifice of his "extension," the limit of his course. His medical adviser was anything but pleased; his successive relapses were ominous. He charged this personage to put out a strong hand and take Doctor Hugh off his mind —it would contribute so much to his being quiet. The agitating name, in his room, was not mentioned again, but his security was a smothered fear, and it was not confirmed by the receipt, at ten o'clock that evening, of a telegram which his servant opened and read for him and to which, with an address in London, the signature of Miss Vernham was attached. "Beseech you to use all influence to make our friend join us here in the morning. Countess much the worse for dreadful journey, but everything may still be saved." The two ladies had gathered themselves up and had been capable in the afternoon of a spiteful revolution. They had started for the capital, and if the elder one, as Miss Vernham had announced, was very ill, she had wished to make it clear that she was proportionately reckless. Poor Dencombe, who was not reckless and who only desired that everything should indeed be "saved," sent this missive straight off to the young man's lodging and had on the morrow the pleasure of knowing that he had quitted Bournemouth by an early train.

Two days later he pressed in with a copy of a literary journal in his hand. He had returned because he was anxious and for the pleasure of flourishing the great review of "The Middle Years." Here at least was something adequate—it rose to the occasion; it was an acclamation, a reparation, a critical attempt to place the author in the niche he had fairly won. Dencombe accepted and submitted; he made neither objection nor inquiry, for old complications had returned and he had had two atrocious days. He was convinced not only that he should never again leave his bed, so that his young friend might pardonably remain, but that the demand he should make on the patience of beholders would be very moderate indeed. Doctor Hugh had been to town, and he tried to find in his eyes some confession that the Countess was pacified and his legacy clinched; but all he could see there was the light of his juvenile joy in two or three of the phrases of the newspaper. Dencombe couldn't read them, but when his visitor had insisted on repeating them more than once he was able to shake an unintoxicated head. "Ah, no; but they would have been true of what I *could* have done!"

"What people 'could have done' is mainly what they've in fact done," Doctor Hugh contended.

"Mainly, yes; but I've been an idiot!" said Dencombe.

Doctor Hugh did remain; the end was coming fast. Two days later Dencombe observed to him, by way of the feeblest of jokes, that there would now be no question whatever of a second chance. At this the young man stared; then he exclaimed: "Why, it has come to pass—it has come to pass! The second chance has been the public's—the chance to find the point of view, to pick up the pearl!"

"Oh, the pearl!" poor Dencombe uneasily sighed. A smile as cold as a winter sunset flickered on his drawn lips as he added: "The pearl is the unwritten—the pearl is the unalloyed, the *rest,* the lost!"

From that moment he was less and less present, heedless to all appearance of what went on around him. His disease was definitely mortal, of an action as relentless, after the short arrest that had enabled him to fall in with Doctor Hugh, as a leak in a great ship. Sinking steadily, though this visitor, a man of rare resources, now cordially approved by his physician, showed endless art in guarding him from pain, poor Dencombe kept no reckoning of favour or neglect, betrayed no symptom of regret or speculation. Yet toward the last he gave a sign of having noticed that for two days Doctor Hugh had not been in his room, a sign that consisted of his suddenly opening his eyes to ask of him if he had spent the interval with the Countess.

"The Countess is dead," said Doctor Hugh. "I knew that in a particular contingency she wouldn't resist. I went to her grave."

Dencombe's eyes opened wider. "She left you 'something handsome'?"

The young man gave a laugh almost too light for a chamber of woe. "Never a penny. She roundly cursed me."

"Cursed you?" Dencombe murmured.

"For giving her up. I gave her up for *you.* I had to choose," his companion explained.

"You chose to let a fortune go?"

"I chose to accept, whatever they might be, the consequences of my infatuation," smiled Doctor Hugh. Then, as a larger pleasantry: "A fortune be hanged! It's your own fault if I can't get your things out of my head."

The immediate tribute to his humour was a long, bewildered moan; after which, for many hours, many days, Dencombe lay motionless and absent. A response so absolute, such a glimpse of a definite result and such a sense of credit worked together in his mind and, producing a strange commotion, slowly altered and transfigured his despair. The sense of cold submersion left him—he seemed to float without an effort. The incident was extraordinary as evidence, and it shed an intenser light. At the last he signed to Doctor Hugh to listen, and, when he was down on his knees by the pillow, brought him very near.

"You've made me think it all a delusion."

"Not your glory, my dear friend," stammered the young man.

"Not my glory—what there is of it! It *is* glory—to have been tested, to have had our little quality and cast our little spell. The thing is to have made somebody care. You happen to be crazy, of course, but that doesn't affect the law."

"You're a great success!" said Doctor Hugh, putting into his young voice the ring of a marriage-bell.

Dencombe lay taking this in; then he gathered strength to speak once more. "A second chance—*that's* the delusion. There never was to be but one. We work in the dark—we do what we can—we give what we have. Our doubt is our passion and our passion is our task. The rest is the madness of art."

"If you've doubted, if you've despaired, you've always 'done' it," his visitor subtly argued.

"We've done something or other," Dencombe conceded.

"Something or other is everything. It's the feasible. It's *you!*"

"Comforter!" poor Dencombe ironically sighed.

"But it's true," insisted his friend.

"It's true. It's frustration that doesn't count."

"Frustration's only life," said Doctor Hugh.

"Yes, it's what passes." Poor Dencombe was barely audible, but he had marked with the words the virtual end of his first and only chance.

Anton Chekhov / 1860–1904

In the Cart

They drove out of the town at half past eight in the morning.

The paved road was dry, a splendid April sun was shedding warmth, but there was still snow in the ditches and in the woods. Winter, evil, dark, long, had ended so recently; spring had arrived suddenly; but neither the warmth nor the languid, transparent woods, warmed by the breath of spring, nor the black flocks flying in the fields over huge puddles that were like lakes, nor this marvelous, immeasurably deep sky, into which it seemed that one would plunge with such joy, offered anything new and interesting to Marya Vasilyevna, who was sitting in the cart. She had been teaching school for thirteen years, and in the course of all those years she had gone to the town for her salary countless times; and whether it was spring, as now, or a rainy autumn evening, or winter, it was all the same to her, and what she always, invariably, longed for was to reach her destination as soon as possible.

She felt as though she had been living in these parts for a long, long time, for a hundred years, and it seemed to her that she knew every stone, every tree on the road from the town to her school. Here was her past and her present, and she could imagine no other future than the school, the road to the town and back, and again the school and again the road.

She had lost the habit of thinking of the time before she became a schoolmistress and had almost forgotten all about it. She had once had a father and mother; they had lived in Moscow in a big apartment near the Red Gate, but all that remained in her memory of that part of her life was something vague and formless like a dream. Her father had died when she was ten years old, and her mother had died soon after. She had a brother, an officer; at first they used to write to each other, then her brother had stopped answering her letters, he had lost the habit. Of her former belongings, all that remained was a photograph of her mother, but the dampness in the school had faded it, and now nothing could be seen on it but the hair and the eyebrows.

When they had gone a couple of miles, old Semyon, who was driving, turned round and said:

"They have nabbed an official in the town. They have sent him away. They say that he and some Germans killed Alexeyev, the mayor, in Moscow."

"Who told you that?"

"They read it in the papers, in Ivan Ionov's teahouse."

And again there was a long silence. Marya Vasilyevna thought of her school, of the examinations that were coming soon, and of the girl and the four boys whom she was sending up for them. And just as she was thinking about the examinations she was overtaken by a landowner named Hanov in a carriage with four horses, the very man who had acted as examiner in her school the previous year. As he drew alongside he recognized her and bowed.

"Good morning," he said. "Are you driving home, madam?"

This Hanov, a man of about forty, with a worn face and a lifeless expression, was beginning to age noticeably, but was still handsome and attractive to women. He lived alone on his large estate, was not in the service, and it was said of him that he did nothing at home but pace from one end of the room to the other, whistling, or play chess with his old footman. It was said, too, that he drank heavily. And indeed, at the examination the previous year the very papers he had brought with him smelt of scent and wine. On that occasion everything he wore was brand-new, and Marya Vasilyevna had found him very attractive and, sitting next to him, had felt embarrassed. She was used to seeing cold, hardheaded examiners at the school, but this one did not remember a single prayer, did not know what questions to ask, was exceedingly polite and considerate, and gave only the highest marks.

"I am on my way to visit Bakvist," he continued, addressing Marya Vasilyevna, "but I wonder if he is at home."

They turned off the highway onto a dirt road, Hanov leading the way and Semyon following. The team of four horses kept to the road, slowly pulling the heavy carriage through the mud. Semyon changed his course continually, leaving the road now to drive over a hillock, now to skirt a meadow, often jumping down from the cart and helping the horse. Marya Vasilyevna kept thinking about the school, and wondering whether the arithmetic problem at the examination would be hard or easy. And she was annoyed with the Zemstvo office, where she had found no one the previous day. What negligence! For the past two years she had been asking them to discharge the janitor, who did nothing, was rude to her, and cuffed the boys, but no one paid any attention to her. It was hard to find the chairman at the office and when you did find him, he would say with tears in his eyes that he had no time; the inspector visited the school once in three years and had no understanding of anything connected with it, since he had formerly been employed in the Finance Department and had obtained the post of school inspector through pull; the School Board met very rarely and no one knew where; the Trustee was a half literate peasant, the owner of a tannery, stupid, coarse, and a bosom friend of the janitor's —and heaven knows to whom she could turn with complaints and inquiries.

"He is really handsome," she thought, glancing at Hanov.

Meanwhile the road was growing worse and worse. They drove into the woods. Here there was no turning off the road, the ruts were deep, and water flowed and gurgled in them. Twigs struck them stingingly in the face.

"How's the road?" asked Hanov, and laughed.

The schoolmistress looked at him and could not understand why this odd fellow lived here. What could his money, his interesting appearance, his refinement get him in this Godforsaken place, with its mud, its boredom? Life granted him no privileges, and here, like

Semyon, he was jogging slowly along over an abominable road and suffering the same discomforts. Why live here, when one had a chance to live in Petersburg or abroad? And it seemed as though it would be a simple matter for a rich man like him to turn this bad road into a good one so as to avoid having to endure this misery and seeing the despair written on the faces of his coachman and Semyon? But he merely laughed, and apparently it was all the same to him, and he asked nothing better of life. He was kind, gentle, naive; he had no grasp of this coarse life, he did not know it, any more than he had known the prayers at the examination. He presented nothing to the schools but globes, and sincerely regarded himself as a useful person and a prominent worker in the field of popular education. And who had need of his globes here?

"Hold on, Vasilyevna!" said Semyon.

The cart lurched violently and was about to turn over; something heavy fell on Marya Vasilyevna's feet—it was her purchases. There was a steep climb uphill over a clayey road; noisy rivulets were flowing in winding ditches; the water had gullied the road; and how could one drive here! The horses breathed heavily. Hanov got out of the carriage and walked at the edge of the road in his long coat. He was hot.

"How's the road?" he repeated, and laughed. "This is the way to smash your carriage."

"But who tells you to go driving in such weather?" asked Semyon in a surly voice. "You ought to stay home."

"I'm bored at home, grandfather. I don't like staying home."

Next to old Semyon he seemed well-built and vigorous, but there was something barely perceptible in his gait which betrayed him as a weak creature, already blighted, approaching its end. And suddenly it seemed as though there were a whiff of liquor in the woods. Marya Vasilyevna felt frightened and was filled with pity for this man who was going to pieces without rhyme or reason, and it occurred to her that if she were his wife or his sister she would devote her whole life to his rescue. His wife! Life was so ordered that here he was living in his great house alone, while she was living in a Godforsaken village alone, and yet for some reason the mere thought that he and she might meet on an equal footing and become intimate seemed impossible, absurd. Fundamentally, life was so arranged and human relations were complicated so utterly beyond all understanding that when you thought about it you were terrified and your heart sank.

"And you can't understand," she thought, "why God gives good looks, friendliness, charming, melancholy eyes to weak, unhappy, useless people—why they are so attractive."

"Here we must turn off to the right," said Hanov, getting into his carriage. "Good-by! All good wishes!"

And again she thought of her pupils, of the examination, of the janitor, of the School Board; and when the wind brought her the sound of the receding carriage these thoughts mingled with others. She wanted to think of beautiful eyes, of love, of the happiness that would never be. . . .

His wife? It is cold in the morning, there is no one to light the stove, the janitor has gone off somewhere; the children come in as soon as it is light, bringing in snow and mud and making a noise; it is all so uncomfortable, so unpleasant. Her quarters consist of one little room and a kitchen close by. Every day when school is over she has a headache and after dinner she has heartburn. She has to collect money from the children for firewood and to pay the janitor, and to turn it over to the Trustee, and then to implore him—that overfed, insolent peasant—for God's sake to send her firewood. And at night she dreams of examinations, peasants, snowdrifts. And this life has aged and coarsened her, making her homely, angular, and clumsy, as though they had poured lead into her. She is afraid of everything, and in the presence of a member of the Zemstvo Board or of the Trustee, she gets up and does not dare sit down again. And she uses obsequious expressions when she mentions any one of them. And no one likes her, and life is passing drearily, without warmth, without friendly sympathy, without interesting acquaintances. In her position how terrible it would be if she were to fall in love!

"Hold on, Vasilyevna!"

Another steep climb.

She had begun to teach school from necessity, without feeling called to it; and she had never thought of a call, of the need for enlightenment; and it always seemed to her that what was most important in her work was not the children, not enlightenment, but the examinations. And when did she have time to think of a call, of enlightenment? Teachers, impecunious physicians, doctors' assistants, for all their terribly hard work, do not even have the comfort of thinking that they are serving an ideal or the people, because their heads are always filled with thoughts of their daily bread, of firewood, of bad roads, of sickness. It is a hard, humdrum existence, and only stolid cart horses like Marya Vasilyevna can bear it a long time; lively, alert, impressionable people who talk about their calling and about serving the ideal are soon weary of it and give up the work.

Semyon kept on picking out the driest and shortest way, traveling now across a meadow, now behind the cottages, but in one place the peasants would not let them pass and in another the land belonged to the priest and so they could not cross it, in yet another Ivan Ionov had bought a plot from the landowner and had dug a ditch round it. They kept turning back.

They reached Nizhneye Gorodishche. Near the teahouse, on the dung-strewn, snowy ground, there stood wagons loaded with great bottles of oil of vitriol. There were a great many people in the teahouse, all drivers, and it smelled of vodka, tobacco, and sheepskins. The place was noisy with loud talk and the banging of the door which was provided with a pulley. In the shop next door someone was playing an accordion steadily. Marya Vasilyevna was sitting down, having tea, while at the next table some peasants were drinking vodka and beer, sweaty with the tea they had had and the bad air.

"Hey, Kuzma!" people kept shouting confusedly. "What's doing?" "The Lord bless us!" "Ivan Dementyich, that I can do for you!" "See here, friend!"

A little pockmarked peasant with a black beard, who was quite drunk, was suddenly taken aback by something and began using foul language.

"What are you cursing about, you there?" Semyon, who was sitting some way off, remarked angrily. "Don't you see the young lady?"

"The young lady!" someone jeered in another corner.

"The swine!"

"I didn't mean nothing—" The little peasant was embarrassed. "Excuse me. I pays my money and the young lady pays hers. How-de-do, ma'am?"

"How do you do?" answered the schoolmistress.

"And I thank you kindly."

Marya Vasilyevna drank her tea with pleasure, and she, too, began turning red like the peasants, and again she fell to thinking about firewood, about the janitor. . . .

"Wait, brother," came from the next table. "It's the school-ma'am from Vyazovye. I know; she's a good sort."

"She's all right!"

The door was banging continually, some coming in, others going out. Marya Vasilyevna went on sitting there, thinking of the same things all the time, while the accordion went on playing and playing behind the wall. There had been patches of sunlight on the floor, they shifted to the counter, then to the wall, and finally disappeared altogether; this meant that it was past midday. The peasants at the next table were getting ready to leave. The little peasant went up to Marya Vasilyevna somewhat unsteadily and shook hands with her; following his example, the others shook hands with her at parting, and filed out singly, and the door squeaked and slammed nine times.

"Vasilyevna, get ready," Semyon called to her.

They drove off. And again they went at a walking pace.

"A little while back they were building a school here at this Nizhneye Gorodishche," said Semyon, turning round. "There were wicked doings then!"

"Why, what?"

"They say the chairman pocketed a cool thousand, and the Trustee another thousand, and the teacher five hundred."

"The whole school only cost a thousand. It's wrong to slander people, grandfather. That's all nonsense."

"I don't know. I only repeat what folks say."

But it was clear that Semyon did not believe the schoolmistress. The peasants did not believe her. They always thought she received too large a salary, twenty-one rubles a month (five would have been enough), and that she kept for herself the greater part of the money that she received for firewood and for the janitor's wages. The Trustee thought as the peasants did, and he himself made something on the firewood and received a salary from the peasants for acting as Trustee —without the knowledge of the authorities.

The woods, thank God, were behind them, and now it would be clear, level ground all the way to Vyazovye, and they had not far to go now. All they had to do was to cross the river and then the railway line, and then they would be at Vyazovye.

"Where are you going?" Marya Vasilyevna asked Semyon. "Take the road to the right across the bridge."

"Why, we can go this way just as well, it's not so deep."

"Mind you don't drown the horse."

"What?"

"Look, Hanov is driving to the bridge, too," said Marya Vasilyevna, seeing the four-horse team far away to the right. "I think it's he."

"It's him all right. So he didn't find Bakvist in. What a blockhead he is. Lord have mercy on us! He's driving over there, and what for? It's all of two miles nearer this way."

They reached the river. In summer it was a shallow stream, easily forded and usually dried up by August, but now, after the spring floods, it was a river forty feet wide, rapid, muddy, and cold; on the bank, and right up to the water, there were fresh wheel tracks, so it had been crossed there.

"Giddap!" shouted Semyon angrily and anxiously, tugging violently at the reins and flapping his elbows as a bird does its wings. "Giddap!"

The horse went into the water up to its belly and stopped, but at once went on again, straining its muscles, and Marya Vasilyevna felt a sharp chill in her feet.

"Giddap!" she shouted, too, standing up. "Giddap!"

They got to the bank.

"Nice mess, Lord have mercy on us!" muttered Semyon, setting the harness straight. "It's an affliction, this Zemstvo."

Her shoes and rubbers were full of water, the lower edge of her dress and of her coat and one sleeve were wet and dripping; the sugar and flour had got wet, and that was the worst of it, and Marya Vasilyevna only struck her hands together in despair and said:

"Oh, Semyon, Semyon! What a fellow you are, really!"

The barrier was down at the railway crossing. An express was coming from the station. Marya Vasilyevna stood at the crossing waiting for the train to pass, and shivering all over with cold. Vyazovye was in sight now, and the school with the green roof, and the church with its blazing crosses that reflected the setting sun; and the station windows were aflame, too, and a pink smoke rose from the engine. . . . And it seemed to her that everything was shivering with cold.

Here was the train; the windows, like the crosses on the church, reflected the blazing light; it hurt her eyes to look at them. On the platform of one of the first-class carriages a lady was standing, and Marya Vasilyevna glanced at her as she flashed by. Her mother! What a resemblance! Her mother had had just such luxuriant hair, just such a forehead and that way of holding her head. And with amazing distinctness, for the first time in those thirteen years, she imagined vividly her mother, her father, her brother, their apartment in Moscow, the aquarium with the little fishes, everything down to the smallest detail; she suddenly heard the piano playing, her father's voice; she felt as then, young, good-looking, well-dressed, in a bright warm room among her own people. A feeling of joy and happiness suddenly overwhelmed her, she pressed her hands to her temples in ecstasy, and called softly, imploringly:

"Mama!"

And she began to cry, she did not know why. Just at that moment Hanov drove up with his team of four horses, and seeing him she imagined such happiness as had never been, and smiled and nodded to him as an equal and an intimate, and it seemed to her that the sky, the windows, the trees, were glowing with her happiness, her triumph. No, her father and mother had never died, she had never been a schoolmistress, that had been a long, strange, oppressive dream, and now she had awakened. . . .

"Vasilyevna, get in!"

And suddenly it all vanished. The barrier was slowly rising. Marya

Vasilyevna, shivering and numb with cold, got into the cart. The carriage with the four horses crossed the railway track, Semyon followed. The guard at the crossing took off his cap.

"And this is Vyazovye. Here we are."

Translated by Avrahm Yarmolinsky

Miguel de Unamuno / 1864–1936

Saint Manuel Bueno,[1] *Martyr*

If in this life only we have hope in Christ, we are of all men most miserable.

SAINT PAUL, I Corinthians 15:19

Now that the bishop of the diocese of Renada, to which my dear village of Valverde de Lucerna belongs, is said to be working for the beatification of our Don Manuel, or rather Saint Manuel Bueno, who was parish priest in this place, I wish to leave on record by way of a confession, to what end God alone knows, for I don't, all that I know and remember about that matriarchal figure, who filled all the innermost life of my soul, and was my true spiritual father, the father of my spirit, of Angela Carballino's spirit.

I hardly knew my other father, the temporal father of my own flesh and blood, as he died when I was a little girl. I know that he had arrived, a stranger, in our Valverde de Lucerna, and that he settled down here on marrying my mother. He brought with him a few books, *Don Quixote,* classical plays, some novels, stories, *Bertoldo,*[2] all mixed up, and, as a child, I fed on dreams from those

---

[1] The Good.

[2] *Bertoldo, Bertoldino and Cacasenno,* an early-eighteenth-century Italian poem in twenty cantos, each by a different author, based on two comic prose romances set in an imaginary Italian court by Guilio Cesare Croce (1550–1609) and a third, a sequel by Adriano Banchieri (1567–1634). A Spanish translation was published in Madrid in 1745.

books, almost the only ones there were in the whole village. My good mother hardly ever told me of anything my father had said or done. The deeds and words of Don Manuel, whom she, like all the village, adored and with whom she was in love (of course most chastely), had erased the memory of those of her husband, whom she commended fervently to God each day when she told her beads.

I remember our Don Manuel as if it were yesterday, when I was a child of ten, before I was taken to the Convent School in the cathedral city of Renada. Our saint would then be about thirty-seven. He was tall, thin, erect; he carried his head as our Vulture's Crag carries its crest, and there was in his eyes all the blue depth of our lake. All eyes would be drawn to him and, with them, all hearts, and when he looked at us, he seemed to see through our flesh as through a glass and look into our hearts. We all loved him, but the children most of all. What things he said to us! They were things, not words. The village began to sense the saintliness in him; it felt itself filled and intoxicated with its aura.

It was then that my brother Lázaro, who was in America and regularly sent us money, with which we lived a decent, comfortable life, made my mother send me to the Convent School, to complete my education outside the village. He did this although he, Lázaro, did not care for nuns. "But as in your district," he wrote to us, "there are not up to now, that I know of, any secular progressive schools, and least of all for girls, we must make do with what there is. The important thing is that Angelita should be refined and not go on living among those rough village girls." And so I entered the school, thinking at first of becoming a teacher, but afterwards I could not stomach pedagogy.

At the school I got to know girls of the town and became very friendly with some of them. But I continued to take an interest in the things and people in our village, from which I received frequent news and occasionally a visitor. The fame of our parish priest reached even the school, and they began to talk about him in the episcopal city. The nuns did nothing but question me about him.

From a very early age, for some reason or other, I cherished feelings of curiosity, worry and uneasiness, due, in part at least, to that jumble of books of my father's. All this thrived at school, particularly in my dealings with one fellow pupil who grew inordinately fond of me. Sometimes she proposed that we should both enter the same convent at the same time, swearing perpetual sisterhood, and even signing the oath in our blood; and at other times she would talk to me, with her eyes half-shut, of lovers and romantic marriages. By the way, I have never again heard of her or what became of her. However, whenever Don Manuel was mentioned, or whenever my mother told me something about him in her letters (and that was in nearly all of them) and I read them to my friend, she would exclaim as if in raptures: "You lucky thing, being able to live near a saint like that, a live saint of flesh and blood, and being able to kiss his hand! When you go back to your village write to me often, and tell me about him."

I spent about five years at school, years which are now lost like an early-morning dream in the distance of memory, and at fifteen I returned to my Valverde de Lucerna. By now it consisted entirely of Don Manuel; Don Manuel, with the lake and the mountain. I arrived eager to know him, to submit myself to his guidance, for him to mark out the course of my life.

It was said that he had entered the Seminary to become a priest, in order to care for the children of a sister of his recently widowed, and to act as a father to them. At the Seminary he had distinguished himself by the keenness of his mind and by his gifts. It was said, moreover, that he had refused offers of a brilliant ecclesiastical career because he wished to belong only to his Valverde de Lucerna, to his village lying like a brooch between the lake and the mountain that is reflected in it.

How he loved his flock! His life consisted of reconciling married couples in discord, of making unruly children submit to their parents, or the parents to their children, and especially of comforting the embittered and the wearied, and helping everyone to make a happy death.

I remember, among other things, when Tía Rabona's unfortunate daughter came back from the city. She had gone astray and returned, unmarried and an outcast, bringing a little son with her. Don Manuel did not rest until he had made a former sweetheart, Perote, marry her and recognise the baby as his, saying:

"Come! Give a father to this poor child who has none except in Heaven."

"But, Don Manuel, I am not to blame."

"Who knows, my son, who knows! . . . And besides, it isn't a question of blame."

Today poor Perote, an invalid, paralysed, has as the support and comfort of his life that son whom he, infected with Don Manuel's saintliness, recognised as his own, although he was not.

. . .

On Midsummer's Eve, the shortest night in the year, there used to be a gathering at the lake, and there still is, of all the poor wretched women, and not a few wretched men, who believe themselves possessed of a devil, and who it seems are nothing but hysterics and sometimes epileptics. Don Manuel undertook the task of acting as a lake, a healing spring, and of trying to relieve and, if possible, cure them. Such was the effect of his presence, of his glance, and above all such was the most gentle authority of his words and especially of his voice—what a miracle of a voice!—that he achieved surprising cures. With this, his fame grew and attracted to the lake and to him all the sick from round about. Once a mother arrived asking him to work a miracle in her son, but to this he replied smiling sadly:

"I haven't my lord bishop's licence to work miracles."

He was particularly concerned that everyone should be clean. If anyone had a tear in his clothing, he would say to him: "Go and see the sacristan, and let him mend that." The sacristan was a tailor. And when, on the first day in the year, people went to greet him, for it was his saint's day—his patron saint being Our Lord Jesus Himself—Don Manuel wished everyone to appear in a new shirt, and to those that were without he himself presented one.

He showed the same affection for all, and if he gave preference to any it was to the most unfortunate and to those who appeared most refractory. As there was in the village a poor idiot from birth, daft Blasillo, it was he whom the priest treated with most kindness and to whom he even succeeded in teaching things which it seemed a miracle for him to have been able to learn. What happened was that the small glimmer of intelligence which still remained in the idiot was kindled as he imitated Don Manuel like a poor monkey.

The wonderful thing about him was his voice, a divine voice, that made people weep. When, officiating at High or Solemn Mass, he chanted the preface, the church trembled and all who heard him felt moved within themselves. His chant, issuing from the temple, came to rest upon the lake and at the foot of the mountain. When in his Good Friday sermon he cried the words: "My God, my God! Why hast Thou forsaken Me?" a deep shudder passed over the whole village just as it passes over the waters of the lake on days when the north wind whips it. It was as if they heard Our Lord Jesus Christ Himself, as if the voice broke forth from that old crucifix at whose feet so many generations of mothers had laid their grief. So that once, when his, Don Manuel's, mother heard him, she could not contain herself, and, from the body of the church where she was sitting, cried out, "My son!" And there was an outburst of weeping all round. It seemed as though the mother's cry had come from the parted lips of that Mater Dolo-rosa[3]—her heart pierced with seven swords—which stood in one of the chapels in the church. Then daft Blasillo went about the lanes repeating in a pathetic tone and like an echo, "My God, my God! Why hast Thou forsaken Me?" and in such a way that, when people heard him, the tears started to their eyes, to the idiot's great joy at his successful imitation.

His effect on people was such that no one dared tell a lie in front of him, and everyone, without having to go to the confessional, confessed themselves to him. It came to the point that, when once a repulsive crime took place in a nearby village, the judge, a senseless man who little knew Don Manuel, called him and said:

"Let us see if you, Don Manuel, can manage to make this bandit declare the truth."

"So that you can then punish him for it?" replied the holy man. "No, judge, no. I don't draw out of anyone a truth that may perhaps lead him to his death. There between him and God . . . Human justice does not concern me. 'Judge not that ye be not judged,' said Our Lord."

"But I, father . . ."

"I understand. You, judge, render unto Caesar the things that are Caesar's, for I shall render unto God the things that are God's."

And as he left, gazing at the suspect, he said to him:

"Make sure that God has forgiven you, for that is the only thing that matters."

In the village everyone used to attend Mass, even though it were only to hear him and see him at the altar, where he seemed to become transfigured, his face lighting up. There was a holy practice which he introduced into the people's worship and it was that, gathering the whole village together in the church, men and women, old people and children, about a thousand persons, we used to recite the Creed in unison, all together: "I believe in one God the Father Almighty, Maker of Heaven and Earth . . ." and so on. It was not a chorus but a single voice, a simple and united voice, all voices fused into one and forming a sort of mountain, whose summit, lost at times in the clouds, was Don Manuel. And on reaching the words: "I believe in the resurrection of the body and the life everlasting," Don Manuel's voice would be drowned, as in a lake, in the voice of the whole village, and it was because he fell silent. I used to hear the bells of the town which is said here to lie submerged on the bed of the lake—these, it is said,

[3] The sorrowing mother of Christ, as represented in Roman Catholic art.

can also be heard on Midsummer's Eve—and they were the bells of the town submerged in the spiritual lake of our village; I used to hear the voice of our dead who in us came to life again in the communion of saints. Afterwards, when I came to know our saint's secret, I realised that it was as if a caravan were on the march across the desert, and their leader having collapsed as they approached their journey's end, his men took him on their shoulders to carry his lifeless body into the land of promise.

Most people were reluctant to die except clinging to his hand as to an anchor.

Never in his sermons did he begin to declaim against the impious, masons, liberals or heretics. Why, if there were none in the village? Still less did he speak against the bad press. On the other hand, one of the most frequent themes for his sermons was against an evil tongue. For he made excuses for everything and everyone. He would not believe that anyone had evil intentions.

"Envy," he liked to repeat, "is fostered by those who persist in believing themselves envied, and most persecutions are the effect of persecution mania, rather than of the mania for persecuting."

"But just see, Don Manuel, what he meant . . ."

And he would reply:

"We must not mind so much what people mean to say as what they say without meaning to . . ."

His life was active and not contemplative, and he avoided as far as possible not having anything to do. When he heard the saying that idleness is the mother of all vices, he replied: "And of the worst of all, which is idle thinking." As I once asked him what that meant, he answered me: "Idle thinking is thinking to avoid doing anything, or thinking too much about what has been done and not about what there is to do. It's no use crying over spilt milk: go on to something else, for there is nothing worse than remorse without remedy." Action! Action! I well understood from then on that Don Manuel fled from idle and solitary thinking, that some thought haunted him.

So it was that he was always busy, and not infrequently busy inventing occupations. He wrote very little for himself, so that he has left us scarcely any writings or notes; but, on the other hand, he acted as chronicler for the others, and for the mothers especially he drafted the letters to their absent sons.

He also did manual work, helping with his own hands in certain tasks in the village. At harvest-time he went to the threshing-floor to thresh and winnow, and he admonished them or amused them the while. Sometimes, when someone was ill, he would replace him at his work. One day in the bitterest winter weather he met a boy, perished with cold, whose father was sending him to fetch a cow from a long way off in the mountains.

"Look," he said to the child, "go back home, and tell your father that I am going to do the errand."

When he came back with the cow he met the father, all confusion, who was going to meet him. In winter he chopped firewood for the poor. When that magnificent walnut tree withered—"a matriarchal walnut tree" he called it—in whose shade he had played as a child and with whose nuts he had for so many years regaled himself, he asked for the trunk and took it home. After cutting six boards out of it, which he kept at the foot of his bed, he made the rest into firewood to warm the poor. He also used to make the balls for the lads to play with and not a few toys for the children.

He used to accompany the doctor on his visits, and emphasised the latter's prescriptions. He was particularly interested in pregnancies and in the rearing of children. The death of children moved him deeply.

"A stillborn child or a newborn child that dies and a suicide," he once said to me, "are for me among the most terrible mysteries: a child on the cross!"

When once, as someone had taken his own life, the suicide's father, a stranger, asked him if he would bury him in consecrated ground, he replied:

"Of course, for at the last moment, in the second of agony, he repented without any doubt."

He also often went to the school to help the master, to teach with him, and not only the catechism. He was fleeing from idleness and solitude. So that in order to be with the people, and above all with the young people and children, he used to go to the dances. And more than once he began to play the drum there for the lads and lasses to dance, and that which in another would have seemed a grotesque profanation of the priesthood, in him took on a sacred character and became something of a religious rite. The Angelus rang, he left the drum and the drumstick, bared his head and everyone with him, and prayed: "The Angel of the Lord declared unto Mary: Hail Mary . . ." And then: "And now to rest for tomorrow."

"The first thing," he would say, "is that the people should be content, that everyone should be content with life. Contentment with life is the first thing of all. No one ought to wish to die until God wills it."

"Well, I do," a woman recently widowed once said to him. "I want to follow my husband . . ."

"And why?" he replied. "Stay here to commend his soul to God."

At a wedding he once said: "Ah, if only I could change all the water in our lake into wine, into a good wine which always cheered without ever making one drunk however much one took . . . or which at least made one cheerfully drunk!"

Once there passed through the village a band of poor strolling players. The leader of them, who arrived with his wife seriously ill and pregnant, and with three sons who assisted him, took the part of a clown. While he, in the village square, was making the children and even the grown-ups laugh, she, suddenly feeling seriously indisposed, had to withdraw and withdrew accompanied by a look of anguish from the clown and a burst of laughter from the children. And escorted by Don Manuel, who later, in a corner of the stable at the inn, helped her to make a happy death. When, the performance over, the village and the clown learnt of the tragedy, they all went to the inn, and the poor man, saying in a broken voice, "They are right, father, when they say you are a real saint," approached him wanting to take his hand and kiss it. But Don Manuel came forward and taking the clown's hand declared before everyone:

"You are the saint, honest clown; I saw you perform and realised that you do it not only to give your children bread but also to bring joy to other people's children. I tell you that your wife, the mother of your sons, whom I have sped on her way to God while you worked and gave pleasure, rests in the Lord, and that you will go to join her, so that the angels whom you make laugh with pleasure in heaven may repay you by laughing."

Everyone, children and grown-ups, wept, and wept as much for grief as for a mysterious contentment in which the grief was quenched. Later, remembering that solemn moment, I realised that Don Manuel's imperturbable joy was the temporal and earthly form of an infinite and eternal sadness which, with heroic saintliness, he concealed from the eyes and ears of others.

With that constant activity of his, with that habit of joining in everyone's tasks and pastimes, he seemed to wish to escape from himself, to wish to escape from his solitude. "I fear solitude," he would repeat. But, even so, from time to time he went alone, along the shore of the lake, to the ruins of that old abbey where still seem to rest the souls of the pious Cistercians whom History has buried in oblivion. There is the cell of the so-called Father Captain; and it is said that on its walls there still remain marks of the drops of blood with which he splashed them when scourging himself. What would our Don Manuel think there? What I do remember is that when once, talking about the abbey, I asked him how it was that it had not occurred to him to enter a monastery, he replied:

"It is not particularly because I have, as I do, my widowed sister and my nephews and nieces to support, for God helps the poor, but because I was not born to be a hermit, an anchorite; the solitude would kill my soul, and as for a monastery, my monastery is Valverde de Lucerna. I must not live alone; I must not die alone. I must live for my people; die for my people. How am I going to save my soul if I do not save that of my people?"

"But there have been saints who were hermits, solitaires . . . ," I said to him.

"Yes, to them the Lord gave the grace of solitude which has been denied me, and I must be resigned. I cannot lose my people to save my soul. God has made me thus. I could not bear the temptations in the wilderness. I could not bear the cross of birth alone."

With these reminiscences, on which my faith lives, I have tried to portray Don Manuel as he was when I, a girl of about sixteen, returned from the Convent School in Renada to our monastery of Valverde de Lucerna. I returned to sit at the feet of its abbot.

"Hello, Simona's daughter!" he said, as soon as he saw me, "and you're quite a young woman already, knowing French, and how to embroider and play the piano and goodness knows what else! Now we must prepare you to give us another family. And your brother Lázaro, when is he coming back? He is still in the New World, isn't he?"

"Yes, sir, he is still in America . . ."

"The New World! And we in the Old. Well then, when you write to him, tell him from me, from the priest, that I want to know when he is coming back from the New World to this old one, bringing the news from over there. And tell him that he will find the lake and the mountain as he left them."

When I went to confess myself to him, I was so confused that I did not succeed in uttering a word. I stammered through the *Confiteor,* almost sobbing; and he, who noticed it, said to me:

"But what is the matter, little lamb? What or whom are you afraid of? Because you are not trembling now beneath the weight of your sins nor for fear of God; you are trembling at me, aren't you?"

I began to cry.

"But what have they told you about me? What tales are these?

Perhaps your mother . . . ? Come, come, calm yourself and imagine you are talking to your brother . . ."

I took heart and began to confide to him my worries, my doubts, my sorrows.

"Bah, bah, bah! And where have you read that, Miss Know-all? All that is literature. Don't give yourself up to it too much, not even to St. Teresa.[4] And if you want to amuse yourself, read the *Bertoldo,* which your father used to read."

I came away from my first confession to the holy man deeply comforted. And my first fear, that fear rather than respect, with which I approached him, changed to a deep pity. I was then a young girl, almost a child; but I was beginning to be a woman, I felt deep within me the sap of motherhood, and finding myself in the confessional near the holy man, I sensed something like a silent confession in the submissive murmur of his voice and remembered how, on his crying out in the church the words of Jesus Christ: "My God, my God, why hast Thou forsaken Me?", his, Don Manuel's, mother replied from the nave: "My son!", and I heard this cry which rent the stillness of the church. And I again confessed myself to him to comfort him.

Once in the confessional when I expressed one of those doubts, he answered:

"As for that, you know that piece in the Catechism: 'Do not ask me that, for I am ignorant; Holy Mother Church has doctors who will know how to answer you.' "

"But you are the doctor here, Don Manuel."

"I, I a doctor? A doctor, I? Not by any means! I, little doctor, am nothing more than a poor village priest. And those questions, do you know who insinuates them to you, who directs them to you? Well . . . the Devil!"

And then, becoming bolder, I came out point blank with:

"And if he directed them to you, Don Manuel?"

"To whom? To me? The Devil? We don't know each other, child. We don't know each other."

"And if he did direct them to you?"

"I shouldn't take any notice of him. And that's that, eh? Let us hurry, because some really sick people are waiting for me."

I withdrew, thinking, I don't know why, that our Don Manuel, so famous a healer of those possessed by the Devil, did not believe in the Devil. On my way home I met with daft Blasillo, who happened to be prowling around the church, and who on seeing me, so as to

[4] St. Teresa of Ávila (1515-82), famous mystic and author of meditative works.

entertain me with his talents, repeated—and in such a way!—: "My God, my God, why hast Thou forsaken Me?" I arrived home most distressed and locked myself in my room to cry, until my mother came.

"With all these confessions, Angelita, it looks to me as though you are going to become a nun."

"There's no fear of that, mother," I answered her, "for I have plenty to do here, in the village, which is my convent."

"Until you get married."

"I am not thinking of that," I replied.

And when I met Don Manuel again, I asked him, looking him straight in the eye:

"Is there a hell, Don Manuel?"

And he, without flinching, replied:

"For you, child? No."

"For others, is there one?"

"What does it matter to you, if you haven't to go there?"

"It matters to me because of the others. Is there one?"

"Believe in heaven, in the heaven which we see. Look at it." And he pointed it out to me above the mountain and below, reflected in the lake.

"But we must believe in hell, as in heaven," I replied.

"Yes, we must believe all that our Holy Mother, the Roman Catholic Apostolic Church, believes and teaches. And that is enough!"

I read I know not what deep sadness in his eyes, that were blue like the waters of the lake.

Those years passed like a dream. Don Manuel's image went on growing in me without my realising it, as he was such an everyday man, as much a part of every day as the bread we daily ask for in the Our Father. I helped him when I could in his tasks, I visited his sick, our sick, the girls at the school, I mended the church vestments, I acted as his deaconess, as he himself called me. Invited by a school friend, I went to the city for a few days, and I had to come back, as in the city I was choking, I was missing something, I was thirsting for the sight of the waters of the lake, hungering for the sight of the mountain crags. I missed, above all, my Don Manuel, and I felt as if his absence called me, as if he were in danger away from me, as if he needed me. I began to feel a sort of maternal affection for my spiritual father; I wanted to relieve him of the weight of the cross of birth.

.   .   .

So I reached the age of twenty-four, which is when my brother Lázaro returned from America, with a tidy fortune saved up. He arrived here, in Valverde de Lucerna, with the idea of taking our mother and me to live in the city, perhaps in Madrid.

"In the village," he said, "people become stupid, brutish and poor." And he added:

"Civilisation is the opposite of ruralisation; village ways, no! I didn't make you go to school for you to rot here afterwards, among these rough yokels."

I said nothing, still prepared to resist emigration; but our mother, who was by now past sixty, opposed it from the outset. "At my age, to have a change of water!" she said at first; but afterwards she let it be clearly known that she could not live out of sight of her lake, her mountain, and especially her Don Manuel.

"You are like cats, the way you become attached to the house!" my brother would repeat.

When he realised the full extent of the hold that the evangelic holy man had upon all the village and in particular upon my mother and me, he was roused to anger against him. It seemed to him an example of the dark theocracy in which he supposed Spain to be sunk. He began to babble unceasingly all the old anti-clerical commonplaces and even anti-religious and progressive ones which he had brought in a new form from the New World.

"In this Spain full of henpecked husbands," he would say, "the priests manage the women and the women the men . . . and then the countryside! The countryside! This feudal countryside . . ."

For him feudal was a dreadful term; feudal and medieval were the two epithets which he used liberally when he wished to condemn anything.

He was disconcerted by the negative effect which his diatribes had on us and the almost negative effect which they had on the village, where he was listened to with respectful indifference. "There's nobody can move these yokels." But as he was good, through being intelligent, he soon realised what kind of hold Don Manuel had upon the village, he soon found out about the work of his village priest.

"No, he is not like the others," he said, "he is a saint!"

"But do you know what the other priests are like?" I said to him, and he replied:

"I can imagine it."

But even so he neither went into the church nor stopped making a show of his incredulity everywhere, although he always tried to leave Don Manuel out of it. And by now in the village, somehow or other, people were beginning to anticipate a sort of duel between my brother Lázaro and Don Manuel, or rather they expected the conversion of the former by the latter. No one doubted that in the end the parish priest would carry him off to his parish church. Lázaro, for his part, burned with longing—so he told me later—to go and hear Don Manuel, to see him and hear him in church, to approach him and converse with him, to know the secret of his spiritual hold upon souls. He let himself be pressed, until at last, out of curiosity—he said —he went to hear him.

"Yes, this is quite another thing," he said to me after he had heard him; "he is not like the others, but he can't take me in; he is too intelligent to believe all that he has to teach."

"But do you believe him to be a hypocrite?" I said.

"A hypocrite . . . no! But it is the profession by which he must live."

As for me, my brother insisted that I should read books that he brought and others that he urged me to buy.

"So your brother Lázaro," Don Manuel said to me, "insists on your reading? Then read, my child, read and please him that way. I know that you must only read good things; read, even if it is novels. The stories they call true are not better. It is better that you should read than that you should feed on the gossip and tattle of the village. But read above all devotional books which make you content with life, peacefully and silently content."

Was he content?

About then our mother fell mortally ill and died, and in her last days her repeated request was that Don Manuel should convert Lázaro, whom she hoped to see again one day in heaven, in a corner among the stars whence one could see the lake and the mountain of Valverde de Lucerna. She was going now, to see God.

"You are not going," Don Manuel said to her, "you are staying. Your body here, in this earth, and your soul here too in this house, seeing and hearing your children although they cannot see or hear you."

"But I, father," she said, "am going to God."

"God, my daughter, is here as He is everywhere, and you will see Him from here. And all of us in Him, and Him in us."

"May God reward you," I said to him.

"The contentment in which your mother dies," he said to me, "will be her eternal life."

And turning to my brother Lázaro:

"Her heaven is to go on seeing you, and now is when you must save her. Tell her you will pray for her."

"But . . ."

"But? Tell her you will pray for her, to whom you owe your life, and I know that, once you promise her that, you will pray, and I know that as soon as you pray . . ."

My brother, his eyes brimming with tears, drawing near our dying mother, solemnly promised to pray for her.

"And I in heaven for you, for all of you," answered my mother, and kissing the crucifix and fixing her eyes on Don Manuel's, she gave up her soul to God.

"Into Thy hands I commend my spirit!" prayed the holy man.

My brother and I were left alone in the house. What happened at our mother's death put Lázaro in contact with Don Manuel, who seemed to neglect his other patients, his other needy folk, to attend to my brother. They went for walks in the evenings, on the lake-shore, or towards the ivy-covered ruins of the old Cistercian abbey.

"He is a wonderful man," Lázaro said to me. "You know they say that at the bottom of this lake there is a submerged town and that on Midsummer's Eve, at twelve o'clock, you can hear its church bells ringing."

"Yes," I answered, "a feudal and medieval town."

"And I believe," he added, "that at the bottom of our Don Manuel's soul there is also a town, submerged, drowned, and that sometimes we can hear the ringing of its bells."

"Yes," I said, "that town sunk in Don Manuel's soul—and why not in yours too?—is the cemetery of the souls of our ancestors, the ancestors of our Valverde de Lucerna . . . feudal and medieval!"

My brother ended by always going to Mass, to hear Don Manuel, and when it was said that he would do his duty by the parish, that he would take communion when the others did, an intimate feeling of rejoicing ran through the whole village, which believed it had recovered him. But it was such a rejoicing, so clean, that Lázaro felt neither defeated nor belittled.

The day of his communion arrived, before the whole village, with the whole village. When my brother's turn came, I could see that Don Manuel, as white as the January snow upon the mountain and trembling as the lake trembles when the north wind whips it, approached him with the Sacred Host in his hand, which trembled so as he put it to Lázaro's lips, that, overcome by faintness, he dropped the Host. It was my brother himself who picked up the Host and put it in his mouth. The people, seeing Don Manuel weep, wept, saying to each other: "How he loves him!" And then, as it was early morning, a cock crowed.

When I had returned home and was alone with my brother, I threw my arms round his neck and kissing him said:

"Ah, Lázaro, Lázaro, what joy you have given to us all, to the whole village, to the living and the dead and especially to Mama, to our mother. Did you see? Poor Don Manuel wept for joy. What joy you have given us all!"

"I have done it because of that," he answered.

"Because of that? To give us joy? You will have done it first and foremost because of yourself, because of your conversion."

Then Lázaro, my brother, as pale and trembling as Don Manuel when he gave him communion, made me sit down, in the very arm-chair where our mother used to sit, took a deep breath, and then, as if making an intimate confession of a domestic and family nature, he said to me:

"Look, Angelita, the moment has come to tell you the truth, the whole truth, and I am going to tell it you, because I must; because I cannot and must not keep it from you and because moreover you would, sooner or later, have to guess at it and only guess half the truth, which is worst of all."

And then, serenely and quietly, in a low voice, he told me a story which plunged me into a lake of sadness. How Don Manuel had been working on him, particularly during those walks to the ruins of the old Cistercian abbey, begging him not to give offence, to set a good example, to join in the religious life of the village, to pretend to believe if he did not believe, to conceal his ideas on the subject, but without even trying to catechise him, or to convert him in any other way.

"But is it possible?" I exclaimed, in consternation.

"It is indeed, sister! And when I said to him: 'But is it you, you the priest, who are advising me to pretend?' he replied, stammering: 'Pretend? Not pretend! Take holy water, as someone once said, and you will end by believing.' And as I, looking him in the eye, said: 'And you, by celebrating Mass, have you ended by believing?', he looked down at the lake and his eyes filled with tears. And that is how I wrenched his secret from him."

"Lázaro!" I groaned.

At that moment daft Blasillo passed down the street, calling out his "My God, my God! Why hast Thou forsaken Me?", and Lázaro shuddered, thinking he heard Don Manuel's voice, perhaps that of Our Lord Jesus Christ.

"Then," my brother went on, "I understood his motives and with them his saintliness; because he is a saint, sister, a true saint. When he undertook the task, he did not try to win me for his holy cause—

because it is a holy cause, most holy—to take credit for a triumph, but he did it for the sake of the peace, the happiness, the illusion, if you like, of those entrusted to him. I realised that if he deceives them like that—if it is deception—it is not for his own benefit. I surrendered to his reasoning, and that is my conversion. I shall never forget the day when I said to him: 'But, Don Manuel, the truth, the truth before all else,' and he, trembling, whispered in my ear—and this in spite of our being alone in the heart of the country—'The truth? The truth, Lázaro, is perhaps something terrible, something intolerable, something deadly; simple people could not live with it.' 'And why do you let me glimpse it here and now, as at confession?' I said to him. And he answered: 'Because if I didn't, it would torment me so much, that I would end by shouting it in the middle of the market-place, and that must never happen, never, never. I am here to make the souls of my parishioners live, to make them happy, to make them dream they are immortal, and not to kill them. What is needed here is that they should live healthy lives, that they should live unanimous in feeling, and with the truth, with my truth, they would not live. Let them live. That is what the Church does, it makes them live. True religion? All religions are true, in so far as they make the people who profess them live spiritually, in so far as they console them for having had to be born only to die; and for each people the truest religion is their own, that which has made them. And mine? Mine is to console myself by consoling others, although the consolation I give them may not be mine.' I shall never forget these words of his."

"But your communion has been a sacrilege!" I dared to insinuate, promptly feeling sorry for having insinuated it.

"Sacrilege? And he who gave it to me? And his Masses?"

"What torture!" I exclaimed.

"And now," added my brother, "there is one more to console the people."

"To deceive them?" I said.

"To deceive them, no," he replied, "but to corroborate them in their faith."

"And they, the people," I said, "do they really believe?"

"How am I to know? They believe involuntarily, from habit, from tradition. What is necessary is not to waken them. Let them live in their spiritual poverty, so that they may be kept from the torments of luxury. 'Blessed are the poor in spirit!' "

"You have learnt that, brother, from Don Manuel. And now, tell me, have you kept that promise that you made to our mother when she was about to die, that you would pray for her?"

"As if I shouldn't keep it! But what do you take me for, sister?

Do you believe me capable of breaking my word, a solemn promise, a promise made to a mother on her death-bed?"

"How do I know! . . . You might have meant to deceive her, so that she might die with that consolation."

"If I had not kept the promise I should live unconsoled."

"And so?"

"I kept the promise and I have not ceased to pray for her a single day."

"Only for her?"

"For whom else, then?"

"For yourself! And from now on, for Don Manuel."

We parted to go each one to his own room, I to weep all night, to pray for the conversion of my brother and Don Manuel, and he, Lázaro, I don't quite know what he did.

From that day on I trembled at the thought of finding myself alone with Don Manuel, whom I continued to assist in his errands of mercy. He appeared to notice my innermost state of mind and guess the reason, and when at last I approached him in the confessional—who was the judge and who the offender?—both of us, he and I, bowed our heads in silence and began to weep. It was Don Manuel who broke the tremendous silence, to say to me in a voice which seemed to come from the tomb:

"But you, Angelina, you believe as you did when you were ten years old, don't you? You do believe?"

"Yes, I believe, father."

"Then go on believing. If any doubts arise, keep them from yourself. We must live . . ."

I became bold, and trembling all over I said:

"But you, father, do you believe?"

He hesitated a moment and, recovering himself, said:

"I believe."

"But in what exactly, father? Do you believe in the other life? Do you believe that on our death we do not wholly die? Do you believe we shall see each other and love each other again in another world to come? Do you believe in the other life?"

The poor saint was sobbing.

"Come, child, let us leave this!"

And now, as I write this record, I say to myself: "Why did he not deceive me? Why did he not deceive me then as he deceived the others? Why was he distressed? Because he could not deceive himself, or because he could not deceive me? I want to believe that he was distressed because he could not deceive himself in order to deceive me.

"And now," he added, "pray for me, for your brother, for yourself, for everyone. We must live. And we must give life."

And after a pause:

"And why don't you get married, Angelina?"

"You already know why, father."

"But no, no; you must get married. Between Lázaro and me we'll find you a bridegroom, because it is in your interest to marry, so that those worries may be dispelled."

"Worries, Don Manuel?"

"I know what I am saying. Don't distress yourself too much over others, for everyone has enough to do to have to answer for himself."

"That you should be the one, Don Manuel, to say that to me! to advise me to marry so as to answer for myself and not care about others! That you should be the one!"

"You are right, Angelina, I don't know what I am saying; I don't know what I have been saying since I have been confessing myself to you. Yes, yes, we must live."

When I was about to get up and leave the church, he said to me:

"And now, Angelina, in the people's name, do you absolve me?"

I felt as if I were permeated with a mysterious priesthood and said: "In the name of God the Father, the Son and the Holy Ghost, I absolve you, father."

We left the church, and as we left, my maternal instincts welled up within me.

My brother, now entirely at the service of Don Manuel in his work, was his most assiduous collaborator and companion. They were bound together, moreover, by their mutual secret. He accompanied him on his visits to the sick and to the schools, and put his money at the saintly man's disposition. He very nearly learned to assist him at Mass. And he penetrated more and more deeply into Don Manuel's unfathomable soul.

"What a man!" he would say to me. "Why, yesterday, while walking along the shores of the lake, he said to me: 'This is my greatest temptation.' And as I looked at him enquiringly, he added: 'My poor father, who died when he was almost ninety, spent his life, as he confessed to me, tortured by the temptation to commit suicide, which he had felt as long as he could remember. 'I was born with it,' he would say, in his own defence. And this defence was his life. So as not to yield to such temptation he went to extremes in the care he took to safeguard his life. He told me of terrible scenes. It seemed like madness. And I have inherited it. How this water calls me, as with its apparent calm—the current runs below the surface—it mirrors the sky! My life, Lázaro, is a sort of continuous suicide, a struggle against suicide, which is the same; but let them live, let our people live!' And then he added: 'Here the course of the river is slowed down and forms a lake, and afterwards, descending to the plateau, it rushes in cascades, waterfalls and torrents, through chasms and gullies, close by the city, and thus life is checked, here, in the village. But the temptation to commit suicide is greater here, beside the backwater which mirrors the stars at night, than it is beside the frightening cascades. You see, Lázaro, I have attended poor ignorant, illiterate villagers at their death, people who had scarcely ever left the village, and I have been able to learn from their lips, and if not, guess, the real cause of their mortal illness, and I have been able to see, there, at their deathbed, all the blackness of the abyss of boredom with life. A thousand times worse than hunger! Let us go on then, Lázaro, committing suicide in our work and in our village, and let the village dream its life as the lake dreams the sky.' "

"Another time," my brother also said to me, "when we were coming back here, we saw a lass, a goatherd, who, standing on a spur of rock on the mountain slope, in sight of the lake, was singing in a voice fresher than its waters. Don Manuel stopped me and, pointing to her, said: 'Look, it seems as if time had come to an end, as if this girl had always been there, just as she is, singing as she does, and as if she must go on being like that for ever, as she was before my consciousness began, as she will be when it has ceased. Along with the rocks, the clouds, the trees, the waters, this girl is part of nature and not of history.' How Don Manuel feels nature and gives it life! I shall never forget the day of the snowfall when he said to me: 'Have you seen, Lázaro, a greater mystery than that of the snow falling on the lake and dying in it, while it covers the mountain with its cloak?' "

Don Manuel had to restrain my brother in his zeal and in his inexperience as a neophyte. As he knew that Lázaro was preaching against certain popular superstitions, he had to say:

"Leave them alone! It is so difficult to make them understand where orthodox belief ends and superstition begins. And more so for us. Leave them alone then, so long as they find consolation. It is better that they should believe everything, even things which contradict each other, than that they should believe nothing. That those who believe too much end by believing nothing is a Protestant idea. Let us not protest. Protest kills contentment."

One night when the moon was full—my brother also told me— they were returning to the village along the shore of the lake, whose surface was then ruffled by the mountain breeze, and on the ripples frolicked the shafts of light from the full moon, and Don Manuel said to Lázaro:

"Look, the water is reciting the Litany, and now it says 'ianua caeli, ora pro nobis, gate of heaven, pray for us!' "

And there fell trembling from his eyelashes to the grass two fleeting tears which, like the dew, caught the quivering light of the full moon.

Time passed, and my brother and I observed that Don Manuel's strength began to fail him, that he no longer succeeded in altogether containing the unfathomable sadness which was consuming him, that perhaps some treacherous illness was undermining his body and soul. Lázaro, perhaps to take his mind off things, proposed to him that it would be a good thing to found in the church something like a Catholic Agrarian Union.

"Union?" Don Manuel replied sadly. "Union? And what is that? I know of no other Union but the Church, and you know the saying that 'my kingdom is not of this world.' Our kingdom, Lázaro, is not of this world . . ."

"And of the other?"

Don Manuel bowed his head:

"The other, Lázaro, is here as well, because there are two kingdoms in this world. Or rather, the other world . . . that is, I don't know what I am saying. As for this matter of the Union, in you it is a relic of your progressive period. No, Lázaro, no; religion is not for settling the economic or political conflicts of this world which God gave over to the disputes of men. Let men think and work as they may, let them console themselves for having been born, let them live as contentedly as they can in the illusion that all this has some purpose. I have not come to make the poor submit to the rich, nor to preach to the latter that they should submit to the former. Resignation and charity in all and for all. Because the rich man must also be resigned to his wealth, and to life, and the poor man must also be charitable towards the rich man. The social question? Let it be, it does not concern us. They bring in a new society, in which there are no longer rich or poor, in which wealth is justly shared out, in which everything belongs to everybody, and what then? Don't you think that from the general well-being will arise a greater boredom with life? Yes, I know that one of those leaders of what they call the social revolution has said that religion is the opium of the people.[5] Opium . . . opium . . . opium, yes. Let us give them opium, and let them sleep and dream. I too with my mad activity am administering opium to myself. And I don't manage to

[5] Karl Marx (1818–83).

sleep well, much less dream pleasant dreams . . . This terrible nightmare! I too can say with the Divine Master: 'My soul is weary unto death.' No, Lázaro, no; no Unions where we are concerned. If they form them, I shall think it a good thing, because in this way they will keep themselves amused. Let them play at Unions, if it pleases them."

The whole village observed that Don Manuel's strength was waning, that he was tiring. Even his voice, that voice which was a miracle, took on a certain inner tremor. Tears started to his eyes for no particular reason. Especially when he talked to the people about the other world, the other life, he had to stop at times and shut his eyes. "He can see it," they said. At such moments it was daft Blasillo who wept most brokenheartedly, because now Blasillo cried more than he laughed, and even his laughter sounded like weeping.

When Passion Week came round—the last that Don Manuel kept with us, in our world, in our village—everyone had a presentiment of the end of the tragedy. And how it rang out then, that "My God, my God! Why hast Thou forsaken Me?", the last time that Don Manuel sobbed it in public! And when he repeated the Divine Master's words to the good thief—"All thieves are good," our Don Manuel used to say—the words: "This day shalt thou be with Me in Paradise." And the last general communion which our saint administered! When he came to give it to my brother, this time with a surer hand, after the liturgical ". . . *in vitam aeternam*" he bent over and said in his ear: "There is no eternal life other than this one . . . let them dream that it is eternal . . . eternal for a few years . . ." And when he gave it to me he said: "Pray, my daughter, pray for us." And then, something so extraordinary that I carry it in my heart as the greatest of mysteries, and it was that he said to me in a voice that seemed to belong to another world: ". . . and pray too for Our Lord Jesus Christ . . ."

I arose exhausted, like a sleep-walker. Everything round about seemed like a dream. I thought: "I shall have to pray for the lake and the mountain too." And then: "Can I be possessed of a devil?" Once in the house, I took the crucifix which my mother had held in her hands when she had given up her soul to God, and, looking at it through my tears and remembering the "My God, my God! Why hast Thou forsaken Me?" of our two Christs, that of this Earth and that of our village, I prayed: "Thy will be done in earth as it is in Heaven" first, and afterwards: "and lead us not into temptation, Amen." Then I turned to that image of the Mater Dolorosa, with her heart pierced with seven swords, which had been the most sorrowful comfort to my poor mother, and I prayed, "Holy Mary, Mother of God, pray for us sinners, now and in the hour of our death. Amen." I had scarcely prayed, when I said to myself, "Sinners? Are we sinners? And what is our sin, what is it?" I went about all day troubled by this question.

The following day I went to Don Manuel, who was growing more and more solemn as the hour of his passing approached, and I said:

"Do you remember, father, when years ago, on my asking you a question, you answered: 'Do not ask me that, for I am ignorant; our Holy Mother Church has doctors who will know how to answer you'?"

"Do I remember! . . . and I remember that I told you that those were questions that the Devil dictated to you."

"Well, father, I, who am possessed, have come back today, to ask you another question which my guardian demon dictates to me."

"Ask."

"Yesterday, when you gave me communion, you asked me to pray for us all and even for . . ."

"Well, keep it to yourself and go on."

"I reached home and began to pray, and when I came to the words 'Pray for us sinners, now and in the hour of our death,' an inner voice said to me, 'Sinners? Are we sinners? And what is our sin?' What is our sin, father?"

"What?" he answered me. "A great doctor of the Spanish Catholic Apostolic Church has already said what it is, the great doctor of *La Vida es Sueño.*[6] He said that 'man's greatest crime is to have been born.' That, my daughter, is our sin: to have been born."

"And is there a remedy, father?"

"Go away and pray again! Pray again for us sinners, now and in the hour of our death . . . Yes, in the end the dream has a remedy . . . in the end life has a remedy . . . in the end the cross of birth is taken from us . . . And as Calderón said, good deeds and deceiving people for their good are not lost even in dreams . . ."

And the hour of his death came at last. The whole village saw it coming. And it was his greatest lesson. He did not wish to die alone or idle. He died preaching to the people, in the church. First, before ordering them to take him there, as he could no longer move for paralysis, he called Lázaro and me to his house. And there, with the three of us alone, he said:

"Listen: care for these poor sheep, let them be consoled for living, let them believe what I have been unable to believe. And you, Lázaro, when you must die, die like me, as our Angela will die, in the bosom

---

[6] *Life Is a Dream,* the masterpiece of the Spanish dramatist Don Pedro Calderón de la Barca (1600–81).

of the Holy Roman Catholic Apostolic Mother, of the Holy Mother Church of Valverde de Lucerna, you understand. And we shall never see each other again, since this dream of life is ending . . ."

"Father, father!" I wailed.

"Don't be distressed, Angela, and go on praying for all sinners, for all those who have been born. And let them dream, let them dream. How I long to sleep, to sleep endlessly, to sleep throughout an eternity and without dreaming! Forgetting the dream! When they bury me, let it be in a coffin made from those six boards which I cut out of the old walnut tree, poor thing, in whose shade I played as a child, when I was beginning to dream. Then indeed I believed in everlasting life! That is to say, I imagine now that I believed then. For a child, believing is nothing more than dreaming. And for a village too. Those six boards, which I cut with my own hands, you will find at the foot of my bed."

He gasped for breath, then, having recovered, he went on:

"You will remember that, when we all recited the Creed as one, unanimous in feeling, as a village, on reaching the end I was silent. When the Israelites were reaching the end of their pilgrimage through the desert, the Lord said to Aaron and Moses that, because they had not believed Him, they would not take his people into the promised land. He made them go up into Mount Hor, where Aaron was made to undress by Moses and where he died, and then Moses went up from the plains of Moab to Mount Nebo, to the top of Pisgah, over against Jericho, and the Lord showed him all the land promised to his people, but saying to him: 'Thou shalt not enter therein,' and there Moses died and no one knew his burial-place. And he left Joshua as leader. You, Lázaro, be my Joshua, and if you can stop the sun, stop it and never mind about progress. Like Moses, I have known the Lord, our highest dream, face to face, and you know that the Scriptures say that he who beholds the face of God, he who beholds in the dream the eyes of the face with which He looks at us, dies irrevocably and for ever. While our people live, then, let them not see the face of God, for after death there is nothing to worry about, since they shall see nothing . . ."

"Father, father, father!" I wailed again.

And he answered:

"You, Angela, always pray, go on praying that all sinners may dream, until they die, of the resurrection of the body and the life everlasting . . ."

I waited for his "and who knows . . . ?" when Don Manuel again gasped for breath.

"And now," he added, "now, in the hour of my death, it is time for you to have me carried, in this same armchair, to the church, to take leave there of my people, who are waiting for me."

He was carried to the church and was placed, in the armchair, in the sanctuary at the foot of the altar. He held a crucifix in his hands. My brother and I stood near him, but it was daft Blasillo who drew closest. He wanted to take Don Manuel's hand and kiss it. As some tried to prevent him, Don Manuel reproved them, saying:

"Let him come up to me. Come, Blasillo, give me your hand."

The idiot wept for joy. Then Don Manuel said:

"Very few words, my children, as I feel scarcely strong enough for anything except to die. I have nothing new to tell you. I have already told you all. Live in peace and contentment, in the hope that we shall all see each other some day, in the Valverde de Lucerna which is there, among the stars of the night which are reflected in the lake, above the mountain. And pray, pray to most Holy Mary, pray to Our Lord. Be good, for that is enough. Forgive me the evil I may have done you without meaning to and without knowing it. And now, after I have given you my blessing, all say together the Our Father, the Hail Mary, the Salve, and finally the Creed."

Then, with the crucifix he held in his hand, he gave his blessing to the people, while the women and children and not a few men wept, and immediately the prayers began, and Don Manuel heard them in silence, his hand held by Blasillo, who gradually fell asleep to the sound of the intercessions. First the Our Father with its "Thy will be done in earth as it is in heaven," then the Hail Mary with its "Pray for us sinners, now and in the hour of our death," after that the Salve with its "mourning and weeping in this vale of tears," and finally the Creed. And when we reached the "resurrection of the body and the life everlasting," the whole village felt that its saint had given up his soul to God. We did not have to close his eyes, because he died with them closed. And when we went to waken Blasillo, we found that he had fallen asleep in the Lord for ever. So we had then to bury two bodies.

The whole village went straight away to the saint's house to collect relics, to share out shreds of his clothing, to carry off what they could as a relic and remembrance of the blessed martyr. My brother kept his breviary, between the leaves of which he found, as in a herbarium, a dried pink stuck to a paper, and on this a cross with a date.

Nobody in the village would believe in Don Manuel's death; everybody expected to see him daily, and perhaps they did see him, walking along by the lake and mirrored in it or with the mountain as a background; everybody went on hearing his voice, and everybody came to his tomb, around which quite a cult grew up. The women possessed of a devil came to touch the walnut cross, also made with his own hands from the same tree from which the six boards in which he was buried had been taken. And those who least wished to believe that he had died were my brother and myself.

He, Lázaro, carried on the saint's tradition and began to set down what he had heard from him, notes which I have used for this account of mine.

"He made me a new man, a real Lazarus, one risen from the dead," he would say to me. "He gave me faith."

"Faith?" I interrupted him.

"Yes, faith, faith in consolation for life, faith in contentment with life. He cured me of my progressiveness. Because there are, Angela, two kinds of dangerous and harmful men: those who, convinced of a life beyond the grave and of the resurrection of the body, torment, like the inquisitors they are, their fellow men that they might attain the other life, despising this one as transitory, and there are those who, not believing in any but this . . ."

"Like you perhaps," I said.

"Yes, and like Don Manuel. But, not believing in any world but this, they await some future society or other, and they persist in denying the people the consolation of believing in another . . ."

"So that . . ."

"So that we must make them live on illusion."

The poor priest who came to take Don Manuel's place in the parish came to Valverde de Lucerna overwhelmed by the memory of the saint and put himself into my hands and my brother's for us to guide him. He only wanted to follow in the saint's footsteps. My brother said to him: "Very little theology, eh? Very little theology: religion, religion." And I smiled when I heard him, wondering if what we had was not theology too.

I began at that time to fear for my poor brother. Since Don Manuel died, one could not say that my brother lived. He visited his tomb daily and spent long hours contemplating the lake. He was yearning for true peace.

"Don't look so much at the lake," I said to him.

"No, sister, don't be afraid. It is another lake which calls me: it is another mountain. I can't live without him."

"And contentment with life, Lázaro, what about that?"

"That is for other sinners, not for us, who have seen the face of God, not for us whom the dream of life has looked upon with His eyes."

"What! Are you preparing to go and see Don Manuel?"

"No, sister, no; here and now at home, between ourselves alone, the whole truth, however bitter it may be, bitter as the sea into which the fresh waters of this lake finally make their way, the whole truth for you, who are shielded from it . . ."

"No, no, Lázaro, that is not the truth!"

"Mine, yes."

"Yours, but what about that of . . . ?"

"His also."

"Not now, Lázaro, not now! Now he believes something else, now he believes . . ."

"Look, Angela, on one of the occasions when Don Manuel told me that there are things which, although one says them to oneself, one ought to keep secret from others, I replied that he was telling me that because he said those same things to himself. He ended by confessing to me that he believed that more than one of the greatest saints, perhaps the greatest of all, had died without believing in the other life."

"Is it possible?"

"It is indeed possible! And now, sister, take care that they don't even suspect our secret here in the village."

"Suspect it?" I said to him. "If I tried, out of sheer madness, to explain it to them, they would not understand it. The village understands nothing of words; the village has understood nothing but your works. To attempt to expound that to them would be like reading to children of eight several pages of St. Thomas Aquinas[7] . . . in Latin."

"Well then, when I go, pray for me and for him and for everyone!"

And at last his hour came too. An illness which was undermining his robust constitution seemed to be aggravated by Don Manuel's death.

"It is not so much that I am sorry to have to die," he said to me in his last days, "as that with me there dies another piece of Don Manuel's soul. But the rest of him will live on with you. Until one day even we dead shall die completely."

When he lay dying, the people from the village came in, as is the custom in our hamlets, to see him die, and commended his soul to Don Manuel, to Saint Manuel Bueno, the martyr. My brother said nothing to them, he no longer had anything to say; he had said everything, all that has been said. He was yet another link between the two Valverdes de Lucerna, the one at the bottom of the lake and the one which is reflected on its surface; he was now one of the dead in our life, and also, in his way, one of our saints.

[7] Most famous of the scholastic philosophers (1225–74), author of the *Summa Theologica*.

I was left more than disconsolate, but in my village and with my village. And now, having lost my Saint Manuel, the father of my soul, and my Lázaro, my even more than earthly, my spiritual, brother, it is now that I realise that I have grown old and how I have grown old. But, have I lost them? Have I grown old? Am I approaching my death?

We must live! And he taught me to live, he taught us to live, to feel life, to feel the meaning of life, to merge into the soul of the mountain, the soul of the lake, the soul of the people of the village, to lose ourselves in them in order to remain in them. He taught me by his life to lose myself in the life of the people of my village, and I felt the passing of the hours, and the days and the years no more than the passing of the water of the lake. It seemed as if my life had always to be the same. I did not feel myself growing old. I no longer lived in myself, but in my village and my village in me. I wanted to say what they, my own people, said spontaneously. I went out into the street, which was the highroad, and, as I knew everyone, I lived in them and forgot myself, while in Madrid, where I was once with my brother, as I knew no one, I felt terribly lonely and tortured by so many strangers.

And now, as I write this record, this intimate confession of my experience of another's saintliness, I believe that Don Manuel Bueno, my Saint Manuel, and my brother Lázaro died believing that they did not believe what concerns us most, but without believing that they believed it, they did believe it in an active and resigned desolation.

But, why—I have often asked myself—did Don Manuel not try to convert my brother too with a deception, with a lie, pretending to be a believer without being one? I have realised that it was because he realised he would not deceive him, that deceit was of no use in his case, that only with the truth, his truth, would he convert him; that he would have achieved nothing if he had attempted to act a play—or rather a tragedy—the one he acted to save the village. And so he won him over, in short, for his pious fraud; won him over with the truth of death to the reason for living. And so he won me, and I never let others have the faintest notion of his divine, his most holy game. It is that I believed and do believe that God our Lord, for I know not what sacred and inscrutable designs, made them believe themselves to be incredulous. And that perhaps at the end of their passing over the bandage fell from their eyes. And I, do I believe?

As I write this now, here in my mother's old house, at the age of fifty-odd, when my memories are beginning to whiten with my hair, it is snowing, snowing on the lake, snowing on the mountain, snowing on the memories of my father, the stranger, of my mother, of my brother Lázaro, of my village, of my Saint Manuel, and also on the memory of poor Blasillo, my Saint Blasillo, and may he protect me from there in heaven. This snow blots out corners and shadows, for even at night the snow gives light. I do not know what is true and what is false, nor what I saw and what I only dreamed—or rather what I dreamed and what I only saw—nor what I knew, nor what I believed. I do not know whether I am committing to this paper, that is as white as the snow, my conscience which must remain there, when I am left without it. What use is it to me anyway? . . .

Do I know anything? Do I believe anything? Has this, which I am relating here, happened and has it happened exactly as I am relating it? Can these things happen? Is all this anything more than a dream dreamed within another dream? Shall I, Angela Carballino, now in my fifties, be the only person in this village assailed by these thoughts foreign to the rest? And these, the others, those around me, do they believe? What is this believing? At least they live. And now they believe in Saint Manuel Bueno, the martyr, who, without hoping for immortality, sustained their hopes of it.

It appears that the most Illustrious Lord Bishop who has begun to work for the beatification of our saint of Valverde de Lucerna, proposes to write his life, a sort of manual of the perfect parish priest, and is gathering for it all kinds of information. He has asked me for some insistently, he has had interviews with me, I have given him all sorts of data, but I have always kept to myself the tragic secret of Don Manuel and of my brother. It is curious that he has not suspected it. I trust that all that I have left recorded in this account does not come to his knowledge. I fear the authorities of the earth, the temporal authorities, even though they may be those of the Church.

But there it is, whatever its fate may be.

How did this document, this account of Angela Carballino's, come into my hands? This is something, reader, which I must keep secret. I give it to you exactly as it came to me, without doing anything to it, except to correct a few, very few details of style. It is very similar to other things I have written. This proves nothing against its objectivity, its originality. And do I know, moreover, whether I have not created outside myself real, true beings, with an immortal soul? Do I know whether that Augusto Pérez, in my novel *Niebla,*[8] was not right when he claimed to be more real, more objective than myself, who believed that I had invented him? It does not occur to me to doubt the reality

[8] Unamuno's tragi-comic novel *Mist* (1914).

of this Saint Manuel Bueno, the martyr, just as his disciple and spiritual daughter Angela Carballino has revealed him to me. I believe in this reality more than the saint himself did; I believe in it more than I believe in my own reality.

And now, before I close this epilogue, I want to remind you, patient reader, of the ninth verse of the Epistle of the forgotten Apostle Saint Jude—what a name can do!—where we are told how my celestial patron, Saint Michael the Archangel—Michael means "Who like God?" and archangel, archmessenger—disputed with the Devil—Devil means accuser, prosecutor—about the body of Moses and would not allow him to carry it away into the judgement of railing speech, but said to the Devil: "The Lord rebuke thee." And he who would understand, let him understand.

Since Angela Carballino put her own feelings into her account, and I do not know how anything else is possible, I also wish to comment here on what she said about the people not understanding if Don Manuel and his disciple Lázaro had confessed to them the state of their belief. They would not have believed them, I add. They would have believed their actions and not their words, because words are of no use in backing up actions, but the actions are sufficient in themselves. And for a village like Valverde de Lucerna there is no confession other than conduct. The village neither knows what faith is, nor perhaps does it very much care.

I well know that in the course of this account, novelistic if you will —and the novel is the most intimate, the truest, kind of story, for which reason I cannot understand that there should be people who are annoyed that the Gospel should be called a novel, which actually raises it above the level of any ordinary chronicle—I well know that in the course of this account nothing happens; but I hope that it is because in it everything is enduring, as are the lakes and the mountains and the holy simple souls settled beyond faith and despair, who sheltered among them, among the lakes and the mountains, outside history, in a divine novel.

Translated by Francisco de Segovia and Jean Pérez

Luigi Pirandello / 1867–1936

War

The passengers who had left Rome by the night express had had to
stop until dawn at the small station of Fabriano in order to continue
their journey by the small old-fashioned local joining the main line
with Sulmona.

At dawn, in a stuffy and smoky second-class carriage in which five
people had already spent the night, a bulky woman in deep mourning
was hoisted in—almost like a shapeless bundle. Behind her, puffing
and moaning, followed her husband—a tiny man, thin and weakly,
his face death-white, his eyes small and bright and looking shy and
uneasy.

Having at last taken a seat he politely thanked the passengers who
had helped his wife and who had made room for her; then he turned
round to the woman trying to pull down the collar of her coat, and
politely inquired:

"Are you all right, dear?"

The wife, instead of answering, pulled up her collar again to her
eyes, so as to hide her face.

"Nasty world," muttered the husband with a sad smile.

And he felt it his duty to explain to his traveling companions that
the poor woman was to be pitied, for the war was taking away from
her her only son, a boy of twenty to whom both had devoted their
entire life, even breaking up their home at Sulmona to follow him to
Rome, where he had to go as a student, then allowing him to volunteer for war with an assurance, however, that at least for six months
he would not be sent to the front and now, all of a sudden, receiving
a wire saying that he was due to leave in three days' time and asking
them to go and see him off.

The woman under the big coat was twisting and wriggling, at times
growling like a wild animal, feeling certain that all those explanations
would not have aroused even a shadow of sympathy from those people
who—most likely—were in the same plight as herself. One of them,
who had been listening with particular attention, said:

"You should thank God that your son is only leaving now for the front. Mine has been sent there the first day of the war. He has already come back twice wounded and been sent back again to the front."

"What about me? I have two sons and three nephews at the front," said another passenger.

"Maybe, but in our case it is our *only* son," ventured the husband.

"What difference can it make? You may spoil your only son with excessive attentions, but you cannot love him more than you would all your other children if you had any. Paternal love is not like bread that can be broken into pieces and split amongst the children in equal shares. A father gives *all* his love to each one of his children without discrimination, whether it be one or ten, and if I am suffering now for my two sons, I am not suffering half for each of them but double . . ."

"True . . . true . . ." sighed the embarrassed husband, "but suppose (of course we all hope it will never be your case) a father has two sons at the front and he loses one of them, there is still one left to console him . . . while . . ."

"Yes," answered the other, getting cross, "a son left to console him but also a son left for whom he must survive, while in the case of the father of an only son if the son dies the father can die too and put an end to his distress. Which of the two positions is the worse? Don't you see how my case would be worse than yours?"

"Nonsense," interrupted another traveler, a fat, red-faced man with bloodshot eyes of the palest gray.

He was panting. From his bulging eyes seemed to spurt inner violence of an uncontrolled vitality which his weakened body could hardly contain.

"Nonsense," he repeated, trying to cover his mouth with his hand so as to hide the two missing front teeth. "Nonsense. Do we give life to our children for our own benefit?"

The other travelers stared at him in distress. The one who had had his son at the front since the first day of the war sighed: "You are right. Our children do not belong to us, they belong to the Country. . . ."

"Bosh," retorted the fat traveler. "Do we think of the Country when we give life to our children? Our sons are born because . . . well, because they must be born and when they come to life they take our own life with them. This is the truth. We belong to them but they never belong to us. And when they reach twenty they are exactly what we were at their age. We too had a father and mother, but there were so many other things as well . . . girls, cigarettes, illusions, new ties . . . and the Country, of course, whose call we would have answered—when we were twenty—even if father and mother had said no. Now at our age, the love of our Country is still great, of course, but stronger than it is the love for our children. Is there any one of us here who wouldn't gladly take his son's place at the front if he could?"

There was a silence all round, everybody nodding in approval.

"Why then," continued the fat man, "shouldn't we consider the feelings of our children when they are twenty? Isn't it natural that at their age they should consider the love for their Country (I am speaking of decent boys, of course) even greater than the love for us? Isn't it natural that it should be so, as after all they must look upon us as upon old boys who cannot move any more and must stay at home? If Country exists, if Country is a natural necessity, like bread, of which each of us must eat in order not to die of hunger, somebody must go to defend it. And our sons go, when they are twenty, and they don't want tears, because if they die, they die inflamed and happy (I am speaking, of course, of decent boys). Now, if one dies young and happy, without having the ugly sides of life, the boredom of it, the pettiness, the bitterness of disillusion . . . what more can we ask for him? Everyone should stop crying; everyone should laugh, as I do . . . or at least thank God—as I do—because my son, before dying, sent me a message saying that he was dying satisfied at having ended his life in the best way he could have wished. That is why, as you see, I do not even wear mourning. . . ."

He shook his light fawn coat as to show it; his livid lip over his missing teeth was trembling, his eyes were watery and motionless, and soon after he ended with a shrill laugh which might well have been a sob.

"Quite so . . . quite so . . ." agreed the others.

The woman who, bundled in a corner under her coat, had been sitting and listening had—for the last three months—tried to find in the words of her husband and her friends something to console her in her deep sorrow, something that might show her how a mother should resign herself to send her son not even to death but to a probably dangerous life. Yet not a word had she found amongst the many which had been said . . . and her grief had been greater in seeing that nobody—as she thought—could share her feelings.

But now the words of the traveler amazed and almost stunned her. She suddenly realized that it wasn't the others who were wrong and could not understand her but herself who could not rise up to the same height of those fathers and mothers willing to resign themselves, without crying, not only to the departure of their sons but even to their death.

She lifted her head, she bent over from her corner trying to listen with great attention to the details which the fat man was giving to his companions about the way his son had fallen as a hero, for his King and his Country, happy and without regrets. It seemed to her that she had stumbled into a world she had never dreamt of, a world so far unknown to her and she was so pleased to hear everyone joining in congratulating that brave father who could so stoically speak of his child's death.

Then, suddenly, just as if she had heard nothing of what had been said and almost as if waking up from a dream, she turned to the old man, asking him:

"Then . . . is your son really dead?"

Everybody stared at her. The old man, too, turned to look at her, fixing his great, bulging, horribly watery light gray eyes, deep in her face. For some little time he tried to answer, but words failed him. He looked and looked at her, almost as if only then—at that silly, incongruous question—he had suddenly realized at last that his son was really dead—gone for ever—for ever. His face contracted, became horribly distorted, then he snatched in haste a handkerchief from his pocket and, to the amazement of everyone, broke into harrowing, heart-rending, uncontrollable sobs.

Translated by Michael Pettinati

Thomas Mann / 1875-1955

Little Lizzy

There are marriages which the imagination, even the most practised literary one, cannot conceive. You must just accept them, as you do in the theatre when you see the ancient and doddering married to the beautiful and gay, as the given premises on which the farce is mechanically built up.

Yes, the wife of Jacoby the lawyer was lovely and young, a woman of unusual charm. Some years—shall we say thirty years?—ago, she had been christened with the names of Anna, Margarete, Rosa, Amalie; but the name she went by was always Amra, composed of the initials of her four real ones; it suited to perfection her somewhat exotic personality. Her soft, heavy hair, which she wore parted on one side and brushed straight back above her ears from the narrow temples, had only the darkness of the glossy chestnut; but her skin displayed the dull, dark sallowness of the south and clothed a form which southern suns must have ripened. Her slow, voluptuous, indolent presence suggested the harem; each sensuous, lazy movement of her body strengthened the impression that with her the head was entirely subordinate to the heart. She needed only to have looked at you once, with her artless brown eyes, lifting her brows in the pathetically narrow forehead, horizontally, in a quaint way she had, for you to be certain of that. But she herself was not so simple as not to know it too. Quite simply, she avoided exposing herself, she spoke seldom and little—and what is there to say against a woman who is both beautiful and silent? Yes, the word "simple" is probably the last which should be applied to her. Her glance was artless; but also it had a kind of luxurious cunning—you could see that she was not dull, also that she might be a mischief-maker. In profile her nose was rather too thick; but her full, large mouth was utterly lovely, if also lacking in any expression save sensuality.

This disturbing phenomenon was the wife of Jacoby the lawyer, a man of forty. Whoever looked at him was bound to be amazed at the fact. He was stout, Jacoby the lawyer; but stout is not the word, he was a perfect colossus of a man! His legs, in their columnar clumsiness and the slate-grey trousers he always wore, reminded one of an elephant's. His round, fat-upholstered back was that of a bear; and over the vast round of his belly his funny little grey jacket was held by a single button strained so tight that when it was unbuttoned the jacket came wide open with a pop. Scarcely anything which could be called a neck united this huge torso with the little head atop. The head had narrow watery eyes, a squabby nose, and a wee mouth between cheeks drooping with fullness. The upper lip and the round head were covered with harsh, scanty, light-coloured bristles that showed the naked skin, as on an overfed dog. There was no doubt that Jacoby's fatness was not of a healthy kind. His gigantic body, tall as well as stout, was not muscular, but flabby. The blood would sometimes rush to his puffy face, then ebb away leaving it of a yellowish pallor; the mouth would be drawn and sour.

Jacoby's practice was a limited one; but he was well-to-do, partly from his wife's side; and the childless pair lived in a comfortable apartment in the Kaiserstrasse and entertained a good deal. This must have been Frau Amra's taste, for it is unthinkable that the lawyer could have cared for it; he participated with an enthusiasm of a peculiarly painful kind. This fat man's character was the oddest in the world. No human being could have been politer, more accommodating, more complaisant than he. But you unconsciously knew that this over-obligingness was somehow forced, that its true source was an inward insecurity and cowardice—the impression it gave was not very pleasant. A man who despises himself is a very ugly sight; worse still when vanity combines with his cowardice to make him wish to please. This was the case, I should say, with Jacoby: his obsequiousness was almost crawling, it went beyond the bounds of personal decency. He was quite capable of saying to a lady as he escorted her to table: "My dear lady, I am a disgusting creature, but will you do me the honour?" No humour would be mingled with the remark; it was simply cloying, bitter, self-tortured—in a word, disgusting, as he said.

The following once actually happened: the lawyer was taking a walk, and a clumsy porter with a hand-cart ran over his foot. Too late the man stopped his cart and turned round—whereupon Jacoby, quite pale and dazed, his cheeks shaking up and down, took off his hat and stuttered: "I b-beg your pardon." A thing like that is infuriating. But this extraordinary colossus seemed perpetually to suffer from a plague of conscience. When he took a walk with his wife on the Lerchenberg, the Corso[1] of the little city, he would roll his eyes round at Amra, walking with her wonderful elastic gait at his side, and bow so anxiously, diligently, and zealously in all directions that he seemed to be begging pardon of all the lieutenants they met for being in unworthy possession of such a beautiful wife. His mouth had a pathetically ingratiating expression, as though he wanted to disarm their scorn.

I have already hinted that the reason why Amra married Jacoby is unfathomable. As for him, he was in love with her; ardently, as people of his physical make-up seldom are, and with such anxious humility as fitted the rest of his character. Sometimes, late in the evening, he would enter their large sleeping-chamber with its high windows and flowered hangings—softly, so softly that there was no sound, only the slow shaking of floor and furniture. He would come up to Amra's massive bed, where she already lay, kneel down, and with

[1] Main street.

infinite caution take her hand. She would lift her brows in a level line, in the quaint way she had, and look at her husband, abject before her in the dim light, with a look of malice and sensuality combined. With his puffy, trembling hands he would softly stroke back the sleeve and press his tragic fat face into the soft brown flesh of her wrist, where little blue veins stood out. And he would speak to her, in a shaking, half-smothered voice, as a sensible man in everyday life never speaks:

"Amra, my dear Amra! I am not disturbing you? You were not asleep yet? Dear God! I have been thinking all day how beautiful you are and how much I love you. I beg you to listen, for it is so very hard to express what I feel: I love you so much that sometimes my heart contracts and I do not know where to turn. I love you beyond my strength. You do not understand that, I know; but you believe it, and you must say, just one single time, that you are a little grateful to me. For, you see, such a love as mine to you is precious, it has its value in this life of ours. And that you will never betray or deceive me, even if you cannot love me, just out of gratitude for this love. I have come to you to beg you, as seriously, as fervently as I can . . ." here the lawyer's speech would be dissolved in sobs, in low, bitter weeping, as he knelt. Amra would feel moved; she would stroke her husband's bristles and say over and over, in the soothing, contemptuous sing-song one uses to a dog who comes to lick one's feet: "Yes, yes, good doggy, good doggy!"

And this behaviour of Amra's was certainly not that of a moral woman. For to relieve my mind of the truth which I have so far withheld, she did already deceive her husband; she betrayed him for the embraces of a gentleman named Alfred Läutner, a gifted young musician, who at twenty-seven had made himself a small reputation with amusing little compositions. He was a slim young chap with a provocative face, a flowing blond mane, and a sunny smile in his eyes, of which he was quite aware. He belonged to the present-day race of small artists, who do not demand the utmost of themselves, whose first requirement is to be jolly and happy, who employ their pleasing little talents to heighten their personal charms. It pleases them to play in society the rôle of the naïve genius. Consciously childlike, entirely unmoral and unscrupulous, merry and self-satisfied as they are, and healthy enough to enjoy even their disorders, they are agreeable even in their vanity, so long as that has not been wounded. But woe to these wretched little poseurs when serious misfortune befalls them, with which there is no coquetting, and when they can no longer be pleasant in their own eyes. They will not know how to be wretched decently and in order, they do not know how to attack the problem of suffering. They will be destroyed. All that is a story in itself. But Herr Alfred Läutner wrote pretty things, mostly waltzes and mazurkas. They would have been rather too gay and popular to be considered music as I understand it, if each of them had not contained a passage of some originality, a modulation, a harmonic phrasing, some sort of bold effect that betrayed wit and invention, which was evidently the point of the whole and which made it interesting to genuine musicians. Often these two single measures would have a strange plaintive, melancholy tone which would come out abruptly in the midst of a piece of dance-music and as suddenly be gone.

Amra Jacoby was on fire with guilty passion for this young man, and as for him he had not enough moral fibre to resist her seductions. They met here, they met there, and for some years an immoral relation had subsisted between them, known to the whole town, who laughed at it behind the lawyer's back. But what did he think? Amra was not sensitive enough to betray herself on account of a guilty conscience, so we must take it as certain that, however heavy the lawyer's heart, he could cherish no definite suspicions.

Spring had come, rejoicing all hearts; and Amra conceived the most charming idea.

"Christian," said she—Jacoby's name was Christian—"let us give a party, a beer party to celebrate the new beer—of course quite simply, but let's have a lot of people."

"Certainly," said the lawyer, "but could we not have it a little later?"

To which Amra made no reply, having passed on to the consideration of details.

"It will be so large that we cannot have it here, we must hire a place, some sort of outdoor restaurant where there is plenty of room and fresh air. You see that, of course. The place I am thinking of is Wendelin's big hall at the foot of the Lerchenberg. The hall is independent of the restaurant and brewery, connected by a passage only. We can decorate it for the occasion and set up long tables, drink our bock, and dance—we must have music and even perhaps some sort of entertainment. There is a little stage, as I happen to know, that makes it very suitable. It will be a very original party and no end of fun."

The lawyer's face had gone a pale yellow as she spoke, and the corners of his mouth went down. He said:

"My dear Amra! How delightful it will be! I can leave it all to you, you are so clever. Make any arangements you like."

. . .

And Amra made her arrangements. She took counsel of various ladies and gentlemen, she went in person to hire the hall, she even formed a committee of people who were invited or who volunteered to co-operate in the entertainment. These were exclusively men, except for the wife of Herr Hildebrandt, an actor at the Hoftheater, who was herself a singer. Then there was Herr Hildebrandt, an Assessor Witznagel, a young painter, Alfred Läutner the musician, and some students brought in by Herr Witznagel, who were to do Negro dances.

A week after Amra had made her plan, this committee met in Amra's drawing-room in the Kaiserstrasse—a small, crowded, over-heated room, with a heavy carpet, a sofa with quantities of cushions, a fan palm, English leather chairs, and a splay-legged mahogany table with a velvet cover, upon which rested several large illustrated morocco-bound volumes. There was a fireplace too, with a small fire still burning, and on the marble chimney-top were plates of dainty sandwiches, glasses, and two decanters of sherry. Amra reclined in one corner of the sofa under the fan palm, with her legs crossed. She had the beauty of a warm summer night. A thin blouse of light-coloured silk covered her bosom, but her skirt was of heavy dark stuff embroidered with large flowers. Sometimes she put up one hand to brush back the chestnut hair from her narrow forehead. Frau Hildebrandt sat beside her on the sofa; she had red hair and wore riding clothes. Opposite the two all the gentlemen formed a semicircle—among them Jacoby himself, in the lowest chair he could find. He looked unutterably wretched, kept drawing a long breath and swallowing as though struggling against increasing nausea. Herr Alfred Läutner was in tennis clothes—he would not take a chair, but leaned decoratively against the chimney-piece, saying merrily that he could not sit still so long.

Herr Hildebrandt talked sonorously about English songs. He was a most respectable gentleman, in a black suit, with a Roman head and an assured manner—in short a proper actor for a court theatre, cultured, knowledgeable, and with enlightened tastes. He liked to hold forth in condemnation of Ibsen, Zola, and Tolstoi, all of whom had the same objectionable aims. But today he was benignly interested in the small affair under discussion.

"Do you know that priceless song 'That's Maria!'?" he asked. "Perhaps it is a little racy—but very effective. And then" so-and-so—he suggested other songs, upon which they came to an agreement and Frau Hildebrandt said that she would sing them. The young painter, who had sloping shoulders and a very blond beard, was to give a burlesque conjuring turn. Herr Hildebrandt offered to impersonate various famous characters. In short, everything was developing nicely, the programme was apparently arranged, when Assessor Witznagel, who had command of fluent gesture and a good many duelling scars, suddenly took the word.

"All very well, ladies and gentlemen, it looks like being most amusing. But if I may say so, it still lacks something; it wants some kind of high spot, a climax as it were, something a bit startling, perhaps, to round the thing off. I leave it to you, I have nothing particular in mind, I only think . . ."

"That is true enough!" Alfred Läutner's tenor voice came from the chimney-piece where he leaned. "Witznagel is right. We need a climax. Let us put our heads together!" He settled his red belt and looked engagingly about him.

"Well, if we do not consider the famous characters as the high spot," said Herr Hildebrandt. Everybody agreed with the Assessor. Something piquant was wanted for the principal number. Even Jacoby nodded, and murmured: "Yes, yes, something jolly and striking. . . ." They all reflected.

At the end of a minute's pause, which was broken only by stifled exclamations, an extraordinary thing happened. Amra was sitting reclined among the cushions, gnawing as busily as a mouse at the pointed nail of her little finger. She had a very odd look on her face: a vacant, almost an irresponsible smile, which betrayed a sensuality both tormented and cruel. Her eyes, very bright and wide, turned slowly to the chimney-piece, where for a second they met the musician's. Then suddenly she jerked her whole body to one side as she sat, in the direction of her husband. With both hands in her lap she stared into his face with an avid and clinging gaze, her own growing visibly paler, and said in her rich, slow voice:

"Christian, suppose you come on at the end as a *chanteuse,* in a red satin baby frock, and do a dance."

The effect of these few words was tremendous. The young painter essayed to laugh good-humouredly; Herr Hildebrandt, stony-faced, brushed a crumb from his sleeve; his wife coloured up, a rare thing for her; the students coughed and used their handkerchiefs loudly; and Herr Assessor Witznagel simply left the field and got himself a sandwich. The lawyer sat huddled on his little chair, yellow in the face, with a terrified smile. He looked all round the circle, and stammered:

"But, my God . . . I—I—I am not up to—not that I—I beg pardon, but . . ."

Alfred Läutner had lost his insouciant expression; he even seemed to have reddened a little, and he thrust out his neck to peer searchingly into Amra's face. He looked puzzled and upset.

But she, Amra, holding the same persuasive pose, went on with the same impressiveness:

"And you must sing, too, Christian, a song which Herr Läutner shall compose, and he can accompany you on the piano. We could not have a better or more effective climax."

There was a pause, an oppressive pause. Then this extraordinary thing happened, that Herr Läutner, as it were seized upon and carried away by his excitement, took a step forward and his voice fairly trembled with enthusiasm as he said:

"Herr Jacoby, that is a priceless idea, and I am more than ready to compose something. You must have a dance and song, anything else is unthinkable as a wind-up to our affair. You will see, it will be the best thing I have ever written or ever shall write. In a red satin baby frock. Oh, your wife is an artist, only an artist could have hit upon the idea! Do say yes, I beg of you. I will do my part, you will see, it will be an achievement."

Here the circle broke up and the meeting became lively. Out of politeness, or out of malice, the company began to storm the lawyer with entreaties—Frau Hildebrandt went so far as to say, quite loudly, in her Brünnhilde[2] voice:

"Herr Jacoby, after all, you are such a jolly and entertaining man!"

But the lawyer had pulled himself together and spoke, a little yellow, but with a strong effort at resolution:

"But listen to me, ladies and gentlemen—what can I say to you? It isn't my line, believe me. I have no comic gift, and besides . . . in short, no, it is quite impossible, alas!"

He stuck obstinately to his refusal, and Amra no longer insisted, but sat still with her absent look. Herr Läutner was silent too, staring in deep abstraction at a pattern in the rug. Herr Hildebrandt changed the subject, and presently the committee meeting broke up without coming to a final decision about the "climax."

On the evening of the same day Amra had gone to bed and was lying there with her eyes wide open; her husband came lumbering into the bedroom, drew a chair up beside the bed, dropped into it, and said, in a low, hesitating voice:

"Listen, Amra; to be quite frank, I am feeling very disturbed. I refused them today—I did not mean to be offensive—goodness knows I did not mean that. Or do you seriously feel that—I beg you to tell me."

Amra was silent for a moment, while her brows rose slowly. Then she shrugged her shoulders and said:

[2] The principal valkyrie in Richard Wagner's operatic tetralogy *Ring of the Nibelungs*; a powerful soprano.

"I do not know, my dear friend, how to answer you. You behaved in a way I should not have expected from you. You were unfriendly, you refused to support our enterprise in a way which they flatteringly considered to be indispensable to it. To put it mildly, you disappointed everybody and upset the whole company with your rude lack of compliance. Whereas it was your duty as host—"

The lawyer hung his head and sighed heavily. He said:

"Believe me, Amra, I had no intention to be disobliging. I do not like to offend anybody; if I have behaved badly I am ready to make amends. It is only a joke, after all, an innocent little dressing-up— why not? I will not upset the whole affair, I am ready to . . ."

The following afternoon Amra went out again to "make preparations." She drove to Number 78 Holzstrasse and went up to the second storey, where she had an appointment. And when she lay relaxed by the expression of her love she pressed her lover's head passionately to her breast and whispered:

"Write it for four hands. We will accompany him together while he sings and dances. I will see to the costume myself."

And an extraordinary shiver, a suppressed and spasmodic burst of laughter went through the limbs of both.

For anyone who wants to give a large party out of doors Herr Wendelin's place on the slope of the Lerchenberg is to be recommended. You enter it from the pretty suburban street through a tall trellised gateway and pass into the parklike garden, in the centre of which stands a large hall, connected only by a narrow passage with restaurant, kitchen, and brewery. It is a large, brightly painted wooden hall, in an amusing mixture of Chinese and Renaissance styles. It has folding doors which stand open in good weather to admit the woodland air, and it will hold a great many people.

On this evening as the carriages rolled up they were greeted from afar by the gleam of coloured lights. The whole gateway, the trees, and the hall itself were set thick with lanterns, while the interior made an entrancing sight. Heavy garlands were draped across the ceiling and studded with paper lanterns. Hosts of electric lights hung among the decorations of the walls, which consisted of pine boughs, flags, and artificial flowers; the whole hall was brilliantly lighted. The stage had foliage plants grouped on either side, and a red curtain with a painted design of a presiding genius hovering in the air. A long row of decorated tables ran almost the whole length of the hall. And at these tables the guests of Attorney Jacoby were doing themselves well on cold roast veal and bock beer. There were certainly more than a hundred and fifty people: officers, lawyers, business men, artists, upper officials, with their wives and daughters. They were quite simply dressed, in black coats and light spring toilettes, for this was a jolly, informal occasion. The gentlemen carried their mugs in person to the big casks against one of the walls; the spacious, festive, brightly lighted room was filled with a heavy sweetish atmosphere of evergreen boughs, flowers, beer, food, and human beings; and there was a clatter and buzz of laughter and talk—the loud, simple talk and the high, good-natured, unrestrained, carefree laughter of the sort of people there assembled.

The attorney sat shapeless and helpless at one end of the table, near the stage. He drank little and now and then addressed a laboured remark to his neighbour, Frau Regierungsrat Havermann.[3] He breathed offensively, the corners of his mouth hung down, he stared fixedly with his bulging watery eyes into the lively scene, with a sort of melancholy remoteness, as though there resided in all this noisy merriment something inexpressibly painful and perplexing.

Large fruit tarts were now being handed round for the company to cut from; they drank sweet wine with these, and the time for the speeches arrived. Herr Hildebrandt celebrated the new brew in a speech almost entirely composed of classical quotations, even Greek. Herr Witznagel, with florid gestures and ingenious turns of phrase, toasted the ladies, taking a handful of flowers from the nearest vase and comparing each flower to some feminine charm. Amra Jacoby, who sat opposite him in a pale-yellow silk frock, he called "a lovelier sister of the Maréchal Niel." [4]

Then she nodded meaningfully to her husband, brushing back her hair from her forehead; whereupon the fat man arose and almost ruined the whole atmosphere by stammering a few words with painful effort, smiling a repulsive smile. Some half-hearted bravos rewarded him, then there was an oppressive pause, after which jollity resumed its sway. All smoking, all a little elevated by drink, they rose from table and with their own hands and a great deal of noise removed the tables from the hall to make way for the dancing.

It was after eleven and high spirits reigned supreme. Some of the guests streamed out into the brightly lighted garden to get the fresh air; others stood about the hall in groups, smoking, chatting, drawing beer from the kegs, and drinking it standing. Then a loud trumpet call sounded from the stage, summoning everybody to the entertainment. The band arrived and took its place before the curtains; rows of chairs were put in place and red programmes distributed on them;

[3] Mrs. Councilor Havermann. (That is, her husband is a government official.)
[4] A handsome yellow climbing rose.

the gentlemen ranged themselves along the walls. There was an expectant hush.

The band played a noisy overture, and the curtains parted to reveal a row of Negroes horrifying to behold in their barbaric costumes and their blood-red lips, gnashing their teeth and emitting savage yells.

Certainly the entertainment was the crowning success of Amra's party. As it went on, the applause grew more and more enthusiastic. Frau Hildebrandt came on in a powdered wig, pounded with a shepherdess' crook on the floor and sang—in too large a voice—"That's Maria!" A conjuror in a dress coat covered with orders performed the most amazing feats; Herr Hildebrandt impersonated Goethe, Bismarck, and Napoleon in an amazingly lifelike manner; and a newspaper editor, Dr. Wiesensprung, improvised a humorous lecture which had as its theme bock beer and its social significance. And now the suspense reached its height, for it was time for the last, the mysterious number which appeared on the programme framed in a laurel wreath and was entitled: "*Little Lizzy*. Song and Dance. Music by Alfred Läutner."

A movement swept through the hall, and people's eyes met as the band sat down at their instruments and Alfred Läutner came from the doorway where he had been lounging with a cigarette between his pouting lips to take his place beside Amra Jacoby at the piano, which stood in the centre of the stage in front of the curtains. Herr Läutner's face was flushed and he turned over his manuscript score nervously; Amra for her part was rather pale. She leaned one arm on the back of her chair and looked loweringly at the audience. The bell rang, the pianists played a few bars of an insignificant accompaniment, the curtains parted, little Lizzy appeared.

The whole audience stiffened with amazement as that tragic and bedizened bulk shambled with a sort of bear-dance into view. It was Jacoby. A wide, shapeless garment of crimson satin, without folds, fell to his feet; it was cut out above to make a repulsive display of the fat neck, stippled with white powder. The sleeves consisted merely of a shoulder puff, but the flabby arms were covered by long lemon-coloured gloves; on the head perched a high blond wig with a swaying green feather. And under the wig was a face, a puffy, pasty, unhappy, and desperately mirthful face, with cheeks that shook pathetically up and down and little red-rimmed eyes that strained in anguish towards the floor and saw nothing else at all. The fat man hoisted himself with effort from one leg to the other, while with his hands he either held up his skirts or else weakly raised his index fingers—these two gestures he had and knew no others. In a choked and gasping voice he sang, to the accompaniment of the piano.

The lamentable figure exhaled more than ever a cold breath of anguish. It killed every light-hearted enjoyment and lay like an oppressive weight upon the assembled audience. Horror was in the depths of all these spellbound eyes, gazing at this pair at the piano and at that husband there. The monstrous, unspeakable scandal lasted five long minutes.

Then came a moment which none of those present will forget as long as they live. Let us picture to ourselves what happened in that frightful and frightfully involved little instant of time.

You know of course the absurd little jingle called "Lizzy." And you remember the lines:

> *I can polka until I am dizzy,*
> *I can waltz with the best and beyond,*
> *I'm the popular pet, little Lizzy,*
> *Who makes all the menfolks so fond—*

which form the trivial and unlovely refrain to three longish stanzas. Alfred Läutner had composed a new setting to the verses I have quoted, and it was, as he had said it would be, his masterpiece. He had, that is, brought to its highest pitch his little artifice of introducing into a fairly vulgar and humorous piece of hackwork a sudden phrase of genuine creative art. The melody, in C-sharp major, had been in the first bars rather pretty and perfectly banal. At the beginning of the refrain the rhythm became livelier and dissonances occurred, which by means of the constant accentuation of a B-natural made one expect a transition into F-sharp major. These dissonances went on developing until the word "beyond"; and after the "I'm the" a culmination into F-sharp major should have followed. Instead of which the most surprising thing happened. That is, through a harsh turn, by means of an inspiration which was almost a stroke of genius, the key changed to F-major, and this little interlude which followed, with the use of both pedals on the long-drawn-out first syllable of the word "Lizzy," was indescribably, almost gruesomely effective. It was a complete surprise, an abrupt assault on the nerves, it shivered down the back, it was a miracle, a revelation, it was like a curtain suddenly torn away to reveal something nude.

And on the F-major chord Attorney Jacoby stopped dancing. He stood still, he stood as though rooted to the stage with his two forefingers lifted, one a little lower than the other. The word "Lizzy" stuck in his throat, he was dumb; almost at the same time the accompaniment broke sharp off, and the incredible, absurd, and ghastly figure stood there frozen, with his head thrust forward like a steer's, staring with inflamed eyes straight before him. He stared into the brightly lighted, decorated, crowded hall, in which, like an exhalation from all these people, the scandal hung and thickened into visibility. He stared at all these upturned faces, foreshortened and distorted by the lighting, into these hundreds of pairs of eyes all directed with the same knowing expression upon himself and the two at the piano. In a frightful stillness, unbroken by the smallest sound, his gaze travelled slowly and uneasily from the pair to the audience, from the audience to the pair, while his eyes widened more and more. Then knowledge seemed to flash across his face, like a sudden rush of blood, making it red as the frock he wore, only to give way to a waxen yellow pallor—and the fat man collapsed, making the platform creak beneath his weight.

For another moment the stillness reigned. Then there came shrieks, hubbub ensued, a few gentlemen took heart to spring upon the platform, among them a young doctor—and the curtains were drawn together.

Amra Jacoby and Alfred Läutner still sat at the piano. They had turned a little away from each other, and he, with his head bent, seemed to be listening to the echo of his F-major chord, while she, with her birdlike brain, had not yet grasped the situation, but gazed round her with vacant face.

The young doctor came back presently. He was a little Jewish gentleman with a serious face and a small pointed beard. Some people surrounded him at the door with questions—to which he replied with a shrug of the shoulders and the words:

"All over."

Translated by H. T. Lowe-Porter

The Egg

My father was, I am sure, intended by nature to be a cheerful, kindly man. Until he was thirty-four years old he worked as a farmhand for a man named Thomas Butterworth whose place lay near the town of Bidwell, Ohio. He had then a horse of his own, and on Saturday evenings drove into town to spend a few hours in social intercourse with other farmhands. In town he drank several glasses of beer and stood about in Ben Head's saloon—crowded on Saturday evenings with visiting farmhands. Songs were sung and glasses thumped on the bar. At ten o'clock father drove home along a lonely country road, made his horse comfortable for the night, and himself went to bed, quite happy in his position in life. He had at that time no notion of trying to rise in the world.

It was in the spring of his thirty-fifth year that father married my mother, then a country school-teacher, and in the following spring I came wriggling and crying into the world. Something happened to the two people. They became ambitious. The American passion for getting up in the world took possession of them.

It may have been that mother was responsible. Being a school-teacher she had no doubt read books and magazines. She had, I presume, read of how Garfield, Lincoln, and other Americans rose from poverty to fame and greatness, and as I lay beside her—in the days of her lying-in—she may have dreamed that I would some day rule men and cities. At any rate she induced father to give up his place as a farmhand, sell his horse, and embark on an independent enterprise of his own. She was a tall silent woman with a long nose and troubled gray eyes. For herself she wanted nothing. For father and myself she was incurably ambitious.

The first venture into which the two people went turned out badly. They rented ten acres of poor stony land on Griggs's Road, eight miles from Bidwell, and launched into chicken-raising. I grew into boyhood on the place and got my first impressions of life there. From the beginning they were impressions of disaster, and if, in my turn, I am a gloomy man inclined to see the darker side of life, I attribute it to the fact that what should have been for me the happy joyous days of childhood were spent on a chicken farm.

One unversed in such matters can have no notion of the many and tragic things that can happen to a chicken. It is born out of an egg, lives for a few weeks as a tiny fluffy thing such as you will see pictured on Easter cards, then becomes hideously naked, eats quantities of corn and meal bought by the sweat of your father's brow, gets diseases called pip, cholera, and other names, stands looking with stupid eyes at the sun, becomes sick and dies. A few hens and now and then a rooster, intended to serve God's mysterious ends, struggle through to maturity. The hens lay eggs out of which come other chickens and the dreadful cycle is thus made complete. It is all unbelievably complex. Most philosophers must have been raised on chicken farms. One hopes for so much from a chicken and is so dreadfully disillusioned. Small chickens, just setting out on the journey of life, look so bright and alert and they are in fact so dreadfully stupid. They are so much like people they mix one up in one's judgments of life. If disease does not kill them, they wait until your expectations are thoroughly aroused and then walk under the wheels of a wagon— to go squashed and dead back to their maker. Vermin infest their youth, and fortunes must be spent for curative powders. In later life I have seen how a literature has been built up on the subject of fortunes to be made out of the raising of chickens. It is intended to be read by the gods who have just eaten of the tree of the knowledge of good and evil. It is a hopeful literature and declares that much may be done by simple ambitious people who own a few hens. Do not be led astray by it. It was not written for you. Go hunt for gold on the frozen hills of Alaska, put your faith in the honesty of a politician, believe if you will that the world is daily growing better and that good will triumph over evil, but do not read and believe the literature that is written concerning the hen. It was not written for you.

I, however, digress. My tale does not primarily concern itself with the hen. If correctly told it will center on the egg. For ten years my father and mother struggled to make our chicken farm pay and then they gave up that struggle and began another. They moved into the town of Bidwell, Ohio, and embarked in the restaurant business. After ten years of worry with incubators that did not hatch, and with tiny— and in their own way lovely—balls of fluff that passed on into seminaked pullethood and from that into dead henhood, we threw all aside and, packing our belongings on a wagon, drove down Griggs's Road toward Bidwell, a tiny caravan of hope looking for a new place from which to start on our upward journey through life.

We must have been a sad-looking lot, not, I fancy, unlike refugees fleeing from a battlefield. Mother and I walked in the road. The wagon that contained our goods had been borrowed for the day from Mr. Albert Griggs, a neighbor. Out of its sides stuck the legs of cheap chairs, and at the back of the pile of beds, tables, and boxes filled with kitchen utensils was a crate of live chickens, and on top of that the baby carriage in which I had been wheeled about in my infancy. Why we stuck to the baby carriage I don't know. It was unlikely other children would be born and the wheels were broken. People who have few possessions cling tightly to those they have. That is one of the facts that make life so discouraging.

Father rode on top of the wagon. He was then a bald-headed man of forty-five, a little fat, and from long association with mother and the chickens he had become habitually silent and discouraged. All during our ten years on the chicken farm he had worked as a laborer on neighboring farms and most of the money he had earned had been spent for remedies to cure chicken diseases, on Wilmer's White Wonder Cholera Cure or Professor Bidlow's Egg Producer or some other preparations that mother found advertised in the poultry papers. There were two little patches of hair on father's head just above his ears. I remember that as a child I used to sit looking at him when he had gone to sleep in a chair before the stove on Sunday afternoons in the winter. I had at that time already begun to read books and have notions of my own, and the bald path that led over the top of his head was, I fancied, something like a broad road, such a road as Caesar might have made on which to lead his legions out of Rome and into the wonders of an unknown world. The tufts of hair that grew above father's ears were, I thought, like forests. I fell into a half-sleeping, half-waking state and dreamed I was a tiny thing going along the road into a far beautiful place where there were no chicken farms and where life was a happy eggless affair.

One might write a book concerning our flight from the chicken farm into town. Mother and I walked the entire eight miles—she to be sure that nothing fell from the wagon and I to see the wonders of the world. On the seat of the wagon beside father was his greatest treasure. I will tell you of that.

On a chicken farm, where hundreds and even thousands of chickens come out of eggs, surprising things sometimes happen. Grotesques are born out of eggs as out of people. The accident does not often occur—perhaps once in a thousand births. A chicken is, you see, born that has four legs, two pairs of wings, two heads, or what not. The things do not live. They go quickly back to the hand of their maker that has for a moment trembled. The fact that the poor little things could not live was one of the tragedies of life to father. He had some sort of notion that if he could but bring into henhood or roosterhood a five-legged hen or a two-headed rooster his fortune would be made. He dreamed of taking the wonder about the county fairs and of growing rich by exhibiting it to other farmhands.

At any rate, he saved all the little monstrous things that had been born on our chicken farm. They were preserved in alcohol and put each in its own glass bottle. These he had carefully put into a box, and on our journey into town it was carried on the wagon seat beside him. He drove the horses with one hand and with the other clung to the box. When we got to our destination, the box was taken down at once and the bottles removed. All during our days as keepers of a restaurant in the town of Bidwell, Ohio, the grotesques in their little glass bottles sat on a shelf back of the counter. Mother sometimes protested, but father was a rock on the subject of his treasure. The grotesques were, he declared, valuable. People, he said, liked to look at strange and wonderful things.

Did I say that we embarked in the restaurant business in the town of Bidwell, Ohio? I exaggerated a little. The town itself lay at the foot of a low hill and on the shore of a small river. The railroad did not run through the town and the station was a mile away to the north at a place called Pickleville. There had been a cider mill and pickle factory at the station, but before the time of our coming they had both gone out of business. In the morning and in the evening busses came down to the station along a road called Turner's Pike from the hotel on the main street of Bidwell. Our going to the out-of-the-way place to embark in the restaurant business was mother's idea. She talked of it for a year and then one day went off and rented an empty store building opposite the railroad station. It was her idea that the restaurant would be profitable. Traveling men, she said, would be always waiting around to take trains out of town and town people would come to the station to await incoming trains. They would come to the restaurant to buy pieces of pie and drink coffee. Now that I am older I know that she had another motive in going. She was ambitious for me. She wanted me to rise in the world, to get into a town school and become a man of the towns.

At Pickleville father and mother worked hard, as they always had done. At first there was the necessity of putting our place into shape to be a restaurant. That took a month. Father built a shelf on which he put tins of vegetables. He painted a sign on which he put his name in large red letters. Below his name was the sharp command—"EAT HERE"—that was so seldom obeyed. A showcase was bought and filled with cigars and tobacco. Mother scrubbed the floor and the walls of the room. I went to school in the town and was glad to be away from the farm and from the presence of the discouraged, sad-looking chickens. Still I was not very joyous. In the evening I walked home from school along Turner's Pike and remembered the children I had seen playing in the town school yard. A troop of little girls had gone hopping about and singing. I tried that. Down along the frozen road I went hopping solemnly on one leg. "Hippity Hop To The Barber Shop," I sang shrilly. Then I stopped and looked doubtfully about. I was afraid of being seen in my gay mood. It must have seemed to me that I was doing a thing that should not be done by one who, like myself, had been raised on a chicken farm where death was a daily visitor.

Mother decided that our restaurant should remain open at night. At ten in the evening a passenger train went north past our door followed by a local freight. The freight crew had switching to do in Pickleville, and when the work was done they came to our restaurant for hot coffee and food. Sometimes one of them ordered a fried egg. In the morning at four they returned north-bound and again visited us. A little trade began to grow up. Mother slept at night and during the day tended the restaurant and fed our boarders while father slept. He slept in the same bed mother had occupied during the night and I went off to the town of Bidwell and to school. During the long nights, while mother and I slept, father cooked meats that were to go into sandwiches for the lunch baskets of our boarders. Then an idea in regard to getting up in the world came into his head. The American spirit took hold of him. He also became ambitious.

In the long nights when there was little to do, father had time to think. That was his undoing. He decided that he had in the past been an unsuccessful man because he had not been cheerful enough and that in the future he would adopt a cheerful outlook on life. In the early morning he came upstairs and got into bed with mother. She woke and the two talked. From my bed in the corner I listened.

It was father's idea that both he and mother should try to entertain the people who came to eat at our restaurant. I cannot now remember his words, but he gave the impression of one about to become in some obscure way a kind of public entertainer. When people, particularly young people from the town of Bidwell, came into our place, as on very rare occasions they did, bright entertaining conversation was to be made. From father's words I gathered that something of the jolly innkeeper effect was to be sought. Mother must have been doubtful from the first, but she said nothing discouraging. It was father's notion that a passion for the company of himself and mother would spring up in the breasts of the younger people of the town of Bidwell. In the evening bright happy groups would come singing down

Turner's Pike. They would troop shouting with joy and laughter into our place. There would be song and festivity. I do not mean to give the impression that father spoke so elaborately of the matter. He was, as I have said, an uncommunicative man. "They want some place to go. I tell you they want some place to go," he said over and over. That was as far as he got. My own imagination has filled in the blanks.

For two or three weeks this notion of father's invaded our house. We did not talk much, but in our daily lives tried earnestly to make smiles take the place of glum looks. Mother smiled at the boarders and I, catching the infection, smiled at our cat. Father became a little feverish in his anxiety to please. There was, no doubt, lurking somewhere in him, a touch of the spirit of the showman. He did not waste much of his ammunition on the railroad men he served at night, but seemed to be waiting for a young man or woman from Bidwell to come in to show what he could do. On the counter in the restaurant there was a wire basket kept always filled with eggs, and it must have been before his eyes when the idea of being entertaining was born in his brain. There was something pre-natal about the way eggs kept themselves connected with the development of his idea. At any rate, an egg ruined his new impulse in life. Late one night I was awakened by a roar of anger coming from father's throat. Both mother and I sat upright in our beds. With trembling hands she lighted a lamp that stood on a table by her head. Downstairs the front door of our restaurant went shut with a bang and in a few minutes father tramped up the stairs. He held an egg in his hand and his hand trembled as though he were having a chill. There was a half-insane light in his eyes. As he stood glaring at us I was sure he intended throwing the egg at either mother or me. Then he laid it gently on the table beside the lamp and dropped on his knees beside mother's bed. He began to cry like a boy, and I, carried away by his grief, cried with him. The two of us filled the little upstairs room with our wailing voices. It is ridiculous, but of the picture we made I can remember only the fact that mother's hand continually stroked the bald path that ran across the top of his head. I have forgotten what mother said to him and how she induced him to tell her of what had happened downstairs. His explanation also has gone out of my mind. I remember only my own grief and fright and the shiny path over father's head glowing in the lamplight as he knelt by the bed.

As to what happened downstairs. For some unexplainable reason I know the story as well as though I had been a witness to my father's discomfiture. One in time gets to know many unexplainable things. On that evening young Joe Kane, son of a merchant of Bidwell, came to Pickleville to meet his father, who was expected on the ten o'clock evening train from the South. The train was three hours late and Joe came into our place to loaf about and to wait for its arrival. The local freight train came in and the freight crew were fed. Joe was left alone in the restaurant with father.

From the moment he came into our place the Bidwell young man must have been puzzled by my father's actions. It was his notion that father was angry at him for hanging around. He noticed that the restaurant-keeper was apparently disturbed by his presence and he thought of going out. However, it began to rain and he did not fancy the long walk to town and back. He bought a five-cent cigar and ordered a cup of coffee. He had a newspaper in his pocket and took it out and began to read. "I'm waiting for the evening train. It's late," he said apologetically.

For a long time father, whom Joe Kane had never seen before, remained silently gazing at his visitor. He was no doubt suffering from an attack of stage fright. As so often happens in life he had thought so much and so often of the situation that now confronted him that he was somewhat nervous in its presence.

For one thing, he did not know what to do with his hands. He thrust one of them nervously over the counter and shook hands with Joe Kane. "How-de-do," he said. Joe Kane put his newspaper down and stared at him. Father's eyes lighted on the basket of eggs that sat on the counter and he began to talk. "Well," he began hesitatingly, "well, you have heard of Christopher Columbus, eh?" He seemed to be angry. "That Christopher Columbus was a cheat," he declared emphatically. "He talked of making an egg stand on its end. He talked, he did, and then he went and broke the end of the egg."

My father seemed to his visitor to be beside himself at the duplicity of Christopher Columbus. He muttered and swore. He declared it was wrong to teach children that Christopher Columbus was a great man when, after all, he cheated at the critical moment. He had declared he would make an egg stand on end and then, when his bluff had been called, he had done a trick. Still grumbling at Columbus, father took an egg from the basket on the counter and began to walk up and down. He rolled the egg between the palms of his hands. He smiled genially. He began to mumble words regarding the effect to be produced on an egg by the electricity that comes out of the human body. He declared that, without breaking its shell and by virtue of rolling it back and forth in his hands, he could stand the egg on its end. He explained that the warmth of his hands and the gentle rolling movement he gave the egg created a new center of gravity, and Joe Kane was mildly interested. "I have handled thousands of eggs," father said. "No one knows more about eggs than I do."

He stood the egg on the counter and it fell on its side. He tried the trick again and again, each time rolling the egg between the palms of his hands and saying the words regarding the wonders of electricity and the laws of gravity. When after a half-hour's effort he did succeed in making the egg stand for a moment, he looked up to find that his visitor was no longer watching. By the time he had succeeded in calling Joe Kane's attention to the success of his effort, the egg had again rolled over and lay on its side.

Afire with the showman's passion and at the same time a good deal disconcerted by the failure of his first effort, father now took the bottles containing the poultry monstrosities down from their place on the shelf and began to show them to his visitor. "How would you like to have seven legs and two heads like this fellow?" he asked, exhibiting the most remarkable of his treasures. A cheerful smile played over his face. He reached over the counter and tried to slap Joe Kane on the shoulder as he had seen men do in Ben Head's saloon when he was a young farmhand and drove to town on Saturday evenings. His visitor was made a little ill by the sight of the body of the terribly deformed bird floating in the alcohol in the bottle and got up to go. Coming from behind the counter, father took hold of the young man's arm and led him back to his seat. He grew a little angry and for a moment had to turn his face away and force himself to smile. Then he put the bottles back on the shelf. In an outburst of generosity he fairly compelled Joe Kane to have a fresh cup of coffee and another cigar at his expense. Then he took a pan and filling it with vinegar, taken from a jug that sat beneath the counter, he declared himself about to do a new trick. "I will heat this egg in this pan of vinegar," he said. "Then I will put it through the neck of a bottle without breaking the shell. When the egg is inside the bottle it will resume its normal shape and the shell will become hard again. Then I will give the bottle with the egg in it to you. You can take it about with you wherever you go. People will want to know how you got the egg in the bottle. Don't tell them. Keep them guessing. That is the way to have fun with this trick."

Father grinned and winked at his visitor. Joe Kane decided that the man who confronted him was mildly insane but harmless. He drank the cup of coffee that had been given him and began to read his paper again. When the egg had been heated in vinegar, father carried it on a spoon to the counter and going into a back room got an empty bottle. He was angry because his visitor did not watch him as he began to do his trick, but nevertheless went cheerfully to work. For a long time he struggled, trying to get the egg to go through the neck of the bottle. He put the pan of vinegar back on the stove, intending to reheat the egg, then picked it up and burned his fingers. After a second bath in the hot vinegar, the shell of the egg had been softened a little, but not enough for his purpose. He worked and worked and a spirit of desperate determination took possession of him. When he thought that at last the trick was about to be consummated, the delayed train came in at the station and Joe Kane started to go nonchalantly out at the door. Father made a last desperate effort to conquer the egg and make it do the thing that would establish his reputation as one who knew how to entertain guests who came into his restaurant. He worried the egg. He attempted to be somewhat rough with it. He swore and the sweat stood out on his forehead. The egg broke under his hand. When the contents spurted over his clothes, Joe Kane, who had stopped at the door, turned and laughed.

A roar of anger rose from my father's throat. He danced and shouted a string of inarticulate words. Grabbing another egg from the basket on the counter, he threw it, just missing the head of the young man as he dodged through the door and escaped.

Father came upstairs to mother and me with an egg in his hand. I do not know what he intended to do. I imagine he had some idea of destroying it, of destroying all eggs, and that he intended to let mother and me see him begin. When, however, he got into the presence of mother, something happened to him. He laid the egg gently on the table and dropped on his knees by the bed as I have already explained. He later decided to close the restaurant for the night and to come upstairs and get into bed. When he did so, he blew out the light and after much muttered conversation both he and mother went to sleep. I suppose I went to sleep also, but my sleep was troubled. I awoke at dawn and for a long time looked at the egg that lay on the table. I wondered why eggs had to be and why from the egg came the hen who again laid the egg. The question got into my blood. It has stayed there, I imagine, because I am the son of my father. At any rate, the problem remains unsolved in my mind. And that, I conclude, is but another evidence of the complete and final triumph of the egg—at least as far as my family is concerned.

Counterparts

The bell rang furiously and, when Miss Parker went to the tube, a furious voice called out in a piercing North of Ireland accent:

"Send Farrington here!"

Miss Parker returned to her machine, saying to a man who was writing at a desk:

"Mr. Alleyne wants you upstairs."

The man muttered *"Blast* him!" under his breath and pushed back his chair to stand up. When he stood up he was tall and of great bulk. He had a hanging face, dark wine-coloured, with fair eyebrows and moustache: his eyes bulged forward slightly and the whites of them were dirty. He lifted up the counter and, passing by the clients, went out of the office with a heavy step.

He went heavily upstairs until he came to the second landing, where a door bore a brass plate with the inscription *Mr. Alleyne.* Here he halted, puffing with labour and vexation, and knocked. The shrill voice cried:

"Come in!"

The man entered Mr. Alleyne's room. Simultaneously Mr. Alleyne, a little man wearing gold-rimmed glasses on a clean-shaven face, shot his head up over a pile of documents. The head itself was so pink and hairless it seemed like a large egg reposing on the papers. Mr. Alleyne did not lose a moment:

"Farrington? What is the meaning of this? Why have I always to complain of you? May I ask you why you haven't made a copy of that contract between Bodley and Kirwan? I told you it must be ready by four o'clock."

"But Mr. Shelley said, sir——"

"Mr. Shelley said, sir. . . . Kindly attend to what I say and not to what *Mr. Shelley says, sir.* You have always some excuse or another for shirking work. Let me tell you that if the contract is not copied before this evening I'll lay the matter before Mr. Crosbie. . . . Do you hear me now?"

"Yes, sir."

"Do you hear me now? . . . Ay and another little matter! I might as well be talking to the wall as talking to you. Understand once for all that you get a half an hour for your lunch and not an hour and a half. How many courses do you want, I'd like to know. . . . Do you mind me now?"

"Yes, sir."

Mr. Alleyne bent his head again upon his pile of papers. The man stared fixedly at the polished skull which directed the affairs of Crosbie & Alleyne, gauging its fragility. A spasm of rage gripped his throat for a few moments and then passed, leaving after it a sharp sensation of thirst. The man recognised the sensation and felt that he must have a good night's drinking. The middle of the month was passed and, if he could get the copy done in time, Mr. Alleyne might give him an order on the cashier. He stood still, gazing fixedly at the head upon the pile of papers. Suddenly Mr. Alleyne began to upset all the papers, searching for something. Then, as if he had been unaware of the man's presence till that moment, he shot up his head again, saying:

"Eh? Are you going to stand there all day? Upon my word, Farrington, you take things easy!"

"I was waiting to see . . ."

"Very good, you needn't wait to see. Go downstairs and do your work."

The man walked heavily towards the door and, as he went out of the room, he heard Mr. Alleyne cry after him that if the contract was not copied by evening Mr. Crosbie would hear of the matter.

He returned to his desk in the lower office and counted the sheets which remained to be copied. He took up his pen and dipped it in the ink but he continued to stare stupidly at the last words he had written: *In no case shall the said Bernard Bodley be* . . . The evening was falling and in a few minutes they would be lighting the gas: then he could write. He felt that he must slake the thirst in his throat. He stood up from his desk and, lifting the counter as before, passed out of the office. As he was passing out the chief clerk looked at him inquiringly.

"It's all right, Mr. Shelley," said the man, pointing with his finger to indicate the objective of his journey.

The chief clerk glanced at the hat-rack, but, seeing the row complete, offered no remark. As soon as he was on the landing the man pulled a shepherd's plaid cap out of his pocket, put it on his head and ran quickly down the rickety stairs. From the street door he walked on furtively on the inner side of the path towards the corner and all at once dived into a doorway. He was now safe in the dark snug of O'Neill's shop, and filling up the little window that looked into the bar with his inflamed face, the colour of dark wine or dark meat, he called out:

"Here, Pat, give us a g.p., like a good fellow."

The curate brought him a glass of plain porter. The man drank it at a gulp and asked for a caraway seed. He put his penny on the counter and, leaving the curate to grope for it in the gloom, retreated out of the snug as furtively as he had entered it.

Darkness, accompanied by a thick fog, was gaining upon the dusk of February and the lamps in Eustace Street had been lit. The man went up by the houses until he reached the door of the office, wondering whether he could finish his copy in time. On the stairs a moist pungent odour of perfumes saluted his nose: evidently Miss Delacour had come while he was out in O'Neill's. He crammed his cap back again into his pocket and re-entered the office, assuming an air of absentmindedness.

"Mr. Alleyne has been calling for you," said the chief clerk severely. "Where were you?"

The man glanced at the two clients who were standing at the counter as if to intimate that their presence prevented him from answering. As the clients were both male the chief clerk allowed himself a laugh.

"I know that game," he said. "Five times in one day is a little bit . . . Well, you better look sharp and get a copy of our correspondence in the Delacour case for Mr. Alleyne."

This address in the presence of the public, his run upstairs and the porter he had gulped down so hastily confused the man and, as he sat down at his desk to get what was required, he realised how hopeless was the task of finishing his copy of the contract before half past five. The dark damp night was coming and he longed to spend it in the bars, drinking with his friends amid the glare of gas and the clatter of glasses. He got out the Delacour correspondence and passed out of the office. He hoped Mr. Alleyne would not discover that the last two letters were missing.

The moist pungent perfume lay all the way up to Mr. Alleyne's room. Miss Delacour was a middle-aged woman of Jewish appearance. Mr. Alleyne was said to be sweet on her or on her money. She came to the office often and stayed a long time when she came. She was sitting beside his desk now in an aroma of perfumes, smoothing the handle of her umbrella and nodding the great black feather in her hat. Mr. Alleyne had swivelled his chair round to face her and thrown his right foot jauntily upon his left knee. The man put the correspondence on the desk and bowed respectfully but neither Mr. Alleyne nor Miss Delacour took any notice of his bow. Mr. Alleyne tapped a finger on the correspondence and then flicked it towards him as if to say: "*That's all right: you can go.*"

The man returned to the lower office and sat down again at his desk. He stared intently at the incomplete phrase: *In no case shall the said Bernard Bodley be* . . . and thought how strange it was that the last three words began with the same letter. The chief clerk began to hurry Miss Parker, saying she would never have the letters typed in time for post. The man listened to the clicking of the machine for a few minutes and then set to work to finish his copy. But his head was not clear and his mind wandered away to the glare and rattle of the public-house. It was a night for hot punches. He struggled on with his copy, but when the clock struck five he had still fourteen pages to write. Blast it! He couldn't finish it in time. He longed to execrate aloud, to bring his fist down on something violently. He was so enraged that he wrote *Bernard Bernard* instead of *Bernard Bodley* and had to begin again on a clean sheet.

He felt strong enough to clear out the whole office singlehanded. His body ached to do something, to rush out and revel in violence. All the indignities of his life enraged him. . . . Could he ask the cashier privately for an advance? No, the cashier was no good, no damn good: he wouldn't give an advance. . . . He knew where he would meet the boys: Leonard and O'Halloran and Nosey Flynn. The barometer of his emotional nature was set for a spell of riot.

His imagination had so abstracted him that his name was called twice before he answered. Mr. Alleyne and Miss Delacour were standing outside the counter and all the clerks had turned round in anticipation of something. The man got up from his desk. Mr. Alleyne began a tirade of abuse, saying that two letters were missing. The man answered that he knew nothing about them, that he had made a faithful copy. The tirade continued: it was so bitter and violent that the man could hardly restrain his fist from descending upon the head of the manikin before him:

"I know nothing about any other two letters," he said stupidly.

"*You—know—nothing*. Of course you know nothing," said Mr. Alleyne. "Tell me," he added, glancing first for approval to the lady beside him, "do you take me for a fool? Do you think me an utter fool?"

The man glanced from the lady's face to the little egg-shaped head and back again; and, almost before he was aware of it, his tongue had found a felicitous moment:

"I don't think, sir," he said, "that that's a fair question to put to me."

There was a pause in the very breathing of the clerks. Everyone was astounded (the author of the witticism no less than his neighbours) and Miss Delacour, who was a stout amiable person, began to smile broadly. Mr. Alleyne flushed to the hue of a wild rose and his mouth twitched with a dwarf's passion. He shook his fist in the man's face till it seemed to vibrate like the knob of some electric machine:

"You impertinent ruffian! You impertinent ruffian! I'll make short work of you! Wait till you see! You'll apologise to me for your impertinence or you'll quit the office instanter! You'll quit this, I'm telling you, or you'll apologise to me!"

He stood in a doorway opposite the office watching to see if the cashier would come out alone. All the clerks passed out and finally the cashier came out with the chief clerk. It was no use trying to say a word to him when he was with the chief clerk. The man felt that his position was bad enough. He had been obliged to offer an abject apology to Mr. Alleyne for his impertinence but he knew what a hornet's nest the office would be for him. He could remember the way in which Mr. Alleyne had hounded little Peake out of the office in order to make room for his own nephew. He felt savage and thirsty and revengeful, annoyed with himself and with everyone else. Mr. Alleyne would never give him an hour's rest; his life would be a hell to him. He had made a proper fool of himself this time. Could he not keep his tongue in his cheek? But they had never pulled together from the first, he and Mr. Alleyne, ever since the day Mr. Alleyne had overheard him mimicking his North of Ireland accent to amuse Higgins and Miss Parker: that had been the beginning of it. He might have tried Higgins for the money, but sure Higgins never had anything for himself. A man with two establishments to keep up, of course he couldn't. . . .

He felt his great body again aching for the comfort of the public-house. The fog had begun to chill him and he wondered could he touch Pat in O'Neill's. He could not touch him for more than a bob —and a bob was no use. Yet he must get money somewhere or other: he had spent his last penny for the g.p. and soon it would be too late for getting money anywhere. Suddenly, as he was fingering his watch-chain, he thought of Terry Kelly's pawn-office in Fleet Street. That was the dart! Why didn't he think of it sooner?

He went through the narrow alley of Temple Bar quickly, muttering to himself that they could all go to hell because he was going to have a good night of it. The clerk in Terry Kelly's said *A crown!* but the consignor held out for six shillings; and in the end the six shillings was allowed him literally. He came out of the pawn-office joyfully, making a little cylinder of the coins between his thumb and fingers.

In Westmoreland Street the footpaths were crowded with young men and women returning from business and ragged urchins ran here and there yelling out the names of the evening editions. The man passed through the crowd, looking on the spectacle generally with proud satisfaction and staring masterfully at the office-girls. His head was full of the noises of tram-gongs and swishing trolleys and his nose already sniffed the curling fumes of punch. As he walked on he preconsidered the terms in which he would narrate the incident to the boys:

"So, I just looked at him—coolly, you know, and looked at her. Then I looked back at him again—taking my time, you know. 'I don't think that that's a fair question to put to me,' says I."

Nosey Flynn was sitting up in his usual corner of Davy Byrne's and, when he heard the story, he stood Farrington a half-one, saying it was as smart a thing as ever he heard. Farrington stood a drink in his turn. After a while O'Halloran and Paddy Leonard came in and the story was repeated to them. O'Halloran stood tailors of malt, hot, all round and told the story of the retort he had made to the chief clerk when he was in Callan's of Fownes's Street; but, as the retort was after the manner of the liberal shepherds in the eclogues, he had to admit that it was not as clever as Farrington's retort.[1] At this Farrington told the boys to polish off that and have another.

Just as they were naming their poisons who should come in but Higgins! Of course he had to join in with the others. The men asked him to give his version of it, and he did so with great vivacity for the sight of five small hot whiskies was very exhilarating. Everyone roared laughing when he showed the way in which Mr. Alleyne shook his fist in Farrington's face. Then he imitated Farrington, saying, *"And here was my nabs, as cool as you please,"* while Farrington looked at the company out of his heavy dirty eyes, smiling and at times drawing forth stray drops of liquor from his moustache with the aid of his lower lip.

When that round was over there was a pause. O'Halloran had money but neither of the other two seemed to have any; so the whole party left the shop somewhat regretfully. At the corner of Duke Street

[1] This probably refers to the Queen's speech about Ophelia in *Hamlet* (IV.vii.169-72):

> There with fantastic garlands did she come
> Of crowflowers, nettles, daisies, and long purples
> That liberal shepherds give a grosser name,
> But our cold maids do dead-men's-fingers call them.

Liberal here means "licentious in talk"; O'Halloran's retort was scabrous rather than witty.

Higgins and Nosey Flynn bevelled off to the left while the other three turned back towards the city. Rain was drizzling down on the cold streets and, when they reached the Ballast Office, Farrington suggested the Scotch House. The bar was full of men and loud with the noise of tongues and glasses. The three men pushed past the whining match-sellers at the door and formed a little party at the corner of the counter. They began to exchange stories. Leonard introduced them to a young fellow named Weathers who was performing at the Tivoli as an acrobat and knockabout *artiste*. Farrington stood a drink all round. Weathers said he would take a small Irish and Apollinaris. Farrington, who had definite notions of what was what, asked the boys would they have an Apollinaris too; but the boys told Tim to make theirs hot. The talk became theatrical. O'Halloran stood a round and then Farrington stood another round, Weathers protesting that the hospitality was too Irish. He promised to get them in behind the scenes and intro-duce them to some nice girls. O'Halloran said that he and Leonard would go, but that Farrington wouldn't go because he was a married man; and Farrington's heavy dirty eyes leered at the company in token that he understood he was being chaffed. Weathers made them all have just one little tincture at his expense and promised to meet them later on at Mulligan's in Poolbeg Street.

When the Scotch House closed they went round to Mulligan's. They went into the parlour at the back and O'Halloran ordered small hot specials all round. They were all beginning to feel mellow. Far-rington was just standing another round when Weathers came back. Much to Farrington's relief he drank a glass of bitter this time. Funds were getting low but they had enough to keep them going. Presently two young women with big hats and a young man in a check suit came in and sat at a table close by. Weathers saluted them and told the company that they were out of the Tivoli. Farrington's eyes wan-dered at every moment in the direction of one of the young women. There was something striking in her appearance. An immense scarf of peacock-blue muslin was wound round her hat and knotted in a great bow under her chin; and she wore bright yellow gloves, reaching to the elbow. Farrington gazed admiringly at the plump arm which she moved very often and with much grace; and when, after a little time, she answered his gaze he admired still more her large dark brown eyes. The oblique staring expression in them fascinated him. She glanced at him once or twice and, when the party was leaving the room, she brushed against his chair and said *"O, pardon!"* in a London accent. He watched her leave the room in the hope that she would look back at him, but he was disappointed. He cursed his want of money and cursed all the rounds he had stood, particularly all the whiskies and Apollinaris which he had stood to Weathers. If there was one thing that he hated it was a sponge. He was so angry that he lost count of the conversation of his friends.

When Paddy Leonard called him he found that they were talking about feats of strength. Weathers was showing his biceps muscle to the company and boasting so much that the other two had called on Farrington to uphold the national honour. Farrington pulled up his sleeve accordingly and showed his biceps muscle to the company. The two arms were examined and compared and finally it was agreed to have a trial of strength. The table was cleared and the two men rested their elbows on it, clasping hands. When Paddy Leonard said *"Go!"* each was to try to bring down the other's hand on to the table. Farrington looked very serious and determined.

The trial began. After about thirty seconds Weathers brought his opponent's hand slowly down on to the table. Farrington's dark wine-coloured face flushed darker still with anger and humiliation at having been defeated by such a stripling.

"You're not to put the weight of your body behind it. Play fair," he said.

"Who's not playing fair?" said the other.

"Come on again. The two best out of three."

The trial began again. The veins stood out on Farrington's forehead, and the pallor of Weathers' complexion changed to peony. Their hands and arms trembled under the stress. After a long struggle Weathers again brought his opponent's hand slowly on to the table. There was a murmur of applause from the spectators. The curate, who was standing beside the table, nodded his red head towards the victor and said with stupid familiarity:

"Ah! that's the knack!"

"What the hell do you know about it?" said Farrington fiercely, turning on the man. "What do you put in your gab for?"

"Sh, sh!" said O'Halloran, observing the violent expression of Farrington's face. "Pony up, boys. We'll have just one little smahan more and then we'll be off."

A very sullen-faced man stood at the corner of O'Connell Bridge waiting for the little Sandymount tram to take him home. He was full of smouldering anger and revengefulness. He felt humiliated and discontented; he did not even feel drunk; and he had only twopence in his pocket. He cursed everything. He had done for himself in the office, pawned his watch, spent all his money; and he had not even got drunk. He began to feel thirsty again and he longed to be back again in the hot reeking public-house. He had lost his reputation as a strong man, having been defeated twice by a mere boy. His heart swelled with fury and, when he thought of the woman in the big hat who had brushed against him and said *Pardon!* his fury nearly choked him.

His tram let him down at Shelbourne Road and he steered his great body along in the shadow of the wall of the barracks. He loathed returning to his home. When he went in by the side-door he found the kitchen empty and the kitchen fire nearly out. He bawled upstairs:

"Ada! Ada!"

His wife was a little sharp-faced woman who bullied her husband when he was sober and was bullied by him when he was drunk. They had five children. A little boy came running down the stairs.

"Who is that?" said the man, peering through the darkness.

"Me, pa."

"Who are you? Charlie?"

"No, pa. Tom."

"Where's your mother?"

"She's out at the chapel."

"That's right. . . . Did she think of leaving any dinner for me?"

"Yes, pa. I——"

"Light the lamp. What do you mean by having the place in darkness? Are the other children in bed?"

The man sat down heavily on one of the chairs while the little boy lit the lamp. He began to mimic his son's flat accent, saying half to himself: *"At the chapel. At the chapel, if you please!"* When the lamp was lit he banged his fist on the table and shouted:

"What's for my dinner?"

"I'm going . . . to cook it, pa," said the little boy.

The man jumped up furiously and pointed to the fire.

"On that fire! You let the fire out! By God, I'll teach you to do that again!"

He took a step to the door and seized the walking-stick which was standing behind it.

"I'll teach you to let the fire out!" he said, rolling up his sleeve in order to give his arm free play.

The little boy cried *"O pa!"* and ran whimpering round the table, but the man followed him and caught him by the coat. The little boy looked about him wildly but, seeing no way of escape, fell upon his knees.

"Now, you'll let the fire out the next time!" said the man, striking at him vigorously with the stick. "Take that, you little whelp!"

The boy uttered a squeal of pain as the stick cut his thigh. He clasped his hands together in the air and his voice shook with fright.

"O, pa!" he cried. "Don't beat me, pa! And I'll . . . I'll say a *Hail Mary* for you. . . . I'll say a *Hail Mary* for you, pa, if you don't beat me. . . . I'll say a *Hail Mary*. . . ."

Franz Kafka / 1883–1924

A Hunger Artist

During these last decades the interest in professional fasting has markedly diminished. It used to pay very well to stage such great performances under one's own management, but today that is quite impossible. We live in a different world now. At one time the whole town took a lively interest in the hunger artist; from day to day of his fast the excitement mounted; everybody wanted to see him at least once a day; there were people who bought season tickets for the last few days and sat from morning till night in front of his small barred cage; even in the nighttime there were visiting hours, when the whole effect was heightened by torch flares; on fine days the cage was set out in the open air, and then it was the children's special treat to see the hunger artist; for their elders he was often just a joke that happened to be in fashion, but the children stood open-mouthed, holding each other's hands for greater security, marveling at him as he sat there pallid in black tights, with his ribs sticking out so prominently, not even on a seat but down among straw on the ground, sometimes giving a courteous nod, answering questions with a constrained smile, or perhaps stretching an arm through the bars so that one might feel how thin it was, and then again withdrawing deep into himself, paying no attention to anyone or anything, not even to the all-important striking of the clock that was the only piece of furniture in his cage, but merely staring into vacancy with half-shut eyes, now and then taking a sip from a tiny glass of water to moisten his lips.

Besides casual onlookers there were also relays of permanent watchers selected by the public, usually butchers, strangely enough, and it was their task to watch the hunger artist day and night, three of them at a time, in case he should have some secret recourse to nourishment. This was nothing but a formality, instituted to reassure the masses, for the initiates knew well enough that during his fast the artist would never in any circumstances, not even under forcible compulsion, swallow the smallest morsel of food; the honor of his profession forbade it. Not every watcher, of course, was capable of understanding this, there were often groups of night watchers who were very lax in carrying out their duties and deliberately huddled together in a retired corner to play cards with great absorption, obviously intending to give the hunger artist the chance of a little refreshment, which they supposed he could draw from some private hoard. Nothing annoyed the artist more than such watchers; they made him miserable; they made his fast seem unendurable; sometimes he mastered his feebleness sufficiently to sing during their watch for as long as he could keep going, to show them how unjust their suspicions were. But that was of little use; they only wondered at his cleverness in being able to fill his mouth even while singing. Much more to his taste were the watchers who sat close up to the bars, who were not content with the dim night lighting of the hall but focused him in the full glare of the electric pocket torch given them by the impresario. The harsh light did not trouble him at all, in any case he could never sleep properly, and he could always drowse a little, whatever the light, at any hour, even when the hall was thronged with noisy onlookers. He was quite happy at the prospect of spending a sleepless night with such watchers; he was ready to exchange jokes with them, to tell them stories out of his nomadic life, anything at all to keep them awake and demonstrate to them again that he had no eatables in his cage and that he was fasting as not one of them could fast. But his happiest moment was when the morning came and an enormous breakfast was brought them, at his expense, on which they flung themselves with the keen appetite of healthy men after a weary night of wakefulness. Of course there were people who argued that this breakfast was an unfair attempt to bribe the watchers, but that was going rather too far, and when they were invited to take on a night's vigil without a breakfast, merely for the sake of the cause, they made themselves scarce, although they stuck stubbornly to their suspicions.

Such suspicions, anyhow, were a necessary accompaniment to the profession of fasting. No one could possibly watch the hunger artist continuously, day and night, and so no one could produce first-hand evidence that the fast had really been rigorous and continuous; only the artist himself could know that, he was therefore bound to be the sole completely satisfied spectator of his own fast. Yet for other reasons he was never satisfied; it was not perhaps mere fasting that had brought him to such skeleton thinness that many people had regretfully to keep away from his exhibitions, because the sight of him was too much for them, perhaps it was dissatisfaction with himself that had worn him down. For he alone knew, what no other initiate knew, how easy it was to fast. It was the easiest thing in the world. He made no secret of this, yet people did not believe him, at the best they set him down as modest; most of them, however, thought he was out for publicity or else was some kind of cheat who found it easy to fast because he had discovered a way of making it easy, and then had the impudence to admit the fact, more or less. He had to put up with all that, and in the course of time had got used to it, but his inner dissatisfaction always rankled, and never yet, after any term of fasting— this must be granted to his credit—had he left the cage of his own free will. The longest period of fasting was fixed by his impresario at forty days, beyond that term he was not allowed to go, not even in great cities, and there was good reason for it, too. Experience had proved that for about forty days the interest of the public could be stimulated by a steadily increasing pressure of advertisement, but after that the town began to lose interest, sympathetic support began notably to fall off; there were of course local variations as between one town and another or one country and another, but as a general rule forty days marked the limit. So on the fortieth day the flower-bedecked cage was opened, enthusiastic spectators filled the hall, a military band played, two doctors entered the cage to measure the results of the fast, which were announced through a megaphone, and finally two young ladies appeared, blissful at having been selected for the honor, to help the hunger artist down the few steps leading to a small table on which was spread a carefully chosen invalid repast. And at this very moment the artist always turned stubborn. True, he would entrust his bony arms to the outstretched helping hands of the ladies bending over him, but stand up he would not. Why stop fasting at this particular moment, after forty days of it? He had held out for a long time, an illimitably long time; why stop now, when he was in his best fasting form, or rather, not yet quite in his best fasting form? Why should he be cheated of the fame he would get for fasting longer, for being not only the record hunger artist of all time, which presumably he was already, but for beating his own record by a performance beyond human imagination, since he felt that there were no limits to his capacity for fasting? His public pretended to admire him so much, why should it have so little patience with him; if he could endure fasting longer, why shouldn't the public endure it? Besides, he was tired, he was comfortable sitting in the straw, and now he was supposed to lift himself to his full height and go down to a meal the very thought of which gave him a nausea that only the presence of the ladies kept him from betraying, and even that with an effort. And he looked up into the eyes of the ladies who were apparently so friendly and in reality so cruel, and shook his head, which felt too heavy on its strengthless neck. But then there happened yet again what always happened. The impresario came forward, without a word—for the band made speech impossible—lifted his arms in the air above the artist, as if inviting Heaven to look down upon its creature here in the straw, this suffering martyr, which indeed he was, although in quite another sense; grasped him round the emaciated waist, with exaggerated caution, so that the frail condition he was in might be appreciated; and committed him to the care of the blenching ladies, not without secretly giving him a shaking so that his legs and body tottered and swayed. The artist now submitted completely; his head lolled on his breast as if it had landed there by chance; his body was hollowed out; his legs in a spasm of self-preservation clung close to each other at the knees, yet scraped on the ground as if it were not really solid ground, as if they were only trying to find solid ground; and the whole weight of his body, a featherweight after all, relapsed onto one of the ladies, who, looking round for help and panting a little—this post of honor was not at all what she had expected it to be—first stretched her neck as far as she could to keep her face at least free from contact with the artist, then finding this impossible, and her more fortunate companion not coming to her aid but merely holding extended on her own trembling hand the little bunch of knucklebones that was the artist's, to the great delight of the spectators burst into tears and had to be replaced by an attendant who had long been stationed in readiness. Then came the food, a little of which the impresario managed to get between the artist's lips, while he sat in a kind of half-fainting trance, to the accompaniment of cheerful patter designed to distract the public's attention from the artist's condition; after that, a toast was drunk to the public, supposedly prompted by a whisper from the artist in the impresario's ear; the band confirmed it with a mighty flourish, the spectators melted away, and no one had any cause to be dissatisfied with the proceedings, no one except the hunger artist himself, he only, as always.

So he lived for many years, with small regular intervals of recuperation, in visible glory, honored by the world, yet in spite of that troubled in spirit, and all the more troubled because no one would take his trouble seriously. What comfort could he possibly need? What more could he possibly wish for? And if some good-natured person, feeling sorry for him, tried to console him by pointing out that his melancholy was probably caused by fasting, it could happen, especially when he had been fasting for some time, that he reacted with an outburst of fury and to the general alarm began to shake the bars of his cage like a wild animal. Yet the impresario had a way of punishing these outbreaks which he rather enjoyed putting into operation. He would apologize publicly for the artist's behavior, which was only to be excused, he admitted, because of the irritability caused by fasting; a condition hardly to be understood by well-fed people; then by natural transition he went on to mention the artist's equally incomprehensible boast that he could fast for much longer than he was doing; he praised the high ambition, the good will, the great self-denial undoubtedly implicit in such a statement; and then quite simply countered it by bringing out photographs, which were also on sale to the public, showing the artist on the fortieth day of a fast lying in bed almost dead from exhaustion. This perversion of the truth, familiar to the artist though it was, always unnerved him afresh and proved too much for him. What was a consequence of the premature ending of his fast was here presented as the cause of it! To fight against this lack of understanding, against a whole world of non-understanding, was impossible. Time and again in good faith he stood by the bars listening to the impresario, but as soon as the photographs appeared he always let go and sank with a groan back on to his straw, and the reassured public could once more come close and gaze at him.

A few years later when the witnesses of such scenes called them to mind, they often failed to understand themselves at all. For meanwhile the aforementioned change in public interest had set in; it seemed to happen almost overnight; there may have been profound causes for it, but who was going to bother about that; at any rate the pampered hunger artist suddenly found himself deserted one fine day by the amusement seekers, who went streaming past him to other more favored attractions. For the last time the impresario hurried him over half Europe to discover whether the old interest might still survive here and there; all in vain; everywhere, as if by secret agreement, a positive revulsion from professional fasting was in evidence. Of course it could not really have sprung up so suddenly as all that, and many premonitory symptoms which had not been sufficiently remarked or suppressed during the rush and glitter of success now came retrospectively to mind, but it was now too late to take any countermeasures. Fasting would surely come into fashion again at some future date, yet that was no comfort for those living in the present. What, then, was the hunger artist to do? He had been applauded by thousands in his time and could hardly come down to showing himself in a street booth at village fairs, and as for adopting another profession, he was not only too old for that but too fanatically devoted to fasting. So he took leave of the impresario, his partner in an unparalleled career, and hired himself to a large circus; in order to spare his own feelings he avoided reading the conditions of his contract.

A large circus with its enormous traffic in replacing and recruiting men, animals and apparatus can always find a use for people at any time, even for a hunger artist, provided of course that he does not ask too much, and in this particular case anyhow it was not only the artist who was taken on but his famous and long-known name as well, indeed considering the peculiar nature of his performance, which was not impaired by advancing age, it could not be objected that here was an artist past his prime, no longer at the height of his professional skill, seeking a refuge in some quiet corner of a circus, on the contrary, the hunger artist averred that he could fast as well as ever, which was entirely credible, he even alleged that if he were allowed to fast as he liked, and this was at once promised him without more ado, he could astound the world by establishing a record never yet achieved, a statement which certainly provoked a smile among the other professionals, since it left out of account the change in public opinion, which the hunger artist in his zeal conveniently forgot.

He had not, however, actually lost his sense of the real situation and took it as a matter of course that he and his cage should be stationed, not in the middle of the ring as a main attraction, but outside, near the animal cages, on a site that was after all easily accessible. Large and gaily painted placards made a frame for the cage and announced what was to be seen inside it. When the public came thronging out in the intervals to see the animals, they could hardly avoid passing the hunger artist's cage and stopping there for a moment, perhaps they might even have stayed longer had not those pressing behind them in the narrow gangway, who did not understand why they should be held up on their way towards the excitements of the menagerie, made it impossible for anyone to stand gazing quietly for any length of time. And that was the reason why the hunger artist, who had of course been looking forward to these visiting hours as the main achievement of his life, began instead to shrink from them. At first he could hardly wait for the intervals; it was exhilarating to watch the crowds come streaming his way, until only too soon—not even the most obstinate self-deception, clung to almost consciously, could hold out against the fact—the conviction was borne in upon him that these people, most of them, to judge from their actions, again and again, without exception, were all on their way to the menagerie. And the first sight of them from the distance remained the best. For when they reached his cage he was at once deafened by the storm of shouting and abuse that arose from the two contending factions, which renewed themselves continuously, of those who wanted to stop and stare at him—he soon began to dislike them more than the others—not out of real interest but only out of obstinate self-assertiveness, and those who wanted to go straight on to the animals. When the first great rush was past, the stragglers came along, and these, whom nothing could have prevented from stopping to look at him as long as they had breath, raced past with long strides, hardly even glancing at him, in their haste to get to the menagerie in time. And all too rarely did it happen that he had a stroke of luck, when some father of a family fetched up before him with his children, pointed a finger at the hunger artist and explained at length what the phenomenon meant, telling stories of earlier years when he himself had watched similar but much more thrilling performances, and the children, still rather uncomprehending, since neither inside nor outside school had they been sufficiently prepared for this lesson—what did they care about fasting?—yet showed by the brightness of their intent eyes that new and better times might be coming. Perhaps, said the hunger artist to himself many a time, things would be a little better if his cage were set not quite so near the menagerie. That made it too easy for people to make their choice, to say nothing of what he suffered from the stench of the menagerie, the animals' restlessness by night, the carrying past of raw lumps of flesh for the beasts of prey, the roaring at feeding times, which depressed him continually. But he did not dare to lodge a complaint with the management; after all, he had the animals to thank for the troops of people who passed his cage, among whom there might always be one here and there to take an interest in him, and who could tell where they might seclude him if he called attention to his existence and thereby to the fact that, strictly speaking, he was only an impediment on the way to the menagerie.

A small impediment, to be sure, one that grew steadily less. People grew familiar with the strange idea that they could be expected, in times like these, to take an interest in a hunger artist, and with this familiarity the verdict went out against him. He might fast as much as he could, and he did so; but nothing could save him now, people passed him by. Just try to explain to anyone the art of fasting! Anyone who has no feeling for it cannot be made to understand it. The fine placards grew dirty and illegible, they were torn down; the little notice board telling the number of fast days achieved, which at first was changed carefully every day, had long stayed at the same figure, for after the first few weeks even this small task seemed pointless to the staff; and so the artist simply fasted on and on, as he had once dreamed of doing, and it was no trouble to him, just as he had always foretold, but no one counted the days, no one, not even the artist himself, knew what records he was already breaking, and his heart grew heavy. And when once in a time some leisurely passer-by stopped, made merry over the old figure on the board and spoke of swindling, that was in its way the stupidest lie ever invented by indifference and inborn malice, since it was not the hunger artist who was cheating, he was working honestly, but the world was cheating him of his reward.

Many more days went by, however, and that too came to an end. An overseer's eye fell on the cage one day and he asked the attendants why this perfectly good stage should be left standing there unused with dirty straw inside it; nobody knew, until one man, helped out by the notice board, remembered about the hunger artist. They poked into the straw with sticks and found him in it. "Are you still fasting?" asked the overseer, "when on earth do you mean to stop?" "Forgive me, everybody," whispered the hunger artist; only the overseer, who had his ear to the bars, understood him. "Of course," said the overseer, and tapped his forehead with a finger to let the attendants know what state the man was in, "we forgive you." "I always wanted you to admire my fasting," said the hunger artist. "We do admire it," said the overseer, affably. "But you shouldn't admire it," said the hunger artist. "Well then we don't admire it," said the overseer, "but why shouldn't we admire it?" "Because I have to fast, I can't help it," said the hunger artist. "What a fellow you are," said the overseer, "and why can't you help it?" "Because," said the hunger artist, lifting his head a little and speaking, with his lips pursed, as if for a kiss, right into the overseer's ear, so that no syllable might be lost, "because I couldn't find the food I liked. If I had found it, believe me, I should have made no fuss and stuffed myself like you or anyone else." These were his last words, but in his dimming eyes remained the firm though no longer proud persuasion that he was still continuing to fast.

"Well, clear this out now!" said the overseer, and they buried the hunger artist, straw and all. Into the cage they put a young panther. Even the most insensitive felt it refreshing to see this wild creature leaping around the cage that had so long been dreary. The panther was all right. The food he liked was brought him without hesitation by the attendants; he seemed not even to miss his freedom; his noble body, furnished almost to the bursting point with all that it needed, seemed to carry freedom around with it too; somewhere in his jaws it seemed to lurk; and the joy of life streamed with such ardent passion from his throat that for the onlookers it was not easy to stand the shock of it. But they braced themselves, crowded round the cage, and did not want ever to move away.

Translated by Willa and Edwin Muir

D. H. Lawrence / 1885–1930

You Touched Me

The Pottery House was a square, ugly, brick house girt in by the wall that enclosed the whole grounds of the pottery itself. To be sure, a privet hedge partly masked the house and its ground from the pottery-yard and works: but only partly. Through the hedge could be seen the desolate yard, and the many-windowed, factory-like pottery, over the hedge could be seen the chimneys and the out-houses. But inside the hedge, a pleasant garden and lawn sloped down to a willow pool, which had once supplied the works.

The Pottery itself was now closed, the great doors of the yard permanently shut. No more the great crates with yellow straw showing through stood in stacks by the packing-shed. No more the drays drawn by great horses rolled down the hill with a high load. No more the pottery-lasses in their clay-coloured overalls, their faces and hair splashed with grey fine mud, shrieked and larked with the men. All that was over.

"We like it much better—oh, much better—quieter," said Matilda Rockley.

"Oh, yes," assented Emmie Rockley, her sister.

"I'm sure you do," agreed the visitor.

But whether the two Rockley girls liked it better, or whether they only imagined they did, is a question. Certainly their lives were much more grey and dreary now that the grey clay had ceased to spatter its mud and silt its dust over the premises. They did not quite realise how they missed the shrieking, shouting lasses, whom they had known all their lives and disliked so much.

Matilda and Emmie were already old maids. In a thorough industrial district, it is not easy for the girls who have expectations above the common to find husbands. The ugly industrial town was full of men, young men who were ready to marry. But they were all colliers or pottery-hands, mere workmen. The Rockley girls would have about ten thousand pounds each when their father died: ten thousand pounds' worth of profitable house-property. It was not to be sneezed at: they felt so themselves, and refrained from sneezing away such a fortune on any mere member of the proletariat. Consequently, bank-clerks or non-conformist clergymen or even school-teachers having failed to come forward, Matilda had begun to give up all idea of ever leaving the Pottery House.

Matilda was a tall, thin, graceful, fair girl, with a rather large nose. She was the Mary to Emmie's Martha: that is, Matilda loved painting and music, and read a good many novels, whilst Emmie looked after the housekeeping. Emmie was shorter, plumper than her sister, and she had no accomplishments. She looked up to Matilda, whose mind was naturally refined and sensible.

In their quiet, melancholy way, the two girls were happy. Their mother was dead. Their father was ill also. He was an intelligent man who had had some education, but preferred to remain as if he were one with the rest of the working people. He had a passion for music and played the violin pretty well. But now he was getting old, he was very ill, dying of a kidney disease. He had been rather a heavy whisky-drinker.

This quiet household, with one servant-maid, lived on year after year in the Pottery House. Friends came in, the girls went out, the father drank himself more and more ill. Outside in the street there was a continual racket of the colliers and their dogs and children. But inside the pottery wall was a deserted quiet.

In all this ointment there was one little fly. Ted Rockley, the father of the girls, had had four daughters, and no son. As his girls grew, he felt angry at finding himself always in a household of women. He went off to London and adopted a boy out of a Charity Institution. Emmie was fourteen years old and Matilda sixteen, when their father arrived home with his prodigy, the boy of six, Hadrian.

Hadrian was just an ordinary boy from a Charity Home, with ordinary brownish hair and ordinary bluish eyes and of ordinary rather Cockney speech. The Rockley girls—there were three at home at the time of his arrival—had resented his being sprung on them. He, with his watchful, charity-institution instinct, knew this at once. Though he was only six years old, Hadrian had a subtle, jeering look on his face when he regarded the three young women. They insisted he should address them as Cousin: Cousin Flora, Cousin Matilda, Cousin Emmie. He complied, but there seemed a mockery in his tone.

The girls, however, were kind-hearted by nature. Flora married and left home. Hadrian did very much as he pleased with Matilda and Emmie, though they had certain strictnesses. He grew up in the Pottery House and about the Pottery premises, went to an elementary school, and was invariably called Hadrian Rockley. He regarded Cousin Matilda and Cousin Emmie with a certain laconic indifference, was quiet and reticent in his ways. The girls called him sly, but that was unjust. He was merely cautious, and without frankness. His uncle, Ted Rockley, understood him tacitly, their natures were somewhat akin. Hadrian and the elderly man had a real but unemotional regard for one another.

When he was thirteen years old the boy was sent to a High School in the County town. He did not like it. His Cousin Matilda had longed to make a little gentleman of him, but he refused to be made. He would give a little contemptuous curve to his lip, and take on a shy, charity-boy grin, when refinement was thrust upon him. He played truant from the High School, sold his books, his cap with its badge, even his very scarf and pocket-handkerchief, to his school-fellows, and went raking off heaven knows where with the money. So he spent two very unsatisfactory years.

When he was fifteen he announced that he wanted to leave England to go to the Colonies. He had kept touch with the Home. The Rockleys knew that, when Hadrian made a declaration, in his quiet, half-jeering manner, it was worse than useless to oppose him. So at last the boy departed, going to Canada under the protection of the Institution to which he had belonged. He said good-bye to the Rockleys, without a word of thanks, and parted, it seemed, without a pang. Matilda and Emmie wept often to think of how he left them: even on their father's face a queer look came. But Hadrian wrote fairly regularly from Canada. He had entered some electricity works near Montreal, and was doing well.

At last, however, the war came. In his turn, Hadrian joined up and came to Europe. The Rockleys saw nothing of him. They lived on, just the same, in the Pottery House. Ted Rockley was dying of a sort of dropsy, and in his heart he wanted to see the boy. When the Armistice was signed, Hadrian had a long leave, and wrote that he was coming home to the Pottery House.

The girls were terribly fluttered. To tell the truth, they were a little afraid of Hadrian. Matilda, tall and thin, was frail in her health, both girls were worn with nursing their father. To have Hadrian, a young man of twenty-one, in the house with them, after he had left them so coldly five years before, was a trying circumstance.

They were in a flutter. Emmie persuaded her father to have his bed made finally in the morning-room downstairs, whilst his room up-stairs was prepared for Hadrian. This was done, and preparations were going on for the arrival, when, at ten o'clock in the morning, the young man suddenly turned up, quite unexpectedly. Cousin Emmie, with her hair bobbed up in absurd little bobs round her forehead, was busily polishing the stair-rods, while Cousin Matilda was in the kitchen washing the drawing-room ornaments in a lather, her sleeves rolled back on her thin arms, and her head tied up oddly and coquet-tishly in a duster.

Cousin Matilda blushed deep with mortification when the self-possessed young man walked in with his kit-bag, and put his cap on the sewing-machine. He was little and self-confident, with a curious neatness about him that still suggested the Charity Institution. His face was brown, he had a small moustache, he was vigorous enough in his smallness.

"*Well,* is it Hadrian!" exclaimed Cousin Matilda, wringing the lather off her hand. "We didn't expect you till to-morrow."

"I got off Monday night," said Hadrian, glancing round the room.

"Fancy!" said Cousin Matilda. Then, having dried her hands, she went forward, held out her hand, and said:

"How are you?"

"Quite well, thank you," said Hadrian.

"You're quite a man," said Cousin Matilda.

Hadrian glanced at her. She did not look her best: so thin, so large-nosed, with that pink-and-white checked duster tied round her head. She felt her disadvantage. But she had had a good deal of suffering and sorrow, she did not mind any more.

The servant entered—one that did not know Hadrian.

"Come and see my father," said Cousin Matilda.

In the hall they roused Cousin Emmie like a partridge from cover. She was on the stairs pushing the bright stair-rods into place. In-stinctively her hand went to the little knobs, her front hair bobbed on her forehead.

"Why!" she exclaimed, crossly. "What have you come to-day for?"

"I got off a day earlier," said Hadrian, and his man's voice so deep and unexpected was like a blow to Cousin Emmie.

"Well, you've caught us in the midst of it," she said, with resent-ment. Then all three went into the middle room.

Mr. Rockley was dressed—that is, he had on his trousers and

socks—but he was resting on the bed, propped up just under the window, from whence he could see his beloved and resplendent garden, where tulips and apple trees were ablaze. He did not look as ill as he was, for the water puffed him up, and his face kept its colour. His stomach was much swollen.

He glanced round swiftly, turning his eyes without turning his head. He was the wreck of a handsome, well-built man.

Seeing Hadrian, a queer, unwilling smile went over his face. The young man greeted him sheepishly.

"You wouldn't make a life-guardsman,"[1] he said. "Do you want something to eat?"

Hadrian looked round—as if for the meal.

"I don't mind," he said.

"What shall you have—egg and bacon?" asked Emmie shortly.

"Yes, I don't mind," said Hadrian.

The sisters went down to the kitchen, and sent the servant to finish the stairs.

"Isn't he *altered?*" said Matilda, *sotto voce.*

"Isn't he!" said Cousin Emmie. "*What* a little man!"

They both made a grimace, and laughed nervously.

"Get the frying pan," said Emmie to Matilda.

"But he's as cocky as ever," said Matilda, narrowing her eyes and shaking her head knowingly, as she handed the frying-pan.

"Mannie!" said Emmie sarcastically. Hadrian's new-fledged, cock-sure manliness evidently found no favour in her eyes.

"Oh, he's not bad," said Matilda. "You don't want to be prejudiced against him."

"I'm not prejudiced against him, I think he's all right for looks," said Emmie, "but there's too much of the little mannie about him."

"Fancy catching us like this," said Matilda.

"They've no thought for anything," said Emmie with contempt. "You go up and get dressed, our Matilda. I don't care about him. I can see to things, and you can talk to him. I shan't."

"He'll talk to my father," said Matilda, meaningful.

"*Sly*——!" exclaimed Emmie, with a grimace.

The sisters believed that Hadrian had come hoping to get something out of their father—hoping for a legacy. And they were not at all sure he would not get it.

Matilda went upstairs to change. She had thought it all out how she would receive Hadrian, and impress him. And he had caught her with her head tied up in a duster, and her thin arms in a basin of

[1] A member of the Life Guards, two regiments of the British cavalry assigned to the Royal household.

lather. But she did not care. She now dressed herself most scrupu-lously, carefully folded her long, beautiful, blonde hair, touched her pallor with a little rouge, and put her long string of exquisite crystal beads over her soft green dress. Now she looked elegant, like a heroine in a magazine illustration, and almost as unreal.

She found Hadrian and her father talking away. The young man was short of speech as a rule, but he could find his tongue with his 'uncle'. They were both sipping a glass of brandy, and smoking, and chatting like a pair of old cronies. Hadrian was telling about Canada. He was going back there when his leave was up.

"You wouldn't like to stop in England, then?" said Mr. Rockley.

"No, I wouldn't stop in England," said Hadrian.

"How's that? There's plenty of electricians here," said Mr. Rockley.

"Yes. But there's too much difference between the men and the employers over here—too much of that for me," said Hadrian.

The sick man looked at him narrowly, with oddly smiling eyes.

"That's it, is it?" he replied.

Matilda heard and understood. "So that's your big idea, is it, my little man," she said to herself. She had always said of Hadrian that he had no proper *respect* for anybody or anything, that he was sly and *common*. She went down to the kitchen for a *sotto voce* confab with Emmie.

"He thinks a rare lot of himself!" she whispered.

"He's somebody, he is!" said Emmie with contempt.

"He thinks there's too much difference between masters and men over here," said Matilda.

"Is it any different in Canada?" asked Emmie.

"Oh yes—democratic," replied Matilda. "He thinks they're all on a level over there."

"Ay, well, he's over here now," said Emmie dryly, "so he can keep his place."

As they talked they saw the young man sauntering down the garden, looking casually at the flowers. He had his hands in his pockets, and his soldier's cap neatly on his head. He looked quite at his ease, as if in possession. The two women, fluttered, watched him through the window.

"We know what he's come for," said Emmie, churlishly. Matilda looked a long time at the neat khaki figure. It had something of the charity-boy about it still; but now it was a man's figure, laconic, charged with plebeian energy. She thought of the derisive passion in his voice as he had declaimed against the propertied classes, to her father.

"You don't know, Emmie. Perhaps he's not come for that," she rebuked her sister. They were both thinking of the money.

They were still watching the young soldier. He stood away at the bottom of the garden, with his back to them, his hands in his pockets, looking into the water of the willow pond. Matilda's dark blue eyes had a strange, full look in them, the lids, with the faint blue veins showing, dropped rather low. She carried her head light and high, but she had a look of pain. The young man at the bottom of the garden turned and looked up the path. Perhaps he saw them through the window. Matilda moved into shadow.

That afternoon their father seemed weak and ill. He was easily exhausted. The doctor came, and told Matilda that the sick man might die suddenly at any moment—but then he might not. They must be prepared.

So the day passed, and the next. Hadrian made himself at home. He went about in the morning in his brownish jersey and his khaki trousers, collarless, his bare neck showing. He explored the pottery premises, as if he had some secret purpose in so doing, he talked with Mr. Rockley, when the sick man had strength. The two girls were always angry when the two men sat talking together like cronies. Yet it was chiefly a kind of politics they talked.

On the second day after Hadrian's arrival, Matilda sat with her father in the evening. She was drawing a picture which she wanted to copy. It was very still, Hadrian was gone out somewhere, no one knew where, and Emmie was busy. Mr. Rockley reclined on his bed, looking out in silence over his evening-sunny garden.

"If anything happens to me, Matilda," he said, "you won't sell this house—you'll stop here——"

Matilda's eyes took their slightly haggard look as she stared at her father.

"Well, we couldn't do anything else," she said.

"You don't know what you might do," he said. "Everything is left to you and Emmie, equally. You do as you like with it—only don't sell this house, don't part with it."

"No," she said.

"And give Hadrian my watch and chain, and a hundred pounds out of what's in the bank—and help him if he ever wants helping. I haven't put his name in the will."

"Your watch and chain, and a hundred pounds—yes. But you'll be here when he goes back to Canada, father."

"You never know what'll happen," said her father.

Matilda sat and watched him, with her full, haggard eyes, for a long time, as if tranced. She saw that he knew he must go soon—she saw like a clairvoyant.

Later on she told Emmie what her father had said about the watch and chain and the money.

"What right has *he*"—*he*—meaning Hadrian—"to my father's watch and chain—what has it to do with him? Let him have the money, and get off," said Emmie. She loved her father.

That night Matilda sat late in her room. Her heart was anxious and breaking, her mind seemed entranced. She was too much entranced even to weep, and all the time she thought of her father, only her father. At last she felt she must go to him.

It was near midnight. She went along the passage and to his room. There was a faint light from the moon outside. She listened at his door. Then she softly opened and entered. The room was faintly dark. She heard a movement on the bed.

"Are you asleep?" she said softly, advancing to the side of the bed.

"Are you asleep?" she repeated gently, as she stood at the side of the bed. And she reached her hand in the darkness to touch his forehead. Delicately, her fingers met the nose and the eyebrows, she laid her fine, delicate hand on his brow. It seemed fresh and smooth—very fresh and smooth. A sort of surprise stirred her, in her entranced state. But it could not waken her. Gently, she leaned over the bed and stirred her fingers over the low-growing hair on his brow.

"Can't you sleep to-night?" she said.

There was a quick stirring in the bed. "Yes, I can," a voice answered. It was Hadrian's voice. She started away. Instantly she was wakened from her late-at-night trance. She remembered that her father was downstairs, that Hadrian had his room. She stood in the darkness as if stung.

"Is it you, Hadrian?" she said. "I thought it was my father." She was so startled, so shocked, that she could not move. The young man gave an uncomfortable laugh, and turned in his bed.

At last she got out of the room. When she was back in her own room, in the light, and her door was closed, she stood holding up her hand that had touched him, as if it were hurt. She was almost too shocked, she could not endure.

"Well," said her calm and weary mind, "it was only a mistake, why take any notice of it."

But she could not reason her feelings so easily. She suffered, feeling herself in a false position. Her right hand, which she had laid so gently on his face, on his fresh skin, ached now, as if it were really injured. She could not forgive Hadrian for the mistake: it made her dislike him deeply.

Hadrian too slept badly. He had been awakened by the opening of the door, and had not realised what the question meant. But the soft, straying tenderness of her hand on his face startled something out of his soul. He was a charity boy, aloof and more or less at bay. The fragile exquisiteness of her caress startled him most, revealed unknown things to him.

In the morning she could feel the consciousness in his eyes, when she came downstairs. She tried to bear herself as if nothing at all had happened, and she succeeded. She had the calm self-control, self-indifference, of one who has suffered and borne her suffering. She looked at him from her darkish, almost drugged blue eyes, she met the spark of consciousness in his eyes, and quenched it. And with her long, fine hand she put the sugar in his coffee.

But she could not control him as she thought she could. He had a keen memory stinging his mind, a new set of sensations working in his consciousness. Something new was alert in him. At the back of his reticent, guarded mind he kept his secret alive and vivid. She was at his mercy, for he was unscrupulous, his standard was not her standard.

He looked at her curiously. She was not beautiful, her nose was too large, her chin was too small, her neck was too thin. But her skin was clear and fine, she had a high-bred sensitiveness. This queer, brave, high-bred quality she shared with her father. The charity boy could see it in her tapering fingers, which were white and ringed. The same glamour that he knew in the elderly man he now saw in the woman. And he wanted to possess himself of it, he wanted to make himself master of it. As he went about through the old pottery-yard, his secretive mind schemed and worked. To be master of that strange soft delicacy such as he had felt in her hand upon his face—this was what he set himself towards. He was secretly plotting.

He watched Matilda as she went about, and she became aware of his attention, as of some shadow following her. But her pride made her ignore it. When he sauntered near her, his hands in his pockets, she received him with that same commonplace kindliness which mastered him more than any contempt. Her superior breeding seemed to control him. She made herself feel towards him exactly as she had always felt: he was a young boy who lived in the house with them, but was a stranger. Only, she dared not remember his face under her hand. When she remembered that, she was bewildered. Her hand had offended her, she wanted to cut it off. And she wanted, fiercely, to cut off the memory in him. She assumed she had done so.

One day, when he sat talking with his 'uncle', he looked straight into the eyes of the sick man, and said:

"But I shouldn't like to live and die here in Rawsley."

"No—well—you needn't," said the sick man.

"Do you think Cousin Matilda likes it?"

"I should think so."

"I don't call it much of a life," said the youth. "How much older is she than me, Uncle?"

The sick man looked at the young soldier.

"A good bit," he said.

"Over thirty?" said Hadrian.

"Well, not so much. She's thirty-two."

Hadrian considered a while.

"She doesn't look it," he said.

Again the sick father looked at him.

"Do you think she'd like to leave here?" said Hadrian.

"Nay, I don't know," replied the father, restive.

Hadrian sat still, having his own thoughts. Then in a small, quiet voice, as if he were speaking from inside himself, he said:

"I'd marry her if you wanted me to."

The sick man raised his eyes suddenly and stared. He stared for a long time. The youth looked inscrutably out of the window.

"*You!*" said the sick man, mocking, with some contempt. Hadrian turned and met his eyes. The two men had an inexplicable understanding.

"If you wasn't against it," said Hadrian.

"Nay," said the father, turning aside, "I don't think I'm against it. I've never thought of it. But—but Emmie's the youngest."

He had flushed, and looked suddenly more alive. Secretly he loved the boy.

"You might ask her," said Hadrian.

The elder man considered.

"Hadn't you better ask her yourself?" he said.

"She'd take more notice of you," said Hadrian.

They were both silent. Then Emmie came in.

For two days Mr. Rockley was excited and thoughtful. Hadrian went about quietly, secretly, unquestioning. At last the father and daughter were alone together. It was very early morning, the father had been in much pain. As the pain abated, he lay still thinking.

"Matilda!" he said suddenly, looking at his daughter.

"Yes, I'm here," she said.

"Ay! I want you to do something——"

She rose in anticipation.

"Nay, sit still. I want you to marry Hadrian——"

She thought he was raving. She rose, bewildered and frightened.

"Nay, sit you still, sit you still. You hear what I tell you."

"But you don't know what you're saying, father."

"Ay, I know well enough. I want you to marry Hadrian, I tell you."

She was dumbfounded. He was a man of few words.

"You'll do what I tell you," he said.

She looked at him slowly.

"What put such an idea in your mind?" she said proudly.

"He did."

Matilda almost looked her father down, her pride was so offended.

"Why, it's disgraceful," she said.

"Why?"

She watched him slowly.

"What do you ask me for?" she said. "It's disgusting."

"The lad's sound enough," he replied testily.

"You'd better tell him to clear out," she said coldly.

He turned and looked out of the window. She sat flushed and erect for a long time. At length her father turned to her, looking really malevolent.

"If you won't," he said, "you're a fool, and I'll make you pay for your foolishness, do you see?"

Suddenly a cold fear gripped her. She could not believe her senses. She was terrified and bewildered. She stared at her father, believing him to be delirious, or mad, or drunk. What could she do?

"I tell you," he said. "I'll send for Whittle to-morrow if you don't. You shall neither of you have anything of mine."

Whittle was the solicitor. She understood her father well enough: he would send for his solicitor, and make a will leaving all his property to Hadrian: neither she nor Emmie should have anything. It was too much. She rose and went out of the room, up to her own room, where she locked herself in.

She did not come out for some hours. At last, late at night, she confided in Emmie.

"The sliving[2] demon, he wants the money," said Emmie. "My father's out of his mind."

The thought that Hadrian merely wanted the money was another blow to Matilda. She did not love the impossible youth—but she had not yet learned to think of him as a thing of evil. He now became hideous to her mind.

Emmie had a little scene with her father next day.

"You don't mean what you said to our Matilda yesterday, do you, father?" she asked aggressively.

"Yes," he replied.

[2] Nottinghamshire dialect for *sly, deceitful.*

"What, that you'll alter your will?"

"Yes."

"You won't," said his angry daughter.

But he looked at her with a malevolent little smile.

"Annie!" he shouted. "Annie!"

He had still power to make his voice carry. The servant maid came in from the kitchen.

"Put your things on, and go down to Whittle's office, and say I want to see Mr. Whittle as soon as he can, and will he bring a will-form."

The sick man lay back a little—he could not lie down. His daughter sat as if she had been struck. Then she left the room.

Hadrian was pottering about in the garden. She went straight down to him.

"Here," she said. "You'd better get off. You'd better take your things and go from here, quick."

Hadrian looked slowly at the infuriated girl.

"Who says so?" he asked.

"*We* say so—get off, you've done enough mischief and damage."

"Does Uncle say so?"

"Yes, he does."

"I'll go and ask him."

But like a fury Emmie barred his way.

"No, you needn't. You needn't ask him nothing at all. We don't want you, so you can go."

"Uncle's boss here."

"A man that's dying, and you crawling round and working on him for his money!—you're not fit to live."

"Oh!" he said. "Who says I'm working for his money?"

"I say. But my father told our Matilda, and *she* knows what you are. *She* knows what you're after. So you might as well clear out, for all you'll get—guttersnipe!"

He turned his back on her, to think. It had not occurred to him that they would think he was after the money. He *did* want the money—badly. He badly wanted to be an employer himself, not one of the employed. But he knew, in his subtle, calculating way, that it was not for money he wanted Matilda. He wanted both the money and Matilda. But he told himself the two desires were separate, not one. He could not do with Matilda, *without* the money. But he did not want her *for* the money.

When he got this clear in his mind, he sought for an opportunity to tell it her, lurking and watching. But she avoided him. In the evening the lawyer came. Mr. Rockley seemed to have a new access of strength—a will was drawn up, making the previous arrangements wholly conditional. The old will held good, if Matilda would consent to marry Hadrian. If she refused then at the end of six months the whole property passed to Hadrian.

Mr. Rockley told this to the young man, with malevolent satisfaction. He seemed to have a strange desire, quite unreasonable, for revenge upon the women who had surrounded him for so long, and served him so carefully.

"Tell her in front of me," said Hadrian.

So Mr. Rockley sent for his daughters.

At last they came, pale, mute, stubborn. Matilda seemed to have retired far off, Emmie seemed like a fighter ready to fight to the death. The sick man reclined on the bed, his eyes bright, his puffed hand trembling. But his face had again some of its old, bright handsomeness. Hadrian sat quiet, a little aside: the indomitable, dangerous charity boy.

"There's the will," said their father, pointing them to the paper.

The two women sat mute and immovable, they took no notice.

"Either you marry Hadrian, or he has everything," said the father with satisfaction.

"Then let him have everything," said Matilda coldly.

"He's not! He's not!" cried Emmie fiercely. "He's not going to have it. The guttersnipe!"

An amused look came on her father's face.

"You hear that, Hadrian," he said.

"I didn't offer to marry Cousin Matilda for the money," said Hadrian, flushing and moving on his seat.

Matilda looked at him slowly, with her dark blue, drugged eyes. He seemed a strange little monster to her.

"Why, you liar, you know you did," cried Emmie.

The sick man laughed. Matilda continued to gaze strangely at the young man.

"She knows I didn't," said Hadrian.

He too had his courage, as a rat has indomitable courage in the end. Hadrian had some of the neatness, the reserve, the underground quality of the rat. But he had perhaps the ultimate courage, the most unquenched courage of all.

Emmie looked at her sister.

"Oh, well," she said. "Matilda—don't you bother. Let him have everything, we can look after ourselves."

"I know he'll take everything," said Matilda, abstractedly.

Hadrian did not answer. He knew in fact that if Matilda refused him he would take everything, and go off with it.

"A clever little mannie——!" said Emmie, with a jeering grimace.

The father laughed noiselessly to himself. But he was tired. . . .

"Go on, then," he said. "Go on, let me be quiet."

Emmie turned and looked at him.

"You deserve what you've got," she said to her father bluntly.

"Go on," he answered mildly. "Go on."

Another night passed—a night nurse sat up with Mr. Rockley. Another day came. Hadrian was there as ever, in his woollen jersey and coarse khaki trousers and bare neck. Matilda went about, frail and distant, Emmie black-browed in spite of her blondness. They were all quiet, for they did not intend the mystified servant to learn anything.

Mr. Rockley had very bad attacks of pain, he could not breathe. The end seemed near. They all went about quiet and stoical, all unyielding. Hadrian pondered within himself. If he did not marry Matilda he would go to Canada with twenty thousand pounds. This was itself a very satisfactory prospect. If Matilda consented he would have nothing—she would have her own money.

Emmie was the one to act. She went off in search of the solicitor and brought him home with her. There was an interview, and Whittle tried to frighten the youth into withdrawal—but without avail. The clergyman and relatives were summoned—but Hadrian stared at them and took no notice. It made him angry, however.

He wanted to catch Matilda alone. Many days went by, and he was not successful: she avoided him. At last, lurking, he surprised her one day as she came to pick gooseberries, and he cut off her retreat. He came to the point at once.

"You don't want me, then?" he said, in his subtle, insinuating voice.

"I don't want to speak to you," she said, averting her face.

"You put your hand on me, though," he said. "You shouldn't have done that, and then I should never have thought of it. You shouldn't have touched me."

"If you were anything decent, you'd know that was a mistake, and forget it," she said.

"I know it was a mistake—but I shan't forget it. If you wake a man up, he can't go to sleep again because he's told to."

"If you had any decent feeling in you, you'd have gone away," she replied.

"I didn't want to," he replied.

She looked away into the distance. At last she asked:

"What do you persecute me for, if it isn't for the money? I'm old enough to be your mother. In a way I've been your mother."

"Doesn't matter," he said. "You've been no mother to me. Let us marry and go out to Canada—you might as well—you've touched me."

She was white and trembling. Suddenly she flushed with anger.

"It's so *indecent*," she said.

"How?" he retorted. "You touched me."

But she walked away from him. She felt as if he had trapped her. He was angry and depressed, he felt again despised.

That same evening she went into her father's room.

"Yes," she said suddenly. "I'll marry him."

Her father looked up at her. He was in pain, and very ill.

"You like him now, do you?" he said, with a faint smile.

She looked down into his face, and saw death not far off. She turned and went coldly out of the room.

The solicitor was sent for, preparations were hastily made. In all the interval Matilda did not speak to Hadrian, never answered him if he addressed her. He approached her in the morning.

"You've come round to it, then?" he said, giving her a pleasant look from his twinkling, almost kindly eyes. She looked down at him and turned aside. She looked down on him both literally and figuratively. Still he persisted, and triumphed.

Emmie raved and wept, the secret flew abroad. But Matilda was silent and unmoved, Hadrian was quiet and satisfied, and nipped with fear also. But he held out against his fear. Mr. Rockley was very ill, but unchanged.

On the third day the marriage took place. Matilda and Hadrian drove straight home from the registrar, and went straight into the room of the dying man. His face lit up with a clear twinkling smile.

"Hadrian—you've got her?" he said, a little hoarsely.

"Yes," said Hadrian, who was pale round the gills.

"Ay, my lad, I'm glad you're mine," replied the dying man. Then he turned his eyes closely on Matilda.

"Let's look at you, Matilda," he said. Then his voice went strange and unrecognisable. "Kiss me," he said.

She stooped and kissed him. She had never kissed him before, not since she was a tiny child. But she was quiet, very still.

"Kiss him," the dying man said.

Obediently, Matilda put forward her mouth and kissed the young husband.

"That's right! That's right!" murmured the dying man.

He

Life was very hard for the Whipples. It was hard to feed all the hungry mouths, it was hard to keep the children in flannels during the winter, short as it was: "God knows what would become of us if we lived north," they would say: keeping them decently clean was hard. "It looks like our luck won't never let up on us," said Mr. Whipple, but Mrs. Whipple was all for taking what was sent and calling it good, anyhow when the neighbors were in earshot. "Don't ever let a soul hear us complain," she kept saying to her husband. She couldn't stand to be pitied. "No, not if it comes to it that we have to live in a wagon and pick cotton around the country," she said, "nobody's going to get a chance to look down on us."

Mrs. Whipple loved her second son, the simple-minded one, better than she loved the other two children put together. She was forever saying so, and when she talked with certain of her neighbors, she would even throw in her husband and her mother for good measure.

"You needn't keep on saying it around," said Mr. Whipple, "you'll make people think nobody else has any feelings about Him but you."

"It's natural for a mother," Mrs. Whipple would remind him. "You know yourself it's more natural for a mother to be that way. People don't expect so much of fathers, some way."

This didn't keep the neighbors from talking plainly among themselves. "A Lord's pure mercy if He should die," they said. "It's the sins of the fathers," they agreed among themselves. "There's bad blood and bad doings somewhere, you can bet on that." This behind the Whipples' backs. To their faces everybody said, "He's not so bad off. He'll be all right yet. Look how He grows!"

Mrs. Whipple hated to talk about it, she tried to keep her mind off it, but every time anybody set foot in the house, the subject always came up, and she had to talk about Him first, before she could get on to anything else. It seemed to ease her mind. "I wouldn't have anything happen to Him for all the world, but it just looks like I can't keep Him out of mischief. He's so strong and active, He's always into everything; He was like that since He could walk. It's actually funny sometimes, the way He can do anything; it's laughable to see Him up to His tricks. Emly has more accidents; I'm forever tying up her bruises, and Adna can't fall a foot without cracking a bone. But He can do anything and not get a scratch. The preacher said such a nice thing once when he was here. He said, and I'll remember it to my dying day, 'The innocent walk with God—that's why He don't get hurt.'" Whenever Mrs. Whipple repeated these words, she always felt a warm pool spread in her breast, and the tears would fill her eyes, and then she could talk about something else.

He did grow and He never got hurt. A plank blew off the chicken house and struck Him on the head and He never seemed to know it. He had learned a few words, and after this He forgot them. He didn't whine for food as the other children did, but waited until it was given Him; He ate squatting in the corner, smacking and mumbling. Rolls of fat covered Him like an overcoat, and He could carry twice as much wood and water as Adna. Emly had a cold in the head most of the time—"she takes that after me," said Mrs. Whipple—so in bad weather they gave her the extra blanket off His cot. He never seemed to mind the cold.

Just the same, Mrs. Whipple's life was a torment for fear something might happen to Him. He climbed the peach trees much better than Adna and went skittering along the branches like a monkey, just a regular monkey. "Oh, Mrs. Whipple, you hadn't ought to let Him do that. He'll lose His balance sometime. He can't rightly know what He's doing."

Mrs. Whipple almost screamed out at the neighbor. "He *does* know what He's doing! He's as able as any other child! Come down out of there, you!" When He finally reached the ground she could hardly keep her hands off Him for acting like that before people, a grin all over His face and her worried sick about Him all the time.

"It's the neighbors," said Mrs. Whipple to her husband. "Oh, I do mortally wish they would keep out of our business. I can't afford to let Him do anything for fear they'll come nosing around about it. Look at the bees, now. Adna can't handle them, they sting him up so; I haven't got time to do everything, and now I don't dare let Him. But if He gets a sting He don't really mind."

"It's just because He ain't got sense enough to be scared of anything," said Mr. Whipple.

"You ought to be ashamed of yourself," said Mrs. Whipple, "talking that way about your own child. Who's to take up for Him if we don't, I'd like to know? He sees a lot that goes on, He listens to things all the time. And anything I tell Him to do He does it. Don't never let anybody hear you say such things. They'd think you favored the other children over Him."

"Well, now I don't, and you know it, and what's the use of getting all worked up about it? You always think the worst of everything. Just let Him alone, He'll get along somehow. He gets plenty to eat and wear, don't He?" Mr. Whipple suddenly felt tired out. "Anyhow, it can't be helped now."

Mrs. Whipple felt tired too, she complained in a tired voice. "What's done can't never be undone, I know that as good as anybody; but He's my child, and I'm not going to have people say anything. I get sick of people coming around saying things all the time."

In the early fall Mrs. Whipple got a letter from her brother saying he and his wife and two children were coming over for a little visit next Sunday week. "Put the big pot in the little one," he wrote at the end. Mrs. Whipple read this part out loud twice, she was so pleased. Her brother was a great one for saying funny things. "We'll just show him that's no joke," she said, "we'll just butcher one of the sucking pigs."

"It's a waste and I don't hold with waste the way we are now," said Mr. Whipple. "That pig'll be worth money by Christmas."

"It's a shame and a pity we can't have a decent meal's vittles once in a while when my own family comes to see us," said Mrs. Whipple. "I'd hate for his wife to go back and say there wasn't a thing in the house to eat. My God, it's better than buying up a great chance of meat in town. There's where you'd spend the money!"

"All right, do it yourself then," said Mr. Whipple. "Christamighty, no wonder we can't get ahead!"

The question was how to get the little pig away from his ma, a great fighter, worse than a Jersey cow. Adna wouldn't try it: "That sow'd rip my insides out all over the pen." "All right, old fraidy," said Mrs. Whipple, "*He's* not scared. Watch *Him* do it." And she laughed as though it was all a good joke and gave Him a little push towards the pen. He sneaked up and snatched the pig right away from the teat and galloped back and was over the fence with the sow raging at His heels. The little black squirming thing was screeching like a baby in a tantrum, stiffening its back and stretching its mouth to the ears. Mrs. Whipple took the pig with her face stiff and sliced its throat with one stroke. When He saw the blood He gave a great jolting breath and ran away. "But He'll forget and eat plenty, just the same," thought Mrs. Whipple. Whenever she was thinking, her lips moved making words. "He'd eat it all if I didn't stop Him. He'd eat up every mouthful from the other two if I'd let Him."

She felt badly about it. He was ten years old now and a third again as large as Adna, who was going on fourteen. "It's a shame, a shame," she kept saying under her breath, "and Adna with so much brains!"

She kept on feeling badly about all sorts of things. In the first place it was the man's work to butcher; the sight of the pig scraped pink and naked made her sick. He was too fat and soft and pitiful-looking. It was simply a shame the way things had to happen. By the time she had finished it up, she almost wished her brother would stay at home.

Early Sunday morning Mrs. Whipple dropped everything to get Him all cleaned up. In an hour He was dirty again, with crawling under fences after a possum, and straddling along the rafters of the barn looking for eggs in the hayloft. "My Lord, look at you now after all my trying! And here's Adna and Emly staying so quiet. I get tired trying to keep you decent. Get off that shirt and put on another, people will say I don't half dress you!" And she boxed Him on the ears, hard. He blinked and blinked and rubbed His head, and His face hurt Mrs. Whipple's feelings. Her knees began to tremble, she had to sit down while she buttoned His shirt. "I'm just all gone before the day starts."

The brother came with his plump healthy wife and two great roaring hungry boys. They had a grand dinner, with the pig roasted to a crackling in the middle of the table, full of dressing, a pickled peach in his mouth and plenty of gravy for the sweet potatoes.

"This looks like prosperity all right," said the brother; "you're going to have to roll me home like I was a barrel when I'm done."

Everybody laughed out loud; it was fine to hear them laughing all at once around the table. Mrs. Whipple felt warm and good about it. "Oh, we've got six more of these; I say it's as little as we can do when you come to see us so seldom."

He wouldn't come into the dining room, and Mrs. Whipple passed it off very well. "He's timider than my other two," she said. "He'll just have to get used to you. There isn't everybody He'll make up with, you know how it is with some children, even cousins." Nobody said anything out of the way.

"Just like my Alfy here," said the brother's wife. "I sometimes got to lick him to make him shake hands with his own grandmammy."

So that was over, and Mrs. Whipple loaded up a big plate for Him first, before everybody. "I always say He ain't to be slighted, no matter who else goes without," she said, and carried it to Him herself.

"He can chin Himself on the top of the door," said Emly, helping along.

"That's fine, He's getting along fine," said the brother.

They went away after supper. Mrs. Whipple rounded up the dishes, and sent the children to bed and sat down and unlaced her shoes. "You see?" she said to Mr. Whipple. "That's the way my whole family is. Nice and considerate about everything. No out-of-the-way remarks —they *have* got refinement. I get awfully sick of people's remarks. Wasn't that pig good?"

Mr. Whipple said, "Yes, we're out three hundred pounds of pork, that's all. It's easy to be polite when you come to eat. Who knows what they had in their minds all along?"

"Yes, that's like you," said Mrs. Whipple. "I don't expect anything else from you. You'll be telling me next that my own brother will be saying around that we made Him eat in the kitchen! Oh, my God!" She rocked her head in her hands, a hard pain started in the very middle of her forehead. "Now it's all spoiled, and everything was so nice and easy. All right, you don't like them and you never did—all right, they'll not come here again soon, never you mind! But they *can't* say He wasn't dressed every lick as good as Adna—oh, honest, sometimes I wish I was dead!"

"I wish you'd let up," said Mr. Whipple. "It's bad enough as it is."

It was a hard winter. It seemed to Mrs. Whipple that they hadn't ever known anything but hard times, and now to cap it all a winter like this. The crops were about half of what they had a right to expect; after the cotton was in it didn't do much more than cover the grocery bill. They swapped off one of the plow horses, and got cheated, for the new one died of the heaves. Mrs. Whipple kept thinking all the time it was terrible to have a man you couldn't depend on not to get cheated. They cut down on everything, but Mrs. Whipple kept saying there are things you can't cut down on, and they cost money. It took a lot of warm clothes for Adna and Emly, who walked four miles to school during the three-months session. "He sets around the fire a lot, He won't need so much," said Mr. Whipple. "That's so," said Mrs. Whipple, "and when He does the outdoor chores He can wear your tarpaullion coat. I can't do no better, that's all."

In February He was taken sick, and lay curled up under His blanket looking very blue in the face and acting as if He would choke. Mr. and Mrs. Whipple did everything they could for Him for two days, and then they were scared and sent for the doctor. The doctor told them they must keep Him warm and give Him plenty of milk and eggs. "He isn't as stout as He looks, I'm afraid," said the doctor. "You've got to watch them when they're like that. You must put more cover onto Him, too."

"I just took off His big blanket to wash," said Mrs. Whipple, ashamed. "I can't stand dirt."

"Well, you'd better put it back on the minute it's dry," said the doctor, "or He'll have pneumonia."

Mr. and Mrs. Whipple took a blanket off their own bed and put His cot in by the fire. "They can't say we didn't do everything for Him," she said, "even to sleeping cold ourselves on His account."

When the winter broke He seemed to be well again, but He walked as if His feet hurt Him. He was able to run a cotton planter during the season.

"I got it all fixed up with Jim Ferguson about breeding the cow next time," said Mr. Whipple. "I'll pasture the bull this summer and give Jim some fodder in the fall. That's better than paying out money when you haven't got it."

"I hope you didn't say such a thing before Jim Ferguson," said Mrs. Whipple. "You oughtn't to let him know we're so down as all that."

"Godamighty, that ain't saying we're down. A man is got to look ahead sometimes. He can lead the bull over today. I need Adna on the place."

At first Mrs. Whipple felt easy in her mind about sending Him for the bull. Adna was too jumpy and couldn't be trusted. You've got to be steady around animals. After He was gone she started thinking, and after a while she could hardly bear it any longer. She stood in the lane and watched for Him. It was nearly three miles to go and a hot day, but He oughtn't to be so long about it. She shaded her eyes and stared until colored bubbles floated in her eyeballs. It was just like everything else in life, she must always worry and never know a moment's peace about anything. After a long time she saw Him turn into the side lane, limping. He came on very slowly, leading the big hulk of an animal by a ring in the nose, twirling a little stick in His hand, never looking back or sideways, but coming on like a sleep-walker with His eyes half shut.

Mrs. Whipple was scared sick of bulls; she had heard awful stories about how they followed on quietly enough, and then suddenly pitched on with a bellow and pawed and gored a body to pieces. Any second now that black monster would come down on Him, my God, He'd never have sense enough to run.

She mustn't make a sound nor a move; she mustn't get the bull started. The bull heaved his head aside and horned the air at a fly. Her voice burst out of her in a shriek, and she screamed at Him to come on, for God's sake. He didn't seem to hear her clamor, but kept on twirling His switch and limping on, and the bull lumbered along behind him as gently as a calf. Mrs. Whipple stopped calling and ran towards the house, praying under her breath: "Lord, don't let anything happen to Him. Lord, you *know* people will say we oughtn't to have sent Him. You *know* they'll say we didn't take care of Him. Oh, get Him home, safe home, safe home, and I'll look out for Him better! Amen."

She watched from the window while He led the beast in, and tied him up in the barn. It was no use trying to keep up, Mrs. Whipple couldn't bear another thing. She sat down and rocked and cried with her apron over her head.

From year to year the Whipples were growing poorer and poorer. The place just seemed to run down of itself, no matter how hard they worked. "We're losing our hold," said Mrs. Whipple. "Why can't we do like other people and watch for our best chances? They'll be calling us poor white trash next."

"When I get to be sixteen I'm going to leave," said Adna. "I'm going to get a job in Powell's grocery store. There's money in that. No more farm for me."

"I'm going to be a schoolteacher," said Emly. "But I've got to finish the eighth grade, anyhow. Then I can live in town. I don't see any chances here."

"Emly takes after my family," said Mrs. Whipple. "Ambitious every last one of them, and they don't take second place for anybody."

When fall came Emly got a chance to wait on table in the railroad eating-house in the town near by, and it seemed such a shame not to take it when the wages were good and she could get her food too, that Mrs. Whipple decided to let her take it, and not bother with school until the next session. "You've got plenty of time," she said. "You're young and smart as a whip."

With Adna gone too, Mr. Whipple tried to run the farm with just Him to help. He seemed to get along fine, doing His work and part of Adna's without noticing it. They did well enough until Christmas time, when one morning He slipped on the ice coming up from the barn. Instead of getting up He thrashed round and round, and when Mr. Whipple got to Him, He was having some sort of fit.

They brought Him inside and tried to make Him sit up, but He blubbered and rolled, so they put Him to bed and Mr. Whipple rode to town for the doctor. All the way there and back he worried about where the money was to come from: it sure did look like he had about all the troubles he could carry.

From then on He stayed in bed. His legs swelled up double their size, and the fits kept coming back. After four months, the doctor said, "It's no use, I think you'd better put Him in the County Home for treatment right away. I'll see about it for you. He'll have good care there and be off your hands."

"We don't begrudge Him any care, and I won't let Him out of my sight," said Mrs. Whipple. "I won't have it said I sent my sick child off among strangers."

"I know how you feel," said the doctor. "You can't tell me anything about that, Mrs. Whipple. I've got a boy of my own. But you'd better listen to me. I can't do anything more for Him, that's the truth."

Mr. and Mrs. Whipple talked it over a long time that night after they went to bed. "It's just charity," said Mrs. Whipple, "that's what we've come to, charity! I certainly never looked for this."

"We pay taxes to help support the place just like everybody else," said Mr. Whipple, "and I don't call that taking charity. I think it would be fine to have Him where He'd get the best of everything . . . and besides, I can't keep up with these doctor bills any longer."

"Maybe that's why the doctor wants us to send Him—he's scared he won't get his money," said Mrs. Whipple.

"Don't talk like that," said Mr. Whipple, feeling pretty sick, "or we won't be able to send Him."

"Oh, but we won't keep Him there long," said Mrs. Whipple. "Soon's He's better, we'll bring Him right back home."

"The doctor has told you and told you time and again He can't ever get better, and you might as well stop talking," said Mr. Whipple.

"Doctors don't know everything," said Mrs. Whipple, feeling almost happy. "But anyhow, in the summer Emly can come home for a vacation, and Adna can get down for Sundays: we'll all work together and get on our feet again, and the children will feel they've got a place to come to."

All at once she saw it full summer again, with the garden going fine, and new white roller shades up all over the house, and Adna and Emly home, so full of life, all of them happy together. Oh, it could happen, things would ease up on them.

They didn't talk before Him much, but they never knew just how much He understood. Finally the doctor set the day and a neighbor who owned a double-seated carryall offered to drive them over. The hospital would have sent an ambulance, but Mrs. Whipple couldn't stand to see Him going away looking so sick as all that. They wrapped Him in blankets, and the neighbor and Mr. Whipple lifted Him into the back seat of the carryall beside Mrs. Whipple, who had on her black shirt waist. She couldn't stand to go looking like charity.

"You'll be all right, I guess I'll stay behind," said Mr. Whipple. "It don't look like everybody ought to leave the place at once."

"Besides, it ain't as if He was going to stay forever," said Mrs. Whipple to the neighbor. "This is only for a little while."

They started away, Mrs. Whipple holding to the edges of the blankets to keep Him from sagging sideways. He sat there blinking and blinking. He worked His hands out and began rubbing His nose with His knuckles, and then with the end of the blanket. Mrs. Whipple couldn't believe what she saw; He was scrubbing away big tears that rolled out of the corners of His eyes. He sniveled and made a gulping noise. Mrs. Whipple kept saying, "Oh, honey, you don't feel so bad, do you? You don't feel so bad, do you?" for He seemed to be accusing her of something. Maybe He remembered that time she boxed His ears, maybe He had been scared that day with the bull, maybe He had slept cold and couldn't tell her about it; maybe He knew they were sending Him away for good and all because they were too poor to keep Him. Whatever it was, Mrs. Whipple couldn't bear to think of it. She began to cry, frightfully, and wrapped her arms tight around Him. His head rolled on her shoulder: she had loved Him as much as she possibly could, there were Adna and Emly who had to be thought of too, there was nothing she could do to make up to Him for His life. Oh, what a mortal pity He was ever born.

They came in sight of the hospital, with the neighbor driving very fast, not daring to look behind him.

F. Scott Fitzgerald / 1896–1940

Babylon Revisited

"And where's Mr. Campbell?" Charlie asked.

"Gone to Switzerland. Mr. Campbell's a pretty sick man, Mr. Wales."

"I'm sorry to hear that. And George Hardt?" Charlie inquired.

"Back in America, gone to work."

"And where is the Snow Bird?"

"He was in here last week. Anyway, his friend, Mr. Schaeffer, is in Paris."

Two familiar names from the long list of a year and a half ago. Charlie scribbled an address in his notebook and tore out the page.

"If you see Mr. Schaeffer, give him this," he said. "It's my brother-in-law's address. I haven't settled on a hotel yet."

He was not really disappointed to find Paris was so empty. But the stillness in the Ritz bar was strange and portentous. It was not an American bar any more—he felt polite in it, and not as if he owned it. It had gone back into France. He felt the stillness from the moment he got out of the taxi and saw the doorman, usually in a frenzy of activity at this hour, gossiping with a *chasseur*[1] by the servants' entrance.

Passing through the corridor, he heard only a single, bored voice in the once-clamorous women's room. When he turned into the bar he traveled the twenty feet of green carpet with his eyes fixed straight ahead by old habit; and then, with his foot firmly on the rail, he turned and surveyed the room, encountering only a single pair of eyes that fluttered up from a newspaper in the corner. Charlie asked for the head barman, Paul, who in the latter days of the bull market had come to work in his own custom-built car—disembarking, however, with due nicety at the nearest corner. But Paul was at his country house today and Alix giving him information.

"No, no more," Charlie said, "I'm going slow these days."

Alix congratulated him: "You were going pretty strong a couple of years ago."

"I'll stick to it all right," Charlie assured him. "I've stuck to it for over a year and a half now."

"How do you find conditions in America?"

"I haven't been to America for months. I'm in business in Prague, representing a couple of concerns there. They don't know about me down there."

Alix smiled.

"Remember the night of George Hardt's bachelor dinner here?" said Charlie. "By the way, what's become of Claude Fessenden?"

Alix lowered his voice confidentially: "He's in Paris, but he doesn't come here any more. Paul doesn't allow it. He ran up a bill of thirty thousand francs, charging all his drinks and his lunches, and usually his dinner, for more than a year. And when Paul finally told him he had to pay, he gave him a bad check."

Alix shook his head sadly.

[1] Porter.

"I don't understand it, such a dandy fellow. Now he's all bloated up—" He made a plump apple of his hands.

Charlie watched a group of strident queens installing themselves in a corner.

"Nothing affects them," he thought. "Stocks rise and fall, people loaf or work, but they go on forever." The place oppressed him. He called for the dice and shook with Alix for the drink.

"Here for long, Mr. Wales?"

"I'm here for four or five days to see my little girl."

"Oh-h! You have a little girl?"

Outside, the fire-red, gas-blue, ghost-green signs shone smokily through the tranquil rain. It was late afternoon and the streets were in movement; the *bistros* gleamed. At the corner of the Boulevard des Capucines he took a taxi. The Place de la Concorde moved by in pink majesty; they crossed the logical Seine, and Charlie felt the sudden provincial quality of the left bank.

Charlie directed his taxi to the Avenue de l'Opera, which was out of his way. But he wanted to see the blue hour spread over the magnificent façade, and imagine that the cab horns, playing endlessly the first few bars of *Le Plus que Lent,* were the trumpets of the Second Empire. They were closing the iron grill in front of Brentano's Book-store, and people were already at dinner behind the trim little bourgeois hedge of Duval's. He had never eaten at a really cheap restaurant in Paris. Five-course dinner, four francs fifty, eighteen cents, wine included. For some odd reason he wished that he had.

As they rolled on to the Left Bank and he felt its sudden provincialism, he thought, "I spoiled this city for myself. I didn't realize it, but the days came along one after another, and then two years were gone, and everything was gone, and I was gone."

He was thirty-five, and good to look at. The Irish mobility of his face was sobered by a deep wrinkle between his eyes. As he rang his brother-in-law's bell in the Rue Palatine, the wrinkle deepened till it pulled down his brows; he felt a cramping sensation in his belly. From behind the maid who opened the door darted a lovely little girl of nine who shrieked "Daddy!" and flew up, struggling like a fish, into his arms. She pulled his head around by one ear and set her cheek against his.

"My old pie," he said.

"Oh, daddy, daddy, daddy, daddy, dads, dads, dads!"

She drew him into the salon, where the family waited, a boy and a girl his daughter's age, his sister-in-law and her husband. He greeted Marion with his voice pitched carefully to avoid either feigned enthusiasm or dislike, but her response was more frankly tepid, though she minimized her expression of unalterable distrust by directing her regard toward his child. The two men clasped hands in a friendly way and Lincoln Peters rested his for a moment on Charlie's shoulder.

The room was warm and comfortably American. The three children moved intimately about, playing through the yellow oblongs that led to other rooms; the cheer of six o'clock spoke in the eager smacks of the fire and the sounds of French activity in the kitchen. But Charlie did not relax; his heart sat up rigidly in his body and he drew confidence from his daughter, who from time to time came close to him, holding in her arms the doll he had brought.

"Really extremely well," he declared in answer to Lincoln's question. "There's a lot of business there that isn't moving at all, but we're doing even better than ever. In fact, damn well. I'm bringing my sister over from America next month to keep house for me. My income last year was bigger than it was when I had money. You see, the Czechs——"

His boasting was for a specific purpose; but after a moment, seeing a faint restiveness in Lincoln's eye, he changed the subject:

"Those are fine children of yours, well brought up, good manners."

"We think Honoria's a great little girl too."

Marion Peters came back from the kitchen. She was a tall woman with worried eyes, who had once possessed a fresh American loveliness. Charlie had never been sensitive to it and was always surprised when people spoke of how pretty she had been. From the first there had been an instinctive antipathy between them.

"Well, how do you find Honoria?" she asked.

"Wonderful. I was astonished how much she's grown in ten months. All the children are looking well."

"We haven't had a doctor for a year. How do you like being back in Paris?"

"It seems very funny to see so few Americans around."

"I'm delighted," Marion said vehemently. "Now at least you can go into a store without their assuming you're a millionaire. We've suffered like everybody, but on the whole it's a good deal pleasanter."

"But it was nice while it lasted," Charlie said. "We were a sort of royalty, almost infallible, with a sort of magic around us. In the bar this afternoon"—he stumbled, seeing his mistake—"there wasn't a man I knew."

She looked at him keenly. "I should think you'd have had enough of bars."

"I only stayed a minute. I take one drink every afternoon, and no more."

"Don't you want a cocktail before dinner?" Lincoln asked.

"I take only one drink every afternoon, and I've had that."

"I hope you keep to it," said Marion.

Her dislike was evident in the coldness with which she spoke, but Charlie only smiled; he had larger plans. Her very aggressiveness gave him an advantage, and he knew enough to wait. He wanted them to initiate the discussion of what they knew had brought him to Paris.

At dinner he couldn't decide whether Honoria was most like him or her mother. Fortunate if she didn't combine the traits of both that had brought them to disaster. A great wave of protectiveness went over him. He thought he knew what to do for her. He believed in character; he wanted to jump back a whole generation and trust in character again as the eternally valuable element. Everything else wore out.

He left soon after dinner, but not to go home. He was curious to see Paris by night with clearer and more judicious eyes than those of other days. He bought a *strapontin*[2] for the Casino and watched Josephine Baker[3] go through her chocolate arabesques.

After an hour he left and strolled toward Montmartre, up the Rue Pigalle into the Place Blanche. The rain had stopped and there were a few people in evening clothes disembarking from taxis in front of cabarets, and *cocottes* prowling singly or in pairs, and many Negroes. He passed a lighted door from which issued music, and stopped with the sense of familiarity; it was Bricktop's, where he had parted with so many hours and so much money. A few doors farther on he found another ancient rendezvous and incautiously put his head inside. Immediately an eager orchestra burst into sound, a pair of professional dancers leaped to their feet and a maître d'hôtel swooped toward him, crying, "Crowd just arriving, sir!" But he withdrew quickly.

"You have to be damn drunk," he thought.

Zelli's was closed, the bleak and sinister cheap hotels surrounding it were dark; up in the Rue Blanche there was more light and a local, colloquial French crowd. The Poet's Cave had disappeared, but the two great mouths of the Café of Heaven and the Café of Hell still yawned—even devoured, as he watched, the meager contents of a tourist bus—a German, a Japanese, and an American couple who glanced at him with frightened eyes.

So much for the effort and ingenuity of Montmartre. All the catering to vice and waste was on an utterly childish scale, and he suddenly realized the meaning of the word "dissipate"—to dissipate into thin air; to make nothing out of something. In the little hours of the night

---

[2] Seat.

[3] A famous American Negro entertainer in Paris.

every move from place to place was an enormous human jump, an increase of paying for the privilege of slower and slower motion.

He remembered thousand-franc notes given to an orchestra for playing a single number, hundred-franc notes tossed to a doorman for calling a cab.

But it hadn't been given for nothing.

It had been given, even the most wildly squandered sum, as an offering to destiny that he might not remember the things most worth remembering, the things that now he would always remember—his child taken from his control, his wife escaped to a grave in Vermont.

In the glare of a *brasserie*[4] a woman spoke to him. He bought her some eggs and coffee, and then, eluding her encouraging stare, gave her a twenty-franc note and took a taxi to his hotel.

2

He woke upon a fine fall day—football weather. The depression of yesterday was gone and he liked the people on the streets. At noon he sat opposite Honoria at Le Grand Vatel, the only restaurant he could think of not reminiscent of champagne dinners and long luncheons that began at two and ended in a blurred and vague twilight.

"Now, how about vegetables? Oughtn't you to have some vegetables?"

"Well, yes."

"Here's *épinards* and *chou-fleur* and carrots and *haricots*." [5]

"I'd like *chou-fleur*."

"Wouldn't you like to have two vegetables?"

"I usually only have one at lunch."

The waiter was pretending to be inordinately fond of children. *"Qu'elle est mignonne la petite! Elle parle exactement comme une Française."* [6]

"How about dessert? Shall we wait and see?"

The waiter disappeared. Honoria looked at her father expectantly.

"What are we going to do?"

"First, we're going to that toy store in the Rue Saint-Honoré and buy you anything you like. And then we're going to the vaudeville at the Empire."

She hesitated. "I like it about the vaudeville, but not the toy store."

"Why not?"

"Well, you brought me this doll." She had it with her. "And I've got lots of things. And we're not rich any more, are we?"

4 A bar.
5 Spinach, cauliflower, beans.
6 "How adorable this little one is! She speaks just like a French person."

"We never were. But today you are to have anything you want."

"All right," she agreed resignedly.

When there had been her mother and a French nurse he had been inclined to be strict; now he extended himself, reached out for a new tolerance; he must be both parents to her and not shut any of her out of communication.

"I want to get to know you," he said gravely. "First let me introduce myself. My name is Charles J. Wales, of Prague."

"Oh, daddy!" her voice cracked with laughter.

"And who are you, please?" he persisted, and she accepted a rôle immediately: "Honoria Wales, Rue Palatine, Paris."

"Married or single?"

"No, not married. Single."

He indicated the doll. "But I see you have a child, madame."

Unwilling to disinherit it, she took it to her heart and thought quickly: "Yes, I've been married, but I'm not married now. My husband is dead."

He went on quickly, "And the child's name?"

"Simone. That's after my best friend at school."

"I'm very pleased that you're doing so well at school."

"I'm third this month," she boasted. "Elsie"—that was her cousin—"is only about eighteenth, and Richard is about at the bottom."

"You like Richard and Elsie, don't you?"

"Oh, yes. I like Richard quite well and I like her all right."

Cautiously and casually he asked: "And Aunt Marion and Uncle Lincoln—which do you like best?"

"Oh, Uncle Lincoln, I guess."

He was increasingly aware of her presence. As they came in, a murmur of ". . . adorable" followed them, and now the people at the next table bent all their silences upon her, staring as if she were something no more conscious than a flower.

"Why don't I live with you?" she asked suddenly. "Because mamma's dead?"

"You must stay here and learn more French. It would have been hard for daddy to take care of you so well."

"I don't really need much taking care of any more. I do everything for myself."

Going out of the restaurant, a man and a woman unexpectedly hailed him.

"Well, the old Wales!"

"Hello there, Lorraine. . . . Dunc."

Sudden ghosts out of the past: Duncan Schaeffer, a friend from college. Lorraine Quarrles, a lovely, pale blonde of thirty; one of a crowd who had helped them make months into days in the lavish times of three years ago.

"My husband couldn't come this year," she said, in answer to his question. "We're poor as hell. So he gave me two hundred a month and told me I could do my worst on that. . . . This your little girl?"

"What about coming back and sitting down?" Duncan asked.

"Can't do it." He was glad for an excuse. As always, he felt Lorraine's passionate, provocative attraction, but his own rhythm was different now.

"Well, how about dinner?" she asked.

"I'm not free. Give me your address and let me call you."

"Charlie, I believe you're sober," she said judicially. "I honestly believe he's sober, Dunc. Pinch him and see if he's sober."

Charlie indicated Honoria with his head. They both laughed.

"What's your address?" said Duncan skeptically.

He hesitated, unwilling to give the name of his hotel.

"I'm not settled yet. I'd better call you. We're going to see the vaudeville at the Empire."

"There! That's what I want to do," Lorraine said. "I want to see some clowns and acrobats and jugglers. That's just what we'll do, Dunc."

"We've got to do an errand first," said Charlie. "Perhaps we'll see you there."

"All right, you snob. . . . Good-by, beautiful little girl."

"Good-by."

Honoria bobbed politely

Somehow, an unwelcome encounter. They liked him because he was functioning, because he was serious; they wanted to see him, because he was stronger than they were now, because they wanted to draw a certain sustenance from his strength.

At the Empire, Honoria proudly refused to sit upon her father's folded coat. She was already an individual with a code of her own, and Charlie was more and more absorbed by the desire of putting a little of himself into her before she crystallized utterly. It was hopeless to try to know her in so short a time.

Between the acts they came upon Duncan and Lorraine in the lobby where the band was playing.

"Have a drink?"

"All right, but not up at the bar. We'll take a table."

"The perfect father."

Listening abstractedly to Lorraine, Charlie watched Honoria's eyes leave their table, and he followed them wistfully about the room, wondering what they saw. He met her glance and she smiled.

"I liked that lemonade," she said.

What had she said? What had he expected? Going home in a taxi afterward, he pulled her over until her head rested against his chest.

"Darling, do you ever think about your mother?"

"Yes, sometimes," she answered vaguely.

"I don't want you to forget her. Have you got a picture of her?"

"Yes, I think so. Anyhow, Aunt Marion has. Why don't you want me to forget her?"

"She loved you very much."

"I loved her too."

They were silent for a moment.

"Daddy, I want to come and live with you," she said suddenly.

His heart leaped; he had wanted it to come like this.

"Aren't you perfectly happy?"

"Yes, but I love you better than anybody. And you love me better than anybody, don't you, now that mummy's dead?"

"Of course I do. But you won't always like me best, honey. You'll grow up and meet somebody your own age and go marry him and forget you ever had a daddy."

"Yes, that's true," she agreed tranquilly.

He didn't go in. He was coming back at nine o'clock and he wanted to keep himself fresh and new for the thing he must say then.

"When you're safe inside, just show yourself in that window."

"All right. Good-by, dads, dads, dads, dads."

He waited in the dark street until she appeared, all warm and glowing, in the window above and kissed her fingers out into the night.

3

They were waiting. Marion sat behind the coffee service in a dignified black dinner dress that just faintly suggested mourning. Lincoln was walking up and down with the animation of one who had already been talking. They were as anxious as he was to get into the question. He opened it almost immediately:

"I suppose you know what I want to see you about—why I really came to Paris."

Marion played with the black stars on her necklace and frowned.

"I'm awfully anxious to have a home," he continued. "And I'm awfully anxious to have Honoria in it. I appreciate your taking in Honoria for her mother's sake, but things have changed now"—he hesitated and then continued more forcibly—"changed radically with me, and I want to ask you to reconsider the matter. It would be silly for me to deny that about three years ago I was acting badly——"

Marion looked up at him with hard eyes.

"—but all that's over. As I told you, I haven't had more than a drink a day for over a year, and I take that drink deliberately, so that the idea of alcohol won't get too big in my imagination. You see the idea?"

"No," said Marion succinctly.

"It's a sort of stunt I set myself. It keeps the matter in proportion."

"I get you," said Lincoln. "You don't want to admit it's got any attraction for you."

"Something like that. Sometimes I forget and don't take it. But I try to take it. Anyhow, I couldn't afford to drink in my position. The people I represent are more than satisfied with what I've done, and I'm bringing my sister over from Burlington to keep house for me, and I want awfully to have Honoria too. You know that even when her mother and I weren't getting along well we never let anything that happened touch Honoria. I know she's fond of me and I know I'm able to take care of her and—well, there you are. How do you feel about it?"

He knew that now he would have to take a beating. It would last an hour or two hours, and it would be difficult, but if he modulated his inevitable resentment to the chastened attitude of the reformed sinner, he might win his point in the end.

Keep your temper, he told himself. You don't want to be justified. You want Honoria.

Lincoln spoke first: "We've been talking it over ever since we got your letter last month. We're happy to have Honoria here. She's a dear little thing, and we're glad to be able to help her, but of course that isn't the question——"

Marion interrupted suddenly. "How long are you going to stay sober, Charlie?" she asked.

"Permanently, I hope."

"How can anybody count on that?"

"You know I never did drink heavily until I gave up business and came over here with nothing to do. Then Helen and I began to run around with——"

"Please leave Helen out of it. I can't bear to hear you talk about her like that."

He stared at her grimly; he had never been certain how fond of each other the sisters were in life.

"My drinking only lasted about a year and a half—from the time we came over until I—collapsed."

"It was time enough."

"It was time enough," he agreed.

"My duty is entirely to Helen," she said. "I try to think what she would have wanted me to do. Frankly, from the night you did that terrible thing you haven't really existed for me. I can't help that. She was my sister."

"Yes."

"When she was dying she asked me to look out for Honoria. If you hadn't been in a sanitarium then, it might have helped matters."

He had no answer.

"I'll never in my life be able to forget the morning when Helen knocked at my door, soaked to the skin and shivering and said you'd locked her out."

Charlie gripped the sides of the chair. This was more difficult than he expected; he wanted to launch out into a long expostulation and explanation, but he only said: "The night I locked her out—" and she interrupted, "I don't feel up to going over that again."

After a moment's silence Lincoln said: "We're getting off the subject. You want Marion to set aside her legal guardianship and give you Honoria. I think the main point for her is whether she has confidence in you or not."

"I don't blame Marion," Charlie said slowly, "but I think she can have entire confidence in me. I had a good record up to three years ago. Of course, it's within human possibilities I might go wrong any time. But if we wait much longer I'll lose Honoria's childhood and my chance for a home." He shook his head, "I'll simply lose her, don't you see?"

"Yes, I see," said Lincoln.

"Why didn't you think of all this before?" Marion asked.

"I suppose I did, from time to time, but Helen and I were getting along badly. When I consented to the guardianship, I was flat on my back in a sanitarium and the market had cleaned me out. I knew I'd acted badly, and I thought if it would bring any peace to Helen, I'd agree to anything. But now it's different. I'm functioning, I'm behaving damn well, so far as——"

"Please don't swear at me," Marion said.

He looked at her, startled. With each remark the force of her dislike became more and more apparent. She had built up all her fear of life into one wall and faced it toward him. This trivial reproof was possibly the result of some trouble with the cook several hours before. Charlie became increasingly alarmed at leaving Honoria in this atmosphere of hostility against himself; sooner or later it would come out, in a word here, a shake of the head there, and some of that distrust would be irrevocably implanted in Honoria. But he pulled his temper down out of his face and shut it up inside him; he had won a point, for Lincoln realized the absurdity of Marion's remark and asked her lightly since when she had objected to the word "damn."

"Another thing," Charlie said: "I'm able to give her certain advantages now. I'm going to take a French governess to Prague with me. I've got a lease on a new apartment——"

He stopped, realizing that he was blundering. They couldn't be expected to accept with equanimity the fact that his income was again twice as large as their own.

"I suppose you can give her more luxuries than we can," said Marion. "When you were throwing away money we were living along watching every ten francs. . . . I suppose you'll start doing it again."

"Oh, no," he said. "I've learned. I worked hard for ten years, you know—until I got lucky in the market, like so many people. Terribly lucky. It won't happen again."

There was a long silence. All of them felt their nerves straining, and for the first time in a year Charlie wanted a drink. He was sure now that Lincoln Peters wanted him to have his child.

Marion shuddered suddenly; part of her saw that Charlie's feet were planted on the earth now, and her own maternal feeling recognized the naturalness of his desire; but she had lived for a long time with a prejudice—a prejudice founded on a curious disbelief in her sister's happiness, and which, in the shock of one terrible night, had turned to hatred for him. It had all happened at a point in her life where the discouragement of ill health and adverse circumstances made it necessary for her to believe in tangible villainy and a tangible villain.

"I can't help what I think!" she cried out suddenly. "How much you were responsible for Helen's death, I don't know. It's something you'll have to square with your own conscience."

An electric current of agony surged through him; for a moment he was almost on his feet, an unuttered sound echoing in his throat. He hung on to himself for a moment, another moment.

"Hold on there," said Lincoln uncomfortably. "I never thought you were responsible for that."

"Helen died of heart trouble," Charlie said dully.

"Yes, heart trouble." Marion spoke as if the phrase had another meaning for her.

Then, in the flatness that followed her outburst, she saw him plainly and she knew he had somehow arrived at control over the situation. Glancing at her husband, she found no help from him, and as abruptly as if it were a matter of no importance, she threw up the sponge.

"Do what you like!" she cried, springing up from her chair. "She's your child. I'm not the person to stand in your way. I think if it were my child I'd rather see her—" She managed to check herself. "You two decide it. I can't stand this. I'm sick. I'm going to bed."

She hurried from the room; after a moment Lincoln said:

"This has been a hard day for her. You know how strongly she feels—" His voice was almost apologetic: "When a woman gets an idea in her head."

"Of course."

"It's going to be all right. I think she sees now that you—can provide for the child, and so we can't very well stand in your way or Honoria's way."

"Thank you, Lincoln."

"I'd better go along and see how she is."

"I'm going."

He was still trembling when he reached the street, but a walk down the Rue Bonaparte to the *quais* set him up, and as he crossed the Seine, fresh and new by the *quai* lamps, he felt exultant. But back in his room he couldn't sleep. The image of Helen haunted him. Helen whom he had loved so until they had senselessly begun to abuse each other's love, tear it into shreds. On that terrible February night that Marion remembered so vividly, a slow quarrel had gone on for hours. There was a scene at the Florida, and then he attempted to take her home, and then she kissed young Webb at a table; after that there was what she had hysterically said. When he arrived home alone he turned the key in the lock in wild anger. How could he know she would arrive an hour later alone, that there would be a snowstorm in which she wandered about in slippers, too confused to find a taxi? Then the aftermath, her escaping pneumonia by a miracle, and all the attendant horror. They were "reconciled," but that was the beginning of the end, and Marion, who had seen with her own eyes and who imagined it to be one of many scenes from her sister's martyrdom, never forgot.

Going over it again brought Helen nearer, and in the white, soft light that steals upon half sleep near morning he found himself talking to her again. She said that he was perfectly right about Honoria and that she wanted Honoria to be with him. She said she was glad he was being good and doing better. She said a lot of other things—very friendly things—but she was in a swing in a white dress, and swinging faster and faster all the time, so that at the end he could not hear clearly all that she said.

4

He woke up feeling happy. The door of the world was open again. He made plans, vistas, futures for Honoria and himself, but suddenly he grew sad, remembering all the plans he and Helen had made. She had not planned to die. The present was the thing—work to do and someone to love. But not to love too much, for he knew the injury that a father can do to a daughter or a mother to a son by attaching them too closely: afterward, out in the world, the child would seek in the marriage partner the same blind tenderness and, failing probably to find it, turn against love and life.

It was another bright, crisp day. He called Lincoln Peters at the bank where he worked and asked if he could count on taking Honoria when he left for Prague. Lincoln agreed that there was no reason for delay. One thing—the legal guardianship. Marion wanted to retain that a while longer. She was upset by the whole matter, and it would oil things if she felt that the situation was still in her control for another year. Charlie agreed, wanting only the tangible, visible child.

Then the question of a governess. Charles sat in a gloomy agency and talked to a cross Béarnaise and to a buxom Breton peasant, neither of whom he could have endured. There were others whom he would see tomorrow.

He lunched with Lincoln Peters at Griffons, trying to keep down his exultation.

"There's nothing quite like your own child," Lincoln said. "But you understand how Marion feels too."

"She's forgotten how hard I worked for seven years there," Charlie said. "She just remembers one night."

"There's another thing." Lincoln hesitated. "While you and Helen were tearing around Europe throwing money away, we were just getting along. I didn't touch any of the prosperity because I never got ahead enough to carry anything but my insurance. I think Marion felt there was some kind of injustice in it—you not even working toward the end, and getting richer and richer."

"It went just as quick as it came," said Charlie.

"Yes, a lot of it stayed in the hands of *chasseurs* and saxophone players and maîtres d'hôtel—well, the big party's over now. I just said that to explain Marion's feeling about those crazy years. If you drop in about six o'clock tonight before Marion's too tired, we'll settle the details on the spot."

Back at his hotel, Charlie found a *pneumatique*[7] that had been redirected from the Ritz bar where Charlie had left his address for the purpose of finding a certain man.

"DEAR CHARLIE: You were so strange when we saw you the other day that I wondered if I did something to offend you. If so, I'm not

[7] A postal or telegraphic message sent by compressed air through a tubular system common in European cities.

conscious of it. In fact, I have thought about you too much for the last year, and it's always been in the back of my mind that I might see you if I came over here. We *did* have such good times that crazy spring, like the night you and I stole the butcher's tricycle, and the time we tried to call on the president and you had the old derby rim and the wire cane. Everybody seems so old lately, but I don't feel old a bit. Couldn't we get together some time today for old time's sake? I've got a vile hang-over for the moment, but will be feeling better this afternoon and will look for you about five in the sweatshop at the Ritz.

"Always devotedly,
"LORRAINE."

His first feeling was one of awe that he had actually, in his mature years, stolen a tricycle and pedaled Lorraine all over the Étoile between the small hours and dawn. In retrospect it was a nightmare. Locking out Helen didn't fit in with any other act of his life, but the tricycle incident did—it was one of many. How many weeks or months of dissipation to arrive at that condition of utter irresponsibility?

He tried to picture how Lorraine had appeared to him then—very attractive; Helen was unhappy about it, though she said nothing. Yesterday, in the restaurant, Lorraine had seemed trite, blurred, worn away. He emphatically did not want to see her, and he was glad Alix had not given away his hotel address. It was a relief to think, instead, of Honoria, to think of Sundays spent with her and of saying good morning to her and of knowing she was there in his house at night, drawing her breath in the darkness.

At five he took a taxi and bought presents for all the Peters—a piquant cloth doll, a box of Roman soldiers, flowers for Marion, big linen handkerchiefs for Lincoln.

He saw, when he arrived in the apartment, that Marion had accepted the inevitable. She greeted him now as though he were a recalcitrant member of the family, rather than a menacing outsider. Honoria had been told she was going; Charlie was glad to see that her tact made her conceal her excessive happiness. Only on his lap did she whisper her delight and the question "When?" before she slipped away with the other children.

He and Marion were alone for a minute in the room, and on an impulse he spoke out boldly:

"Family quarrels are bitter things. They don't go according to any rules. They're not like aches or wounds; they're more like splits in the skin that won't heal because there's not enough material. I wish you and I could be on better terms."

"Some things are hard to forget," she answered. "It's a question of confidence." There was no answer to this and presently she asked, "When do you propose to take her?"

"As soon as I can get a governess. I hoped the day after tomorrow."

"That's impossible. I've got to get her things in shape. Not before Saturday."

He yielded. Coming back into the room, Lincoln offered him a drink.

"I'll take my daily whisky," he said.

It was warm here, it was a home, people together by a fire. The children felt very safe and important; the mother and father were serious, watchful. They had things to do for the children more important than his visit here. A spoonful of medicine was, after all, more important than the strained relations between Marion and himself. They were not dull people, but they were very much in the grip of life and circumstances. He wondered if he couldn't do something to get Lincoln out of his rut at the bank.

A long peal at the door-bell; the *bonne à tout faire*[8] passed through and went down the corridor. The door opened upon another long ring, and then voices, and the three in the salon looked up expectantly; Richard moved to bring the corridor within his range of vision, and Marion rose. Then the maid came back along the corridor, closely followed by the voices, which developed under the light into Duncan Schaeffer and Lorraine Quarrles.

They were gay, they were hilarious, they were roaring with laughter. For a moment Charlie was astounded; unable to understand how they ferreted out the Peters' address.

"Ah-h-h!" Duncan wagged his finger roguishly at Charlie. "Ah-h-h!"

They both slid down another cascade of laughter. Anxious and at a loss, Charlie shook hands with them quickly and presented them to Lincoln and Marion. Marion nodded, scarcely speaking. She had drawn back a step toward the fire; her little girl stood beside her, and Marion put an arm about her shoulder.

With growing annoyance at the intrusion, Charlie waited for them to explain themselves. After some concentration Duncan said:

"We came to invite you out to dinner. Lorraine and I insist that all this shishi, cagy business 'bout your address got to stop."

Charlie came closer to them, as if to force them backward down the corridor.

"Sorry, but I can't. Tell me where you'll be and I'll phone you in half an hour."

This made no impression. Lorraine sat down suddenly on the side

[8] Maid-of-all-work.

of a chair, and focusing her eyes on Richard, cried, "Oh, what a nice little boy! Come here, little boy." Richard glanced at his mother, but did not move. With a perceptible shrug of her shoulders, Lorraine turned back to Charlie:

"Come and dine. Sure your cousins won' mine. See you so sel'om. Or solemn."

"I can't," said Charlie sharply. "You two have dinner and I'll phone you."

Her voice became suddenly unpleasant. "All right, we'll go. But I remember once when you hammered on my door at four A.M. I was enough of a good sport to give you a drink. Come on, Dunc."

Still in slow motion, with blurred, angry faces, with uncertain feet, they retired along the corridor.

"Good night," Charlie said.

"Good night!" responded Lorraine emphatically.

When he went back into the salon Marion had not moved, only now her son was standing in the circle of her other arm. Lincoln was still swinging Honoria back and forth like a pendulum from side to side.

"What an outrage!" Charlie broke out. "What an absolute outrage!"

Neither of them answered. Charlie dropped into an armchair, picked up his drink, set it down again and said:

"People I haven't seen for two years having the colossal nerve——"

He broke off. Marion had made the sound "Oh!" in one swift, furious breath, turned her body from him with a jerk and left the room.

Lincoln set down Honoria carefully.

"You children go in and start your soup," he said, and when they obeyed, he said to Charlie:

"Marion's not well and she can't stand shocks. That kind of people make her really physically sick."

"I didn't tell them to come here. They wormed your name out of somebody. They deliberately——"

"Well, it's too bad. It doesn't help matters. Excuse me a minute."

Left alone, Charlie sat tense in his chair. In the next room he could hear the children eating, talking in monosyllables, already oblivious to the scene between their elders. He heard a murmur of conversation from a farther room and then the ticking bell of a telephone receiver picked up, and in a panic he moved to the other side of the room and out of earshot.

In a minute Lincoln came back. "Look here, Charlie. I think we'd better call off dinner for tonight. Marion's in bad shape."

"Is she angry with me?"

"Sort of," he said, almost roughly. "She's not strong and——"

"You mean she's changed her mind about Honoria?"

"She's pretty bitter right now. I don't know. You phone me at the bank tomorrow."

"I wish you'd explain to her I never dreamed these people would come here. I'm just as sore as you are."

"I couldn't explain anything to her now."

Charlie got up. He took his coat and hat and started down the corridor. Then he opened the door of the dining room and said in a strange voice, "Good night, children."

Honoria rose and ran around the table to hug him.

"Good night, sweetheart," he said vaguely, and then trying to make his voice more tender, trying to conciliate something, "Good night, dear children."

5

Charlie went directly to the Ritz bar with the furious idea of finding Lorraine and Duncan, but they were not there, and he realized that in any case there was nothing he could do. He had not touched his drink at the Peters, and now he ordered a whisky-and-soda. Paul came over to say hello.

"It's a great change," he said sadly. "We do about half the business we did. So many fellows I hear about back in the States lost everything, maybe not in the first crash, but then in the second. Your friend George Hardt lost every cent, I hear. Are you back in the States?"

"No, I'm in business in Prague."

"I heard that you lost a lot in the crash."

"I did," and he added grimly, "but I lost everything I wanted in the boom."

"Selling short."

"Something like that."

Again the memory of those days swept over him like a nightmare —the people they had met travelling; then people who couldn't add a row of figures or speak a coherent sentence. The little man Helen had consented to dance with at the ship's party, who had insulted her ten feet from the table; the women and girls carried screaming with drink or drugs out of public places—

—The men who locked their wives out in the snow, because the snow of twenty-nine wasn't real snow. If you didn't want it to be snow, you just paid some money.

He went to the phone and called the Peters' apartment; Lincoln answered.

"I called up because this thing is on my mind. Has Marion said anything definite?"

"Marion's sick," Lincoln answered shortly. "I know this thing isn't altogether your fault, but I can't have her go to pieces about it. I'm afraid we'll have to let it slide for six months; I can't take the chance of working her up to this state again."

"I see."

"I'm sorry, Charlie."

He went back to his table. His whisky glass was empty, but he shook his head when Alix looked at it questioningly. There wasn't much he could do now except send Honoria some things; he would send her a lot of things tomorrow. He thought rather angrily that this was just money—he had given so many people money. . . .

"No, no more," he said to another waiter. "What do I owe you?"

He would come back some day; they couldn't make him pay forever. But he wanted his child, and nothing was much good now, beside that fact. He wasn't young any more, with a lot of nice thoughts and dreams to have by himself. He was absolutely sure Helen wouldn't have wanted him to be so alone.

William Faulkner / 1897–1962

A Rose for Emily

When Miss Emily Grierson died, our whole town went to her funeral: the men through a sort of respectful affection for a fallen monument, the women mostly out of curiosity to see the inside of her house, which no one save an old man-servant—a combined gardener and cook—had seen in at least ten years.

It was a big, squarish frame house that had once been white, decorated with cupolas and spires and scrolled balconies in the heavily lightsome style of the seventies, set on what had once been our most select street. But garages and cotton gins had encroached and obliterated even the august names of that neighborhood; only Miss Emily's house was left, lifting its stubborn and coquettish decay above the cotton wagons and the gasoline pumps—an eyesore among eyesores. And now Miss Emily had gone to join the representatives of those august names where they lay in the cedar-bemused cemetery among the ranked and anonymous graves of Union and Confederate soldiers who fell at the battle of Jefferson.

Alive, Miss Emily had been a tradition, a duty, and a care; a sort of hereditary obligation upon the town, dating from that day in 1894 when Colonel Sartoris, the mayor—he who fathered the edict that no Negro woman should appear on the streets without an apron—remitted her taxes, the dispensation dating from the death of her father on into perpetuity. Not that Miss Emily would have accepted charity. Colonel Sartoris invented an involved tale to the effect that Miss Emily's father had loaned money to the town, which the town, as a matter of business, preferred this way of repaying. Only a man of Colonel Sartoris' generation and thought could have invented it, and only a woman could have believed it.

When the next generation, with its more modern ideas, became mayors and aldermen, this arrangement created some little dissatisfaction. On the first of the year they mailed her a tax notice. February came, and there was no reply. They wrote her a formal letter, asking her to call at the sheriff's office at her convenience. A week later the mayor wrote her himself, offering to call or to send his car for her, and received in reply a note on paper of an archaic shape, in a thin, flowing calligraphy in faded ink, to the effect that she no longer went out at all. The tax notice was also enclosed, without comment.

They called a special meeting of the Board of Aldermen. A deputation waited upon her, knocked at the door through which no visitor had passed since she ceased giving china-painting lessons eight or ten years earlier. They were admitted by the old Negro into a dim hall from which a stairway mounted into still more shadow. It smelled of dust and disuse—a close, dank smell. The Negro led them into the parlor. It was furnished in heavy, leather-covered furniture. When the Negro opened the blinds of one window, they could see that the leather was cracked; and when they sat down, a faint dust rose sluggishly about their thighs, spinning with slow motes in the single sun-ray. On a tarnished gilt easel before the fireplace stood a crayon portrait of Miss Emily's father.

They rose when she entered—a small, fat woman in black, with a thin gold chain descending to her waist and vanishing into her belt, leaning on an ebony cane with a tarnished gold head. Her skeleton was small and spare; perhaps that was why what would have been merely plumpness in another was obesity in her. She looked bloated, like a body long submerged in motionless water, and of that pallid hue. Her eyes, lost in the fatty ridges of her face, looked like two small pieces of coal pressed into a lump of dough as they moved from one face to another while the visitors stated their errand.

She did not ask them to sit. She just stood in the door and listened quietly until the spokesman came to a stumbling halt. Then they could hear the invisible watch ticking at the end of the gold chain.

Her voice was dry and cold. "I have no taxes in Jefferson. Colonel Sartoris explained it to me. Perhaps one of you can gain access to the city records and satisfy yourselves."

"But we have. We are the city authorities, Miss Emily. Didn't you get a notice from the sheriff, signed by him?"

"I received a paper, yes," Miss Emily said. "Perhaps he considers himself the sheriff . . . I have no taxes in Jefferson."

"But there is nothing on the books to show that, you see. We must go by the—"

"See Colonel Sartoris. I have no taxes in Jefferson."

"But, Miss Emily—"

"See Colonel Sartoris." (Colonel Sartoris had been dead almost ten years.) "I have no taxes in Jefferson. Tobe!" The Negro appeared. "Show these gentlemen out."

2

So she vanquished them, horse and foot, just as she had vanquished their fathers thirty years before about the smell. That was two years after her father's death and a short time after her sweetheart—the one we believed would marry her—had deserted her. After her father's death she went out very little; after her sweetheart went away, people hardly saw her at all. A few of the ladies had the temerity to call, but were not received, and the only sign of life about the place was the Negro man—a young man then—going in and out with a market basket.

"Just as if a man—any man—could keep a kitchen properly," the ladies said; so they were not surprised when the smell developed. It was another link between the gross, teeming world and the high and mighty Griersons.

A neighbor, a woman, complained to the mayor, Judge Stevens, eighty years old.

"But what will you have me do about it, madam?" he said.

"Why, send her word to stop it," the woman said. "Isn't there a law?"

"I'm sure that won't be necessary," Judge Stevens said. "It's probably just a snake or a rat that nigger of hers killed in the yard. I'll speak to him about it."

The next day he received two more complaints, one from a man who came in diffident deprecation. "We really must do something about it, Judge. I'd be the last one in the world to bother Miss Emily, but we've got to do something." That night the Board of Aldermen met—three graybeards and one younger man, a member of the rising generation.

"It's simple enough," he said. "Send her word to have her place cleaned up. Give her a certain time to do it in, and if she don't . . ."

"Dammit, sir," Judge Stevens said, "will you accuse a lady to her face of smelling bad?"

So the next night, after midnight, four men crossed Miss Emily's lawn and slunk about the house like burglars, sniffing along the base of the brickwork and at the cellar openings while one of them performed a regular sowing motion with his hand out of a sack slung from his shoulder. They broke open the cellar door and sprinkled lime there, and in all the outbuildings. As they recrossed the lawn, a window that had been dark was lighted and Miss Emily sat in it, the light behind her, and her upright torso motionless as that of an idol. They crept quietly across the lawn and into the shadow of the locusts that lined the street. After a week or two the smell went away.

That was when people had begun to feel really sorry for her. People in our town, remembering how old lady Wyatt, her great-aunt, had gone completely crazy at last, believed that the Griersons held themselves a little too high for what they really were. None of the young men were quite good enough for Miss Emily and such. We had long thought of them as a tableau, Miss Emily a slender figure in white in the background, her father a spraddled silhouette in the foreground, his back to her and clutching a horsewhip, the two of them framed by the back-flung front door. So when she got to be thirty and was still single, we were not pleased exactly, but vindicated; even with insanity in the family she wouldn't have turned down all of her chances if they had really materialized.

When her father died, it got about that the house was all that was left to her; and in a way, people were glad. At last they could pity Miss Emily. Being left alone, and a pauper, she had become humanized. Now she too would know the old thrill and the old despair of a penny more or less.

The day after his death all the ladies prepared to call at the house and offer condolence and aid, as is our custom. Miss Emily met them at the door, dressed as usual and with no trace of grief on her face. She told them that her father was not dead. She did that for three days, with the ministers calling on her, and the doctors, trying to persuade her to let them dispose of the body. Just as they were about to resort to law and force, she broke down, and they buried her father quickly.

We did not say she was crazy then. We believed she had to do that. We remembered all the young men her father had driven away, and we knew that with nothing left, she would have to cling to that which had robbed her, as people will.

3

She was sick for a long time. When we saw her again, her hair was cut short, making her look like a girl, with a vague resemblance to those angels in colored church windows—sort of tragic and serene.

The town had just let the contracts for paving the sidewalks, and in the summer after her father's death they began the work. The construction company came with niggers and mules and machinery, and a foreman named Homer Barron, a Yankee—a big, dark, ready man, with a big voice and eyes lighter than his face. The little boys would follow in groups to hear him cuss the niggers, and the niggers singing in time to the rise and fall of picks. Pretty soon he knew everybody in town. Whenever you heard a lot of laughing anywhere about the square, Homer Barron would be in the center of the group. Presently we began to see him and Miss Emily on Sunday afternoons driving in the yellow-wheeled buggy and the matched team of bays from the livery stable.

At first we were glad that Miss Emily would have an interest, because the ladies all said, "Of course a Grierson would not think seriously of a Northerner, a day laborer." But there were still others, older people, who said that even grief could not cause a real lady to forget *noblesse oblige*—without calling it *noblesse oblige*. They just said, "Poor Emily. Her kinsfolk should come to her." She had some kin in Alabama; but years ago her father had fallen out with them over the estate of old lady Wyatt, the crazy woman, and there was no communication between the two families. They had not even been represented at the funeral.

And as soon as the old people said, "Poor Emily," the whispering began. "Do you suppose it's really so?" they said to one another. "Of course it is. What else could . . ." This behind their hands; rustling of craned silk and satin behind jalousies closed upon the sun of Sunday afternoon as the thin, swift clop-clop-clop of the matched team passed: "Poor Emily."

She carried her head high enough—even when we believed that she was fallen. It was as if she demanded more than ever the recognition of her dignity as the last Grierson; as if it had wanted that touch of earthiness to reaffirm her imperviousness. Like when she bought the rat poison, the arsenic. That was over a year after they had begun to say "Poor Emily," and while the two female cousins were visiting her.

"I want some poison," she said to the druggist. She was over thirty then, still a slight woman, though thinner than usual, with cold, haughty black eyes in a face the flesh of which was strained across the temples and about the eye-sockets as you imagine a lighthouse-keeper's face ought to look. "I want some poison," she said.

"Yes, Miss Emily. What kind? For rats and such? I'd recom—"

"I want the best you have. I don't care what kind."

The druggist named several. "They'll kill anything up to an elephant. But what you want is—"

"Arsenic," Miss Emily said. "Is that a good one?"

"Is . . . arsenic? Yes, ma'am. But what you want—"

"I want arsenic."

The druggist looked down at her. She looked back at him, erect, her face like a strained flag. "Why, of course," the druggist said. "If that's what you want. But the law requires you to tell what you are going to use it for."

Miss Emily just stared at him, her head tilted back in order to look him eye for eye, until he looked away and went and got the arsenic and wrapped it up. The Negro delivery boy brought her the package; the druggist didn't come back. When she opened the package at home there was written on the box, under the skull and bones: "For rats."

4

So the next day we all said, "She will kill herself"; and we said it would be the best thing. When she had first begun to be seen with Homer Barron, we had said, "She will marry him." Then we said, "She will persuade him yet," because Homer himself had remarked—he liked men, and it was known that he drank with the younger men in the Elks' Club—that he was not a marrying man. Later we said, "Poor Emily" behind the jalousies as they passed on Sunday afternoon in the glittering buggy, Miss Emily with her head high and Homer Barron with his hat cocked and a cigar in his teeth, reins and whip in a yellow glove.

Then some of the ladies began to say that it was a disgrace to the town and a bad example to the young people. The men did not want to interfere, but at last the ladies forced the Baptist minister—Miss Emily's people were Episcopal—to call upon her. He would never divulge what happened during that interview, but he refused to go back again. The next Sunday they again drove about the streets, and the following day the minister's wife wrote to Miss Emily's relations in Alabama.

So she had blood-kin under her roof again and we sat back to watch developments. At first nothing happened. Then we were sure that they were to be married. We learned that Miss Emily had been to the jeweler's and ordered a man's toilet set in silver, with the letters H. B. on each piece. Two days later we learned that she had bought a complete outfit of men's clothing, including a nightshirt, and we said, "They are married." We were really glad. We were glad because the two female cousins were even more Grierson than Miss Emily had ever been.

So we were not surprised when Homer Barron—the streets had been finished some time since—was gone. We were a little disappointed that there was not a public blowing-off, but we believed that he had gone on to prepare for Miss Emily's coming, or to give her a chance to get rid of the cousins. (By that time it was a cabal, and we were all Miss Emily's allies to help circumvent the cousins.) Sure enough, after another week they departed. And, as we had expected all along, within three days Homer Barron was back in town. A neighbor saw the Negro man admit him at the kitchen door at dusk one evening.

And that was the last we saw of Homer Barron. And of Miss Emily for some time. The Negro man went in and out with the market basket, but the front door remained closed. Now and then we would see her at a window for a moment, as the men did that night when they sprinkled the lime, but for almost six months she did not appear on the streets. Then we knew that this was to be expected too; as if that quality of her father which had thwarted her woman's life so many times had been too virulent and too furious to die.

When we next saw Miss Emily, she had grown fat and her hair was turning gray. During the next few years it grew grayer and grayer until it attained an even pepper-and-salt iron-gray, when it ceased turning. Up to the day of her death at seventy-four it was still that vigorous iron-gray, like the hair of an active man.

From that time on her front door remained closed, save for a period of six or seven years, when she was about forty, during which she gave lessons in china-painting. She fitted up a studio in one of the downstairs rooms, where the daughters and granddaughters of Colonel Sartoris' contemporaries were sent to her with the same regularity and in the same spirit that they were sent to church on Sundays with a twenty-five-cent piece for the collection plate. Meanwhile her taxes had been remitted.

Then the newer generation became the backbone and the spirit of the town, and the painting pupils grew up and fell away and did not send their children to her with boxes of color and tedious brushes and pictures cut from the ladies' magazines. The front door closed upon the last one and remained closed for good. When the town got free postal delivery, Miss Emily alone refused to let them fasten the metal numbers above her door and attach a mailbox to it. She would not listen to them.

Daily, monthly, yearly we watched the Negro grow grayer and more stooped, going in and out with the market basket. Each December we sent her a tax notice, which would be returned by the post office a week later, unclaimed. Now and then we would see her in one of the downstairs windows—she had evidently shut up the top floor of the house—like the carven torso of an idol in a niche, looking or not looking at us, we could never tell which. Thus she passed from generation to generation—dear, inescapable, impervious, tranquil, and perverse.

And so she died. Fell ill in the house filled with dust and shadows, with only a doddering Negro man to wait on her. We did not even know she was sick; we had long since given up trying to get any information from the Negro. He talked to no one, probably not even to her, for his voice had grown harsh and rusty, as if from disuse.

She died in one of the downstairs rooms, in a heavy walnut bed with a curtain, her gray head propped on a pillow yellow and moldy with age and lack of sunlight.

5

The Negro met the first of the ladies at the front door and let them in, with their hushed, sibilant voices and their quick, curious glances, and then he disappeared. He walked right through the house and out the back and was not seen again.

The two female cousins came at once. They held the funeral on the second day, with the town coming to look at Miss Emily beneath a mass of bought flowers, with the crayon face of her father musing profoundly above the bier and the ladies sibilant and macabre; and the very old men—some in their brushed Confederate uniforms—on the porch and the lawn, talking of Miss Emily as if she had been a contemporary of theirs, believing that they had danced with her and courted her perhaps, confusing time with its mathematical progression, as the old do, to whom all the past is not a diminishing road but, instead, a huge meadow which no winter ever quite touches, divided from them now by the narrow bottle-neck of the most recent decade of years.

Already we knew that there was one room in that region above stairs which no one had seen in forty years, and which would have to be forced. They waited until Miss Emily was decently in the ground before they opened it.

The violence of breaking down the door seemed to fill this room with pervading dust. A thin, acrid pall as of the tomb seemed to lie everywhere upon this room decked and furnished as for a bridal: upon the valance curtains of faded rose color, upon the rose-shaded lights, upon the dressing table, upon the delicate array of crystal and the man's toilet things backed with tarnished silver, silver so tarnished that the monogram was obscured. Among them lay a collar and tie, as if they had just been removed, which, lifted, left upon the surface a pale crescent in the dust. Upon a chair hung the suit, carefully folded; beneath it the two mute shoes and the discarded socks.

The man himself lay in the bed.

For a long while we just stood there, looking down at the profound and fleshless grin. The body had apparently once lain in the attitude of an embrace, but now the long sleep that outlasts love, that conquers even the grimace of love, had cuckolded him. What was left of him, rotted beneath what was left of the nightshirt, had become inextricable from the bed in which he lay; and upon him and upon the pillow beside him lay that even coating of the patient and biding dust.

Then we noticed that in the second pillow was the indentation of a head. One of us lifted something from it, and leaning forward, that faint and invisible dust dry and acrid in the nostrils, we saw a long strand of iron-gray hair.

Soldier's Home

Krebs went to the war from a Methodist college in Kansas. There is a picture which shows him among his fraternity brothers, all of them wearing exactly the same height and style collar. He enlisted in the Marines in 1917 and did not return to the United States until the second division returned from the Rhine in the summer of 1919.

There is a picture which shows him on the Rhine with two German girls and another corporal. Krebs and the corporal look too big for their uniforms. The German girls are not beautiful. The Rhine does not show in the picture.

By the time Krebs returned to his home town in Oklahoma the greeting of heroes was over. He came back much too late. The men from the town who had been drafted had all been welcomed elaborately on their return. There had been a great deal of hysteria. Now the reaction had set in. People seemed to think it was rather ridiculous for Krebs to be getting back so late, years after the war was over.

At first Krebs, who had been at Belleau Wood, Soissons, the Champagne, St. Mihiel and in the Argonne, did not want to talk about the war at all. Later he felt the need to talk but no one wanted to hear about it. His town had heard too many atrocity stories to be thrilled by actualities. Krebs found that to be listened to at all he had to lie, and after he had done this twice he, too, had a reaction against the war and against talking about it. A distaste for everything that had happened to him in the war set in because of the lies he had told. All of the times that had been able to make him feel cool and clear inside himself when he thought of them; the times so long back when he had done the one thing, the only thing for a man to do, easily and naturally, when he might have done something else, now lost their cool, valuable quality and then were lost themselves.

His lies were quite unimportant lies and consisted in attributing to himself things other men had seen, done or heard of, and stating as facts certain apocryphal incidents familiar to all soldiers. Even his lies were not sensational at the pool room. His acquaintances, who had heard detailed accounts of German women found chained to machine guns in the Argonne forest and who could not comprehend, or were barred by their patriotism from interest in, any German machine gunners who were not chained, were not thrilled by his stories.

Krebs acquired the nausea in regard to experience that is the result of untruth or exaggeration, and when he occasionally met another man who had really been a soldier and they talked a few minutes in the dressing room at a dance he fell into the easy pose of the old soldier among other soldiers: that he had been badly, sickeningly frightened all the time. In this way he lost everything.

During this time, it was late summer, he was sleeping late in bed, getting up to walk down town to the library to get a book, eating lunch at home, reading on the front porch until he became bored and then walking down through the town to spend the hottest hours of the day in the cool dark of the pool room. He loved to play pool.

In the evening he practised on his clarinet, strolled down town, read and went to bed. He was still a hero to his two young sisters. His mother would have given him breakfast in bed if he had wanted it. She often came in when he was in bed and asked him to tell her about the war, but her attention always wandered. His father was non-committal.

Before Krebs went away to the war he had never been allowed to drive the family motor car. His father was in the real estate business and always wanted the car to be at his command when he required it to take clients out into the country to show them a piece of farm property. The car always stood outside the First National Bank building where his father had an office on the second floor. Now, after the war, it was still the same car.

Nothing was changed in the town except that the young girls had grown up. But they lived in such a complicated world of already defined alliances and shifting feuds that Krebs did not feel the energy or the courage to break into it. He liked to look at them, though. There were so many good-looking young girls. Most of them had their hair cut short. When he went away only little girls wore their hair like that or girls that were fast. They all wore sweaters and shirt waists with round Dutch collars. It was a pattern. He liked to look at them from the front porch as they walked on the other side of the street. He liked to watch them walking under the shade of the trees. He liked the round Dutch collars above their sweaters. He liked their silk stockings and flat shoes. He liked their bobbed hair and the way they walked.

When he was in town their appeal to him was not very strong. He did not like them when he saw them in the Greek's ice cream parlor. He did not want them themselves really. They were too complicated. There was something else. Vaguely he wanted a girl but he did not want to have to work to get her. He would have liked to have a girl but he did not want to have to spend a long time getting her. He did not want to get into the intrigue and the politics. He did not want to have to do any courting. He did not want to tell any more lies. It wasn't worth it.

He did not want any consequences. He did not want any consequences ever again. He wanted to live along without consequences. Besides he did not really need a girl. The army had taught him that. It was all right to pose as though you had to have a girl. Nearly everybody did that. But it wasn't true. You did not need a girl. That was the funny thing. First a fellow boasted how girls mean nothing to him, that he never thought of them, that they could not touch him. Then a fellow boasted that he could not get along without girls, that he had to have them all the time, that he could not go to sleep without them.

That was all a lie. It was all a lie both ways. You did not need a girl unless you thought about them. He learned that in the army. Then sooner or later you always got one. When you were really ripe for a girl you always got one. You did not have to think about it. Sooner or later it would come. He had learned that in the army.

Now he would have liked a girl if she had come to him and not wanted to talk. But here at home it was all too complicated. He knew he could never get through it all again. It was not worth the trouble. That was the thing about French girls and German girls. There was not all this talking. You couldn't talk much and you did not need to talk. It was simple and you were friends. He thought about France and then he began to think about Germany. On the whole he had liked Germany better. He did not want to leave Germany. He did not want to come home. Still, he had come home. He sat on the front porch.

He liked the girls that were walking along the other side of the street. He liked the look of them much better than the French girls or the German girls. But the world they were in was not the world he was in. He would like to have one of them. But it was not worth it. They were such a nice pattern. He liked the pattern. It was exciting. But he would not go through all the talking. He did not want one badly enough. He liked to look at them all, though. It was not worth it. Not now when things were getting good again.

He sat there on the porch reading a book on the war. It was a history and he was reading about all the engagements he had been in. It was the most interesting reading he had ever done. He wished there were more maps. He looked forward with a good feeling to reading all the really good histories when they would come out with good detail maps. Now he was really learning about the war. He had been a good soldier. That made a difference.

One morning after he had been home about a month his mother came into his bedroom and sat on the bed. She smoothed her apron.

"I had a talk with your father last night, Harold," she said, "and he is willing for you to take the car out in the evenings."

"Yeah?" said Krebs, who was not fully awake. "Take the car out? Yeah?"

"Yes. Your father has felt for some time that you should be able to take the car out in the evenings whenever you wished but we only talked it over last night."

"I'll bet you made him," Krebs said.

"No. It was your father's suggestion that we talk the matter over."

"Yeah. I'll bet you made him," Krebs sat up in bed.

"Will you come down to breakfast, Harold?" his mother said.

"As soon as I get my clothes on," Krebs said.

His mother went out of the room and he could hear her frying something downstairs while he washed, shaved and dressed to go down into the dining-room for breakfast. While he was eating breakfast his sister brought in the mail.

"Well, Hare," she said. "You old sleepy-head. What do you ever get up for?"

Krebs looked at her. He liked her. She was his best sister.

"Have you got the paper?" he asked.

She handed him *The Kansas City Star* and he shucked off its brown wrapper and opened it to the sporting page. He folded *The Star* open and propped it against the water pitcher with his cereal dish to steady it, so he could read while he ate.

"Harold," his mother stood in the kitchen doorway, "Harold, please don't muss up the paper. Your father can't read his *Star* if it's been mussed."

"I won't muss it," Krebs said.

His sister sat down at the table and watched him while he read.

"We're playing indoor over at school this afternoon," she said. "I'm going to pitch."

"Good," said Krebs. "How's the old wing?"

"I can pitch better than lots of the boys. I tell them all you taught me. The other girls aren't much good."

"Yeah?" said Krebs.

"I tell them all you're my beau. Aren't you my beau, Hare?"

"You bet."

"Couldn't your brother really be your beau just because he's your brother?"

"I don't know."

"Sure you know. Couldn't you be my beau, Hare, if I was old enough and if you wanted to?"

"Sure. You're my girl now."

"Am I really your girl?"

"Sure."

"Do you love me?"

"Uh, huh."

"Will you love me always?"

"Sure."

"Will you come over and watch me play indoor?"

"Maybe."

"Aw, Hare, you don't love me. If you loved me, you'd want to come over and watch me play indoor."

Krebs's mother came into the dining-room from the kitchen. She carried a plate with two fried eggs and some crisp bacon on it and a plate of buckwheat cakes.

"You run along, Helen," she said. "I want to talk to Harold."

She put the eggs and bacon down in front of him and brought in a jug of maple syrup for the buckwheat cakes. Then she sat down across the table from Krebs.

"I wish you'd put down the paper a minute, Harold," she said.

Krebs took down the paper and folded it.

"Have you decided what you are going to do yet, Harold?" his mother said, taking off her glasses.

"No," said Krebs.

"Don't you think it's about time?" His mother did not say this in a mean way. She seemed worried.

"I hadn't thought about it," Krebs said.

"God has some work for every one to do," his mother said. "There can be no idle hands in His Kingdom."

"I'm not in His Kingdom," Krebs said.

"We are all of us in His Kingdom."

Krebs felt embarrassed and resentful as always.

"I've worried about you so much, Harold," his mother went on. "I know the temptations you must have been exposed to. I know how weak men are. I know what your own dear grandfather, my own father, told us about the Civil War and I have prayed for you. I pray for you all day long, Harold."

Krebs looked at the bacon fat hardening on his plate.

"Your father is worried, too," his mother went on. "He thinks you have lost your ambition, that you haven't got a definite aim in life. Charley Simmons, who is just your age, has a good job and is going to be married. The boys are all settling down; they're all determined to get somewhere; you can see that boys like Charley Simmons are on their way to being really a credit to the community."

Krebs said nothing.

"Don't look that way, Harold," his mother said. "You know we love you and I want to tell you for your own good how matters stand. Your father does not want to hamper your freedom. He thinks you should be allowed to drive the car. If you want to take some of the nice girls out riding with you, we are only too pleased. We want you to enjoy yourself. But you are going to have to settle down to work, Harold. Your father doesn't care what you start in at. All work is honorable as he says. But you've got to make a start at something. He asked me to speak to you this morning and then you can stop in and see him at his office."

"Is that all?" Krebs said.

"Yes. Don't you love your mother, dear boy?"

"No," Krebs said.

His mother looked at him across the table. Her eyes were shiny. She started crying.

"I don't love anybody," Krebs said.

It wasn't any good. He couldn't tell her, he couldn't make her see it. It was silly to have said it. He had only hurt her. He went over and took hold of her arm. She was crying with her head in her hands.

"I didn't mean it," he said. "I was just angry at something. I didn't mean I didn't love you."

His mother went on crying. Krebs put his arm on her shoulder.

"Can't you believe me, mother?"

His mother shook her head.

"Please, please, mother. Please believe me."

"All right," his mother said chokily. She looked up at him. "I believe you, Harold."

Krebs kissed her hair. She put her face up to him.

"I'm your mother," she said. "I held you next to my heart when you were a tiny baby."

Krebs felt sick and vaguely nauseated.

"I know, Mummy," he said. "I'll try and be a good boy for you."

"Would you kneel and pray with me, Harold?" his mother asked.

They knelt down beside the dining-room table and Krebs's mother prayed.

"Now, you pray, Harold," she said.

"I can't," Krebs said.

"Try, Harold."

"I can't."

"Do you want me to pray for you?"

"Yes."

So his mother prayed for him and then they stood up and Krebs
kissed his mother and went out of the house. He had tried so to keep
his life from being complicated. Still, none of it had touched him. He
had felt sorry for his mother and she had made him lie. He would go
to Kansas City and get a job and she would feel all right about it.
There would be one more scene maybe before he got away. He would
not go down to his father's office. He would miss that one. He wanted
his life to go smoothly. It had just gotten going that way. Well, that
was all over now, anyway. He would go over to the schoolyard and
watch Helen play indoor baseball.

Jean-Paul Sartre / 1905–

The Room

Mme. Darbedat held a *rahat-loukoum*[1] between her fingers. She
brought it carefully to her lips and held her breath, afraid that the
fine dust of sugar that powdered it would blow away. "Just right,"
she told herself. She bit quickly into its glassy flesh and a scent of
stagnation filled her mouth. "Odd how illness sharpens the sensations."
She began to think of mosques, of obsequious Orientals (she had been
to Algeria for her honeymoon) and her pale lips started in a smile:
the *rahat-loukoum* was obsequious too.

Several times she had to pass the palm of her hand over the pages
of her book, for in spite of the precaution she had taken they were
covered with a thin coat of white powder. Her hand made the little
grains of sugar slide and roll, grating on the smooth paper: "That
makes me think of Arcachon, when I used to read on the beach." She
had spent the summer of 1907 at the seashore. Then she wore a big

[1] Turkish delight.

straw hat with a green ribbon; she sat close to the jetty, with a novel by Gyp or Colette Yver.[2] The wind made swirls of sand rain down upon her knees, and from time to time she had to shake the book, holding it by the corners. It was the same sensation: only the grains of sand were dry while the small bits of sugar stuck a little to the ends of her fingers. Again she saw a band of pearl grey sky above a black sea. "Eve wasn't born yet." She felt herself all weighted down with memories and precious as a coffer of sandalwood. The name of the book she used to read suddenly came back to mind: it was called *Petite Madame,* not at all boring. But ever since an unknown illness had confined her to her room she preferred memories and historical works.

She hoped that suffering, heavy readings, a vigilant attention to her memories and the most exquisite sensations would ripen her as a lovely hothouse fruit.

She thought, with some annoyance, that her husband would soon be knocking at her door. On other days of the week he came only in the evening, kissed her brow in silence and read *Le Temps,*[3] sitting in the armchair across from her. But Thursday was M. Darbedat's *day:* he spent an hour with his daughter, generally from three to four. Before going he stopped in to see his wife and both discussed their son-in-law with bitterness. These Thursday conversations, predictable to their slightest detail, exhausted Mme. Darbedat. M. Darbedat filled the quiet room with his presence. He never sat, but walked in circles about the room. Each of his outbursts wounded Mme. Darbedat like a glass splintering. This particular Thursday was worse than usual: at the thought that it would soon be necessary to repeat Eve's confessions to her husband, and to see his great terrifying body convulse with fury, Mme. Darbedat broke out in a sweat. She picked up a *loukoum* from the saucer, studied it for a while with hesitation, then sadly set it down: she did not like her husband to see her eating *loukoums.*

She heard a knock and started up. "Come in," she said weakly.

M. Darbedat entered on tiptoe. "I'm going to see Eve," he said, as he did every Thursday. Mme. Darbedat smiled at him. "Give her a kiss for me."

M. Darbedat did not answer and his forehead wrinkled worriedly: every Thursday at the same time, a muffled irritation mingled with the load of his digestion. "I'll stop in and see Franchot after leaving her, I wish he'd talk to her seriously and try to convince her."

He had made frequent visits to Dr. Franchot. But in vain. Mme.

[2] Pseudonyms of two popular early-twentieth-century female novelists, Sibylle Martel de Janville and Antoinette Huzard.
[3] A conservative Parisian newspaper.

Darbedat raised her eyebrows. Before, when she was well, she shrugged her shoulders. But since sickness had weighted down her body, she replaced the gestures which would have tired her by plays of emotion in the face: she said *yes* with her eyes, *no* with the corners of her mouth: she raised her eyebrows instead of her shoulders.

"There should be some way to take him away from her by force."

"I told you already it was impossible. And besides, the law is very poorly drawn up. Only the other day Franchot was telling me that they have a tremendous amount of trouble with the families: people who can't make up their mind, who want to keep the patient at home; the doctors' hands are tied. They can give their advice, period. That's all. He would," he went on, "have to make a public scandal or else she would have to ask to have him put away herself."

"And that," said Mme. Darbedat, "isn't going to happen tomorrow."

"No." He turned to the mirror and began to comb his fingers through his beard. Mme. Darbedat looked at the powerful red neck of her husband without affection.

"If she keeps on," said M. Darbedat, "she'll be crazier than he is. It's terribly unhealthy. She doesn't leave his side, she only goes out to see you. She has no visitors. The air in their room is simply unbreathable. She never opens the window because Pierre doesn't want it open. As if you should ask a sick man. I believe they burn incense, some rubbish in a little pan, you'd think it was a church. Really, sometimes I wonder . . . she's got a funny look in her eyes, you know."

"I haven't noticed," Mme. Darbedat said. "I find her quite normal. She looks sad, obviously."

"She has a face like an unburied corpse. Does she sleep? Does she eat? But we aren't supposed to ask her about those things. But I should think that with a fellow like Pierre next to her, she wouldn't sleep a wink all night." He shrugged his shoulders. "What I find amazing is that we, her parents, don't have the right to protect her against herself. Understand that Pierre would be much better cared for by Franchot. There's a big park. And besides, I think," he added, smiling a little, "he'd get along much better with people of his own type. People like that are children, you have to leave them alone with each other; they form a sort of freemasonry. That's where he should have been put the first day and for his own good, I'd say. Of course it's in his own best interest."

After a moment, he added, "I tell you I don't like to know she's alone with Pierre, especially at night. Suppose something happened. Pierre has a very sly way about him."

"I don't know," Mme. Darbedat said, "if there's any reason to worry. He always looked like that. He always seemed to be making fun of the world. Poor boy," she sighed, "to have had his pride and then come to that. He thought he was cleverer than all of us. He had a way of saying 'You're right' simply to end the argument . . . It's a blessing for him that he can't see the state he's in."

She recalled with displeasure the long, ironic face, always turned a little to the side. During the first days of Eve's marriage, Mme. Darbedat asked nothing more than a little intimacy with her son-in-law. But he had discouraged her: he almost never spoke, he always agreed quickly and absentmindedly.

M. Darbedat pursued his idea. "Franchot let me visit his place," he said. "It was magnificent. The patients have private rooms with leather armchairs, if you please, and day-beds. You know, they have a tennis court and they're going to build a swimming pool."

He was planted before the window, looking out, rocking a little on his bent legs. Suddenly he turned lithely on his heel, shoulders lowered, hands in his pockets. Mme. Darbedat felt she was going to start perspiring: it was the same thing every time: now he was pacing back and forth like a bear in a cage and his shoes squeaked at every step.

"Please, please won't you sit down. You're tiring me." Hesitating, she added, "I have something important to tell you."

M. Darbedat sat in the armchair and put his hands on his knees; a slight chill ran up Mme. Darbedat's spine: the time had come, she had to speak.

"You know," she said with an embarrassed cough, "I saw Eve on Tuesday."

"Yes."

"We talked about a lot of things, she was very nice, she hadn't been so confiding for a long time. Then I questioned her a little, I got her to talk about Pierre. Well, I found out," she added, again embarrassed, "that she is *very* attached to him."

"I know that too damned well," said M. Darbedat.

He irritated Mme. Darbedat a little: she always had to explain things in such detail. Mme. Darbedat dreamed of living in the company of fine and sensitive people who would understand her slightest word.

"But I mean," she went on, "that she is attached to him *differently* than we imagined."

M. Darbedat rolled furious, anxious eyes, as he always did when he never completely grasped the sense of an allusion or something new.

"What does that all mean?"

"Charles," said Mme. Darbedat, "don't tire me. You should understand a mother has difficulty in telling certain things."

"I don't understand a damned word of anything you say," M. Darbedat said with irritation. "You can't mean . . ."

"Yes," she said.

"They're still . . . now, still . . . ?"

"Yes! Yes! Yes!" she said, in three annoyed and dry little jolts.

M. Darbedat spread his arms, lowered his head and was silent.

"Charles," his wife said, worriedly, "I shouldn't have told you. But I couldn't keep it to myself."

"Our child," he said slowly. "With this madman! He doesn't even recognize her any more. He calls her Agatha. She must have lost all sense of her own dignity."

He raised his head and looked at his wife severely. "You're sure you aren't mistaken?"

"No possible doubt. Like you," she added quickly, "I couldn't believe her and I still can't. The mere idea of being touched by that wretch . . . So . . ." she sighed, "I suppose that's how he holds on to her."

"Do you remember what I told you," M. Darbedat said, "when he came to ask for her hand? I told you I thought he pleased Eve *too much*. You wouldn't believe me." He struck the table suddenly, blushing violently. "It's perversity! He takes her in his arms, kisses her and calls her Agatha, selling her on a lot of nonsense about flying statues and God knows what else! Without a word from her! But what in heaven's name's between those two? Let her be sorry for him, let her put him in a sanatorium and see him every day,—fine. But I never thought . . . I considered her a widow. Listen, Jeannette," he said gravely, "I'm going to speak frankly to you; if she had any sense, I'd rather see her take a lover!"

"Be quiet, Charles!" Mme. Darbedat cried.

M. Darbedat wearily took his hat and the cane he had left on the stool. "After what you've just told me," he concluded, "I don't have much hope left. In any case, I'll have a talk with her because it's my duty."

Mme. Darbedat wished he would go quickly.

"You know," she said to encourage him, "I think Eve is more headstrong than . . . than anything. She knows he's incurable but she's obstinate, she doesn't want to be in the wrong."

M. Darbedat stroked his beard absently.

"Headstrong? Maybe so. If you're right, she'll finally get tired of it. He's not always pleasant and he doesn't have much to say. When I say hello to him he gives me a flabby handshake and doesn't say a word. As soon as they're alone, I think they go back to his obsessions:

she tells me sometimes he screams as though his throat were being cut because of his hallucinations. He sees statues. They frighten him because they buzz. He says they fly around and make fishy eyes at him."

He put on his gloves and continued, "She'll get tired of it, I'm not saying she won't. But suppose she goes crazy before that? I wish she'd go out a little, see the world: she'd meet some nice young man—well, someone like Schroeder, an engineer with Simplon, somebody with a future, she could see him a little here and there and she'd get used to the idea of making a new life for herself."

Mme. Darbedat did not answer, afraid of starting the conversation up again. Her husband bent over her.

"So," he said, "I've got to be on my way."

"Goodbye, Papa," Mme. Darbedat said, lifting her forehead up to him. "Kiss her for me and tell her for me she's a poor dear."

Once her husband had gone, Mme. Darbedat let herself drift to the bottom of the armchair and closed her eyes, exhausted. "What vitality," she thought reproachfully. As soon as she got a little strength back, she quietly stretched out her pale hand and took a *loukoum* from the saucer, groping for it without opening her eyes.

Eve lived with her husband on the sixth floor of an old building on the Rue du Bac. M. Darbedat slowly climbed the 112 steps of the stairway. He was not even out of breath when he pushed the bell. He remembered with satisfaction the words of Mlle. Dormoy: "Charles, for your age, you're simply marvelous." Never did he feel himself stronger and healthier than on Thursday, especially after these invigorating climbs.

Eve opened the door: that's right, she doesn't have a maid. No girls *can* stay with her. I can put myself in their place. He kissed her. "Hello, poor darling."

Eve greeted him with a certain coldness.

"You look a little pale," M. Darbedat said, touching her cheek. "You don't get enough exercise."

There was a moment of silence.

"Is Mamma well?" Eve asked.

"Not good, not too bad. You saw her Tuesday? Well, she's just the same. Your Aunt Louise came to see her yesterday, that pleased her. She likes to have visitors, but they can't stay too long. Aunt Louise came to Paris for that mortgage business. I think I told you about it, a very odd sort of affair. She stopped in at the office to ask my advice. I told her there was only one thing to do: sell. She found a taker, by the way: Bretonnel! You remember Bretonnel. He's retired from business now."

He stopped suddenly: Eve was hardly listening. He thought sadly that nothing interested her any more. It's like the books. Before you had to tear them away from her. Now she doesn't even read any more.

"How is Pierre?"

"Well," Eve said. "Do you want to see him?"

"Of course," M. Darbedat said gaily, "I'd like to pay him a little call."

He was full of compassion for this poor young man, but he could not see him without repugnance. *I detest unhealthy people.* Obviously, it was not Pierre's fault: his heredity was terribly loaded down. M. Darbedat sighed: *All the precautions are taken in vain, you find out those things too late.* No, Pierre was not responsible. But still he had always carried that fault in him; it formed the base of his character; it wasn't like cancer or tuberculosis, something you could always put aside when you wanted to judge a man as he is. His nervous grace, the subtlety which pleased Eve so much when he was courting her were the flowers of madness. He was already mad when he married her only you couldn't tell.

It makes you wonder, thought M. Darbedat, *where responsibility begins, or rather, where it ends.* In any case, he was always analysing himself too much, always turned in on himself. But was it the cause or effect of his sickness? He followed his daughter through a long, dim corridor.

"This apartment is too big for you," he said. "You ought to move out."

"You say that every time, Papa," Eve answered, "but I've already told you Pierre doesn't want to leave his room."

Eve was amazing. Enough to make you wonder if she realized her husband's state. He was insane enough to be in a strait-jacket and she respected his decisions and advice as if he still had good sense.

"What I'm saying is for your own good." M. Darbedat went on, somewhat annoyed, "It seems to me that if I were a woman I'd be afraid of these badly lighted old rooms. I'd like to see you in a bright apartment, the kind they're putting up near Auteuil, three airy little rooms. They lowered the rents because they couldn't find any tenants; this would be just the time."

Eve quietly turned the doorknob and they entered the room. M. Darbedat's throat tightened at the heavy odor of incense. The curtains were drawn. In the shadows he made out a thin neck above the back of an armchair: Pierre's back was turned. He was eating.

"Hello, Pierre," M. Darbedat said, raising his voice. "How are we today?" He drew near him: the sick man was seated in front of a small table: he looked sly.

"I see we had soft boiled eggs," M. Darbedat said, raising his voice higher. "That's good!"

"I'm not deaf," Pierre said quietly.

Irritated, M. Darbedat turned his eyes toward Eve as his witness. But Eve gave him a hard glance and was silent. M. Darbedat realized he had hurt her. Too bad for her. It was impossible to find just the right tone for this boy. He had less sense than a child of four and Eve wanted him treated like a man. M. Darbedat could not keep himself from waiting with impatience for the moment when all this ridiculous business would be finished. Sick people annoyed him a little—especially madmen because they were wrong. Poor Pierre, for example, was wrong all along the line, he couldn't speak a reasonable word and yet it would be useless to expect the least humility from him, or even temporary recognition of his errors.

Eve cleared away the eggshells and the cup. She put a knife and fork in front of Pierre.

"What's he going to eat now," M. Darbedat said jovially.

"A steak."

Pierre had taken the fork and held it in the ends of his long, pale fingers. He inspected it minutely and then gave a slight laugh.

"I can't use it this time," he murmured, setting it down, "I was warned."

Eve came in and looked at the fork with passionate interest.

"Agatha," Pierre said, "give me another one."

Eve obeyed and Pierre began to eat. She had taken the suspect fork and held it tightly in her hands, her eyes never leaving it; she seemed to make a violent effort. How suspicious all their gestures and relationships are! thought M. Darbedat.

He was uneasy.

"Be careful, Pierre, take it by the middle because of the prongs."

Eve sighed and laid the fork on the serving table. M. Darbedat felt his gall rising. He did not think it well to give in to all this poor man's whims—even from Pierre's viewpoint it was pernicious. Franchot had said: "One must never enter the delirium of a madman." Instead of giving him another fork, it would have been better to have reasoned quietly and made him understand that the first was like all the others.

He went to the serving table, took the fork ostentatiously and tested the prongs with a light finger. Then he turned to Pierre. But the latter was cutting his meat peacefully: he gave his father-in-law a gentle, inexpressive glance.

"I'd like to have a little talk with you," M. Darbedat said to Eve.

She followed him docilely into the salon. Sitting on the couch, M.

Darbedat realized he had kept the fork in his hand. He threw it on the table.

"It's much better here," he said.

"I never come here."

"All right to smoke?"

"Of course, Papa," Eve said hurriedly. "Do you want a cigar?"

M. Darbedat preferred to roll a cigarette. He thought eagerly of the discussion he was about to begin. Speaking to Pierre he felt as embarrassed about his reason as a giant about his strength when playing with a child. All his qualities of clarity, sharpness, precision, turned against him; *I must confess it's somewhat the same with my poor Jeannette*. Certainly Mme. Darbedat was not insane, but this illness had . . . stultified her. Eve, on the other hand, took after her father . . . a straight, logical nature; discussion with her was a pleasure; *that's why I don't want them to ruin her*. M. Darbedat raised his eyes. Once again he wanted to see the fine intelligent features of his daughter. He was disappointed with this face; once so reasonable and transparent, there was now something clouded and opaque in it. Eve had always been beautiful. M. Darbedat noticed she was made up with great care, almost with pomp. She had blued her eyelids and put mascara on her long lashes. This violent and perfect make-up made a painful impression on her father.

"You're green beneath your rouge," he told her. "I'm afraid you're getting sick. And the way you make yourself up now! You used to be so discreet."

Eve did not answer and for an embarrassed moment M. Darbedat considered this brilliant, worn-out face beneath the heavy mass of black hair. He thought she looked like a tragedian. *I even know who she looks like. That women . . . that Roumanian who played* Phèdre[4] *in French at the Mur d'Orange*. He regretted having made so disagreeable a remark: *It escaped me! Better not worry her with little things*.

"Excuse me," he said smiling. "You know I'm an old purist. I don't like all these creams and paints women stick on their face today. But I'm in the wrong. You must live in your time."

Eve smiled amiably at him. M. Darbedat lit a cigarette and drew several puffs.

"My child," he began, "I wanted to talk with you: the two of us are going to talk the way we used to. Come, sit down and listen to me nicely; you must have confidence in your old Papa."

[4] The title and heroine of Jean Racine's classic tragedy (1677).

"I'd rather stand," Eve said. "What did you want to tell me?"

"I am going to ask you a single question," M. Darbedat said a little more dryly. "Where will all this lead you?"

"All this?" Eve asked astonished.

"Yes . . . all this whole life you've made for yourself. Listen," he went on, "don't think I don't understand you (he had a sudden illumination) but what you want to do is beyond human strength. You want to live solely by imagination, isn't that it? You don't want to admit he's sick. You don't want to see the Pierre of today, do you? You have eyes only for the Pierre of before. My dear, my darling little girl, it's an impossible bet to win," M. Darbedat continued. "Now I'm going to tell you a story which perhaps you don't know. When we were at Sables-d'Olonne—you were three years old—your mother made the acquaintance of a charming young woman with a superb little boy. You played on the beach with this little boy, you were thick as thieves, you were engaged to marry him. A while later, in Paris, your mother wanted to see this young woman again; she was told she had had a terrible accident. That fine little boy's head was cut off by a car. They told your mother, 'Go and see her, but above all don't talk to her about the death of her child, she *will not* believe he is dead.' Your mother went, she found a half-mad creature: she lived as though her boy was still alive; she spoke to him, she set his place at the table. She lived in such a state of nervous tension that after six months they had to take her away by force to a sanatorium where she was obliged to stay three years. No, my child," M. Darbedat said, shaking his head, "these things are impossible. It would have been better if she had recognized the truth courageously. She would have suffered once, then time would have erased with its sponge. There is nothing like looking things in the face, believe me."

"You're wrong," Eve said with effort. "I know very well that Pierre is . . ."

The word did not escape. She held herself very straight and put her hands on the back of the armchair: there was something dry and ugly in the lower part of her face.

"So . . . ?" asked M. Darbedat, astonished.

"So . . . ?"

"You . . . ?"

"I love him as he is," said Eve rapidly and with an irritated look.

"Not true," M. Darbedat said forcefully. "It isn't true: you don't love him, you can't love him. You can only feel that way about a healthy, normal person. You pity Pierre, I don't doubt it, and surely you have the memory of three years of happiness he gave you. But don't tell me you love him. I won't believe you."

Eve remained wordless, staring at the carpet absently.

"You could at least answer me," M. Darbedat said coldly. "Don't think this conversation has been any less painful for me than it has for you."

"More than you think."

"Well then, if you love him," he cried, exasperated, "it is a great misfortune for you, for me and for your poor mother because I'm going to tell you something I would rather have hidden from you: before three years Pierre will be sunk in complete dementia, he'll be like a beast."

He watched his daughter with hard eyes: he was angry at her for having compelled him, by stubbornness, to make this painful revelation.

Eve was motionless; she did not so much as raise her eyes.

"I knew."

"Who told you?" he asked stupefied.

"Franchot. I knew six months ago."

"And I told him to be careful with you," said M. Darbedat with bitterness. "Maybe it's better. But under those circumstances you must understand that it would be unpardonable to keep Pierre with you. The struggle you have undertaken is doomed to failure, his illness won't spare him. If there were something to be done, if we could save him by care, I'd say yes. But look: you're pretty, intelligent, gay, you're destroying yourself willingly and without profit. I know you've been admirable, but now it's over . . . done, you've done your duty and more; now it would be immoral to continue. We also have duties to ourselves, child. And then you aren't thinking about us. You must," he repeated, hammering the words, "send Pierre to Franchot's clinic. Leave this apartment where you've had nothing but sorrow and come home to us. If you want to be useful and ease the sufferings of someone else, you have your mother. The poor woman is cared for by nurses, she needs someone closer to her, and *she*," he added, "can appreciate what you do for her and be grateful."

There was a long silence. M. Darbedat heard Pierre singing in the next room. It was hardly a song, rather a sort of sharp, hasty recitative. M. Darbedat raised his eyes to his daughter.

"It's no then?"

"Pierre will stay with me," she said quietly. "I get along well with him."

"By living like an animal all day long?"

Eve smiled and shot a glance at her father, strange, mocking and almost gay. *It's true.* M. Darbedat thought furiously, *that's not all they do; they sleep together.*

"You are completely mad," he said, rising.

Eve smiled sadly and murmured, as if to herself, "Not enough so."

"Not enough? I can only tell you one thing, my child. You frighten me."

He kissed her hastily and left. Going down the stairs he thought: *we should send out two strong-arm men who'd take the poor imbecile away and stick him under a shower without asking his advice on the matter.*

It was a fine autumn day, calm and without mystery; the sunlight gilded the faces of the passers-by. M. Darbedat was struck with the simplicity of the faces; some weather-beaten, others smooth, but they reflected all the happiness and care with which he was so familiar.

I know exactly what I resent in Eve, he told himself, entering the Boulevard St. Germain. *I resent her living outside the limits of human nature. Pierre is no longer a human being: in all the care and all the love she gives him she deprives human beings of a little. We don't have the right to refuse ourselves to the world; no matter what, we live in society.*

He watched the faces of the passers-by with sympathy; he loved their clear, serious looks. In these sunlit streets, in the midst of mankind, one felt secure, as in the midst of a large family.

A woman stopped in front of an open-air display counter. She was holding a little girl by the hand.

"What's that?" the little girl asked, pointing to a radio set.

"Mustn't touch," her mother said. "It's a radio; it plays music."

They stood for a moment without speaking, in ecstasy. Touched, M. Darbadet bent down to the little girl and smiled.

2

"He's gone." The door closed with a dry snap. Eve was alone in the salon. *I wish he'd die.*

She twisted her hands around the back of the armchair: she had just remembered her father's eyes. M. Darbedat had bent over Pierre with a competent air; he had said "That's good!" the way someone says when they speak to invalids. He had looked and Pierre's face had been painted in the depths of his sharp, bulging eyes. *I hate him when he looks at him because I think he sees him.*

Eve's hands slid along the armchair and she turned to the window. She was dazzled. The room was filled with sunlight, it was everywhere, in pale splotches on the rug, in the air like a blinding dust. Eve was not accustomed to this diligent, indiscreet light which darted from everywhere, scouring all the corners, rubbing the furniture like a busy housewife and making it glisten. However, she went to the window and raised the muslin curtain which hung against the pane. Just at that moment M. Darbedat left the building; Eve suddenly caught sight of his broad shoulders. He raised his head and looked at the sky, blinking, then with the stride of a young man he walked away. *He's straining himself,* thought Eve, *soon he'll have a stitch in the side.* She hardly hated him any longer: there was so little in that head; only the tiny worry of appearing young. Yet rage took her again when she saw him turn the corner of the Boulevard St. Germain and disappear. *He's thinking about Pierre.* A little of their life had escaped from the closed room and was being dragged through the streets, in the sun, among the people. *Can they never forget about us?*

The Rue du Bac was almost deserted. An old lady crossed the street with mincing steps; three girls passed, laughing. Then men, strong, serious men carrying briefcases and talking among themselves. *Normal people,* thought Eve, astonished at finding such a powerful hatred in herself. A handsome, fleshy woman ran heavily toward an elegant gentleman. He took her in his arms and kissed her on the mouth. Eve gave a hard laugh and let the curtain fall.

Pierre sang no more but the woman on the fourth floor was playing the piano; she played a Chopin Etude. Eve felt calmer; she took a step toward Pierre's room but stopped almost immediately and leaned against the wall in anguish; each time she left the room, she was panic-stricken at the thought of going back. Yet she knew she could live nowhere else: she loved the room. She looked around it with cold curiosity as if to gain a little time: this shadowless, odorless room where she waited for her courage to return. *You'd think it was a dentist's waiting room.* Armchairs of pink silk, the divan, the tabourets were somber and discreet, a little fatherly; man's best friends. Eve imagined those grave gentlemen dressed in light suits, all like the ones she saw at the window, entering the room, continuing a conversation already begun. They did not even take time to reconnoiter, but advanced with firm step to the middle of the room; one of them, letting his hand drag behind him like a wake in passing knocked over cushions, objects on the table, and was never disturbed by their contact. And when a piece of furniture was in their way, these poised men, far from making a detour to avoid it, quietly changed its place. Finally they sat down, still plunged in their conversation, without even glancing behind them. *A living-room for normal people,* thought Eve. She stared at the knob of the closed door and anguish clutched her throat: *I must go back. I never leave him alone so long.* She would have to open the door, then stand for a moment on the threshold, trying to accustom her eyes to the shadow and the room would push her back with all its strength. Eve would have to triumph over this resistance and enter all the way into the heart of the room. Suddenly she wanted violently to see Pierre; she would have liked to make fun of M. Darbedat with him. But Pierre had no need of her; Eve could not foresee the welcome he had in store for her. Suddenly she thought with a sort of pride that she had no place anywhere. *Normal people think I belong with them. But I couldn't stay an hour among them. I need to live out there, on the other side of the wall. But they don't want me out there.*

A profound change was taking place around her. The light had grown old and greying: it was heavy, like the water in a vase of flowers that hasn't been changed since the day before. In this aged light Eve found a melancholy she had long forgotten: the melancholy of an autumn afternoon that was ending. She looked around her, hesitant, almost timid: all that was so far away: there was neither day nor night nor season nor melancholy in the room. She vaguely recalled autumns long past, autumns of her childhood, then suddenly she stiffened: she was afraid of memories.

She heard Pierre's voice. "Agatha! Where are you?"

"Coming!" she cried.

She opened the door and entered the room.

The heavy odor of incense filled her mouth and nostrils as she opened her eyes and stretched out her hands—for a long time the perfume and the gloom had meant nothing more to her than a single element, acrid and heavy, as simple, as familiar as water, air or fire— and she prudently advanced toward a pale stain which seemed to float in the fog. It was Pierre's face: Pierre's clothing (he dressed in black ever since he had been sick) melted in obscurity. Pierre had thrown back his head and closed his eyes. He was handsome. Eve looked at his long, curved lashes, then sat close to him on the low chair. *He seems to be suffering,* she thought. Little by little her eyes grew used to the darkness. The bureau emerged first, then the bed, then Pierre's personal things: scissors, the pot of glue, books, the herbarium which shed its leaves onto the rug near the armchair.

"Agatha?"

Pierre had opened his eyes. He was watching her, smiling. "You know, that fork?" he said. "I did it to frighten that fellow. There was *almost* nothing the matter with it."

Eve's apprehensions faded and she gave a light laugh. "You succeeded," she said, "You drove him completely out of his mind."

Pierre smiled. "Did you see? He played with it a long time, he held it right in his hands. The trouble is," he said, "they don't know how to take hold of things; they grab them."

"That's right," Eve said.

Pierre tapped the palm of his left hand lightly with the index of his right.

"They take with that. They reach out their fingers and when they catch hold of something they crack down on it to knock it out."

He spoke rapidly and hardly moving his lips; he looked puzzled.

"I wonder what they want," he said at last, "that fellow has already been here. Why did they send him to me? If they wanted to know what I'm doing all they have to do is read it on the screen, they don't even need to leave the house. They make mistakes. They have the power but they make mistakes. I never make any, that's my trump card. *Hoffka!*" he said. He shook his long hands before his forehead. "The bitch Hoffka, Paffka! Suffka! Do you want any more?"

"Is it the bell?" asked Eve.

"Yes. It's gone." He went on severely. "This fellow, he's just a subordinate. You know him, you went into the living room with him."

Eve did not answer.

"What did he want?" asked Pierre. "He must have told you."

She hesitated an instant, then answered brutally. "He wanted you locked up."

When the truth was told quietly to Pierre he distrusted it. He had to be dealt with violently in order to daze and paralyze his suspicions. Eve preferred to brutalize him rather than lie: when she lied and he acted as if he believed it she could not avoid a very slight feeling of superiority which made her horrified at herself.

"Lock me up!" Pierre repeated ironically. "They're crazy. What can walls do to me. Maybe they think that's going to stop me. I sometimes wonder if there aren't two groups. The real one, the negro—and then a bunch of fools trying to stick their noses in and making mistake after mistake."

He made his hand jump up from the arm of the chair and looked at it happily.

"I can get through walls. What did you tell them?" he asked, turning to Eve with curiosity.

"Not to lock you up."

He shrugged. "You shouldn't have said that. You made a mistake too . . . unless you did it on purpose. You've got to call their bluff."

He was silent. Eve lowered her head sadly: *They grab things!* *How scornfully he said that—and he was right. Do I grab things too? It doesn't do any good to watch myself, I think most of my movements annoy him. But he doesn't say anything.* Suddenly she felt as miserable as when she was fourteen and Mme. Darbedat told her, "You don't know what to do with your hands." She didn't dare make a move and just at that time she had an irresistible desire to change her position. Quietly she put her feet under the chair, barely touching the rug. She watched the lamp on the table—the lamp whose base Pierre had painted black—and the chess set. Pierre had left only the black pawns on the board. Sometimes he would get up, go to the table and take the pawns in his hands one by one. He spoke to them, called them Robots and they seemed to stir with a mute life under his fingers. When he set them down, Eve went and touched them in her turn (she always felt somewhat ridiculous about it). They had become little bits of dead wood again but something vague and incomprehensible stayed in them, something like understanding. *These are* his *things,* she thought. *There is nothing of mine in the room.* She had had a few pieces of furniture before; the mirror and the little inlaid dresser handed down from her grandmother and which Pierre jokingly called "*your* dresser." Pierre had carried them away with him; things showed their true face to Pierre alone. Eve could watch them for hours: they were unflaggingly stubborn and determined to deceive her, offering her nothing but their appearance—as they did to Dr. Franchot and M. Darbedat. *Yet,* she told herself with anguish, *I don't see them quite like my father. It isn't possible for me to see them exactly like him.*

She moved her knees a little: her legs felt as though they were crawling with ants. Her body was stiff and taut and hurt her; she felt it too alive, too demanding. *I would like to be invisible and stay here seeing him without his seeing me. He doesn't need me; I am useless in this room.* She turned her head slightly and looked at the wall above Pierre. Threats were written on the wall. Eve knew it but she could not read them. She often watched the big red roses on the wallpaper until they began to dance before her eyes. The roses flamed in shadow. Most of the time the threat was written near the ceiling, a little to the left of the bed; but sometimes it moved. *I must get up. I can't . . . I can't sit down any longer.* There were also white discs on the wall that looked like slices of onion. The discs spun and Eve's hands began to tremble: *Sometimes I think I'm going mad. But no,* she thought, *I can't* go mad. I get nervous, *that's all.*

Suddenly she felt Pierre's hand on hers.

"Agatha," Pierre said tenderly.

He smiled at her but he held her hand by the ends of his fingers with a sort of revulsion, as though he had picked up a crab by the back and wanted to avoid its claws.

"Agatha," he said. "I would so much like to have confidence in you."

She closed her eyes and her breast heaved. *I mustn't answer anything, if I do he'll get angry, he won't say anything more.*

Pierre had dropped her hand. "I like you, Agatha," he said, "but I can't understand you. Why do you stay in the room all the time?"

Eve did not answer.

"Tell me why."

"You know I love you," she said dryly.

"I don't believe you," Pierre said. "Why should you love me? I must frighten you: I'm haunted." He smiled but suddenly became serious. "There is a wall between you and me. I see you, I speak to you, but you're on the other side. What keeps us from loving? I think it was easier before. In Hamburg."

"Yes," Eve said sadly. Always Hamburg. He never spoke of their real past. Neither Eve nor he had ever been to Hamburg.

"We used to walk along the canal. There was a barge, remember? The barge was black; there was a dog on the deck."

He made it up as he went along; it sounded false.

"I held your hand. You had another skin. I believed all you told me. Be quiet!" he shouted.

He listened for a moment. "They're coming," he said mournfully.

Eve jumped up. "They're coming? I thought they wouldn't ever come again."

Pierre had been calmer for the past three days; the statues did not come. Pierre was terribly afraid of the statues even though he would never admit it. Eve was not afraid: but when they began to fly, buzzing, around the room, she was afraid of Pierre.

"Give me the ziuthre," Pierre said.

Eve got up and took the ziuthre[5]: it was a collection of pieces of cardboard Pierre had glued together; he used it to conjure the statues. The ziuthre looked like a spider. On one of the cardboards Pierre had written "Power over ambush" and on the other, "Black." On a third he had drawn a laughing face with wrinkled eyes: it was Voltaire.[6]

Pierre seized the ziuthre by one end and looked at it darkly.

"I can't use it any more," he said.

"Why?"

"They turned it upside down."

"Will you make another?"

He looked at her for a long while. "You'd like me to, wouldn't you," he said between his teeth.

Eve was angry at Pierre. *He's warned every time they come: how does he do it? He's never wrong.*

[5] A word that Pierre has made up for his invention.
[6] Pseudonym of François Marie Arouet (1694–1778), French philosopher and man of letters.

The ziuthre dangled pitifully from the ends of Pierre's fingers. *He always finds a good reason not to use it. Sunday when they came he pretended he'd lost it but I saw it behind the paste pot and he couldn't fail to see it. I wonder if he isn't the one who brings them.* One could never tell if he were completely sincere. Sometimes Eve had the impression that despite himself Pierre was surrounded by a swarm of unhealthy thoughts and visions. But at other times Pierre seemed to invent them. *He suffers. But how much does he believe in the statues and the negro. Anyhow, I know he doesn't see the statues, he only hears them: when they pass he turns his head away; but he still says he sees them; he describes them.* She remembered the red face of Dr. Franchot: "But my dear madame, all mentally unbalanced persons are liars; you're wasting your time if you're trying to distinguish between what they really feel and what they pretend to feel." She gave a start. *What is Franchot doing here? I don't want to start thinking like him.*

Pierre had gotten up. He went to throw the ziuthre into the wastebasket: *I want to think like you,* she murmured. He walked with tiny steps, on tiptoe, pressing his elbows against his hips so as to take up the least possible space. He came back and sat down and looked at Eve with a closed expression.

"We'll have to put up black wallpaper," he said. "There isn't enough black in this room."

He was crouched in the armchair. Sadly Eve watched his meagre body, always ready to withdraw, to shrink: the arms, legs and head looked like retractable organs. The clock struck six. The piano downstairs was silent. Eve sighed: the statues would not come right away; they had to wait for them.

"Do you want me to turn on the light?"

She would rather not wait for them in darkness.

"Do as you please," Pierre said.

Eve lit the small lamp on the bureau and a red mist filled the room. Pierre was waiting too.

He did not speak but his lips were moving, making two dark stains in the red mist. Eve loved Pierre's lips. Before, they had been moving and sensual; but they had lost their sensuality. They were wide apart, trembling a little, coming together incessantly, crushing against each other only to separate again. They were the only living things in this blank face; they looked like two frightened animals. Pierre could mutter like that for hours without a sound leaving his mouth and Eve often let herself be fascinated by this tiny, obstinate movement. *I love his mouth.* He never kissed her any more; he was horrified at contacts; at night they touched him—the hands of men, hard and dry, pinched him all over; the long-nailed hands of women caressed him. Often he went to bed with his clothes on but the hands slipped under the clothes and tugged at his shirt. Once he heard laughter and puffy lips were placed on his mouth. He never kissed Eve after that night.

"Agatha," Pierre said, "don't look at my mouth."

Eve lowered her eyes.

"I am not unaware that people can learn to read lips," he went on insolently.

His hand trembled on the arm of the chair. The index finger stretched out, tapped three times on the thumb and the other fingers curled: this was a spell. *It's going to start,* she thought. She wanted to take Pierre in her arms.

Pierre began to speak at the top of his voice in a very sophisticated tone.

"Do you remember São Paulo?"

No answer. Perhaps it was a trap.

"I met you there," he said, satisfied. "I took you away from a Danish sailor. We almost fought but I paid for a round of drinks and he let me take you away. All that was only a joke."

He's lying, he doesn't believe a word of what he says. He knows my name isn't Agatha. I hate him when he lies. But she saw his staring eyes and her rage melted. *He isn't lying,* she thought, *he can't stand it any more. He feels them coming; he's talking to keep from hearing them.* Pierre dug both hands into the arm of the chair. His face was pale; he was smiling.

"These meetings are often strange," he said, "but I don't believe it's by chance. I'm not asking who sent you. I know you wouldn't answer. Anyhow, you've been smart enough to bluff me."

He spoke with great difficulty, in a sharp, hurried voice. There were words he could not pronounce and which left his mouth like some soft and shapeless substance.

"You dragged me away right in the middle of the party, between the rows of black automobiles, but behind the cars there was an army with red eyes which glowed as soon as I turned my back. I think you made signs to them, all the time hanging on my arm, but I didn't see a thing. I was too absorbed by the great ceremonies of the Coronation."

He looked straight ahead, his eyes wide open. He passed his hand over his forehead very rapidly, in one spare gesture, without stopping his talking. He did not want to stop talking.

"It was the Coronation of the Republic," he said stridently, "an impressive spectacle of its kind because of all the species of animals that the colonies sent for the ceremony. You were afraid to get lost among the monkeys. I said among the monkeys," he repeated arrogantly, looking around him, "I could say *among the negroes!* The abortions sliding under the tables, trying to pass unseen, are discovered and nailed to the spot by my Look. The password is silence. To be silent. Everything in place and attention for the entrance of the statues, that's the countersign. Tralala . . ." he shrieked and cupped his hands to his mouth. "Tralalala, tralalalala!"

He was silent and Eve knew that the statues had come into the room. He was stiff, pale and distrustful. Eve stiffened too and both waited in silence. Someone was walking in the corridor: it was Marie the house-cleaner, she had undoubtedly just arrived. Eve thought, *I have to give her money for the gas.* And then the statues began to fly; they passed between Eve and Pierre.

Pierre went "Ah!" and sank down in the armchair, folding his legs beneath him. He turned his face away; sometimes he grinned, but drops of sweat pearled his forehead. Eve could stand the sight no longer, this pale cheek, this mouth deformed by a trembling grimace; she closed her eyes. Gold threads began to dance on the red background of her eyelids; she felt old and heavy. Not far from her Pierre was breathing violently. *They're flying, they're buzzing, they're bending over him.* She felt a slight tickling, a pain in the shoulder and right side. Instinctively her body bent to the left as if to avoid some disagreeable contact, as if to let a heavy, awkward object pass. Suddenly the floor creaked and she had an insane desire to open her eyes, to look to her right, sweeping the air with her hand.

She did nothing: she kept her eyes closed and a bitter joy made her tremble: *I am afraid too,* she thought. Her entire life had taken refuge in her right side. She leaned towards Pierre without opening her eyes. The slightest effort would be enough and she would enter this tragic world for the first time. *I'm afraid of the statues,* she thought. It was a violent, blind affirmation, an incantation. She wanted to believe in their presence with all her strength. She tried to make a new sense, a sense of touch out of the anguish which paralysed her right side. She *felt* their passage in her arm, in her side and shoulder.

The statues flew low and gently; they buzzed. Eve knew that they had an evil look and that eyelashes stuck out from the stone around their eyes; but she pictured them badly. She knew, too, that they were not quite alive but that slabs of flesh, warm scales appeared on their great bodies; the stone peeled from the ends of their fingers and their palms were eaten away. Eve could not *see* all that: she simply thought of enormous women sliding against her, solemn and grotesque, with a human look and compact heads of stone. *They are bending over Pierre*—Eve made such a violent effort that her hands began trembling—*they are bending over me.* A horrible cry suddenly chilled her.

They had touched him. She opened her eyes: Pierre's head was in his hands, he was breathing heavily. Eve felt exhausted: *a game,* she thought with remorse; *it was only a game. I didn't sincerely believe it for an instant. And all that time he suffered as if it were real.*

Pierre relaxed and breathed freely. But his pupils were strangely dilated and he was perspiring.

"Did you see them?" he asked.

"I can't see them."

"Better for you. They'd frighten you," he said. "I am used to them."

Eve's hands were still shaking and the blood had rushed to her head. Pierre took a cigarette from his pocket and brought it up to his mouth. But he did not light it:

"I don't care whether I see them or not," he said, "but I don't want them to touch me: I'm afraid they'll give me pimples."

He thought for an instant, then asked, "Did you hear them?"

"Yes," Eve said, "it's like an airplane engine." (Pierre had told her this the previous Sunday.)

Pierre smiled with condescension. "You exaggerate," he said. But he was still pale. He looked at Eve's hands. "Your hands are trembling. That made quite an impression on you, my poor Agatha. But don't worry. They won't come back again before tomorrow." Eve could not speak. Her teeth were chattering and she was afraid Pierre would notice it. Pierre watched her for a long time.

"You're tremendously beautiful," he said, nodding his head. "It's too bad, too bad."

He put out his hand quickly and toyed with her ear. "My lovely devil-woman. You disturb me a little, you are too beautiful: that distracts me. If it weren't a question of recapitulation . . ."

He stopped and looked at Eve with surprise.

"That's not the word . . . it came . . . it came," he said, smiling vaguely. "I had another on the tip of my tongue . . . but this one . . . came in its place. I forget what I was telling you."

He thought for a moment, then shook his head.

"Come," he said, "I want to sleep." He added in a childish voice, "You know, Agatha, I'm tired. I can't collect my thoughts any more."

He threw away his cigarette and looked at the rug anxiously. Eve slipped a pillow under his head.

"You can sleep too," he told her, "they won't be back." . . . *Recapitulation . . .*

Pierre was asleep, a candid, half-smile on his face; his head was turned to one side: one might have thought he wanted to caress his cheek with his shoulder. Eve was not sleepy, she was thoughtful: *Recapitulation.* Pierre had suddenly looked stupid and the word had slipped out of his mouth, long and whitish. Pierre had stared ahead of him in astonishment, as if he had seen the word and didn't recognize it; his mouth was open, soft: something seemed broken in it. He stammered. *That's the first time it ever happened to him: he noticed it, too. He said he couldn't collect his thoughts any more.* Pierre gave a voluptuous little whimper and his hand made a vague movement. Eve watched him harshly: *how is he going to wake up.* It gnawed at her. As soon as Pierre was asleep she had to think about it. She was afraid he would wake up wild-eyed and stammering. *I'm stupid,* she thought, *it can't start before a year; Franchot said so.* But the anguish did not leave her; a year: a winter, a springtime, a summer, the beginning of another autumn. One day his features would grow confused, his jaw would hang loose, he would half open his weeping eyes. Eve bent over Pierre's hand and pressed her lips against it: *I'll kill you before that.*

Translated by Lloyd Alexander

Yukio Mishima / 1925–

Onnagata[1]

Masuyama had been overwhelmed by Mangiku's artistry; that was how it happened that, after getting a degree in classical Japanese literature, he had chosen to join the kabuki theatre staff. He had been entranced by seeing Mangiku Sanokawa perform.

Masuyama's addiction to kabuki began when he was a high-school student. At the time, Mangiku, still a fledgling *onnagata,* was appearing in such minor roles as the ghost butterfly in *Kagami Jishi* or, at

[1] In the kabuki theater of Japan—a theater highly stylized and often violently melodramatic—the female roles are played by intensely trained male actors, and such actors are called *onnagata.* The literal meaning of the word is "female form."

best, the waiting maid Chidori in *The Disowning of Genta*. Mangiku's acting was unassertive and orthodox; nobody suspected he would achieve his present eminence. But even in those days Masuyama sensed the icy flames given off by this actor's aloof beauty. The general public, needless to say, noticed nothing. For that matter, none of the drama critics had ever called attention to the peculiar quality of Mangiku, like shoots of flame visible through the snow, which illuminated his performances from very early in his career. Now everyone spoke as if Mangiku had been a personal discovery.

Mangiku Sanokawa was a true *onnagata,* a species seldom encountered nowadays. Unlike most contemporary *onnagata,* he was quite incapable of performing successfully in male roles. His stage presence was colorful, but with dark overtones; his every gesture was the essence of delicacy. Mangiku never expressed anything—not even strength, authority, endurance, or courage—except through the single medium open to him, feminine expression, but through this medium he could filter every variety of human emotion. That is the way of the true *onnagata,* but in recent years this breed has become rare indeed. Their tonal coloring, produced by a particular, exquisitely refined musical instrument, cannot be achieved by playing a normal instrument in a minor key, nor, for that matter, is it produced by a mere slavish imitation of real women.

Yukihime, the Snow Princess, in *Kinkakuji* was one of Mangiku's most successful roles. Masuyama remembered having seen Mangiku perform Yukihime ten times during a single month, but no matter how often he repeated this experience, his intoxication did not diminish. Everything symbolizing Sanokawa Mangiku may be found in this play, the elements entwined, beginning with the opening words of the narrator: "The Golden Pavilion, the mountain retreat of Lord Yoshimitsu, Prime Minister and Monk of the Deer Park, stands three stories high, its garden graced with lovely sights: the night-lodging stone, the water trickling below the rocks, the flow of the cascade heavy with spring, the willows and cherry trees planted together; the capital now is a vast, many-hued brocade." The dazzling brilliance of the set, depicting cherry trees in blossom, a waterfall, and the glittering Golden Pavilion; the drums, suggesting the dark sound of the waterfall and contributing a constant agitation to the stage; the pale, sadistic face of the lecherous Daizen Matsunaga, the rebel general; the miracle of the magic sword which shines in morning sunlight with the holy image of Fudō,[2] but shows a dragon's form when pointed at the setting sun; the radiance of the sunset glow on the waterfall and

---

[2] A god of fire.

cherry trees; the cherry blossoms scattering down petal by petal—
everything in the play exists for the sake of one woman, the beautiful,
aristocratic Yukihime. There is nothing unusual about Yukihime's
costume, the crimson silk robe customarily worn by young princesses.
But a ghostly presence of snow, befitting her name, hovers about this
granddaughter of the great painter Sesshū, and the landscapes of
Sesshū, permeated with snow, may be sensed across the breadth of
the scene; this phantom snow gives Yukihime's crimson robe its dazzling brilliance.

Masuyama loved especially the scene where the princess, bound
with ropes to a cherry tree, remembers the legend told of her grandfather, and with her toes draws in the fallen blossoms a rat, which
comes to life and gnaws through the ropes binding her. It hardly
needs be said that Mangiku Sanokawa did not adopt the puppetlike
movements favored by some *onnagata* in this scene. The ropes fasten-
ing him to the tree made Mangiku look lovelier than ever: all the
artificial arabesques of this *onnagata*—the delicate gestures of the
body, the play of the fingers, the arch of the hand—contrived though
they might appear when employed for the movements of daily life,
took on a strange vitality when used by Yukihime, bound to a tree.
The intricate, contorted attitudes imposed by the constraint of the
rope made of each instant an exquisite crisis, and the crises seemed to
flow, one into the next, with the irresistible energy of successive waves.

Mangiku's performances unquestionably possessed moments of diabolic power. He used his lovely eyes so effectively that often with one
flash he could create in an entire audience the illusion that the character of a scene had completely altered: when his glance embraced the
stage from the *hanamichi*[3] or the *hanamichi* from the stage, or when
he darted one upward look at the bell in *Dōjōji*. In the palace scene
from *Imoseyama*, Mangiku took the part of Omiwa, whose lover was
stolen from her by Princess Tachibana and who has been cruelly
mocked by the court ladies. At the end Omiwa rushes out onto the
hanamichi, all but wild with jealousy and rage; just then she hears the
voices of the court ladies at the back of the stage saying, "A groom
without peer has been found for our princess! What joy for us all!"
The narrator, seated at the side of the stage, declaims in powerful
tones, "Omiwa, hearing this, at once looks back." At this moment
Omiwa's character is completely transformed, and her face reveals
the marks of a possessive attachment.

Masuyama felt a kind of terror every time he witnessed this mo-

[3] A raised runway that passes through the kabuki theater from the back to the
stage and by means of which the actors enter and exit.

ment. For an instant a diabolic shadow had swept over both the bright stage with its splendid set and beautiful costumes and over the thousands of intently watching spectators. This force clearly emanated from Mangiku's body, but at the same time transcended his flesh. Masuyama sensed in such passages something like a dark spring welling forth from this figure on the stage, this figure so imbued with softness, fragility, grace, delicacy, and feminine charms. He could not identify it, but he thought that a strange evil presence, the final residue of the actor's fascination, a seductive evil which leads men astray and makes them drown in an instant of beauty, was the true nature of the dark spring he had detected. But one explains nothing merely by giving it a name.

Omiwa shakes her head and her hair tumbles in disarray. On the stage, to which she now returns from the *hanamichi,* Funashichi's blade is waiting to kill her.

"The house is full of music, an autumn sadness in its tone," declaims the narrator.

There is something terrifying about the way Omiwa's feet hurry forward to her doom. The bare white feet, rushing ahead toward disaster and death, kicking the lines of her kimono askew, seem to know precisely when and where on the stage the violent emotions now urging her forward will end, and to be pressing toward the spot, rejoicing and triumphant even amidst the tortures of jealousy. The pain she reveals outwardly is backed with joy like her robe, on the outside dark and shot with gold thread, but bright with variegated silken strands within.

2

Masuyama's original decision to take employment at the theatre had been inspired by his absorption with kabuki, and especially with Mangiku; he realized also he could never escape his bondage unless he became thoroughly familiar with the world behind the scenes. He knew from what others had told him of the disenchantment to be found backstage, and he wanted to plunge into that world and taste for himself genuine disillusion.

But the disenchantment he expected somehow never came. Mangiku himself made this impossible. Mangiku faithfully maintained the injunctions of the eighteenth-century *onnagata*'s manual *Ayamegusa,* "An *onnagata,* even in the dressing room, must preserve the attitudes of an *onnagata.* He should be careful when he eats to face away from other people, so that they cannot see him." Whenever Mangiku was obliged to eat in the presence of visitors, not having the time to leave his dressing room, he would turn toward his table with a word of apology and race through his meal, so skillfully that the visitors could not even guess from behind that he was eating.

Undoubtedly, the feminine beauty displayed by Mangiku on the stage had captivated Masuyama as a man. Strangely enough, however, this spell was not broken even by close observation of Mangiku in the dressing room. Mangiku's body, when he had removed his costume, was delicate but unmistakably a man's. Masuyama, as a matter of fact, found it rather unnerving when Mangiku, seated at his dressing table, too scantily clad to be anything but a man, directed polite, feminine greetings toward some visitor, all the while applying a heavy coating of powder to his shoulders. If even Masuyama, long a devotee of kabuki, experienced eerie sensations on his first visits to the dressing room, what would have been the reactions of people who dislike kabuki, because the *onnagata* make them uncomfortable, if shown such a sight?

Masuyama, however, felt relief rather than disenchantment when he saw Mangiku after a performance, naked except for the gauzy underclothes he wore in order to absorb perspiration. The sight in itself may have been grotesque, but the nature of Masuyama's fascination—its intrinsic quality, one might say—did not reside in any surface illusion, and there was accordingly no danger that such a revelation would destroy it. Even after Mangiku had disrobed, it was apparent that he was still wearing several layers of splendid costumes beneath his skin; his nakedness was a passing manifestation. Something which could account for his exquisite appearance on stage surely lay concealed within him.

Masuyama enjoyed seeing Mangiku when he returned to the dressing room after performing a major role. The flush of the emotions of the part he had been enacting still hovered over his entire body, like sunset glow or the moon in the sky at dawn. The grand emotions of classical tragedy—emotions quite unrelated to our mundane lives—may seem to be guided, at least nominally, by historical facts—the world of disputed successions, campaigns of pacification, civil warfare, and the like—but in reality they belong to no period. They are the emotions appropriate to a stylized, grotesquely tragic world, luridly colored in the manner of a late woodblock print. Grief that goes beyond human bounds, superhuman passions, searing love, terrifying joy, the brief cries of people trapped by circumstances too tragic for human beings to endure: such were the emotions which a moment before had lodged in Mangiku's body. It was amazing that Mangiku's slender frame could hold them and that they did not break from that delicate vessel.

Be that as it may, Mangiku a moment before had been living amidst these grandiose feelings, and he had radiated light on the stage precisely because the emotions he portrayed transcended any known to his audience. Perhaps this is true of all characters on the stage, but among present-day actors none seemed to be so honestly living stage emotions so far removed from daily life.

A passage in *Ayamegusa* states, "Charm is the essence of the *onnagata*. But even the *onnagata* who is naturally beautiful will lose his charm if he strains to impress by his movements. If he consciously attempts to appear graceful, he will seem thoroughly corrupt instead. For this reason, unless the *onnagata* lives as a woman in his daily life, he is unlikely ever to be considered an accomplished *onnagata*. When he appears on stage, the more he concentrates on performing this or that essentially feminine action, the more masculine he will seem. I am convinced that the essential thing is how the actor behaves in real life."

How the actor behaves in real life . . . yes, Mangiku was utterly feminine in both the speech and bodily movements of his real life. If Mangiku had been more masculine in his daily life, those moments when the flush from the *onnagata* role he had been performing gradually dissolved like the high-water mark on a beach into the femininity of his daily life—itself an extension of the same make-believe—would have become an absolute division between sea and land, a bleak door shut between dream and reality. The make-believe of his daily life supported the make-believe of his stage performances. This, Masuyama was convinced, marked the true *onnagata*. An *onnagata* is the child born of the illicit union between dream and reality.

3

Once the celebrated veteran actors of the previous generation had all passed away, one on the heels of the other, Mangiku's authority backstage became absolute. His *onnagata* disciples waited on him like personal servants; indeed, the order of seniority they observed when following Mangiku on stage as maids in the wake of his princess or great lady was exactly the same they observed in the dressing room.

Anyone pushing apart the door curtains dyed with the crest of the Sanokawa family and entering Mangiku's dressing room was certain to be struck by a strange sensation: this charming sanctuary contained not a single man. Even members of the same troupe felt inside this room that they were in the presence of the opposite sex. Whenever

Masuyama went to Mangiku's dressing room on some errand, he had only to brush apart the door curtains to feel—even before setting foot inside—a curiously vivid, carnal sensation of being a male.

Sometimes Masuyama had gone on company business to the dressing rooms of chorus girls backstage at revues. The rooms were filled with an almost suffocating femininity and the rough-skinned girls, sprawled about like animals in the zoo, threw bored glances at him, but he never felt so distinctly alien as in Mangiku's dressing room; nothing in these real women made Masuyama feel particularly masculine.

The members of Mangiku's entourage exhibited no special friendliness toward Masuyama. On the contrary, he knew that they secretly gossiped about him, accusing him of being disrespectful or of giving himself airs merely because he had gone through some university. He knew too that sometimes they professed irritation at his pedantic insistence on historical facts. In the world of kabuki, academic learning unaccompanied by artistic talent is considered of no value.

Masuyama's work had its compensations too. It would happen when Mangiku had a favor to ask of someone—only, of course, when he was in a good mood—that he twisted his body diagonally from his dressing table and gave a little nod and a smile; the indescribable charm in his eyes at such moments made Masuyama feel that he wished for nothing more than to slave like a dog for this man. Mangiku himself never forgot his dignity: he never failed to maintain a certain distance, though he obviously was aware of his charms. If he had been a real woman, his whole body would have been filled with the allure in his eyes. The allure of an *onnagata* is only a momentary glimmer, but that is enough for it to exist independently and to display the eternal feminine.

Mangiku sat before the mirror after the performance of *The Castle of the Lord Protector of Hachijin,* the first item of the program. He had removed the costume and wig he wore as Lady Hinaginu, and changed to a bathrobe, not being obliged to appear in the middle work of the program. Masuyama, informed that Mangiku wanted to see him, had been waiting in the dressing room for the curtain of *Hachijin.* The mirror suddenly burst into crimson flames as Mangiku returned to the room, filling the entrance with the rustle of his robes. Three disciples and costumers joined to remove what had to be removed and store it away. Those who were to leave departed, and now no one remained except for a few disciples around the hibachi in the next room. The dressing room had all at once fallen still. From a loudspeaker in the corridor issued the sounds of stage assistants hammering as they dismantled the set for the play which had just ended. It was late November, and steam heat clouded the windowpanes, bleak as in a hospital ward. White chrysanthemums bent gracefully in a cloisonné vase placed beside Mangiku's dressing table. Mangiku, perhaps because his stage name meant literally "ten thousand chrysanthemums," was fond of this flower.

Mangiku sat on a bulky cushion of purple silk, facing his dressing table. "I wonder if you'd mind telling the gentleman from Sakuragi Street?" (Mangiku, in the old-fashioned manner, referred to his dancing and singing teachers by the names of the streets where they lived.) "It'd be hard for me to tell him." He gazed directly into the mirror as he spoke. Masuyama could see from where he sat by the wall the nape of Mangiku's neck and the reflections in the mirror of his face still made up for the part of Hinaginu. The eyes were not on Masuyama; they were squarely contemplating his own face. The flush from his exertions on the stage still glowed through the powder on his cheeks, like the morning sun through a thin sheet of ice. He was looking at Hinaginu.

Indeed, he actually saw her in the mirror—Hinaginu, whom he had just been impersonating, Hinaginu, the daughter of Mori Sanzaemon Yoshinari and the bride of the young Satō Kazuenosuke. Her marriage ties with her husband having been broken because of his feudal loyalty, Hinaginu killed herself so that she might remain faithful to a union "whose ties were so faint we never shared the same bed." Hinaginu had died on stage of a despair so extreme she could not bear to live any longer. The Hinaginu in the mirror was a ghost. Even that ghost, Mangiku knew, was at this very moment slipping from his body. His eyes pursued Hinaginu. But as the glow of the ardent passions of the role subsided, Hinaginu's face faded away. He bade it farewell. There were still seven performances before the final day. Tomorrow again Hinaginu's features would no doubt return to the pliant mold of Mangiku's face.

Masuyama, enjoying the sight of Mangiku in this abstracted state, all but smiled with affection. Mangiku suddenly turned toward him. He had been aware all along of Masuyama's gaze, but with the nonchalance of the actor accustomed to the public's stares, he continued with his business. "It's those instrumental passages. They're simply not long enough. I don't mean I can't get through the part if I hurry, but it makes everything so ugly." Mangiku was referring to the music for the new dance-play which would be presented the following month. "Mr. Masuyama, what do *you* think?"

"I quite agree. I'm sure you mean the passage after 'How slow the day ends by the Chinese bridge at Seta.'"

"Yes, that's the place. Ho-ow slo-ow the da-ay . . ." Mangiku sang the passage in question, beating time with his delicate fingers.

"I'll tell him. I'm sure that the gentleman from Sakuragi Street will understand."

"Are you sure you don't mind? I feel so embarrassed about making a nuisance of myself all the time."

Mangiku was accustomed to terminate a conversation by standing, once his business had been dealt with. "I'm afraid I must bathe now," he said. Masuyama drew back from the narrow entrance to the dressing room and let Mangiku pass. Mangiku, with a slight bow of the head, went out into the corridor, accompanied by a disciple. He turned back obliquely toward Masuyama and, smiling, bowed again. The rouge at the corners of his eyes had an indefinable charm. Masuyama sensed that Mangiku was well aware of his affection.

4

The troupe to which Masuyama belonged was to remain at the same theatre through November, December, and January, and the program for January had already become the subject of gossip. A new work by a playwright of the modern theatre was to be staged. The man, whose sense of his own importance accorded poorly with his youth, had imposed innumerable conditions, and Masuyama was kept frantically busy with complicated negotiations intended to bring together not only the dramatist and the actors but the management of the theatre as well. Masuyama was recruited for this job because the others considered him to be an intellectual.

One of the conditions laid down by the playwright was that the direction of the play be confided to a talented young man whom he trusted. The management accepted this condition. Mangiku also agreed, but without enthusiasm. He conveyed his doubts in this manner: "I don't really know, of course, but if this young man doesn't understand kabuki very well, and makes unreasonable demands on us, it will be so hard explaining." Mangiku was hoping for an older, more mature—by which he meant a more compliant—director.

The new play was a dramatization in modern language of the twelfth-century novel *If Only I Could Change Them!* The managing director of the company, deciding not to leave the production of this new work to the regular staff, announced it would be in Masuyama's hands. Masuyama grew tense at the thought of the work ahead of him, but convinced that the play was first-rate, he felt that it would be worth the trouble.

As soon as the scripts were ready and the parts assigned, a preliminary meeting was held one mid-December morning in the reception room adjoining the office of the theatre owner. The meeting was attended by the executive in charge of production, the playwright, the director, the stage designer, the actors, and Masuyama. The room was warmly heated and sunlight poured through the windows. Masuyama always felt happiest at preliminary meetings. It was like spreading out a map and discussing a projected outing: Where do we board the bus and where do we start walking? Is there drinking water where we're going? Where are we going to eat lunch? Where is the best view? Shall we take the train back? Or would it be better to allow enough time to return by boat?

Kawasaki, the director, was late. Masuyama had never seen a play directed by Kawasaki, but he knew of him by reputation. Kawasaki had been selected, despite his youth, to direct Ibsen and modern American plays for a repertory company, and in the course of a year had done so well, with the latter especially, that he was awarded a newspaper drama prize.

The others (except for Kawasaki) had all assembled. The designer, who could never bear waiting a minute before throwing himself into his work, was already jotting down in a large notebook especially brought for the purpose suggestions made by the others, frequently tapping the end of his pencil on the blank pages, as if bursting with ideas. Eventually the executive began to gossip about the absent director. "He may be as talented as they say, but he's still young, after all. The actors will have to help out."

At this moment there was a knock at the door and a secretary showed in Kawasaki. He entered the room with a dazed look, as if the light were too strong for him and, without uttering a word, stiffly bowed toward the others. He was rather tall, almost six feet, with deeply etched, masculine—but highly sensitive—features. It was a cold winter day, but Kawasaki wore a rumpled, thin raincoat. Underneath, as he presently disclosed, he had on a brick-colored corduroy jacket. His long, straight hair hung down so far—to the tip of his nose—that he was frequently obliged to push it back. Masuyama was rather disappointed by his first impression. He had supposed that a man who had been singled out for his abilities would have attempted to distinguish himself somehow from the stereotypes of society, but this man dressed and acted exactly in the way one would expect of the typical young man of the modern theatre.

Kawasaki took the place offered him at the head of the table. He did not make the usual polite protests against the honor. He kept his eyes on the playwright, his close friend, and when introduced to each of the actors he uttered a word of greeting, only to turn back at once to the playwright. Masuyama could remember similar experiences.

It is not easy for a man trained in the modern theatre, where most of the actors are young, to establish himself on easy terms with the kabuki actors, who are likely to prove to be imposing old gentlemen when encountered off stage.

The actors assembled for this preliminary meeting managed in fact to convey somehow their contempt for Kawasaki, all with a show of the greatest politeness and without an unfriendly word. Masuyama happened to glance at Mangiku's face. He modestly kept to himself, refraining from any demonstration of self-importance; he displayed no trace of the others' contempt. Masuyama felt greater admiration and affection than ever for Mangiku.

Now that everyone was present, the author described the play in outline. Mangiku, probably for the first time in his career—leaving aside parts he took as a child—was to play a male role. The plot told of a certain Grand Minister with two children, a boy and a girl. By nature they are quite unsuited to their sexes and are therefore reared accordingly: the boy (actually the girl) eventually becomes General of the Left, and the girl (actually the boy) becomes chief lady-in-waiting in the Senyōden, the palace of the Imperial concubines. Later, when the truth is revealed, they revert to lives more appropriate to the sex of their birth: the brother marries the fourth daughter of the Minister of the Right, the sister a Middle Counselor, and all ends happily.

Mangiku's part was that of the girl who is in reality a man. Although this was a male role, Mangiku would appear as a man only in the few moments of the final scene. Up to that point, he was to act throughout as a true *onnagata* in the part of a chief lady-in-waiting at the Senyōden. The author and director were agreed in urging Mangiku not to make any special attempt even in the last scene to suggest that he was in fact a man.

An amusing aspect of the play was that it inevitably had the effect of satirizing the kabuki convention of the *onnagata*. The lady-in-waiting was actually a man; so, in precisely the same manner, was Mangiku in the role. That was not all. In order for Mangiku, at once an *onnagata* and a man, to perform this part, he would have to unfold on two levels his actions of real life, a far cry from the simple case of the actor who assumes female costume during the course of a play so as to work some deception. The complexities of the part intrigued Mangiku.

Kawasaki's first words to Mangiku were, "I would be glad if you played the part throughout as a woman. It doesn't make the least difference if you act like a woman even in the last scene." His voice had a pleasant, clear ring.

"Really? If you don't mind my acting the part that way, it'll make it ever so much easier for me."

"It won't be easy in any case. Definitely not," said Kawasaki decisively. When he spoke in this forceful manner his cheeks glowed red as if a lamp had been lit inside. The sharpness of his tone cast something of a pall over the gathering. Masuyama's eyes wandered to Mangiku. He was giggling good-naturedly, the back of his hand pressed to his mouth. The others relaxed to see Mangiku had not been offended.

"Well, then," said the author, "I shall read the book." He lowered his protruding eyes, which looked double behind his thick spectacles, and began to read the script on the table.

5

Two or three days later the rehearsal by parts began, whenever the different actors had free time. Full-scale rehearsals would only be possible during the few days in between the end of this month and the beginning of next month's program. Unless everything that needed tightening were attended to by then, there would be no time to pull the performance together.

Once the rehearsal of the parts began it became apparent to everyone that Kawasaki was like a foreigner strayed among them. He had not the smallest grasp of kabuki, and Masuyama found himself obliged to stand beside him and explain word by word the technical language of the kabuki theatre, making Kawasaki extremely dependent on him. The instant the first rehearsal was over Masuyama invited Kawasaki for a drink.

Masuyama knew that for someone in his position it was generally speaking a mistake to ally himself with the director, but he felt he could easily understand what Kawasaki must be experiencing. The young man's views were precisely defined, his mental attitudes were wholesome, and he threw himself into his work with boyish enthusiasm. Masuyama could see why Kawasaki's character should have so appealed to the playwright; he felt as if Kawasaki's genuine youthfulness were a somehow purifying element, a quality unknown in the world of kabuki. Masuyama justified his friendship with Kawasaki in terms of attempting to turn this quality to the advantage of kabuki.

Full-scale rehearsals began at last on the day after the final performances of the December program. It was two days after Christmas. The year-end excitement in the streets could be sensed even through the windows in the theatre and the dressing rooms. A battered old desk had been placed by a window in the large rehearsal room. Kawasaki and one of Masuyama's seniors on the staff—the stage manager—sat with their backs to the window. Masuyama was behind Kawasaki. The actors sat on the *tatami*[4] along the wall. Each would go up center when his turn came to recite his lines. The stage manager supplied forgotten lines.

Sparks flew repeatedly between Kawasaki and the actors. "At this point," Kawasaki would say, "I'd like you to stand as you say, 'I wish I could go to Kawachi and have done with it.' Then you're to walk up to the pillar at stage right."

"That's one place I simply can't stand up."

"Please try doing it my way." Kawasaki forced a smile, but his face visibly paled with wounded pride.

"You can ask me to stand up from now until next Christmas, but I still can't do it. I'm supposed at this place to be mulling over something. How can I walk across stage when I'm thinking?"

Kawasaki did not answer, but he betrayed his extreme irritation at being addressed in such terms.

But things were quite different when it came Mangiku's turn. If Kawasaki said, "Sit!" Mangiku would sit, and if he said, "Stand!" Mangiku stood. He obeyed unresistingly every direction given by Kawasaki. It seemed to Masuyama that Mangiku's fondness for the part did not fully explain why he was so much more obliging than was his custom at rehearsals.

Masuyama was forced to leave this rehearsal on business just as Mangiku, having run through his scene in the first act, was returning to his seat by the wall. When Masuyama got back, he was met by the following sight: Kawasaki, all but sprawled over the desk, was intently following the rehearsal, not bothering even to push back the long hair falling over his eyes. He was leaning on his crossed arms, the shoulders beneath the corduroy jacket shaking with suppressed rage. To Masuyama's right was a white wall interrupted by a window, through which he could see a balloon swaying in the northerly wind, its streamer proclaiming an end-of-the-year sale. Hard, wintry clouds looked as if they had been blocked in with chalk against the pale blue of the sky. He noticed a shrine to Inari[5] and a tiny vermilion torii[6] on the roof of an old building near by. Farther to his right, by the wall, Mangiku sat erect in Japanese style on the *tatami*. The script lay open on his lap, and the lines of his greenish-gray kimono were perfectly straight. From where Masuyama stood at the door he could not see Mangiku's full face; but the eyes, seen in profile, were utterly tranquil, the gentle gaze fixed unwaveringly on Kawasaki.

---

[4] Straw matting.
[5] A Shinto demi-god of the harvest.
[6] The gateway to a Shinto shrine.

Masuyama felt a momentary shudder of fear. He had set one foot inside the rehearsal room, but it was now almost impossible to go in.

6

Later in the day Masuyama was summoned to Mangiku's dressing room. He felt an unaccustomed emotional block when he bent his head, as so often before, to pass through the door curtains. Mangiku greeted him, all smiles, from his perch on the purple cushion and offered Masuyama some cakes he had been given by a visitor.

"How do you think the rehearsal went today?"

"Pardon me?" Masuyama was startled by the question. It was not like Mangiku to ask his opinion on such matters.

"How did it seem?"

"If everything continues to go as well as it did today, I think the play'll be a hit."

"Do you really think so? I feel terribly sorry for Mr. Kawasaki. It's so hard for him. The others have been treating him in such a high-handed way that it's made me quite nervous. I'm sure you could tell from the rehearsal that I've made up my mind to play the part exactly as Mr. Kawasaki says. That's the way I'd like to play it myself anyway, and I thought it might make things a little easier for Mr. Kawasaki, even if nobody else helps. I can't very well tell the others, but I'm sure they'll notice if I do exactly what I'm told. They know how difficult I usually am. That's the least I can do to protect Mr. Kawasaki. It'd be a shame, when he's trying so hard, if nobody helped."

Masuyama felt no particular surge of emotion as he listened to Mangiku. Quite likely, he thought, Mangiku himself was unaware that he was in love: he was so accustomed to portraying love on a more heroic scale. Masuyama, for his part, considered that these sentiments—however they were to be termed—which had formed in Mangiku's heart were most inappropriate. He expected of Mangiku a far more transparent, artificial, aesthetic display of emotions.

Mangiku, most unusually for him, sat rather informally, imparting a kind of languor to his delicate figure. The mirror reflected the cluster of crimson asters arranged in the cloisonné vase and the recently shaved nape of Mangiku's neck.

Kawasaki's exasperation had become pathetic by the day before stage rehearsals began. As soon as the last private rehearsal ended, he invited Masuyama for a drink, looking as if he had reached the end of his tether. Masuyama was busy at the moment, but two hours later he found Kawasaki in the bar where they had arranged to meet, still waiting for him. The bar was crowded, though it was the night before New Year's Eve, when bars are usually deserted. Kawasaki's face looked pale as he sat drinking alone. He was the kind who only gets paler the more he has had to drink. Masuyama, catching sight of Kawasaki's ashen face as soon as he entered the bar, felt that the young man had saddled him with an unfairly heavy spiritual burden. They lived in different worlds; there was no reason why courtesy should demand that Kawasaki's uncertainties and anguish should fall so squarely on his shoulders.

Kawasaki, as he rather expected, immediately engaged him with a good-natured taunt, accusing him of being a double agent. Masuyama took the charge with a smile. He was only five or six years older than Kawasaki, but he possessed the self-confidence of a man who had dwelt among people who "knew the score." At the same time, he felt a kind of envy of this man who had never known hardship, or at any rate, enough hardship. It was not exactly a lack of moral integrity which had made Masuyama indifferent to most of the backstage gossip directed against him, now that he was securely placed in the kabuki hierarchy; his indifference demonstrated that he had nothing to do with the kind of sincerity which might destroy him.

Kawasaki spoke. "I'm fed up with the whole thing. Once the curtain goes up on opening night, I'll be only too glad to disappear from the picture. Stage rehearsals beginning tomorrow! That's more than I can take, when I'm feeling so disgusted. This is the worst assignment I've ever had. I've reached my limit. Never again will I barge into a world that's not my own."

"But isn't that what you more or less expected from the outset? Kabuki's not the same as the modern theatre, after all." Masuyama's voice was cold.

Kawasaki's next words came as a surprise. "Mangiku's the hardest to take. I really dislike him. I'll never stage another play with him." Kawasaki stared at the curling wisps of smoke under the low ceiling, as if into the face of an invisible enemy.

"I wouldn't have guessed it. It seems to me he's doing his best to be co-operative."

"What makes you think so? What's so good about him? It doesn't bother me too much when the other actors don't listen to me during rehearsals or try to intimidate me, or even when they sabotage the whole works, but Mangiku's more than I can figure out. All he does is stare at me with that sneer on his face. At bottom he's absolutely uncompromising, and he treats me like an ignorant little squirt. That's why he does everything exactly as I say. He's the only one of them who obeys my directions, and that burns me up all the more. I can tell just what he's thinking: 'If that's the way you want it, that's the way I'll do it, but don't expect me to take any responsibility for what happens in the performance.' That's what he keeps flashing at me, without saying a word, and it's the worst sabotage I know. He's the nastiest of the lot."

Masuyama listened in astonishment, but he shrank from revealing the truth to Kawasaki now. He hesitated even to let Kawasaki know that Mangiku was intending to be friendly, much less the whole truth. Kawasaki was baffled as to how he should respond to the entirely unfamiliar emotions of this world into which he had suddenly plunged; if he were informed of Mangiku's feelings, he might easily suppose they represented just one more snare laid for him. His eyes were too clear: for all his grasp of the principles of theatre, he could not detect the dark, aesthetic presence lurking behind the texts.

7

The New Year came and with it the first night of the new program.

Mangiku was in love. His sharp-eyed disciples were the first to gossip about it. Masuyama, a frequent visitor to Mangiku's dressing room, sensed it in the atmosphere almost immediately. Mangiku was wrapped in his love like a silkworm in its cocoon, soon to emerge as a butterfly. His dressing room was the cocoon of his love. Mangiku was of a retiring disposition in any case, but the contrast with the New Year's excitement elsewhere gave his dressing room a peculiarly solemn hush.

Opening night, Masuyama, noticing as he passed Mangiku's dressing room that the door was wide open, decided to take a look inside. He saw Mangiku from behind, seated before the mirror in full costume, waiting for his signal to go on. His eyes took in the pale lavender of Mangiku's robe, the gentle slope of the powdered and half-exposed shoulders, the glossy, lacquer-black wig. Mangiku at such moments in the deserted dressing room looked like a woman absorbed in her spinning; she was spinning her love, and would continue spinning forever, her mind elsewhere.

Masuyama intuitively understood that the mold for this *onnagata*'s love had been provided by the stage alone. The stage was present all day long, the stage where love was incessantly shouting, grieving, shedding blood. Music celebrating the sublime heights of love sounded perpetually in Mangiku's ears, and each exquisite gesture of his body was constantly employed on stage for the purposes of love. To the tips of his fingers, nothing about Mangiku was alien to love. His toes encased in white *tabi*,[7] the seductive colors of his under kimono barely

---

[7] The socks, fitted for the toes, that are worn with Oriental sandals.

glimpsed through the openings in his sleeves, the long, swanlike nape of his neck were all in the service of love.

Masuyama did not doubt but that Mangiku would obtain guidance in pursuing his love from the grandiose emotions of his stage roles. The ordinary actor is apt to enrich his performances by infusing them with the emotions of his real life, but not Mangiku. The instant that Mangiku fell in love, the loves of Yukihime, Omiwa, Hinaginu, and the other tragic heroines came to his support.

The thought of Mangiku in love took Masuyama aback, however. Those tragic emotions for which he had yearned so fervently since his days as a high-school student, those sublime emotions which Mangiku always evoked through his corporeal presence on stage, encasing his sensual faculties in icy flames, Mangiku was now visibly nurturing in real life. But the object of these emotions—granted that he had some talent—was an ignoramus as far as kabuki was concerned; he was merely a young, commonplace-looking director whose only qualification as the object of Mangiku's love consisted in being a foreigner in this country, a young traveler who would soon depart the world of kabuki and never return.

8

If Only I Could Change Them! was well received. Kawasaki, despite his announced intention of disappearing after opening night, came to the theatre every day to complain of the performance, to rush back and forth incessantly through the subterranean passages under the stage, to finger with curiosity the mechanisms of the trap door or the *hanamichi.* Masuyama thought this man had something childish about him.

The newspaper reviews praised Mangiku. Masuyama made it a point to show them to Kawasaki, but he merely pouted, like an obstinate child, and all but spat out the words, "They're all good at acting. But there wasn't any *direction.*" Masuyama naturally did not relay to Mangiku these harsh words, and Kawasaki himself was on his best behavior when he actually met Mangiku. It nevertheless irritated Masuyama that Mangiku, who was utterly blind when it came to other people's feelings, should not have questioned that Kawasaki was aware of his good will. But Kawasaki was absolutely insensitive to what other people might feel. This was the one trait that Kawasaki and Mangiku had in common.

A week after the first performance Masuyama was summoned to Mangiku's dressing room. Mangiku displayed on his table amulets and charms from the shrine where he regularly worshipped, as well as some small New Year's cakes. The cakes would no doubt be distributed later among his disciples. Mangiku pressed some sweets on Masuyama, a sign that he was in a good mood. "Mr. Kawasaki was here a little while ago," he said.

"Yes, I saw him out front."

"I wonder if he's still in the theatre."

"I imagine he'll stay until *If Only* is over."

"Did he say anything about being busy afterward?"

"No, nothing particular."

"Then, I have a little favor I'd like to ask you."

Masuyama assumed as businesslike an expression as he could muster. "What might it be?"

"Tonight, you see, when the performance is over . . . I mean, tonight . . ." The color had mounted in Mangiku's cheeks. His voice was clearer and higher-pitched than usual. "Tonight, when the performance is over, I thought I'd like to have dinner with him. Would you mind asking if he's free?"

"I'll ask him."

"It's dreadful of me, isn't it, to ask you such a thing."

"That's quite all right." Masuyama sensed that Mangiku's eyes at that moment had stopped roving and were trying to read his expression. He seemed to expect—and even to desire—some perturbation on Masuyama's part. "Very well," Masuyama said, rising at once, "I'll inform him."

Hardly had Masuyama gone into the lobby than he ran into Kawasaki, coming from the opposite direction; this chance meeting amidst the crowd thronging the lobby during intermission seemed like a stroke of fate. Kawasaki's manner poorly accorded with the festive air pervading the lobby. The somehow haughty airs which the young man always adopted seemed rather comic when set amidst a buzzing, gaily dressed crowd, upstanding members of the community in the theatre merely for the pleasure of seeing a play.

Masuyama led Kawasaki to a corner of the lobby and informed him of Mangiku's request.

"I wonder what he wants with me now? Dinner together—that's funny. I have nothing else to do tonight, and there's no reason why I can't go, but I don't see why."

"I suppose there's something he wants to discuss about the play."

"The play! I've said all I want to on that subject."

At this moment a gratuitous desire to do evil, an emotion always associated on the stage with minor villains, took seed within Masuyama's heart, though he did not realize it; he was not aware that he himself was now acting like a character in a play. "Don't you see—being invited to dinner gives you a marvelous opportunity to tell him everything you've got on your mind, this time without mincing words."

"All the same—"

"I don't suppose you've got the nerve to tell him."

The remark wounded the young man's pride. "All right. I'll go. I've known all along that sooner or later I'd have my chance to have it out with him in the open. Please tell him that I'm glad to accept his invitation."

Mangiku appeared in the last work of the program and was not free until the entire performance was over. Once the show ends, actors normally make a quick change of clothes and rush from the theatre, but Mangiku showed no sign of haste as he completed his dressing by putting a cape and a scarf of a muted color over his outer kimono. He waited for Kawasaki. When Kawasaki at last appeared, he curtly greeted Mangiku, not bothering to take his hands from his overcoat pockets.

The disciple who always waited on Mangiku as his "lady's maid" rushed up, as if to announce some major calamity. "It's started to snow," he reported with a bow.

"A heavy snow?" Mangiku touched his cape to his cheek.

"No, just a flurry."

"We'll need an umbrella to the car," Mangiku said. The disciple rushed off for an umbrella.

Masuyama saw them to the stage entrance. The door attendant had politely arranged Mangiku's and Kawasaki's footwear next to each other. Mangiku's disciple stood outside in the thin snow, holding an open umbrella. The snow fell so sparsely that one couldn't be sure one saw it against the dark concrete wall beyond. One or two flakes fluttered onto the doorstep at the stage entrance.

Mangiku bowed to Masuyama. "We'll be leaving now," he said. The smile on his lips could be seen indistinctly behind his scarf. He turned to the disciple, "That's all right. I'll carry the umbrella. I'd like you to go instead and tell the driver we're ready." Mangiku held the umbrella over Kawasaki's head. As Kawasaki in his overcoat and Mangiku in his cape walked off side by side under the umbrella, a few flakes suddenly flew—all but bounced—from the umbrella.

Masuyama watched them go. He felt as though a big, black, wet umbrella were being noisily opened inside his heart. He could tell that the illusion, first formed when as a boy he saw Mangiku perform, an illusion which he had preserved intact even after he joined the kabuki staff, had shattered that instant in all directions, like a delicate piece of crystal dropped from a height. At last I know what disillusion means, he thought. I might as well give up the theatre.

But Masuyama knew that along with disillusion a new sensation was assaulting him, jealousy. He dreaded where this new emotion might lead him.

Translated by Donald Keene

Flannery O'Connor / 1925–1964

Revelation

The doctor's waiting room, which was very small, was almost full when the Turpins entered and Mrs. Turpin, who was very large, made it look even smaller by her presence. She stood looming at the head of the magazine table set in the center of it, a living demonstration that the room was inadequate and ridiculous. Her little bright black eyes took in all the patients as she sized up the seating situation. There was one vacant chair and a place on the sofa occupied by a blond child in a dirty blue romper who should have been told to move over and make room for the lady. He was five or six, but Mrs. Turpin saw at once that no one was going to tell him to move over. He was slumped down in the seat, his arms idle at his sides and his eyes idle in his head; his nose ran unchecked.

Mrs. Turpin put a firm hand on Claud's shoulder and said in a voice that included anyone who wanted to listen, "Claud, you sit in that chair there," and gave him a push down into the vacant one. Claud was florid and bald and sturdy, somewhat shorter than Mrs. Turpin, but he sat down as if he were accustomed to doing what she told him to.

Mrs. Turpin remained standing. The only man in the room besides Claud was a lean stringy old fellow with a rusty hand spread out on each knee, whose eyes were closed as if he were asleep or dead or pretending to be so as not to get up and offer her his seat. Her gaze settled agreeably on a well-dressed grey-haired lady whose eyes met hers and whose expression said: if that child belonged to me, he would have some manners and move over—there's plenty of room there for you and him too.

Claud looked up with a sigh and made as if to rise.

"Sit down," Mrs. Turpin said. "You know you're not supposed to stand on that leg. He has an ulcer on his leg," she explained.

Claud lifted his foot onto the magazine table and rolled his trouser leg up to reveal a purple swelling on a plump marble-white calf.

"My!" the pleasant lady said. "How did you do that?"

"A cow kicked him," Mrs. Turpin said.

"Goodness!" said the lady.

Claud rolled his trouser leg down.

"Maybe the little boy would move over," the lady suggested, but the child did not stir.

"Somebody will be leaving in a minute," Mrs. Turpin said. She could not understand why a doctor—with as much money as they made charging five dollars a day to just stick their head in the hospital door and look at you—couldn't afford a decent-sized waiting room. This one was hardly bigger than a garage. The table was cluttered with limp-looking magazines and at one end of it there was a big green glass ash tray full of cigaret butts and cotton wads with little blood spots on them. If she had had anything to do with the running of the place, that would have been emptied every so often. There were no chairs against the wall at the head of the room. It had a rectangular-shaped panel in it that permitted a view of the office where the nurse came and went and the secretary listened to the radio. A plastic fern in a gold pot sat in the opening and trailed its fronds down almost to the floor. The radio was softly playing gospel music.

Just then the inner door opened and a nurse with the highest stack of yellow hair Mrs. Turpin had ever seen put her face in the crack and called for the next patient. The woman sitting beside Claud grasped the two arms of her chair and hoisted herself up; she pulled her dress free from her legs and lumbered through the door where the nurse had disappeared.

Mrs. Turpin eased into the vacant chair, which held her tight as a corset. "I wish I could reduce," she said, and rolled her eyes and gave a comic sigh.

"Oh, *you* aren't fat," the stylish lady said.

"Ooooo I am too," Mrs. Turpin said. "Claud he eats all he wants to and never weighs over one hundred and seventy-five pounds, but me I just look at something good to eat and I gain some weight," and her stomach and shoulders shook with laughter. "You can eat all you want to, can't you, Claud?" she asked, turning to him.

Claud only grinned.

"Well, as long as you have such a good disposition," the stylish lady said, "I don't think it makes a bit of difference what size you are. You just can't beat a good disposition."

Next to her was a fat girl of eighteen or nineteen, scowling into a thick blue book which Mrs. Turpin saw was entitled *Human Development*. The girl raised her head and directed her scowl at Mrs. Turpin as if she did not like her looks. She appeared annoyed that anyone should speak while she tried to read. The poor girl's face was blue with acne and Mrs. Turpin thought how pitiful it was to have a face like that at that age. She gave the girl a friendly smile but the girl only scowled the harder. Mrs. Turpin herself was fat but she had always had good skin, and, though she was forty-seven years old, there was not a wrinkle in her face except around her eyes from laughing too much.

Next to the ugly girl was the child, still in exactly the same position, and next to him was a thin leathery old woman in a cotton print dress. She and Claud had three sacks of chicken feed in their pump house that was in the same print. She had seen from the first that the child belonged with the old woman. She could tell by the way they sat— kind of vacant and white-trashy, as if they would sit there until Doomsday if nobody called and told them to get up. And at right angles but next to the well-dressed pleasant lady was a lank-faced woman who was certainly the child's mother. She had on a yellow sweat shirt and wine-colored slacks, both gritty-looking, and the rims of her lips were stained with snuff. Her dirty yellow hair was tied behind with a little piece of red paper ribbon. Worse than niggers any day, Mrs. Turpin thought.

The gospel hymn playing was, "When I looked up and He looked down," and Mrs. Turpin, who knew it, supplied the last line mentally, "And wona these days I know I'll we-eara crown."

Without appearing to, Mrs. Turpin always noticed people's feet. The well-dressed lady had on red and grey suede shoes to match her dress. Mrs. Turpin had on her good black patent leather pumps. The ugly girl had on Girl Scout shoes and heavy socks. The old woman had on tennis shoes and the white-trashy mother had on what appeared to be bedroom slippers, black straw with gold braid threaded through them—exactly what you would have expected her to have on.

Sometimes at night when she couldn't go to sleep, Mrs. Turpin would occupy herself with the question of who she would have chosen to be if she couldn't have been herself. If Jesus had said to her before he made her, "There's only two places available for you. You can either be a nigger or white-trash," what would she have said? "Please, Jesus, please," she would have said, "just let me wait until there's another place available," and he would have said, "No, you have to go right now and I have only those two places so make up your mind." She would have wiggled and squirmed and begged and pleaded but it would have been no use and finally she would have said, "All right, make me a nigger then—but that don't mean a trashy one." And he would have made her a neat clean respectable Negro woman, herself but black.

Next to the child's mother was a red-headed youngish woman, reading one of the magazines and working a piece of chewing gum, hell for leather, as Claud would say. Mrs. Turpin could not see the woman's feet. She was not white-trash, just common. Sometimes Mrs. Turpin occupied herself at night naming the classes of people. On the bottom of the heap were most colored people, not the kind she would have been if she had been one, but most of them; then next to them—not above, just away from—were the white-trash; then above them were the home-owners, and above them the home-and-land owners, to which she and Claud belonged. Above she and Claud were people with a lot of money and much bigger houses and much more land. But here the complexity of it would begin to bear in on her, for some of the people with a lot of money were common and ought to be below she and Claud and some of the people who had good blood had lost their money and had to rent and then there were colored people who owned their homes and land as well. There was a colored dentist in town who had two red Lincolns and a swimming pool and a farm with registered white-face cattle on it. Usually by the time she had fallen asleep all the classes of people were moiling and roiling around in her head, and she would dream they were all crammed in together in a box car, being ridden off to be put in a gas oven.

"That's a beautiful clock," she said and nodded to her right. It was a big wall clock, the face encased in a brass sunburst.

"Yes, it's very pretty," the stylish lady said agreeably. "And right on the dot too," she added, glancing at her watch.

The ugly girl beside her cast an eye upward at the clock, smirked, then looked directly at Mrs. Turpin and smirked again. Then she returned her eyes to her book. She was obviously the lady's daughter because, although they didn't look anything alike as to disposition, they both had the same shape of face and the same blue eyes. On the lady they sparkled pleasantly but in the girl's seared face they appeared alternately to smolder and to blaze.

What if Jesus had said, "All right, you can be white-trash or a nigger or ugly"!

Mrs. Turpin felt an awful pity for the girl, though she thought it was one thing to be ugly and another to act ugly.

The woman with the snuff-stained lips turned around in her chair and looked up at the clock. Then she turned back and appeared to look a little to the side of Mrs. Turpin. There was a cast in one of her eyes. "You want to know wher you can get you one of themther clocks?" she asked in a loud voice.

"No, I already have a nice clock," Mrs. Turpin said. Once somebody like her got a leg in the conversation, she would be all over it.

"You can get you one with green stamps," the woman said. "That's most likely wher he got hisn. Save you up enough, you can get you most anythang. I got me some joo'ry."

Ought to have got you a wash rag and some soap, Mrs. Turpin thought.

"I get contour sheets with mine," the pleasant lady said.

The daughter slammed her book shut. She looked straight in front of her, directly through Mrs. Turpin and on through the yellow curtain and the plate glass window which made the wall behind her. The girl's eyes seeemed lit all of a sudden with a peculiar light, an unnatural light like night road signs give. Mrs. Turpin turned her head to see if there was anything going on outside that she should see, but she could not see anything. Figures passing cast only a pale shadow through the curtain. There was no reason the girl should single her out for her ugly looks.

"Miss Finley," the nurse said, cracking the door. The gum-chewing woman got up and passed in front of her and Claud and went into the office. She had on red high-heeled shoes.

Directly across the table, the ugly girl's eyes were fixed on Mrs. Turpin as if she had some very special reason for disliking her.

"This is wonderful weather, isn't it?" the girl's mother said.

"It's good weather for cotton if you can get the niggers to pick it," Mrs. Turpin said, "but niggers don't want to pick cotton any more. You can't get the white folks to pick it and now you can't get the niggers—because they got to be right up there with the white folks."

"They gonna *try* anyways," the white-trash woman said, leaning forward.

"Do you have one of those cotton-picking machines?" the pleasant lady asked.

"No," Mrs. Turpin said, "they leave half the cotton in the field. We don't have much cotton anyway. If you want to make it farming now, you have to have a little of everything. We got a couple of acres of cotton and a few hogs and chickens and just enough white-face that Claud can look after them himself."

"One thang I don't want," the white-trash woman said, wiping her mouth with the back of her hand. "Hogs. Nasty stinking things, a-gruntin and a-rootin all over the place."

Mrs. Turpin gave her the merest edge of her attention. "Our hogs are not dirty and they don't stink," she said. "They're cleaner than some children I've seen. Their feet never touch the ground. We have a pig-parlor—that's where you raise them on concrete," she explained to the pleasant lady, "and Claud scoots them down with the hose every afternoon and washes off the floor." Cleaner by far than that child right there, she thought. Poor nasty little thing. He had not moved except to put the thumb of his dirty hand into his mouth.

The woman turned her face away from Mrs. Turpin. "I know I wouldn't scoot down no hog with no hose," she said to the wall.

You wouldn't have no hog to scoot down, Mrs. Turpin said to herself.

"A-gruntin and a-rootin and a-groanin," the woman muttered.

"We got a little of everything," Mrs. Turpin said to the pleasant lady. "It's no use in having more than you can handle yourself with help like it is. We found enough niggers to pick our cotton this year but Claud he has to go after them and take them home again in the evening. They can't walk that half a mile. No they can't. I tell you," she said and laughed merrily, "I sure am tired of buttering up niggers, but you got to love em if you want em to work for you. When they come in the morning, I run out and I say, 'Hi yawl this morning?' and when Claud drives them off to the field I just wave to beat the band and they just wave back." And she waved her hand rapidly to illustrate.

"Like you read out of the same book," the lady said, showing she understood perfectly.

"Child, yes," Mrs. Turpin said. "And when they come in from the field, I run out with a bucket of icewater. That's the way it's going to be from now on," she said. "You may as well face it."

"One thang I know," the white-trash woman said. "Two thangs I ain't going to do: love no niggers or scoot down no hog with no hose." And she let out a bark of contempt.

The look that Mrs. Turpin and the pleasant lady exchanged indicated they both understood that you had to *have* certain things before you could *know* certain things. But every time Mrs. Turpin exchanged a look with the lady, she was aware that the ugly girl's peculiar eyes were still on her, and she had trouble bringing her attention back to the conversation.

"When you got something," she said, "you got to look after it."

And when you ain't got a thing but breath and britches, she added to herself, you can afford to come to town every morning and just sit on the Court House coping and spit.

A grotesque revolving shadow passed across the curtain behind her and was thrown palely on the opposite wall. Then a bicycle clattered down against the outside of the building. The door opened and a colored boy glided in with a tray from the drug store. It had two large red and white paper cups on it with tops on them. He was a tall, very black boy in discolored white pants and a green nylon shirt. He was chewing gum slowly, as if to music. He set the tray down in the office opening next to the fern and stuck his head through to look for the secretary. She was not in there. He rested his arms on the ledge and waited, his narrow bottom stuck out, swaying slowly to the left and right. He raised a hand over his head and scratched the base of his skull.

"You see that button there, boy?" Mrs. Turpin said. "You can punch that and she'll come. She's probably in the back somewhere."

"Is thas right?" the boy said agreeably, as if he had never seen the button before. He leaned to the right and put his finger on it. "She sometime out," he said and twisted around to face his audience, his elbows behind him on the counter. The nurse appeared and he twisted back again. She handed him a dollar and he rooted in his pocket and made the change and counted it out to her. She gave him fifteen cents for a tip and he went out with the empty tray. The heavy door swung to slowly and closed at length with the sound of suction. For a moment no one spoke.

"They ought to send all them niggers back to Africa," the white-trash woman said. "That's wher they come from in the first place."

"Oh, I couldn't do without my good colored friends," the pleasant lady said.

"There's a heap of things worse than a nigger," Mrs. Turpin agreed. "It's all kinds of them just like it's all kinds of us."

"Yes, and it takes all kinds to make the world go round," the lady said in her musical voice.

As she said it, the raw-complexioned girl snapped her teeth together. Her lower lip turned downwards and inside out, revealing the pale pink inside of her mouth. After a second it rolled back up. It was the ugliest face Mrs. Turpin had ever seen anyone make and for a moment she was certain that the girl had made it at her. She was looking at her as if she had known and disliked her all her life—all of Mrs. Turpin's life, it seemed too, not just all the girl's life. Why, girl, I don't even know you, Mrs. Turpin said silently.

She forced her attention back to the discussion. "It wouldn't be practical to send them back to Africa," she said. "They wouldn't want to go. They got it too good here."

"Wouldn't be what they wanted—if I had anythang to do with it," the woman said.

"It wouldn't be a way in the world you could get all the niggers back over there," Mrs. Turpin said. "They'd be hiding out and lying down and turning sick on you and wailing and hollering and raring and pitching. It wouldn't be a way in the world to get them over there."

"They got over here," the trashy woman said. "Get back like they got over."

"It wasn't so many of them then," Mrs. Turpin explained.

The woman looked at Mrs. Turpin as if here was an idiot indeed but Mrs. Turpin was not bothered by the look, considering where it came from.

"Nooo," she said, "they're going to stay here where they can go to New York and marry white folks and improve their color. That's what they all want to do, every one of them, improve their color."

"You know what comes of that, don't you?" Claud asked.

"No, Claud, what?" Mrs. Turpin said.

Claud's eyes twinkled. "White-faced niggers," he said with never a smile.

Everybody in the office laughed except the white-trash and the ugly girl. The girl gripped the book in her lap with white fingers. The trashy woman looked around her from face to face as if she thought they were all idiots. The old woman in the feed sack dress continued to gaze expressionless across the floor at the high-top shoes of the man opposite her, the one who had been pretending to be asleep when the Turpins came in. He was laughing heartily, his hands still spread out on his knees. The child had fallen to the side and was lying now almost face down in the old woman's lap.

While they recovered from their laughter, the nasal chorus on the radio kept the room from silence.

> *You go to blank blank*
> *And I'll go to mine*
> *But we'll all blank along*
> *To-geth-ther,*
> *And all along the blank*
> *We'll hep eachother out*
> *Smile-ling in any kind of*
> *Weath-ther!*

Mrs. Turpin didn't catch every word but she caught enough to agree with the spirit of the song and it turned her thoughts sober. To help anybody out that needed it was her philosophy of life. She never spared herself when she found somebody in need, whether they were white or black, trash or decent. And of all she had to be thankful for, she was most thankful that this was so. If Jesus had said, "You can be high society and have all the money you want and be thin and svelte-like, but you can't be a good woman with it," she would have had to say, "Well don't make me that then. Make me a good woman and it don't matter what else, how fat or how ugly or how poor!" Her heart rose. He had not made her a nigger or white-trash or ugly! He had made her herself and given her a little of everything. Jesus, thank you! she said. Thank you thank you thank you! Whenever she counted her blessings she felt as buoyant as if she weighed one hundred and twenty-five pounds instead of one hundred and eighty.

"What's wrong with your little boy?" the pleasant lady asked the white-trashy woman.

"He has a ulcer," the woman said proudly. "He ain't give me a minute's peace since he was born. Him and her are just alike," she said, nodding at the old woman, who was running her leathery fingers through the child's pale hair. "Look like I can't get nothing down them two but Co' Cola and candy."

That's all you try to get down em, Mrs. Turpin said to herself. Too lazy to light the fire. There was nothing you could tell her about people like them that she didn't know already. And it was not just that they didn't have anything. Because if you gave them everything, in two weeks it would all be broken or filthy or they would have chopped it up for lightwood. She knew all this from her own experience. Help them you must, but help them you couldn't.

All at once the ugly girl turned her lips inside out again. Her eyes were fixed like two drills on Mrs. Turpin. This time there was no mistaking that there was something urgent behind them.

Girl, Mrs. Turpin exclaimed silently, I haven't done a thing to you! The girl might be confusing her with somebody else. There was no need to sit by and let herself be intimidated. "You must be in college," she said boldly, looking directly at the girl. "I see you reading a book there."

The girl continued to stare and pointedly did not answer.

Her mother blushed at this rudeness. "The lady asked you a question, Mary Grace," she said under her breath.

"I have ears," Mary Grace said.

The poor mother blushed again. "Mary Grace goes to Wellesley College," she explained. She twisted one of the buttons on her dress. "In Massachusetts," she added with a grimace. "And in the summer she just keeps right on studying. Just reads all the time, a real book worm. She's done real well at Wellesley; she's taking English and Math and History and Psychology and Social Studies," she rattled on, "and I think it's too much. I think she ought to get out and have fun."

The girl looked as if she would like to hurl them all through the plate glass window.

"Way up north," Mrs. Turpin murmured and thought, well, it hasn't done much for her manners.

"I'd almost rather to have him sick," the white-trash woman said, wrenching the attention back to herself. "He's so mean when he ain't. Look like some children just take natural to meanness. It's some gets bad when they get sick but he was the opposite. Took sick and turned good. He don't give me no trouble now. It's me waitin to see the doctor," she said.

If I was going to send anybody back to Africa, Mrs. Turpin thought, it would be your kind, woman. "Yes, indeed," she said aloud, but looking up at the ceiling, "it's a heap of things worse than a nigger." And dirtier than a hog, she added to herself.

"I think people with bad dispositions are more to be pitied than anyone on earth," the pleasant lady said in a voice that was decidedly thin.

"I thank the Lord he has blessed me with a good one," Mrs. Turpin said. "The day has never dawned that I couldn't find something to laugh at."

"Not since she married me anyways," Claud said with a comical straight face.

Everybody laughed except the girl and the white-trash.

Mrs. Turpin's stomach shook. "He's such a caution," she said, "that I can't help but laugh at him."

The girl made a loud ugly noise through her teeth.

Her mother's mouth grew thin and tight. "I think the worst thing in the world," she said, "is an ungrateful person. To have everything and not appreciate it. I know a girl," she said, "who has parents who would give her anything, a little brother who loves her dearly, who is getting a good education, who wears the best clothes, but who can never say a kind word to anyone, who never smiles, who just criticizes and complains all day long."

"Is she too old to paddle?" Claud asked.

The girl's face was almost purple.

"Yes," the lady said, "I'm afraid there's nothing to do but leave her to her folly. Some day she'll wake up and it'll be too late."

"It never hurt anyone to smile," Mrs. Turpin said. "It just makes you feel better all over."

"Of course," the lady said sadly, "but there are just some people you can't tell anything to. They can't take criticism."

"If it's one thing I am," Mrs. Turpin said with feeling, "it's grateful. When I think who all I could have been besides myself and what all I got, a little of everything, and a good disposition besides, I just feel like shouting, 'Thank you, Jesus, for making everything the way it is!' It could have been different!" For one thing, somebody else could have got Claud. At the thought of this, she was flooded with gratitude and a terrible pang of joy ran through her. "Oh thank you, Jesus, Jesus, thank you!" she cried aloud.

The book struck her directly over her left eye. It struck almost at the same instant that she realized the girl was about to hurl it. Before she could utter a sound, the raw face came crashing across the table toward her, howling. The girl's fingers sank like clamps into the soft flesh of her neck. She heard the mother cry out and Claud shout, "Whoa!" There was an instant when she was certain that she was about to be in an earthquake.

All at once her vision narrowed and she saw everything as if it were happening in a small room far away, or as if she were looking at it through the wrong end of a telescope. Claud's face crumpled and fell out of sight. The nurse ran in, then out, then in again. Then the gangling figure of the doctor rushed out of the inner door. Magazines flew this way and that as the table turned over. The girl fell with a thud and Mrs. Turpin's vision suddenly reversed itself and she saw everything large instead of small. The eyes of the white-trashy woman were staring hugely at the floor. There the girl, held down on one side by the nurse and on the other by her mother, was wrenching and turning in their grasp. The doctor was kneeling astride her, trying to hold her arm down. He managed after a second to sink a long needle into it.

Mrs. Turpin felt entirely hollow except for her heart which swung from side to side as if it were agitated in a great empty drum of flesh.

"Somebody that's not busy call for the ambulance," the doctor said in the off-hand voice young doctors adopt for terrible occasions.

Mrs. Turpin could not have moved a finger. The old man who had been sitting next to her skipped nimbly into the office and made the call, for the secretary still seemed to be gone.

"Claud!" Mrs. Turpin called.

He was not in his chair. She knew she must jump up and find him but she felt like some one trying to catch a train in a dream, when everything moves in slow motion and the faster you try to run the slower you go.

"Here I am," a suffocated voice, very unlike Claud's, said.

He was doubled up in the corner on the floor, pale as paper, holding his leg. She wanted to get up and go to him but she could not move. Instead, her gaze was drawn slowly downward to the churning face on the floor, which she could see over the doctor's shoulder.

The girl's eyes stopped rolling and focused on her. They seemed a much lighter blue than before, as if a door that had been tightly closed behind them was now open to admit light and air.

Mrs. Turpin's head cleared and her power of motion returned. She leaned forward until she was looking directly into the fierce brilliant eyes. There was no doubt in her mind that the girl did know her, knew her in some intense and personal way, beyond time and place and condition. "What you got to say to me?" she asked hoarsely and held her breath, waiting, as for a revelation.

The girl raised her head. Her gaze locked with Mrs. Turpin's. "Go back to hell where you came from, you old wart hog," she whispered. Her voice was low but clear. Her eyes burned for a moment as if she saw with pleasure that her message had struck its target.

Mrs. Turpin sank back in her chair.

After a moment the girl's eyes closed and she turned her head wearily to the side.

The doctor rose and handed the nurse the empty syringe. He leaned over and put both hands for a moment on the mother's shoulders, which were shaking. She was sitting on the floor, her lips pressed together, holding Mary Grace's hand in her lap. The girl's fingers were gripped like a baby's around her thumb. "Go on to the hospital," he said. "I'll call and make the arrangements."

"Now let's see that neck," he said in a jovial voice to Mrs. Turpin. He began to inspect her neck with his first two fingers. Two little moon-shaped lines like pink fish bones were indented over her windpipe. There was the beginning of an angry red swelling above her eye. His fingers passed over this also.

"Lea' me be," she said thickly and shook him off. "See about Claud. She kicked him."

"I'll see about him in a minute," he said and felt her pulse. He was a thin grey-haired man, given to pleasantries. "Go home and have yourself a vacation the rest of the day," he said and patted her on the shoulder.

Quit your pattin me, Mrs. Turpin growled to herself.

"And put an ice pack over that eye," he said. Then he went and squatted down beside Claud and looked at his leg. After a moment he pulled him up and Claud limped after him into the office.

Until the ambulance came, the only sounds in the room were the tremulous moans of the girl's mother, who continued to sit on the floor. The white-trash woman did not take her eyes off the girl. Mrs. Turpin looked straight ahead at nothing. Presently the ambulance drew up, a long dark shadow, behind the curtain. The attendants came in and set the stretcher down beside the girl and lifted her expertly onto it and carried her out. The nurse helped the mother gather up her things. The shadow of the ambulance moved silently away and the nurse came back in the office.

"That ther girl is going to be a lunatic, ain't she?" the white-trash woman asked the nurse, but the nurse kept on to the back and never answered her.

"Yes, she's going to be a lunatic," the white-trash woman said to the rest of them.

"Po' critter," the old woman murmured. The child's face was still in her lap. His eyes looked idly out over her knees. He had not moved during the disturbance except to draw one leg up under him.

"I thank Gawd," the white-trash woman said fervently, "I ain't a lunatic."

Claud came limping out and the Turpins went home.

As their pick-up truck turned into their own dirt road and made the crest of the hill, Mrs. Turpin gripped the window ledge and looked out suspiciously. The land sloped gracefully down through a field dotted with lavender weeds and at the start of the rise their small yellow frame house, with its little flower beds spread out around it like a fancy apron, sat primly in its accustomed place between two giant hickory trees. She would not have been startled to see a burnt wound between two blackened chimneys.

Neither of them felt like eating so they put on their house clothes and lowered the shade in the bedroom and lay down, Claud with his leg on a pillow and herself with a damp washcloth over her eye. The instant she was flat on her back, the image of a razor-backed hog with warts on its face and horns coming out behind its ears snorted into her head. She moaned, a low quiet moan.

"I am not," she said tearfully, "a wart hog. From hell." But the denial had no force. The girl's eyes and her words, even the tone of her voice, low but clear, directed only to her, brooked no repudiation. She had been singled out for the message, though there was trash in the room to whom it might justly have been applied. The full force of this fact struck her only now. There was a woman there who was neglecting her own child but she had been overlooked. The message had been given to Ruby Turpin, a respectable, hard-working, church-going woman. The tears dried. Her eyes began to burn instead with wrath.

She rose on her elbow and the washcloth fell into her hand. Claud was lying on his back, snoring. She wanted to tell him what the girl had said. At the same time, she did not wish to put the image of herself as a wart hog from hell into his mind.

"Hey, Claud," she muttered and pushed his shoulder.

Claud opened one pale baby blue eye.

She looked into it warily. He did not think about anything. He just went his way.

"Wha, whasit?" he said and closed the eye again.

"Nothing," she said. "Does your leg pain you?"

"Hurts like hell," Claud said.

"It'll quit terreckly," she said and lay back down. In a moment Claud was snoring again. For the rest of the afternoon they lay there. Claud slept. She scowled at the ceiling. Occasionally she raised her fist and made a small stabbing motion over her chest as if she was defending her innocence to invisible guests who were like the comforters of Job, reasonable-seeming but wrong.

About five-thirty Claud stirred. "Got to go after those niggers," he sighed, not moving.

She was looking straight up as if there were unintelligible handwriting on the ceiling. The protuberance over her eye had turned a greenish-blue. "Listen here," she said.

"What?"

"Kiss me."

Claud leaned over and kissed her loudly on the mouth. He pinched her side and their hands interlocked. Her expression of ferocious concentration did not change. Claud got up, groaning and growling, and limped off. She continued to study the ceiling.

She did not get up until she heard the pick-up truck coming back with the Negroes. Then she rose and thrust her feet in her brown oxfords, which she did not bother to lace, and stumped out onto the back porch and got her red plastic bucket. She emptied a tray of ice cubes into it and filled it half full of water and went out into the back yard. Every afternoon after Claud brought the hands in, one of the boys helped him put out hay and the rest waited in the back of the truck until he was ready to take them home. The truck was parked in the shade under one of the hickory trees.

"Hi yawl this evening?" Mrs. Turpin asked grimly, appearing with the bucket and the dipper. There were three women and a boy in the truck.

"Us doin nicely," the oldest woman said. "Hi you doin?" and her gaze stuck immediately on the dark lump on Mrs. Turpin's forehead. "You done fell down, ain't you?" she asked in a solicitous voice. The old woman was dark and almost toothless. She had on an old felt hat of Claud's set back on her head. The other two women were younger and lighter and they both had new bright green sun hats. One of them had hers on her head; the other had taken hers off and the boy was grinning beneath it.

Mrs. Turpin set the bucket down on the floor of the truck. "Yawl hep yourselves," she said. She looked around to make sure Claud had gone. "No. I didn't fall down," she said, folding her arms. "It was something worse than that."

"Ain't nothing bad happen to you!" the old woman said. She said it as if they all knew that Mrs. Turpin was protected in some special way by Divine Providence. "You just had you a little fall."

"We were in town at the doctor's office for where the cow kicked Mr. Turpin," Mrs. Turpin said in a flat tone that indicated they could leave off their foolishness. "And there was this girl there. A big fat girl with her face all broke out. I could look at that girl and tell she was peculiar but I couldn't tell how. And me and her mama were just talking and going along and all of a sudden WHAM! She throws this big book she was reading at me and . . ."

"Naw!" the old woman cried out.

"And then she jumps over the table and commences to choke me."

"Naw!" they all exclaimed, "naw!"

"Hi come she do that?" the old woman asked. "What ail her?"

Mrs. Turpin only glared in front of her.

"Somethin ail her," the old woman said.

"They carried her off in an ambulance," Mrs. Turpin continued, "but before she went she was rolling on the floor and they were trying to hold her down to give her a shot and she said something to me." She paused. "You know what she said to me?"

"What she say?" they asked.

"She said," Mrs. Turpin began, and stopped, her face very dark and heavy. The sun was getting whiter and whiter, blanching the sky overhead so that the leaves of the hickory tree were black in the face of it. She could not bring forth the words. "Something real ugly," she muttered.

"She sho shouldn't said nothin ugly to you," the old woman said. "You so sweet. You the sweetest lady I know."

"She pretty too," the one with the hat on said.

"And stout," the other one said. "I never knowed no sweeter white lady."

"That's the truth befo' Jesus," the old woman said. "Amen! You des as sweet and pretty as you can be."

Mrs. Turpin knew just exactly how much Negro flattery was worth and it added to her rage. "She said," she began again and finished this time with a fierce rush of breath, "that I was an old wart hog from hell."

There was an astounded silence.

"Where she at?" the youngest woman cried in a piercing voice.

"Lemme see her. I'll kill her!"

"I'll kill her with you!" the other one cried.

"She b'long in the sylum," the old woman said emphatically. "You the sweetest white lady I know."

"She pretty too," the other two said. "Stout as she can be and sweet. Jesus satisfied with her!"

"Deed he is," the old woman declared.

Idiots! Mrs. Turpin growled to herself. You could never say anything intelligent to a nigger. You could talk at them but not with them. "Yawl ain't drunk your water," she said shortly. "Leave the bucket in the truck when you're finished with it. I got more to do than just stand around and pass the time of day," and she moved off and into the house.

She stood for a moment in the middle of the kitchen. The dark protuberance over her eye looked like a miniature tornado cloud which might any moment sweep across the horizon of her brow. Her lower lip protruded dangerously. She squared her massive shoulders. Then she marched into the front of the house and out the side door and started down the road to the pig parlor. She had the look of a woman going single-handed, weaponless, into battle.

The sun was a deep yellow now like a harvest moon and was riding westward very fast over the far tree line as if it meant to reach the hogs before she did. The road was rutted and she kicked several good-sized stones out of her path as she strode along. The pig parlor was on a little knoll at the end of a lane that ran off from the side of the barn. It was a square of concrete as large as a small room, with a board fence about four feet high around it. The concrete floor sloped slightly so that the hog wash could drain off into a trench where it was carried to the field for fertilizer. Claud was standing on the outside, on the edge of the concrete, hanging onto the top board, hosing down the floor inside. The hose was connected to the faucet of a water trough nearby.

Mrs. Turpin climbed up beside him and glowered down at the hogs inside. There were seven long-snouted bristly shoats in it—tan with liver-colored spots—and an old sow a few weeks off from farrowing. She was lying on her side grunting. The shoats were running about shaking themselves like idiot children, their little slit pig eyes searching the floor for anything left. She had read that pigs were the most intelligent animal. She doubted it. They were supposed to be smarter than dogs. There had even been a pig astronaut. He had performed his assignment perfectly but died of a heart attack afterwards because they left him in his electric suit, sitting upright throughout his examination when naturally a hog should be on all fours.

A-gruntin and a-rootin and a-groanin.

"Gimme that hose," she said, yanking it away from Claud. "Go on and carry them niggers home and then get off that leg."

"You look like you might have swallowed a mad dog," Claud observed, but he got down and limped off. He paid no attention to her humors.

Until he was out of earshot, Mrs. Turpin stood on the side of the pen, holding the hose and pointing the stream of water at the hind quarters of any shoat that looked as if it might try to lie down. When he had had time to get over the hill, she turned her head slightly and her wrathful eyes scanned the path. He was nowhere in sight. She turned back again and seemed to gather herself up. Her shoulders rose and she drew in her breath.

"What do you send me a message like that for?" she said in a low fierce voice, barely above a whisper but with the force of a shout in its concentrated fury. "How am I a hog and me both? How am I saved and from hell too?" Her free fist was knotted and with the other she gripped the hose, blindly pointing the stream of water in and out of the eye of the old sow whose outraged squeal she did not hear.

The pig parlor commanded a view of the back pasture where their twenty beef cows were gathered around the hay-bales Claud and the boy had put out. The freshly cut pasture sloped down to the highway. Across it was their cotton field and beyond that a dark green dusty wood which they owned as well. The sun was behind the wood, very red, looking over the paling of trees like a farmer inspecting his own hogs.

"Why me?" she rumbled. "It's no trash around here, black or white, that I haven't given to. And break my back to the bone every day working. And do for the church."

She appeared to be the right size woman to command the arena before her. "How am I a hog?" she demanded. "Exactly how am I like them?" and she jabbed the stream of water at the shoats. "There was plenty of trash there. It didn't have to be me.

"If you like trash better, go get yourself some trash then," she railed. "You could have made me trash. Or a nigger. If trash is what you wanted why didn't you make me trash?" She shook her fist with the hose in it and a watery snake appeared momentarily in the air. "I could quit working and take it easy and be filthy," she growled.

"Lounge about the sidewalks all day drinking root beer. Dip snuff and spit in every puddle and have it all over my face. I could be nasty.

"Or you could have made me a nigger. It's too late for me to be a nigger," she said with deep sarcasm, "but I could act like one. Lay down in the middle of the road and stop traffic. Roll on the ground."

In the deepening light everything was taking on a mysterious hue. The pasture was growing a peculiar glassy green and the streak of highway had turned lavender. She braced herself for a final assault and this time her voice rolled out over the pasture. "Go on," she yelled, "call me a hog! Call me a hog again. From hell. Call me a wart hog from hell. Put that bottom rail on top. There'll still be a top and bottom!"

A garbled echo returned to her.

A final surge of fury shook her and she roared, "Who do you think you are?"

The color of everything, field and crimson sky, burned for a moment with a transparent intensity. The question carried over the pasture and across the highway and the cotton field and returned to her clearly like an answer from beyond the wood.

She opened her mouth but no sound came out of it.

A tiny truck, Claud's, appeared on the highway, heading rapidly out of sight. Its gears scraped thinly. It looked like a child's toy. At any moment a bigger truck might smash into it and scatter Claud's and the niggers' brains all over the road.

Mrs. Turpin stood there, her gaze fixed on the highway, all her muscles rigid, until in five or six minutes the truck reappeared, returning. She waited until it had had time to turn into their own road. Then like a monumental statue coming to life, she bent her head slowly and gazed, as if through the very heart of mystery, down into the pig parlor at the hogs. They had settled all in one corner around the old sow who was grunting softly. A red glow suffused them. They appeared to pant with a secret life.

Until the sun slipped finally behind the tree line, Mrs. Turpin remained there with her gaze bent to them as if she were absorbing some abysmal life-giving knowledge. At last she lifted her head. There was only a purple streak in the sky, cutting through a field of crimson and leading, like an extension of the highway, into the descending dusk. She raised her hands from the side of the pen in a gesture hieratic and profound. A visionary light settled in her eyes. She saw the streak as a vast swinging bridge extending upward from the earth through a field of living fire. Upon it a vast horde of souls were rumbling toward heaven. There were whole companies of white-trash, clean for the first time in their lives, and bands of black niggers in white robes, and battalions of freaks and lunatics shouting and clapping and leaping like frogs. And bringing up the end of the procession was a tribe of people whom she recognized at once as those who, like herself and Claud, had always had a little of everything and the God-given wit to use it right. She leaned forward to observe them closer. They were marching behind the others with great dignity, accountable as they had always been for good order and common sense and respectable behavior. They alone were on key. Yet she could see by their shocked and altered faces that even their virtues were being burned away. She lowered her hands and gripped the rail of the hog pen, her eyes small but fixed unblinkingly on what lay ahead. In a moment the vision faded but she remained where she was, immobile.

At length she got down and turned off the faucet and made her slow way on the darkening path to the house. In the woods around her the invisible cricket choruses had struck up, but what she heard were the voices of the souls climbing upward into the starry field and shouting hallelujah.

poems

Anonymous

Western Wind

> Western wind, when wilt thou blow,
> The small rain down can rain?
> Christ, if my love were in my arms,
> And I in my bed again!

William Shakespeare / 1564–1616

When in Disgrace with Fortune and Men's Eyes

> When in disgrace with fortune and men's eyes
> I all alone beweep my outcast state,
> And trouble deaf Heaven with my bootless cries,
> And look upon myself, and curse my fate,
> Wishing me like to one more rich in hope,
> Featured like him, like him with friends possessed,
> Desiring this man's art, and that man's scope,
> With what I most enjoy contented least;
> Yet in these thoughts myself almost despising,
> Haply I think on thee,—and then my state,   10
> Like to the lark at break of day arising
> From sullen earth, sings hymns at Heaven's gate:
> > For thy sweet love remembered such wealth brings
> > That then I scorn to change my state with kings.

sonnet 29

When to the Sessions of Sweet Silent Thought

> When to the sessions of sweet silent thought
> I summon up remembrance of things past,
> I sigh the lack of many a thing I sought,
> And with old woes new wail my dear time's waste:
> Then can I drown an eye, unused to flow,

For precious friends hid in death's dateless[1] night,
And weep afresh love's long since cancelled woe,
And moan the expense of many a vanished sight:
Then can I grieve at grievances foregone,[2]
And heavily from woe to woe tell o'er   10
The sad account of fore-bemoanèd moan,
Which I new pay as if not paid before.
    But if the while I think on thee, dear friend,
    All losses are restored and sorrows end.

sonnet 30

Since Brass, nor Stone, nor Earth, nor Boundless Sea

Since brass, nor stone, nor earth, nor boundless sea,
But sad mortality o'ersways their power,
How with this rage shall beauty hold a plea,
Whose action is no stronger than a flower?
O! how shall summer's honey breath hold out
Against the wrackful[3] siege of battering days,
When rocks impregnable are not so stout,
Nor gates of steel so strong, but Time decays?
O fearful meditation! where, alack,
Shall Time's best jewel from Time's chest[4] lie hid?   10
Or what strong hand can hold his swift foot back?
Or who his spoil of beauty can forbid?
    O! none, unless this miracle have might,
    That in black ink my love may still shine bright.

sonnet 65

✗That Time of Year Thou Mayst in Me Behold

That time of year thou mayst in me behold
When yellow leaves, or none, or few, do hang
Upon those boughs which shake against the cold,
Bare ruined choirs, where late the sweet birds sang.
In me thou see'st the twilight of such day

---

[1] Endless.   [2] Past.   [3] Destructive.   [4] Treasury.

244 / *William Shakespeare*

As after sunset fadeth in the west;
Which by and by black night doth take away,
Death's second self, that seals up all in rest.
In me thou see'st the glowing of such fire,
That on the ashes of his youth doth lie,   10
As the death-bed whereon it must expire,
Consumed with that which it was nourished by.
   This thou perceiv'st, which makes thy love more strong,
   To love that well which thou must leave ere long.

sonnet 73

My Mistress' Eyes Are Nothing like the Sun

My mistress' eyes are nothing like the sun;
Coral is far more red than her lips' red:
If snow be white, why then her breasts are dun;
If hairs be wires, black wires grow on her head.
I have seen roses damasked,[5] red and white,
But no such roses see I in her cheeks;
And in some perfumes is there more delight
Than in the breath that from my mistress reeks.
I love to hear her speak, yet well I know
That music hath a far more pleasing sound: 10
I grant I never saw a goddess go,—
My mistress, when she walks, treads on the ground:
   And yet, by heaven, I think my love as rare
   As any she belied with false compare.

sonnet 130

Song: from The Tempest

Full fathom five thy father lies,
   Of his bones are coral made,
Those are pearls that were his eyes.
   Nothing of him that doth fade
But doth suffer a sea change

---

[5] Of different colors.

Into something rich and strange.
Sea nymphs hourly ring his knell.
BURDEN:[6] Ding-dong.
Hark! Now I hear them,—Ding-dong, bell.

John Donne / 1572?-1631

Song

Go, and catch a falling star,
  Get with child a mandrake[1] root,
Tell me, where all past years are,
  Or who cleft the devil's foot,
Teach me to hear mermaids singing,
Or to keep off envy's stinging,
    And find
    What wind
Serves to advance an honest mind.

If thou be'st born to strange sights,   10
  Things invisible to see,
Ride ten thousand days and nights,
  Till age snow white hairs on thee,
Thou, when thou return'st, wilt tell me
All strange wonders that befell thee,
    And swear
    Nowhere
Lives a woman true, and fair.

If thou find'st one, let me know,
  Such a pilgrimage were sweet;   20
Yet do not, I would not go,
  Though at next door we might meet,
Though she were true, when you met her,
And last, till you write your letter,
    Yet she
    Will be
False, ere I come, to two, or three.

[6] Refrain.

---

[1] The mandragora plant which, with its forked root suggesting the lower part of the human body, was thought to shriek when pulled up.

Woman's Constancy

Now thou hast loved me one whole day,
Tomorrow when thou leav'st, what wilt thou say?
Wilt thou then antedate some new-made vow?
    Or say that now
We are not just those persons, which we were?
Or, that oaths made in reverential fear
Of Love, and his wrath, any may forswear?
Or, as true deaths true marriages untie,
So lovers' contracts, images of those,
Bind but till sleep, death's image, them unloose?   10
    Or, your own end to justify,
For having purposed change, and falsehood, you
Can have no way but falsehood to be true?
Vain lunatic, against these 'scapes[2] I could
    Dispute, and conquer, if I would,
    Which I abstain to do,
For by tomorrow, I may think so too.

A Valediction: Forbidding Mourning

As virtuous men pass mildly away,
   And whisper to their souls, to go,
Whilst some of their sad friends do say,
   The breath goes now, and some say, no:

So let us melt, and make no noise,
   No tear-floods, nor sigh-tempests move,
'Twere profanation of our joys
   To tell the laity our love.

Moving of th' earth brings harms and fears,
   Men reckon what it did and meant,   10
But trepidation of the spheres,
   Though greater far, is innocent.[3]

---

[2] Excuses.
[3] The stanza says that earthquakes are alarming and catastrophic but the much greater movement of the heavenly bodies is harmless.

Dull sublunary lovers' love
   (Whose soul is sense) cannot admit
Absence, because it doth remove
   Those things which elemented it.[4]

But we by a love, so much refined,
   That ourselves know not what it is,
Interassurèd of the mind,
   Care less eyes, lips, and hands to miss.   20

Our two souls therefore, which are one,
   Though I must go, endure not yet
A breach, but an expansion,
   Like gold to airy thinness beat.

If they be two, they are two so
   As stiff twin compasses are two,
Thy soul the fixed foot, makes no show
   To move, but doth, if th' other do.

And though it in the center sit,
   Yet when the other far doth roam,   30
It leans, and hearkens after it,
   And grows erect, as that comes home.

Such wilt thou be to me, who must
   Like th' other foot, obliquely run;
Thy firmness makes my circle just,
   And makes me end, where I begun.

At the Round Earth's Imagined Corners, Blow

At the round earth's imagined corners, blow
Your trumpets, angels, and arise, arise
From death, you numberless infinities
Of souls, and to your scattered bodies go,
All whom the flood did, and fire shall o'erthrow,
All whom war, dearth, age, agues, tyrannies,
Despair, law, chance, hath slain, and you whose eyes
Shall behold God, and never taste death's woe.[5]
But let them sleep, Lord, and me mourn a space,

[4] Which composed it.
[5] Those who are living at the time of the Last Judgment.

For, if above all these, my sins abound, 10
'Tis late to ask abundance of Thy grace,
When we are there; here on this lowly ground,
Teach me how to repent; for that's as good
As if Thou hadst sealed my pardon, with Thy blood.

Holy Sonnet 7

Death Be Not Proud, Though Some Have Callèd Thee

Death be not proud, though some have callèd thee
Mighty and dreadful, for thou art not so,
For those whom thou think'st thou dost overthrow,
Die not, poor Death, nor yet canst thou kill me.
From rest and sleep, which but thy pictures be,
Much pleasure, then from thee, much more must flow,
And soonest our best men with thee do go,
Rest of their bones, and soul's delivery.
Thou art slave to fate, chance, kings, and desperate men,
And dost with poison, war, and sickness dwell, 10
And poppy, or charms can make us sleep as well,
And better than thy stroke; why swell'st thou then?
One short sleep past, we wake eternally,
And Death shall be no more; Death, thou shalt die.

Holy Sonnet 10

Batter My Heart, Three-Personed God; for, You ✕

Batter my heart, three-personed God; for, You
As yet but knock, breathe, shine, and seek to mend;
That I may rise and stand, o'erthrow me, and bend
Your force, to break, blow, burn, and make me new.
I, like an usurped town, to another due,
Labour to admit You, but oh, to no end,
Reason, Your viceroy in me, me should defend,
But is captived, and proves weak or untrue.
Yet dearly I love You, and would be lovèd fain,
But am betrothed unto Your enemy: 10
Divorce me, untie, or break that knot again,
Take me to You, imprison me, for I

Except You enthrall me, never shall be free,
Nor ever chaste, except You ravish me.

Holy Sonnet 14

Ben Jonson / 1572–1637

On My First Son

Farewell, thou child of my right hand, and joy;
   My sin was too much hope of thee, loved boy,
Seven years thou wert lent to me, and I thee pay,
   Exacted by thy fate, on the just day.
O, could I lose all father,[1] now. For why
   Will man lament the state he should envy?
To have so soon 'scaped world's and flesh's rage,
   And, if no other misery, yet age?
Rest in soft peace, and, asked, say here doth lie
   Ben Jonson his best piece of poetry.   10
For whose sake, henceforth, all his vows be such,
   As what he loves may never like too much.

To Heaven

Good and great God! can I not think of Thee,
But it must straight my melancholy be?
Is it interpreted in me disease,
That, laden with my sins, I seek for ease?
O be Thou witness, that the reins[2] dost know
And hearts of all, if I be sad for show;
And judge me after, if I dare pretend
To aught but grace, or aim at other end.
As Thou art all, so be Thou all to me,
First, midst, and last, converted [3] One and Three!   10
My faith, my hope, my love; and, in this state,

---

[1] All sense of being a father.
[2] The kidneys, thought to be the seat of the feelings.
[3] Appearing as.

My judge, my witness, and my advocate!
Where have I been this while exiled from Thee,
And whither rapt,[4] now Thou but stoop'st to me?
Dwell, dwell here still! O, being everywhere,
How can I doubt to find Thee ever here?
I know my state, both full of shame and scorn,
Conceived in sin, and unto labour born,
Standing with fear, and must with horror fall,
And destined unto judgment, after all.   20
I feel my griefs too, and there scarce is ground
Upon my flesh t' inflict another wound;—
Yet dare I not complain or wish for death,
With holy Paul,[5] lest it be thought the breath
Of discontent; or that these prayers be
For weariness of life, not love of Thee.

John Milton / 1608–1674

On Shakespeare

What[1] needs my Shakespeare for his honoured bones
The labour of an age in pilèd stones?
Or that his hallowed reliques should be hid
Under a star-ypointing[2] pyramid?
Dear son of memory, great heir of fame,
What need'st thou such weak witness of thy name?
Thou in our wonder and astonishment
Hast built thyself a livelong monument.
For whilst, to the shame of slow-endeavouring art,
Thy easy numbers flow, and that each heart   10
Hath from the leaves of thy unvalued [3] book
Those Delphic lines[4] with deep impression took,
Then thou, our fancy of itself bereaving,
Dost make us marble with too much conceiving,

[4] Taken.   [5] As he does in Romans 7:24.

[1] Why.
[2] Milton affixed the *y* to *pointing* for the sake of the rhythm.
[3] Invaluable.
[4] Inspired, as by the oracle at Delphi.

And so sepùlchred in such pomp dost lie
That kings for such a tomb would wish to die.[5]

When I Consider How My Light Is Spent

When I consider how my light is spent,
    Ere half my days[6] in this dark world and wide,
    And that one talent which is death to hide[7]
    Lodged with me useless, though my soul more bent
To serve therewith my Maker, and present
    My true account, lest He returning chide,
    "Doth God exact day-labour, light denied?"
    I fondly[8] ask. But Patience, to prevent
That murmur, soon replies, "God doth not need
    Either man's work or His own gifts; who best   10
    Bear His mild yoke, they serve Him best. His state
Is kingly: thousands[9] at His bidding speed,
    And post o'er land and ocean without rest;
    They also serve who only stand and wait."

Methought I Saw My Late Espousèd Saint

Methought I saw my late espousèd saint[10]
    Brought to me like Alcestis from the grave,
    Whom Jove's great son to her glad husband gave,
    Rescued from death by force, though pale and faint.[11]
Mine, as whom washed from spot of child-bed taint
    Purification in the Old Law did save,[12]
    And such as yet once more I trust to have
    Full sight of her in Heaven without restraint,
Came vested all in white, pure as her mind.
    Her face was veiled;[13] yet to my fancied sight   10

---

[5] The last four lines mean that our imagination, so struck by Shakespeare's greater power, leaves us as speechless as marble, and so we become his monument.
[6] Milton was about forty-three when he became totally blind.
[7] See the parable of the talents, Matthew 25:15–30.
[8] Foolishly.   [9] Of angels.
[10] Katherine Woodcock, Milton's second wife, who died in childbirth in 1658.
[11] In Euripides' play, Alcestis dies to save the life of her husband, Admetus, but is brought back from Hades by Heracles.
[12] In Hebrew law a woman underwent a purification ritual after childbirth.
[13] Like Alcestis, but also because Milton had never seen her face.

Love, sweetness, goodness, in her person shined
So clear as in no face with more delight.
But O as to embrace me she inclined,
I waked, she fled, and day brought back my night.

Andrew Marvell / 1621–1678

To His Coy Mistress

Had we but world enough, and time,
This coyness,[1] Lady, were no crime.
We would sit down, and think which way
To walk, and pass our long love's day.
Thou by the Indian Ganges' side
Shouldst rubies find; I by the tide
Of Humber would complain.[2] I would
Love you ten years before the Flood,[3]
And you should, if you please, refuse
Till the conversion of the Jews.   10
My vegetable[4] love should grow
Vaster than empires and more slow;
An hundred years should go to praise
Thine eyes, and on thy forehead gaze;
Two hundred to adore each breast,
But thirty thousand to the rest;
An age at least to every part,
And the last age should show your heart.
For, Lady, you deserve this state,
Nor would I love at lower rate.   20
    But at my back I always hear
Time's wingèd chariot hurrying near;
And yonder all before us lie
Deserts of vast eternity.
Thy beauty shall no more be found,
Nor, in thy marble vault, shall sound
My echoing song; then worms shall try

---

[1] Modesty, inaccessibility.
[2] Make his love complaints beside this river on which his town was situated.
[3] The biblical flood.   [4] Growing like a plant.

That long-preserved virginity,
And your quaint[5] honour turn to dust,
And into ashes all my lust: 30
The grave's a fine and private place,
But none, I think, do there embrace.
    Now therefore, while the youthful hue
Sits on thy skin like morning lew,[6]
And while thy willing soul transpires[7]
At every pore with instant fires,
Now let us sport us while we may,
And now, like amorous birds of prey,
Rather at once our time devour
Than languish in his slow-chapped [8] power.   40
Let us roll all our strength and all
Our sweetness up into one ball,
And tear our pleasures with rough strife
Thorough the iron gates of life;
Thus, though we cannot make our sun
Stand still, yet we will make him run.

The Garden

    How vainly men themselves amaze,[9]
To win the palm, the oak, or bays,
And their incessant labours see
Crowned from some single herb, or tree,
Whose short and narrow-vergèd shade
Does prudently their toils upbraid;
While all the flowers and trees do close
To weave the garlands of repose!

    Fair Quiet, have I found thee here,
And Innocence, thy sister dear?   10
Mistaken long, I sought you then
In busy companies of men.
Your sacred plants, if here below,
Only among the plants will grow;
Society is all but rude
To[10] this delicious solitude.

---

[5] Proud.   [6] Warmth.   [7] Emerges.   [8] Slow-jawed.
[9] Bewilder.   [10] Compared to.

No white nor red [11] was ever seen
So amorous[12] as this lovely green.
Fond lovers, cruel as their flame,
Cut in these trees their mistress' name: 20
Little, alas, they know or heed
How far these beauties hers exceed!
Fair trees, wheresoe'er your barks I wound,
No name shall but your own be found.

When we have run our passion's heat,
Love hither makes his best retreat.
The gods, that mortal beauty chase,
Still in a tree did end their race:
Apollo hunted Daphne so,
Only that she might laurel grow;   30
And Pan did after Syrinx speed,
Not as a nymph, but for a reed.[13]

What wondrous life is this I lead!
Ripe apples drop about my head;
The luscious clusters of the vine
Upon my mouth do crush their wine;
The nectarine and curious[14] peach
Into my hands themselves do reach;
Stumbling on melons, as I pass,
Ensnared with flowers, I fall on grass.   40

Meanwhile the mind, from pleasure less,
Withdraws into its happiness;
The mind, that ocean where each kind
Does straight its own resemblance find;
Yet it creates, transcending these,
Far other worlds, and other seas,
Annihilating all that's made
To a green thought in a green shade.

Here at the fountain's sliding foot,
Or at some fruit-tree's mossy root,   50
Casting the body's vest aside,
My soul into the boughs does glide:

[11] Of a lady's complexion.   [12] Attractive.
[13] In Greek mythology, Apollo pursued Daphne, who turned into a laurel, and
Pan pursued Syrinx, who turned into a clump of reeds from which Pan made his
pipes.
[14] Rare, delicate.

There, like a bird, it sits and sings,
Then whets and combs its silver wings,
And, till prepared for longer flight,
Waves in its plumes the various light.

Such was that happy garden-state,
While man there walked without a mate:
After a place so pure and sweet,
What other help could yet be meet! 60
But 'twas beyond a mortal's share
To wander solitary there:
Two paradises 'twere in one
To live in Paradise alone.

How well the skilful gardener drew
Of flowers and herbs, this dial new;
Where, from above, the milder sun
Does through a fragrant zodiac run;
And, as it works, the industrious bee
Computes its time as well as we! 70
How could such sweet and wholesome hours
Be reckoned but with herbs and flowers?

Edward Taylor / 1642?–1729

Huswifery[1]

Make me, O Lord, Thy spinning wheel complete.
   Thy Holy Word my distaff make for me.
Make mine affections Thy swift fliers neat
   And make my soul Thy holy spool to be.
   My conversation make to be Thy reel
   And reel the yarn thereon spun of Thy wheel.

Make me Thy loom then, knit therein this twine:
   And make Thy Holy Spirit, Lord, wind quills;
Then weave the web Thyself. The yarn is fine.

---

[1] The housewife's work is limited here to the making of homespun clothing. The first stanza deals with the spinning wheel, the second with the loom, and the third with putting on the finished garment.

Thine ordinances[2] make my fulling mills.[3]   10
Then dye the same in heavenly colours choice,
All pinked [4] with varnished [5] flowers of paradise.

Then clothe therewith mine understanding, will,
    Affections, judgment, conscience, memory,
My words, and actions, that their shine may fill
    My ways with glory and Thee glorify.
    Then mine apparel shall display before Ye
That I am clothed in holy robes for glory.

Jonathan Swift / 1667–1745

The Day of Judgment

With a whirl of thought oppressed,
I sunk from reverie to rest.
An horrid vision seized my head;
I saw the graves give up their dead!
Jove, armed with terrors, bursts the skies,
And thunder roars and lightning flies!
Amazed, confused, its fate unknown,
The world stands trembling at his throne!
While each pale sinner hung his head,
Jove, nodding, shook the heavens, and said: 10
"Offending race of humankind,
By nature, reason, *learning,* blind;
You who, through frailty, stepped aside;
And you, who never fell—*through pride:*
You who in different sects were shammed,
And come to see each other damned
(So some folk told you, but they knew
No more of Jove's designs than you)
—The world's mad business now is o'er,
And I resent these pranks no more.   20
—I to such blockheads set my wit!
I damn such fools—Go, go, you're *bit*." [1]

---

[2] The sacraments of the church.
[3] Places where the cloth is cleaned with Fuller's earth or soap.
[4] Decorated.   [5] Polished.

---

[1] An eighteenth-century expression meaning, "You've been had!"

To Lady Mary Wortley Montagu[1]

In beauty, or wit,
No mortal as yet
To question your empire has dared;
But men of discerning
Have thought that in learning,
To yield to a lady was hard.

Impertinent schools,
With musty dull rules,
Have reading to females denied:
So Papists refuse   10
The Bible to use,
Lest flocks should be wise as their guide.

'Twas a woman at first,
(Indeed she was cursed)
In Knowledge that tasted delight,
And sages agree
The laws should decree
To the first possessor the right.

Then bravely, fair Dame,
Resume the old claim,   20
Which to your whole sex does belong;
And let men receive,
From a second bright Eve,
The knowledge of right and of wrong.

But if the first Eve
Hard doom did receive,
When only one apple had she,
What a punishment new
Shall be found out for you,
Who tasting have robbed the whole tree?   30

---

[1] The most famous blue-stocking of the age, with whom Pope had a fantastic
kind of "literary" love affair.

Samuel Johnson / 1709–1784

London

A POEM IN IMITATION OF THE THIRD SATIRE OF JUVENAL

> *Quis ineptae*
> *Tam patiens urbis, tam ferreus ut teneat se?* [1]
>
> JUVENAL

Though grief and fondness in my breast rebel,
When injured THALES[2] bids the town farewell,
Yet still my calmer thoughts his choice commend,
I praise the hermit, but regret the friend,
Resolved at length, from vice and LONDON far,
To breathe in distant fields a purer air,
And, fixed on Cambria's solitary shore,
Give to St. David one true Briton more.
    For who would leave, unbribed, Hibernia's land,
Or change the rocks of Scotland for the Strand? [3]   10
There none are swept by sudden fate away,
But all whom hunger spares, with age decay:
Here malice, rapine, accident, conspire,
And now a rabble rages, now a fire;
Their ambush here relentless ruffians lay,
And here the fell attorney prowls for prey;
Here falling houses thunder on your head,
And here a female atheist talks you dead.
    While THALES waits the wherry that contains
Of dissipated wealth the small remains,   20
On Thames's banks, in silent thought we stood,
Where Greenwich smiles upon the silver flood:
Struck with the seat that gave Eliza[4] birth,

---

[1] "Who can be so tolerant of this unjust city, so made of iron, that he can contain himself?"
[2] Some friend, perhaps Richard Savage.
[3] Cambria is Wales; St. David, the patron saint of Wales; Hibernia, Ireland; and the Strand, a major London thoroughfare.
[4] Elizabeth I, who was born at Greenwich and reigned from 1558 to 1603.

We kneel, and kiss the consecrated earth;
In pleasing dreams the blissful age renew,
And call Britannia's glories back to view;
Behold her cross triumphant on the main,
The guard of commerce, and the dread of Spain,
Ere masquerades debauched, excise oppressed,
Or English honour grew a standing jest. 30

A transient calm the happy scenes bestow,
And for a moment lull the sense of woe.
At length awaking, with contemptuous frown,
Indignant THALES eyes the neighb'ring town.

Since worth, he cries, in these degen'rate days,
Wants even the cheap reward of empty praise;
In those cursed walls, devote to vice and gain,
Since unrewarded science toils in vain;
Since hope but sooths to double my distress,
And every moment leaves my little less; 40
While yet my steady steps no staff sustains,
And life still vig'rous revels in my veins;
Grant me, kind heaven, to find some happier place,
Where honesty and sense are no disgrace;
Some pleasing bank where verdant osiers play,
Some peaceful vale with nature's paintings gay;
Where once the harassed Briton found repose,
And safe in poverty defied his foes;
Some secret cell, ye powers, indulgent give.
Let —— live here, for —— has learned to live.[5] 50
Here let those reign, whom pensions can incite
To vote a patriot black, a courtier white;
Explain their country's dear-bought rights away,
And plead for pirates[6] in the face of day;
With slavish tenets taint our poisoned youth,
And lend a lie the confidence of truth.

Let such raise palaces, and manors buy,
Collect a tax, or farm a lottery,
With warbling eunuchs[7] fill a licensed stage,[8]
And lull to servitude a thoughtless age. 60

[5] These blanks for monosyllabic names cannot be filled.
[6] Spanish searchers of English merchant vessels for illegal trade with Spain's American possessions.
[7] Singers in the then popular Italian operas.
[8] The licensing act for theaters was recent.

Heroes, proceed! what bounds your pride shall hold?
What check restrain your thirst of power and gold?
Behold rebellious virtue quite o'erthrown,
Behold our fame, our wealth, our lives your own.

To such, a groaning nation's spoils are given,
When public crimes inflame the wrath of heaven:
But what, my friend, what hope remains for me,
Who start at theft, and blush at perjury?
Who scarce forbear, though BRITAIN's Court he sing,
To pluck a titled Poet's borrowed wing;[9]   70
A Statesman's logic unconvinced can hear,
And dare to slumber o'er the Gazetteer;[10]
Despise a fool in half his pension dressed,
And strive in vain to laugh at H——y's[11] jest.

Others with softer smiles, and subtler art,
Can sap the principles, or taint the heart;
With more address a lover's note convey,
Or bribe a virgin's innocence away.

Well may they rise, while I, whose rustic tongue
Ne'er knew to puzzle right, or varnish wrong,   80
Spurned as a beggar, dreaded as a spy,
Love unregarded, unlamented die.

For what but social guilt the friend endears?
Who shares Orgilio's[12] crimes, his fortune shares.
But thou, should tempting villainy present
All Marlb'rough hoarded, or all Villiers spent,[13]
Turn from the glitt'ring bribe thy scornful eye,
Nor sell for gold, what gold could never buy,
The peaceful slumber, self-approving day,
Unsullied fame, and conscience ever gay.   90

The cheated nation's happy fav'rites, see!
Mark whom the great caress, who frown on me!
LONDON! the needy villain's gen'ral home,

---

[9] Savage called himself "Volunteer Laureate," to the annoyance of the real Laureate, Colley Cibber.
[10] The official newspaper of the Walpole administration.
[11] John Lord Hervey, supporter of Walpole and confidant of the Queen.
[12] This figure, like the Balbo of line 150, is apparently without any specific prototype in contemporary London, and the names, like the characters, are Johnson's invention.
[13] Duke of Marlborough (1650–1722), famous military commander, thought to have profited from the War of Spanish Succession; George Villiers, 2nd Duke of Buckingham (1628–87), in and out of court favor in the previous century, and noted for his dissolute and reckless life.

The common shore of Paris and of Rome;
With eager thirst, by folly or by fate,
Sucks in the dregs of each corrupted state.
Forgive my transports on a theme like this,
I cannot bear a French metropolis.
　　Illustrious EDWARD! [14] from the realms of day,
The land of heroes and of saints survey;　　　　　　100
Nor hope the British lineaments to trace,
The rustic grandeur, or the surly grace,
But lost in thoughtless ease, and empty show,
Behold the warrior dwindled to a beau;
Sense, freedom, piety, refined away,
Of France the mimic, and of Spain the prey.
　　All that at home no more can beg or steal,
Or like a gibbet better than a wheel;
Hissed from the stage, or hooted from the court,
Their air, their dress, their politics import;　　　　110
Obsequious, artful, voluble and gay,
On Britain's fond credulity they prey.
No gainful trade their industry can 'scape,
They sing, they dance, clean shoes, or cure a clap;
All sciences a fasting Monsieur knows,
And bid him go to hell, to hell he goes.
　　Ah! what avails it, that, from slav'ry far,
I drew the breath of life in English air;
Was early taught a Briton's right to prize,
And lisp the tale of HENRY's[15] victories;　　　　　120
If the gulled conqueror receives the chain,
And flattery subdues when arms are vain?
　　Studious to please, and ready to submit,
The supple Gaul was born a parasite:
Still to his int'rest true, where'er he goes,
Wit, brav'ry, worth, his lavish tongue bestows;
In every face a thousand graces shine,
From every tongue flows harmony divine.
These arts in vain our rugged natives try,
Strain out with falt'ring diffidence a lie,　　　　　130
And get a kick for awkward flattery.
　　Besides, with justice, this discerning age

---

[14] Edward III, who reigned from 1327 to 1377.
[15] Henry V, who reigned from 1415 to 1422.

Admires their wond'rous talents for the stage:
Well may they venture on the mimic's art,
Who play from morn to night a borrowed part;
Practised their master's notions to embrace,
Repeat his maxims, and reflect his face;
With every wild absurdity comply,
And view each object with another's eye;
To shake with laughter ere the jest they hear,   140
To pour at will the counterfeited tear,
And as their patron hints the cold or heat,
To shake in dog-days, in December sweat.

    How, when competitors like these contend,
Can surly virtue hope to fix a friend?
Slaves that with serious impudence beguile,
And lie without a blush, without a smile;
Exalt each trifle, every vice adore,
Your taste in snuff, your judgment in a whore;
Can Balbo's eloquence applaud, and swear   150
He gropes[16] his breeches with a monarch's air.

    For arts like these preferred, admired, caressed,
They first invade your table, then your breast;
Explore your secrets with insidious art,
Watch the weak hour, and ransack all the heart;
Then soon your ill-placed confidence repay,
Commence your lords, and govern or betray.

    By numbers here from shame or censure free,
All crimes are safe, but hated poverty.
This, only this, the rigid law pursues,   160
This, only this, provokes the snarling muse.
The sober trader at a tattered cloak,
Wakes from his dream, and labours for a joke;
With brisker air the silken courtiers gaze,
And turn the varied taunt a thousand ways.
Of all the griefs that harass the distressed,
Sure the most bitter is a scornful jest;
Fate never wounds more deep the gen'rous heart,
Than when a blockhead's insult points the dart.

    Has heaven reserved, in pity to the poor,   170
No pathless waste, or undiscovered shore;
No secret island in the boundless main?

---

[16] Takes hold of.

No peaceful desert yet unclaimed by SPAIN?
Quick let us rise, the happy seats explore,
And bear oppression's insolence no more.
This mournful truth is every where confessed,
SLOW RISES WORTH, BY POVERTY DEPRESSED:
But here more slow, where all are slaves to gold,
Where looks are merchandise, and smiles are sold;
Where won by bribes, by flatteries implored,   180
The groom retails the favours of his lord.

But hark! th' affrighted crowd's tumultuous cries
Roll through the streets, and thunder to the skies;
Raised from some pleasing dream of wealth and power,
Some pompous palace, or some blissful bower,
Aghast you start, and scarce with aching sight
Sustain th' approaching fire's tremendous light;
Swift from pursuing horrors take your way,
And leave your little ALL to flames a prey;
Then through the world a wretched vagrant roam,   190
For where can starving merit find a home?
In vain your mournful narrative disclose,
While all neglect, and most insult your woes.

Should heaven's just bolts Orgilio's wealth confound,
And spread his flaming palace on the ground,
Swift o'er the land the dismal rumour flies,
And public mournings pacify the skies;
The laureat tribe in servile verse relate,
How virtue wars with persecuting fate;
With well-feigned gratitude the pensioned band   200
Refund the plunder of the beggared land.
See! while he builds, the gaudy vassals come,
And crowd with sudden wealth the rising dome;[17]
The price of boroughs and of souls restore,
And raise his treasures higher than before.
Now blessed with all the baubles of the great,
The polished marble, and the shining plate,
Orgilio sees the golden pile aspire
And hopes from angry heaven another fire.

Could'st thou resign the park and play content,   210
For the fair banks of Severn or of Trent;
There might'st thou find some elegant retreat,
Some hireling senator's deserted seat;

[17] Palace.

And stretch thy prospects o'er the smiling land,
For less than rent the dungeons of the Strand;
There prune thy walks, support thy drooping flowers,
Direct thy rivulets, and twine thy bowers;
And, while thy grounds a cheap repast afford,
Despise the dainties of a venal lord:
There every bush with nature's music rings, 220
There every breeze bears health upon its wings;
On all thy hours security shall smile,
And bless thine evening walk and morning toil.
    Prepare for death, if here at night you roam,
And sign your will before you sup from home.
Some fiery fop, with new commission vain,
Who sleeps on brambles till he kills his man;
Some frolic drunkard, reeling from a feast,
Provokes a broil, and stabs you for a jest.
Yet even these heroes, mischievously gay, 230
Lords of the street, and terrors of the way;
Flushed as they are with folly, youth and wine,
Their prudent insults to the poor confine;
Afar they mark the flambeau's bright approach,
And shun the shining train, and golden coach.
    In vain, these dangers past, your doors you close,
And hope the balmy blessings of repose:
Cruel with guilt, and daring with despair,
The midnight murd'rer bursts the faithless bar;
Invades the sacred hour of silent rest, 240
And leaves, unseen, a dagger in your breast.
    Scarce can our fields, such crowds at Tyburn[18] die,
With hemp the gallows and the fleet supply.
Propose your schemes, ye Senatorian band,
Whose Ways and Means[19] support the sinking land;
Lest ropes be wanting in the tempting spring,
To rig another convoy for the k——g.[20]
    A single jail, in ALFRED'S[21] golden reign,
Could half the nation's criminals contain;
Fair Justice then, without constraint adored, 250
Held high the steady scale, but deeped the sword;[22]

[18] London's place of execution.
[19] House of Commons jargon for raising money.
[20] George II's frequent trips to Hanover. George II reigned from 1727 to 1760.
[21] King Alfred's reign, in legend, was ideal.
[22] Justice in her traditional pose, sword pointing down, meaning a suspended sentence.

No spies were paid, no special juries known,
Blest age! but ah! how different from our own!
    Much could I add,—but see the boat at hand,
The tide retiring, calls me from the land:
Farewell!—When youth, and health, and fortune spent,
Thou fly'st for refuge to the wilds of Kent;
And tired like me with follies and with crimes,
In angry numbers warn'st succeeding times;
Then shall thy friend, nor thou refuse his aid,   260
Still foe to vice, forsake his Cambrian shade;
In virtue's cause once more exert his rage,
Thy satire point, and animate thy page.

William Blake / 1757–1827

The Little Black Boy

My mother bore me in the southern wild,
And I am black, but O! my soul is white;
White as an angel is the English child,
But I am black, as if bereaved of light.

My mother taught me underneath a tree,
And, sitting down before the heat of day,
She took me on her lap and kissèd me,
And, pointing to the east, began to say:

"Look on the rising sun: there God does live,
And gives his light, and gives his heat away;   10
And flowers and trees and beasts and men receive
Comfort in morning, joy in the noonday.

"And we are put on earth a little space,
That we may learn to bear the beams of love;
And these black bodies and this sunburnt face
Is but a cloud, and like a shady grove.

"For when our souls have learned the heat to bear,
The cloud will vanish; we shall hear his voice,
Saying: 'Come out from the grove, my love and care,
And round my golden tent like lambs rejoice.' "   20

Thus did my mother say, and kissèd me;
And thus I say to little English boy.
When I from black and he from white cloud free,
And round the tent of God like lambs we joy,

I'll shade him from the heat till he can bear
To lean in joy upon our father's knee;
And then I'll stand and stroke his silver hair,
And be like him, and he will then love me.

The Divine Image

To Mercy, Pity, Peace, and Love
    All pray in their distress;
And to these virtues of delight
    Return their thankfulness.

For Mercy, Pity, Peace, and Love
    Is God, our father dear;
And Mercy, Pity, Peace, and Love
    Is Man, his child and care.

For Mercy has a human heart,
    Pity a human face,   10
And Love, the human form divine;
    And Peace, the human dress.

Then every man, of every clime,
    That prays in his distress,
Prays to the human form divine,
    Love, Mercy, Pity, Peace.

And all must love the human form,
    In heathen, turk, or jew;
Where Mercy, Love, and Pity dwell
    There God is dwelling too.   20

The Tyger

Tyger! Tyger! burning bright
In the forests of the night,
What immortal hand or eye
Could frame thy fearful symmetry?

In what distant deeps or skies
Burnt the fire of thine eyes?
On what wings dare he aspire?
What the hand dare sieze the fire?

And what shoulder, and what art,
Could twist the sinews of thy heart?   10
And when thy heart began to beat,
What dread hand? and what dread feet?

What the hammer? what the chain?
In what furnace was thy brain?
What the anvil? what dread grasp
Dare its deadly terrors clasp?

When the stars threw down their spears,[1]
And watered heaven with their tears,
Did he smile his work to see?
Did he who made the Lamb make thee?   20

Tyger! Tyger! burning bright
In the forests of the night,
What immortal hand or eye,
Dare frame thy fearful symmetry?

Ah! Sun-flower

Ah, Sun-flower! weary of time,
Who countest the steps of the Sun,
Seeking after that sweet golden clime
Where the traveller's journey is done:

Where the Youth pined away with desire,
And the pale Virgin shrouded in snow
Arise from their graves, and aspire[2]
Where my Sun-flower wishes to go.

[1] These stars represent the angels who rebelled against God.
[2] Soar.

The Garden of Love

I went to the Garden of Love,
And saw what I never had seen:
A Chapel was built in the midst,
Where I used to play on the green.

And the gates of this Chapel were shut,
And "Thou shalt not" writ over the door:
So I turned to the Garden of Love
That so many sweet flowers bore;

And I saw it was filled with graves,
And tomb-stones where flowers should be;   10
And Priests in black gowns were walking their rounds,
And binding with briars my joys and desires.

London

I wander through each chartered[3] street,
Near where the chartered Thames does flow,
And mark in every face I meet
Marks of weakness, marks of woe.

In every cry of every Man,
In every Infant's cry of fear,
In every voice, in every ban,[4]
The mind-forged manacles I hear.

How the Chimney-sweeper's cry
Every black'ning Church appalls;   10
And the hapless Soldier's sigh
Runs in blood down Palace walls.

But most through midnight streets I hear
How the youthful Harlot's curse
Blasts[5] the new born Infant's tear,
And blights with plagues the Marriage hearse.

---

[3] This word means both monopoly controlled and mapped.
[4] Curse.   [5] Dries up.

The Human Abstract

Pity would be no more
If we did not make somebody Poor;
And Mercy no more could be
If all were as happy as we.

And mutual fear brings peace,
Till the selfish loves increase:
Then Cruelty knits a snare,
And spreads his baits with care.

He sits down with holy fears,
And waters the ground with tears;   10
Then Humility takes its root
Underneath his foot.

Soon spreads the dismal shade
Of Mystery[6] over his head;
And the Caterpillar and Fly[7]
Feed on the Mystery.

And it bears the fruit of Deceit,
Ruddy and sweet to eat;
And the Raven[8] his nest has made
In its thickest shade.   20

The Gods of the earth and sea
Sought through Nature to find this Tree;
But their search was all in vain:
There grows one in the Human Brain.

A Divine Image

Cruelty has a Human Heart,
And Jealousy a Human Face;
Terror the Human Form Divine,
And Secrecy the Human Dress.

The Human Dress is forged Iron,
The Human Form a fiery Forge,
The Human Face a Furnace sealed,
The Human Heart its hungry Gorge.

[6] Dogmatic religion.   [7] Pests.   [8] Omen of death.

William Wordsworth / 1770–1850

Lines: Composed a Few Miles Above Tintern Abbey[1]

ON REVISITING THE BANKS OF THE WYE DURING A TOUR

Five years have past; five summers, with the length
Of five long winters! and again I hear
These waters, rolling from their mountain-springs
With a soft inland murmur.—Once again
Do I behold these steep and lofty cliffs,
That on a wild secluded scene impress
Thoughts of more deep seclusion; and connect
The landscape with the quiet of the sky.
The day is come when I again repose
Here, under this dark sycamore, and view   10
These plots of cottage-ground, these orchard-tufts,
Which at this season, with their unripe fruits,
Are clad in one green hue, and lose themselves
'Mid groves and copses. Once again I see
These hedge-rows, hardly hedge-rows, little lines
Of sportive wood run wild: these pastoral farms,
Green to the very door; and wreaths of smoke
Sent up, in silence, from among the trees!
With some uncertain notice, as might seem
Of vagrant dwellers in the houseless woods,   20
Or of some Hermit's cave, where by his fire
The Hermit sits alone.

             These beauteous forms,
Through a long absence, have not been to me
As is a landscape to a blind man's eye:
But oft, in lonely rooms, and 'mid the din
Of towns and cities, I have owed to them,
In hours of weariness, sensations sweet,
Felt in the blood, and felt along the heart;
And passing even into my purer mind,
With tranquil restoration:—feelings too   30
Of unremembered pleasure: such, perhaps,
As have no slight or trivial influence
On that best portion of a good man's life,

[1] A ruin by the river Wye.

His little, nameless, unremembered, acts
Of kindness and of love. Nor less, I trust,
To them I may have owed another gift,
Of aspect more sublime; that blessèd mood,
In which the burthen of the mystery,
In which the heavy and the weary weight
Of all this unintelligible world,   40
Is lightened:—that serene and blessèd mood,
In which the affections gently lead us on,—
Until, the breath of this corporeal frame
And even the motion of our human blood
Almost suspended, we are laid asleep
In body, and become a living soul:
While with an eye made quiet by the power
Of harmony, and the deep power of joy,
We see into the life of things.

                If this
Be but a vain belief, yet, oh! how oft—   50
In darkness and amid the many shapes
Of joyless daylight; when the fretful stir
Unprofitable, and the fever of the world,
Have hung upon the beatings of my heart—
How oft, in spirit, have I turned to thee,
O sylvan Wye! thou wanderer through the woods,
How often has my spirit turned to thee!

    And now, with gleams of half-extinguished thought,
With many recognitions dim and faint,
And somewhat of a sad perplexity,   60
The picture of the mind revives again:
While here I stand, not only with the sense
Of present pleasure, but with pleasing thoughts
That in this moment there is life and food
For future years. And so I dare to hope,
Though changed, no doubt, from what I was when first
I came among these hills; when like a roe
I bounded o'er the mountains, by the sides
Of the deep rivers, and the lonely streams,
Wherever nature led: more like a man   70
Flying from something that he dreads, than one
Who sought the thing he loved. For nature then
(The coarser pleasures of my boyish days,
And their glad animal movements all gone by)

To me was all in all.—I cannot paint
What then I was. The sounding cataract
Haunted me like a passion: the tall rock,
The mountain, and the deep and gloomy wood,
Their colours and their forms, were then to me
An appetite; a feeling and a love,   80
That had no need of a remoter charm,
By thought supplied, nor any interest
Unborrowed from the eye.—That time is past,
And all its aching joys are now no more,
And all its dizzy raptures. Not for this
Faint[2] I, nor mourn nor murmur; other gifts
Have followed; for such loss, I would believe,
Abundant recompense. For I have learned
To look on nature, not as in the hour
Of thoughtless youth; but hearing oftentimes   90
The still, sad music of humanity,
Nor harsh nor grating, though of ample power
To chasten and subdue. And I have felt
A presence that disturbs me with the joy
Of elevated thoughts; a sense sublime
Of something far more deeply interfused,
Whose dwelling is the light of setting suns,
And the round ocean and the living air,
And the blue sky, and in the mind of man:
A motion and a spirit, that impels   100
All thinking things, all objects of all thought,
And rolls through all things. Therefore am I still
A lover of the meadows and the woods,
And mountains; and of all that we behold
From this green earth; of all the mighty world
Of eye, and ear,—both what they half create,
And what perceive; well pleased to recognise
In nature and the language of the sense
The anchor of my purest thoughts, the nurse,
The guide, the guardian of my heart, and soul   110
Of all my moral being.
                          Nor perchance,
If I were not thus taught, should I the more
Suffer my genial[3] spirits to decay:
For thou art with me here upon the banks

---

[2] Lose spirit or courage.
[3] Cheerful, enlivening.

Of this fair river; thou my dearest Friend,[4]
My dear, dear Friend; and in thy voice I catch
The language of my former heart, and read
My former pleasures in the shooting lights
Of thy wild eyes. Oh! yet a little while
May I behold in thee what I was once,   120
My dear, dear Sister! and this prayer I make,
Knowing that Nature never did betray
The heart that loved her; 'tis her privilege,
Through all the years of this our life, to lead
From joy to joy: for she can so inform
The mind that is within us, so impress
With quietness and beauty, and so feed
With lofty thoughts, that neither evil tongues,
Rash judgments, nor the sneers of selfish men,
Nor greetings where no kindness is, nor all   130
The dreary intercourse of daily life,
Shall e'er prevail against us, or disturb
Our cheerful faith, that all which we behold
Is full of blessings. Therefore let the moon
Shine on thee in thy solitary walk;
And let the misty mountain-winds be free
To blow against thee: and, in after years,
When these wild ecstasies shall be matured
Into a sober pleasure; when thy mind
Shall be a mansion for all lovely forms,   140
Thy memory be as a dwelling-place
For all sweet sounds and harmonies; oh! then,
If solitude, or fear, or pain, or grief,
Should be thy portion, with what healing thoughts
Of tender joy wilt thou remember me,
And these my exhortations! Nor, perchance—
If I should be where I no more can hear
Thy voice, nor catch from thy wild eyes these gleams
Of past existence—wilt thou then forget
That on the banks of this delightful stream   150
We stood together; and that I, so long
A worshipper of Nature, hither came
Unwearied in that service: rather say
With warmer love—oh! with far deeper zeal
Of holier love. Nor wilt thou then forget

[4] Dorothy Wordsworth, who accompanied her brother on his tour.

That after many wanderings, many years
Of absence, these steep woods and lofty cliffs,
And this green pastoral landscape, were to me
More dear, both for themselves and for thy sake!

A Slumber Did My Spirit Seal

A slumber did my spirit seal;
  I had no human fears:
She seemed a thing that could not feel
  The touch of earthly years.

No motion has she now, no force;
  She neither hears nor sees;
Rolled round in earth's diurnal course,
  With rocks, and stones, and trees.

London, 1802

Milton! thou shouldst be living at this hour:
England hath need of thee: she is a fen
Of stagnant waters: altar, sword, and pen,
Fireside, the heroic wealth of hall and bower,
Have forfeited their ancient English dower
Of inward happiness. We are selfish men;
Oh! raise us up, return to us again;
And give us manners, virtue, freedom, power.
Thy soul was like a Star, and dwelt apart;
Thou hadst a voice whose sound was like the sea: 10
Pure as the naked heavens, majestic, free,
So didst thou travel on life's common way,
In cheerful godliness; and yet thy heart
The lowliest duties on herself did lay.

The World Is Too Much with Us; Late and Soon

The world is too much with us; late and soon,
Getting and spending, we lay waste our powers:
Little we see in Nature that is ours;
We have given our hearts away, a sordid boon!

This Sea that bares her bosom to the moon;
The winds that will be howling at all hours,
And are up-gathered now like sleeping flowers;
For this, for everything, we are out of tune;
It moves us not.—Great God! I'd rather be
A Pagan suckled in a creed outworn;   10
So might I, standing on this pleasant lea,
Have glimpses that would make me less forlorn;
Have sight of Proteus rising from the sea;
Or hear old Triton blow his wreathèd horn.⁵

Samuel Taylor Coleridge / 1772–1834

This Lime-tree Bower My Prison

ADDRESSED TO CHARLES LAMB, OF THE INDIA HOUSE, LONDON

*In the June of 1797 some long-expected friends¹ paid a visit
to the author's cottage; and on the morning of their arrival,
he met with an accident, which disabled him from walking
during the whole time of their stay. One evening, when they
had left him for a few hours, he composed the following lines
in the garden-bower.*

Well, they are gone, and here must I remain,
This lime-tree bower my prison! I have lost
Beauties and feelings, such as would have been
Most sweet to my remembrance even when age
Had dimmed mine eyes to blindness! They, meanwhile,
Friends, whom I never more may meet again,
On springy heath, along the hill-top edge,
Wander in gladness, and wind down, perchance,
To that still roaring dell, of which I told;
The roaring dell, o'erwooded, narrow, deep,   10
And only speckled by the mid-day sun;
Where its slim trunk the ash from rock to rock
Flings arching like a bridge;—that branchless ash,

⁵ In classical mythology, Proteus and Triton are the sons of Neptune, god of the
sea.

¹ William and Dorothy Wordsworth and Charles Lamb.

Unsunned and damp, whose few poor yellow leaves
Ne'er tremble in the gale, yet tremble still,
Fanned by the water-fall! and there my friends
Behold the dark green file of long lank weeds,
That all at once (a most fantastic sight!)
Still nod and drip beneath the dripping edge
Of the blue clay-stone.

     Now, my friends emerge   20
Beneath the wide wide Heaven—and view again
The many-steepled tract magnificent
Of hilly fields and meadows, and the sea,
With some fair bark, perhaps, whose sails light up
The slip of smooth clear blue betwixt two Isles
Of purple shadow! Yes! they wander on
In gladness all; but thou, methinks, most glad,
My gentle-hearted Charles! [2] for thou hast pined
And hungered after Nature, many a year,
In the great City pent, winning thy way   30
With sad yet patient soul, through evil and pain
And strange calamity! [3] Ah! slowly sink
Behind the western ridge, thou glorious Sun!
Shine in the slant beams of the sinking orb,
Ye purple heath-flowers! richlier burn, ye clouds!
Live in the yellow light, ye distant groves!
And kindle, thou blue Ocean! So my friend
Struck with deep joy may stand, as I have stood,
Silent with swimming sense; yea, gazing round
On the wide landscape, gaze till all doth seem   40
Less gross than bodily; and of such hues
As veil the Almighty Spirit, when yet he makes
Spirits perceive his presence.

       A delight
Comes sudden on my heart, and I am glad
As I myself were there! Nor in this bower,
This little lime-tree bower, have I not marked
Much that has soothed me. Pale beneath the blaze
Hung the transparent foliage; and I watched
Some broad and sunny leaf, and loved to see
The shadow of the leaf and stem above   50
Dappling its sunshine! And that walnut-tree

[2] Lamb.
[3] Lamb's sister, Mary, had killed their mother in 1796 during a fit of insanity.

This Lime-tree Bower My Prison / 277

Was richly tinged, and a deep radiance lay
Full on the ancient ivy, which usurps
Those fronting elms, and now, with blackest mass
Makes their dark branches gleam a lighter hue
Through the late twilight: and though now the bat
Wheels silent by, and not a swallow twitters,
Yet still the solitary humble-bee
Sings in the bean-flower! Henceforth I shall know
That Nature ne'er deserts the wise and pure;   60
No plot so narrow, be but Nature there,
No waste so vacant, but may well employ
Each faculty of sense, and keep the heart
Awake to Love and Beauty! and sometimes
'Tis well to be bereft of promised good,
That we may lift the soul, and contemplate
With lively joy the joys we cannot share.
My gentle-hearted Charles! when the last rook
Beat its straight path along the dusky air
Homewards, I blest it! deeming its black wing   70
(Now a dim speck, now vanishing in light)
Had crossed the mighty Orb's dilated glory,
While thou stood'st gazing; or, when all was still,
Flew creeking o'er thy head, and had a charm
For thee, my gentle-hearted Charles, to whom
No sound is dissonant which tells of Life.

Kubla Khan: or, A Vision in a Dream

A FRAGMENT

*In the summer of the year 1797, the Author, then in ill
health, had retired to a lonely farm-house between Porlock
and Linton, on the Exmoor confines of Somerset and Devon-
shire. In consequence of a slight indisposition, an anodyne
had been prescribed, from the effect of which he fell asleep
in his chair at the moment he was reading the following
sentence, or words of the same substance, in "Purchas's Pilgrimage": "Here the Khan Kubla commanded a palace to be
built, and a stately garden thereunto. And thus ten miles of
fertile ground were inclosed with a wall." The Author continued for about three hours in a profound sleep, at least of
the external senses, during which time he has the most vivid*

confidence, that he could not have composed less than from two to three hundred lines; if that indeed can be called composition in which all the images rose up before him as things, with a parallel production of the correspondent expressions, without any sensation or consciousness of effort. On awaking he appeared to himself to have a distinct recollection of the whole, and taking his pen, ink, and paper, instantly and eagerly wrote down the lines that are here preserved. At this moment he was unfortunately called out by a person on business from Porlock, and detained by him above an hour, and on his return to his room, found, to his no small surprise and mortification, that though he still retained some vague and dim recollection of the general purport of the vision, yet, with the exception of some eight or ten scattered lines and images, all the rest had passed away like the images on the surface of a stream into which a stone has been cast, but, alas! without the after restoration of the latter!

> Then all the charm
> Is broken—all that phantom-world so fair
> Vanishes, and a thousand circlets spread,
> And each mis-shape[s] the other. Stay awhile,
> Poor youth! who scarcely dar'st lift up thine eyes—
> The stream will soon renew its smoothness, soon
> The visions will return! And lo, he stays,
> And soon the fragments dim of lively forms
> Come trembling back, unite, and now once more
> The pool becomes a mirror.

[From Coleridge's "The Picture"]

Yet from the still surviving recollections in his mind, the Author has frequently purposed to finish for himself what had been originally, as it were, given to him Αὔριον ἄδιον ἄσω:[4] but the to-morrow is yet to come.

In Xanadu[5] did Kubla Khan
A stately pleasure-dome decree:
Where Alph, the sacred river, ran
Through caverns measureless to man
    Down to a sunless sea.

---

[4] "I will sing you a sweeter song tomorrow" (Theocritus, *Idylls,* I.145).
[5] Xanadu, spelled in several ways by Samuel Purchas, was probably near modern Peking. It was the seat of Kublai Khan (1216–94), grandson of Genghis Khan and founder of the Mongol dynasty in China.

So twice five miles of fertile ground
With walls and towers were girdled round:
And there were gardens bright with sinuous rills,
Where blossomed many an incense-bearing tree;
And here were forests ancient as the hills, 10
Enfolding sunny spots of greenery.

But oh! that deep romantic chasm which slanted
Down the green hill athwart a cedarn cover!
A savage place! as holy and enchanted
As e'er beneath a waning moon was haunted
By woman wailing for her demon-lover!
And from this chasm, with ceaseless turmoil seething,
As if this earth in fast thick pants were breathing,
A mighty fountain momently was forced:
Amid whose swift half-intermitted burst 20
Huge fragments vaulted like rebounding hail,
Or chaffy grain beneath the thresher's flail:
And 'mid these dancing rocks at once and ever
It flung up momently the sacred river.
Five miles meandering with a mazy motion
Through wood and dale the sacred river ran,
Then reached the caverns measureless to man,
And sank in tumult to a lifeless ocean:
And 'mid this tumult Kubla heard from far
Ancestral voices prophesying war! 30
   The shadow of the dome of pleasure
    Floated midway on the waves;
    Where was heard the mingled measure
    From the fountain and the caves.
It was a miracle of rare device,
A sunny pleasure-dome with caves of ice!

    A damsel with a dulcimer
    In a vision once I saw:
    It was an Abyssinian maid,
    And on her dulcimer she played, 40
    Singing of Mount Abora.
    Could I revive within me
    Her symphony and song,
    To such a deep delight 'twould win me,
That with music loud and long,
I would build that dome in air,

That sunny dome! those caves of ice!
And all who heard should see them there,
And all should cry, Beware! Beware!
His flashing eyes, his floating hair!   50
Weave a circle round him thrice,
And close your eyes with holy dread,
For he on honey-dew hath fed,
And drunk the milk of Paradise.

George Gordon, Lord Byron / 1788–1824

When We Two Parted

When we two parted
    In silence and tears,
Half broken-hearted
    To sever for years,
Pale grew thy cheek and cold,
    Colder thy kiss;
Truly that hour foretold
    Sorrow to this.

The dew of the morning
    Sunk chill on my brow—   10
It felt like the warning
    Of what I feel now.
Thy vows are all broken,
    And light is thy fame:
I hear thy name spoken,
    And share in its shame.

They name thee before me,
    A knell to mine ear;
A shudder comes o'er me—
    Why wert thou so dear?   20
They know not I knew thee,
    Who knew thee too well:—
Long, long shall I rue thee,
    Too deeply to tell.

In secret we met—
    In silence I grieve,
That thy heart could forget,
    Thy spirit deceive.
If I should meet thee
    After long years,   30
How should I greet thee?—
    With silence and tears.

So, We'll Go No More A-Roving

So, we'll go no more a-roving
    So late into the night,
Though the heart be still as loving,
    And the moon be still as bright.

For the sword outwears its sheath,
    And the soul outwears the breast,
And the heart must pause to breathe,
    And love itself have rest.

Though the night was made for loving,
    And the day returns too soon,   10
Yet we'll go no more a-roving
    By the light of the moon.

Percy Bysshe Shelley / 1792–1822

Ozymandias

I met a traveller from an antique land
Who said: Two vast and trunkless legs of stone
Stand in the desert . . . Near them, on the sand,
Half sunk, a shattered visage lies, whose frown,
And wrinkled lip, and sneer of cold command,
Tell that its sculptor well those passions read
Which yet survive, stamped on these lifeless things,

The hand that mocked[1] them, and the heart that fed:
And on the pedestal these words appear:
"My name is Ozymandias, king of kings: 10
Look on my works, ye Mighty, and despair!"
Nothing beside remains. Round the decay
Of that colossal wreck, boundless and bare
The lone and level sands stretch far away.

To ——

Music, when soft voices die,
Vibrates in the memory—
Odours, when sweet violets sicken,
Live within the sense they quicken.

Rose leaves, when the rose is dead,
Are heaped for the belovèd's bed;
And so thy thoughts, when thou art gone,
Love itself shall slumber on.

Sonnet: England in 1819

An old, mad, blind, despised, and dying king,—[2]
Princes, the dregs of their dull race, who flow
Through public scorn,—mud from a muddy spring,—
Rulers who neither see, nor feel, nor know,
But leech-like to their fainting country cling,
Till they drop, blind in blood, without a blow,—
A people starved and stabbed in the untilled field,—
An army, which liberticide and prey
Makes as a two-edged sword to all who wield,—
Golden and sanguine laws which tempt and slay;   10
Religion Christless, Godless—a book sealed;
A Senate,—Time's worst statute unrepealed,—[3]
Are graves, from which a glorious Phantom[4] may
Burst, to illumine our tempestuous day.

---

[1] Both imitated and derided.
[2] George III (1760–1820) became hopelessly insane in 1810.
[3] The law that restricted civil liberties of Roman Catholics; repealed in 1829.
[4] Liberty.

Two Fragments on the Moon

1

And like a dying lady, lean and pale,
Who totters forth, wrapped in a gauzy veil,
Out of her chamber, led by the insane
And feeble wanderings of her fading brain,
The moon arose up in the murky east,
A white and shapeless mass.

2

Art thou pale for weariness
Of climbing heaven and gazing on the earth,
Wandering companionless
Among the stars that have a different birth,
And ever changing, like a joyless eye
That finds no object worth its constancy? . . .

John Keats / 1795–1821

On First Looking into Chapman's Homer[1]

Much have I travelled in the realms of gold,
And many goodly states and kingdoms seen;
Round many western islands have I been
Which bards in fealty to Apollo[2] hold.
Oft of one wide expanse had I been told
That deep-browed Homer ruled as his demesne;
Yet did I never breathe its pure serene
Till I heard Chapman speak out loud and bold:
Then felt I like some watcher of the skies
When a new planet swims into his ken;   10
Or like stout Cortez[3] when with eagle eyes
He stared at the Pacific—and all his men
Looked at each other with a wild surmise—
Silent, upon a peak in Darien.[4]

[1] George Chapman (1559?–1634), Elizabethan poet and translator of classics.
[2] God of poetry and music.
[3] Balboa, not Cortez.
[4] Eastern part of the Isthmus of Panama.

La Belle Dame sans Merci[5]

O, what can ail thee, knight-at-arms,
    Alone and palely loitering?
The sedge has withered from the lake,
    And no birds sing.

O, what can ail thee, knight-at-arms,
    So haggard and so woe-begone?
The squirrel's granary is full,
    And the harvest's done.

I see a lily on thy brow,
    With anguish moist and fever dew,   10
And on thy cheeks a fading rose
    Fast withereth too.

I met a lady in the meads,
    Full beautiful—a faery's child,
Her hair was long, her foot was light,
    And her eyes were wild.

I made a garland for her head,
    And bracelets too, and fragrant zone;[6]
She looked at me as she did love,
    And made sweet moan.   20

I set her on my pacing steed,
    And nothing else saw all day long,
For sidelong would she bend and sing
    A faery's song.

She found me roots of relish sweet,
    And honey wild, and manna dew,
And sure in language strange she said,
    "I love thee true."

She took me to her elfin grot,
    And there she wept and sighed full sore,   30
And there I shut her wild wild eyes
    With kisses four.

And there she lullèd me asleep
    And there I dreamed—Ah! woe betide!

---

[5] Keats took his title, "The Beautiful Lady Without Pity," from a medieval French poem by Alain Chartier.
[6] Girdle.

The latest dream I ever dreamed
  On the cold hill side.

I saw pale kings and princes too,
  Pale warriors, death-pale were they all;
They cried, "La Belle Dame sans Merci
  Hath thee in thrall!"   40

I saw their starved lips in the gloam
  With horrid warning gapèd wide,
And I awoke and found me here
  On the cold hill's side.

And this is why I sojourn here
  Alone and palely loitering,
Though the sedge is withered from the lake,
  And no birds sing.

Ode on a Grecian Urn

Thou still unravished bride of quietness,
  Thou foster-child of silence and slow time,
Sylvan historian, who canst thus express
  A flowery tale more sweetly than our rhyme:
What leaf-fringed legend haunts about thy shape
  Of deities or mortals, or of both,
    In Tempe or the dales of Arcady? [7]
  What men or gods are these? What maidens loth?
What mad pursuit? What struggle to escape?
    What pipes and timbrels? What wild ecstasy?   10

Heard melodies are sweet, but those unheard
  Are sweeter; therefore, ye soft pipes, play on;
Not to the sensual ear,[8] but, more endeared,
  Pipe to the spirit ditties of no tone:
Fair youth, beneath the trees, thou canst not leave
  Thy song, nor ever can those trees be bare;
    Bold Lover, never, never canst thou kiss,
Though winning near the goal—yet, do not grieve;
  She cannot fade, though thou hast not thy bliss,
    For ever wilt thou love, and she be fair!   20

[7] Tempe is a valley in Thessaly; Arcady is a mountainous region in Greece celebrated in pastoral poetry.
[8] The physical sense of hearing.

Ah, happy, happy boughs! that cannot shed
   Your leaves, nor ever bid the Spring adieu;
And, happy melodist, unwearièd,
   For ever piping songs for ever new;
More happy love! more happy, happy love!
   For ever warm and still to be enjoyed,
     For ever panting, and for ever young;
All breathing human passion far above,
   That leaves a heart high-sorrowful and cloyed,
     A burning forehead, and a parching tongue.   30

Who are these coming to the sacrifice?
   To what green altar, O mysterious priest,
Lead'st thou that heifer lowing at the skies,
   And all her silken flanks with garlands drest?
What little town[9] by river or sea shore,
   Or mountain-built with peaceful citadel,
     Is emptied of this folk, this pious morn?
And, little town, thy streets for evermore
   Will silent be; and not a soul to tell
     Why thou art desolate, can e'er return.   40

O Attic[10] shape! Fair attitude! with brede[11]
   Of marble men and maidens overwrought,
With forest branches and the trodden weed;
   Thou, silent form, dost tease us out of thought
As doth eternity: Cold Pastoral! [12]
   When old age shall this generation waste,
     Thou shalt remain, in midst of other woe
Than ours, a friend to man, to whom thou say'st,
   "Beauty is truth, truth beauty,—that is all
     Ye know on earth, and all ye need to know." [13]   50

[9] The town is not pictured on the urn. Keats imagines it is "desolate" because the people on the urn can never return to it.
[10] From Attica, or Athens.   [11] Embroidery.
[12] A pastoral scene, removed from life, forever fixed.
[13] Scholars disagree about whether the end quotation marks belong here or after the fifth word in line 49.

Ulysses

It little profits that an idle king,
By this still hearth, among these barren crags,
Matched with an agèd wife, I mete and dole
Unequal laws unto a savage race,
That hoard, and sleep, and feed, and know not me.
I cannot rest from travel: I will drink
Life to the lees: all times I have enjoyed
Greatly, have suffered greatly, both with those
That loved me, and alone; on shore, and when
Through scudding drifts the rainy Hyades[1]   10
Vext the dim sea: I am become a name;
For always roaming with a hungry heart
Much have I seen and known,—cities of men
And manners, climates, councils, governments,
Myself not least, but honoured of them all,—
And drunk delight of battle with my peers,
Far on the ringing plains of windy Troy.
I am a part of all that I have met;
Yet all experience is an arch wherethrough
Gleams that untravelled world, whose margin fades   20
For ever and for ever when I move.
How dull it is to pause, to make an end,
To rust unburnished, not to shine in use!
As though to breathe were life! Life piled on life
Were all too little, and of one to me
Little remains; but every hour is saved
From that eternal silence, something more,
A bringer of new things; and vile it were
For some three suns to store and hoard myself,
And this gray spirit yearning in desire   30
To follow knowledge like a sinking star,
Beyond the utmost bound of human thought.
    This is my son, mine own Telemachus,
To whom I leave the sceptre and the isle,—
Well-loved of me, discerning to fulfil
This labour, by slow prudence to make mild

---

[1] A group of stars in the constellation Taurus, associated with the rainy season.

A rugged people, and through soft degrees
Subdue them to the useful and the good.
Most blameless is he, centred in the sphere
Of common duties, decent not to fail   40
In offices of tenderness, and pay
Meet adoration to my household gods,
When I am gone. He works his work, I mine.
   There lies the port: the vessel puffs her sail:
There gloom the dark broad seas. My mariners,
Souls that have toiled, and wrought, and thought with me,—
That ever with a frolic welcome took
The thunder and the sunshine, and opposed
Free hearts, free foreheads,—you and I are old;
Old age hath yet his honour and his toil.   50
Death closes all: but something ere the end,
Some work of noble note, may yet be done,
Not unbecoming men that strove with Gods.
The lights begin to twinkle from the rocks:
The long day wanes: the slow moon climbs: the deep
Moans round with many voices. Come, my friends,
'Tis not too late to seek a newer world.
Push off, and sitting well in order smite
The sounding furrows; for my purpose holds
To sail beyond the sunset, and the baths[2]   60
Of all the western stars, until I die.
It may be that the gulfs[3] will wash us down:
It may be we shall touch the Happy Isles,[4]
And see the great Achilles,[5] whom we knew.
Though much is taken, much abides; and though
We are not now that strength which in old days
Moved earth and heaven, that which we are, we are,—
One equal temper of heroic hearts,
Made weak by time and fate, but strong in will
To strive, to seek, to find, and not to yield.   70

---

[2] Seas into which the stars descend.   [3] Whirlpools.   [4] Elysium.
[5] Tennyson's dead friend, Arthur Hallam?

The Splendour Falls on Castle Walls

The splendour falls on castle walls
And snowy summits old in story:
The long light shakes across the lakes,
And the wild cataract leaps in glory.
Blow, bugle, blow, set the wild echoes flying,
Blow, bugle; answer, echoes, dying, dying, dying.

O hark, O hear! how thin and clear,
And thinner, clearer, farther going!
O sweet and far from cliff and scar
The horns of Elfland faintly blowing!   10
Blow, let us hear the purple glens replying:
Blow, bugle; answer, echoes, dying, dying, dying.

O love, they die in yon rich sky,
They faint on hill or field or river:
Our echoes roll from soul to soul,
And grow for ever and for ever.
Blow, bugle, blow, set the wild echoes flying,
And answer, echoes, answer, dying, dying, dying.

from *O That 'Twere Possible*

O that 'twere possible
After long grief and pain
To find the arms of my true love
Round me once again! . . .

A shadow flits before me,
Not thou, but like to thee:
Ah, Christ! that it were possible
For one short hour to see
The souls we loved, that they might tell us
What and where they be! . . .

Robert Browning / 1812–1889

My Last Duchess

FERRARA

That's my last Duchess painted on the wall,
Looking as if she were alive. I call
That piece a wonder, now: Frà Pandolf's[1] hands
Worked busily a day, and there she stands.
Will't please you sit and look at her? I said
"Frà Pandolf" by design, for never read
Strangers like you that pictured countenance,
The depth and passion of its earnest glance,
But to myself they turned (since none puts by
The curtain I have drawn for you, but I)   10
And seemed as they would ask me, if they durst,
How such a glance came there; so, not the first
Are you to turn and ask thus. Sir,[2] 'twas not
Her husband's presence only, called that spot
Of joy into the Duchess' cheek: perhaps
Frà Pandolf chanced to say, "Her mantle laps
Over my Lady's wrist too much," or "Paint
Must never hope to reproduce the faint
Half-flush that dies along her throat": such stuff
Was courtesy, she thought, and cause enough   20
For calling up that spot of joy. She had
A heart—how shall I say?—too soon made glad,
Too easily impressed: she liked whate'er
She looked on, and her looks went everywhere.
Sir, 'twas all one! My favour at her breast,
The dropping of the daylight in the West,
The bough of cherries some officious fool
Broke in the orchard for her, the white mule
She rode with round the terrace—all and each
Would draw from her alike the approving speech,   30
Or blush, at least. She thanked men,—good! but thanked
Somehow—I know not how—as if she ranked
My gift of a nine-hundred-years-old name

---

[1] An imaginary artist who was a friar.
[2] The ambassador of another nobleman with whom the Duke is negotiating for another wife.

With anybody's gift. Who'd stoop to blame
This sort of trifling? Even had you skill
In speech—(which I have not)—to make your will
Quite clear to such an one, and say, "Just this
Or that in you disgusts me; here you miss,
Or there exceed the mark"—and if she let
Herself be lessoned so, nor plainly set   40
Her wits to yours, forsooth, and made excuse,
—E'en then would be some stooping; and I choose
Never to stoop. Oh, Sir, she smiled, no doubt
Whene'er I passed her; but who passed without
Much the same smile? This grew; I gave commands;
Then all smiles stopped together. There she stands
As if alive. Will't please you rise? We'll meet
The company below, then. I repeat,
The Count your master's known munificence
Is ample warrant that no just pretence   50
Of mine for dowry will be disallowed;
Though his fair daughter's self, as I avowed
At starting, is my object. Nay, we'll go
Together down, Sir! Notice Neptune,[3] though,
Taming a sea-horse, thought a rarity,
Which Claus of Innsbruck[4] cast in bronze for me!

The Lost Leader[5]

Just for a handful of silver[6] he left us,
   Just for a riband[7] to stick in his coat—
Found the one gift of which fortune bereft us,
   Lost all the others she lets us devote;
They, with the gold to give, doled him out silver,
   So much was theirs who so little allowed;
How all our copper had gone for his service!
   Rags—were they purple, his heart had been proud!
We that had loved him so, followed him, honoured him,
   Lived in his mild and magnificent eye,   10
Learned his great language, caught his clear accents,
   Made him our pattern to live and to die!

[3] God of the sea.
[4] An imaginary artist from a city noted for its bronze work.
[5] William Wordsworth.
[6] The Civil List pension he accepted in 1842.
[7] The laureateship he accepted the next year.

Shakespeare was of us, Milton was for us,
    Burns, Shelley were with us—they watch from their graves!
He alone breaks from the van and the freemen,
    —He alone sinks to the rear and the slaves!

We shall march prospering—not through his presence;
    Songs may inspirit us—not from his lyre;
Deeds will be done—while he boasts his quiescence,
    Still bidding crouch whom the rest bade aspire;   20
Blot out his name, then, record one lost soul more,
    One task more declined, one more footpath untrod,
One more devils' triumph and sorrow for angels,
    One wrong more to man, one more insult to God!
Life's night begins; let him never come back to us!
    There would be doubt, hesitation, and pain,
Forced praise on our part—the glimmer of twilight,
    Never glad confident morning again!
Best fight on well, for we taught him—strike gallantly,
    Menace our heart ere we master his own;   30
Then let him receive the new knowledge and wait us,
    Pardoned in heaven, the first by the throne!

Memorabilia

    Ah, did you once see Shelley plain,
        And did he stop and speak to you,
    And did you speak to him again?
        How strange it seems and new!

    But you were living before that,
        And also you are living after;
    And the memory I started at—
        My starting moves your laughter!

    I crossed a moor, with a name of its own
        And a certain use in the world no doubt,   10
    Yet a handsbreadth of it shines alone
        'Mid the blank miles round about;

    For there I picked up on the heather,
        And there I put inside my breast
    A molted feather, an eagle feather!
        Well, I forget the rest.

There Was a Child Went Forth

There was a child went forth every day,
And the first object he looked upon, that object he became,
And that object became part of him for the day or a certain part of
the day,
Or for many years or stretching cycles of years.

The early lilacs became part of this child,
And grass and white and red morning-glories, and white and red clover,
and the song of the phoebe-bird,
And the Third-month lambs and the sow's pink-faint litter, and the
mare's foal and the cow's calf,
And the noisy brood of the barnyard or by the mire of the pond-side,
And the fish suspending themselves so curiously below there, and the
beautiful curious liquid,
And the water-plants with their graceful flat heads, all became part of
him.   10

The field-sprouts of Fourth-month and Fifth-month became part of
him,
Winter-grain sprouts and those of the light-yellow corn, and the escu-
lent roots of the garden,
And the apple-trees covered with blossoms and the fruit afterward, and
wood-berries, and the commonest weeds by the road,
And the old drunkard staggering home from the outhouse of the tavern
whence he had lately risen,
And the schoolmistress that passed on her way to the school,
And the friendly boys that passed, and the quarrelsome boys,
And the tidy and fresh-cheeked girls, and the barefoot negro boy and
girl,
And all the changes of city and country wherever he went.

His own parents, he that had fathered him and she that had conceived
him in her womb and birthed him,
They gave this child more of themselves than that,   20
They gave him afterward every day, they became part of him.

The mother at home quietly placing the dishes on the supper-table,
The mother with mild words, clean her cap and gown, a wholesome
odor falling off her person and clothes as she walks by,

The father, strong, self-sufficient, manly, mean, angered, unjust,
The blow, the quick loud word, the tight bargain, the crafty lure,
The family usages, the language, the company, the furniture, the yearn-
ing and swelling heart,
Affection that will not be gainsayed, the sense of what is real, the
thought if after all it should prove unreal,
The doubts of day-time and the doubts of night-time, the curious
whether and how,
Whether that which appears so is so, or is it all flashes and specks?
Men and women crowding fast in the streets, if they are not flashes
and specks what are they?   30
The streets themselves and the façades of houses, and goods in the
windows,
Vehicles, teams, the heavy-planked wharves, the huge crossing at the
ferries,
The village on the highland seen from afar at sunset, the river between,
Shadows, aureola and mist, the light falling on roofs and gables of
white or brown two miles off,
The schooner near by sleepily dropping down the tide, the little boat
slack-towed astern,
The hurrying tumbling waves, quick-broken crests, slapping,
The strata of colored clouds, the long bar of maroon-tint away solitary
by itself, the spread of purity it lies motionless in,
The horizon's edge, the flying sea-crow, the fragrance of salt marsh
and shore mud,
These became part of that child who went forth every day, and who
now goes, and will always go forth every day.

Out of the Cradle Endlessly Rocking

Out of the cradle endlessly rocking,
Out of the mocking-bird's throat, the musical shuttle,
Out of the Ninth-month midnight,
Over the sterile sands and the fields beyond, where the child leaving
his bed wandered alone, bareheaded, barefoot,
Down from the showered halo,
Up from the mystic play of shadows twining and twisting as if they
were alive,
Out from the patches of briers and blackberries,
From the memories of the bird that chanted to me,
From your memories sad brother, from the fitful risings and fallings
I heard,

From under that yellow half-moon late-risen and swollen as if with
    tears, ⁱ⁰
From those beginning notes of yearning and love there in the mist,
From the thousand responses of my heart never to cease,
From the myriad thence-aroused words,
From the word stronger and more delicious than any,
From such as now they start the scene revisiting,
As a flock, twittering, rising, or overhead passing,
Borne hither, ere all eludes me, hurriedly,
A man, yet by these tears a little boy again,
Throwing myself on the sand, confronting the waves,
I, chanter of pains and joys, uniter of here and hereafter, 20
Taking all hints to use them, but swiftly leaping beyond them,
A reminiscence sing.

Once Paumanok,[1]
When the lilac-scent was in the air and Fifth-month grass was
    growing,
Up this seashore in some briers,
Two feathered guests from Alabama, two together,
And their nest, and four light-green eggs spotted with brown,
And every day the he-bird to and fro near at hand,
And every day the she-bird crouched on her nest, silent, with bright
    eyes,
And every day I, a curious boy, never too close, never disturbing
    them, 30
Cautiously peering, absorbing, translating.

Shine! shine! shine!
Pour down your warmth, great sun!
While we bask, we two together,

Two together!
Winds blow south, or winds blow north,
Day come white, or night come black,
Home, or rivers and mountains from home,
Singing all time, minding no time,
While we two keep together. 40

Till of a sudden,
May-be killed, unknown to her mate,

[1] Indian name for Long Island, where Whitman grew up.

One forenoon the she-bird crouched not on the nest,
Nor returned that afternoon, nor the next,
Nor ever appeared again.

And thenceforward all summer in the sound of the sea,
And at night under the full of the moon in calmer weather,
Over the hoarse surging of the sea,
Or flitting from brier to brier by day,
I saw, I heard at intervals the remaining one, the he-bird,   50
The solitary guest from Alabama.

Blow! blow! blow!
Blow up sea-winds along Paumanok's shore;
I wait and I wait till you blow my mate to me.

Yes, when the stars glistened,
All night long on the prong of a moss-scalloped stake,
Down almost amid the slapping waves,
Sat the lone singer wonderful causing tears.

He called on his mate,
He poured forth the meanings which I of all men know.   60

Yes my brother I know,
The rest might not, but I have treasured every note,
For more than once dimly down to the beach gliding,
Silent, avoiding the moonbeams, blending myself with the shadows,
Recalling now the obscure shapes, the echoes, the sounds and sights
       after their sorts,
The white arms out in the breakers tirelessly tossing,
I, with bare feet, a child, the wind wafting my hair,
Listened long and long.

Listened to keep, to sing, now translating the notes,
Following you my brother.   70

Soothe! soothe! soothe!
Close on its wave soothes the wave behind,
And again another behind embracing and lapping, every one close,
But my love soothes not me, not me.

Low hangs the moon, it rose late,
It is lagging—O I think it is heavy with love, with love.

O madly the sea pushes upon the land,
With love, with love.

O night! do I not see my love fluttering out among the breakers?
What is that little black thing I see there in the white? 80

Loud! loud! loud!
Loud I call to you, my love!
High and clear I shoot my voice over the waves,
Surely you must know who is here, is here,
You must know who I am, my love.

Low-hanging moon!
What is that dusky spot in your brown yellow?
O it is the shape, the shape of my mate!
O moon do not keep her from me any longer.

Land! land! O land! 90
Whichever way I turn, O I think you could give me my mate back
      again if you only would,
For I am almost sure I see her dimly whichever way I look.

O rising stars!
Perhaps the one I want so much will rise, will rise with some of you.

O throat! O trembling throat!
Sound clearer through the atmosphere!
Pierce the woods, the earth,
Somewhere listening to catch you must be the one I want.

Shake out carols!
Solitary here, the night's carols! 100
Carols of lonesome love! death's carols!
Carols under that lagging, yellow, waning moon!
O under that moon where she droops almost down into the sea!
O reckless despairing carols.

But soft! sink low!
Soft! let me just murmur,
And do you wait a moment you husky-noised sea,
For somewhere I believe I heard my mate responding to me,
So faint, I must be still, be still to listen,
But not altogether still, for then she might not come immediately
      to me. 110

Hither my love!
Here I am! here!
With this just-sustained note I announce myself to you,
This gentle call is for you my love, for you.

Do not be decoyed elsewhere,
That is the whistle of the wind, it is not my voice,
That is the fluttering, the fluttering of the spray,
Those are the shadows of leaves.

O darkness! O in vain!
O I am very sick and sorrowful.   120

O brown halo in the sky near the moon, drooping upon the sea!
O troubled reflection in the sea!
O throat! O throbbing heart!
And I singing uselessly, uselessly all the night.

O past! O happy life! O song of joy!
In the air, in the woods, over fields,
Loved! loved! loved! loved!
But my mate no more, no more with me!
We two together no more.

The aria sinking,   130
All else continuing, the stars shining,
The winds blowing, the notes of the bird continuous echoing,
With angry moans the fierce old mother incessantly moaning,
On the sands of Paumanok's shore gray and rustling,
The yellow half-moon enlarged, sagging down, drooping, the face
    of the sea almost touching,
The boy ecstatic, with his bare feet the waves, with his hair the
    atmosphere dallying,
The love in the heart long pent, now loose, now at last tumultuously
    bursting,
The aria's meaning, the ears, the soul, swiftly depositing,
The strange tears down the cheeks coursing,
The colloquy there, the trio, each uttering,   140
The undertone, the savage old mother incessantly crying,
To the boy's soul's questions sullenly timing, some drowned secret
    hissing,
To the outsetting bard.

Demon or bird! (said the boy's soul,)
Is it indeed toward your mate you sing? or is it really to me?
For I, that was a child, my tongue's use sleeping, now I have heard
you,
Now in a moment I know what I am for, I awake,
And already a thousand singers, a thousand songs, clearer, louder
and more sorrowful than yours,
A thousand warbling echoes have started to life within me, never to
die.

O you singer solitary, singing by yourself, projecting me,   150
O solitary me listening, never more shall I cease perpetuating you,
Never more shall I escape, never more the reverberations,
Never more the cries of unsatisfied love be absent from me,
Never again leave me to be the peaceful child I was before what
there in the night,
By the sea under the yellow and sagging moon,
The messenger there aroused, the fire, the sweet hell within,
The unknown want, the destiny of me.

O give me the clew! (it lurks in the night here somewhere,)
O if I am to have so much, let me have more!

A word then, (for I will conquer it,)   160
The word final, superior to all,
Subtle, sent up—what is it?—I listen;
Are you whispering it, and have been all the time, you sea waves?
Is that it from your liquid rims and wet sands?

Whereto answering, the sea,
Delaying not, hurrying not,
Whispered me through the night, and very plainly before daybreak,
Lisped to me the low and delicious word death,
And again death, death, death, death,
Hissing melodious, neither like the bird nor like my aroused child's
heart,   170
But edging near as privately for me rustling at my feet,
Creeping thence steadily up to my ears and laving me softly all over.
Death, death, death, death, death.

Which I do not forget,
But fuse the song of my dusky demon and brother,

That he sang to me in the moonlight on Paumanok's gray beach,
With the thousand responsive songs at random,
My own songs awaked from that hour,
And with them the key, the word up from the waves,
The word of the sweetest song and all songs, 180
That strong and delicious word which, creeping to my feet,
(Or like some old crone rocking the cradle, swathed in sweet garments, bending aside,)
The sea whispered me.

The Dalliance of the Eagles

Skirting the river road, (my forenoon walk, my rest,)
Skyward in air a sudden muffled sound, the dalliance of the eagles,
The rushing amorous contact high in space together,
The clinching interlocking claws, a living, fierce, gyrating wheel,
Four beating wings, two beaks, a swirling mass tight grappling,
In tumbling turning clustering loops, straight downward falling,
Till o'er the river poised, the twain yet one, a moment's lull,
A motionless still balance in the air, then parting, talons loosing,
Upward again on slow-firm pinions slanting, their separate diverse flight,
She hers, he his, pursuing. 10

Matthew Arnold / 1822–1888

To Marguerite

Yes! in the sea of life enisled,
With echoing straits between us thrown,
Dotting the shoreless watery wild,
We mortal millions live *alone*.
The islands feel the enclasping flow,
And then their endless bounds they know.

But when the moon their hollows lights,
And they are swept by balms of spring,
And in their glens, on starry nights,

The nightingales divinely sing;
And lovely notes, from shore to shore,
Across the sounds and channels pour—

Oh! then a longing like despair
Is to their farthest caverns sent;
For surely once, they feel, we were
Parts of a single continent!
Now round us spreads the watery plain—
Oh might our marges meet again!

Who ordered, that their longing's fire
Should be, as soon as kindled, cooled?
Who renders vain their deep desire?—
A God, a God their severance ruled!
And bade betwixt their shores to be
The unplumbed, salt, estranging sea.

Requiescat

Strew on her roses, roses,
   And never a spray of yew!
In quiet she reposes:
   Ah! would that I did too!

Her mirth the world required:
   She bathed it in smiles of glee.
But her heart was tired, tired,
   And now they let her be.

Her life was turning, turning,
   In mazes of heat and sound.
But for peace her soul was yearning,
   And now peace laps her round.

Her cabined,[1] ample spirit,
   It fluttered and failed for breath.
To-night it doth inherit
   The vasty hall of death.

[1] Confined.

Dover Beach ✳

The sea is calm to-night.
The tide is full, the moon lies fair
Upon the straits;—on the French coast, the light
Gleams, and is gone; the cliffs of England stand,
Glimmering and vast, out in the tranquil bay.
Come to the window, sweet is the night-air!
Only, from the long line of spray
Where the sea meets the moon-blanched land,
Listen! you hear the grating roar
Of pebbles which the waves draw back, and fling,   10
At their return, up the high strand,
Begin, and cease, and then again begin,
With tremulous cadence slow, and bring
The eternal note of sadness in.

Sophocles long ago
Heard it on the Aegean, and it brought
Into his mind the turbid ebb and flow
Of human misery; we
Find also in the sound a thought,
Hearing it by this distant northern sea.   20

The Sea of Faith
Was once, too, at the full, and round earth's shore
Lay like the folds of a bright girdle furled.
But now I only hear
Its melancholy, long, withdrawing roar,
Retreating, to the breath
Of the night-wind down the vast edges drear
And naked shingles[2] of the world.

Ah, love, let us be true
To one another! for the world, which seems   30
To lie before us like a land of dreams,
So various, so beautiful, so new,
Hath really neither joy, nor love, nor light,
Nor certitude, nor peace, nor help for pain;
And we are here as on a darkling plain
Swept with confused alarms of struggle and flight,
Where ignorant armies clash by night.

[2] The coarse gravel of beaches.

George Meredith / 1828–1909

Mark Where the Pressing Wind Shoots Javelin-like

Mark where the pressing wind shoots javelin-like
Its skeleton shadow on the broad-backed wave!
Here is a fitting spot to dig Love's grave;
Here where the ponderous breakers plunge and strike,
And dart their hissing tongues high up the sand:
In hearing of the ocean, and in sight
Of those ribbed wind-streaks running into white.
If I the death of Love had deeply planned,
I never could have made it half so sure,
As by the unblest kisses which upbraid   10
The full-waked sense; or failing that, degrade!
'Tis morning: but no morning can restore
What we have forfeited. I see no sin:
The wrong is mixed. In tragic life, God wot,[1]
No villain need be! Passions spin the plot:
We are betrayed by what is false within.

Thus Piteously Love Closed What He Begat

Thus piteously Love closed what he begat:
The union of this ever-diverse pair!
These two were rapid falcons in a snare,
Condemned to do the flitting of the bat.
Lovers beneath the singing sky of May,
They wandered once; clear as the dew on flowers:
But they fed not on the advancing hours:
Their hearts held cravings for the buried day.
Then each applied to each that fatal knife,
Deep questioning, which probes to endless dole.   10
Ah, what a dusty answer gets the soul
When hot for certainties in this our life!—
In tragic hints here see what evermore
Moves dark as yonder midnight ocean's force,
Thundering like ramping hosts of warrior horse,
To throw that faint thin line upon the shore!

[1] Knows.

Lucifer in Starlight

On a starred night Prince Lucifer uprose.
Tired of his dark dominion swung the fiend
Above the rolling ball[2] in cloud part screened,
Where sinners hugged their spectre of repose.
Poor prey to his hot fit of pride were those.
And now upon his western wing he leaned,
Now his huge bulk o'er Afric's sands careened,
Now the black planet shadowed Arctic snows.
Soaring through wider zones that pricked his scars
With memory of the old revolt from Awe,[3]   10
He reached a middle height, and at the stars,
Which are the brain of heaven, he looked, and sank.
Around the ancient track marched, rank on rank,
The army of unalterable law.

Emily Dickinson / 1830–1886

I Never Hear the Word "Escape"

I never hear the word "escape"
Without a quicker blood,
A sudden expectation,
A flying attitude!

I never hear of prisons broad
By soldiers battered down,
But I tug childish at my bars
Only to fail again!

I'm Nobody! Who Are You?

I'm Nobody! Who are you?
Are you—Nobody—Too?
Then there's a pair of us?
Don't tell! they'd advertise—you know!

[2] The earth.
[3] Satan's rebellion against God.

How dreary—to be—Somebody!
How public—like a Frog—
To tell one's name—the livelong June—
To an admiring Bog!

The Soul Selects Her Own Society

The Soul selects her own Society—
Then—shuts the Door—
To her divine Majority—
Present no more—

Unmoved—she notes the Chariots—pausing—
At her low Gate—
Unmoved—an Emperor be kneeling
Upon her Mat—

I've known her—from an ample nation—
Choose One—   10
Then—close the Valves of her attention—
Like Stone—

Much Madness Is Divinest Sense

Much Madness is divinest Sense—
To a discerning Eye—
Much Sense—the starkest Madness—
'Tis the Majority
In this, as All, prevail—
Assent—and you are sane—
Demur—you're straightway dangerous—
And handled with a Chain—

This Is My Letter to the World

This is my letter to the World
That never wrote to Me—
The simple News that Nature told—
With tender Majesty

Her Message is committed
To Hands I cannot see—
For love of Her—Sweet—countrymen—
Judge tenderly—of Me

I Took My Power in My Hand

I took my Power in my Hand—
And went against the World—
'Twas not so much as David—had—
But I—was twice as bold—

I aimed my Pebble—but Myself
Was all the one that fell—
Was it Goliah—was too large—
Or was myself—too small?

We Outgrow Love, like Other Things

We outgrow love, like other things
And put it in the Drawer—
Till it an Antique fashion shows—
Like Costumes Grandsires wore.

The Bustle in a House

The Bustle in a House
The Morning after Death
Is solemnest of industries
Enacted upon Earth—

The Sweeping up the Heart
And putting Love away
We shall not want to use again
Until Eternity.

Hap[1]

[handwritten: Sonnet]
[handwritten: Note gramatical construction]

If but some vengeful god would call to me
From up the sky, and laugh: "Thou suffering thing,
Know that thy sorrow is my ecstasy,
That thy love's loss is my hate's profiting!"

Then would I bear it, clench myself, and die,
Steeled by the sense of ire unmerited;
Half-eased in that a Powerfuller than I
Had willed and meted me the tears I shed.

But not so. How arrives it joy lies slain,
And why unblooms the best hope ever sown?   10
—Crass Casualty obstructs the sun and rain,
And dicing Time for gladness casts a moan. . .
These purblind Doomsters had as readily strown
Blisses about my pilgrimage as pain.

The Subalterns

"Poor wanderer," said the leaden sky,
    "I fain would lighten thee,
But there are laws in force on high
    Which say it must not be."

—"I would not freeze thee, shorn one," cried
    The North, "knew I but how
To warm my breath, to slack my stride;
    But I am ruled as thou."

—"To-morrow I attack thee, wight,"
    Said Sickness. "Yet I swear   10
I bear thy little ark no spite,
    But am bid enter there."

—"Come hither, Son," I heard Death say;
    "I did not will a grave
Should end thy pilgrimage to-day,
    But I, too, am a slave!"

[1] Chance, accident.

We smiled upon each other then,
    And life to me had less
Of that fell look it wore ere when
    They owned their passiveness.   20

In Tenebris: II ²

*Considerabam ad dexteram, et videbam; et non erat qui cognosceret
    me. . . .*
*Non est qui requirat animam meam.*³

Psalm cxlii

When the clouds' swoln bosoms echo back the shouts of the many
    and strong
That things are all as they best may be, save a few to be right ere long,
And my eyes have not the vision in them to discern what to these is
    so clear,
The blot seems straightway in me alone; one better he were not here.

The stout upstanders say, All's well with us; ruers have nought to rue!
And what the potent say so oft, can it fail to be somewhat true?
Breezily go they, breezily come; their dust smokes around their career,
Till I think I am one born out of due time, who has no calling here.

Their dawns bring lusty joys, it seems; their evenings all that is sweet;
Our times are blessed times, they cry: Life shapes it as is most meet,
And nothing is much the matter; there are many smiles to a tear;   11
Then what is the matter is I, I say. Why should such an one be
    here? . . .

Let him in whose ears the low-voiced Best is killed by the clash of
    the First,
Who holds that if way to the Better there be, it exacts a full look at
    the Worst,
Who feels that delight is a delicate growth cramped by crookedness,
    custom, and fear,
Get him up and be gone as one shaped awry; he disturbs the order
    here.

---

² In darkness.
³ "Look on my right hand, and see; For there is no man that knoweth me: . . .
No man careth for my soul."

Channel Firing

That night your great guns, unawares,
Shook all our coffins as we lay,
And broke the chancel window-squares,
We thought it was the Judgment-day

And sat upright. While drearisome
Arose the howl of wakened hounds:
The mouse let fall the altar-crumb,
The worms drew back into the mounds,

The glebe[4] cow drooled. Till God called, "No;
It's gunnery practice out at sea   10
Just as before you went below;
The world is as it used to be:

"All nations striving strong to make
Red war yet redder. Mad as hatters
They do no more for Christés sake
Than you who are helpless in such matters.

"That this is not the judgment-hour
For some of them's a blessed thing,
For if it were they'd have to scour
Hell's floor for so much threatening. . . .   20

"Ha, ha. It will be warmer when
I blow the trumpet (if indeed
I ever do; for you are men,
And rest eternal sorely need)."

So down we lay again. "I wonder,
Will the world ever saner be,"
Said one, "than when He sent us under
In our indifferent century!"

And many a skeleton shook his head.
"Instead of preaching forty year,"   30
My neighbour Parson Thirdly said,
"I wish I had stuck to pipes and beer."

Again the guns disturbed the hour,
Roaring their readiness to avenge,

---

[4] A glebe in earlier times meant a small portion of land assigned to a clergyman as part of his benefice.

As far inland as Stourton Tower,
And Camelot, and starlit Stonehenge.[5]

Gerard Manley Hopkins / 1844–1889

God's Grandeur

The world is charged with the grandeur of God.
　It will flame out, like shining from shook foil;
　It gathers to a greatness, like the ooze of oil
Crushed. Why do men then now not reck his rod?
Generations have trod, have trod, have trod;
　And all is seared with trade; bleared, smeared with toil;
　And wears man's smudge and shares man's smell: the soil
Is bare now, nor can foot feel, being shod.

And for all this, nature is never spent;
　There lives the dearest freshness deep down things;　　　10
And though the last lights off the black West went
　Oh, morning, at the brown brink eastward, springs—
Because the Holy Ghost over the bent
　World broods with warm breast and with ah! bright wings.

Spring and Fall: To a Young Child

Márgarét, are you gríeving
Over Goldengrove unleaving?
Leáves, líke the things of man, you
With your fresh thoughts care for, can you?
Áh! ás the heart grows older
It will come to such sights colder
By and by, nor spare a sigh
Though worlds of wanwood leafmeal[1] lie;
And yet you wíll weep and know why.
Now no matter, child, the name:　　　10
Sórrow's spríngs áre the same.

[5] Names that evoke ancient British history.

[1] *Wanwood* and *leafmeal* are Hopkins' neologisms.

Nor mouth had, no nor mind, expressed
What heart heard of, ghost guessed:
It ís the blight man was born for,
It is Margaret you mourn for.

Yes. Whý Do We Áll, Seeing of a Soldier, Bless Him?

Yes. Whý do we áll, seeing of a soldier, bless him? bless
Our redcoats, our tars? Both these being, the greater part,
But frail clay, nay but foul clay. Here it is: the heart,
Since, proud, it calls the calling manly, gives a guess
That, hopes that, makesbelieve, the men must be no less;
It fancies, feigns, deems, dears the artist after his art;
And fain will find as sterling all as all is smart,
And scarlet wear the spirit of wár thére express.

Mark Christ our King. He knows war, served this soldiering
     through;
He of all can reeve a rope best. There he bides in bliss   10
Now, and séeing somewhére some mán do all that man can do,
For love he leans forth, needs his neck must fall on, kiss,
And cry "O Christ-done deed! So God-made-flesh does too:
Were I come o'er again" cries Christ "it should be this."

No Worst, There Is None

No worst, there is none. Pitched past pitch of grief,
More pangs will, schooled at forepangs, wilder wring.
Comforter, where, where is your comforting?
Mary, mother of us, where is your relief?
My cries heave, herds-long;[2] huddle in a main, a chief
Woe, world-sorrow; on an age-old anvil wince and sing—
Then lull, then leave off. Fury had shrieked "No ling-
ering! Let me be fell: force I must be brief."

     O the mind, mind has mountains; cliffs of fall
Frightful, sheer, no-man-fathomed. Hold them cheap   10
May who ne'er hung there. Nor does long our small
Durance deal with that steep or deep. Here! creep,
Wretch, under a comfort serves in a whirlwind: all
Life death does end and each day dies with sleep.

[2] Like the cries of whole herds.

Thou Art Indeed Just, Lord

Justus quidem tu es, Domine, si disputem tecum: verumtamen
justa loquar ad te: Quare via impiorum prosperatur? etc.[3]

Thou art indeed just, Lord, if I contend
With thee; but, sir, so what I plead is just.
Why do sinners' ways prosper? and why must
Disappointment all I endeavour end?
  Wert thou my enemy, O thou my friend,
How wouldst thou worse, I wonder, than thou dost
Defeat, thwart me? Oh, the sots and thralls of lust
Do in spare hours more thrive than I that spend,
Sir, life upon thy cause. See, banks and brakes
Now, leavèd how thick! lacèd they are again   10
With fretty chervil, look, and fresh wind shakes
Them; birds build—but not I build; no, but strain,
Time's eunuch, and not breed one work that wakes.
Mine, O thou lord of life, send my roots rain.

A. E. Housman / 1859–1936

On Wenlock Edge the Wood's in Trouble

On Wenlock Edge the wood's in trouble;
  His forest fleece the Wrekin heaves;
The gale, it plies the saplings double,
  And thick on Severn snow the leaves.[1]

'Twould blow like this through holt and hangar
  When Uricon[2] the city stood:
'Tis the old wind in the old anger,
  But then it threshed another wood.

Then, 'twas before my time, the Roman
  At yonder heaving hill would stare: 10

---

[3] "Righteous art thou, O Jehovah, when I contend with thee; yet would I reason the cause with thee; wherefore doth the way of the wicked prosper?" (Jeremiah 12:1).

---

[1] Place names in the borough of Shropshire, England.
[2] Once a Roman legionary fortress, later a town.

The blood that warms an English yeoman,
    The thoughts that hurt him, they were there.

There, like the wind through woods in riot,
    Through him the gale of life blew high;
The tree of man was never quiet:
    Then 'twas the Roman, now 'tis I.

The gale, it plies the saplings double,
    It blows so hard, 'twill soon be gone:
To-day the Roman and his trouble
    Are ashes under Uricon.   20

To an Athlete Dying Young

The time you won your town the race
We chaired you through the market-place;
Man and boy stood cheering by,
And home we brought you shoulder-high.

To-day, the road all runners come,
Shoulder-high we bring you home,
And set you at your threshold down,
Townsman of a stiller town.

Smart lad, to slip betimes away
From fields where glory does not stay   10
And early though the laurel grows
It withers quicker than the rose.

Eyes the shady night has shut
Cannot see the record cut,
And silence sounds no worse than cheers
After earth has stopped the ears:

Now you will not swell the rout
Of lads that wore their honours out,
Runners whom renown outran
And the name died before the man.   20

So set, before its echoes fade,
The fleet foot on the sill of shade,
And hold to the low lintel up
The still-defended challenge-cup.

And round that early-laurelled head
Will flock to gaze the strengthless dead,
And find unwithered on its curls
The garland briefer than a girl's.

William Butler Yeats / 1865–1939

A Coat

I made my song a coat
Covered with embroideries
Out of old mythologies
From heel to throat;
But the fools caught it,
Wore it in the world's eyes
As though they'd wrought it.
Song, let them take it,
For there's more enterprise   10
In walking naked.

Easter 1916 [1]

I have met them at close of day
Coming with vivid faces
From counter or desk among grey
Eighteenth-century houses.
I have passed with a nod of the head
Or polite meaningless words,
Or have lingered awhile and said
Polite meaningless words,
And thought before I had done
Of a mocking tale or a gibe   10
To please a companion
Around the fire at the club,
Being certain that they and I

[1] The Easter Rising, an Irish nationalist insurrection put down by the English; fifteen men were executed, including the four mentioned in the poem.

But lived where motley is worn:
All changed, changed utterly:
A terrible beauty is born.

That woman's[2] days were spent
In ignorant good-will,
Her nights in argument
Until her voice grew shrill.   20
What voice more sweet than hers
When, young and beautiful,
She rode to harriers?
This man[3] had kept a school
And rode our wingèd horse;
This other[4] his helper and friend
Was coming into his force;
He might have won fame in the end,
So sensitive his nature seemed,
So daring and sweet his thought.   30
This other man[5] I had dreamed
A drunken, vainglorious lout.
He had done most bitter wrong
To some who are near my heart,
Yet I number him in the song;
He, too, has resigned his part
In the casual comedy;
He, too, has been changed in his turn,
Transformed utterly:
A terrible beauty is born.   40

Hearts with one purpose alone
Through summer and winter seem
Enchanted to a stone
To trouble the living stream.
The horse that comes from the road,
The rider, the birds that range
From cloud to tumbling cloud,
Minute by minute they change;
A shadow of cloud on the stream
Changes minute by minute;   50
A horse-hoof slides on the brim,

[2] Countess Markiewicz (Constance Gore-Booth), sentenced to life imprisonment.
[3] Patrick Pearse, a poet and leader in the Gaelic language movement.
[4] Thomas MacDonagh, a writer.
[5] Major John MacBride, husband of Maud Gonne, whom Yeats had unsuccessfully courted for years.

And a horse plashes within it;
The long-legged moor-hens dive,
And hens to moor-cocks call;
Minute by minute they live:
The stone's in the midst of all.

Too long a sacrifice
Can make a stone of the heart.
O when may it suffice?
That is Heaven's part, our part   60
To murmur name upon name,
As a mother names her child
When sleep at last has come
On limbs that had run wild.
What is it but nightfall?
No, no, not night but death;
Was it needless death after all?
For England may keep faith
For all that is done and said.
We know their dream; enough   70
To know they dreamed and are dead;
And what if excess of love
Bewildered them till they died?
I write it out in a verse—
MacDonagh and MacBride
And Connolly⁶ and Pearse
Now and in time to be,
Wherever green is worn,
Are changed, changed utterly:
A terrible beauty is born.   80

The Leaders of the Crowd

They must to keep their certainty accuse
All that are different of a base intent;
Pull down established honour; hawk for news
Whatever their loose fantasy invent
And murmur it with bated breath, as though
The abounding gutter had been Helicon⁷

⁶ James Connolly, with Pearse a leader in the insurrection.
⁷ In Greek mythology, a mountain thought to be the source of poetic inspiration;
from it flowed streams associated with the muses.

Or calumny a song. How can they know
Truth flourishes where the student's lamp has shone,
And there alone, that have no solitude?
So the crowd come they care not what may come.　　10
They have loud music, hope every day renewed
And heartier loves; that lamp is from the tomb.

The Second Coming

Turning and turning in the widening gyre[8]
The falcon cannot hear the falconer;
Things fall apart; the centre cannot hold;
Mere anarchy is loosed upon the world,
The blood-dimmed tide is loosed, and everywhere
The ceremony of innocence is drowned;
The best lack all conviction, while the worst
Are full of passionate intensity.

Surely some revelation is at hand;
Surely the Second Coming is at hand.　　10
The Second Coming! Hardly are those words out
When a vast image out of *Spiritus Mundi*[9]
Troubles my sight: somewhere in sands of the desert
A shape with lion body and the head of a man,
A gaze blank and pitiless as the sun,
Is moving its slow thighs, while all about it
Reel shadows of the indignant desert birds.
The darkness drops again; but now I know
That twenty centuries of stony sleep
Were vexed to nightmare by a rocking cradle,　　20
And what rough beast, its hour come round at last,
Slouches towards Bethlehem to be born?

Leda and the Swan

A sudden blow: the great wings beating still
Above the staggering girl, her thighs caressed

[8] That phase of history now closing.
[9] Spirit of the universe, the universal memory which contains all individual memories of the past.

By the dark webs, her nape caught in his bill,
He holds her helpless breast upon his breast.

How can those terrified vague fingers push
The feathered glory from her loosening thighs?
And how can body, laid in that white rush,
But feel the strange heart beating where it lies?

A shudder in the loins engenders there
The broken wall, the burning roof and tower
And Agamemnon dead.[10]
                    Being so caught up,
So mastered by the brute blood of the air,
Did she put on his knowledge with his power
Before the indifferent beak could let her drop?

Sailing to Byzantium[11] – 1928

1

That is no country[12] for old men. The young
In one another's arms, birds in the trees
—Those dying generations—at their song,
The salmon-falls, the mackerel-crowded seas,
Fish, flesh, or fowl, commend all summer long
Whatever is begotten, born, and dies.
Caught in that sensual music all neglect
Monuments of unaging intellect.

2

An aged man is but a paltry thing,
A tattered coat upon a stick, unless
Soul clap its hands and sing, and louder sing
For every tatter in its mortal dress,
Nor is there singing school but studying
Monuments of its own magnificence;
And therefore I have sailed the seas and come
To the holy city of Byzantium.

[10] In Greek mythology, Zeus, in the form of a swan, raped Leda. The abduction of Helen, the child of this union, brought on the Trojan War.
[11] Byzantium refers to the capital of the Eastern Roman Empire and the holy city of Greek Orthodox Christianity. In the poem it represents the ideal city of the spirit.
[12] The natural world, as opposed to Byzantium; life versus art.

O sages standing in God's holy fire
As in the gold mosaic of a wall,
Come from the holy fire, perne[13] in a gyre,
And be the singing-masters of my soul.   20
Consume my heart away; sick with desire
And fastened to a dying animal
It knows not what it is; and gather me
Into the artifice of eternity.

4

Once out of nature I shall never take
My bodily form from any natural thing,
But such a form as Grecian goldsmiths make[14]
Of hammered gold and gold enamelling
To keep a drowsy emperor awake;
Or set upon a golden bough to sing   30
To lords and ladies of Byzantium
Of what is past, or passing, or to come.

Byzantium - 1929

The unpurged images of day recede;
The Emperor's drunken soldiery are abed;
Night resonance recedes, night-walkers' song
After great cathedral gong;
A starlit or a moonlit dome disdains
All that man is,
All mere complexities,
The fury and the mire of human veins.

Before me floats an image, man or shade,
Shade more than man, more image than a shade;   10
For Hades' bobbin bound in mummy-cloth
May unwind the winding path;
A mouth that has no moisture and no breath
Breathless mouths may summon;

---

[13] Literally, *perne* means *spool;* the poet sees the saints descend in a whirling spiral.
[14] In the Emperor's palace there was a gold and silver tree from which artificial birds sang.

I hail the superhuman;
I call it death-in-life and life-in-death.[15]

Miracle, bird or golden handiwork,
More miracle than bird or handiwork,
Planted on the star-lit golden bough,
Can like the cocks of Hades crow,   20
Or, by the moon embittered, scorn aloud
In glory of changeless metal
Common bird or petal
And all complexities of mire or blood.

At midnight on the Emperor's pavement flit
Flames that no faggot feeds, nor steel has lit,
Nor storm disturbs, flames begotten of flame,
Where blood-begotten spirits come
And all complexities of fury leave,
Dying into a dance,   30
An agony of trance,
An agony of flame that cannot singe a sleeve.

Astraddle on the dolphin's mire and blood,
Spirit after spirit! The smithies break the flood,
The golden smithies of the Emperor!
Marbles of the dancing floor
Break bitter furies of complexity,
Those images that yet
Fresh images beget,
That dolphin-torn, that gong-tormented sea.   40

[15] "Only the idea of a ghost, equipped not even with a ghost's substantiality, 'Hades' bobbin,' the thing that had once been a man, the purified spirit which has already unwound the winding path of its human incarnations and has dreamed itself back to its elemental form, this 'image' may breathlessly summon the breathless mouths of those spirits about to be freed from life's complexity and the round of reincarnations. . . . this superhuman form . . . is the powerful force which will call to the Byzantine dancing place those unpurged spirits from beyond the gong-tormented sea" (John Unterecker, *Reader's Guide to William Butler Yeats*, Farrar, Straus, 1959).

 *Vacillation*[16]

1

Between extremities
Man runs his course;
A brand, or flaming breath,
Comes to destroy
All those antinomies
Of day and night;
The body calls it death,
The heart remorse.
But if these be right
What is joy?   10

2

A tree there is that from its topmost bough
Is half all glittering flame and half all green
Abounding foliage moistened with the dew;
And half is half and yet is all the scene;
And half and half consume what they renew,
And he that Attis' image[17] hangs between
That staring fury and the blind lush leaf
May know not what he knows, but knows not grief.

3

Get all the gold and silver that you can,
Satisfy ambition, animate   20
The trivial days and ram them with the sun,
And yet upon these maxims meditate:
All women dote upon an idle man
Although their children need a rich estate;
No man has ever lived that had enough
Of children's gratitude or woman's love.

---

[16] The movement back and forth between all the dualities, "antinomies," of human experience—heart and soul, body and spirit, the natural and the supernatural, etc. These are symbolized by the tree of stanza #2, half foilage, half flame, rooted in earth and reaching through air to heaven. The problem is not to choose between these opposites but to resolve them into a unity, as in the tree itself.

[17] A vegetation god of pagan antiquity at whose festival it was a priest's function to hang the god's image on a sacred tree; here priest is poet, and the image represents works of art—art, which unifies the dualities.

No longer in Lethean[18] foliage caught
Begin the preparation for your death
And from the fortieth winter by that thought
Test every work of intellect or faith, 30
And everything that your own hands have wrought,
And call those works extravagance of breath
That are not suited for such men as come
Proud, open-eyed and laughing to the tomb.

4

My fiftieth year had come and gone,
I sat, a solitary man,
In a crowded London shop,
An open book and empty cup
On the marble table-top.

While on the shop and street I gazed 40
My body of a sudden blazed;
And twenty minutes more or less
It seemed, so great my happiness,
That I was blessèd and could bless.

5

Although the summer sunlight gild
Cloudy leafage of the sky,
Or wintry moonlight sink the field
In storm-scattered intricacy,
I cannot look thereon,
Responsibility so weighs me down. 50

Things said or done long years ago,
Or things I did not do or say
But thought that I might say or do,
Weigh me down, and not a day
But something is recalled,
My conscience or my vanity appalled.

6

A rivery field spread out below,
An odour of the new-mown hay
In his nostrils, the great lord of Chou[19]

[18] Lethe, the river of forgetfulness; here, the distracting multiplicity of the natural life.
[19] Chóu-kung, Duke of Chóu, twelfth-century sage.

Cried, casting off the mountain snow
"Let all things pass away." 60

Wheels by milk-white asses drawn
Where Babylon or Nineveh
Rose; some conqueror drew rein
And cried to battle-weary men,
"Let all things pass away."

From man's blood-sodden heart are sprung
Those branches of the night and day
Where the gaudy moon is hung.
What's the meaning of all song? 70
"Let all things pass away."

7

The Soul. Seek out reality, leave things that seem.
The Heart. What, be a singer born and lack a theme?
The Soul. Isaiah's coal,[20] what more can man desire?
The Heart. Struck dumb in the simplicity of fire!
The Soul. Look on that fire, salvation walks within.
The Heart. What theme had Homer but original sin?

8

Must we part, Von Hügel,[21] though much alike, for we
Accept the miracles of the saints and honour sanctity?
The body of Saint Teresa[22] lies undecayed in tomb, 80
Bathed in miraculous oil, sweet odours from it come,
Healing from its lettered slab. Those self-same hands perchance
Eternalised the body of a modern saint that once
Had scooped out Pharaoh's mummy. I—though heart might find relief
Did I become a Christian man and choose for my belief
What seems most welcome in the tomb—play a predestined part.
Homer is my example and his unchristened heart.
The lion and the honeycomb, what has Scripture said? [23]
So get you gone, Von Hügel, though with blessings on your head.

---

[20] *Isaiah* 6:6–7: fire that purifies the spirit.
[21] Baron Friedrich von Hügel (1852–1925), Roman Catholic author of *The Mystical Element of Religion,* whose exaltation of spirit suggests no difference between poetic inspiration and the Christian apprehension of God.
[22] Saint Teresa of Avila (1515–82), the Christian saint whose body was said to have been found uncorrupted when her tomb was opened in the nineteenth century; Yeats suggests that the ghost of an ancient Egyptian embalmer preserved it.
[23] Judges 14:8–14: ". . . out of the strong came forth sweetness"; the transmutation of life and death into art.

The Choice

The intellect of man is forced to choose
Perfection of the life, or of the work,
And if it take the second must refuse
A heavenly mansion, raging in the dark.
When all that story's finished, what's the news?
In luck or out the toil has left its mark:
That old perplexity an empty purse,
Or the day's vanity, the night's remorse.

Crazy Jane Talks with the Bishop

I met the Bishop on the road
And much said he and I.
"Those breasts are flat and fallen now,
Those veins must soon be dry;
Live in a heavenly mansion,
Not in some foul sty."

"Fair and foul are near of kin,
And fair needs foul," I cried.
"My friends are gone, but that's a truth
Nor grave nor bed denied,   10
Learned in bodily lowliness
And in the heart's pride.

"A woman can be proud and stiff
When on love intent;
But Love has pitched his mansion in
The place of excrement;
For nothing can be sole or whole
That has not been rent."

The Spur

You think it horrible that lust and rage
Should dance attention upon my old age;
They were not such a plague when I was young;
What else have I to spur me into song?

Politics

In our time the destiny of man presents its meaning in political terms.

THOMAS MANN

How can I, that girl standing there,
My attention fix
On Roman or on Russian
Or on Spanish politics?
Yet here's a travelled man that knows
What he talks about,
And there's a politician
That has read and thought,
And maybe what they say is true
Of war and war's alarms,   10
But O that I were young again
And held her in my arms!

Edwin Arlington Robinson / 1869–1935

Richard Cory

Whenever Richard Cory went down town,
We people on the pavement looked at him:
He was a gentleman from sole to crown,
Clean favored, and imperially slim.

And he was always quietly arrayed,
And he was always human when he talked;
But still he fluttered pulses when he said,
"Good-morning," and he glittered when he walked.

And he was rich—yes, richer than a king—
And admirably schooled in every grace: 10
In fine, we thought that he was everything
To make us wish that we were in his place.

So on we worked, and waited for the light,
And went without the meat, and cursed the bread;
And Richard Cory, one calm summer night,
Went home and put a bullet through his head.

Why He Was There

Much as he left it when he went from us
Here was the room again where he had been
So long that something of him should be seen,
Or felt—and so it was. Incredulous,
I turned about, loath to be greeted thus,
And there he was in his old chair, serene
As ever, and as laconic and as lean
As when he lived, and as cadaverous.

Calm as he was of old when we were young,
He sat there gazing at the pallid flame   10
Before him. "And how far will this go on?"
I thought. He felt the failure of my tongue,
And smiled: "I was not here until you came;
And I shall not be here when you are gone."

Eros Turannos[1]

She fears him, and will always ask
    What fated her to choose him;
She meets in his engaging mask
    All reasons to refuse him;
But what she meets and what she fears
Are less than are the downward years,
Drawn slowly to the foamless weirs
    Of age, were she to lose him.

Between a blurred sagacity
    That once had power to sound him,   10
And Love, that will not let him be
    The Judas that she found him,
Her pride assuages her almost,
As if it were alone the cost.—
He sees that he will not be lost,
    And waits and looks around him.

A sense of ocean and old trees
    Envelops and allures him;
Tradition, touching all he sees,
    Beguiles and reassures him;   20

[1] King Love.

And all her doubts of what he says
Are dimmed with what she knows of days—
Till even prejudice delays
    And fades, and she secures him.

The falling leaf inaugurates
    The reign of her confusion;
The pounding wave reverberates
    The dirge of her illusion;
And home, where passion lived and died,
Becomes a place where she can hide,   30
While all the town and harbor side
    Vibrate with her seclusion.

We tell you, tapping on our brows,
    The story as it should be,—
As if the story of a house
    Were told, or ever could be;
We'll have no kindly veil between
Her visions and those we have seen,—
As if we guessed what hers have been,
    Or what they are or would be.   40

Meanwhile we do no harm; for they
    That with a god have striven,
Not hearing much of what we say,
    Take what the god has given;
Though like waves breaking it may be,
Or like a changed familiar tree,
Or like a stairway to the sea
    Where down the blind are driven.

Robert Frost / 1874–1963

The Road Not Taken

    Two roads diverged in a yellow wood,
    And sorry I could not travel both
    And be one traveler, long I stood
    And looked down one as far as I could
    To where it bent in the undergrowth;

Then took the other, as just as fair,
And having perhaps the better claim,
Because it was grassy and wanted wear;
Though as for that the passing there
Had worn them really about the same,   10

And both that morning equally lay
In leaves no step had trodden black.
Oh, I kept the first for another day!
Yet knowing how way leads on to way,
I doubted if I should ever come back.

I shall be telling this with a sigh
Somewhere ages and ages hence:
Two roads diverged in a wood, and I—
I took the one less traveled by,
And that has made all the difference.   20

Fire and Ice

Some say the world will end in fire,
Some say in ice.
From what I've tasted of desire
I hold with those who favor fire.
But if it had to perish twice,
I think I know enough of hate
To say that for destruction ice
Is also great
And would suffice.

Stopping by Woods on a Snowy Evening

Whose woods these are I think I know.
His house is in the village though;
He will not see me stopping here
To watch his woods fill up with snow.

My little horse must think it queer
To stop without a farmhouse near
Between the woods and frozen lake
The darkest evening of the year.

He gives his harness bells a shake
To ask if there is some mistake.
The only other sound's the sweep
Of easy wind and downy flake.

The woods are lovely, dark and deep,
But I have promises to keep,
And miles to go before I sleep,
And miles to go before I sleep.

Spring Pools

These pools that, though in forests, still reflect
The total sky almost without defect,
And like the flowers beside them, chill and shiver,
Will like the flowers beside them soon be gone,
And yet not out by any brook or river,
But up by roots to bring dark foliage on.

The trees that have it in their pent-up buds
To darken nature and be summer woods—
Let them think twice before they use their powers
To blot out and drink up and sweep away
These flowery waters and these watery flowers
From snow that melted only yesterday.

Design

I found a dimpled spider, fat and white,
On a white heal-all, holding up a moth
Like a white piece of rigid satin cloth—
Assorted characters of death and blight
Mixed ready to begin the morning right,
Like the ingredients of a witches' broth—
A snow-drop spider, a flower like a froth,
And dead wings carried like a paper kite.

What had that flower to do with being white,
The wayside blue and innocent heal-all?
What brought the kindred spider to that height,
Then steered the white moth thither in the night?
What but design of darkness to appall?—
If design govern in a thing so small.

Wallace Stevens / 1879-1955

Thirteen Ways of Looking at a Blackbird

1

Among twenty snowy mountains,
The only moving thing
Was the eye of the blackbird.

2

I was of three minds,
Like a tree
In which there are three blackbirds.

3

The blackbird whirled in the autumn winds.
It was a small part of the pantomime.

4

A man and a woman
Are one.   10
A man and a woman and a blackbird
Are one.

5

I do not know which to prefer,
The beauty of inflections
Or the beauty of innuendoes,
The blackbird whistling
Or just after.

6

Icicles filled the long window
With barbaric glass.
The shadow of the blackbird   20
Crossed it, to and fro.
The mood
Traced in the shadow
An indecipherable cause.

7

O thin men of Haddam,[1]
Why do you imagine golden birds?

[1] A small Connecticut town southeast of Hartford, the poet's home.

Do you not see how the blackbird
Walks around the feet
Of the women about you?

8

I know noble accents   30
And lucid, inescapable rhythms;
But I know, too,
That the blackbird is involved
In what I know.

9

When the blackbird flew out of sight,
It marked the edge
Of one of many circles.

10

At the sight of blackbirds
Flying in a green light,
Even the bawds of euphony   40
Would cry out sharply.

11

He rode over Connecticut
In a glass coach.
Once, a fear pierced him,
In that he mistook
The shadow of his equipage
For blackbirds.

12

The river is moving.
The blackbird must be flying.

13

It was evening all afternoon.   50
It was snowing
And it was going to snow.
The blackbird sat
In the cedar-limbs

The Emperor of Ice-Cream

Call the roller of big cigars,
The muscular one, and bid him whip
In kitchen cups concupiscent curds.
Let the wenches dawdle in such dress
As they are used to wear, and let the boys
Bring flowers in last month's newspapers.
Let be be finale of seem.
The only emperor is the emperor of ice-cream.

Take from the dresser of deal,
Lacking the three glass knobs, that sheet   10
On which she embroidered fantails once
And spread it so as to cover her face.
If her horny feet protrude, they come
To show how cold she is, and dumb.
Let the lamp affix its beam.
The only emperor is the emperor of ice-cream.

William Carlos Williams / 1883–1963

Spring and All

By the road to the contagious hospital
under the surge of the blue
mottled clouds driven from the
northeast—a cold wind. Beyond, the
waste of broad, muddy fields
brown with dried weeds, standing and fallen

patches of standing water
the scattering of tall trees

All along the road the reddish
purplish, forked, upstanding, twiggy   10
stuff of bushes and small trees
with dead, brown leaves under them
leafless vines—

Lifeless in appearance, sluggish
dazed spring approaches—

They enter the new world naked,
cold, uncertain of all
save that they enter. All about them
the cold, familiar wind—

Now the grass, tomorrow 20
the stiff curl of wildcarrot leaf
One by one objects are defined—
It quickens: clarity, outline of leaf

But now the stark dignity of
entrance—Still, the profound change
has come upon them: rooted they
grip down and begin to awaken

Smell!

Oh strong-ridged and deeply hollowed
nose of mine! what will you not be smelling?
What tactless asses we are, you and I boney nose
always indiscriminate, always unashamed,
and now it is the souring flowers of the bedraggled
poplars: a festering pulp on the wet earth
beneath them. With what deep thirst
we quicken our desires
to that rank odor of a passing springtime!
Can you not be decent? Can you not reserve your ardors 10
for something less unlovely? What girl will care
for us, do you think, if we continue in these ways?
Must you taste everything? Must you know everything?
Must you have a part in everything?

D. H. Lawrence / 1885–1930

River Roses

By the Isar,[1] in the twilight
We were wandering and singing,

[1] A river in Bavaria.

By the Isar, in the evening
We climbed the huntsman's ladder and sat swinging
In the fir-tree overlooking the marshes,
While river met with river, and the ringing
Of their pale-green glacier water filled the evening.

By the Isar, in the twilight
We found the dark wild roses
Hanging red at the river; and simmering   10
Frogs were singing, and over the river closes
Was savour of ice and of roses; and glimmering
Fear was abroad. We whispered: "No one knows us.
Let it be as the snake disposes
Here in this simmering marsh."

Piano

Softly, in the dusk, a woman is singing to me;
Taking me back down the vista of years, till I see
A child sitting under the piano, in the boom of the tingling strings
And pressing the small, poised feet of a mother who smiles as she sings.

In spite of myself, the insidious mastery of song
Betrays me back, till the heart of me weeps to belong
To the old Sunday evenings at home, with winter outside
And hymns in the cosy parlour, the tinkling piano our guide.

So now it is vain for the singer to burst into clamour
With the great black piano appassionato. The glamour   10
Of childish days is upon me, my manhood is cast
Down in the flood of remembrance, I weep like a child for the past.

Won't It Be Strange———?

Won't it be strange, when the nurse brings the new-born infant
to the proud father, and shows its little, webbed greenish feet
made to smite the waters behind it?
or the round, wild vivid eye of a wild-goose staring
out of fathomless skies and seas?
or when it utters that undaunted little bird-cry
of one who will settle on icebergs, and honk across the Nile?—

And when the father says: This is none of mine!
Woman, where got you this little beast?—
will there be a whistle of wings in the air, and an icy draught?   10
will the singing of swans, high up, high up, invisible
break the drums of his ears
and leave him forever listening for the answer?

The English Are So Nice!

The English are so nice
so awfully nice
they are the nicest people in the world.

And what's more, they're very nice about being nice
about your being nice as well!
If you're not nice they soon make you feel it.

Americans and French and Germans and so on
they're all very well
but they're not *really* nice, you know.
They're not nice in *our* sense of the word, are they now?   10

That's why one doesn't have to take them seriously.
We must be nice to them, of course,
of course, naturally—
But it doesn't really matter what you say to them,
they don't really understand
you can just say anything to them:
be nice, you know, just nice
but you must never take them seriously, they wouldn't understand.
just be nice, you know! oh, fairly nice,
not too nice of course, they take advantage   20
but nice enough, just nice enough
to let them feel they're not quite as nice as they might be.

Silet[1]

When I behold how black, immortal ink
Drips from my deathless pen—ah, well-away!
Why should we stop at all for what I think?
There is enough in what I chance to say.

It is enough that we once came together;
What is the use of setting it to rime?
When it is autumn do we get spring weather,
Or gather may of harsh northwindish time?

It is enough that we once came together;
What if the wind have turned against the rain?   10
It is enough that we once came together;
Time has seen this, and will not turn again.

And who are we, who know that last intent,
To plague to-morrow with a testament!

Portrait d'une Femme

Your mind and you are our Sargasso Sea,
London has swept about you this score years
And bright ships left you this or that in fee:
Ideas, old gossip, oddments of all things,
Strange spars of knowledge and dimmed wares of price.
Great minds have sought you—lacking someone else.
You have been second always. Tragical?
No. You preferred it to the usual thing:
One dull man, dulling and uxorious,
One average mind—with one thought less, each year.   10
Oh, you are patient. I have seen you sit
Hours, where something might have floated up.
And now you pay one. Yes, you richly pay.
You are a person of some interest, one comes to you
And takes strange gain away:
Trophies fished up; some curious suggestion;

[1] Silent.

Fact that leads nowhere; and a tale for two,
Pregnant with mandrakes, or with something else
That might prove useful and yet never proves,
That never fits a corner or shows use, 20
Or finds its hour upon the loom of days:
The tarnished, gaudy, wonderful old work;
Idols, and ambergris and rare inlays.
These are your riches, your great store; and yet
For all this sea-hoard of deciduous things,
Strange woods half sodden, and new brighter stuff:
In the slow float of differing light and deep,
No! there is nothing! In the whole and all,
Nothing that's quite your own.

> Yet this is you.

The Rest

O helpless few in my country,
O remnant enslaved!

Artists broken against her,
A-stray, lost in the villages
Mistrusted, spoken-against,

Lovers of beauty, starved,
Thwarted with systems,
Helpless against the control;

You who can not wear yourselves out
By persisting to successes, 10
You who can only speak,
Who cannot steel yourselves into reiteration;

You of the finer sense,
Broken against false knowledge,
You who can know at first hand,
Hated, shut in, mistrusted:

Take thought:
I have weathered the storm,
I have beaten out my exile.

The Horses ✳

Barely a twelvemonth after
The seven days war that put the world to sleep,
Late in the evening the strange horses came.
By then we had made our covenant with silence,
But in the first few days it was so still
We listened to our breathing and were afraid.
On the second day
The radios failed; we turned the knobs; no answer.
On the third day a warship passed us, heading north,
Dead bodies piled on the deck. On the sixth day   10
A plane plunged over us into the sea. Thereafter
Nothing. The radios dumb;
And still they stand in corners of our kitchens,
And stand, perhaps, turned on, in a million rooms
All over the world. But now if they should speak,
If on a sudden they should speak again,
If on the stroke of noon a voice should speak,
We would not listen, we would not let it bring
That old bad world that swallowed its children quick
At one great gulp. We would not have it again.   20
Sometimes we think of the nations lying asleep,
Curled blindly in impenetrable sorrow,
And then the thought confounds us with its strangeness.
The tractors lie about our fields; at evening
They look like dank sea-monsters couched and waiting.
We leave them where they are and let them rust:
"They'll moulder away and be like other loam."
We make our oxen drag our rusty ploughs,
Long laid aside. We have gone back
Far past our fathers' land.
                And then, that evening   30
Late in the summer the strange horses came.
We heard a distant tapping on the road,
A deepening drumming; it stopped, went on again
And at the corner changed to hollow thunder.
We saw the heads
Like a wild wave charging and were afraid.
We had sold our horses in our fathers' time

To buy new tractors. Now they were strange to us
As fabulous steeds set on an ancient shield
Or illustrations in a book of knights.   40
We did not dare go near them. Yet they waited,
Stubborn and shy, as if they had been sent
By an old command to find our whereabouts
And that long-lost archaic companionship.
In the first moment we had never a thought
That they were creatures to be owned and used.
Among them were some half-a-dozen colts
Dropped in some wilderness of the broken world,
Yet new as if they had come from their own Eden.   49
Since then they have pulled our ploughs and borne our loads,
But that free servitude still can pierce our hearts.
Our life is changed; their coming our beginning.

Edith Sitwell / 1887–1964

Aubade

Jane, Jane,
Tall as a crane,
The morning light creaks down again;

Comb your cockscomb-ragged hair,
Jane, Jane, come down the stair.

Each dull blunt wooden stalactite
Of rain creaks, hardened by the light,

Sounding like an overtone
From some lonely world unknown.

But the creaking empty light   10
Will never harden into sight,

Will never penetrate your brain
With overtones like the blunt rain.

The light would show (if it could harden)
Eternities of kitchen garden,

Cockscomb flowers that none will pluck,
And wooden flowers that 'gin to cluck.

In the kitchen you must light
Flames as staring, red and white,

As carrot or as turnips, shining,   20
Where the cold dawn light lies whining.

Cockscomb hair on the cold wind
Hangs limp, turns the milk's weak mind. . . .

      Jane, Jane,
      Tall as a crane,
      The morning light creaks down again!

Dirge for the New Sunrise

(Fifteen minutes past eight o'clock, on the morning of Monday, the 6th of August, 1945.)[1]

Bound to my heart as Ixion to the wheel,[2]
Nailed to my heart as the Thief upon the Cross,
I hang between our Christ and the gap where the world was lost

And watch the phantom Sun in Famine Street—
The ghost of the heart of man . . . red Cain,
And the more murderous brain
Of Man, still redder Nero that conceived the death
Of his mother Earth, and tore
Her womb, to know the place where he was conceived.

But no eyes grieved—   10
For none were left for tears:
They were blinded as the years
Since Christ was born. Mother or Murderer, you have given or taken
    life—
Now all is one!

[1] On this day the atomic bomb was dropped on Hiroshima.
[2] A legendary Greek king, who was bound to an eternally revolving wheel in Tartarus as punishment by Zeus for his love of Hera.

There was a morning when the holy Light
Was young. . . . The beautiful First Creature came
To our water-springs, and thought us without blame.

Our hearts seemed safe in our breasts and sang to the Light—
The marrow in the bone   19
We dreamed was safe . . . the blood in the veins, the sap in the tree
Were springs of Deity.

But I saw the little Ant-men as they ran
Carrying the world's weight of the world's filth
And the filth in the heart of Man—
Compressed till those lusts and greeds had a greater heat than that of
    the Sun.

And the ray from that heat came soundless, shook the sky
As if in search for food, and squeezed the stems
Of all that grows on the earth till they were dry—
And drank the marrow of the bone:
The eyes that saw, the lips that kissed, are gone—   30
Or black as thunder lie and grin at the murdered Sun.

The living blind and seeing Dead together lie
As if in love. . . . There was no more hating then,
And no more love: Gone is the heart of Man.

Marianne Moore / 1887–

Poetry

I, too, dislike it: there are things that are important beyond all this
    fiddle.
  Reading it, however, with a perfect contempt for it, one discovers in
  it after all, a place for the genuine.
    Hands that can grasp, eyes
    that can dilate, hair that can rise
      if it must, these things are important not because a

high-sounding interpretation can be put upon them but because they
    are

useful. When they become so derivative as to become unintelligible,
the same thing may be said for all of us, that we
　　do not admire what　　　　　　　　　　　　　　　　10
　　we cannot understand: the bat
　　　　holding on upside down or in quest of something to

eat, elephants pushing, a wild horse taking a roll, a tireless wolf under
a tree, the immovable critic twitching his skin like a horse that feels
　　　a flea, the base-
　　ball fan, the statistician—
　　　　nor is it valid
　　　　　to discriminate against "business documents and

school-books"; all these phenomena are important. One must make a
　　　distinction
　　however: when dragged into prominence by half poets, the result
　　　is not poetry,
　　nor till the poets among us can be　　　　　　　　20
　　　"literalists of
　　　the imagination"—above
　　　　insolence and triviality and can present

for inspection, imaginary gardens with real toads in them, shall we
　　have
　　it. In the meantime, if you demand on the one hand,
　　the raw material of poetry in
　　　all its rawness and
　　　that which is on the other hand
　　　　genuine, then you are interested in poetry.

What Are Years?

　　　　　　What is our innocence,
　　　　what is our guilt? All are
　　　　　naked, none is safe. And whence
　　　　is courage: the unanswered question,
　　　　the resolute doubt,—
　　　　dumbly calling, deafly listening—that
　　　　in misfortune, even death,
　　　　　　encourages others
　　　　　　and in its defeat, stirs

the soul to be strong? He
sees deep and is glad, who
 accedes to mortality
and in his imprisonment rises
upon himself as
the sea in a chasm, struggling to be
free and unable to be,
 in its surrendering
 finds its continuing.

So he who strongly feels,
behaves. The very bird,
 grown taller as he sings, steels
his form straight up. Though he is captive,
his mighty singing
says, satisfaction is a lowly
thing, how pure a thing is joy.
 This is mortality.
 this is eternity.

The Mind Is an Enchanting Thing

is an enchanted thing
 like the glaze on a
katydid-wing
 subdivided by sun
 till the nettings are legion.
Like Gieseking playing Scarlatti;[1]

like the apteryx-awl
 as a beak, or the
kiwi's rain-shawl
 of haired feathers, the mind
 feeling its way as though blind,
walks along with its eyes on the ground.

It has memory's ear
 that can hear without
having to hear.
 Like the gyroscope's fall,
 truly unequivocal
because trued by regnant certainty,

[1] Walter Gieseking (1895–1956), great concert pianist; Guiseppe Domenico Scarlatti (1683–1757), composer of many brilliant sonatas for the harpsichord.

it is a power of
        strong enchantment. It   20
is like the dove-
            neck animated by
            sun; it is memory's eye;
it's conscientious inconsistency.

It tears off the veil; tears
        the temptation, the
mist the heart wears,
            from its eyes,—if the heart
            has a face; it takes apart
dejection. It's fire in the dove-neck's   30

iridescence; in the
        inconsistencies
of Scarlatti.
            Unconfusion submits
            its confusion to proof; it's
not a Herod's oath[2] that cannot change.

T. S. Eliot / 1888–1965

The Love Song of J. Alfred Prufrock

> S'io credesse che mia risposta fosse
> A persona che mai tornasse al mondo,
> Questa fiamma staria senza piu scosse.
> Ma perciocche giammai di questo fondo
> Non torno vivo alcun, s'i'odo il vero,
> Senza tema d'infamia ti rispondo.[1]

Let us go then, you and I,
When the evening is spread out against the sky
Like a patient etherised upon a table;

[2] Herod, king of Judea, pleased with Salome's entertainment, promised her on oath anything she asked for; she asked for the head of John the Baptist, and Herod, although reluctant, was obliged to abide by his oath (Matthew 14:1–12 and Mark 6:14–29).

[1] Dante, Inferno, XXVII.61–66: Dante asks one of the damned souls its name, and it replies, "If I thought my answer were to one who could return to the world, I would not reply, but since none ever returned alive from this depth, I answer you without fear of infamy."

Let us go, through certain half-deserted streets,
The muttering retreats
Of restless nights in one-night cheap hotels
And sawdust restaurants with oyster-shells:
Streets that follow like a tedious argument
Of insidious intent
To lead you to an overwhelming question . . .   10
Oh, do not ask, "What is it?"
Let us go and make our visit.

In the room the women come and go
Talking of Michelangelo.[2]

The yellow fog that rubs its back upon the window-panes,
The yellow smoke that rubs its muzzle on the window-panes
Licked its tongue into the corners of the evening,
Lingered upon the pools that stand in drains,
Let fall upon its back the soot that falls from chimneys,
Slipped by the terrace, made a sudden leap,   20
And seeing that it was a soft October night,
Curled once about the house, and fell asleep.

And indeed there will be time
For the yellow smoke that slides along the street,
Rubbing its back upon the window-panes;
There will be time, there will be time
To prepare a face to meet the faces that you meet;
There will be time to murder and create,
And time for all the works and days of hands
That lift and drop a question on your plate;   30
Time for you and time for me,
And time yet for a hundred indecisions,
And for a hundred visions and revisions,
Before the taking of a toast and tea.

In the room the women come and go
Talking of Michelangelo.

And indeed there will be time
To wonder, "Do I dare?" and, "Do I dare?"
Time to turn back and descend the stair,
With a bald spot in the middle of my hair—   40

[2] The allusions throughout to heroic and passionate artists—Dante, Michelangelo, Marvell ("To His Coy Mistress"), and Shakespeare (lines 52, cf. the opening lines of *Twelfth Night,* and 111)—point up the opposite character, enervated, indecisive, of Prufrock.

[They will say: "How his hair is growing thin!"]
My morning coat, my collar mounting firmly to the chin,
My necktie rich and modest, but asserted by a simple pin—
[They will say: "But how his arms and legs are thin!"]
Do I dare
Disturb the universe?
In a minute there is time
For decisions and revisions which a minute will reverse.

For I have known them all already, known them all:—
Have known the evenings, mornings, afternoons,   50
I have measured out my life with coffee spoons;
I know the voices dying with a dying fall
Beneath the music from a farther room.
　　So how should I presume?

And I have known the eyes already, known them all—
The eyes that fix you in a formulated phrase,
And when I am formulated, sprawling on a pin,
When I am pinned and wriggling on the wall,
Then how should I begin
To spit out all the butt-ends of my days and ways?   60
　　And how should I presume?

And I have known the arms already, known them all—
Arms that are braceleted and white and bare
[But in the lamplight, downed with light brown hair!]
Is it perfume from a dress
That makes me so digress?
Arms that lie along a table, or wrap about a shawl.
　　And should I then presume?
　　And how should I begin?

　　　　　　　　·　·　·　·　·

Shall I say, I have gone at dusk through narrow streets   70
And watched the smoke that rises from the pipes
Of lonely men in shirt-sleeves, leaning out of windows? . . .

　　I should have been a pair of ragged claws
Scuttling across the floors of silent seas.

　　　　　　　　·　·　·　·　·

And the afternoon, the evening, sleeps so peacefully!
Smoothed by long fingers,

Asleep . . . tired . . . or it malingers,
Stretched on the floor, here beside you and me.
Should I, after tea and cakes and ices,
Have the strength to force the moment to its crisis?   80
But though I have wept and fasted, wept and prayed,
Though I have seen my head [grown slightly bald] brought in
        upon a platter,
I am no prophet[3]—and here's no great matter;
I have seen the moment of my greatness flicker,
And I have seen the eternal Footman hold my coat, and
        snicker,
And in short, I was afraid.

And would it have been worth it, after all,
After the cups, the marmalade, the tea,
Among the porcelain, among some talk of you and me,
Would it have been worth while,   90
To have bitten off the matter with a smile,
To have squeezed the universe into a ball
To roll it toward some overwhelming question,
To say: "I am Lazarus, come from the dead,[4]
Come back to tell you all, I shall tell you all"—
If one, settling a pillow by her head,
        Should say: "That is not what I meant at all.
        That is not it, at all."

And would it have been worth it, after all,
Would it have been worth while,   100
After the sunsets and the dooryards and the sprinkled streets,
After the novels, after the teacups, after the skirts that trail
        along the floor—
And this, and so much more?—
It is impossible to say just what I mean!
But as if a magic lantern threw the nerves in patterns on a
        screen:
Would it have been worth while
If one, settling a pillow or throwing off a shawl,
And turning toward the window, should say:
        "That is not it at all,
        That is not what I meant, at all."   110

                .   .   .   .   .

[3] Matthew 14:1–12; Mark 6:14–29.   [4] John 12:1.

No! I am not Prince Hamlet, nor was meant to be;
Am an attendant lord, one that will do
To swell a progress, start a scene or two,
Advise the prince; no doubt, an easy tool,
Deferential, glad to be of use,
Politic, cautious, and meticulous;
Full of high sentence, but a bit obtuse;
At times, indeed, almost ridiculous—
Almost, at times, the Fool.

I grow old . . . I grow old . . .   120
I shall wear the bottoms of my trousers rolled.

Shall I part my hair behind? Do I dare to eat a peach?
I shall wear white flannel trousers, and walk upon the beach.
I have heard the mermaids singing, each to each.

I do not think that they will sing to me.

I have seen them riding seaward on the waves
Combing the white hair of the waves blown back
When the wind blows the water white and black.

We have lingered in the chambers of the sea
By sea-girls wreathed with seaweed red and brown   130
Till human voices wake us, and we drown.

Little Gidding[5]

1

Midwinter spring is its own season
Sempiternal though sodden towards sundown,
Suspended in time, between pole and tropic.
When the short day is brightest, with frost and fire,
The brief sun flames the ice, on pond and ditches,
In windless cold that is the heart's heat,
Reflecting in a watery mirror
A glare that is blindness in the early afternoon.
And glow more intense than blaze of branch, or brazier,
Stirs the dumb spirit: no wind, but pentecostal fire   10
In the dark time of the year. Between melting and freezing

[5] A chapel in Huntingdonshire, a religious retreat destroyed by Cromwell and restored in the nineteenth century; the poet has come there to pray.

The soul's sap quivers. There is no earth smell
Or smell of living thing. This is the spring time
But not in time's covenant. Now the hedgerow
Is blanched for an hour with transitory blossom
Of snow, a bloom more sudden
Than that of summer, neither budding nor fading,
Not in the scheme of generation.
Where is the summer, the unimaginable
Zero summer?

If you came this way, 20
Taking the route you would be likely to take
From the place you would be likely to come from,
If you came this way in may time, you would find the hedges
White again, in May, with voluptuary sweetness.
It would be the same at the end of the journey,
If you came at night like a broken king,[6]
If you came by day not knowing what you came for,
It would be the same, when you leave the rough road
And turn behind the pig-sty to the dull façade
And the tombstone. And what you thought you came for 30
Is only a shell, a husk of meaning
From which the purpose breaks only when it is fulfilled
If at all. Either you had no purpose
Or the purpose is beyond the end you figured
And is altered in fulfilment. There are other places
Which also are the world's end, some at the sea jaws,
Or over a dark lake, in a desert or a city—
But this is the nearest, in place and time,
Now and in England.

If you came this way,
Taking any route, starting from anywhere, 40
At any time or at any season,
It would always be the same: you would have to put off
Sense and notion. You are not here to verify,
Instruct yourself, or inform curiosity
Or carry report. You are here to kneel
Where prayer has been valid. And prayer is more
Than an order of words, the conscious occupation
Of the praying mind, or the sound of the voice praying.

[6] Charles I (reigned from 1625 to 1649), who sought refuge there after his
defeat by Cromwell in 1646.

And what the dead had no speech for, when living,
They can tell you, being dead: the communication
Of the dead is tongued with fire[7] beyond the language of the living.
Here, the intersection of the timeless moment
Is England and nowhere. Never and always.

2

Ash on an old man's sleeve
Is all the ash the burnt roses leave.
Dust in the air suspended
Marks the place where a story ended.
Dust inbreathed was a house—
The wall, the wainscot and the mouse.
The death of hope and despair,
    This is the death of air.

   There are flood and drouth
Over the eyes and in the mouth,
Dead water and dead sand
Contending for the upper hand.
The parched eviscerate soil
Gapes at the vanity of toil,
Laughs without mirth.
    This is the death of earth.

   Water and fire succeed
The town, the pasture and the weed.
Water and fire deride
The sacrifice that we denied.
Water and fire shall rot
The marred foundations we forgot,
Of sanctuary and choir.
    This is the death of water and fire.

  In the uncertain hour before the morning[8]
    Near the ending of interminable night

---

[7] Fire provides the central symbolism of this poem, and it suggests both Heaven and Hell: the fiery pentecostal descent of the Dove, the purifying flames of Purgatory and the punishing flames of Hell, the fires of Divine Love.

[8] An encounter like many in Dante, and with a peculiarly Dantesque treatment, begins here. The "dead master" physically suggests Brunetto Lantini of *Inferno*, XV.25–30, and there are buried allusions as well to Virgil, Mallarmé, Swift, and Shakespeare; but the figure chiefly suggests Yeats, and the lines beginning with 111 and ending with 146 should be compared with his poem *Vacillation* (page 322) particularly.

At the recurrent end of the unending
After the dark dove with the flickering tongue
Had passed below the horizon of his homing
While the dead leaves still rattled on like tin
Over the asphalt where no other sound was
Between three districts whence the smoke arose
I met one walking, loitering and hurried
As if blown towards me like the metal leaves
Before the urban dawn wind unresisting.
And as I fixed upon the down-turned face
That pointed scrutiny with which we challenge
The first-met stranger in the waning dusk
I caught the sudden look of some dead master
Whom I had known, forgotten, half recalled
Both one and many; in the brown baked features
The eyes of a familiar compound ghost
Both intimate and unidentifiable.
So I assumed a double part, and cried
And heard another's voice cry: "What! are *you* here?"
Although we were not. I was still the same,
Knowing myself yet being someone other—
And he a face still forming; yet the words sufficed
To compel the recognition they preceded.
And so, compliant to the common wind,
Too strange to each other for misunderstanding,
In concord at this intersection time
Of meeting nowhere, no before and after,
We trod the pavement in a dead patrol.
I said: "The wonder that I feel is easy,
Yet ease is cause of wonder. Therefore speak:
I may not comprehend, may not remember."
And he: "I am not eager to rehearse
My thought and theory which you have forgotten.
These things have served their purpose: let them be.
So with your own, and pray they be forgiven
By others, as I pray you to forgive
Both bad and good. Last season's fruit is eaten
And the fullfed beast shall kick the empty pail.
For last year's words belong to last year's language
And next year's words await another voice.
But, as the passage now presents no hindrance
To the spirit unappeased and peregrine
Between two worlds become much like each other,

So I find words I never thought to speak
   In streets I never thought I should revisit
   When I left my body on a distant shore.
Since our concern was speech, and speech impelled us
   To purify the dialect of the tribe
   And urge the mind to aftersight and foresight,
Let me disclose the gifts reserved for age
   To set a crown upon your lifetime's effort.   130
   First, the cold friction of expiring sense
Without enchantment, offering no promise
   But bitter tastelessness of shadow fruit
   As body and soul begin to fall asunder.
Second, the conscious impotence of rage
   At human folly, and the laceration
   Of laughter at what ceases to amuse.
And last, the rending pain of re-enactment
   Of all that you have done, and been; the shame
   Of motives late revealed, and the awareness   140
Of things ill done and done to others' harm
   Which once you took for exercise of virtue.
   Then fools' approval stings, and honour stains.
From wrong to wrong the exasperated spirit
   Proceeds, unless restored by that refining fire
   Where you must move in measure, like a dancer."
The day was breaking. In the disfigured street
   He left me, with a kind of valediction,
   And faded on the blowing of the horn.

3

There are three conditions which often look alike   150
Yet differ completely, flourish in the same hedgerow:
Attachment to self and to things and to persons, detachment
From self and from things and from persons; and, growing between
     them, indifference
Which resembles the others as death resembles life,
Being between two lives—unflowering, between
The live and the dead nettle. This is the use of memory:
For liberation—not less of love but expanding
Of love beyond desire, and so liberation
From the future as well as the past. Thus, love of a country
Begins as attachment to our own field of action   160
And comes to find that action of little importance
Though never indifferent. History may be servitude,

History may be freedom. See, now they vanish,
The faces and places, with the self which, as it could, loved them,
To become renewed, transfigured, in another pattern.

Sin is Behovely, but[9]
All shall be well, and
All manner of thing shall be well.
If I think, again, of this place,
And of people, not wholly commendable,   170
Of no immediate kin or kindness,
But some of peculiar genius,
All touched by a common genius,
United in the strife which divided them;
If I think of a king at nightfall,[10]
Of three men,[11] and more, on the scaffold
And a few who died forgotten
In other places, here and abroad,[12]
And of one who died blind and quiet,[13]
Why should we celebrate   180
These dead men more than the dying?
It is not to ring the bell backward
Nor is it an incantation
To summon the spectre of a Rose.
We cannot revive old factions
We cannot restore old policies
Or follow an antique drum.
These men, and those who opposed them
And those whom they opposed
Accept the constitution of silence   190
And are folded in a single party.
Whatever we inherit from the fortunate
We have taken from the defeated
What they had to leave us—a symbol:
A symbol perfected in death.
And all shall be well and
All manner of thing shall be well

[9] Lines 166–68, like the lines at the close of this section and the final lines of the poem, are echoes of a famous passage in the mystical Juliana of Norwich's (1343–1443) *Revelations,* meditations on the love of God. The Middle English word *behovely* (cf. our *behoove*) is used in the sense of "inevitable."
[10] Charles I again.
[11] Charles, Archbishop Laud, the Earl of Strafford, all executed by Cromwell.
[12] Possibly Richard Crashaw (1613–49), religious poet, is one of those alluded to here.
[13] John Milton.

By the purification of the motive
In the ground of our beseeching.

4

The dove descending breaks the air   200
With flame of incandescent terror
Of which the tongues declare
The one discharge from sin and error.
The only hope, or else despair
   Lies in the choice of pyre or pyre—
   To be redeemed from fire by fire.

   Who then devised the torment? Love.
Love is the unfamiliar Name
Behind the hands that wove
The intolerable shirt of flame   210
Which human power cannot remove.
   We only live, only suspire
   Consumed by either fire or fire.

5

What we call the beginning is often the end
And to make an end is to make a beginning.
The end is where we start from. And every phrase
And sentence that is right (where every word is at home,
Taking its place to support the others,
The word neither diffident nor ostentatious,
An easy commerce of the old and the new,   220
The common word exact without vulgarity,
The formal word precise but not pedantic,
The complete consort dancing together)
Every phrase and every sentence is an end and a beginning,
Every poem an epitaph. And any action
Is a step to the block, to the fire, down the sea's throat
Or to an illegible stone: and that is where we start.
We die with the dying:
See, they depart, and we go with them.
We are born with the dead: 230
See, they return, and bring us with them.
The moment of the rose and the moment of the yew-tree
Are of equal duration. A people without history
Is not redeemed from time, for history is a pattern
Of timeless moments. So, while the light fails

On a winter's afternoon, in a secluded chapel
History is now and England.
With the drawing of this Love and the voice of this Calling[14]

We shall not cease from exploration
And the end of all our exploring   240
Will be to arrive where we started
And know the place for the first time.
Through the unknown, remembered gate
When the last of earth left to discover
Is that which was the beginning;
At the source of the longest river
The voice of the hidden waterfall
And the children in the apple-tree
Not known, because not looked for
But heard, half-heard, in the stillness   250
Between two waves of the sea.
Quick now, here, now, always—
A condition of complete simplicity
(Costing not less than everything)
And all shall be well and
All manner of thing shall be well
When the tongues of flame are in-folded
Into the crowned knot of fire
And the fire and the rose are one.

Conrad Aiken / 1889–

The Wedding[1]

At noon, Tithonus, withered by his singing,
Climbing the oatstalk with his hairy legs,
Met grey Arachne, poisoned and shrunk down
By her own beauty; pride had shrivelled both.

[14] This line comes from the anonymous fourteenth-century mystical treatise *The Cloud of Unknowing* and underlines the point that history provides the stage for spiritual events.

[1] In Greek legend Tithonus, a beautiful Trojan, was changed into a grasshopper; Arachne, in quite a different Greek story and for quite different reasons, was changed into a spider. This poem, in its bittersweet way, brings these two characters—and stories—together.

In the white web—where seven flies hung wrapped—
She heard his footstep; hurried to him; bound him;
Enshrouded him in silk; then poisoned him.
Twice shrieked Tithonus, feebly; then was still.
Arachne loved him. Did he love Arachne?
She watched him with red eyes, venomous sparks,   10
And the furred claws outspread . . . "O sweet Tithonus!
Darling! Be kind, and sing that song again!
Shake the bright web again with that deep fiddling!
Are you much poisoned? sleeping? do you dream?
Darling Tithonus!"

      And Tithonus, weakly
Moving one hairy shin against the other
Within the silken sack, contrived to fiddle
A little tune, half-hearted: "Shrewd Arachne!
Whom pride in beauty withered to this shape
As pride in singing shrivelled me to mine—   20
Unwrap me, let me go—and let me limp,
With what poor strength your venom leaves me, down
This oatstalk, and away."

      Arachne, angry,
Stung him again, twirling him with rough paws,
The red eyes keen. "What! You would dare to leave me?
Unkind Tithonus! Sooner I'll kill and eat you
Than let you go. But sing that tune again—
So plaintive was it!"

      And Tithonus faintly
Moved the poor fiddles, which were growing cold,
And sang: "Arachne, goddess envied of gods,   30
Beauty's eclipse eclipsed by angry beauty,
Have pity, do not ask the withered heart
To sing too long for you! My strength goes out,
Too late we meet for love. O be content
With friendship, which the noon sun once may kindle
To give one flash of passion, like a dewdrop,
Before it goes! . . . Be reasonable,—Arachne!"

Arachne heard the song grow weaker, dwindle
To first a rustle, and then half a rustle,
And last a tick, so small no ear could hear it   40
Save hers, a spider's ear. And her small heart,
(Rusted away, like his, to a pinch of dust,)

Gleamed once, like his, and died. She clasped him tightly
And sunk her fangs in him. Tithonus dead,
She slept awhile, her last sensation gone;
Woke from the nap, forgetting him; and ate him.

Wilfred Owen / 1893–1918

Dulce et Decorum Est[1]

Bent double, like old beggars under sacks,
Knock-kneed, coughing like hags, we cursed through sludge,
Till on the haunting flares we turned our backs,
And towards our distant rest began to trudge.
Men marched asleep. Many had lost their boots,
But limped on, blood-shod. All went lame, all blind;
Drunk with fatigue; deaf even to the hoots
Of gas-shells dropping softly behind.

Gas! Gas! Quick, boys!—An ecstasy of fumbling,
Fitting the clumsy helmets just in time,   10
But someone still was yelling out and stumbling
And flound'ring like a man in fire or lime.
Dim through the misty panes and thick green light,
As under a green sea, I saw him drowning.

In all my dreams before my helpless sight
He plunges at me, guttering, choking, drowning.

If in some smothering dreams, you too could pace
Behind the wagon that we flung him in,
And watch the white eyes writhing in his face,
His hanging face, like a devil's sick of sin,   20
If you could hear, at every jolt, the blood
Come gargling from the froth-corrupted lungs
Bitter as the cud
Of vile, incurable sores on innocent tongues,—
My friend, you would not tell with such high zest
To children ardent for some desperate glory,
The old lie: *Dulce et decorum est*
Pro patria mori.

[1] "It is sweet and proper [to die for one's country]."

What passing-bells for these who die as cattle?
  Only the monstrous anger of the guns.
Only the stuttering rifles' rapid rattle
  Can patter out their hasty orisons.
No mockeries for them from prayers or bells,
  Nor any voice of mourning save the choirs,—
The shrill, demented choirs of wailing shells;
  And bugles calling for them from sad shires.

What candles may be held to speed them all?
  Not in the hands of boys, but in their eyes
Shall shine the holy glimmers of good-byes.
  The pallor of girls' brows shall be their pall;
Their flowers the tenderness of silent minds,
And each slow dusk a drawing-down of blinds.

10

E. E. Cummings / 1894-1962

anyone lived in a pretty how town

anyone lived in a pretty how town
(with up so floating many bells down)
spring summer autumn winter
he sang his didn't he danced his did.

Women and men(both little and small)
cared for anyone not at all
they sowed their isn't they reaped their same
sun moon stars rain

children guessed(but only a few
and down they forgot as up they grew
autumn winter spring summer)
that noone loved him more by more

10

when by now and tree by leaf
she laughed his joy she cried his grief
bird by snow and stir by still
anyone's any was all to her

someones married their everyones
laughed their cryings and did their dance
(sleep wake hope and then)they
said their nevers they slept their dream

stars rain sun moon
(and only the snow can begin to explain
how children are apt to forget to remember
with up so floating many bells down)

one day anyone died i guess
(and noone stooped to kiss his face)
busy folk buried them side by side
little by little and was by was

all by all and deep by deep
and more by more they dream their sleep

noone and anyone earth by april
wish by spirit and if by yes.

Women and men(both dong and ding)
summer autumn winter spring
reaped their sowing and went their came
sun moon stars rain

my father moved through dooms of love

my father moved through dooms of love
through sames of am through haves of give,
singing each morning out of each night
my father moved through depths of height

this motionless forgetful where
turned at his glance to shining here;
that if(so timid air is firm)
under his eyes would stir and squirm

newly as from unburied which
floats the first who,his april touch

drove sleeping selves to swarm their fates
woke dreamers to their ghostly roots

and should some why completely weep
my father's fingers brought her sleep:

vainly no smallest voice might cry
for he could feel the mountains grow.

Lifting the valleys of the sea
my father moved through griefs of joy;
praising a forehead called the moon
singing desire into begin   20

joy was his song and joy so pure
a heart of star by him could steer
and pure so now and now so yes
the wrists of twilight would rejoice

keen as midsummer's keen beyond
conceiving mind of sun will stand,
so strictly(over utmost him
so hugely)stood my father's dream

his flesh was flesh his blood was blood:
no hungry man but wished him food;   30
no cripple wouldn't creep one mile
uphill to only see him smile.

Scorning the pomp of must and shall
my father moved through dooms of feel;
his anger was as right as rain
his pity was as green as grain

septembering arms of year extend
less humbly wealth to foe and friend
than he to foolish and to wise
offered immeasurable is   40

proudly and(by octobering flame
beckoned)as earth will downward climb,
so naked for immortal work
his shoulders marched against the dark

his sorrow was as true as bread:
no liar looked him in the head;
if every friend became his foe
he'd laugh and build a world with snow.

My father moved through theys of we,
singing each new leaf out of each tree   50
(and every child was sure that spring
danced when she heard my father sing)

then let men kill which cannot share,
let blood and flesh be mud and mire,
scheming imagine,passion willed,
freedom a drug that's bought and sold

giving to steal and cruel kind,
a heart to fear,to doubt a mind,
to differ a disease of same,
conform the pinnacle of am   60

though dull were all we taste as bright,
bitter all utterly things sweet,
maggoty minus and dumb death
all we inherit,all bequeath

and nothing quite so least as truth
—i say though hate were why men breathe—
because my father lived his soul
love is the whole and more than all

Robert Graves / 1895–

Ulysses[1]

To the much-tossed Ulysses, never done
  With woman whether gowned as wife or whore,
Penelope and Circe seemed as one:
She like a whore made his lewd fancies run,
  And wifely she a hero to him bore.

  Their counter-changings terrified his way:
  They were the clashing rocks, Symplegades,
Scylla and Charybdis too were they;
Now they were storms frosting the sea with spray
  And now the lotus island's drunken ease.   10

They multiplied into the Sirens' throng,
  Forewarned by fear of whom he stood bound fast
Hand and foot helpless to the vessel's mast,

[1] This poem alludes to some well-known episodes in Homer's *Odyssey*, which tells of Ulysses' adventures on his return to Ithaca following the Trojan War.

Yet would not stop his ears: daring their song
   He groaned and sweated till that shore was past.

One, two and many: flesh had made him blind,
   Flesh had one pleasure only in the act,
Flesh set one purpose only in the mind—
Triumph of flesh and afterwards to find
   Still those same terrors wherewith flesh was racked.   20

His wiles were witty and his fame far known,
Every king's daughter sought him for her own,
   Yet he was nothing to be won or lost.
   All hands to him with Ithaca: love-tossed
He loathed the fraud, yet would not bed alone.

Down, Wanton, Down!

Down, wanton, down! Have you no shame
That at the whisper of Love's name,
Or Beauty's, presto! up you raise
Your angry head and stand at gaze?

Poor bombard-captain, sworn to reach
The ravelin and effect a breach—
Indifferent what you storm or why,
So be that in the breach you die!

Love may be blind, but Love at least
Knows what is man and what mere beast;   10
Or Beauty wayward, but requires
More delicacy from her squires.

Tell me, my witless, whose one boast
Could be your staunchness at the post,
When were you made a man of parts
To think fine and profess the arts?

Will many-gifted Beauty come
Bowing to your bald rule of thumb,
Or Love swear loyalty to your crown?
Be gone, have done! Down, wanton, down!   20

To Emily Dickinson

You who desired so much—in vain to ask—
Yet fed your hunger like an endless task,
Dared dignify the labor, bless the quest—
Achieved that stillness ultimately best,

Being, of all, least sought for: Emily, hear!
O sweet, dead Silencer, most suddenly clear
When singing that Eternity possessed
And plundered momently in every breast;

—Truly no flower yet withers in your hand,
The harvest you descried and understand   10
Needs more than wit to gather, love to bind.
Some reconcilement of remotest mind—

Leaves Ormus rubyless, and Ophir chill.[1]
Else tears heap all within one clay-cold hill.

Emblems of Conduct

By a peninsula the wanderer sat and sketched
The uneven valley graves. While the apostle gave
Alms to the meek the volcano burst
With sulphur and aureate rocks . . .
For joy rides in stupendous coverings
Luring the living into spiritual gates.

Orators follow the universe
And radio the complete laws to the people.
The apostle conveys thought through discipline.
Bowls and cups fill historians with adorations,—   10
Dull lips commemorating spiritual gates.

The wanderer later chose this spot of rest
Where marble clouds support the sea
And where was finally borne a chosen hero.
By that time summer and smoke were past.

---

[1] West Asian settlements, one (Hormuz) famous for its rubies, the other for its gold.

Dolphins still played, arching the horizons,
But only to build memories of spiritual gates.

Allen Tate / 1899–

Mr. Pope

When Alexander Pope strolled in the city
Strict was the glint of pearl and gold sedans.
Ladies leaned out, more out of fear than pity;
For Pope's tight back was rather a goat's than man's.

One often thinks the urn should have more bones
Than skeletons provide for speedy dust;
The urn gets hollow, cobwebs brittle as stones
Weave to the funeral shell a frivolous rust.

And he who dribbled couplets like the snake
Coiled to a lithe precision in the sun,   10
Is missing. The jar is empty; you may break
It only to find that Mr. Pope is gone.

What requisitions of a verity
Prompted the wit and rage between his teeth
One cannot say: around a crooked tree
A moral climbs whose name should be a wreath.

C. Day Lewis / 1904–

Yes, Why Do We All, Seeing a Red, Feel Small?

Yes, why do we all, seeing a Red, feel small? That small
Catspaw ruffles our calm—how comes it? That touch of storm
Brewing, shivers the torches even in this vault? And the shame
Unsettles a high esteem? Here it is. There fall
From him shadows of what he is building: bold and tall—
For his sun has barely mastered the misted horizon—they seem.
Indeed he casts a shadow, as among the dead will some

Living one. It is the future walking to meet us all.
Mark him. He is only what we are, mortal. Yet from the night
Of history, where we lie dreaming still, he is wide awake: 10
Weak, liable to ill luck—yet rock where we are slight
Eddies, and amid us islands the spring tide beginning to make.
Mark him, workers and all who wish the world aright:
He is what your sons could be, the road these times should take.

Howard Baker / 1905–

The End of the Year 1939

Gray is the sky, and black the tree
That breaks above the muddy field.
The year ends. Eyes cannot foresee
What the stark twigs in time may yield.

Blind too is the denuded heart.
Europe in its own guile is caught;
The Orient still writhes apart;
Russia has stirred too deep for thought.

Upon the sky the twigs scratch lines.
The earth to simplest lines returns,   10
Till the rude sap itself defines
What leaf, what blossom in it burns.

Robert Penn Warren / 1905–

Original Sin: A Short Story

Nodding, its great head rattling like a gourd,
And locks like seaweed strung on the stinking stone,
The nightmare stumbles past, and you have heard
It fumble your door before it whimpers and is gone:
It acts like the old hound that used to snuffle your door and moan.

You thought you had lost it when you left Omaha,
For it seemed connected then with your grandpa, who
Had a wen on his forehead and sat on the veranda
To finger the precious protuberance, as was his habit to do,
Which glinted in sun like rough garnet or the rich old brain bulging
    through.   10

But you met it in Harvard Yard as the historic steeple
Was confirming the midnight with its hideous racket,
And you wondered how it had come, for it stood so imbecile,
With empty hands, humble, and surely nothing in pocket:
Riding the rods, perhaps—or grandpa's will paid the ticket.

You were almost kindly then, in your first homesickness,
As it tortured its stiff face to speak, but scarcely mewed;
Since then you have outlived all your homesickness,
But have met it in many another distempered latitude:
Oh, nothing is lost, ever lost! at last you understood.   20

But it never came in the quantum glare of sun
To shame you before your friends, and had nothing to do
With your public experience or private reformation:
But it thought no bed too narrow—it stood with lips askew
And shook its great head sadly like the abstract Jew.

Never met you in the lyric arsenical meadows
When children call and your heart goes stone in the bosom;
At the orchard anguish never, nor ovoid horror,
Which is furred like a peach or avid like the delicious plum.
It takes no part in your classic prudence or fondled axiom.   30

Not there when you exclaimed: "Hope is betrayed by
Disastrous glory of sea-capes, sun-torment of whitecaps
—There must be a new innocence for us to be stayed by."
But there it stood, after all the timetables, all the maps,
In the crepuscular clutter of *always, always,* or *perhaps.*

You have moved often and rarely left an address,
And hear of the deaths of friends with a sly pleasure,
A sense of cleansing and hope, which blooms from distress;
But it has not died, it comes, its hand childish, unsure,
Clutching the bribe of chocolate or a toy you used to treasure.   40

It tries the lock; you hear, but simply drowse:
There is nothing remarkable in that sound at the door.
Later you may hear it wander the dark house
Like a mother who rises at night to seek a childhood picture;
Or it goes to the backyard and stands like an old horse cold in the
pasture.

W. H. Auden / 1907–

Petition

Sir, no man's enemy, forgiving all
But will its negative inversion, be prodigal:
Send to us power and light, a sovereign touch
Curing the intolerable neural itch,
The exhaustion of weaning, the liar's quinsy,
And the distortions of ingrown virginity.
Prohibit sharply the rehearsed response
And gradually correct the coward's stance;
Cover in time with beams those in retreat
That, spotted, they turn though the reverse were great;   10
Publish each healer that in city lives
Or country houses at the end of drives;
Harrow the house of the dead; look shining at
New styles of architecture, a change of heart.

September 1, 1939 [1]

I sit in one of the dives
On Fifty-second Street
Uncertain and afraid
As the clever hopes expire
Of a low dishonest decade:
Waves of anger and fear
Circulate over the bright
And darkened lands of the earth,
Obsessing our private lives;

[1] On this day the German invasion of Poland unleashed World War II.

The unmentionable odour of death
Offends the September night.

Accurate scholarship can
Unearth the whole offence
From Luther until now
That has driven a culture mad,
Find what occurred at Linz,
What huge imago made
A psychopathic god: [2]
I and the public know
What all schoolchildren learn,
Those to whom evil is done
Do evil in return.

Exiled Thucydides[3] knew
All that a speech can say
About Democracy,
And what dictators do,
The elderly rubbish they talk
To an apathetic grave;
Analysed all in his book,
The enlightenment driven away,
The habit-forming pain,
Mismanagement and grief:
We must suffer them all again.

Into this neutral air
Where blind skyscrapers use
Their full height to proclaim
The strength of Collective Man,
Each language pours its vain
Competitive excuse:
But who can live for long
In an euphoric dream;
Out of the mirror they stare,
Imperialism's face
And the international wrong.

[2] In 1938 Adolf Hitler at Linz, the town where he had been an unhappy school-boy, declared the Austrian Republic at an end and absorbed it into the German Reich. He thus brought to its climax an historical process that began with Luther and the separation of the German states from the Holy Roman Empire. That process was at once to create the possibility of the all-powerful State and the reality of all-powerful individuals in the form of demented dictators.
[3] Greek historian of Athens (460?–400? B.C.).

Faces along the bar
Cling to their average day:
The lights must never go out,
The music must always play,
All the conventions conspire
To make this fort assume   50
The furniture of home;
Lest we should see where we are,
Lost in a haunted wood,
Children afraid of the night
Who have never been happy or good.

The windiest militant trash
Important Persons shout
Is not so crude as our wish:
What mad Nijinsky wrote
About Diaghilev[4]   60
Is true of the normal heart;
For the error bred in the bone
Of each woman and each man
Craves what it cannot have,
Not universal love
But to be loved alone.

From the conservative dark
Into the ethical life
The dense commuters come,
Repeating their morning vow;   70
"I *will* be true to the wife,
I'll concentrate more on my work,"
And helpless governors wake
To resume their compulsory game:
Who can release them now,
Who can reach the deaf,
Who can speak for the dumb?

All I have is a voice
To undo the folded lie,
The romantic lie in the brain   80
Of the sensual man-in-the-street
And the lie of Authority

[4] Vaslav Nijinsky (1890–1950) was one of the world's greatest ballet dancers; his career was cut short by insanity. Sergei Pavlovich Diaghilev (1872–1929) was the impresario who fostered that career.

Whose buildings grope the sky:
There is no such thing as the State
And no one exists alone;
Hunger allows no choice
To the citizen or the police;
We must love one another or die.[5]

Defenceless under the night
Our world in stupor lies;
Yet, dotted everywhere,
Ironic points of light
Flash out wherever the Just
Exchange their messages:
May I, composed like them
Of Eros and of dust,[6]
Beleaguered by the same
Negation and despair,
Show an affirming flame.

90

In Memory of W. B. Yeats

(d. Jan. 1939)

1

He disappeared in the dead of winter:
The brooks were frozen, the airports almost deserted,
And snow disfigured the public statues;
The mercury sank in the mouth of the dying day.
O all the instruments agree
The day of his death was a dark cold day.

Far from his illness
The wolves ran on through the evergreen forests,
The peasant river was untempted by the fashionable quays;
By mourning tongues
The death of the poet was kept from his poems.

10

But for him it was his last afternoon as himself,
An afternoon of nurses and rumours;

[5] This line was later changed to read, "We must love one another and die"; but, still unsatisfied, the poet subsequently deleted the entire stanza beginning with line 78 and, ultimately, the entire poem from his preferred work.
[6] The sex (or life) impulse, intertwined with Thanatos, the death impulse (Freud).

The provinces of his body revolted,
The squares of his mind were empty,
Silence invaded the suburbs,
The current of his feeling failed: he became his admirers.

Now he is scattered among a hundred cities
And wholly given over to unfamiliar affections;
To find his happiness in another kind of wood   20
And be punished under a foreign code of conscience.
The words of a dead man
Are modified in the guts of the living.

But in the importance and noise of tomorrow
When the brokers are roaring like beasts on the floor of the Bourse,
And the poor have the sufferings to which they are fairly accustomed,
And each in the cell of himself is almost convinced of his freedom;
A few thousand will think of this day
As one thinks of a day when one did something slightly unusual.

O all the instruments agree   30
The day of his death was a dark cold day.

2

You were silly like us: [7] your gift survived it all;
The parish of rich women, physical decay,
Yourself; mad Ireland hurt you into poetry.
Now Ireland has her madness and her weather still,
For poetry makes nothing happen: it survives
In the valley of its saying where executives
Would never want to tamper; it flows south
From ranches of isolation and the busy griefs,
Raw towns that we believe and die in; it survives,   40
A way of happening, a mouth.

3

Earth, receive an honoured guest;
William Yeats is laid to rest:
Let the Irish vessel lie
Emptied of its poetry.

[7] Auden may be thinking of Yeats's late, somewhat fascistic political inclinations, or of his spiritualistic and cabalistic "system"-building, or of certain personal habits and proclivities.

Time that is intolerant
Of the brave and innocent,
And indifferent in a week
To a beautiful physique,

Worships language and forgives   50
Everyone by whom it lives;
Pardons cowardice, conceit,
Lays its honours at their feet.

Time that with this strange excuse
Pardoned Kipling[8] and his views,
And will pardon Paul Claudel,[9]
Pardons him for writing well.

In the nightmare of the dark
All the dogs of Europe bark,
And the living nations wait,   60
Each sequestered in its hate;

Intellectual disgrace
Stares from every human face,
And the seas of pity lie
Locked and frozen in each eye.

Follow, poet, follow right
To the bottom of the night,
With your unconstraining voice
Still persuade us to rejoice;

With the farming of a verse   70
Make a vineyard of the curse,
Sing of human unsuccess
In a rapture of distress;

In the deserts of the heart
Let the healing fountain start,
In the prison of his days
Teach the free man how to praise.

[8] Rudyard Kipling (1865–1936), English poet, story writer, and apologist for British imperialism.
[9] French Roman Catholic poet (1868–1955), violently anti-Protestant, and long unrecognized.

To T. S. Eliot on His Sixtieth Birthday

(1948)

When things began to happen to our favorite spot,
A key missing, a library bust defaced,
    Then on the tennis-court one morning,
    Outrageous, the bloody corpse and always,

Blank day after day, the unheard-of drought, it was you
Who, not speechless from shock but finding the right
    Language for thirst and fear, did much to
    Prevent a panic. It is the crime that

Counts, you will say. We know, but would gratefully add,
Today as we wait for the Law to take its course,   10
    (And which of us shall escape whipping?)
    That your sixty years have not been wasted.

Elegy for J. F. K.

(November 22nd, 1963)

Why *then*, why *there*,
Why *thus*, we cry, did he die?
The heavens are silent.

What he was, he was:
What he is fated to become
Depends on us.

Remembering his death,
How we choose to live
Will decide its meaning.

When a just man dies,   10
Lamentation and praise,
Sorrow and joy, are one.

Louis MacNeice / 1907–1963

Babel

There was a tower that went before a fall.
    Can't we ever, my love, speak in the same language?
Its nerves grew worse and worse as it grew tall.
    Have we no aims in common?

As children we were bickering over beads—
    Can't we ever, my love, speak in the same language?
The more there are together, Togetherness recedes.
    Have we no aims in common?

Exiles all as we are in a foreign city,
    Can't we ever, my love, speak in the same language?   10
We cut each other's throats out of our great self-pity—
    Have we no aims in common?

Patriots, dreamers, die-hards, theoreticians, all,
    Can't we ever, my love, speak in the same language,
Or shall we go, still quarrelling over words, to the wall?
    Have we no aims in common?

Epitaph for Liberal Poets[1]

If in the latter
End—which is fairly soon—our way of life goes west
And some shall say So What and some What Matter,
Ready under new names to exploit or be exploited,
What, though better unsaid, would we have history say
Of us who walked in our sleep and died on our Quest?

We who always had, but never admitted, a master,
Who were expected—and paid—to be ourselves,
Conditioned to think freely, how can we   9
Patch up our broken hearts and modes of thought in plaster
And glorify in chromium-plated stories
Those who shall supersede us and cannot need us—
The tight-lipped technocratic Conquistadores?

---

[1] MacNeice's contemporaries and associates—Auden, Day Lewis, Spender, etc.—
as young men held Left political convictions, which were much qualified by the
actualities of European political developments in the late 1930's.

The Individual has died before; Catullus[2]
Went down young, gave place to those who were born old
And more adaptable and were not even jealous
Of his wild life and lyrics. Though our songs
Were not so warm as his, our fate is no less cold.

Such silence then before us, pinned against the wall,
Why need we whine? There is no way out, the birds   20
Will tell us nothing more; we shall vanish first,
Yet leave behind us certain frozen words
Which some day, though not certainly, may melt
And, for a moment or two, accentuate a thirst.

Theodore Roethke / 1908–1963

Poem [I Knew a Woman, Lovely in Her Bones]

I knew a woman, lovely in her bones,
When small birds sighed, she would sigh back at them;
Ah, when she moved, she moved more ways than one:
The shapes a bright container can contain!
Of her choice virtues only gods should speak,
Or English poets who grew up on Greek
(I'd have them sing in chorus, cheek to cheek).

How well her wishes went! She stroked my chin,
She taught me Turn, and Counter-turn, and Stand;
She taught me Touch, that undulant white skin;   10
I nibbled meekly from her proffered hand;
She was the sickle; I, poor I, the rake,
Coming behind her for her pretty sake
(But what prodigious mowing we did make).

Love likes a gander, and adores a goose:
Her full lips pursed, the errant note to seize;
She played it quick, she played it light and loose;
My eyes, they dazzled at her flowing knees;
Her several parts could keep a pure repose,
Or one hip quiver with a mobile nose   20
(She moved in circles, and those circles moved).

[2] Great Latin lyricist (84?–54? B.C.).

Let seed be grass, and grass turn into hay:
I'm martyr to a motion not my own;
What's freedom for? To know eternity.
I swear she cast a shadow white as stone.
But who would count eternity in days?
These old bones live to learn her wanton ways:
(I measure time by how a body sways).

Reply to a Lady Editor

If the Poem (beginning "I knew a woman, lovely in her bones") in *The London Times Literary Supplement* has not appeared here, we offer you $75 for it. Could you wire us collect your answer?

Sincerely yours,
Allice S. Morris
Literary Editor, *Harper's Bazaar*

Sweet Alice S. Morris, I *am* pleased, of course,
You take the *Times Supplement,* and read its verse,
And know that True Love is more than a Life-Force
—And so like my poem called *Poem.*

Dan Cupid, I tell you's a braw laddie-buck;
A visit from him is a piece of pure luck,
And should he arrive, why just lean yourself back
—And recite him my poem called *Poem.*

O print it, my dear, do publish it, yes,
That ladies their true natures never suppress,   10
When they come, dazedly, to the pretty pass
—Of acting my poem called *Poem.*

My darling, my dearest, most-honest-alive,
Just send me along that sweet seventy-five;
I'll continue to think on the nature of love,
—As I dance to my poem called *Poem.*

What I Expected

What I expected, was
Thunder, fighting,
Long struggles with men
And climbing.
After continual straining
I should grow strong;
Then the rocks would shake,
And I rest long.

What I had not foreseen
Was the gradual day   10
Weakening the will
Leaking the brightness away,
The lack of good to touch,
The fading of body and soul
—Smoke before wind,
Corrupt, unsubstantial.

The wearing of Time,
And the watching of cripples pass
With limbs shaped like questions
In their odd twist,   20
The pulverous grief
Melting the bones with pity,
The sick falling from earth—
These, I could not foresee.

Expecting always
Some brightness to hold in trust,
Some final innocence
Exempt from dust,
That, hanging solid,
Would dangle through all,   30
Like the created poem,
Or faceted crystal.

Man and Woman

> Through man's love and woman's love
> Moons and tides move
> Which fuse those islands, lying face to face.
> Mixing in naked passion
> Those who naked new life fashion
> Are themselves reborn in naked grace.

One More New Botched Beginning

> Their voices heard, I stumble suddenly,
> Choking in undergrowth. I'm torn
> Mouth pressed against the thorns,
>   remembering
>   Ten years ago here in Geneva,
>
> I walked with Merleau-Ponty[1] by the lake.
> Upon his face I saw his intellect.
> The energy of the sun-interweaving
> Waves, electric, danced on him. His eyes
> Smiled with their gay logic through   10
> Black coins thrown down from leaves. He who
> Was Merleau-Ponty that day is no more
> Irrevocable than the I that day who was
> Beside him—I'm still living!
>
>   Also that summer
> My son stayed up the valley in the mountains.
> One day I went to see him, and he stood
> Not seeing me, watching some hens.
> Doing so, he was absorbed
> In their wire-netted world. He danced   20
> On one leg. Leaning forward, he became
> A bird-boy. I am there
> Still seeing him. To him,
> That moment—unselfknowing even then—
> Is drowned in the oblivious earliness . . .
>
>   Such pasts
>   Are not diminished distances, perspective

---

[1] Maurice Merleau-Ponty (1908–61), French existentialist associated with Jean-Paul Sartre and Simone de Beauvoir on *Le Temps moderne*.

Vanishing points, but doors
Burst open suddenly by gusts
That seek to blow the heart out. 30

Today, I see
Three undergraduates standing talking in
A college quad. They show each other poems—
Louis MacNeice, Bernard Spencer, and I.
Louis caught cold in the rain, Bernard fell
From a train door.

Their lives are now those poems that were
Pointers to the poems to be their lives.
We read there in the college quad, each poem
Is still a new beginning. If 40
They had been finished though, they would have died
Before they died. Being alive
Is when each moment's a new start, with past
And future shuffled between fingers
For a new game. I'm dealing out
My hand to them, one more new botched beginning
There, where we still stand talking in the quad.

Josephine Miles / 1911–

Son

Men have their alien sons and love them,
The dear fist clenched in theirs,
The foreign taste fed at their table,
The wayward walking in their name.
They love their handsome son.

But they hate the foreign, though an open
Five-fingered hand like theirs,
The gall taste deep as another nation,
The ugly accent in an alien name.
Hate all but him, dear father, and dear son. 10

Oedipus[1]

The gang wanted to give Oedipus Rex a going away present.
He had been a good hard-working father and king.
And besides it is the custom in this country
To give gifts on departure.

But we didn't know what to give Oedipus; he had everything.
Even in his loss, he had more than average.
So we gave him a travelling case, fitted, which we personally
Should have liked to receive.

John Berryman / 1914–

There Sat Down, Once, a Thing on Henry's Heart

There sat down, once, a thing on Henry's[1] heart
só heavy, if he had a hundred years
& more, & weeping, sleepless, in all them time
Henry could not make good.
Starts again always in Henry's ears
the little cough somewhere, an odour, a chime.

And there is another thing he has in mind
like a grave Sienese face[2] a thousand years
would fail to blur the still profiled reproach of. Ghastly,
with open eyes, he attends, blind.   10
All the bells say: too late. This is not for tears;
thinking.

But never did Henry, as he thought he did,
end anyone and hacks her body up
and hide the pieces, where they may be found.
He knows: he went over everyone, & nobody's missing.
Often he reckons, in the dawn, them up.
Nobody is ever missing.

[1] Self-exiled tragic hero of Greek myth.

---

[1] Henry Pussy-cat, a minstrel show Negro, the principal persona in *77 Dream Songs*, the sequence from which this poem is taken.
[2] The austere, reproachful look in the faces of the pre-Renaissance iconic portraits of the Siena school of painters.

Twenty-four Years

Twenty-four years remind the tears of my eyes.
(Bury the dead for fear that they walk to the grave in labour.)
In the groin of the natural doorway I crouched like a tailor
Sewing a shroud for a journey
By the light of the meat-eating sun.
Dressed to die, the sensual strut begun,
With my red veins full of money,
In the final direction of the elementary town
I advance for as long as forever is.

In My Craft or Sullen Art

In my craft or sullen art
Exercised in the still night
When only the moon rages
And the lovers lie abed
With all their griefs in their arms,
I labour by singing light
Not for ambition or bread
Or the strut and trade of charms
On the ivory stages
But for the common wages   10
Of their most secret heart.

Not for the proud man apart
From the raging moon I write
On these spindrift pages
Nor for the towering dead
With their nightingales and psalms
But for the lovers, their arms
Round the griefs of the ages,
Who pay no praise or wages
Nor heed my craft or art.   20

A Refusal to Mourn the Death, by Fire, of a Child in London

Never until the mankind making
Bird beast and flower
Fathering and all humbling darkness
Tells with silence the last light breaking
And the still hour
Is come of the sea tumbling in harness

And I must enter again the round
Zion of the water bead
And the synagogue of the ear of corn
Shall I let pray the shadow of a sound   10
Or sow my salt seed
In the least valley of sackcloth to mourn

The majesty and burning of the child's death.
I shall not murder
The mankind of her going with a grave truth
Nor blaspheme down the stations of the breath
With any further
Elegy of innocence and youth.

Deep with the first dead lies London's daughter,
Robed in the long friends,   20
The grains beyond age, the dark veins of her mother,
Secret by the unmourning water
Of the riding Thames.
After the first death, there is no other.

Do Not Go Gentle into That Good Night

Do not go gentle into that good night,
Old age should burn and rave at close of day;
Rage, rage against the dying of the light.

Though wise men at their end know dark is right,
Because their words had forked no lightning they
Do not go gentle into that good night.

Good men, the last wave by, crying how bright
Their frail deeds might have danced in a green bay,
Rage, rage against the dying of the light.

Wild men who caught and sang the sun in flight,   ¹⁰
And learn, too late, they grieved it on its way,
Do not go gentle into that good night.

Grave men, near death, who see with blinding sight
Blind eyes could blaze like meteors and be gay,
Rage, rage against the dying of the light.

And you, my father, there on the sad height,
Curse, bless, me now with your fierce tears, I pray.
Do not go gentle into that good night.
Rage, rage against the dying of the light.

Robert Lowell / 1917–

Children of Light

Our fathers wrung their bread from stocks and stones
And fenced their gardens with the Redman's bones;
Embarking from the Nether Land of Holland,
Pilgrims unhouseled by Geneva's night,
They planted here the Serpent's seeds of light;
And here the pivoting searchlights probe to shock
The riotous glass houses built on rock,
And candles gutter by an empty altar,
And light is where the landless blood of Cain
Is burning, burning the unburied grain.   10

For the Union Dead

"Relinquunt Omnia Servare Rem Publicam." [1]

The old South Boston Aquarium stands
in a Sahara of snow now. Its broken windows are boarded.
The bronze weathervane cod has lost half its scales.
The airy tanks are dry.

---

[1] "They give up everything to save the republic." The inscription on the frieze
that the poem describes is nearly identical: "Omnia relinquit" ("He gives up everything") etc.

Once my nose crawled like a snail on the glass;
my hand tingled
to burst the bubbles
drifting from the noses of the cowed, compliant fish.

My hand draws back. I often sigh still
for the dark downward and vegetating kingdom   10
of the fish and reptile. One morning last March,
I pressed against the new barbed and galvanized

fence on the Boston Common. Behind their cage,
yellow dinosaur steamshovels were grunting
as they cropped up tons of mush and grass
to gouge their underworld garage.

Parking spaces luxuriate like civic
sandpiles in the heart of Boston.
A girdle of orange, Puritan-pumpkin colored girders
braces the tingling Statehouse,   20

shaking over the excavations, as it faces Colonel Shaw[2]
and his bell-cheeked Negro infantry
on St. Gaudens' [3] shaking Civil War relief,
propped by a plank splint against the garage's earthquake.

Two months after marching through Boston,
half the regiment was dead;
at the dedication,
William James[4] could almost hear the bronze Negroes breathe.

Their monument sticks like a fishbone
in the city's throat.   30
Its Colonel is as lean
as a compass-needle.

He has an angry wrenlike vigilance,
a greyhound's gentle tautness;
he seems to wince at pleasure,
and suffocate for privacy.

He is out of bounds now. He rejoices in man's lovely,
peculiar power to choose life and die—

[2] Colonel Robert G. Shaw, shown leading his Negro troops on horseback.
[3] Augustus Saint-Gaudens (1848–1907), of French-Irish parentage, became the foremost sculptor in nineteenth-century America.
[4] Harvard pragmatic philosopher and psychologist (1842–1910), who delivered the address at the unveiling of the Shaw monument.

when he leads his black soldiers to death,
he cannot bend his back.   40

On a thousand small town New England greens,
the old white churches hold their air
of sparse, sincere rebellion; frayed flags
quilt the graveyards of the Grand Army of the Republic.

The stone statues of the abstract Union Soldier
grow slimmer and younger each year—
wasp-waisted, they doze over muskets
and muse through their sideburns . . .

Shaw's father wanted no monument
except the ditch,   50
where his son's body was thrown
and lost with his "niggers."

The ditch is nearer.
There are no statues for the last war here;
on Boylston Street, a commercial photograph
shows Hiroshima boiling

over a Mosler Safe, the "Rock of Ages"
that survived the blast. Space is nearer.
When I crouch to my television set,
the drained faces of Negro school-children rise like
      balloons.

Colonel Shaw
is riding on his bubble,
he waits
for the blessèd break.

The Aquarium is gone. Everywhere,
giant finned cars nose forward like fish;
a savage servility
slides by on grease.

Museum Piece

The good gray guardians of art
Patrol the halls on spongy shoes,
Impartially protective, though
Perhaps suspicious of Toulouse.

Here dozes one against the wall,
Disposed upon a funeral chair.
A Degas dancer pirouettes
Upon the parting of his hair.

See how she spins! The grace is there,
But strain as well is plain to see.   10
Degas loved the two together:
Beauty joined to energy.

Edgar Degas purchased once
A fine El Greco, which he kept
Against the wall beside his bed
To hang his pants on while he slept.

Advice to a Prophet

When you come, as you soon must, to the streets of our city,
Mad-eyed from stating the obvious,
Not proclaiming our fall but begging us
In God's name to have self-pity,

Spare us all word of the weapons, their force and range,
The long numbers that rocket the mind;
Our slow, unreckoning hearts will be left behind,
Unable to fear what is too strange.

Nor shall you scare us with talk of the death of the race.
How should we dream of this place without us?—   10
The sun mere fire, the leaves untroubled about us,
A stone look on the stone's face?

Speak of the world's own change. Though we cannot conceive
Of an undreamt thing, we know to our cost

How the dreamt cloud crumbles, the vines are blackened by
    frost,
How the view alters. We could believe,

If you told us so, that the white-tailed deer will slip
Into perfect shade, grown perfectly shy,
The lark avoid the reaches of our eye,
The jack-pine lose its knuckled grip   20

On the cold ledge, and every torrent burn
As Xanthus[1] once, its gliding trout
Stunned in a twinkling. What should we be without
The dolphin's arc, the dove's return,

These things in which we have seen ourselves and spoken?
Ask us, prophet, how we shall call
Our natures forth when that live tongue is all
Dispelled, that glass obscured or broken

In which we have said the rose of our love and the clean
Horse of our courage, in which beheld   30
The singing locust of the soul unshelled,
And all we mean or wish to mean.

Ask us, ask us whether with the worldless rose
Our hearts shall fail us; come demanding
Whether there shall be lofty or long standing
When the bronze annals of the oak-tree close.

Philip Larkin / 1922–

_____

Poetry of Departures

    Sometimes you hear, fifth-hand,
    As epitaph:
    He chucked up everything
    And just cleared off,
    And always the voice will sound
    Certain you approve

[1] A city in Asia Minor on a river of the same name, sacked and burned by the
Romans in 42 B.C. All its inhabitants perished.

This audacious, purifying,
Elemental move.

And they are right, I think.
We all hate home
And having to be there:
I detest my room,
Its specially-chosen junk,
The good books, the good bed,
And my life, in perfect order:
So to hear it said

He walked out on the whole crowd
Leaves me flushed and stirred,
Like *Then she undid her dress*
Or *Take that you bastard;*
Surely I can, if he did?
And that helps me stay
Sober and industrious.
But I'd go today,

Yes, swagger the nut-strewn roads,
Crouch in the fo'c'sle
Stubbly with goodness, if
It weren't so artificial,
Such a deliberate step backwards
To create an object:
Books; china; a life
Reprehensibly perfect.

The Large Cool Store

The large cool store selling cheap clothes
Set out in simple sizes plainly
(Knitwear, Summer Casuals, Hose,
In browns and greys, maroon and navy)
Conjures the weekday world of those

Who leave at dawn low terraced houses
Timed for factory, yard and site.
But past the heaps of shirts and trousers
Spread the stands of Modes For Night:
Machine-embroidered, thin as blouses,

Lemon, sapphire, moss-green, rose
Bri-Nylon Baby-Dolls and Shorties
Flounce in clusters. To suppose
They share that world, to think their sort is
Matched by something in it, shows

How separate and unearthly love is,
Or women are, or what they do,
Or in our young unreal wishes
Seem to be: synthetic, new,
And natureless in ecstasies.   20

Kingsley Amis / 1922–

New Approach Needed

Should you revisit us,
Stay a little longer,
And get to know the place.
Experience hunger,
Madness, disease and war.
You heard about them, true,
The last time you came here;
It's different having them.
And what about a go
At sex, marriage, children?   10
All good, but bringing some
Risk of remorse and pain
And fear of an odd sort:
A sort one should, again,
Feel, not just hear about,
To be qualified as
A human-race expert.
On local life, we trust
The resident witness,
Not the royal tourist.   20

People have suffered worse
And more durable wrongs
Than you did on that cross
(I know—you won't get me

Up on one of those things)
Without much prospect of
Ascending good as new
On the third day, without
"I die, but man shall live"
As a nice cheering thought.   30

So, next time, come off it,
And get some service in,
Jack, long before you start
To lay down the old law:
If you still want to then.
Tell your dad that from me.

James Dickey / 1923–

The Fiend

He has only to pass by a tree   moodily walking   head down
A worried accountant   not with it   and he is swarming
He is gliding up the underside light of leaves   upfloating
In a seersucker suit   passing window after window of her building.
He finds her at last, chewing gum   talking on the telephone.
The wind sways him softly   comfortably sighing   she must bathe
Or sleep.   She gets up, and he follows her along the branch
Into another room.   She stands there for a moment   and the teddy
   bear
On the bed feels its guts spin as she takes it by the leg and tosses
It off.   She touches one button at her throat, and rigor mortis   10
Slithers into his pockets, making everything there—keys, pen
and secret love—stand up.   He brings from those depths the knife
And flicks it open   it glints on the moon one time   carries
Through the dead walls   making a wormy static on the TV screen.
He parts the swarm of gnats that live excitedly at this perilous level
Parts the rarified light high windows give out into inhabited trees
Opens his lower body to the moon.   This night the apartments are
   sinking

To ground level   burying their sleepers in the soil   burying all floors
But the one where a sullen shopgirl gets ready to take a shower,

Her hair in rigid curlers, and the rest.   When she gives up
Her aqua terry-cloth robe the wind quits in mid-tree   the birds
Freeze to their perches round his head   a purely human light
Comes out of a one-man oak   around her an energy field   she stands
Rooted   not turning to anything else   then begins to move like a saint
Her stressed nipples rising like things about to crawl off her   as he gets
A hold on himself.   With that clasp she changes   senses   something

Some breath through the fragile walls   some all-seeing eye
Of God   some touch that enfolds her body   some hand come up
    out of roots
That carries her as she moves   swaying   at this rare height.   She
    wraps
The curtain around her and streams.   The room fades.   Then coming
Forth magnificently   the window blurred from within   she moves
    in a cloud   31
Chamber   the tree in the oak currents sailing   in clear air keeping
    pace
With her white breathless closet—he sees her mistily part her lips
As if singing to him   come up from river-fog   almost hears her as if
She sang alone in a cloud   its warmed light streaming into his branches
Out through the gauze glass of the window.   She takes off her bathing
    cap
The tree with him ascending   himself and the birds all moving
In darkness together   sleep crumbling the bark in their claws.
By this time he holds in his awkward, subtle limbs the limbs   39

Of a hundred understanding trees.   He has learned what a plant is like
When it moves near a human habitation   moving closer the later it is
Unfurling its leaves near bedrooms   still keeping its wilderness life
Twigs covering his body with only one way out   for his eyes into
    inner light
Of a chosen window   living with them night after night   watching
Watching with them at times their favorite TV shows   learning—
Though now and then he hears a faint sound: gunshot, bombing,
Building-fall—how to read lips: the lips of laconic cowboys
Bank robbers   old and young doctors tense-faced   gesturing savagely
In wards and corridors   like reading the lips of the dead

The lips of men interrupting the program at the wrong time   50
To sell you a good used car on the Night Owl Show   men silently
    reporting
The news out the window.   But the living as well, three-dimensioned,

Silent as the small gray dead, must sleep at last   must save their lives
By taking off their clothes. It is his beholding that saves them:
God help the dweller in windowless basements   the one obsessed
With drawing curtains this night. At three o'clock in the morning
He descends   a medium-sized shadow   while that one sleeps and turns
In her high bed in loss   as he goes limb by limb   quietly down
The trunk with one lighted side. Ground upon which he could not explain
His presence he walks with toes uncurled from branches, his
   bird-movements   60
Dying hard. At the sidewalk he changes   gains weight   a solid
   citizen

Once more.   At apartments there is less danger from dogs, but he has
For those a super-quiet hand   a hand to calm sparrows and rivers,
And watchdogs in half-tended bushes lie with him watching their women
Undress   the dog's honest eyes and the man's the same pure beast's
Comprehending the same essentials. Not one of these beheld would ever give
Him a second look   but he gives them all a first look that goes
On and on   conferring immortality while it lasts   while the suburb's leaves
Hold still enough   while whatever dog he has with him holds its breath
Yet seems to thick-pant   impatient as he with the indifferent men   70
Drifting in and out of the rooms   or staying on, too tired to move
Reading the sports page   dozing   plainly unworthy   for what women want
Dwells in bushes and trees: what they want is to look outward,

To look with the light streaming into the April limbs   to stand straighter
While their husbands' lips dry out   feeling that something is there
That could dwell in no earthly house: that in poplar trees or beneath
The warped roundabout of the clothesline   in the sordid disorder
Of communal backyards   some being is there in the shrubs
Sitting comfortably on a child's striped rubber ball filled with rainwater
Muffling his glasses with a small studious hand against a sudden   80
Flash of houselight from within   or flash from himself   a needle's eye
Uncontrollable   blaze of uncompromised being. Ah, the lingerie
Hung in the bathroom! The domestic motions of single girls living together
A plump girl girding her loins against her moon-summoned blood:

In that moon he stands   the only male lit by it, covered with
    leaf-shapes.
He coughs, and the smallest root responds   and in his lust he is set
By the wind in motion. That movement can restore the green eyes
Of middle age   looking   renewed   through the qualified light
Not quite reaching him where he stands again on the usual branch
Of his oldest love   his tie not loosened   a plastic shield   90
In his breast pocket full of pencils and ballpoint pens given him by
    salesmen
His hat correctly placed to shade his eyes   a natural gambler's tilt
And in summer wears an eyeshade   a straw hat Caribbean style.
In some guise or other he is near them when they are weeping without
    sound
When the teen-age son has quit school   when the girl has broken up
With the basketball star   when the banker walks out on his wife.
He sees mothers counsel desperately with pulsing girls face down
On beds full of overstuffed beasts   sees men dress as women
In ante-bellum costumes with bonnets   sees doctors come, looking
    oddly   99
Like himself   though inside the houses   worming a medical arm
Up under the cringing covers   sees children put angrily to bed
Sees one told an invisible fairy story   with lips moving silently as his
Are also moving   the book's few pages bright. It will take years
But at last he will shed his leaves   burn his roots   give up
Invisibility   will step out   will make himself known to the one
He cannot see loosen her blouse   take off luxuriously   with lips
Compressed against her mouth-stain   her dress   her stockings
Her magic underwear.   To that one he will come   up frustrated pines
Down alleys   through window blinds   blind windows   kitchen doors
On summer evenings. It will be something small that sets him off: 110
Perhaps a pair of lace pants on a clothesline   gradually losing
Water to the sun   filling out in the warm light with a well-rounded
Feminine wind as he watches   having spent so many sleepless nights
Because of her   because of her hand on a shade always coming down
In his face   not leaving even a shadow   stripped naked upon the
    brown paper
Waiting for her now in a green outdated car with a final declaration
Of love   pretending to read   and when she comes and takes down
Her pants, he will casually follow her in   like a door-to-door salesman
The godlike movement of trees stiffening with him   the light   119
Of a hundred favored windows   gone wrong somewhere in his glasses
Where his knocked-off panama hat was   in his painfully vanishing
    hair.

In California

Here I am, troubling the dream coast
With my New York face,
Bearing among the realtors
And tennis-players my dark preoccupation.

There once was an epical clatter—
Voices and banjos, Tennessee, Ohio,
Rising like incense in the sight of heaven.
Today, there is an angel in the gate.

Lie back, Walt Whitman,
There, on the fabulous raft with the King and the Duke![1]   10
For the white row of the Marina
Faces the Rock.[2] Turn round the wagons here.

Lie back! We cannot bear
The stars any more, those infinite spaces.
Let the realtors divide the mountain,
For they have already subdivided the valley.

Rectangular city blocks astonished
Herodotus in Babylon,[3]
Cortez in Tenochtitlan,[4]
And here's the same old city-planner, death.   20

We cannot turn or stay.
For though we sleep, and let the reins fall slack,
The great cloud-wagons move
Outward still, dreaming of a Pacific.

---

[1] The poet of "the open road" and author of "Pioneers! O Pioneers!" associated with the scheming tramps on Huck's raft in Mark Twain's *Huckleberry Finn*.
[2] Alcatraz prison.
[3] Greek historian (485?–425? B.C.), who traveled extensively in Asia and Africa collecting materials.
[4] Hernando Cortez (1485–1547), Spanish conqueror of Mexico, at Montezuma's royal seat.

The Broken Home

Crossing the street,
I saw the parents and the child
At their window, gleaming like fruit
With evening's mild gold leaf.

In a room on the floor below,
Sunless, cooler—a brimming
Saucer of wax, marbly and dim—
I have lit what's left of my life.

I have thrown out yesterday's milk
And opened a book of maxims.   10
The flame quickens. The word stirs.

Tell me, tongue of fire,
That you and I are as real
At least as the people upstairs.

My father, who had flown in World War I,
Might have continued to invest his life
In cloud banks well above Wall Street and wife.
But the race was run below, and the point was to win.

Too late now, I make out in his blue gaze
(Through the smoked glass of being thirty-six)   20
The soul eclipsed by twin black pupils, sex
And business; time was money in those days.

Each thirteenth year he married. When he died
There were already several chilled wives
In sable orbit—rings, cars, permanent waves.
We'd felt him warming up for a green bride.

He could afford it. He was "in his prime"
At three score ten. But money was not time.

When my parents were younger this was a popular act: 29
A veiled woman would leap from an electric, wine-dark car
To the steps of no matter what—the Senate or the Ritz Bar—
And bodily, at newsreel speed, attack

No matter whom—Al Smith[1] or José Maria Sert[2]
Or Clemenceau[3]—veins standing out on her throat
As she yelled *War mongerer! Pig! Give us the vote!,*
And would have to be hauled away in her hobble skirt.

What had the man done? Oh, made history.
Her business (he had implied) was giving birth,
Tending the house, mending the socks.

Always that same old story—   40
Father Time and Mother Earth,
A marriage on the rocks.

One afternoon, red, satyr-thighed
Michael, the Irish setter, head
Passionately lowered, led
The child I was to a shut door. Inside,

Blinds beat sun from the bed.
The green-gold room throbbed like a bruise.
Under a sheet, clad in taboos
Lay whom we sought, her hair undone, outspread,   50

And of a blackness found, if ever now, in old
Engravings where the acid bit.
I must have needed to touch it
Or the whiteness—was she dead?
Her eyes flew open, startled strange and cold.
The dog slumped to the floor. She reached for me. I fled.

Tonight they have stepped out onto the gravel.
The party is over. It's the fall
Of 1931. They love each other still.

SHE: Charlie, I can't stand the pace.   60
HE: Come on, honey—why, you'll bury us all!

A lead soldier guards my windowsill:
Khaki rifle, uniform, and face.
Something in me grows heavy, silvery, pliable.

[1] Alfred E. Smith (1873–1944), governor of New York.
[2] Spanish painter (1874–1945), commissioned in 1932 to execute murals for Rockefeller Center.
[3] Georges Clemenceau (1841–1929), French statesman and premier.

How intensely people used to feel!
Like metal poured at the close of a proletarian novel,
Refined and glowing from the crucible,
I see those two hearts, I'm afraid,
Still. Cool here in the graveyard of good and evil,
They are even so to be honored and obeyed.

. . . Obeyed, at least, inversely. Thus
I rarely buy a newspaper, or vote.
To do so, I have learned, is to invite
The tread of a stone guest within my house.

Shooting this rusted bolt, though, against him,
I trust I am no less time's child than some
Who on the heath impersonate Poor Tom[4]
Or on the barricades risk life and limb.

Nor do I try to keep a garden, only
An avocado in a glass of water—   80
Roots pallid, gemmed with air. And later,

When the small gilt leaves have grown
Fleshy and green, I let them die, yes, yes,
And start another. I am earth's no less.

A child, a red dog roam the corridors,
Still, of the broken home. No sound. The brilliant
Rag runners halt before wide-open doors.
My old room! Its wallpaper—cream, medallioned
With pink and brown—brings back the first nightmares,
Long summer colds, and Emma, sepia-faced,   90
Perspiring over broth carried upstairs
Aswim with golden fats I could not taste.

The real house became a boarding-school.
Under the ballroom ceiling's allegory
Someone at last may actually be allowed
To learn something; or, from my window, cool
With the unstiflement of the entire story,
Watch a red setter stretch and sink in cloud.

[4] Edgar, feigning madness, in *King Lear,* III.iv.

"Blackie, the Electric Rembrandt"

We watch through the shop-front while
Blackie draws stars—an equal

concentration on his and
the youngster's faces. The hand

is steady and accurate;
but the boy does not see it

for his eyes follow the point
that touches (quick, dark movement!)

a virginal arm beneath
his rolled sleeve: he holds his breath.   10

. . . Now that it is finished, he
hands a few bills to Blackie

and leaves with a bandage on
his arm, under which gleam ten

stars, hanging in a blue thick
cluster. Now he is starlike.

Modes of Pleasure

New face, strange face, for my unrest.
I hunt your look, and lust marks time
Dark in his doubtful uniform,
Preparing once more for the test.

You do not know you are observed:
Apart, contained, you wait on chance,
Or seem to, till your callous glance
Meets mine, as callous and reserved.

And as it does we recognize
That sharing an anticipation   10
Amounts to a collaboration—
A warm game for a warmer prize.

Yet when I've had you once or twice
I may not want you any more:
A single night is plenty for
Every magnanimous device.

Why should that matter? Why pretend
Love must accompany erection?
This is a momentary affection,
A curiosity bound to end,   20

Which as good-humored muscle may
Against the muscle try its strength
—Exhausted into sleep at length—
And will not last long into day.

Ted Hughes / 1930–

The Thought-Fox

I imagine this midnight moment's forest:
Something else is alive
Beside the clock's loneliness
And this blank page where my fingers move.

Through the window I see no star:
Something more near
Though deeper within darkness
Is entering the loneliness:

Cold, delicately as the dark snow,
A fox's nose touches twig, leaf;   10
Two eyes serve a movement, that now
And again now, and now, and now

Sets neat prints into the snow
Between trees, and warily a lame
Shadow lags by stump and in hollow
Of a body that is bold to come

Across clearings, an eye,
A widening deepening greenness,
Brilliantly, concentratedly,
Coming about its own business   20

Till, with a sudden sharp hot stink of fox
It enters the dark hole of the head.
The window is starless still; the clock ticks,
The page is printed.

Sylvia Plath / 1932–1963

Daddy

You do not do, you do not do
Any more, black shoe
In which I have lived like a foot
For thirty years, poor and white,
Barely daring to breathe or Achoo.

Daddy, I have had to kill you.
You died before I had time——
Marble-heavy, a bag full of God,
Ghastly statue with one grey toe
Big as a Frisco seal   10

And a head in the freakish Atlantic
Where it pours bean green over blue
In the waters off beautiful Nauset.
I used to pray to recover you.
Ach, du.[1]

In the German tongue, in the Polish town
Scraped flat by the roller
Of wars, wars, wars.
But the name of the town is common.
My Polack friend   20

Says there are a dozen or two.
So I never could tell where you
Put your foot, your root,
I never could talk to you.
The tongue stuck in my jaw.

It stuck in a barb wire snare.
Ich,[2] ich, ich, ich,

[1] Oh, you.   [2] I.

I could hardly speak.
I thought every German was you.
And the language obscene

30

An engine, an engine
Chuffing me off like a Jew.
A Jew to Dachau, Auschwitz, Belsen.[3]
I began to talk like a Jew.
I think I may well be a Jew.

The snows of the Tyrol, the clear beer of Vienna
Are not very pure or true.
With my gypsy ancestress and my weird luck
And my Taroc pack[4] and my Taroc pack
I may be a bit of a Jew.

40

I have always been scared of *you,*
With your Luftwaffe, your gobbledygoo.
And your neat moustache
And your Aryan eye, bright blue.
Panzer-man,[5] panzer-man, O You——

Not God but a swastika
So black no sky could squeak through.
Every woman adores a Fascist,
The boot in the face, the brute
Brute heart of a brute like you.

50

You stand at the blackboard, daddy,
In the picture I have of you,
A cleft in your chin instead of your foot
But no less a devil for that, no not
Any less the black man who

Bit my pretty red heart in two.
I was ten when they buried you.
At twenty I tried to die[6]
And get back, back, back to you.
I thought even the bones would do.

60

---

[3] The most notorious Nazi extermination camps.
[4] An old kind of playing-card deck, used for fortune-telling, more commonly called Tarot.
[5] In World War II, *panzer* meant German mechanized troops or troops using armored tanks.
[6] Sylvia Plath attempted suicide several times before 1963.

But they pulled me out of the sack,
And they stuck me together with glue.
And then I knew what to do.
I made a model of you,
A man in black with a Meinkampf[7] look

And a love of the rack and the screw.
And I said I do, I do.
So daddy, I'm finally through.
The black telephone's off at the root,
The voices just can't worm through.   70

If I've killed one man, I've killed two——
The vampire who said he was you
And drank my blood for a year,
Seven years, if you want to know.
Daddy, you can lie back now.

There's a stake in your fat black heart
And the villagers never liked you.
They are dancing and stamping on you.
They always *knew* it was you.
Daddy, daddy, you bastard, I'm through.   80

[7] *Mein Kampf* (1925), Adolf Hitler's autobiography and political testament.

plays

The Trojan Women

EDITOR'S NOTE

The Background of the Play

Euripides staged *The Trojan Women* in 415 B.C., when Athens was nominally at peace but was preparing for a massive, unprovoked, and ultimately disastrous campaign to conquer Sicily. Just a few months earlier, the Athenians had slaughtered the men of Melos, a neutral city, and enslaved its women and children after Melos refused to join Athens as an ally. The Sicilian campaign was to be the second phase of the great war between Athens and Sparta. The first phase had ended—after ten years of indecisive fighting—a few years before *The Trojan Women* was presented. Thus, though the play deals with the Trojan War, which had taken place some 800 years earlier, it was clearly Euripides' commentary on the contemporary situation.

Euripides' audience knew all about the Trojan War, for it was celebrated in their great epic poems. The modern reader may find some preparation for the play useful. Here, in brief, is the story.

Paris, son of the Trojan king Priam, fell in love with Helen, wife of the Spartan king Menelaus, and carried her off to Troy. An army of Greeks, led by Menelaus' brother Agamemnon, sailed for Troy to bring Helen back. The Greek siege of Troy lasted for ten years, and in the final year of the war Achilles, greatest of the Greek heroes, killed Hector, another son of Priam, and then was killed in turn by Paris. The Greeks finally gained entry to Troy by hiding inside a huge wooden horse, which the Trojans—thinking it an offering to Athena—brought inside the city walls. In the night, the Greeks stole out of the horse, opened the gates to their compatriots, and took Troy.

The Trojan Women opens after the Trojan force has been destroyed; only the sorrowing women remain.

The stage and scene directions have been supplied by the translator, since Greek plays had none. The following list of characters has been added by the editor.

CHARACTERS

POSEIDON, *god of the sea; brother of the supreme god, Zeus*

ATHENA, *goddess of wisdom, war, and arts and crafts; patron goddess of Athens; daughter of Zeus*

HECUBA, *wife of Priam, king of Troy; mother of Hector, Troilus, Paris, Cassandra, Polyxena, and others*

TALTHYBIUS, *a Greek herald*

CASSANDRA, *prophetess and priestess; daughter of Priam and Hecuba*

ANDROMACHE, *wife of Hector; mother of Astyanax*

ASTYANAX, *infant son of Hector and Andromache*

MENELAUS, *king of Sparta, brother of Agamemnon*

HELEN, *wife of Menelaus*

CHORUS, *consisting of Trojan women*

GREEK SOLDIERS

The scene is a space of waste ground except for a few huts to right and left, where the women selected for the Greek leaders are housed. Far in the background Troy, the wall in ruins, is slowly burning, as yet more smoke than flame. In front a woman with white hair lies on the ground. It is just before dawn. A tall dim figure is seen, back of the woman.

POSEIDON. I am the sea god. I have come
    up from the salt sea depths of the Aegean,
    from where the sea nymphs' footsteps fall,
    weaving the lovely measures of the dance.
    For since that day I built the towers of stone
    around this town of Troy, Apollo[1] with me,
    —and straight we raised them, true by line and plummet—
    good will for them has never left my heart,
    my Trojans and their city.
    City? Smoke only—all is gone,   10
    perished beneath Greek spears.
    A horse was fashioned, big with arms.
    Parnassus was the workman's home,
    in Phocia, and his name Epeius.
    The skill he had Athena gave him.
    He sent it through the walls—it carried death.
    The wooden horse, so men will call it always,

[1] God of the sun, life, healing, and prophecy.

which held and hid those spears.
A desert now where groves were. Blood drips down
from the gods' shrines. Beside his hearth   20
Priam lies dead upon the altar steps
of Zeus, the hearth's protector.
While to the Greek ships pass the Trojan treasure,
gold, gold in masses, armor, clothing,
stripped from the dead.
The Greeks who long since brought war to the town,
—ten times the seed was sown before Troy fell—
wait now for a fair wind for home,
the joyful sight of wife and child again.
Myself defeated by the Argive goddess   30
Hera and by Athena, both in league together—[2]
I too must take my leave of glorious Troy,
forsake my altars. When a town is turned
into a desert, things divine fall sick.
Not one to do them honor.
Scamander's stream[3] is loud with lamentation,
so many captive women weeping.
Their masters drew lots for them. Some will go
to Arcady and some to Thessaly.
Some to the lords of Athens, Theseus' sons.   40
Huts here hold others spared the lot, but chosen
for the great captains.
With them, like them a captive of the spear,
the Spartan woman, Helen.
But if a man would look on misery,
it is here to see—Hecuba lies there
before the gates. She weeps.
Many tears for many griefs.
And one still hidden from her.
But now upon Achilles' grave her daughter   50
was killed—Polyxena. So patiently she died.
Gone is her husband, gone her sons, all dead.
One daughter whom the Lord Apollo loved,

[2] The mythical background tells that Paris acted as a judge of the beauty of three goddesses—Athena, Hera, and Aphrodite (Venus). Each offered him a bribe, and he accepted Aphrodite's—the person of Helen. Later in the play (lines 978–1007), Helen recounts this tale to Menelaus in self-justification, and Hecuba derides it (lines 1032–60). Poseidon's opening speech suggests, however, that Hera and Athena, in jealous revenge, assisted the Greeks in the destruction of the city.
[3] Troy stood on a triangular plateau between two rivers identified as the Scamander and the Simois.

yet spared her wild virginity, Cassandra,
Agamemnon, in the dark, will force upon his bed.
No thought for what was holy and was God's.
O city happy once, farewell.
O shining towers, crumbling now
beneath Athena's hand, the child of God,
or you would still stand firm on deep foundations.   60
    (*As he turns to go the goddess* PALLAS ATHENA *enters.*)
ATHENA.   Am I allowed to speak to one who is
my father's nearest kinsman,
a god among gods honored, powerful?
If I put enmity aside, will he?
POSEIDON.   He will, most high Athena. We are kin,
old comrades too, and these have magic power.
ATHENA.   Thanks for your gentleness. What I would say
touches us both, great king.
POSEIDON.   A message from the gods? A word from Zeus?
Some spirit, surely?   70
ATHENA.   No, but for Troy's sake, where we stand, I seek
your power to join my own with it.
POSEIDON.   What! Now—at last? Has that long hatred left you?
Pity—when all is ashes—burned to ashes?
ATHENA.   The point first, please. Will you make common cause
with me? What I wish done will you wish, too?
POSEIDON.   Gladly. But what you wish I first must know.
You come to me for Troy's sake or for Greece?
ATHENA.   I wish to make my Trojan foes rejoice,
and give the Greeks a bitter home-coming.   80
POSEIDON.   The way you change! Here—there—then back again.
Now hate, now love—no limit ever.
ATHENA.   You know how I was outraged and my temple.
POSEIDON.   Oh that—when Ajax[4] dragged Cassandra out?
ATHENA.   And not one Greek to punish him—not one to blame him.
POSEIDON.   Even though your power ruined Troy for them.
ATHENA.   Therefore with you I mean to hurt them.
POSEIDON.   Ready for all you wish. But—hurt them? How?
ATHENA.   Give them affliction for their coming home.
POSEIDON.   Held here, you mean? Or out on the salt sea?   90
ATHENA.   Whenever the ships sail.
Zeus shall send rain, unending rain, and sleet,
and darkness blown from heaven.

---

[4] The ruffianly Greek warrior violated Athena's temple by seizing its attendant, Priam's virginal daughter, the prophetess protected by Zeus.

He will give me—he has promised—his thunderbolt,
to strike the ships with fire. They shall burn.
Your part, to make your sea-roads roar—
wild waves and whirlwinds,
while dead men choke the winding bay.
So Greeks shall learn to reverence my house
and dread all gods.   100
POSEIDON.   These things shall be. No need of many words
to grant a favor. I will stir the sea,
the wide Aegean. Shores and reefs and cliffs
will hold dead men, bodies of many dead.
Off to Olympus with you now, and get
those fiery arrows from the hand of Zeus.
Then when a fair wind sends the Greeks to sea,
watch the ships sail.
          (*Exit* ATHENA.)
Oh, fools, the men who lay a city waste,
giving to desolation temples, tombs,   110
the sanctuaries of the dead—so soon
to die themselves.
          (*Exit* POSEIDON.)
          (*The two gods have been talking before daylight, but now
          the day begins to dawn and the woman lying on the ground
          in front moves. She is* HECUBA, *the aged queen of Troy.*)
HECUBA.   Up from the ground—O weary head, O breaking neck.
This is no longer Troy. And we are not
the lords of Troy.
Endure. The ways of fate are the ways of the wind.
Drift with the stream—drift with fate.
No use to turn the prow to breast the waves.
Let the boat go as it chances.
Sorrow, my sorrow.   120
What sorrow is there that is not mine,
grief to weep for.
Country lost and children and husband.
Glory of all my house brought low.
All was nothing—nothing, always.

Keep silent? Speak?
Weep then? Why? For what?
          (*She begins to get up.*)
Oh, this aching body—this bed—
it is very hard. My back pressed to it—

Oh, my side, my brow, my temples.   130
Up! Quick, quick. I must move.
Oh, I'll rock myself this way, that way,
to the sound of weeping, the song of tears,
dropping down forever.
The song no feet will dance to ever,
for the wretched, the ruined.

O ships, O prows, swift oars,
out from the fair Greek bays and harbors,
over the dark shining sea,
you found your way to our holy city,   140
and the fearful music of war was heard,
the war song sung to flute and pipe,
as you cast on the shore your cables,
ropes the Nile dwellers twisted and coiled,
and you swung, oh, my grief, in Troy's waters.

What did you come for? A woman?
A thing of loathing, of shame,
to husband, to brother, to home.
She slew Priam, the king,
father of fifty sons,   150
she wrecked me upon
the reef of destruction.

Who am I that I wait[5]
here at a Greek king's door?
A slave that men drive on,
an old gray woman that has no home.
Shaven head brought low in dishonor.
O wives of the bronze-armored men who fought,
and maidens, sorrowing maidens,
plighted to shame,   160
see—only smoke left where was Troy.
Let us weep for her.
As a mother bird cries to her feathered brood,
so will I cry.
Once another song I sang
when I leaned on Priam's scepter,

[5] This is the way Professor Murray translates the line and the one following.
The translation is so simple and beautiful, I cannot bear to give it up for a
poorer one of my own. TRANSLATOR'S NOTE.

and the beat of dancing feet
marked the music's measure.
Up to the gods
the song of Troy rose at my signal.   170
  (*The door of one of the huts opens and a* WOMAN *steals out,*
  then another, and another.)
FIRST WOMAN. Your cry, O Hecuba—oh, such a cry—
What does it mean? There in the tent
we heard you call so piteously,
and through our hearts flashed fear.
In the tent we were weeping, too,
for we are slaves.
HECUBA. Look, child, there where the Greek ships lie—
ANOTHER WOMAN. They are moving. The men hold oars.
ANOTHER. O God, what will they do? Carry me off
over the sea in a ship far from home?   180
HECUBA. You ask and I know nothing,
but I think ruin is here.
ANOTHER WOMAN. Oh, we are wretched. We shall hear the summons.
Women of Troy, go forth from your home,
for the Greeks set sail.
HECUBA. But not Cassandra, oh, not her.
She is mad—she has been driven mad. Leave her within.
Not shamed before the Greeks—not that grief too.
I have enough.
  O Troy, unhappy Troy, you are gone   190
and we, the unhappy, leave you,
we who are living and we who are dead.
  (*More* WOMEN *now come out from a second hut.*)
A WOMAN. Out of the Greek king's tent
trembling I come, O Queen,
to hear my fate from you.
Not death— They would not think of death
for a poor woman.
ANOTHER. The sailors—they are standing on the prow.
Already they are running out the oars.
ANOTHER. (*She comes out of a third hut and several follow her.*) It
  is so early—but a terror woke me.   200
   My heart beats so.
ANOTHER. Has a herald come from the Greek camp?
Whose slave shall I be? I—bear that?
HECUBA. Wait for the lot drawing. It is near.
ANOTHER. Argos shall it be, or Phthia?

or an island of the sea?
A Greek soldier lead me there,
far, far from Troy?
HECUBA.   And I a slave—to whom—where—how?
You old gray woman, patient to endure,   210
you bee without a sting,
only an image of what was alive.
or the ghost of one dead.
I watch a master's door?
I nurse his children?
Once I was queen in Troy.
ONE WOMAN TO ANOTHER.   Poor thing. What are your tears
to the shame before you?
THE OTHER.   The shuttle will still pass through my hands,
but the loom will not be in Troy.   220
ANOTHER.   My dead sons. I would look at them once more.
Never again.
ANOTHER.   Worse to come.
A Greek's bed—and I—
ANOTHER.   A night like that? Oh, never—
oh, no—not that for me.
ANOTHER.   I see myself a water carrier,
dipping my pitcher in the great Pierian spring.
ANOTHER.   The land of Theseus, Athens, it is known
to be a happy place. I wish I could go there.   230
ANOTHER.   But not to the Eurotas, hateful river,
where Helen lived. Not there, to be a slave
to Menelaus who sacked Troy.
ANOTHER.   Oh, look. A man from the Greek army—
a herald. Something strange has happened,
he comes so fast. To tell us—what?
What will he say? Only Greek slaves are here,
waiting for orders.
        (*Enter* TALTHYBIUS *with* SOLDIERS.)
TALTHYBIUS.   You know me, Hecuba. I have often come
with messages to Troy from the Greek camp.   240
Talthybius—these many years you've known me.
I bring you news.
HECUBA.   It has come, women of Troy. Once we only feared it.
TALTHYBIUS.   The lots are drawn, if that is what you feared.
HECUBA.   Who—where? Thessaly? Phthia? Thebes?
TALTHYBIUS.   A different man takes each. You're not to go together.
HECUBA.   Then which takes which? Has any one good fortune?

TALTHYBIUS.   I know, but ask about each one, not all at once.

HECUBA.   My daughter, who—who drew her? Tell me—

    Cassandra. She has had so much to bear.   250

TALTHYBIUS.   King Agamemnon chose her out from all.

HECUBA.   Oh! but—of course—to serve his Spartan wife?

TALTHYBIUS.   No, no—but for the king's own bed at night.

HECUBA.   Oh, never. She is God's, a virgin, always.

    That was God's gift to her for all her life.

TALTHYBIUS.   He loved her for that same strange purity.[6]

HECUBA.   Throw away, daughter, the keys of the temple.

    Take off the wreath and the sacred stole.

TALTHYBIUS.   Well, now—a king's bed is not so bad.

HECUBA.   My other child you took from me just now?   260

TALTHYBIUS (*speaking with constraint*).   Polyxena, you mean? Or someone else?

HECUBA.   Her. Who drew her?

TALTHYBIUS.   They told her off to watch Achilles' tomb.

HECUBA.   To watch a tomb? My daughter?

    That a Greek custom?

    What strange ritual is that, my friend?

TALTHYBIUS (*speaking fast and trying to put her off*).   Just think of her as happy—all well with her.

HECUBA.   Those words— Why do you speak like that?

    She is alive?

TALTHYBIUS (*determined not to tell her*).   What happened was—well, she is free from trouble.   270

HECUBA (*wearily giving the riddle up*).   Then Hector's wife—my Hector, wise in war—

    Where does she go, poor thing—Andromache?

TALTHYBIUS.   Achilles' son[7] took her. He chose her out.

HECUBA.   And I, old gray head, whose slave am I,

    creeping along with my crutch?

TALTHYBIUS.   Slave of the king of Ithaca, Odysseus.

HECUBA.   Beat, beat my shorn head! Tear, tear my cheek!

    His slave—vile lying man. I have come to this—

    There is nothing good he does not hurt—a lawless beast.

    He twists and turns, this way and that, and back again.   280

    A double tongue, as false in hate as false in love.

    Pity me, women of Troy,

    I have gone. I am lost—oh, wretched.

---

[6] This line, too, is Professor Murray's, and retained here for the reason given above. TRANSLATOR'S NOTE.

[7] Neoptolemus.

An evil fate fell on me,
a lot the hardest of all.

A WOMAN. You know what lies before you, Queen, but I—
What man among the Greeks owns me?

TALTHYBIUS (*to the* SOLDIERS). Off with you. Bring Cassandra here.
Be quick,
you fellows. We must give her to the chief,
into his very hand. And then these here   290
to all the other generals. But what's that—
that flash of light inside there?

(*Light shines through the crevices of one of the huts.*)
Set fire to the huts—is that their plan,
these Trojan women? Burn themselves to death
rather than sail to Greece. Choosing to die instead.
How savagely these days the yoke bears down
on necks so lately free.
Open there, open the door. (*Aside*) As well for them perhaps,
but for the Greeks—they'd put the blame on me.

HECUBA. No, no, there is nothing burning. It is my daughter,   300
Cassandra. She is mad.

(CASSANDRA *enters from the hut dressed like a priestess, a
wreath in her hair, a torch in her hand. She does not seem
to see anyone.*)

CASSANDRA. Lift it high—in my hand—light to bring.
I praise him. I bear a flame.
With my torch I touch to fire
this holy place.
Hymen,[8] O Hymen.
Blessed the bridegroom,
blessed am I
to lie with a king in a king's bed in Argos.
Hymen, O Hymen.   310
Mother, you weep
tears for my father dead,
mourning for the beloved
country lost.
I for my bridal here
lift up the fire's flame
to the dawn, to the splendor,
to you, O Hymen.
Queen of night,

---

[8] God of marriage.

give your starlight
to a virgin bed,
as of old you did.
Fly, dancing feet.
Up with the dance.
   Oh, joy, oh, joy!
Dance for my father dead,
   most blest to die.
Oh, holy dance!
Apollo—you?
Lead on then.
There in the laurel grove
I served your altar.
   Dance, Mother, come.
   Keep step with me.
Dear feet with my feet
   tracing the measure
   this way and that.
Sing to the Marriage god,
oh, joyful song.
Sing for the bride, too,
joyously all.
Maidens of Troy,
dressed in your best,
honor my marriage.
Honor too him
whose bed fate drives me to share.

A WOMAN.   Hold her fast, Queen, poor frenzied girl.
   She might rush straight to the Greek camp.

HECUBA.   O fire, fire, when men make marriages
   you light the torch, but this flame flashing here
   is for grief only. Child, such great hopes once I had.
   I never thought that to your bridal bed
   Greek spears would drive you.
   Give me your torch. You do not hold it straight,
   you move so wildly. Your sufferings, my child,
   have never taught you wisdom.
   You never change. Here! someone take the torch
   into the hut. This marriage needs no songs,
   but only tears.

CASSANDRA.   O Mother, crown my triumph with a wreath.
   Be glad, for I am married to a king.
   Send me to him, and if I shrink away,

drive me with violence. If Apollo lives,
my marriage shall be bloodier than Helen's.
Agamemnon, the great, the glorious lord of Greece—
I shall kill him, Mother, lay his house as low
as he laid ours, make him pay for all
he made my father suffer, brothers, and—
But no. I must not speak of that—that axe
which on my neck—on others' too—   370
nor of that murder of a mother.
All, all because he married me and so
pulled his own house down.
But I will show you. This town now, yes, Mother,
is happier than the Greeks. I know that I am mad,
but Mother, dearest, now, for this one time
I do not rave.
One woman they came hunting, and one love,
Helen, and men by tens of thousands died.
Their king, so wise, to get what most he hated   380
destroyed what most he loved,
his joy at home, his daughter, killing her[9]
for a brother's sake, to get him back a woman
who had fled because she wished—not forced to go.
And when they came to the banks of the Scamander
those thousands died. And why?
No man had moved their landmarks
or laid siege to their high-walled towns.
But those whom war took never saw their children.
No wife with gentle hands shrouded them for their grave.   390
They lie in a strange land. And in their homes
are sorrows, too, the very same.
Lonely women who died, old men who waited
for sons that never came—no son left to them
to make the offering at their graves.
That was the glorious victory they won.
But we—we Trojans died to save our people,
no glory greater. All those the spear slew,
friends bore them home and wrapped them in their shroud
with dutiful hands. The earth of their own land   400
covered them. The rest, through the long days they fought,

---

[9] The Greeks were at first prevented from sailing to Troy by contrary winds. A
prophet declared that the winds had been raised by the goddess Artemis, who
would be appeased only by the sacrifice of Agamemnon's daughter Iphigenia.
Agamemnon deceived Iphigenia and had her killed to free his fleet.

had wife and child at hand, not like the Greeks,
whose joys were far away.
And Hector's pain—your Hector. Mother, hear me.
This is the truth: he died, the best, a hero.
Because the Greeks came, he died thus.
Had they stayed home, we never would have known him.
This truth stands firm: the wise will fly from war.
But if war comes, to die well is to win
the victor's crown.   410
The only shame is not to die like that.
So, Mother, do not pity Troy,
or me upon my bridal bed.

TALTHYBIUS (*has been held awestruck through all this, but can bear
          no more*).   Now if Apollo had not made you mad
     I would have paid you for those evil words,
     bad omens, and my general sailing soon.
          (*Grumbles to himself*)
     The great, who seem so wise, have no more sense
     than those who rank as nothing.
     Our king, the first in Greece, bows down
     before this mad girl, loves her, chooses her   420
     out of them all. Well, I am a poor man,
     but I'd not go to bed with her.
          (*Turns to* CASSANDRA)
     Now you—you know your mind is not quite right.
     So all you said against Greece and for Troy,
     I never heard—the wind blew it away.
     Come with me to the ship now.
          (*Aside*)
     A grand match for our general, she is.
          (*To* HECUBA, *gently*)
     And you, do follow quietly when Odysseus' men come.
     His wife's a good, wise woman, so they say.

CASSANDRA (*seeming to see* TALTHYBIUS *for the first time and looking
          him over haughtily*).   A strange sort of slave, surely.   430
     Heralds such men are called,
     hated by all, for they are tyrants' tools.
     You say my mother goes to serve Odysseus?
          (*She turns away and speaks to herself.*)
     But where then is Apollo's word, made clear
     to me, that death will find her here?
     And—no, that shame I will not speak of.
     Odysseus! wretched—but he does not know.

Soon all these sorrows, mine and Troy's, will seem
compared to his like golden hours.
Ten years behind him here, ten years before him. 440
Then only, all alone, will he come home,
and there find untold trouble has come first.
But his cares—why let fly one word at him?
Come, let us hasten to my marriage.
We two shall rest, the bridegroom and the bride,
within the house of death.
O Greek king, with your dreams of grandeur yet to come,
vile as you are, so shall your end be,
in darkness—all light gone.
And me—a cleft in the hills, 450
washed by winter rains,
his tomb near by.
There—dead—cast out—naked—
and wild beasts seeking food—
It is I there—I myself—Apollo's servant.
O flowers of the God I love, mysterious wreaths,
away. I have forgotten temple festival,
I have forgotten joy.
Off. I tear them from my neck.
Swift winds will carry them 460
up to you, O God of truth.
My flesh still clean, I give them back to you.
Where is the ship? How do I go on board?
Spread the sail—the wind comes swift.
Those who bring vengeance—three are they,
And one of them goes with you on the sea.
Mother, my Mother, do not weep. Farewell,
dear City. Brothers, in Troy's earth laid, my father,
a little time and I am with you.
You dead, I shall come to you a victor. 470
Those ruined by my hand who ruined us.

(*She goes out with* TALTHYBIUS *and the* SOLDIERS. HECUBA,
motionless for a moment, falls.)

A WOMAN.   The Queen! See—see—she is falling.
Oh, help! She cannot speak.
Miserable slaves, will you leave her on the ground,
old as she is. Up—lift her up.
HECUBA.   Let me be. Kindness not wanted is unkindness.
I cannot stand. Too much is on me.

Anguish here and long since and to come—
O God— Do I call to you? You did not help.
But there is something that cries out for God   480
when trouble comes.
Oh, I will think of good days gone,
days to make a song of,
crowning my sorrow by remembering.
We were kings and a king I married.
Sons I bore him, many sons.
That means little—but fine, brave lads.
They were the best in all Troy.
No woman, Trojan, Greek, or stranger,
had sons like mine to be proud of.   490
I saw them fall beneath Greek spears.
My hair I shore at the grave of the dead.
Their father—I did not learn from others
that I must weep for him—these eyes beheld him.
I, my own self, saw him fall murdered
upon the altar, when his town was lost.
My daughters, maidens reared to marry kings,
are torn from me. For the Greeks I reared them.
All gone—no hope that I shall look upon
their faces any more, or they on mine.   500
And now the end—no more can lie beyond—
an old gray slave woman I go to Greece.
The tasks they know for my age hardest, mine.
The door to shut and open, bowing low
—I who bore Hector—meal to grind; upon
the ground lay this old body down that once
slept in a royal bed; torn rags around me,
torn flesh beneath.
And all this misery and all to come
because a man desired a woman.   510
Daughter, who knew God's mystery and joy,
what strange chance lost you your virginity?
And you, Polyxena—where are you gone?
No son, no daughter, left to help my need,
and I had many, many—
Why lift me up? What hope is there to hold to?

This slave that once went delicately in Troy,
take her and cast her on her bed of clay,
rocks for her pillow, there to fall and die,

wasted with tears. Count no one happy,
however fortunate, before he dies.
CHORUS.   Sing me, O Muse, a song for Troy,
  a strange song sung to tears,
  a music for the grave.
  O lips, sound forth a melody
      for Troy.

A four-wheeled cart brought the horse to the gates,
brought ruin to me,
    captured, enslaved me.
Gold was the rein and the bridle,   530
deadly the arms within,
and they clashed loud to heaven as the threshold was passed.

High on Troy's rock the people cried,
"Rest at last, trouble ended.
Bring the carven image in.
Bear it to Athena,
fit gift for the child of God."

Who of the young but hurried forth?
Who of the old would stay at home?
With song and rejoicing they brought death in,   540
treachery and destruction.

All that were in Troy,
hastening to the gate,
drew that smooth-planed horse of wood
carven from a mountain pine,
where the Greeks were hiding,
where was Troy's destruction,
gave it to the goddess,
gift for her, the virgin,
driver of the steeds that never die.   550

With ropes of twisted flax,
as a ship's dark hull is drawn to land,
they brought it to her temple of stone,
to her floor that soon would run with blood,
    to Pallas Athena.

    On their toil and their joy
the dark of evening fell,
but the lutes of Egypt still rang out
    to the songs of Troy.

And girls with feet light as air   560
dancing, sang happy songs.
The houses blazed with light
through the dark splendor,
    and sleep was not.
A GIRL.   I was among the dancers.
I was singing to the maiden of Zeus,
the goddess of the hills.
A shout rang out in the town,
a cry of blood through the houses,
and a frightened child caught his mother's skirt   570
and hid himself in her cloak.
Then War came forth from his hiding place—
Athena, the virgin, devised it.
Around the altars they slaughtered us.
Within on their beds lay headless men,
young men cut down in their prime.
This was the triumph-crown of Greece.
We shall bear children for her to rear,
    grief and shame to our country.
        (*A chariot approaches, loaded with spoils. In it sits a* WOMAN
        and a CHILD.)
A WOMAN.   Look, Hecuba, it is Andromache.   580
See, in the Greek car yonder.
Her breast heaves with her sobs and yet
the baby sleeps there, dear Astyanax,
    the son of Hector.
ANOTHER.   Most sorrowful of women, where do you go?
Beside you the bronze armor that was Hector's,
the spoil of the Greek spear, stripped from the dead.
Will Achilles' son use it to deck his temples?
ANDROMACHE.   I go where my Greek masters take me.
HECUBA.   Oh, our sorrow—our sorrow.   590
ANDROMACHE.   Why should you weep? This sorrow is mine.
HECUBA.   O God—
ANDROMACHE.   What has come to me is mine.
HECUBA.   My children—
ANDROMACHE.   Once we lived, not now.
HECUBA.   Gone—gone—happiness—Troy—
ANDROMACHE.   And you bear it.
HECUBA.   Sons, noble sons, all lost.
ANDROMACHE.   Oh, sorrow is here.
HECUBA.   For me—for me.   600

ANDROMACHE.   For the city, in its shroud of smoke.
　　Come to me, O my husband.
HECUBA.   What you cry to lies in the grave.
　　My son, wretched woman, mine.
ANDROMACHE.   Defend me—me, your wife.
HECUBA.   My son, my eldest son,
　　whom I bore to Priam,
　　whom the Greeks used shamefully,[10]
　　come to me, lead me to death.
ANDROMACHE.   Death—oh, how deep a desire.　　　　　610
HECUBA.   Such is our pain—
ANDROMACHE.   For a city that has fallen, fallen.
HECUBA.   For anguish heaped upon anguish.
ANDROMACHE.   For the anger of God against Paris,
　　your son, who fled from death,
　　who laid Troy's towers low
　　　　to win an evil love.
　　Dead men—bodies—blood—
　　vultures hovering—
　　Oh, Athena the goddess is there, be sure,　　　　620
　　and the slave's yoke is laid upon Troy.
HECUBA.   O country, desolate, empty.
ANDROMACHE.   My tears fall for you.
HECUBA.   Look and see the end—
ANDROMACHE.   Of the house where I bore my children.
HECUBA.   O children, your mother has lost her city,
　　and you—you have left her alone.
　　Only grief is mine and mourning.
　　Tears and more tears, falling, falling.
　　The dead—they have forgotten their pain.　　　　630
　　They weep no more.
A WOMAN (*aside to another*).   Tears are sweet in bitter grief,
　　and sorrow's song is lamentation.
ANDROMACHE.   Mother of him whose spear of old brought death
　　to Greeks unnumbered, you see what is here.
HECUBA.   I see God's hand that casts the mighty down
　　and sets on high the lowly.
ANDROMACHE.   Driven like cattle captured in a raid,
　　my child and I—the free changed to a slave.
　　Oh, changed indeed.　　　　　　　　　　　　　640

---

[10] Achilles killed Hector and then dragged his body to the Greek camp.

HECUBA.   It is fearful to be helpless. Men just now
    have taken Cassandra—forced her from me.
ANDROMACHE.   And still more for you—more than that—
HECUBA.   Number my sorrows, will you? Measure them?
    One comes—the next one rivals it.
ANDROMACHE.   Polyxena lies dead upon Achilles' tomb,
    a gift to a corpse, to a lifeless thing.
HECUBA.   My sorrow! That is what Talthybius meant—
    I could not read his riddle. Oh, too plain.
ANDROMACHE.   I saw her there and left the chariot   650
    and covered her dead body with my cloak,
    and beat my breast.
HECUBA.   Murdered—my child. Oh, wickedly!
    Again I cry to you. Oh, cruelly slain!
ANDROMACHE.   She has died her death, and happier by far
    dying than I alive.
HECUBA.   Life cannot be what death is, child.
    Death is empty—life has hope.
ANDROMACHE.   Mother, O Mother, hear a truer word.
    Now let me bring joy to your heart.   660
    I say to die is only not to be,
    and rather death than life with bitter grief.
    They have no pain, they do not feel their wrongs.
    But the happy who has come to wretchedness,
    his soul is a lost wanderer,
    the old joys that were once, left far behind.
    She is dead, your daughter—to her the same
    as if she never had been born.
    She does not know the wickedness that killed her.
    While I—I aimed my shaft at good repute.   670
    I gained full measure—then missed happiness.
    For all that is called virtuous in a woman
    I strove for and I won in Hector's house.
    Always, because we women, whether right or wrong,
    are spoken ill of
    unless we stay within our homes, my longing
    I set aside and kept the house.
    Light talk, glib women's words,
    could never gain an entrance there.
    My own thoughts were enough for me,   680
    best of all teachers to me in my home.
    Silence, a tranquil eye, I brought my husband,

knew well in what I should rule him,
and when give him obedience.
And this report of me came to the Greeks
for my destruction. When they captured me
Achilles' son would have me.
I shall be a slave to those who murdered—
O Hector, my beloved—shall I thrust him aside,
open my heart to the man that comes to me,   690
and be a traitor to the dead?
And yet to shrink in loathing from him
and make my masters hate me—
One night, men say, one night in a man's bed
will make a woman tame—
Oh, shame! A woman throw her husband off
and in a new bed love another—
Why, a young colt will not run in the yoke
with any but her mate—not a dumb beast
that has no reason, of a lower nature.   700
O Hector, my beloved, you were all to me,
wise, noble, mighty, in wealth, in manhood, both.
No man had touched me when you took me,
took me from out my father's home
and yoked a girl fast to you.
And you are dead, and I, with other plunder,
am sent by sea to Greece. A slave's yoke there.
Your dead Polyxena you weep for,
what does she know of pain like mine?
The living must have hope. Not I, not any more.   710
I will not lie to my own heart. No good will ever come.
But oh, to think it would be sweet.

A WOMAN.   We stand at the same point of pain. You mourn your ruin,
and in your words I hear my own calamity.

HECUBA.   Those ships—I never have set foot on one,
but I have heard of them, seen pictures of them.
I know that when a storm comes which they think
they can ride out, the sailors do their best,
one by the sail, another at the helm,
and others bailing.   720
But if great ocean's raging overwhelms them,
they yield to fate.
They give themselves up to the racing waves.
So in my many sorrows I am dumb.
I yield, I cannot speak.

The great wave from God has conquered me.
But, O dear child, let Hector be,
and let be what has come to him.
Your tears will never call him back.
Give honor now to him who is your master. 730
Your sweet ways—use them to allure him.
So doing you will give cheer to your friends.
Perhaps this child, my own child's son,
you may rear to manhood and great aid for Troy,
and if ever you should have more children,
they might build her again. Troy once more be a city!
Oh—one thought leads another on.
But why again that servant of the Greeks?
I see him coming. Some new plan is here.
> (*Enter* TALTHYBIUS *with* SOLDIERS. *He is troubled and advances hesitatingly.*)
TALTHYBIUS.   Wife of the noblest man that was in Troy, 740
O wife of Hector, do not hate me.
Against my will I come to tell you.
The people and the kings have all resolved—
ANDROMACHE.   What is it? Evil follows words like those.
TALTHYBIUS.   This child they order— Oh, how can I say it—
ANDROMACHE.   Not that he does not go with me to the same master—
TALTHYBIUS.   No man in Greece shall ever be his master.
ANDROMACHE.   But—leave him here—all that is left of Troy?
TALTHYBIUS.   I don't know how to tell you. What is bad,
words can't make better— 750
ANDROMACHE.   I feel you kind. But you have not good news.
TALTHYBIUS.   Your child must die. There, now you know
the whole, bad as it is.
ANDROMACHE.   Oh, I have heard an evil worse
than a slave in her master's bed.
TALTHYBIUS.   It was Odysseus had his way. He spoke
to all the Greeks.
ANDROMACHE.   O God. There is no measure to my pain.
TALTHYBIUS.   He said a hero's son must not grow up—
ANDROMACHE.   God, on his own sons may that counsel fall. 760
TALTHYBIUS.   —but from the towering wall of Troy be thrown.
Now, now— let it be done— that's wiser.
Don't cling so to him. Bear your pain
the way a brave woman suffers.
You have no strength—don't look to any help.
There's no help for you anywhere. Think—think.

The city gone—your husband too. And you
a captive and alone, one woman—how
can you do battle with us? For your own good
I would not have you try, and draw   770
hatred down on you and be shamed.
Oh, hush—never a curse upon the Greeks.
If you say words that make the army angry
the child will have no burial, and without pity—
Silence now. Bear your fate as best you can.
So then you need not leave him dead without a grave,
and you will find the Greeks more kind.

ANDROMACHE.   Go die, my best beloved, my own, my treasure,
in cruel hands, leaving your mother comfortless.
Your father was too noble. That is why   780
they kill you. He could save others,
he could not save you for his nobleness.
My bed, my bridal—all for misery—
when long ago I came to Hector's halls
to bear my son—oh, not for Greeks to slay,
but for a ruler over teeming Asia.
Weeping, my little one? There, there.
You cannot know what waits for you.
Why hold me with your hands so fast, cling so fast to me?
You little bird, flying to hide beneath my wings.   790
And Hector will not come—he will not come,
up from the tomb, great spear in hand, to save you.
Not one of all his kin, of all the Trojan might.
How will it be? Falling down—down—oh, horrible.
And his neck—his breath—all broken.
And none to pity. You little thing,
curled in my arms, you dearest to your mother,
how sweet the fragrance of you.
All nothing then—this breast from where
your baby mouth drew milk, my travail too,   800
my cares, when I grew wasted watching you.
Kiss me— Never again. Come, closer, closer.
Your mother who bore you—put your arms around my neck.
Now kiss me, lips to lips.
O Greeks, you have found out ways to torture
that are not Greek.
A little child, all innocent of wrong—
you wish to kill him.

O Helen, evil growth, that was sown by Tyndareus,[11]
you are no child of Zeus, as people say.   810
Many the fathers you were born of,
Madness, Hatred, Red Death, whatever poison
the earth brings forth—no child of Zeus,
but Greece's curse and all the world's.
God curse you, with those beautiful eyes
that brought to shame and ruin
Troy's far-famed plains.
Quick! take him—seize him—cast him down—
if so you will. Feast on his flesh.
God has destroyed me, and I cannot—   820
I cannot save my child from death.
Oh hide my head for shame and fling me
into the ship.
  (*She falls, then struggles to her knees.*)
My fair bridal—I am coming—
Oh, I have lost my child, my own.
A WOMAN. O wretched Troy, tens of thousands lost
  for a woman's sake, a hateful marriage bed.
TALTHYBIUS (*drawing the* CHILD *away*). Come, boy, let go. Unclasp
  those loving hands,
poor mother.
Come now, up, up, to the very height,   830
where the towers of your fathers crown the wall,
and where it is decreed that you must die.
  (*To the* SOLDIERS)
Take him away.
A herald who must bring such orders
should be a man who feels no pity,
and no shame either—not like me.
HECUBA. Child, son of my poor son, whose toil was all in vain,
  we are robbed, your mother and I, oh, cruelly—
robbed of your life. How bear it?
What can I do for you, poor piteous child?   840
Beat my head, my breast—all I can give you.
Troy lost, now you—all lost.
The cup is full. Why wait? For what?
Hasten on—swiftly on to death.
  (*The* SOLDIERS, *who have waited while* HECUBA *speaks, go out*

[11] Husband of Leda, and real or putative father of Helen. Andromache is here
denying the legend that Zeus, in the form of a swan, begot her.

with the CHILD and TALTHYBIUS. *One of them takes* ANDROM-
ACHE *to the chariot and drives off with her.*)
CHORUS.   The waves make a ring around Salamis.[12]
The bees are loud in the island.
King Telamon built him a dwelling.
It fronted the holy hills,
where first the gray gleaming olive
Athena showed to men,   850
the glory of shining Athens,
her crown from the sky.
He joined himself to the bowman,
the son of Alcmena, for valorous deeds.
Troy, Troy he laid waste, my city,
long ago when he went forth from Greece.
When he led forth from Greece the bravest
in his wrath for the steeds withheld,
and by fair-flowing Simois stayed his oar
that had brought him over the sea.   860
Cables there made the ship fast.
In his hand was the bow that never missed.
It brought the king to his death.
Walls of stone that Phoebus[13] had built
he wrecked with the red breath of fire.
He wasted the plain of Troy.
Twice her walls have fallen. Twice
a blood-stained spear struck her down,
laid her in ruin.

· · ·

[12] This choral passage (lines 845-901) alludes to the first destruction of Troy,
when Telamon of Salamis, the principal city of Cypress, assisted Hercules, "the
bowman," in its sacking. Gilbert Murray (in his translation of *The Trojan
Women,* Oxford, 1915) paraphrased this "rather difficult lyric" as follows:

This is not the first time Troy has been taken. Long ago Heracles [Hercules]
made war against the old king Laomedon, because he had not given him the
immortal steeds that he promised. And Telamon joined him; Telamon who
might have been happy in his island of Salamis, among the bees and the
pleasant waters, looking over the strait to the olive-laden hills of Athens, the
beloved City! And they took ship and slew Laomedon. Yea, twice Zeus has
destroyed Ilion [Troy]!
Is it all in vain that our Trojan princes have been loved by the Gods?
Ganymêdês [son of Tros and cup-bearer to Zeus] pours the nectar of
Zeus in his banquets, his face never troubled, though his motherland is burned
with fire! And, to say nothing of Zeus, how can the Goddess of Morning rise
and shine upon us uncaring? She loved Tithônus, son of Laomedon, and bore
him up from us in a chariot to be her husband in the skies. But all that once
made them love us is gone!

[13] Apollo as god of the sun. See lines 5–6.

In vain, O you who move   870
with delicate feet where the wine-cups are gold,
son of that old dead king,
who fill with wine the cup Zeus holds,
service most fair—
she who gave you birth is afire.
The shores of the sea are wailing for her.
As a bird cries over her young,
women weep for husbands, for children,
for the old, too, who gave them birth.
Your dewy baths are gone,   880
and the race-course where you ran.
Yet your young face keeps the beauty of peace
in joy, by the throne of Zeus.
While Priam's land
lies ruined by Greek spearsmen.

Love, O Love,
once you came to the halls of Troy,
and your song rose up to the dwellers in heaven.
How did you then exalt Troy high,
binding her fast to the gods, by a union—   890
No—I will not speak blame of Zeus.
But the light of white-winged Dawn, dear to men,
is deadly over the land this day,
shining on fallen towers.
And yet Dawn keeps in her bridal bower
her children's father, a son of Troy.
Her chariot bore him away to the sky.
It was gold, and four stars drew it.
Hope was high then for our town.
But the magic that brought her the love of the gods   900
has gone from Troy.

    (*As the song ends* MENELAUS *enters with a bodyguard of*
    SOLDIERS.)

MENELAUS.   How bright the sunlight is today—
this day, when I shall get into my power
Helen, my wife. For I am Menelaus,
the man of many wrongs.
I came to Troy and brought with me my army,
not for that woman's sake, as people say,
but for the man who from my house,
and he a guest there, stole away my wife.

Ah, well, with God's help he has paid the price,   910
he and his country, fallen beneath Greek spears.
I am come to get her—wretch—I cannot speak her name
who was my wife once.
In a hut here, where they house the captives,
she is numbered with the other Trojan women.
The men who fought and toiled to win her back,
have given her to me—to kill, or else,
if it pleases me, to take her back to Argos.
And it has seemed to me her death in Troy
is not the way. I will take her overseas,   920
with swift oars speeding on the ship,
and there in Greece give her to those to kill
whose dearest died because of her.

> (*To his men*)

Attention! Forward to the huts.
Seize her and drag her out by that long blood-drenched hair—

> (*Stops suddenly and controls himself*)

And when fair winds come, home with her to
Greece.

> (SOLDIERS *begin to force the door of one of the huts.*)

HECUBA (*comes slowly forward*).   O thou who dost uphold the world,
whose throne is high above the world,
thou, past our seeking hard to find, who art thou?   930
God, or Necessity of what must be,
or Reason of our reason?
Whate'er thou art, I pray to thee,
seeing the silent road by which
all mortal things are led by thee to justice.

MENELAUS.   What have we here? A queer prayer that.

HECUBA. (*She comes still nearer to him and he recognizes her.*)   Kill
her, Menelaus? You will? Oh, blessings on you!
But—shun her, do not look at her.
Desire for her will seize you, conquer you.
For through men's eyes she gets them in her power.   940
She ruins them and ruins cities too.
Fire comes from her to burn homes,
magic for death. I know her—so do you,
and all these who have suffered.

> (HELEN *enters from the hut. The* SOLDIERS *do not touch her.*
> *She is very gentle and undisturbed.*)

HELEN (*with sweet, injured dignity. Not angry at all*).   Menelaus,
these things might well make a woman fear.

Your men with violence have driven me from my room,
have laid their hands upon me.
Of course I know—almost I know—you hate me,
but yet I ask you, what is your decision,
yours and the Greeks? Am I to live or not?   950

MENELAUS.   Nothing more clear. Unanimous, in fact.
Not one who did not vote you should be given me,
whom you have wronged, to kill you.

HELEN.   Am I allowed to speak against the charge?
To show you if I die that I shall die
most wronged and innocent?

MENELAUS.   I have come to kill you, not to argue with you.

HECUBA.   Oh, hear her. She must never die unheard.
Then. Menelaus, let me answer her.
The evil that she did in Troy, you do not know.   960
But I will tell the story. She will die.
She never can escape.

MENELAUS.   That means delay. Still—if she wants to speak,
she can. I grant her this because of what you say,
not for her sake. She can be sure of that.

HELEN.   And perhaps, no matter if you think I speak
the truth or not, you will not talk to me,
since you believe I am your enemy.
Still, I will try to answer what I think
you would say if you spoke your mind,   970
and my wrongs shall be heard as well as yours.
First: who began these evils? She, the day
when she gave birth to Paris. Who next was guilty?
The old king who decreed the child should live,[14]
and ruined Troy and me—Paris, the hateful,
the firebrand.
What happened then? Listen and learn.
This Paris—he was made the judge for three,
all yoked together in a quarrel—goddesses.
Athena promised he should lead the Trojans   980
to victory and lay all Greece in ruins.
And Hera said if he thought her the fairest
she would make him lord of Europe and of Asia.
But Aphrodite—well, she praised my beauty—

[14] Priam and Hecuba had been warned that if Paris grew to manhood he would
ruin his country, but they did not kill the child. The story of Paris was the subject
of Euripides' *Alexandros,* the first play in the trilogy that ended with *The Trojan
Women.*

astonishing, she said—and promised him
that she would give me to him if he judged
that she was loveliest. Then, see what happened.
She won, and so my bridal brought all Greece
great good. No strangers rule you,
no foreign spears, no tyrant.   990
Oh, it was well for Greece, but not for me,
sold for my beauty and reproached besides
when I deserved a crown.
But—to the point. Is that what you are thinking?
Why did I go—steal from your house in secret?
That man, Paris, or any name you like to call him,
his mother's curse—oh, when he came to me
a mighty goddess walked beside him.
And you, poor fool, you spread your sails for Crete,
left Sparta—left him in your house.   1000
Ah well— Not you, but my own self I ask,
what was there in my heart that I went with him,
a strange man, and forgot my home and country?
Not I, but Aphrodite. Punish her,
be mightier than Zeus who rules
the other gods, but is her slave.
She is my absolution—
One thing with seeming justice you might say.
When Paris died and went down to the grave,
and when no god cared who was in my bed,   1010
I should have left his house—gone to the Greeks.
Just what I tried to do—oh, many times.
I have witnesses—the men who kept the gates,
the watchmen on the walls. Not once, but often
they found me swinging from a parapet,
a rope around this body, stealthily
feeling my way down.
The Trojans then no longer wanted me,
but the man who next took me—and by force—
would never let me go.   1020
My husband, must I die, and at your hands?
You think that right? Is that your justice?
I was forced—by violence. I lived a life
that had no joy, no triumph. In bitterness
I lived a slave.
Do you wish to set yourself above the gods?
Oh, stupid, senseless wish!

A WOMAN.   O Queen, defend your children and your country.
      Her soft persuasive words are deadly.
      She speaks so fair and is so vile.
      A fearful thing.
HECUBA.   Her goddesses will fight on my side while
      I show her for the liar that she is.
      Not Hera, not virgin Athena, do I think
      would ever stoop to folly great enough
      to sell their cities. Hera sell her Argos,
      Athena Athens, to be the Trojan's slave!
      playing like silly children there on Ida,[15]
      and each one in her insolence demanding
      the prize for beauty. Beauty—why was Hera   1040
      so hot for it? That she might get herself
      a better mate than Zeus?
      Athena—who so fled from marriage that she begged
      one gift from Zeus, virginity.
      But she would have the prize, you say. And why?
      To help her hunt some god to marry her?
      Never make gods out fools to whitewash your own evil.
      No one with sense will listen to you.
      And Aphrodite, did you say—who would not laugh?
      —must take my son to Menelaus' house?   1050
      Why? Could she not stay quietly in heaven
      and send you on—and all your town—to Troy?
      My son was beautiful exceedingly.
      You saw him—your own desire was enough.
      No need of any goddess.
      Men's follies—they are Aphrodite.
      She rose up from the sea-foam; where the froth
      and foam of life are, there she is.
      It was my son. You saw him in his Eastern dress
      all bright with gold, and you were mad with love.   1060
      Such little things had filled your mind in Argos,
      busied with this and that.
      Once free of Sparta and in Troy where gold,
      you thought, flowed like a river, you would spend
      and spend, until your spendthrift hand
      had drowned the town.
      Your luxuries, your insolent excesses,

[15] A mountain in Asia Minor near Troy from which the gods witnessed the Trojan War. It was also the site where Paris passed judgment on the three rival goddesses.

Menelaus' halls had grown too small for them.
Enough of that. By force you say he took you?
You cried out? Where? No one in Sparta heard you. ¹⁰⁷⁰
Young Castor was there and his brother too,
not yet among the stars.[16]
And when you came to Troy and on your track the Greeks,
and death and agony in battle,
if they would tell you, "Greece has won today,"
you would praise this man here, Menelaus,
to vex my son, who feared him as a rival.
Then Troy had victories, and Menelaus
was nothing to you.
Looking to the successful side—oh yes, ¹⁰⁸⁰
you always followed there.
There was no right or wrong side in your eyes.
And now you talk of ropes—letting your body down
in secret from the wall, longing to go.
Who found you so?
Was there a noose around your neck?
A sharp knife in your hand? Such ways
as any honest woman would have found,
who loved the husband she had lost?
Often and often I would tell you, Go, ¹⁰⁹⁰
my daughter. My sons will find them other wives.
I will help you. I will send you past the lines
to the Greek ships. Oh, end this war
between our foes and us. But this was bitter to you.
In Paris' house you had your insolent way.
You liked to see the Eastern men fall at your feet.
These were great things to you.
Look at the dress you wear, your ornaments.
Is that the way to meet your husband?
You should not dare to breathe the same air with him. ¹¹⁰⁰
Oh, men should spit upon you.
Humbly, in rags, trembling and shivering,
with shaven head—so you should come,
with shame at last, instead of shamelessness,
for all the wickedness you did.
King, one word more and I am done.
Give Greece a crown, be worthy of yourself.
Kill her. So shall the law stand for all women,

[16] Castor and Pollux were the twin sons of Leda and the brothers of Helen. Zeus placed them among the stars.

that she who plays false to her husband's bed,
shall die.   1110

A WOMAN.   O son of an ancient house, O King, now show
that you are worthy of your fathers.
The Greeks called you a woman, shamed you
with that reproach. Be strong. Be noble. Punish her.

MENELAUS (*impatiently*).   I see it all as you do. We agree.
She left my house because she wanted to—
went to a stranger's bed. Her talk of Aphrodite—
big words, no more. (*Turns to* HELEN) Go. Death is near.
Men there are waiting for you. In their hands are stones.
Die—a small price for the Greeks' long suffering.   1120
You shall not any more dishonor me.

HELEN (*kneeling and clinging to him*).   No! No! Upon my knees—
see, I am praying to you.
It was the gods, not me. Oh, do not kill me.
Forgive.

HECUBA.   The men she murdered. Think of those
who fought beside you—of their children too.
Never betray them. Hear that prayer.

MENELAUS (*roughly*).   Enough, old woman. She is nothing to me.
Men, take her to the ships and keep her safe
until she sails.   1130

HECUBA.   But not with you! She must not set foot on your ship.

MENELAUS (*bitterly*).   And why? Her weight too heavy for it?

HECUBA.   A lover once, a lover always.

MENELAUS (*pauses a moment to think*).   Not so when what he loved
has gone.
But it shall be as you would have it.
Not on the same ship with me. The advice is good.
And when she gets to Argos she shall die
a death hard as her heart.
So in the end she will become a teacher,
teach women chastity—no easy thing,   1140
but yet her utter ruin will strike terror
into their silly hearts,
even women worse than she.

CHORUS.   And so your temple in Ilium,
your altar of frankincense,
are given to the Greek,
the flame from the honey, the corn and the oil,
the smoke from the myrrh floating upward,
the holy citadel.

And Ida, the mountain where the ivy grows, 1150
and rivers from the snows rush through the glens,
and the boundary wall of the world
where the first sunlight falls,
the blessed home of the dawn.

The sacrifice is gone, and the glad call
of dancers, and the prayers at evening to the gods
that last the whole night long.
Gone too the golden images,
and the twelve Moons, to Trojans holy.
Do you care, do you care, do you heed these things, 1160
O God, from your throne in high heaven?
My city is perishing,
ending in fire and onrushing flame.

A WOMAN.   O dear one, O my husband,
you are dead, and you wander
unburied, uncared for, while over-seas
the ships shall carry me,
swift-winged ships darting onward,
on to the land the riders love,
Argos, where the towers of stone 1170
built by giants reach the sky.

ANOTHER.   Children, our children.
At the gate they are crying, crying,
calling to us with tears,
Mother, I am all alone.
They are driving me away
to a black ship, and I cannot see you.

ANOTHER.   Where, oh where? To holy Salamis,
with swift oars dipping?
Or to the crest of Corinth, 1180
the city of two seas,
where the gates King Pelops built
for his dwelling stand?

ANOTHER.   Oh, if only, far out to sea,
the crashing thunder of God
would fall down, down on Menelaus' ship,
crashing down upon her oars,
the Aegean's wild-fire light.
He it was drove me from Troy.
He is driving me in tears 1190
over to Greece to slavery.

ANOTHER.   And Helen, too, with her mirrors of gold,
    looking and wondering at herself,
    as pleased as a girl.
    May she never come to the land of her fathers,
    never see the hearth of her home,
    her city, the temple with brazen doors
    of goddess Athena.
    Oh, evil marriage that brought
    shame to Greece, the great,   1200
    and to the waters of Simois
    sorrow and suffering.

        (TALTHYBIUS *approaches with a few* SOLDIERS. *He is carrying*
        the dead CHILD.)

ANOTHER WOMAN.   Before new sufferings are grown old
    come other new.
    Look, unhappy wives of Troy,
    the dead Astyanax.
    They threw him from the tower as one might pitch a ball.
    Oh, bitter killing.
    And now they have him there.

TALTHYBIUS.   (*He gives the body into* HECUBA'S *arms.*)   One ship is
    waiting, Hecuba, to take aboard   1210
    the last of all the spoil Achilles' son was given,
    and bear it with the measured beat of oars
    to Thessaly's high headlands.
    The chief himself has sailed because of news
    he heard, his father's father
    driven from his land by his own son.
    So, more for haste even than before,
    he went and with him went Andromache.
    She drew tears from me there upon the ship
    mourning her country, speaking to Hector's grave,   1220
    begging a burial for her child, your Hector's son,
    who thrown down from the tower lost his life.
    And this bronze-fronted shield, the dread of many a Greek,
    which Hector used in battle,
    that it should never, so she prayed,
    hang in strange halls, her grief before her eyes,
    nor in that bridal chamber where she must be a wife,
    Andromache, this dead boy's mother.
    She begged that he might lie upon it in his grave,
    instead of cedar wood or vault of stone.   1230

And in your arms she told me I must lay him,
for you to cover the body, if you still
have anything, a cloak left—
And to put flowers on him if you could,
since she has gone. Her master's haste
kept her from burying her child.
So now, whenever you have laid him out,
we'll heap the earth above him, then
up with the sails!
Do all as quickly as you can. One trouble   1240
I saved you. When we passed Scamander's stream
I let the water run on him and washed his wounds.
I am off to dig his grave now, break up the hard earth.
Working together, you and I,
will hurry to the goal, oars swift for home.

HECUBA.   Set the shield down—the great round shield of Hector.
I wish I need not look at it.

       (TALTHYBIUS *goes out with the* SOLDIERS.)
You Greeks, your spears are sharp but not your wits.
You feared a child. You murdered him.
Strange murder. You were frightened, then? You thought   1250
he might build up our ruined Troy? And yet
when Hector fought and thousands at his side,
we fell beneath you. Now, when all is lost,
the city captured and the Trojans dead,
a little child like this made you afraid.
The fear that comes when reason goes away—
Myself, I do not wish to share it.

       (*She dismisses the Greeks and their ways.*)
Beloved, what a death has come to you.
If you had fallen fighting for the city,
if you had known strong youth and love   1260
and godlike power, if we could think
you had known happiness—if there is
happiness anywhere—
But now—you saw and knew, but with your soul
you did not know, and what was in your house
you could not use.
Poor little one. How savagely our ancient walls,
Apollo's towers, have torn away the curls
your mother's fingers wound and where she pressed
her kisses—here where the broken bone grins white—   1270
Oh no—I cannot—

Dear hands, the same dear shape your father's had,
how loosely now you fall. And dear proud lips
forever closed. False words you spoke to me
when you would jump into my bed, call me sweet names
and tell me, Grandmother, when you are dead,
I'll cut off a great lock of hair and lead my soldiers all
to ride out past your tomb.
Not you, but I, old, homeless, childless,
must lay you in your grave, so young,   1280
so miserably dead.
Dear God. How you would run to greet me.
And I would nurse you in my arms, and oh,
so sweet to watch you sleep. All gone.
What could a poet carve upon your tomb?
"A child lies here whom the Greeks feared and slew."
Ah, Greece should boast of that.
Child, they have taken all that was your father's,
but one thing, for your burying, you shall have,
the bronze-barred shield.   1290
It kept safe Hector's mighty arm, but now
it has lost its master.
The grip of his own hand has marked it—dear to me then—
His sweat has stained the rim. Often and often
in battle it rolled down from brows and beard
while Hector held the shield close.
Come, bring such covering for the pitiful dead body
as we still have. God has not left us much
to make a show with. Everything I have
I give you, child.   1300
      O men, secure when once good fortune comes—
fools, fools. Fortune's ways—
here now, there now. She springs
away—back—and away, an idiot's dance.
No one is ever always fortunate.
      (*The* WOMEN *have come in with coverings and garlands.*)
A WOMAN.   Here, for your hands, they bring you clothing for the dead,
      got from the spoils of Troy.
HECUBA (*shrouding the body and putting garlands beside it*).   Oh, not
      because you conquered when the horses raced,
      or with the bow outdid your comrades,
      your father's mother lays these wreaths beside you,   1310
      and of all that was yours, gives you this covering.
      A woman whom God hates has robbed you,

taken your life, when she had taken your treasure
and ruined all your house.

A WOMAN.   Oh, my heart! As if you touched it—touched it.
Oh, this was once our prince, great in the city.

HECUBA.   So on your wedding day I would have dressed you,
the highest princess of the East your bride.
Now on your body I must lay the raiment,
all that is left of the splendor that was Troy's.   1320
And the dear shield of Hector, glorious in battle,
mother of ten thousand triumphs won,
it too shall have its wreath of honor,
undying it will lie beside the dead.
More honorable by far than all the armor
Odysseus won, the wicked and the wise.

A WOMAN.   You, O child, our bitter sorrow,
earth will now receive.
Mourn, O Mother.

HECUBA.   Mourn, indeed.   1330

A WOMAN.   Weeping for all the dead.

HECUBA.   Bitter tears.

A WOMAN.   Your sorrows that can never be forgotten.

(*The funeral rite is now begun,* HECUBA *symbolically healing
the wounds.*)

HECUBA.   I heal your wounds; with linen I bind them.
Ah, in words only, not in truth—
a poor physician.
But soon among the dead your father
will care for you.

A WOMAN.   Beat, beat your head.
Lift your hands and let them fall,   1340
moving in measure.

HECUBA.   O Women. Dearest—

A WOMAN.   Oh, speak to us. Your cry—what does it mean?

HECUBA.   Only this the gods would have,
pain for me and pain for Troy,
those they hated bitterly.
Vain, vain, the bulls we slew.[17]
And yet—had God not bowed us down,
not laid us low in dust,
none would have sung of us or told our wrongs   1350
in stories men will listen to forever.

---

[17] In traditional sacrifices.

Go: lay our dead in his poor grave,
with these last gifts of death given to him.
I think those that are gone care little
how they are buried. It is we, the living,
our vanity.

(WOMEN *lift the shield with the body on it and carry it out.*)

A WOMAN.   Poor mother—her high hopes were stayed on you
and they are broken.
They called you happy at your birth,
a good man's son.   1360
Your death was miserable exceedingly.

ANOTHER.   Oh, see, see—
On the crested height of Troy
fiery hands. They are flinging torches.
Can it be
some new evil?
Something still unknown?

TALTHYBIUS (*stops as he enters and speaks off stage*).   Captains, attention. You have been given charge
to burn this city. Do not let your torches sleep.
Hurry the fire on.   1370
When once the town is level with the ground
then off for home and glad goodbye to Troy.
And you, you Women—I will arrange for you
as well, one speech for everything—
whenever a loud trumpet-call is sounded,
go to the Greek ships, to embark.
Old woman, I am sorriest for you,
follow. Odysseus' men are here to get you.
He drew you—you must leave here as his slave.

HECUBA.   The end then. Well—the height of sorrow, I stand there.
Troy is burning—I am going.   1381
But—hurry, old feet, if you can,
a little nearer—here, where I can see
my poor town, say goodbye to her.
You were so proud a city, in all the East
the proudest. Soon your name the whole world knew,
will be taken from you. They are burning you
and leading us away, their slaves.
O God— What makes me say that word?
The gods— I prayed, they never listened.   1390
Quick, into the fire— Troy, I will die with you.
Death then—oh, beautiful.

TALTHYBIUS. Out of your head, poor thing, with all you've suffered.
Lead her away— Hold her, don't be too gentle.
She must be taken to Odysseus.
Give her into his hands. She is his—
    (*Shakes his head*)
his prize.
    (*It grows darker.*)

A WOMAN. Ancient of days, our country's Lord,
Father, who made us,
You see your children's sufferings.   1400
Have we deserved them?

ANOTHER. He sees—but Troy has perished, the great city.
No city now, never again.

ANOTHER. Oh, terrible!
The fire lights the whole town up.
The inside rooms are burning.
The citadel—it is all flame now.

ANOTHER. Troy is vanishing.
War first ruined her.
And what was left is rushing up in smoke,   1410
the glorious houses fallen.
First the spear and then the fire.

HECUBA (*She stands up and seems to be calling to someone far away.*)
Children, hear, your mother is calling.

A WOMAN (*gently*). They are dead, those you are speaking to.

HECUBA. My knees are stiff, but I must kneel.
Now, strike the ground with both my hands—

A WOMAN. I too, I kneel upon the ground.
I call to mine down there.
Husband, poor husband.

HECUBA. They are driving us like cattle—taking us away.   1420

A WOMAN. Pain, all pain.

ANOTHER. To a slave's house, from my country.

HECUBA. Priam, Priam, you are dead,
and not a friend to bury you.
The evil that has found me—
do you know?

A WOMAN. No. Death has darkened his eyes.
He was good and the wicked killed him.

HECUBA. O dwellings of the gods and O dear city,
the spear came first and now   1430
only the red flame lives there.

A WOMAN. Fall and be forgotten. Earth is kind.

ANOTHER. The dust is rising, spreading out like a great wing of
smoke.

I cannot see my house.

ANOTHER. The name has vanished from the land,

and we are gone, one here, one there.

And Troy is gone forever.

(*A great crash is heard.*)

HECUBA. Did you hear? Did you know—

A WOMAN. The fall of Troy—

ANOTHER. Earthquake and flood and the city's end—   1440

HECUBA. Trembling body—old weak limbs,

you must carry me on to the new day of slavery.

(*A trumpet sounds.*)

A WOMAN. Farewell, dear city.

Farewell, my country, where once my children lived.

On to the ships—

There below, the Greek ships wait.

(*The trumpet sounds again and the* WOMEN *pass out.*)

Translated by Edith Hamilton

The Three Sisters

CHARACTERS

PROZOROFF, ANDREI SERGEEVICH
NATALIA IVANOVNA, *his fiancée, later his wife*
OLGA ⎱
MASHA ⎰ *his sisters*
IRINA ⎰
KULYGIN, FYODOR ILYICH, *a high-school teacher, husband of Masha*
VERSHININ, ALEXANDER IGNATIEVICH, *Lieutenant Colonel, a battery Commander*
TUSENBACH, NIKOLAI LVOVICH, *Baron, Lieutenant*
SOLYONY, VASILI VASILIEVICH, *Staff Captain*
TCHEBUTYKIN, IVAN ROMANOVICH, *an Army Doctor*
FEDOTIK, ALEXEI PETROVICH, *Second Lieutenant*
RODAY, VLADIMIR KARLOVICH, *Second Lieutenant*
FERAPONT, *porter of the District Board, an old man*
ANFISA, *the nurse, an old woman of eighty*
            ORDERLY, MAIDS, SOLDIERS, MUSICIANS

The action takes place in a provincial town in Russia.

ACT I

In the PROZOROFFS' *house. A drawing room with columns, beyond which a large room is seen. Midday: outside it is sunny and bright. The table in the dining room is being set for lunch.* OLGA, *in the blue uniform of a girls' high-school teacher, is busy correcting school papers, standing and walking to and fro;* MASHA, *in a black dress with her hat on her knees, sits and reads a book;* IRINA, *in a white dress, stands lost in thought.*

OLGA. Father died just a year ago today, on the fifth of May— your saint's day, Irina. It was very cold then and snowing. I thought

I could never live through it; you were lying in a dead faint. But now a year has passed and we can talk of it freely; you've a white dress on, your face is beaming. (*The clock strikes twelve.*) And the clock was striking then too. (*A pause*) I remember as they carried Father along, the band was playing, and at the cemetery they fired a volley. He was a brigadier general; but at that there were very few people walking behind his coffin. It was raining, though, then. Heavy rain and snow.

IRINA.   Why think of it?

(*Behind the columns in the dining room near the table,* BARON TUSENBACH, TCHEBUTYKIN *and* SOLYONY *appear.*)

OLGA.   It's warm today. We can keep the windows wide open, but the birches haven't any leaves yet. Father was given his brigade and left Moscow with us eleven years ago, and I remember distinctly that early in May, at this very time, in Moscow everything is in bloom, it's warm, everything is bathed in sunshine. That's eleven years ago, but I remember it all as if we'd left there yesterday. Oh, God! I woke up this morning, saw a flood of light, saw the spring, and my heart leapt with joy. And I did long passionately to go home again.

TCHEBUTYKIN.   The devil!

TUSENBACH.   Of course, it's all rot.

(MASHA, *brooding over a book, softly whistles a song.*)

OLGA.   Don't whistle, Masha. How can you do that! (*A pause*) I'm at the high school every day giving lessons till evening, that's why my head aches all the time and what thoughts I have might just as as well belong to an old woman and be done with it. These four years I've been teaching in high school, I have felt my strength and youth going out of me day by day, drop by drop. And just one dream grows stronger and stronger. . . .

IRINA.   To go to Moscow. Sell the house, wind up everything here and to Moscow.

OLGA.   Yes! Soon to Moscow.

(TCHEBUTYKIN *and* TUSENBACH *laugh.*)

IRINA.   Brother will be a professor very likely, but all the same he won't live here. The one thing that stops us is poor Masha.

OLGA.   Masha will be coming to Moscow for the whole summer every year.

(MASHA *is softly whistling a song.*)

IRINA.   God grant it all works out! (*Looking out of the window*) The weather is beautiful today. I don't know why my heart's so light! This morning I remembered it was my saint's day and suddenly felt happy, and remembered when I was a child and Mother was still alive. And such wonderful thoughts thrilled me; such thoughts!

OLGA. You look radiant today, lovelier than ever. And Masha is lovely too. Andrei would be good-looking if he hadn't got so heavy, it's not becoming to him. And I've grown older, a lot thinner; it must be because I get cross with the girls. Now that I'm free today and am here at home and my head's not aching, I feel younger than yesterday. I'm only twenty-eight. . . . It's all good, all God's will, but it seems to me if I had married and stayed at home the whole day long, it would have been better. (*A pause*) I'd have loved my husband.

TUSENBACH (*to* SOLYONY). You talk such nonsense that I'm tired of listening to you. (*Entering the drawing room*) Forgot to tell you. Today you'll receive a call from our new Battery Commander Vershinin. (*Sitting down at the piano*)

OLGA. Well, I'll be very glad of it.

IRINA. Is he old?

TUSENBACH. No, not very. Forty or forty-five at most. (*Playing softly*) He seems a nice chap. Not stupid, that's certain. Except that he talks a lot.

IRINA. Is he an interesting person?

TUSENBACH. Yes, quite, only there is a wife, a mother-in-law and two girls. What's more he's married for the second time. He pays calls and says everywhere that he has a wife and two girls. And he'll say so here. The wife is sort of half-crazy, wears long girlish braids, speaks only of lofty matters, philosophizes, and often tries to commit suicide, obviously to plague the husband. I'd have left such a woman long ago myself, but he puts up with her and merely complains.

SOLYONY (*entering the drawing room from the dining room with* TCHEBUTYKIN). With one hand I can lift only fifty pounds, but with both, one hundred eighty, or even two hundred pounds. From this I conclude that two men are not twice as strong as one, but three times, even more. . . .

TCHEBUTYKIN (*reading a newspaper as he comes in*). For falling hair . . . two ounces of naphthalene to half a bottle of spirits. . . . Dissolve and use daily. . . . (*Writing it down in his notebook*) Let's write it down! (*To* SOLYONY) And so, I tell you, a little cork is put in a bottle and through the cork there's a glass tube. . . . Then you take a pinch of plain ordinary alum . . .

IRINA. Ivan Romanovich, dear Ivan Romanovich!

TCHEBUTYKIN. What is it, my child, my sweet?

IRINA. Tell me, why am I so happy today? It's just as if I were going full sail, with the wide blue sky above me and great white birds floating there. Why is that? Why?

TCHEBUTYKIN (*kissing both her hands tenderly*). My white bird . . .

IRINA. This morning when I awoke and got up and bathed, it seemed all at once that everything in this world was clear to me and I knew how one must live. Dear Ivan Romanovich, I know everything. A man must do something, he must toil by the sweat of his brow, no matter who he is; and all the meaning and aim of his life, his happiness, his ecstasies must lie in this only. How good it is to be a workman who gets up at dawn and breaks stones in the street, or a shepherd, or a schoolmaster who teaches children, or an engineer on a railroad. My God! Next to being a man, it's better to be an ox, it's better to be a common horse, if only you do some work, than be a young woman who wakes up at twelve o'clock, has coffee in bed, and then dresses for two hours. . . . Oh, but that's dreadful! Just as on hot days one may have a craving for water, I have a craving for work. And if I don't get up early and go to work, give me up as a friend, Ivan Romanovich.

TCHEBUTYKIN (*tenderly*). I'll give you up, I'll give you up—

OLGA. Father trained us to get up at seven. Now Irina wakes at seven and lies there till at least nine thinking. And looking so serious! (*Laughing*)

IRINA. You are used to thinking of me as a little girl, so it seems strange to you when I look serious. I'm twenty years old.

TUSENBACH. Longing for work. Oh my God, how I understand that! I have never worked in my life. I was born in Petersburg, cold, idle Petersburg, in a family that never knew any sort of work or worry. I remember when I came home from military school the footman pulled off my boots while I fidgeted and my mother looked adoringly at me, and was surprised when the others didn't look at me the same way. I was shielded from work. Though I doubt if they succeeded in shielding me, I doubt it! The time has come, something tremendous is hovering over us all, a vast, healing storm is gathering; it's coming, it's near already, and will soon clear our society of the laziness, the indifference, the prejudice against work, the rotten boredom. I'll work and in another twenty-five or thirty years, every man will be working. Every one!

TCHEBUTYKIN. I shan't work.

TUSENBACH. You don't count.

SOLYONY. Twenty-five years from now you won't even be on earth, thank God! In two or three years you'll die of distemper, or I'll forget myself and put a bullet in your forehead, my angel. (*Taking a phial of perfume from his pocket and sprinkling his chest and hands*)

TCHEBUTYKIN (*laughing*). And I really never did anything. Since I left the University, I haven't lifted a finger, I've not read a single book even, but just read the newspapers. . . . (*Taking another newspaper out of his pocket*) Listen—I know from the newspapers that there was, let's say, a Dobrolyubov,[1] but what he wrote about I don't know. God only knows. (*A knock is heard on the floor from the floor below.*) Listen. . . . They are calling me from downstairs, somebody has come to see me. I'll be back right away. . . . Wait. . . . (*He leaves hurriedly, combing out his beard as he goes.*)

IRINA. He's up to something.

TUSENBACH. Yes. He left with a triumphant face, obviously he will now bring you a present.

IRINA. That's too bad.

OLGA. Yes, it's awful. He always does something childish.

MASHA. By the curved seashore a green oak, a golden chain upon that oak . . . a golden chain upon that oak. (*Getting up and singing softly*)

OLGA. You are not very merry today, Masha.

(MASHA *sings as she puts on her hat.*)

OLGA. Where to?

MASHA. Home.

IRINA. That's strange. . . .

TUSENBACH. To leave a saint's day party!

MASHA. It's all the same. . . . I'll come this evening. Good-by, my pretty . . . (*Kissing* IRINA) I wish you once again good health and happiness. When father was alive, thirty or forty officers used to come to our birthday parties, it was good and noisy; but nowadays there's only a man and a half, and it's quiet as the desert. . . . I'm going. . . . I've got the blues today, I feel depressed, so don't listen to me. (*Laughing through her tears*) We'll talk later on, so good-by now, my dear, I'll go somewhere or other.

IRINA (*vexed*). Oh, you are such a . . .

OLGA (*tearfully*). I understand you, Masha.

SOLYONY. If a man philosophizes, it will be philosophy or sophistry; but if a woman philosophizes, or two women, it will be—like cracking your fingers.

[1] Nikolai Alexandrovich Dobrolyubov (1836–61), influential literary critic of the "socio-utilitarian" school.

MASHA. What are you trying to say, you terribly dreadful man?

SOLYONY. Nothing. Quick as a flash, the bear made a dash. . . . (*A pause*)

MASHA (*to* OLGA, *crossly*). Don't howl.

(ANFISA *enters, and after her,* FERAPONT *with a cake.*)

ANFISA. Here, little Father. Come in, your feet are clean. (*To* IRINA) From the District Board, from Mikhail Ivanovich Protopopov . . . a cake.

IRINA. Thank you. Thank him for me. (*Taking the cake*)

FERAPONT. How's that?

IRINA (*louder*). Thank him for me.

OLGA. Nurse, give him some pie. Go on, Ferapont. They'll give you some pie.

FERAPONT. How's that?

ANFISA. Come on, little Father, Ferapont Spiridonich. Come on. . . . (*Goes out with* FERAPONT)

MASHA. I don't like Protopopov, that Mikhail Potopich or Ivanovich. He should not be invited.

IRINA. I didn't do the inviting.

MASHA. That's fine!

(TCHEBUTYKIN *enters, behind him an* ORDERLY *with a silver samovar; there is a hum of astonishment and displeasure.*)

OLGA (*covering her face with her hands*). A samovar! This is terrible. (*Going to the table in the dining room*)

IRINA. Darling Ivan Romanovich, what are you doing?

TUSENBACH (*laughing*). I told you so.

MASHA. Ivan Romanovich, you're simply shameless.

TCHEBUTYKIN. My darlings, my good little ones, you are all I have, to me you are everything that's most precious in the world. I'll soon be sixty, I'm an old man, a lonely worthless old man. . . . There is nothing good about me but this love for you, and if it weren't for you I'd long ago have stopped living in this world. . . . (*To* IRINA) My dear, my little child, I have known you since the day you were born. . . . I carried you in my arms. . . . I loved your dear mother. . . .

IRINA. But why such expensive presents!

TCHEBUTYKIN (*through his tears, angrily*). Expensive presents! . . . Why, you're completely . . . (*To the* ORDERLY) Carry the samovar in there. . . . (*Mimicking*) Expensive presents . .

(*The* ORDERLY *carries the samovar into the dining room.*)

ANFISA (*passing through the drawing room*). My dears, there's a colonel, a stranger. He's already taken off his overcoat, children, and is coming in here. Irinushka, now be a nice, polite girl. (*As she goes out*) And it was time for lunch long ago. . . . Lord have mercy! . . .

TUSENBACH. It must be Vershinin.

(VERSHININ *enters.*)

TUSENBACH. Lieutenant Colonel Vershinin!

VERSHININ (*to* MASHA *and* IRINA). I have the honor to introduce myself: Vershinin. I'm very, very glad that at last I am in your house. How you've grown! Ay! Ay!

IRINA. Please sit down. We are delighted.

VERSHININ (*gaily*). How glad I am! How glad I am! But you are three sisters. I remember—three girls. Your faces I don't remember now, but your father, Colonel Prozoroff, had three little girls, I remember that perfectly, I saw them with my own eyes. How time does pass! Oh, oh, how time does pass!

TUSENBACH. Alexander Ignatievich is from Moscow.

IRINA. From Moscow. You are from Moscow?

VERSHININ. Yes, from there. Your father was a battery commander there, and I was an officer in the same brigade. (*To* MASHA) It seems to me now I do remember your face rather.

MASHA. And you I—No!

IRINA. Olya! Olya! (*Calling into the dining room*) Olya! Come here. (OLGA *comes in from the dining room.*) Lieutenant Colonel Vershinin, it turns out, is from Moscow.

VERSHININ. You must be Olga Sergeevna, the eldest. . . . And you Maria. . . . And you Irina—the youngest.

OLGA. You are from Moscow?

VERSHININ. Yes. I was at school in Moscow and began my service in Moscow, served there a long time, was finally assigned a battery here—moved here, as you see. I don't remember you, as a matter of fact, but only that you were three sisters. Your father is fresh in my memory; I can close my eyes now and see him as plain as life. I used to pay you calls in Moscow. . . .

OLGA. I thought I remembered everybody, and look, all of a sudden . . .

VERSHININ. My name is Alexander Ignatievich.

IRINA. Alexander Ignatievich, you are from Moscow. What a surprise!

OLGA. We are going to move there, you know.

IRINA. We think by autumn we'll be there. It's our native town, we were born there. . . . In Old Basmanny Street.

(*They both laugh delightedly.*)

MASHA. Unexpectedly we see a fellow countryman. (*Vivaciously*) Now I remember! Do you remember, Olya, at our house they used to say, "The lovesick major." You were a lieutenant then and in love with someone, and they all teased you for some reason as the lovesick major.

VERSHININ (*laughing*). That's right! That's right! The lovesick major. That was it!

MASHA. But you had only a mustache then. . . . Oh, how much older you look! (*Tearfully*) How much older you look!

VERSHININ. Yes, when they called me the lovesick major, I was still young, I was in love. Not so now.

OLGA. But you still haven't a single gray hair. You look older, but you are still not old.

VERSHININ. For all that, I'm in my forty-third year. Is it long since you left Moscow?

IRINA. Eleven years. But why are you crying, Masha, you little fool? (*Through her tears*) I'm starting to cry, too. . . .

MASHA. I'm all right. And in what street did you live?

VERSHININ. In Old Basmanny.

OLGA. And we lived there, too. . . .

VERSHININ. At one time I lived in Nemetzky Street. I used to walk from Nemetzky Street to the Red Barracks. There's a sullen-looking bridge on the way, and under the bridge you hear the water roaring. A lonely man feels sick at heart there. (*A pause*) But here, what a broad, what a superb river! A wonderful river!

OLGA. Yes, except that it's cold. It's cold here and there are mosquitoes. . . .

VERSHININ. How can you! You have such a fine, healthy Russian climate here. Woods, river . . . and birches too. Sweet, modest birches, of all trees I love them best. It's good to live here. And yet, strangely enough, the railway station is thirteen miles away. . . . And nobody knows why that is.

SOLYONY. But I know why it is. (*Everyone looks at him.*) Because if the station were right here then 'twere not off there, and if it is off there, then it's not right here.

(*An awkward silence*)

TUSENBACH. You're a joker, Vasili Vasilievich.

OLGA. Now I remember you too. I remember.

VERSHININ. I knew your mother.

TCHEBUTYKIN. She was a lovely woman . . . bless her soul!

IRINA. Mother is buried in Moscow.

OLGA. In the Novo Devichy. . . .

MASHA. Imagine, I'm already beginning to forget her face. Just as we won't be remembered either. They'll forget us.

VERSHININ. Yes. They'll forget us. Such is our fate, it can't be helped.

What seems to us serious, significant, highly important—the time will come when it will be forgotten or seem unimportant. (*A pause*) And it's an interesting thing, we can't possibly tell now just what will be considered great, or important, and what pitiful, ridiculous. Didn't the discoveries of Copernicus or, let's say, Columbus, seem at first unnecessary, ridiculous, and some shallow nonsense written by a fool seem to be the truth? And it may be that our present life, to which we are so reconciled, will seem very strange some day, uncomfortable, stupid, not pure enough, perhaps even sinful. . . .

TUSENBACH. Who knows? Perhaps our life will be called superior and remembered with respect. Nowadays there are no tortures, no executions, no invasions, though, for all that, there's so much unhappiness!

SOLYONY (*in a high-pitched voice*). Chick, chick, chick. . . . Don't feed the Baron grain, just let him philosophize.

TUSENBACH. Vasili Vasilievich, I beg you leave me alone. (*Sits at another place*) After all, it's tiresome.

SOLYONY (*in a high-pitched voice*). Chick, chick, chick . . .

TUSENBACH (*to* VERSHININ). The unhappiness we see now, however, though there is still so much of it even now—bespeaks a certain moral regeneration that has already reached society. . . .

VERSHININ. Yes, yes, of course.

TCHEBUTYKIN. You just said, Baron, that they will call our present life superior; but, all the same, people are small. . . . (*Standing up*) Look how small I am. It would only be to console me if anybody called my life a superior, understandable thing.

(*Behind the scenes a violin plays.*)

MASHA. It's Andrei playing, our brother.

IRINA. He is the learned member of the family. It looks as if he'd be a professor. Father was a military man, but his son chose for himself a learned career.

MASHA. According to Father's wish.

OLGA. Today we teased him to death. It seems he's a bit in love.

IRINA. With a local girl. She'll be with us today, there's every chance of it.

MASHA. Oh, how she dresses! Not merely ugly and out of style but simply pitiful. Some sort of strange, loud, yellowish skirt with a vulgar fringe and a red blouse. And her cheeks are so scrubbed, scrubbed! Andrei isn't in love—I won't admit it, after all he has taste, he's simply teasing us, he's fooling. I heard yesterday that she is marrying Protopopov, the Chairman of the Board. And that's fine —(*At the side door*) Andrei, come here! Darling, just for a minute!

(ANDREI *enters.*)

OLGA. This is my brother, Andrei Sergeevich.

VERSHININ. Vershinin.

ANDREI. Prozoroff. (*He wipes his perspiring face.*) You are our new Battery Commander?

OLGA. Can you imagine, Alexander Ignatievich is from Moscow.

ANDREI. Yes? Well, I congratulate you, now my little sisters won't give you any peace.

VERSHININ. I have already had time to tire your sisters out.

IRINA. Look at the frame Andrei gave me today! (*Showing the frame*) He made it himself.

VERSHININ (*looking at the frame and not knowing what to say*). Yes. . . . A thing . . .

IRINA. And the frame that's over the piano there, he made that, too.

(ANDREI *waves his hand as if disparagingly and moves away.*)

OLGA. He is not only our learned one, he also plays the violin and he saws various things out of wood. In sum he has a hand for anything. Andrei, don't go away! That's the way he does—he's always leaving us. Come here!

(MASHA *and* IRINA, *laughing, take him by the arms and lead him back.*)

MASHA. Come! Come!

ANDREI. Let me alone, please.

MASHA. How funny he is! Alexander Ignatievich used to be called the lovesick major and he didn't get a bit angry.

VERSHININ. Not a bit.

MASHA. And I want to call you the lovesick violinist!

IRINA. Or the lovesick professor! . . .

OLGA. He's in love! Andrusha's in love!

IRINA (*applauding*). Bravo, bravo! *Bis!* Andrushka is in love!

TCHEBUTYKIN (*comes up behind* ANDREI *and puts both arms around his waist*). For love alone did Nature put us in this world. (*Laughing. All the while he is holding a newspaper.*)

ANDREI. Well, that's enough, that's enough. . . . (*Wiping his face*) I haven't slept all night and now I'm not myself, as they say. Till four o'clock I read, then lay down, but nothing happened. I thought of this and of that, and then, of course, at the crack of dawn here the sun swarms into my bedroom. During the summer while I am here, I want to translate a certain book from English.

VERSHININ. And do you read English?

ANDREI. Yes. Our father—bless his soul!—loaded us down with education. It's ridiculous and stupid, but all the same I must admit that in a year after his death, I began to fill out and get fat like this, as if my body were freed from the load. Thanks to Father, my sisters and I know the French, German and English languages and Irina knows Italian too. But at what a cost!

MASHA. In this town, to know three languages is an unnecessary luxury. It isn't even a luxury, it's a sort of unnecessary appendage like a sixth finger. We know a lot that's useless.

VERSHININ. There we have it! (*Laughing*) You know a lot that is useless! It seems to me there's not and can't be a town so boring and dull that a clever, educated person would be unnecessary in it. Let's suppose that among the hundred thousand inhabitants of this town, which evidently is backward and crude, there are only three such people as you. It is obvious that you cannot triumph over the dark masses that surround you; in the course of your life you'll have to yield little by little and be lost in the crowd of a hundred thousand; life will stifle you, but just the same you'll still be there and not without influence; your kind, after you, will begin to appear, six, perhaps, then twelve, and so on, until finally your kind will get to be the majority. After two or three hundred years, life on earth will be unimaginably beautiful, wonderful. Man needs such a life, and if it is not here yet, he must anticipate it, wait, dream of it, be prepared for it, for it he must see and know more than his grandfather and father saw and knew. (*Laughing*) And you complain of knowing a lot that's useless.

MASHA (*taking off her hat*). I am staying for lunch.

IRINA (*with a sigh*). Really all that should be written down. . . .

(ANDREI *is not to be seen, he has gone out unobserved.*)

TUSENBACH. After many years, you say, life on earth will be beautiful, wonderful. That's true. But to share it now, even from afar, we must prepare ourselves for it, must be doing something. . . .

VERSHININ (*getting up*). Yes. How many flowers you have! (*Looking around*) And a beautiful apartment. I envy you! And all my life I have hung around little apartments with two chairs, a sofa and a stove that always smokes. In my life I have lacked just such flowers . . . (*Rubbing his hands*) Well, nothing can be done about it!

TUSENBACH. Yes, one must work. You probably think the German is getting sentimental. But on my word of honor, I am Russian and don't even speak German. My father was Orthodox. . . .

(*A pause*)

VERSHININ (*walking about the stage*). I often think: what might happen if we began life anew, and did it consciously? If one life, already lived through, had been, as it were the first draft, the other, the final copy! Then each of us, I think, would try above all things not to repeat himself, at least he would create for himself a different setting for his life, would arrange for himself an apartment such as this, with flowers, with a flood of light. . . . I have a wife and two girls; and, at that, the wife is a delicate lady, and so forth and so on, well, and if I were to begin life anew, I would never marry. . . . No. no!

(KULYGIN *enters, in a schoolteacher's uniform.*)

KULYGIN (*going up to* IRINA). My dear sister, allow me to congratulate you on your saint's day and wish you sincerely, from my heart, health and all that could be wished for a girl of your age. And then to present this book to you as a gift. (*Giving her the book*) A history of our high school covering fifty years, written by me. A trifle of a book, written out of nothing else to do, but all the same you must read it. Good morning, gentlemen! (*To* VERSHININ) Kulygin, teacher in the local high school, County Councilor. (*To* IRINA) In this book you will find a list of all the graduates of our high school for the last fifty years. *Feci, quod potui, faciant meliora potentes.*[2]

(*He kisses* MASHA.)

IRINA. But you've already given me a book like that at Easter.

KULYGIN (*laughing*). It couldn't be! In that case give it back, or better still, give it to the Colonel. Take it, Colonel. Read it sometime when you are bored.

VERSHININ. Thank you. (*He is about to leave.*) I am extremely glad I made your acquaintance. . . .

OLGA. You are leaving? No, no!

IRINA. Stay and lunch with us. Please.

OLGA. I beg you!

VERSHININ (*bowing*). It seems I've stumbled on to a saint's day party. Forgive me, I didn't know, didn't congratulate you.

(*Goes with* OLGA *to the dining room*)

KULYGIN. Today is Sunday, gentlemen, a day of rest, let us rest, let us be gay, each one according to his age and position. The rugs should be taken up for the summer and stored till winter. . . . Persian powder or naphthalene. . . . The Romans were healthy because they knew how to work, knew how to rest, they had *mens sana in corpore sano.*[3] Their life flowed on according to fixed forms. Our director says: the principal thing in every life is its

---

[2] "I did what I could, let those who are able do better."
[3] "A sound mind in a sound body."

form. . . . That which loses its form ends itself—and it's the same with our everyday existence. (*Takes* MASHA *by the waist, laughing*) Masha loves me. My wife loves me. And the window curtains, too, together with the rugs. . . . Today, I am gay, in a splendid mood. Masha, at four o'clock today we are to be at the director's. There's a walk being arranged for the teachers and their families.

MASHA. I am not going.

KULYGIN (*aggrieved*). Dear Masha, why?

MASHA. Later on about that. . . . (*Angrily*) Oh, very well, I'll go, but just leave me alone, please. . . . (*Walks away*)

KULYGIN. And then we'll spend the evening at the director's. In spite of his sickly state of health, this man tries above all else to be sociable. A superior, bright personality. A magnificent man. Yesterday, after the teacher's conference, he says to me: "I am tired, Fyodor Ilyich: I am tired!" (*Looks at the clock on the wall, then at his watch*) Your clock is seven minutes fast. Yes, he says, I am tired!

(*Behind the scene a violin is playing.*)

OLGA. Ladies and gentlemen, come to lunch, please! There's a meat-pie.

KULYGIN. Ah, my dear Olga, my dear! Yesterday, I worked from early morning till eleven o'clock in the evening, got tired and today I feel happy. (*Goes into the dining room and up to the table*)

TCHEBUTYKIN (*puts the newspaper in his pocket, combs his beard*). A meat-pie? Splendid!

MASHA (*to* TCHEBUTYKIN, *sternly*). Only, look out: nothing to drink today. Do you hear? Drinking's bad for you.

TCHEBUTYKIN. Oh, go on! I'm past all that. It is two years I've not been on a drunk. (*Impatiently*) Ah, old girl, isn't it all the same?

MASHA. All the same, don't you dare drink. Don't you dare. (*Angrily, but so that her husband doesn't hear*) The Devil take it, to be bored again all evening long at the director's.

TUSENBACH. I wouldn't go if I were in your place. It's very simple.

TCHEBUTYKIN. Don't go, dearie.

MASHA. Yes, don't go. . . . This curst, unbearable life . . . (*Going to the dining room*)

TCHEBUTYKIN (*going with her*). Now!

SOLYONY (*going to the dining room*). Chick, chick, chick. . . .

TUSENBACH. That's enough, Vasili Vasilievich. Drop it!

SOLYONY. Chick, chick, chick. . . .

KULYGIN (*gaily*). Your health, Colonel! I am a pedagogue and here in this house I'm one of the family, Masha's husband. . . . She is kind, very kind. . . .

VERSHININ. I'll have some of that dark vodka. . . . (*Drinking*)
Your health! (*To* OLGA) I feel so good in your house! . . .
(*In the drawing room only* IRINA *and* TUSENBACH *are left.*)

IRINA. Masha is in a bad humor today. She got married at eighteen,
when he seemed to her the most intelligent of men. But now it's
not the same. He's the kindest but not the most intelligent.

OLGA (*impatiently*). Andrei, do come, after all!

ANDREI (*behind the scenes*). This minute. (*Enters and goes to the
table*)

TUSENBACH. What are you thinking about?

IRINA. This: I dislike and I'm afraid of that Solyony of yours.
He talks nothing but nonsense. . . .

TUSENBACH. He is a strange person. I am both sorry for him and
annoyed, but more sorry. It seems to me he's shy. . . . When the
two of us are alone, he's very clever and gentle sometimes; but in
company he is a crude fellow, a bully. Don't go away, let them get
settled at the table. Let me be near you awhile. What are you thinking about? (*A pause*) You are twenty, I am not yet thirty. How
many years there are left for us ahead, a long, long row of days,
full of my love for you. . . .

IRINA. Nikolai Lvovich, don't talk to me of love.

TUSENBACH (*not listening*). I have a passionate thirst for life, struggle, work, and that thirst is mingled in my soul with love for you,
Irina. And it's as though it were by some design that you are beautiful and life seems beautiful to me because of you. What are you
thinking about?

IRINA. You say life is beautiful. Yes, but what if it only seems so!
With us three sisters, life hasn't yet been beautiful, it has stifled us
as weeds do grass. . . . I'm letting my tears fall. I shouldn't
do that. . . . (*Quickly wiping her face, smiling*) We must do
something, must work. That's why we are not happy and look at
life so gloomily—we don't know anything about working. We come
of people who despised work.

(NATALIA IVANOVNA *enters; she has a pink dress with a green
belt.*)

NATASHA. Look, they are already sitting down to lunch. . . . I'm
late. . . . (*She steals a glance at herself in the mirror and tidies
herself up.*) My hair seems to be all right. . . . (*Seeing* IRINA)
Dear Irina Sergeevna, I congratulate you! (*Kissing her vigorously
and long*) You have lots of guests, I really feel shy. . . . How do
you do, Baron!

OLGA (*entering the living room*). Well, and here is Natalia Ivanovna.
Good day, my dear. (*They kiss.*)

NATASHA. Congratulations on the saint's day. You have so much company, I feel awfully that . . .

OLGA. Never mind, it's just the family. (*In an undertone, alarmed*) You have on a green belt! My dear, that's not right!

NATASHA. Is it a sign of something?

OLGA. No, it just doesn't match . . . and somehow it looks odd—

NATASHA (*in a tearful voice*). Yes? But it's not really green, it's more of a neutral color.

> (*Follows* OLGA *into the dining room*)
> (*In the dining room they are sitting down to lunch; there is not a soul in the living room.*)

KULYGIN. I wish you, Irina, a good fiancé! It's time you married.

TCHEBUTYKIN. Natalia Ivanovna, I wish you a fiancé too.

KULYGIN. Natalia Ivanovna already has a fiancé.

MASHA (*strikes her plate with her fork*). I'll take a little drink! What the . . . life is all roses, I'll risk it. . . .

KULYGIN. Your conduct gets C minus.

VERSHININ. And the liqueur tastes good. What's it made of?

SOLYONY. Cockroaches.

IRINA (*in a tearful voice*). Phew! How disgusting! . . .

OLGA. For supper there will be roast turkey and apple pie. Thank the Lord, I'll be at home all day, and in the evening—at home. . . . Everybody must come this evening. . . .

VERSHININ. Allow me, too, to come this evening!

IRINA. Please do.

NATASHA. They are very informal.

TCHEBUTYKIN. For love alone did Nature put us in this world. (*Laughing*)

ANDREI (*angrily*). Stop it, everybody! Aren't you tired of it?

> (FEDOTIK *and* RODAY *enter with a big basket of flowers.*)

FEDOTIK. But say, they are already lunching.

RODAY (*talking loud and affectedly*). Lunching? Yes, already lunching. . . .

FEDOTIK. Wait a minute! (*Taking a snapshot*) One! Wait, just one more. . . . (*Taking another snapshot*) Two! Now, ready!

> (*They pick up the basket and go to the dining room, where they are greeted noisily.*)

RODAY (*in a loud voice*). Congratulations, I wish you everything, everything! The weather today is charming, perfectly magnificent. Today, all morning long, I was walking with the high school boys. I teach gymnastics at the high school. . . .

FEDOTIK. You may move, Irina Sergeevna, you may! (*Taking a snapshot*) You look well today. (*Getting a top out of his pocket*) By the way, see this top. . . . It has an amazing sound. . . .

IRINA.   How delightful!

MASHA.   By the curved seashore a green oak, a golden chain upon that oak. . . . A golden chain upon that oak. . . . (*Tearfully*) Now, why do I say that? This phrase has stuck in my mind ever since morning. . . .

KULYGIN.   Thirteen at the table!

RODAY (*in a loud voice*).   Could it really be, ladies and gentlemen, that you attach importance to these superstitions?
(*Laughing*)

KULYGIN.   Thirteen at the table shows that there are lovers here. It's not you, Ivan Romanovich, by any chance?
(*Laughter*)

TCHEBUTYKIN.   I am an old sinner, but why Natalia Ivanovna should be embarrassed I simply can't understand.
(*Loud laughter;* NATASHA *runs out from the dining room into the living room,* ANDREI *following her.*)

ANDREI.   Come on, don't pay any attention to them! Wait. . . . Stop. . . . I beg you. . . .

NATASHA.   I'm ashamed. . . . I don't know what it's all about and they are making fun of me. It was bad manners for me to leave the table just now, but I can't . . . I can't . . . (*Covers her face with her hands*)

ANDREI.   My dear, I beg you, I entreat you, don't be upset. I assure you they are only joking, they have kind hearts. My darling, my beautiful, they all are gentle, kind-hearted people and they love me and you. Come over here to the window, they can't see us here. . . .
(*He glances around.*)

NATASHA.   I am so unused to being in society! . . .

ANDREI.   Ah, youth, wonderful, beautiful youth! My dear, my darling, don't be so upset! . . . Believe me, believe . . . I feel so happy, my soul is full of love, ecstasy. . . . Oh, they can't see us! They can't see! Why, why I fell in love with you; when I fell in love. My dear, darling, pure one, be my wife! I love you, love . . . as nobody ever. . . .
(*A kiss*)
(*The* TWO OFFICERS *enter and, seeing the pair kissing, stop in astonishment.*)

Curtain

ACT II

The setting is the same as in Act I. It is eight o'clock in the evening. Offstage faintly we hear an accordion, playing in the street. There are no lights.

NATALIA IVANOVNA *enters in a dressing gown, with a candle; she comes in and stops at the door that leads into* ANDREI'S *room.*

NATASHA.   Andrusha, what are you doing? Reading? It's nothing, I just . . . (*Goes and opens another door and after looking in, closes it*) If there's a light . . .

ANDREI (*enters with a book in his hand*).   You what, Natasha?

NATASHA.   Looking to see if there's a light. . . . Now it's Carnival week the servants are beside themselves, we have to look and look, so that nothing goes wrong. Last night at midnight, I passed through the dining room, and a candle was burning there. Who lighted it I couldn't find out. (*Putting down her candle*) What time is it?

ANDREI (*looking at his watch*).   It's a quarter past eight.

NATASHA.   And Olga and Irina not in yet. They haven't come in. Always working, poor girls! Olga at the Teachers' Council, Irina at the telegraph office. . . . (*Sighing*) This morning I say to your sister: "Spare yourself, I say, Irina darling." But she won't listen. Quarter past eight, you say? I am anxious for fear, our Bobik is not at all well. Why is he so cold? Yesterday he had fever, and today he is cold all over. . . . I am so anxious!

ANDREI.   It's nothing, Natasha. The boy is all right.

NATASHA.   Still it's better to put him on a diet. I'm anxious. And tonight, around ten o'clock, they said, the maskers will be here, it would be better if they didn't come, Andrusha.

ANDREI.   Really, I don't know. But they were invited.

NATASHA.   This morning the little fellow wakes up and looks at me and all at once he smiles; so he knew me. "Bobik," I say, "good morning! Good morning, dear!" And he laughs. Children understand, they understand perfectly. So, Andrusha, I'll tell them not to let the maskers in.

ANDREI (*indecisively*).   But that's for my sisters to say, they are mistresses here.

NATASHA.   And they too, I'll tell them. They are kind. . . . (*Going*) For supper I ordered some buttermilk. The doctor says, you're to have nothing but buttermilk or you'll never get any thinner. (*Stopping*) Bobik is cold. I'm afraid he may be cold in that room of his. We ought to—at least till warm weather comes—put him in a different room. For instance, Irina's room is just right for a child; it's dry and sunny too all day long. I must tell her that. For a while at least she could be in the same room with Olga. . . . She's not at home during the day anyhow, she only spends the night. . . . (*A pause*) Andrushanchik, why don't you say something?

ANDREI. I was just thinking— Besides there's nothing to talk about. . . .

NATASHA. Yes. . . . There's something I wanted to tell you. . . . Oh, yes. Ferapont has just come from the District Board, he's asking for you.

ANDREI (*yawning*). Call him in.

(NATASHA *goes out.* ANDREI, *bending over to the candle, which she has forgotten to take along, reads his book.* FERAPONT *enters; he is in a shabby old coat, with the collar turned up, a scarf over his ears.*)

ANDREI. Good evening, my good soul. What have you got to say?

FERAPONT. The Chairman has sent you a book and a paper of some kind. Here. . . . (*He gives the book and an envelope to* ANDREI.)

ANDREI. Thanks. Good! But why did you come so late? It's after eight now?

FERAPONT. How's that?

ANDREI (*louder*). I say you came late, it's now after eight.

FERAPONT. Exactly. I got here when it was still light, but they all wouldn't let me in. The master, they said, is busy. Well, it's like this. You're busy, very busy. I have nowhere to hurry to. (*Thinking that* ANDREI *is asking him something*) How's that?

ANDREI. Nothing. (*Examining the book*) Tomorrow is Friday, we haven't any school, but all the same I'll come, just to be doing something. It's tiresome at home. . . . (*A pause*) Dear Grandpa, how strangely it changes, how life deceives one! Today, out of boredom, out of nothing else to do, I picked up this book here—old university lectures, and I felt like laughing. . . . My God! I'm the secretary of the District Board, that board where Protopopov presides, I am the secretary and the very most I can hope for—is to be a member of the District Board! Me, a member of the local district board, I who dream every night that I'm a professor in Moscow University, a famous scholar whom this Russian land is proud of!

FERAPONT. I wouldn't know. Don't hear well. . . .

ANDREI. If you could hear well, I might not have talked to you. I must talk to somebody, but my wife doesn't understand me, and I am afraid of my sisters somehow, I'm afraid they will laugh at me, make me ashamed. . . . I don't drink, don't like bars; but with what pleasure I could be sitting right now in Moscow at Testoff's or in the Bolshoy Moscoffsky, my dear fellow.

FERAPONT. And in Moscow, so a contractor was saying the other day at the District Board, some merchants were eating bliny;[4] one of them, it seems, ate forty blinies and died. It was either forty or fifty. I wouldn't remember.

ANDREI. You sit in Moscow in a huge room at a restaurant, you don't know anybody, and nobody knows you, but at the same time you don't feel like a stranger. . . . And here you know everybody and everybody knows you, but you are a stranger, a stranger. . . . A stranger and lonely.

FERAPONT. How's that? (*A pause*) And the same contractor was saying—maybe he was just lying—that a rope is stretched all the way across Moscow.

ANDREI. What for?

FERAPONT. I wouldn't know. The contractor said so.

ANDREI. Fiddlesticks. (*Reading*) Were you ever in Moscow?

FERAPONT (*after a pause*). Never was. God didn't grant me that. (*A pause*) Shall I go?

ANDREI. You may go. Good-by. (FERAPONT *goes out.*) Good-by. (*Reading*) Come tomorrow morning and get these papers. . . . Go. . . . (*A pause*) He's gone. (*A bell rings.*) Yes, it's a business— (*Stretching and going slowly into his room*)

> (*Behind the scenes a* NURSE *is singing, rocking a child.* MASHA *and* VERSHININ *enter conversing. In the dining room one of the* MAIDS *is lighting a lamp and the candles.*)

MASHA. I don't know. (*A pause*) I don't know. Of course habit means a lot. For example, after Father's death it took us a long time to get used to not having orderlies in the house. But even apart from habit, I think, common justice makes me say it—in other places it may not be so, but in our town the most decent, the most honorable and well-brought-up people—are the military.

VERSHININ. I'm thirsty. I'd drink some tea.

MASHA (*glancing at the clock*). It will soon be here. They married me off when I was eighteen years old, and I was afraid of my husband because he was a teacher, and that was when I had barely finished my courses. He seemed to me terribly learned then, clever, and important. But now it's not the same, unfortunately.

VERSHININ. So—yes.

MASHA. I am not talking about my husband. I'm used to him, but

---

[4] A small pancake served with caviar.

among the civilians generally there are so many people who are crude and unfriendly and haven't any manners. Rudeness upsets me and offends me, I suffer when I see that a man is not fine enough, gentle enough, polite. When I happen to be among the teachers, my husband's colleagues, I'm simply miserable.

VERSHININ. Yes. . . . But it seems to me it's all the same whether they are civilian or military, they are equally uninteresting, at any rate in this town they are. It's all the same! If you listen to one of the local intelligentsia—civilian or military—what you hear is that he's worn out with his wife, worn out with his home, worn out with his estate, worn out with his horses. . . . A Russian is quite supremely given to lofty ways in thought, but will you tell me why it is that in life he strikes so low? Why?

MASHA. Why?

VERSHININ. Why is he worn out with his children, worn out with his wife? And why are the wife and the children worn out with him?

MASHA. You are not in a very good humor today.

VERSHININ. Perhaps. I haven't had any dinner today, nothing to eat since morning. One of my daughters is not very well, and when my girls are ailing, I am seized with anxiety, and my conscience torments me for their having such a mother. Oh, if you'd seen her today! What a miserable wretch! We began to quarrel at seven o'clock in the morning, and at nine I slammed the door and went out. (*A pause*) I never speak of it, and strangely enough I complain just to you. (*Kissing her hand*) Don't be angry with me. But for you alone, I'd not have anybody—nobody. . . .

(*A pause*)

MASHA. What a noise in the stove! At home, just before Father died, it was howling in the chimney. There, just like that!

VERSHININ. Are you superstitious?

MASHA. Yes.

VERSHININ. That's strange. (*Kissing her hand*) You are a magnificent, wonderful woman. Magnificent, wonderful! It is dark here, but I see the sparkle of your eyes.

MASHA (*moving to another chair*). It's lighter here.

VERSHININ. I love, love, love. . . . Love your eyes, your gestures, I see them in my dreams. . . . Magnificent, wonderful woman!

MASHA (*laughing quietly*). When you talk to me like that, for some reason or other, I laugh, though I'm frightened. Don't do it again, I beg you. . . . (*In a low voice*) But talk, though, it's all the same to me. (*Covering her face with her hands*) It's all the same to me. They're coming here—talk about something else. . . .

(IRINA *and* TUSENBACH *enter from the dining room.*)

TUSENBACH. I have a triple name. I am called Tusenbach—Krone—Altschauer—but I am Russian, Orthodox, like you. There's very little German left in me, perhaps only this patience and stubbornness that I bore you with. I see you home every evening.

IRINA. I'm so tired!

TUSENBACH. And every day I'll come to the telegraph office and see you home, I'll do that for ten, twenty years, for as long as you don't drive me away. . . . (*Seeing* MASHA *and* VERSHININ, *delightedly*) It's you? Good evening.

IRINA. Here I am home at last. (*To* MASHA) Just now a lady came, telegraphed her brother in Saratov that her son died today, and couldn't remember the address at all. So she sent it without the address, simply to Saratov. She was crying. And I was rude to her for no reason whatever. "I haven't got time," I said. 'Twas so silly! Are the maskers coming tonight?

MASHA. Yes.

IRINA. (*She sits down in an armchair.*) I must rest. I'm tired.

TUSENBACH (*smiling*). When you come back from your office, you seem so young, unhappy. . . .

 (*A pause*)

IRINA. I'm tired. No, I don't like the telegraphing, I don't like it.

MASHA. You are thinner. . . . (*She begins to whistle.*) And look younger and your face begins to look like a little boy's.

TUSENBACH. That's from her hair.

IRINA. I must try and find another position, this one is not for me. What I wanted so, what I dreamed of, that's exactly what's not there. Work without poetry, without thoughts. . . . (*A knock on the floor*) The doctor is knocking. . . . (*To* TUSENBACH) Knock back, dear. . . . I can't. . . . I'm tired. . . .

 (TUSENBACH *knocks on the floor.*)

IRINA. He'll come this minute. Something or other will have to be done about it. The doctor and our Andrei were at the club yesterday and lost again. They say Andrei lost two hundred roubles.

MASHA (*indifferently*). So what's there to do now?

IRINA. Two weeks ago he lost, in December he lost. If he'd lose everything soon, perhaps we'd go away from this town. Oh my Lord God, I dream of Moscow every night, I am like someone completely possessed. (*Laughing*) We are moving there in June and from now to June leaves still . . . February, March, April, May. . . . Almost half a year!

MASHA. The only thing is Natasha mustn't some way or other hear of his losses.

IRINA. It's all one to her, I imagine.

(TCHEBUTYKIN, *who has just got out of bed—he has been resting after dinner—enters the dining room combing his beard, then sits down at the table and takes a newspaper from his pocket.*)

MASHA. There he comes. . . . Has he paid anything on his apartment?

IRINA (*laughing*). No. Not a kopeck for eight months. He's forgotten it evidently.

MASHA (*laughing*). How importantly he sits!

(*Everybody laughs; a pause*)

IRINA. Why are you so quiet, Alexander Ignatievich?

VERSHININ. I don't know. What I'd like is some tea. Half my life for a glass of tea! I've eaten nothing since morning. . . .

TCHEBUTYKIN. Irina Sergeevna!

IRINA. What do you want?

TCHEBUTYKIN. Please come here. *Venez ici!* [5] (IRINA *goes and sits down at the table.*) I can't do without you.

(IRINA *lays out the cards for patience.*)

VERSHININ. Well? If they are not giving us any tea, let's at least philosophize.

TUSENBACH. Yes, let's. What about?

VERSHININ. What about? Let's dream . . . for example, of the life that will come after us in two or three hundred years.

TUSENBACH. Well? After us they will fly in balloons, the style of coats will change, they will discover the sixth sense perhaps, and develop it; but life will remain quite the same, a difficult life, mysterious and happy. And after a thousand years, man will be sighing the same: "Ah, how hard it is to live!" and meanwhile, exactly the same as now, he will be afraid of death and not want to die.

VERSHININ (*after a moment's thought*). How shall I put it? It seems to me everything on earth must change little by little and is already changing before our very eyes. In two or three hundred, eventually a thousand, years—it's not a matter of time—a new, happy life will come. We won't share in that life of course, but we are living for it now, working, well—suffering; we are creating it—and in that alone lies the purpose of our being and, if you like, our happiness.

(MASHA *laughs softly.*)

TUSENBACH. What are you laughing at?

MASHA. I don't know. All day today I've been laughing, ever since morning.

[5] "Come here!"

VERSHININ. I was graduated from the same school you were, but was not at the academy; I read a great deal, but don't know how to choose books, and read, perhaps, not at all what I should; and meanwhile the longer I live the more I want to know. My hair is turning gray, I'm almost an old man now, but I know very little, oh, how very little! And yet it does seem to me that what's most important and real I do know, know solidly. And I'd so like to prove to you that there's no happiness, there should not be, and there won't be, for us. . . . We should only work and work, and happiness—that's the lot of our remote descendants. (*A pause*) Not I, but at least the descendants of my descendants.

(FEDOTIK *and* RODAY *appear in the dining room; they sit down and sing softly, strumming a guitar.*)

TUSENBACH. According to you, we are not even to dream of happiness! But what if I'm happy?

VERSHININ. No.

TUSENBACH (*throwing up his hands and laughing*). Obviously we don't understand each other. Well, how can I convince you?

(MASHA *laughs softly.*)

TUSENBACH (*holding up a finger to her*). Laugh! (*To* VERSHININ) Not only in two or three hundred but in a million years, even, life will be just the same as it was; it doesn't change, it stays constant, following its own laws, which are none of our affair, or which, at least, you will never know. Birds of passage, cranes, for example, fly and fly, and no matter what thoughts, great or small, stray through their heads, they will fly just the same and not know why and where. They fly and will fly, no matter what philosophers spring up among them; and they may philosophize as much as they like so long as they fly. . . .

MASHA. Just the same, has it meaning?

TUSENBACH. Meaning. . . . Look, it's snowing. What meaning has that?

(*A pause*)

MASHA. It seems to me a man must be a believer or must seek some belief, otherwise his life is empty, empty. . . . To live and not know why the cranes fly, why children are born, why there are stars in the sky. . . . Either he knows what he's living for, or it's all nonsense, waste.

VERSHININ. Yet it's a shame youth is gone. . . .

MASHA. Gogol [6] says: It is boring to live in this world, gentlemen.

[6] Nikolai Vasilievich Gogol (1809–52), novelist and dramatist.

TUSENBACH. And I say: it is difficult to argue with you, gentlemen! Why you completely. . . .

TCHEBUTYKIN (*reading a newspaper*). Balzac[7] was married in Berdichev. (IRINA *sings softly.*) Really I'll put that in my book. (*Writing*) Balzac was married in Berdichev. (*Reading his newspaper*)

IRINA (*as she lays out cards for patience, musing*). Balzac was married in Berdichev.

TUSENBACH. The die is cast. You know, Maria Sergeevna, I have tendered my resignation.

MASHA. So I heard. And I don't see anything good about that. I don't like civilians.

TUSENBACH. Just the same . . . (*Getting up*) I'm not handsome, what sort of military man am I? Well, well, but all the same, however. . . . I shall work. For just one day in my life, work so that I come home in the evening, drop exhausted into bed and fall asleep right off. (*Going into the dining room*) Workmen must sleep soundly!

FEDOTIK (*to* IRINA). I bought you some crayons on Moscoffsky Street, at Pyjokoff's, and this penknife.

IRINA. You are used to treating me as if I were little, but I'm grown up now. . . . (*She takes the crayons and the penknife, gaily.*) How delightful!

FEDOTIK. And I bought a knife for myself. . . . Look here . . . a blade, and another blade, a third, this to pick the ears, these small scissors, this to clean the nails. . . .

RODAY (*talking very loud*). Doctor, what's your age?

TCHEBUTYKIN. Me? Thirty-two.

(*Laughter*)

FEDOTIK. I'll now show you another game of patience. . . . (*Laying out cards for patience*)

(*The samovar is brought:* ANFISA *is at the samovar; a little later* NATASHA *also comes in and hovers near the table;* SOLYONY *enters and, after greetings, sits down at the table.*)

VERSHININ. But what a wind!

MASHA. Yes. I'm tired of winter. I've already forgotten what summer is like.

IRINA. It's coming out right, the patience, I see. We shall be in Moscow.

FEDOTIK. No, it's not coming out right. Look, the eight falls on the two of spades. (*Laughing*) So you will not be in Moscow.

---

[7] Honoré de Balzac (1799–1850), French novelist.

TCHEBUTYKIN (*reading his newspaper*). Tsitsikar. Smallpox is raging here.

ANFISA (*approaching* MASHA). Masha, have some tea, little one. (*To* VERSHININ) If you please, Your Excellency. . . . Excuse me, dear sir, your name, your family name, I've forgotten. . . .

MASHA. Bring it here, Nurse. I'm not going there.

IRINA. Nurse!

ANFISA. I'm coming!

NATASHA (*to* SOLYONY). Bobik understands beautifully. "Good morning," I say, "Bobik. Good morning, dear!" He gave me a special look somehow. You think I'm only a mother talking, but no, no, I assure you! That's an unusual child.

SOLYONY. If this child were mine, I would have fried him in a skillet and eaten him. (*He goes with his glass into the living room and sits down in the corner.*)

NATASHA (*covering her face with her hands*). Rude, ill-bred man!

MASHA. Happy is he who does not notice whether it's summer now or winter. If I were in Moscow, I think I should scorn the weather. . . .

VERSHININ. The other day I read the diary of a certain French Minister, written in prison. The Minister was convicted of fraud. With what rapture and delight, he mentions the birds he saw through the prison window and had never noticed before when he was a Minister. And now, of course, that he's released, it's the same as it was before, he doesn't notice the birds. Just as you won't notice Moscow when you live there. Happiness we have not and it does not exist, we only long for it.

TUSENBACH (*taking a box from the table*). But where's the candy?

IRINA. Solyony ate it all.

TUSENBACH. All of it?

ANFISA (*serving tea*). A letter for you, dear sir.

VERSHININ. For me? (*Taking the letter*) From my daughter. (*Reading*) Yes, of course. . . . Forgive me, Maria Sergeevna, I'll just slip out. Not any tea for me— (*Getting up very much disturbed*) These eternal messes. . . .

MASHA. What is it? Not a secret?

VERSHININ (*in a low voice*). The wife has taken poison again. Got to go. I'll slip out, won't be seen. Terribly unpleasant, all this. (*Kissing* MASHA'S *hand*) My dear, kind, good woman. . . . I'll slip out of here quietly. . . . (*He goes out.*)

ANFISA. Where is he going now? And I have poured his tea. . . . Such a . . .

MASHA (*losing her temper*). Let it be! Plaguing us around here, there's no rest from you. . . . (*Going to the table with her cup*) I am tired of you, old woman!

ANFISA.   Why are you offended? Darling!

ANDREI'S VOICE.   Anfisa!

ANFISA (*mocking him*).   Anfisa! Sitting there. . . . (*She goes out.*)

MASHA (*in the dining room at the table, angrily*).   Do let me sit down! (*Musses up the cards on the table*) Lounging here with the cards. Drink your tea!

IRINA.   You are spiteful, Masha.

MASHA.   If I'm spiteful, don't talk to me. Don't touch me!

TCHEBUTYKIN (*laughing*).   Don't touch her, don't touch. . . .

MASHA.   You are sixty years old, and you are like a little boy, always prattling the devil knows what.

NATASHA (*sighing*).   Dear Masha, why use such expressions in your conversation? With your beautiful looks you'd be, I'll tell you candidly, simply charming in a decent, well-bred society, if it weren't for these words of yours. *Je vous prie, pardonnez-moi, Marie, mais vous avez des manières un peu grossières.*[8]

TUSENBACH (*suppressing a laugh*).   Give me. . . . Give me. . . . Seems there's some cognac.

NATASHA.   *Il parait que mon Bobik déjà ne dort pas,*[9] he's waked up. He doesn't seem to me very well today. I'm going to him, excuse me. . . . (*She goes out.*)

IRINA.   And where's Alexander Ignatievich gone?

MASHA.   Home. There's something extraordinary the matter with his wife again.

TUSENBACH (*going to* SOLYONY, *with a decanter of cognac*).   You sit by yourself all the time, you are thinking of something—and there's no grasping what it is. Well, let's make peace. Let's drink some cognac. (*Drinking*) I'll have to play the piano all night tonight probably, play all kinds of trash. . . . Come what may!

SOLYONY.   Why make peace? I have not quarreled with you.

TUSENBACH.   You always give me a sort of feeling that something has happened between us. You are a strange character, we must admit.

SOLYONY (*declaiming*).   I am strange, who isn't strange! Don't be angry, Aleko!

TUSENBACH.   But why this Aleko. . . .

(*A pause*)

SOLYONY.   When I am alone with someone I'm all right, I am like

---

[8] "I beg you, pardon me, Marie, but your ways are a little boorish."
[9] "It seems that my Bobik is no longer sleeping."

everybody else, but in company I am gloomy, shy and . . . talk all kinds of rot. Nevertheless, I am more honest and nobler than many, many others are. And I can prove it.

TUSENBACH. I often get sore at you, you are forever plaguing me when we are in company, but just the same you attract me somehow. Come what may, I'll get drunk today. Let's drink!

SOLYONY. Let's do. (*Drinking*) I've never had anything against you, Baron. But I have the disposition of Lermontov.[10] (*In a low voice*) I even resemble Lermontov a little. . . . So they say. . . . (*Getting a bottle of perfume out of his pocket and pouring some of it over his hands*)

TUSENBACH. I am sending in my resignation. *Basta!* For five years I kept pondering it and finally decided. I'm going to work.

SOLYONY (*declaiming*). Don't be angry, Aleko. . . . Forget, forget those dreams of yours. . . .

    (*While they are talking,* ANDREI *comes in quietly with a book and sits down near a candle.*)

TUSENBACH. I'm going to work.

TCHEBUTYKIN (*going into the living room with* IRINA). And the refreshments were real Caucasian too: onion soup, and for the roast —tchehartma, meat.

SOLYONY. Tcheremsha is not meat at all, but a plant something like our onion.

TCHEBUTYKIN. No, my angel . . . Tchehartma is not onion but a mutton roast.

SOLYONY. And I tell you, tcheremsha—onion.

TCHEBUTYKIN. And I tell you, tchehartma—mutton.

SOLYONY. And I tell you, tcheremsha—onion.

TCHEBUTYKIN. But why should I argue with you, you never were in the Caucasus, and never ate tchehartma.

SOLYONY. I haven't eaten it because I can't bear it. Tcheremsha smells exactly like garlic.

ANDREI (*imploringly*). That's enough, gentlemen! I beg you!

TUSENBACH. When are the maskers coming?

IRINA. They promised toward nine; which means, this minute.

TUSENBACH (*embracing* ANDREI. *Singing*). Oh, you porch, my porch, new porch of mine. . . .

ANDREI (*dancing and singing*). New porch of maple. . . .

TCHEBUTYKIN (*dancing*). Made of lattice!

    (*Laughter*)

TUSENBACH (*kissing* ANDREI). The Devil take it, let's have a drink!

---

[10] Mikhail Yurevich Lermontov (1814–41), Russian poet of Scottish extraction.

Andrusha, let us drink with you. And I'll go with you, Andrusha, to Moscow, to the university.

SOLYONY. To which one? In Moscow there are two universities.

ANDREI. In Moscow, there's one university.

SOLYONY. And I tell you—two.

ANDREI. Let there be three even. So much the better!

SOLYONY. In Moscow there are two universities! (*Disapproval and hisses*) In Moscow there are two universities: the old and the new. And if you don't want to listen, if my words irritate you, I can stop talking. I can even go to another room. . . . (*He goes out through one of the doors.*)

TUSENBACH. Bravo, bravo! (*Laughing*) Ladies and gentlemen, begin, I am sitting down to play! Funny this Solyony. . . . (*Sitting down at the piano and playing a waltz*)

MASHA (*waltzing by herself*). The Baron is drunk, the Baron is drunk, the Baron is drunk.

(NATASHA *enters.*)

NATASHA (*to* TCHEBUTYKIN). Ivan Romanovich!

(*She says something to* TCHEBUTYKIN, *then goes out quietly.* TCHEBUTYKIN *touches* TUSENBACH *on the shoulder and whispers something to him.*)

IRINA. What is it?

TCHEBUTYKIN. It's time for us to go.

TUSENBACH. Good night. It's time to go.

IRINA. But look here—what about the maskers?

ANDREI (*embarrassed*). There won't be any maskers. Don't you see, my dear, Natasha says that Bobik isn't quite well, and therefore . . . In sum, I don't know, it's all the same to me, absolutely.

IRINA (*shrugging her shoulders*). Bobik not well!

MASHA. What of it! If they run us out, we must go. (*To* IRINA) It is not Bobik that's sick, but she herself is. . . . Here! (*Tapping her forehead*) Common creature!

(ANDREI *goes through the right door into his room.* TCHEBUTYKIN *follows him: in the dining room good-bys are being said.*)

FEDOTIK. What a pity! I counted on spending the evening, but if the child is sick, of course . . . Tomorrow I'll bring him some toys. . . .

RODAY (*in a loud voice*). I purposely took a nap after dinner today, thought I would dance all night. Why, it's only nine o'clock now.

MASHA. Let's go out in the street: we'll talk things over there. We'll decide what's what.

(*Sounds of:* "Good-by! . . . Farewell! " *You can hear* TUSEN-BACH's *gay laughter. Everyone is gone.* ANFISA *and a* MAID *clear the table, put out the lights. A* NURSE *can be heard singing.* ANDREI *in his coat and hat and* TCHEBUTYKIN *enter quietly.*)

TCHEBUTYKIN. I've had no time to marry because life has flashed by me like lightning, and also because I was madly in love with your mother, who was married. . . .

ANDREI. One shouldn't marry. One shouldn't, it's boring.

TCHEBUTYKIN. That may be so, but the loneliness! You may philosophize as much as you please, but loneliness is a frightful thing, my boy. . . . Though as a matter of fact . . . of course it's absolutely the same.

ANDREI. Let's go quick.

TCHEBUTYKIN. Why hurry? We have time.

ANDREI. I am afraid the wife might stop us.

TCHEBUTYKIN. Ah!

ANDREI. Today I shan't play, but just sit. I don't feel well. . . . What shall I do, Ivan Romanovich, for shortness of breath?

TCHEBUTYKIN. Why ask me? Don't remember, my boy. Don't know.

ANDREI. Let's go through the kitchen.

(*They go out. A ring, then another ring; voices are heard, laughter.* IRINA *enters.*)

IRINA. What is it?

ANFISA (*in a whisper*). The maskers!

(*A ring*)

IRINA. Tell them, Nursey, nobody's at home. They must excuse us.

(ANFISA *goes out.* IRINA *paces the room, thinking things over, she is perturbed.* SOLYONY ENTERS.)

SOLYONY (*in a quandary*). Nobody here. . . . But where are they all?

IRINA. Gone home.

SOLYONY. That's odd. Are you alone here?

IRINA. Alone. (*A pause*) Good-by.

SOLYONY. I behaved without restraint just now, tactlessly. But you are not like the rest of them, you are superior and pure, you can see the truth. . . . Only you alone can understand me. I love you, deeply, love you without end. . . .

IRINA. Good-by! Go away.

SOLYONY. I can't live without you. (*Following her*) Oh, my delight! (*Through his tears*) Oh, happiness! Such glorious, wonderful, marvelous eyes as I have never seen in any other woman. . . .

IRINA (*coldly*). Stop it, Vasili Vasilievich!

SOLYONY. I'm speaking of love to you for the first time and it's as if

I were not on earth but on another planet. (*Rubbing his forehead*)
Well, it's all the same. Love is not to be forced, certainly. . . . But
lucky rivals I cannot have. . . . Cannot. . . . I swear to you by
all that's holy, I'll kill any rival. . . . Oh, wonderful creature!

    (NATASHA *passes by with a candle.*)

NATASHA (*looks in at one door, then at another and passes by the
door leading into her husband's room*). Andrei is there. Let him
read. Excuse me, Vasili Vasilievich, I didn't know you were here.
I'm in my dressing gown.

SOLYONY. It's all the same to me. Good-by! (*He goes out.*)

NATASHA. And you are tired, my dear, poor girl! (*Kissing* IRINA)
You should go to bed a little earlier.

IRINA. Is Bobik asleep?

NATASHA. Asleep. But not sound asleep. By the way, dear, I wanted
to tell you, but you are never here, or else I haven't time. . . . In
the nursery Bobik has now, seems to me it's cold and damp. And
your room is so good for a child. My dear, my own, move in with
Olya for a while!

IRINA (*not understanding*). Where?

    (*A troika with bells is heard driving up to the house.*)

NATASHA. You and Olya will be in one room, for this little while, and
your room will be for Bobik. He's such a darling, today I say to him:
"Bobik, you are mine! Mine!" And he looks at me with his little
eyes. (*A ring*) It must be Olga. How late she is!

    (*A* MAID *comes and whispers in* NATASHA'S *ear.*)

NATASHA. Protopopov? What a queer man! Protopopov has come, he's
asking me to go for a ride with him in a troika. (*Laughing*) How
strange these men are . . . ! (*A ring*) Somebody's come out there.
I might go ride for a quarter of an hour. . . . (*To the* MAID)
Tell him right away— (*A ring*) There's a ring. . . . Olga must
be here. (*She goes out.*)

    (*The* MAID *runs out;* IRINA *sits there thinking.* KULYGIN, OLGA
enter, behind them VERSHININ.)

KULYGIN. There you are! And they said there would be a party.

VERSHININ. Strange, I went away a while ago, half an hour ago, and
they were expecting the maskers. . . .

IRINA. They have all gone.

KULYGIN. And Masha's gone? Where did she go? And why is Protopopov downstairs waiting in the troika? Who's he waiting for?

IRINA. Don't ask questions. . . . I'm tired.

KULYGIN. Well, Miss Caprice . . .

OLGA. The council has just finished. I'm exhausted. Our headmistress
is ill, and I'm taking her place. My head, my head aches, my

head . . . (*Sitting down*) Andrei lost two hundred roubles yesterday at cards. . . . The whole town is talking about it. . . .

KULYGIN. Yes, and I got tired at the council. (*He sits down.*)

VERSHININ. My wife decided just now to scare me, she almost poisoned herself. It all passed over and I'm happy, I'm easy now. . . . The order is we must leave here. So—let me wish you all well. Fyodor Ilyich, go somewhere with me. I can't stay at home, absolutely cannot. . . . Let's go!

KULYGIN. I'm tired. I'm not going. (*Rising*) I'm tired. Has the wife come home?

IRINA. She must have.

KULYGIN (*kissing* IRINA's *hand*). Good-by. Tomorrow and the day after I'll rest all day long. I wish you well. (*Going*) I'd like some tea very much. I counted on spending the evening in pleasant company and—*o, fallacem hominum spem!* [11] Accusative case exclamatory. . . .

VERSHININ. Which means I'm going by myself.

(*He goes out with* KULYGIN, *whistling.*)

OLGA. My head aches, my head . . . Andrei has lost . . . the whole town is talking. . . . I'll go lie down. . . . (*Starting out of the room*) Tomorrow I am free. . . . O Lord, how pleasant it is! Tomorrow is free, day after tomorrow is free. . . . My head aches, my head . . . (*She goes out.*)

IRINA (*alone*). They've all gone. There's nobody here.

(*In the street an accordion is heard, the* NURSE *sings a song.*)

NATASHA (*with a fur coat and cap, passes through the dining room; behind her a* MAID). I'll be home in half an hour. I'll take just a little ride. (*She goes out.*)

IRINA (*left alone, dejected*). To Moscow! To Moscow! To Moscow!

Curtain

ACT III

OLGA'S *and* IRINA'S *room. To the left and to the right are beds, with screens around them. It is going on three o'clock in the morning. Offstage they are ringing the firebell for a fire that began a long time back. Plainly no one in the house has gone to bed yet.* MASHA *lies on the sofa, she wears, as usual, a black dress.* OLGA *and* ANFISA *enter.*

ANFISA. Sitting down there now under the staircase . . . I say—"If you please, come upstairs, as if," I say, "you could sit there like

[11] "Ah, the falseness of men's hope!"

that!"—they are crying, "Daddy," they say, "we don't know where Daddy is. God forbid," they say, "he's burned!" They thought that up! And in the courtyard there are some people. . . . They are undressed too.

OLGA (*taking some dresses out of the closet*). Here, this gray one— take it. . . . And this one here. . . . The blouse too . . . And take the skirt, Nursey. . . . All Kirsanoffsky Street seems to be burned down. . . . Take this. . . . Take this. . . . (*Throws the dresses for her to catch*) The poor Vershinins were frightened. . . . Their house nearly burned up. They must spend the night here. . . . We can't let them go home. . . . At poor Fedotik's everything got burned, there's nothing left. . . .

ANFISA. You'll have to call Ferapont, Olyushka, or I can't carry . . .

OLGA. (*She rings.*) Nobody answers. . . . (*Through the door*) Come here, whoever it is! (*Through the open door she sees a window glowing red with the fire; a fire brigade is heard passing the house.*) How frightful! And how sickening! (FERAPONT *enters.*) Here, take this and carry it downstairs. . . . Down there under the staircase the young Kolotilin girls. . . . Give it to them. And give this. . . .

FERAPONT. Yes, miss. In the year '12, Moscow also burned. Oh my Lord God! The French were astonished.

OLGA. Go on, step along. . . .

FERAPONT. Yes, miss. (*He goes out.*)

OLGA. Nursey, dear, give everything away. We don't need anything. Give everything away! Nursey . . . I'm tired, I can barely stand on my feet. . . . The Vershinins shouldn't be allowed to go home. . . . The girls can sleep in the drawing room, and Alexander Ignatievich downstairs at the Baron's . . . Fedotik too at the Baron's, or let him stay with us in the dining room. . . . The doctor as if he'd done it on purpose, is drunk, terribly drunk, and we mustn't send anyone to him. And Vershinin's wife too in the drawing room.

ANFISA (*wearily*). Olyushka, dear, don't you drive me away! Don't drive me away!

OLGA. You are talking nonsense, Nurse. Nobody's driving you away.

ANFISA (*laying her head on* OLGA'S *breast*). My own, my treasure, I do try, I work. . . . I'll get feeble and everybody will say: get out! And where will I go? Eighty years old. My eighty-second year. . . .

OLGA. You sit down a while, Nursey. . . . You are tired, poor thing. . . . (*Making her sit down*) Rest, my dear good old Nurse. You look so pale!

(NATASHA *enters.*)

NATASHA. They are saying it around that we must form right off a relief society for those who have been burnt out. Why not! It's a fine idea. We must be quick to help poor people, that's the duty of the rich. Bobik and Sofotchka have just gone to sleep, they sleep as if nothing had happened. There are so many people everywhere here that anywhere you go the house is full. There's influenza in town now, I'm afraid the children may catch it.

OLGA (*not listening to her*). In this room you don't see the fire, it's peaceful here. . . .

NATASHA. Yes. . . . I must be very much disheveled. (*In front of the mirror*) They say I have filled out. . . . And it isn't true! Not at all! And Masha's sleeping, exhausted . . . poor thing. . . . (*To* ANFISA, *coldly*) In my presence, don't you dare sit down! Get up! Get out of here! (ANFISA *goes out; a pause*) Why you keep this old woman I don't understand!

OLGA (*taken aback*). Excuse me, I don't understand either. . . .

NATASHA. For no reason at all she's here. She is a peasant, she should live in the country. . . . What a lot of pampering! I like in a house to have order. Useless people shouldn't be in a house. (*Stroking* OLGA's *cheek*) Poor dear, you are tired! Our headmistress is tired. And when my Sofotchka grows up and enters high school, I shall be afraid of you.

OLGA. I shan't be the headmistress.

NATASHA. You will be elected, Olitchka, that's decided.

OLGA. I'll decline it. I can't, I've not the strength for it. (*Drinking some water*) You were so rude just now to Nurse. . . . Forgive me, I'm not in any condition to bear . . . It's getting all black before my eyes. . . .

NATASHA (*disturbed*). Forgive me, Olya, forgive me. . . . I didn't mean to distress you.

(MASHA *gets up, takes a pillow and goes out, angrily.*)

OLGA. Understand, my dear . . . perhaps we were brought up strangely, but I can't bear it. That kind of attitude depresses me, I get sick. . . . I'm just sick at heart!

NATASHA. Forgive me, forgive me. . . . (*Kissing her*)

OLGA. Every rudeness, even the slightest, even a word indelicately spoken, upsets me.

NATASHA. I often talk too much, it's true, but you must agree, my dear, she might very well have lived in the country.

OLGA. She's been these thirty years with us.

NATASHA. But now, though, she can't do anything. It's either that I don't understand or else you don't want to understand me. She is not up to doing any sort of work, she just sleeps and sits.

OLGA. But let her sit.

NATASHA (*surprised*). How let her sit? She's a servant nevertheless. (*Tearfully*) I don't understand you, Olya. I have a nurse, have a wet nurse, we have a maid, a cook. . . . What do we have that old woman too for? What for?

(*Behind the scene the fire-alarm rings.*)

OLGA. I have aged ten years in this one night!

NATASHA. We must come to some sort of understanding, Olya. You are at high school, I'm at home; you have the teaching, I have the housekeeping. And if I say anything about the servants, I know what I'm saying. I know what I'm saying. . . . And by tomorrow there won't be this old thief here, this old hag. (*Stamping her foot*) This witch . . . Don't dare cross me! Don't you dare! (*Catching herself*) Really, if you don't move downstairs, we'll always be quarreling. It's terrible.

(KULYGIN *enters.*)

KULYGIN. Where is Masha? It's quite time to go home. The fire, they say, is subsiding. (*Stretching*) Burnt just one section of the town, in spite of the fact that there was a wind; at first it looked as if the whole town was on fire. (*Sitting down*) I'm tired out, Olitchka, my dear. . . . I often think if there hadn't been Masha, I'd have married you, Olitchka. You are so good. . . . I'm exhausted. (*Listening for something*)

OLGA. What is it?

KULYGIN. As if on purpose, the doctor is drunk, he's terribly drunk. As if on purpose! (*Getting up*) There he is coming here, I imagine . . . Do you hear? Yes, coming . . . (*Laughing*) What a fellow, really . . . I'll hide. (*Going to the cupboard and standing in the corner*) Such a rascal!

OLGA. For two years he hasn't been drinking and here all of a sudden he's gone and got drunk.

(*Following* NATASHA *to the back of the room*)

(TCHEBUTYKIN *enters; without staggering, as if he were sober, he walks across the room, stops, looks around, then goes to the washstand and begins to wash his hands.*)

TCHEBUTYKIN (*crossly*). The Devil take all of 'em, take—They think I'm a doctor, know how to cure any sickness, but I know absolutely nothing, I've forgotten everything I ever knew, remember nothing, absolutely nothing. (OLGA *and* NATASHA *go out, unnoticed by him.*) The Devil take it! Last Wednesday, I treated a woman at Zasip—she died, and I'm to blame for her dying. Yes . . . I knew a little something twenty-five years ago, but now I don't remember anything. Nothing. Perhaps I'm not even a man, but only give the appearance here of having hands and legs and a head; perhaps I don't even exist, and it only seems to me that I walk and eat and sleep. (*Crying*) Oh, that I didn't exist! (*No longer crying, crossly*) The Devil knows . . . ! Three days ago there was a conversation at the club, they were talking about Shakespeare, Voltaire[12] . . . I hadn't read them, hadn't read them at all, but I looked as if I had read them. And the others did too, just as I did. The banality of it! The meanness! And that woman I killed Wednesday came back to me . . . And everything came back to me, and it weighed on my soul, crooked, foul, disgusting . . . I went and got drunk. . . .

> (IRINA, VERSHININ *and* TUSENBACH *enter;* TUSENBACH *wears civilian clothes, new and stylish.*)

IRINA. Let's sit here. Nobody's coming here.

VERSHININ. If it were not for the soldiers, the whole town would be burnt up. Brave boys! (*Rubbing his hands with pleasure*) Salt of the earth! Ah, what brave boys!

KULYGIN. What's the time, gentlemen?

TUSENBACH. Going on four by now. It's getting light.

IRINA. Everybody is sitting in the dining room, nobody is going out. And that Solyony of yours is sitting . . . (*To* TCHEBUTYKIN) Doctor, you should have gone to sleep.

TCHEBUTYKIN. Not at all . . . Thank you . . . (*Combing his beard*)

KULYGIN (*laughing*). You got a little tipsy, Ivan Romanovich! (*Slapping him on the shoulder*) Bravo! *In vino veritas,*[13] said the ancients.

TUSENBACH. They keep asking me to arrange a concert for the benefit of the refugees.

IRINA. Well, who is there to . . . ?

TUSENBACH. It could be arranged if we wanted to do it. Maria Sergeevna, in my opinion, plays the piano wonderfully.

KULYGIN. She does play wonderfully!

IRINA. She has forgotten how by now. It's three years since she's played. . . . Or four.

TUSENBACH. Here in this town absolutely nobody understands music, not one soul; but I, I do understand it, and on my word of honor, I assure you that Maria Sergeevna plays magnificently, almost with genius.

KULYGIN. You are right, Baron. I love her very much, I love my Masha. She's sweet.

TUSENBACH. Think of being able to play so splendidly and at the

---

[12] Pseudonym of François Marie Arouet (1694–1778), French philosopher and man of letters.
[13] "In wine there's truth."

same time know quite well that nobody, nobody, understands you!

KULYGIN (*sighing*). Yes . . . But is it proper for her to take part in a concert? (*A pause*) Really, gentlemen, I don't know anything about that. Perhaps it would be a good thing. I must admit our director is a fine man, in fact, very fine, of the brainiest; but he has such views that . . . Of course, it's not his affair, but just the same, if you like, I might talk with him.

(TCHEBUTYKIN *is taking up a china clock in both hands and examining it.*)

VERSHININ. I got all covered with dirt at the fire—I'm not presentable. (*A pause*) Yesterday I heard in passing that they might transfer our brigade somewhere far away. Some say to the Kingdom of Poland, others—that it looks like Chita.

TUSENBACH. I heard that too. And so what? The town will be completely empty then.

IRINA. And we shall go away!

TCHEBUTYKIN. (*He drops the clock, shattering it.*) All to pieces!

(*A pause; everyone is distressed and embarrassed.*)

KULYGIN (*picks up the pieces*). To break such a precious thing— Oh, Ivan Romanovich, Ivan Romanovich! Minus zero to you for conduct.

IRINA. That clock was our dear mother's.

TCHEBUTYKIN. Perhaps . . . Mother's, then, mother's. Perhaps I didn't break it but only seemed to break it. Perhaps it only seems to us that we exist, and we don't really. I don't know anything, nobody knows anything. (*By the door*) What are you looking at? Natasha has an affair with Protopopov, and you don't see it. . . . There you sit and see nothing, and Natasha has an affair with Protopopov. . . . (*Singing*) How do you like swallowing that dose . . . ? (*He goes out.*)

VERSHININ. Yes. . . . (*Laughing*) How strange all this is at bottom! (*A pause*) When the fire began, I ran home fast; got there, looked . . . our house was unharmed and out of danger, but my two girls stood at the door in nothing but their underclothes, the mother wasn't there, people were scurrying about, horses running around, and dogs, and on my girls' faces was all that anxiety, terror, entreaty, who knows what; my heart was wrung when I saw those faces. My God, I thought, what more will these girls have to go through, in a long life! I grabbed them, ran and kept thinking one thing: What more will they have to live through in this world! (*Fire-alarm; a pause*) I came this way and the mother was here, shouting, angry.

(MASHA *enters with a pillow and sits down on the sofa.*)

VERSHININ. And while my girls were standing at the door in nothing but their underclothes and the street was red with the fire, the noise was terrible, I reflected that something like that used to happen when the enemy made a sudden raid, plundering and burning as they went. Meanwhile what a difference there is essentially between what is and what was! And a little more time will pass, some two or three hundred years, and they will look on this life of ours now with fear and derision, everything now will seem then to be all angles and heavy and most inconvenient and strange. Oh, what a life that will be, what a life! (*Laughing*) Forgive me, I'm philosophizing again. Allow me to continue, ladies and gentlemen. I'd like awfully to philosophize, now that I'm in such a mood for it. (*A pause*) It's as if everybody were asleep. And so I say: What a life it will be! You can just imagine. . . . Here in town there are only three of your kind now, but in coming generations there will be more, always more and more; a time will come when everything will veer to you, they will live like you, and then, too, later on you'll get antiquated, there'll be people springing up who are better than you. . . . (*Laughing*) I am in a most singular mood today. I want like the devil to live. . . . (*Singing*) Unto love all ages bow, its pangs are blest. . . .

MASHA. Tram-tum-tum. . . .

VERSHININ. Tum-tum. . . .

MASHA. Tra-ra-ra?

VERSHININ. Tra-ta-ta. (Laughing)

(FEDOTIK enters.)

FEDOTIK (*dancing*). Burnt out, burnt out! Absolutely everything! (*Laughter*)

IRINA. What sort of a joke is that? Is it all gone?

FEDOTIK (*laughing*). Absolutely everything. There's nothing left. And the guitar burned, and the photography outfit burned, and all my letters. . . . And I wanted to present you with a notebook . . . it burned up too.

(SOLYONY *enters.*)

IRINA. No. Please go away, Vasili Vasilievich. You can't come in here.

SOLYONY. But why is it the Baron can and I can't?

VERSHININ. We must go, really. How's the fire?

SOLYONY. They say it's subsiding. No, it's decidedly strange to me, why is it the Baron can and I can't? (*Taking out the perfume bottle and sprinkling himself*)

VERSHININ. Tram-tum-tum.

MASHA. Tram-tum.

VERSHININ (*laughing, to* SOLYONY). Let's go to the dining room.

SOLYONY. Very well, I'll make a note of it so. This thought could be made more clear, but 'twould annoy the geese, I fear. . . . (*Looking at* TUSENBACH) Chick, chick, chick. . . .

    (*He goes out with* VERSHININ *and* FEDOTIK.)

IRINA. How that Solyony has smoked things up. (*With surprise*) The Baron is asleep! Baron! Baron!

TUSENBACH (*waking up*). I'm tired, however. . . . The brickyard. . . . I'm not saying this in my sleep, for it's a fact that I'll soon be going to the brickyard to start work. . . . It's already been discussed. (*To* IRINA, *tenderly*) You are so pale, beautiful, bewitching. . . . It seems to me your paleness brightens the dark air like light. . . . You are sad, you are not satisfied with life. . . . Oh, come along with me, let's go to work together!

MASHA. Nikolai Lvovich, do go on out of here!

TUSENBACH (*laughing*). You here? I didn't see you. (*Kissing* IRINA'S *hand*) Good-by, I'm going. . . . I'm looking at you now and am reminded of how long ago once on your saint's day you were all so gay and happy, talking of the joy of work. . . . And what a happy life I dreamed of then! Where is it? (*Kissing her hand*) You have tears in your eyes. Go to bed. . . . It's getting light now . . . morning has begun. . . . If only it were granted me to give my life for you!

MASHA. Nikolai Lvovich, go on! Why, really, what . . .

TUSENBACH. I'm going. . . . (*He goes out.*)

MASHA (*lying down*). Are you asleep, Fyodor?

KULYGIN. Eh?

MASHA. You ought to go home.

KULYGIN. My darling Masha, my dear Masha. . . .

IRINA. She's tired. . . . You ought to let her rest, Fedya.

KULYGIN. I'm going right away. . . . My good wife, darling . . . I love you, my one and only. . . .

MASHA (*bored and cross*). *Amo, amas, amat, amamus, amatis, amant.*[14]

KULYGIN (*laughing*). No, really, she's amazing. I've been married to you for seven years; but it seems as if we'd married only yesterday. Word of honor! No, really, you are an amazing woman. I am content, I am content, I am content!

MASHA. Bored, bored, bored. . . . (*She sits up, and speaks sitting.*) It just won't go out of my head. . . . It's simply shocking. It's there like a nail in my head. I can't stay silent. I mean about Andrei. . . . He's mortgaged this house to the bank and his wife grabbed

[14] Conjugation of the Latin verb *amare,* "to love."

all the money, but the house belongs not just to him, but to the four of us! He ought to know that if he's a decent man.

KULYGIN.   What do you care, Masha! Why should you? Andrusha is in debt all round, well, God reward him!

MASHA.   Anyhow it's shocking. (*She lies back down.*)

KULYGIN.   You and I are not poor. I work, I go to the high school, and then give private lessons. . . . I'm an honest man. Simple. . . . *Omnia mea mecum porto,*[15] as they say.

MASHA.   I don't need anything. But injustice makes me furious. (*A pause*) Go on, Fyodor!

KULYGIN (*kissing her*).   You are tired, rest about half an hour, and I'll sit and wait out there. Sleep. . . . (*Going*) I am content, I am content, I am content. (*He goes out.*)

IRINA.   How small our Andrei has grown, how he has dried up and aged beside that woman! There was a time when he was preparing for a professorship, and yesterday he was bragging that at last he could become a member of the District Board. He a member of the board and Protopopov chairman. . . . The whole town's talking, is laughing, and he's the only one who knows nothing and sees nothing. And now, everybody has rushed off to the fire, but he sits there in his room and pays not the least attention to it. He just plays the violin. (*Nervously*) Oh, it's awful, awful, awful! (*Crying*) I can't, I can't bear any more! . . . I can't—I can't!

(OLGA *enters. She tidies up her dressing table.*)

IRINA (*sobbing aloud*).   Cast me out, cast me out, I can't stand any more! . . .

OLGA (*alarmed*).   What is it, what is it? Darling!

IRINA (*sobbing*).   Where? Where is it all gone? Where is it? Oh, my God, my God! I've forgotten everything, I've forgotten . . . it's muddled in my head. . . . I don't remember what in Italian *window* is, or the ceiling there. . . . I'm forgetting everything, every day forgetting, and life slips away and will never return, never, we'll never go to Moscow. . . . I can see we'll never go.

OLGA.   Darling, darling. . . .

IRINA (*restraining herself*).   Oh, I'm miserable. . . . I can't work and won't work. I'm sick of it, sick of it! I was a telegraph operator, and now have a place with the Town Board, and hate and despise everything they give me to do. . . . I'm going on twenty-four and have already been working a long time, and my brain's drying up, I'm getting thin, losing my looks, getting old, and there's nothing,

---

[15] "All my things I carry with me. . . ."

nothing—no satisfaction of any kind—and time is passing, and it all seems to be moving away from any real, beautiful life, all moving away farther and farther into some abyss. . . . I'm in despair, and how I'm alive, how it is I haven't killed myself, I can't understand. . . .

OLGA. Don't cry, my own little girl, don't cry. . . .

IRINA. I am not crying, not crying. . . . I'm sick of it. . . . Now look—I am not crying any more. I'm sick of it. . . . I'm sick of it!

OLGA. Darling, I'm telling you as a sister, as a friend, if you want my advice, marry the Baron!

(IRINA *weeps silently.*)

OLGA. Why, you respect him, you value him highly. It's true he's not good-looking, but he's so decent and clean. . . . Why, one doesn't marry for love but to do one's duty. At least, I think so, and I would marry without being in love. At any rate I'd marry anyone who proposed to me so long as he was an honorable man. I'd marry even an old man. . . .

IRINA. I kept expecting us to move to Moscow; there I'd meet my real beloved, I dreamed of him, loved him. But it turned out just foolishness, just foolishness! . . .

OLGA (*embracing her sister*). My dear, lovely sister, I understand it all; when Baron Nikolai Lvovich left the military service and came to see us in civilian clothes, he seemed to me so homely that I even cried. He asked, "Why are you crying?" How could I tell him! But if God should grant he married you, I'd be happy. Now, that's different, quite different!

(NATASHA *crosses the stage from the right door to the left, without speaking, a candle in her hand.*)

MASHA (*sitting up*). She walks as if she had been the one to start the fire.

OLGA. Masha, you are silly! The silliest one in our family is you. Forgive me, please.

(*A pause*)

MASHA. I want to confess, my dear sisters. I'm tired in my soul. I'll confess to you and then to nobody else, never. . . . I'll say it this minute. (*Quietly*) It's my secret, but you must know everything. . . . I can't be silent. . . . (*A pause*) I love, love . . . I love that man. . . . You just saw him. . . . Well, there it is. In one word, I love Vershinin. . . .

OLGA (*going behind her screen*). Stop that. At any rate I'm not hearing.

MASHA. What is there to do about it? (*Clutching her head*) At first he seemed to me strange, then I felt sorry for him. . . . Then I began to love him . . . began to love him with his voice, his words, his misfortunes, his two girls. . . .

OLGA (*behind the screen*). I'm not hearing you at any rate. Whatever silly things you say, at any rate I'm not hearing you!

MASHA. Oh, Olya, you are silly. I love—such, that is to say, is my fate. That is to say my lot is such. . . . And he loves me. . . . All that is frightening. Yes? Is it wrong? (*Taking* IRINA *by the hand and drawing her to her*) Oh, my darling . . . how are we going to live our life, what's to become of us? . . . When one reads some novel, all this seems old and all of it so understandable, but when you fall in love yourself, you begin to see that nobody knows anything and everybody must decide for himself. . . . My darlings, my sisters. . . . I confessed to you, now I'll be silent. . . . I'll be now like Gogol's madman . . . silence . . . silence. . . .

(ANDREI *enters, followed by* FERAPONT.)

ANDREI (*annoyed*). What do you want? I don't understand.

FERAPONT (*standing in the door, impatiently*). Andrei Sergeevich, I have already told you ten times.

ANDREI. First, I am not Andrei Sergeevich to you but Your Excellency!

FERAPONT. The firemen, Your Excellentness, ask your permission to go to the river through your garden. As it is, they are driving round and round—it's pure punishment.

ANDREI. Very well. Tell them, very well. (FERAPONT *goes out*.) That's enough of them. Where's Olga? (OLGA *comes out from behind the screen*.) I've come to ask you to give me the key to the cupboard. I've lost mine. You have one of the little keys. (OLGA *gives him the key without speaking.* IRINA *goes behind her screen; a pause*) And what a tremendous fire! It's starting to die down now. The devil take it, that Ferapont's made me lose my temper. I said a stupid thing to him. . . . Your Excellency. . . . (*A pause*) But why are you silent, Olya? (*A pause*) It's high time to stop this silliness and stop pouting for no reason at all. . . . You are here, Masha, Irina's here, well, that's fine—let's have it out once and for all. What have you got against me? Now what?

OLGA. Let it rest, Andrusha. Tomorrow we'll have it out. (*Anxiously*) What a night of torment!

ANDREI. (*He is very much confused.*) Don't be upset. I ask you absolutely in cold blood: what have you got against me? Speak right out.

VERSHININ'S VOICE. Tram-tum-tum!

MASHA (*rising, in a loud voice*). Tra-ta-ta! (*To* OLGA) Good-by

Olya, God be with you! (*She goes behind the screen, kisses* IRINA.)
Sleep well. . . . Good-by, Andrei. Go on away, they are tired.
. . . Tomorrow you will have it out. (*She goes out.*)

OLGA. Indeed, Andrusha, let's put it off till tomorrow. . . . (*She
goes behind her screen.*) It's time to go to sleep.

ANDREI. I'll just say it and go. Right away. . . . In the first place,
you have something against Natasha, my wife, and that I have
noticed from the very day of my wedding. Natasha is a splendid,
honest person, straightforward, and honorable—in my opinion. I
love and respect my wife, understand, I respect her and demand
that others respect her too. I repeat, she is an honest, honorable
person, and all your dissatisfactions, excuse me, are simply caprices.
. . . (*A pause*) In the second place, you seem to be angry because
of the fact that I am not a professor, don't occupy myself with
learning. But I serve in the Zemstvo,[16] I am a member of the District Board, and this service of mine I consider just as sacred and
lofty as service to learning. I'm a member of the District Board
and I'm proud of it, if you want to know. . . . (*A pause*) In
the third place, I have something else to say . . . : I mortgaged
the house without asking your permission. . . . Of that I am guilty,
yes, and ask you to forgive me. I was forced to it by debts. . . .
Thirty-five thousand. . . . I don't play cards any more, gave it
up long ago, but the chief thing I can say in my own justification,
is that you—girls, as of the privileged sex, you receive a pension,
while I didn't have . . . my earnings, so to speak. . . . (*A pause*)

KULYGIN (*at the door*). Masha not here? (*Perturbed*) But where
is she? That's strange. . . . (*He goes out.*)

ANDREI. They don't listen. Natasha is a superior, honest person.
(*Walks up and down the stage in silence, then stops*) When I
married, I thought we should be happy . . . everybody happy
. . . but, my God . . . ! (*Crying*) My dear sisters, darling sisters,
don't believe me, don't believe . . . (*He goes out.*)

KULYGIN (*at the door, anxiously*). Where is Masha? Masha's not
here? What an astonishing business! (*He goes out.*)

(*Fire-alarm; the stage is empty.*)

IRINA (*behind the screen*). Olya! Who is that knocking on the floor?

OLGA. It's the doctor, Ivan Romanovich. He's drunk.

IRINA. What a torn-up night! (*A pause*) Olya! (*Looking out from
behind the screen*) Did you hear? They are taking the brigade from
us, transferring it somewhere far away.

OLGA. That's only a rumor.

16 County council.

IRINA. We'll be left alone. . . . Olya!

OLGA. Well?

IRINA. Darling, precious, I respect, I value the Baron, he's a marvelous person, I'll marry him, I consent, only let's go to Moscow! I beg you, let's go! There's nothing in the world better than Moscow! Let's go, Olya! Let's go!

Curtain

ACT IV

An old garden in front of the PROZOROFFS' *house. A long alley of fir trees, at the end of which a river is seen. On the other side of the river, a wood. To the right a terrace of the house and on it a table with bottles and glasses; you can see they have just been drinking champagne. Twelve o'clock noon. Now and then on their way from the street to the river,* PEOPLE *cross the garden; four or five* SOLDIERS *pass that way, walking fast.* TCHEBUTYKIN, *in an amiable mood, which does not leave him during the entire Act, sits in an easy chair, in the garden, waiting to be called; he wears a military cap and carries a stick.* IRINA, KULYGEN *with a decoration around his neck, with no mustache, and* TUSENBACH, *are standing on the terrace, saying good-by to* FEDOTIK *and* RODAY, *who are going down the steps; both officers are in campaign uniform.*

TUSENBACH (*exchanging kisses with* FEDOTIK). You are a good fellow, we lived like good friends. (*Exchanging kisses with* RODAY) Once again. . . . Good-by, my dear boy. . . .

IRINA. Till we meet again.

FEDOTIK. It's not meet again, but good-by, we shall never meet again.

KULYGIN. Who knows! (*Wiping his eyes, smiling*) There, I'm beginning to cry too.

IRINA. Some day we'll run across each other.

FEDOTIK. In ten or fifteen years maybe? But by then we'll scarcely know each other, we'll greet each other coldly. . . . (*Taking a snapshot*) Stand still. . . . Once more, for the last time.

RODAY (*embracing* TUSENBACH). We won't meet again. . . . (*Kissing* IRINA'S *hand*) Thank you for everything, for everything!

FEDOTIK (*vexed*). Oh, wait a little!

TUSENBACH. God grant we meet. Write us though. Without fail write.

RODAY (*casting a glance around the garden*). Good-by, trees! (*Shouting*) Yoo hoo! (*A pause*) Good-by, echo!

KULYGIN. I am afraid you'll marry there in Poland. . . . The Polish wife will embrace you and say: *"Kochany!"* [17] (*Laughing*)

FEDOTIK (*looking at his watch*). There's less than an hour left. Out of our battery only Solyony is going on the barge, we are with the rank and file. Three battery divisions are going today, tomorrow three more—and quiet and peace will reign in the town. . . .

TUSENBACH. And terrible boredom.

RODAY. And where is Maria Sergeevna?

KULYGIN. Masha is in the garden.

FEDOTIK. We must say good-by to her.

RODAY. Good-by, I must go or I'll be crying. . . . (*He hurriedly embraces* TUSENBACH *and* KULYGIN, *kisses* IRINA'S *hand.*) It was fine living here.

FEDOTIK (*to* KULYGIN). This is a memento for you. . . . A notebook with a pencil. . . . We'll go this way to the river. . . .
(*They move off, both look back.*)

RODAY (*shouts*). Yoo hoo!

KULYGIN (*shouts*). Good-by!
(*At the rear of the stage* FEDOTIK *and* RODAY *meet* MASHA *and bid her good-by. She walks away with them.*)

IRINA. They are gone. . . . (*Sitting down on the bottom step of the terrace*)

TCHEBUTYKIN. And forgot to say good-by to me.

IRINA. And what about you?

TCHEBUTYKIN. And I forgot too somehow. Anyway I'll soon see them, I'm leaving tomorrow. Yes. . . . One more short day is left. In a year they will retire me, I'll come back here and live out my little span near you. Just one short year is left before my pension. (*He puts one newspaper in his pocket and takes out another.*) I'll come here to you and change my life from the very roots. I'll become so quiet, right—right-minded, respectable.

IRINA. And you really should change your life, dovey. You should somehow.

TCHEBUTYKIN. Yes, I feel so. (*Singing softly*) Ta-ra-ra-boom-de-aye. . . . Sit on a curb I may. . . .

KULYGIN. You're incorrigible, Ivan Romanovich! You're incorrigible!

TCHEBUTYKIN. Now then, if you'd only teach me! Then I'd be reformed.

IRINA. Fyodor has shaved off his mustache. I can't bear to look at him.

[17] "Darling!"

KULYGIN.   Why not?

TCHEBUTYKIN.   I could say what your physiognomy looks like now, but I can't.

KULYGIN.   Well! It's the accepted thing, it is *modus vivendi.*[18] Our director shaved off his mustache, and as soon as I became inspector, I shaved clean too. Nobody likes it, but that's all the same to me. I am content. I may be with a mustache, or without a mustache, but I'm equally content. . . . (*Sitting down*)

   (*At the rear of the stage* ANDREI *passes, wheeling a baby-carriage with a child asleep in it.*)

IRINA.   Ivan Romanovich, my own darling, I am terribly disturbed. You were on the boulevard yesterday, tell me what happened there?

TCHEBUTYKIN.   What happened? Nothing. Fiddlesticks. (*Reading the newspaper*) All the same!

KULYGIN.   What they are saying is that Solyony and the Baron met yesterday on the boulevard near the theatre. . . .

TUSENBACH.   Stop it! Well, what really. . . . (*With a wave of his hand he goes into the house.*)

KULYGIN.   Near the theatre . . . Solyony began picking on the Baron, and he wouldn't tolerate it, he said something insulting. . . .

TCHEBUTYKIN.   I don't know. It's all nonsense.

KULYGIN.   In a certain theological seminary a teacher wrote on a composition paper, "Nonsense" and the pupil read "consensus"—thought it was written in Latin. (*Laughing*) Amazingly funny. It's said that Solyony is in love with Irina, and that he's begun to hate the Baron. . . . That's understandable. Irina is a very nice girl. She even resembles Masha, just as thoughtful. It's merely that you have a gentle character, Irina. Though Masha, too, has a very fine character, I love her, my Masha.

   (*At the rear of the garden offstage:* "Yoo, hoo!")

IRINA (*shivering*).   Somehow everything frightens me today. (*A pause*) I have everything all ready, after dinner I'm sending off my things. The Baron and I are getting married tomorrow, and tomorrow we are leaving for the brickyard, and day after tomorrow I'll be at the school, a new life is beginning. Somehow God will help me! When I passed my teacher's examination I cried for pure joy . . . so happy. (*A pause*) The cart will soon be here for my things. . . .

KULYGIN.   That's all very well, only somehow it's not serious. Just

---

[18] Manner of living.

ideas—and very little seriousness. However, I wish you luck with all my heart.

TCHEBUTYKIN (*tenderly*). My darling, my dear child. . . . My treasure. . . . You have gone far away. I can't catch up with you. I'm left behind, like a bird of passage that has grown old, that can't fly. Fly on, my dears, fly on and God be with you! (*A pause*) It's too bad, Fyodor Ilyich, you shaved off your mustache.

KULYGIN. That'll do from you! (*Sighing*) Well, today the officers are leaving and everything will go on again as of old. Whatever they may say, Masha is a good, honest woman and I love her very much and I am thankful for my fate. People's fate differs. . . . In the excise office here a certain Kozyroff works. He went to school with me, was expelled from the fifth class at high school because he just couldn't understand *ut consecutivum*.[19] Now he is terribly poor, ill, and when we meet I say to him: "Greetings, *ut consecutivum!*" Yes, he says, that's it, *consecutivum* . . . and then coughs. . . . And here I am, all my life I've been successful, I am happy, I have the Order of Stanislav, Second Degree, and am teaching others myself now that *ut consecutivum*. Of course, I am a clever man, cleverer than many others, but happiness doesn't consist in that. . . .

(*In the house they are playing "The Maiden's Prayer" on the piano.*)

IRINA. And tomorrow evening I won't be hearing that "Maiden's Prayer" any more, and won't be meeting Protopopov. . . . (*A pause*) And Protopopov is sitting there in the drawing room now; he came again today. . . .

KULYGIN. The headmistress has not come yet?

IRINA. No. They have sent for her. If only you knew how hard it is for me to live here alone, without Olya. . . . She lives at the high school; she's the headmistress, busy all day long with her duties, and I'm alone, I am bored with nothing to do, and the very room I live in is hateful. . . . So I have made up my mind: If it isn't my lot to be in Moscow, then let it be so. That's my lot. There's nothing to be done. All is God's will, that's the truth. Nikolai Lvovich proposed to me. . . . Well, then? I thought it over and made up my mind. He is a good man, it is really amazing how good. . . . And suddenly as if wings had grown on my soul, I grew happier, relieved, and felt once more the desire for work, work. . . . Except that something happened yesterday, there's something hidden that's hanging over me. . . .

---

[19] A Latin rhetorical principle.

TCHEBUTYKIN. Consensus. Nonsense.

NATASHA (*at the window*). The headmistress!

KULYGIN. The headmistress has arrived. Let's go.

> (*He goes with* IRINA *into the house.*)

TCHEBUTYKIN (*reading the newspaper, softly singing to himself*). Ta-ra-ra-boom-de-aye. . . . Sit on the curb I may. . . .

> (MASHA *approaches; in the background* ANDREI *is seen pushing the baby-carriage.*)

MASHA. There he sits, all settled.

TCHEBUTYKIN. And what?

MASHA (*sitting down*). Nothing. . . . (*A pause*) Did you love my mother?

TCHEBUTYKIN. Very much.

MASHA. And did she love you?

TCHEBUTYKIN (*after a pause*). That I no longer remember.

MASHA. Is "mine" here? Our cook Marfa used to talk about her policeman like that: mine. Is "mine" here?

TCHEBUTYKIN. Not yet.

MASHA. When you get happiness in snatches, in bits, and you lose it, like me, then little by little you harden, you grow bitter. (*Pointing to her breast*) Right here I'm boiling. . . . (*Looking at her brother* ANDREI *pushing the baby-carriage*) There's Andrei, our little brother. . . . All our hopes gone. . . . Once upon a time thousands of people were hoisting a bell, a lot of effort and money were spent, and then suddenly it fell and broke. Suddenly for neither one reason nor another. The same with Andrei.

ANDREI. And when will they finally quiet down in the house? Such noise!

TCHEBUTYKIN. Soon. (*Looking at his watch*) I have a very old watch, with chimes. . . . (*Winding the watch; it chimes.*) The first, second, and fifth batteries are going at one o'clock sharp. (*A pause*) And I tomorrow.

ANDREI. For good?

TCHEBUTYKIN. I don't know. I might return in a year. Though the devil knows . . . it's all the same. . . .

> (*Somewhere far off a harp and violin are playing.*)

ANDREI. The town will be dead. As if they had covered it with a cowl. (*A pause*) Something happened yesterday near the theatre; everybody is talking about it, but I don't know what it was.

TCHEBUTYKIN. Nothing. Nonsense. Solyony began to pick on the Baron and he lost his temper and insulted him, and it got finally to the point where Solyony had to challenge him to a duel. (*Looks at his watch*) It's time now, I believe. At half-past twelve, in the

State forest there, the one we see from here, beyond the river. . . . Piff—paff. (*Laughing*) Solyony imagines he is Lermontov and even writes verses. Now jokes are jokes, but it is the third duel for him.

MASHA. For whom?

TCHEBUTYKIN. For Solyony.

MASHA. And for the Baron?

TCHEBUTYKIN. What for the Baron?

(*A pause*)

MASHA. I'm all confused in the head. All the same, I say it shouldn't be allowed. He might wound the Baron or even kill him.

TCHEBUTYKIN. The Baron is a good man but one baron more, one less—isn't it all the same? Let them! All the same! (*Beyond the garden there are shouts:* "Yoo hoo." *Answering the shout*) You can wait. (*To* MASHA) That's Skvortzoff shouting, the second. He's sitting in a boat.

(*A pause*)

ANDREI. To my mind either to engage in a duel or to be present at one even in the capacity of doctor, is simply immoral.

TCHEBUTYKIN. That only seems so. . . . We are not here, there is nothing in the world, we don't exist, but it only seems that we exist. . . . And isn't it all the same!

MASHA. Just like that . . . all day long they talk, talk. . . . (*Going*) To live in such a climate, be afraid it will snow any minute, and still to have these conversations— (*Stopping*) I'm not going into the house, I can't. . . . When Vershinin comes let me know— (*She goes down the alley.*) And the birds of passage are flying already. . . . (*Looking up*) Swans or geese. . . . My dear ones, my happy ones—! (*She goes out.*)

ANDREI. Our house will be empty. The officers will go, you will go, my sister will be married, and I'll be left alone in the house.

TCHEBUTYKIN. And your wife?

(FERAPONT *enters with some papers.*)

ANDREI. A wife is a wife. She is honest, decent, well—kind, but along with all that there's something in her that reduces her to the level of some sort of petty, blind, coarse animal. In any case, she's not a human being. I say this to you as to a friend, the only man I can open my soul to. I love Natasha, it's true, but at times she seems to me amazingly vulgar, and then I lose my wits, I don't understand, what for or why, I love her so or, at least, did love. . . .

TCHEBUTYKIN (*getting up*). Brother, I'm going away tomorrow, we may never see each other again, so here is my advice to you. You know, put on your hat, take a walking-stick in your hands and be off— Be off, and go, go without looking back. And the farther you get the better.

(SOLYONY *walks by at the rear of the stage with two* OFFICERS; *seeing* TCHEBUTYKIN *he turns toward him; the* OFFICERS *walk on.*)

SOLYONY. Doctor, it's time! Half-past twelve. (*Greeting* ANDREI)

TCHEBUTYKIN. Directly. I've had enough of you all. (*To* ANDREI) If anybody asks for me, Andrusha, say that I—directly . . . (*Sighing*) Oho-ho-ho—

SOLYONY (*starting off with* TCHEBUTYKIN). Quick as a flash the bear made a dash— Why are you grunting, old man?

TCHEBUTYKIN. Get out!

SOLYONY. How's your health?

TCHEBUTYKIN (*angrily*). Smooth as butter.

SOLYONY. The old man is needlessly upset. I'll indulge myself a little, I'll only wing him like a snipe. (*Takes out the perfume and sprinkles it on his hands*) There, I've poured a whole bottle out today and they still smell. My hands smell of a corpse. (*A pause*) So . . . Do you remember the poem? "And, rebellious, he seeks the storm, as if in storms were peace." . . .

TCHEBUTYKIN. Yes. Quick as a flash, the bear made a dash!

(*He goes out with* SOLYONY.)

(*Shouts are heard:* "Yoo hoo!" ANDREI *and* FERAPONT *enter.*)

FERAPONT. The papers to sign. . . .

ANDREI (*nervously*). Leave me alone! Leave me! I beg of you! (*He walks away with the baby-carriage.*)

FERAPONT. But that's what papers are for, so they can be signed. (*He goes to the rear of the stage.*)

(*Enter* IRINA *and* TUSENBACH, TUSENBACH *in a straw hat,* KULYGIN *crosses the stage, calling* "Ah-oo, Masha, Ah-oo.")

TUSENBACH. That seems to be the only man in town who's glad the officers are leaving.

IRINA. That's understandable. (*A pause*) Our town will be empty now.

TUSENBACH. Dear, I'll come right back.

IRINA. Where are you going?

TUSENBACH. I have to go to town, then . . . to see my comrades off.

IRINA. It's not true. . . . Nikolai, why are you so distraught today? (*A pause*) What happened yesterday near the theatre?

TUSENBACH (*with an impatient gesture*). In an hour I'll be back and will be with you again. (*Kissing her hand*) My beloved. . . . (*Looking into her face*) It's five years now I've loved you, and somehow I can't get used to it, and you seem always more beautiful to me. What lovely, wonderful hair! What eyes! I'll take you away tomorrow, we will work, we'll be rich, my dreams will come true. You shall be happy. Only there is one thing, one thing: You don't love me.

IRINA. That's not in my power! I'll be your wife, faithful and obedient, but it's not love, what is there to do! (Crying) I have never been in love—not once in my life. Oh, I've dreamed so of love, I've dreamed of it a long time now, day and night, but my soul is like some fine piano that's locked and the key is lost. (*A pause*) You have a restless look.

TUSENBACH. I haven't slept all night. There is nothing in my life so terrible that it could frighten me, and only that lost key tortures my soul—won't let me sleep. Say something to me. (*A pause*) Say something to me. . . .

IRINA. What? What shall I say? What?

TUSENBACH. Something.

IRINA. That's enough! That's enough!

(*A pause*)

TUSENBACH. What nothings sometimes in life, what foolish trifles will take on meaning suddenly, for no reason at all. You laugh at them as you've always done, you consider them nothings, and yet you go on and feel that you haven't the strength to stop. Oh, let's not talk about that! I feel gay. I see these firs, maples, birches now as if I were seeing them for the first time and they are all looking at me curiously and waiting. What beautiful trees and what a beautiful life there should be under them! (*A shout:* "Yoo hoo!") I must go. It's time. . . . There's a tree that's dead, but it still waves with the others in the wind. So it seems to me even if I die, I'll still share in life somehow or other. Good-by, my dearest. . . . (*Kissing her hands*) The papers you gave me are lying on my table, under the calendar.

IRINA. But I'm going with you.

TUSENBACH (*alarmed*). No, no! (*Going quickly, stopping in the alley*) Irina!

IRINA. What?

TUSENBACH (*not knowing what to say*). I didn't drink any coffee today. Tell them, so that they'll make me some. . . . (*He goes quickly out.*)

(IRINA *stands thinking, then goes to the rear of the stage and sits down in the swing.* ANDREI *comes in with the baby-carriage;* FERAPONT *appears.*)

FERAPONT. But Andrei Sergeevich, the papers aren't mine, they are official. I didn't think them up.

ANDREI. Oh, where is it, where is gone my past, when I was young and gay and clever, when my dreams and thoughts were full of grace, and the present and future bright with hope? Why is it that when we have barely begun to live we grow dull, gray, uninteresting, lazy, indifferent, useless, unhappy. . . . Our town has been in existence now for two hundred years, a hundred thousand people living in it, and there's not one who's not just like the others, not one that's outstanding either in the past or in the present, not one scholar, not one artist, not one who's even faintly remarkable, and would arouse envy or any passionate desire to imitate him. They just eat, drink, sleep, and then die. . . . Others are born and they, too, eat, drink, sleep and to keep from sinking into the torpor of boredom, vary their lives with foul gossip, vodka, cards, chicanery, and the wives deceive the husbands, while the husbands lie, pretend not to see anything, hear anything, and an unavoidably banal influence weighs on the children, and the divine spark dies in them and they become just as pitiful, identical corpses as their fathers and mothers were. . . . (*To* FERAPONT, *crossly*) What do you want?

FERAPONT. Hey? Papers to sign.

ANDREI. I've had enough of you.

FERAPONT (*handing over the papers*). Just now the doorman from the State Chamber was saying . . . It appears he says, this winter in Petersburg there was a frost of two hundred degrees.

ANDREI. The present is hateful, but on the other hand, when I think of the future— Oh, how good it is! I begin to feel so easy, so free; and in the distance a light dawns, I see freedom, I see how my children and I are freed from idleness, from kvass,[20] from goose with cabbage, from naps after dinner, from despicable sloth. . . .

FERAPONT. Two thousand people were frozen, it appears. The people, they say, were horrified. It was either in Petersburg, or it was in Moscow—I can't remember.

ANDREI (*seized with a tender feeling*). My dear sisters, my wonderful sisters. (*Tearfully*) Masha, my sister. . . .

NATASHA (*in the window*). Who is it talking so loud out here? Is it you, Andrusha? You will wake up Sofia. *Il ne faut pas faire du bruit, la Sofie est dormie déjà. Vous êtes un ours.*[21] (*Getting angry*) If you want to talk, give the carriage and child to somebody else. Ferapont, take the carriage from your master.

FERAPONT. Yes, ma'am. (*He takes the carriage.*)

ANDREI (*embarrassed*). I'm speaking low.

[20] Beer.
[21] "You mustn't be noisy, Sophie is still asleep. You're a bear."

NATASHA (*behind the window, caressing her child*). Bobik! Mischievous Bobik! Naughty Bobik!

ANDREI (*glancing through the papers*). Very well, I'll look through them and sign what's necessary, and you can take them back to the Board. . . .

(*He goes into the house, reading the papers;* FERAPONT *pushes the baby-carriage toward the rear of the garden.*)

NATASHA (*behind the window*). Bobik, what is your Mama's name? Darling, darling! And who is this? This is Aunt Olya. Say to Auntie: "How do you do, Olya!"

(*Some wandering* MUSICIANS, *a man and a girl, begin to play a violin and a harp;* VERSHININ, OLGA *and* ANFISA *emerge from the house, and listen quietly for a moment.* IRINA *joins them.*)

OLGA. Our garden's like a lot opening into several streets, they walk and drive through it. Nurse, give these musicians something!

ANFISA (*giving money to the* MUSICIANS). Good-by, my dear souls! (*The* MUSICIANS *bow and go away.*) Hard lives they have! When you're full you don't play. (*To* IRINA) Good morning, Irisha! (*Kissing her*) M-m-m-m, child, how I live! How I live! At the high school in a Government apartment, with Olyushka—God has granted me that for my old age. Not since I was born, sinner that I am, have I lived so. . . . A large apartment, the Government's, and a whole room for me and a little bed. All the Government's. I wake up in the night and—Oh Lord, Mother of God, there's nobody happier than I am.

VERSHININ (*looking at his watch*). We are going now, Olga Sergeevna. It's time. (*A pause*) I wish you everything, everything. . . . Where's Maria Sergeevna?

IRINA. She's somewhere in the garden. I'll go look for her.

VERSHININ. Kindly, I'm in a hurry.

ANFISA. I'll go, too, and look for her. (*Calling*) Mashenka. Ah, oo-oo! (*Going away with* IRINA *to the rear of the garden*) Ah, oo-oo! Ah, oo-oo!

VERSHININ. Everything has its end. And here we are parting. (*Looking at his watch*) The town gave our company a sort of lunch, we drank champagne, the Mayor made a speech, I ate and listened, but in my heart I was here with you all— (*Looking around the garden*) I've grown used to you. . . .

OLGA. Are we ever to see each other again?

VERSHININ. Most likely not. (*A pause*) My wife and my two girls are leaving here in about two months; please, if anything happens, if anything is needed. . . .

OLGA. Yes, yes, of course. Be sure of that. (*A pause*) By tomorrow there won't be an officer in town; it will all be a memory and for us, of course, a new life will begin. . . . (*A pause*) Everything turns out not as we'd like to have it. I didn't want to be a head-mistress and yet I became one. Which means we are not to be in Moscow.

VERSHININ. Well. . . . Thank you for everything. Forgive me, if anything was not quite. . . . Much, much too much, I've talked —forgive me for that, too, don't bear me any grudge.

OLGA (*wiping her eyes*). Now why doesn't Masha come. . . .

VERSHININ. What else can I say to you as we part? What shall I philosophize about? . . . (*Laughing*) Life is difficult. It presents itself to many of us as blank and hopeless, and yet, one must admit, it gets always clearer and easier, and the day is not far off, apparently, when it will be wholly bright. (*Looking at his watch*) It's time for me to go, it's time! Once humanity was occupied with wars, filling its whole existence with marches, invasions, conquests, whereas now all of that is outlived, leaving behind it an enor-mous empty space which so far there is nothing to fill; humanity is searching passionately and, of course, will find it. Ah, if only it were quicker! (*A pause*) You know, if culture were added to industry and industry to culture. . . . (*Looking at his watch*) However, it's time for me. . . .

OLGA. There she comes.

(MASHA *enters*.)

VERSHININ. I came to say good-by. . . .

(OLGA *moves a little away so as not to disturb their farewell*.)

MASHA (*looking into his face*). Good-by. . . .

(*A long kiss*)

OLGA. Now, now. . . .

(MASHA *sobs violently*.)

VERSHININ. Write to me. . . . Don't forget me! Let me go . . . it's time. . . . Olga Sergeevna, take her, I'm all ready—it's time . . . late—

(*Deeply moved, he kisses* OLGA'S *hand, then embraces* MASHA *again and goes quickly out*.)

OLGA. There, Masha! Stop, darling! . . .

(KULYGIN *enters*.)

KULYGIN (*embarrassed*). No matter, let her cry, let her. . . . My good Masha, my kind Masha. . . . You are my wife and I am happy whatever happens. . . . I don't complain. . . . I don't make you a single reproach. And here's Olga to witness. . . . We'll begin to live again as we used to, and I won't say one word to you, not a breath. . . .

MASHA (*stifling her sobs*). By the curved seashore a green oak, a golden chain upon that oak. . . . A golden chain upon that oak. . . . I'm going out of my mind. . . . By the curved seashore . . . a green oak. . . .

OLGA. Be calm, Masha. . . . Be calm. . . . Give her some water.

MASHA. I am not crying any more.

KULYGIN. She is not crying now. . . . She's good. . . .

(*A shot is heard, faintly, from a distance.*)

MASHA. By the curved seashore a green oak, a golden chain upon that oak. . . . The cat's green . . . the oak's green. . . . I am mixing it up. . . . (*Taking a drink of water*) My life is a failure. I don't want anything now. I'll soon be calm. It's all the same. . . . What does it mean: "By the curved seashore"? Why does this word keep running through my head? My thoughts are all mixed up.

(IRINA *enters.*)

OLGA. Be calm, Masha. Now, that's a good girl. . . . Let's go in. . . .

MASHA (*angrily*). I'm not going in there. (*Sobbing, but checking herself at once*) I don't go in the house any more, so I won't do it now.

IRINA. Let's sit down together just quietly. Well, tomorrow I'm going away. . . .

(*A pause*)

KULYGIN. In the third grade yesterday I took this mustache and beard from a boy, see— (*Putting on the mustache and beard*) I look like the German teacher. . . . (*Laughing*) Isn't that so? Funny, these boys. . . .

MASHA. Really you do look like your German.

OLGA (*laughing*). Yes.

(MASHA *weeps.*)

IRINA. There, Masha!

KULYGIN. A lot like. . . .

(NATASHA *enters.*)

NATASHA (*to the* MAID). What? Protopopov will sit with Sofotchka, Mikhail Ivanovich, and let Andrei Sergeevich wheel Bobik. There's so much bother with children. . . . (*To* IRINA) Irina, you are going away tomorrow—it's such a pity! Stay at least another week. (*Seeing* KULYGIN *she gives a shriek; he laughs and takes off the mustache and beard.*) Why, look at you, you scared me! (*To* IRINA) I am used to you and do you think parting with you will be easy for me? I'll give orders to put Andrei in your room, with his violin—let him saw away there!—and in his room we'll put Sofotchka. Marvelous, wonderful child! What a girl! Today she looked at me with such eyes, and—"Mama!"

KULYGIN. Beautiful child, that's true.

NATASHA. And so tomorrow I'll be all alone here. (*Sighing*) First of all, I'll give orders to chop down this alley of fir trees, then this maple here. . . . In the evening it looks so ugly. . . . (*To* IRINA) Dear, that belt doesn't suit you at all. . . . It's in very poor taste. You need something light. . . . And I'll order flowers planted, everywhere, flowers, and there'll be a fragrance . . . (*Severely*) What's a fork doing here on the bench? (*She goes into the house, to the* MAID.) What's a fork doing here on the bench, I'd like to know? (*Shouting*) Shut up!

KULYGIN. She's off again.

(*Behind the scenes a band is playing a march; everybody listens.*)

OLGA. They are leaving.

(TCHEBUTYKIN *enters.*)

MASHA. Our friends are going. Well, then. . . . A pleasant journey to them! (*To her husband*) We must go home. . . . Where are my hat and cape?

KULYGIN. I carried them in the house . . . I'll get them right away.

OLGA. Yes, now we can all go home. It's time.

TCHEBUTYKIN. Olga Sergeevna!

OLGA. What? (*A pause*) What?

TCHEBUTYKIN. Nothing. . . . Don't know how to tell you. . . . (*Whispering in her ear*)

OLGA (*alarmed*). It's not possible!

TCHEBUTYKIN. Yes. . . . What a story. . . . I'm tired, completely exhausted, don't want to talk any more. (*Irritably*) However, it's all the same!

MASHA. What happened?

OLGA (*embracing* IRINA). It's a terrible day today. . . . I don't know how to tell you, my darling. . . .

IRINA. What? Say it quick. . . . What? For God's sake! (*Crying*)

TCHEBUTYKIN. The Baron was killed just now in a duel.

IRINA (*weeping quietly*). I knew, I knew. . . .

TCHEBUTYKIN (*sitting down on a bench to the rear of the stage*). I'm tired. . . . (*Taking a newspaper out of his pocket*) Let them cry a little. . . . (*Singing softly*) Ta-ra-ra-boom-de-aye. . . . Sit on a curb I may. . . . As if it weren't all the same!

(*The three sisters stand with their arms around one another.*)

MASHA. Oh, how the music is playing! They are leaving us, one has gone entirely, entirely, forever. We'll be left alone to begin our life over again. We must live. . . . We must live. . . .

IRINA (*putting her head on* OLGA's *breast*). The time will come when all will know why all this is, what these sufferings are for, there will be no secrets—but meanwhile we must live—must work, only work! Tomorrow I'm going away alone, I'll teach in the school and give my whole life to those who need it perhaps. It's autumn now; winter will soon come and cover everything with snow, and I'll work, work. . . .

OLGA (*embracing both her sisters*). The music plays so gaily, bravely, and one wants to live. Oh, Lord! Time will pass and we shall be gone forever, they will forget us, they will forget our faces, voices, and how many of us there were, but our sufferings will turn into joy for those who will be living after us, happiness and peace will come on earth, and they will remember with some gentle word those who live now and will bless them. Oh, dear sisters, our life isn't over yet. We shall live! The music plays so gaily, so joyously, and it looks as if a little more and we shall know why we live, why we suffer. . . . If we only knew, if we only knew!

(*The music plays always softer and softer;* KULYGIN, *smiling and gay, brings the hat and cape,* ANDREI *is pushing the baby-carriage with Bobik in it.*)

TCHEBUTYKIN (*singing softly*). Ta-ra-ra-boom-de-aye. . . . Sit on a curb I may. . . . (*Reading the newspaper*) It's all the same! It's all the same!

OLGA. If we only knew, if we only knew!

Curtain

Translated by Stark Young

Tiger at the Gates[1]

CHARACTERS

ANDROMACHE	TWO MESSENGERS
CASSANDRA	PEACE
LAUNDRESS	TROILUS
HECTOR	ABNEOS
PARIS	BUSIRIS
1st OLD MAN	GUARD
2nd OLD MAN	AJAX
PRIAM	ULYSSES[2]
DEMOKOS	A TOPMAN
HECUBA	OLPIDES
MATHEMATICIAN	SERVANT
SERVANT	SENATOR
POLYXENE	TWO SAILORS
HELEN	IRIS

OLD MEN, MESSENGERS, GUARDS, CROWD

ACT I

[*The terrace of a rampart dominated by a terrace and dominating other ramparts.*]

ANDROMACHE. There's not going to be a Trojan War, Cassandra!

CASSANDRA. I shall take that bet, Andromache.

ANDROMACHE. The Greeks are quite right to protest. We are going to receive their ambassador very civilly. We shall wrap up his little Helen and give her back to him.

CASSANDRA. We shall receive him atrociously. We shall refuse to give Helen back. And there *will* be a Trojan War.

[1] You may find it useful to read the editor's note and annotated list of characters on pages 407–08 before you read this play.
[2] The Latin name for Odysseus.

ANDROMACHE. Yes, if Hector were not here. But he is here, Cassandra, he is home again. You can hear the trumpets. At this moment he is marching into the city, victorious. And Hector is certainly going to have something to say. When he left, three months ago, he promised me this war would be the last.

CASSANDRA. It is the last. The next is still ahead of him.

ANDROMACHE. Doesn't it ever tire you to see and prophesy only disasters?

CASSANDRA. I see nothing. I prophesy nothing. All I ever do is to take account of two great stupidities: the stupidity of men, and the wild stupidity of the elements.

ANDROMACHE. Why should there be a war? Paris and Helen don't care for each other any longer.

CASSANDRA. Do you think it will matter if Paris and Helen don't care for each other any longer? Has destiny ever been interested in whether things were still true or not?

ANDROMACHE. I don't know what destiny is.

CASSANDRA. I'll tell you. It is simply the relentless logic of each day we live.

ANDROMACHE. I don't understand abstractions.

CASSANDRA. Never mind. We can try a metaphor. Imagine a tiger. You can understand that? It's a nice, easy metaphor. A sleeping tiger.

ANDROMACHE. Let it sleep.

CASSANDRA. There's nothing I should like better. But certain cocksure statements have been prodding him out of his sleep. For some considerable time Troy has been full of them.

ANDROMACHE. Full of what?

CASSANDRA. Of cocksure statements, a confident belief that the world, and the supervision of the world, is the province of mankind in general, and Trojan men and women in particular.

ANDROMACHE. I don't follow you.

CASSANDRA. Hector at this very moment is marching into Troy.

ANDROMACHE. Yes. Hector at this very moment has come home to his wife.

CASSANDRA. And Hector's wife is going to have a child?

ANDROMACHE. Yes; I am going to have a child.

CASSANDRA. Don't you call these statements a little overconfident?

ANDROMACHE. Don't frighten me, Cassandra.

(*A young* LAUNDRESS *goes past with an armful of linen.*)

LAUNDRESS. What a beautiful day, miss!

CASSANDRA. Does it seem so, indeed?

LAUNDRESS. It's the most beautiful Spring day Troy has seen this year.
   (*Exit.*)
CASSANDRA. Even the laundrymaid is confident!
ANDROMACHE. And so she should be, Cassandra. How can you talk
   of a war on a day like this? Happiness is falling on us out of the sky.
CASSANDRA. Like a blanket of snow.
ANDROMACHE. And beauty, as well. Look at the sunshine. It is finding
   more mother-of-pearl on the rooftops of Troy than was ever dragged
   up from the bed of the sea. And do you hear the sound coming up
   from the fishermen's houses, and the movement of the trees, like
   the murmuring of sea shells? If ever there were a chance to see men
   finding a way to live in peace, it is today. To live in peace, in
   humility. And to be immortal.
CASSANDRA. Yes, I am sure those cripples who have been carried
   out to lie in their doorways feel how immortal they are.
ANDROMACHE. And to be good. Do you see that horseman, in the
   advance-guard, leaning from his saddle to stroke a cat on the battlements? Perhaps this is also going to be the first day of true fellow-
   ship between men and the animals.
CASSANDRA. You talk too much. Destiny, the tiger, is getting restive,
   Andromache!
ANDROMACHE. Restive, maybe, in young girls looking for husbands;
   but not otherwise.
CASSANDRA. You are wrong. Hector has come home in triumph to
   the wife he adores. The tiger begins to rouse, and opens one eye.
   The incurables lie out on their benches in the sun and feel immortal.
   The tiger stretches himself. Today is the chance for peace to en-
   throne herself over all the world. The tiger licks his lips. And An-
   dromache is going to have a son! And the horsemen have started
   leaning from their saddles to stroke tom-cats on the battlements! The
   tiger starts to prowl.
ANDROMACHE. Be quiet!
CASSANDRA. He climbs noiselessly up the palace steps. He pushes open
   the doors with his snout. And here he is, here he is!
   (HECTOR'S *voice:* Andromache!)
ANDROMACHE. You are lying! It is Hector!
CASSANDRA. Whoever said it was not?
   (*Enter* HECTOR.)
ANDROMACHE. Hector!
HECTOR. Andromache!
   (*They embrace.*)
   And good morning to you, too, Cassandra. Ask Paris to come to
   me, if you will. As soon as he can.

(CASSANDRA *lingers.*)

Have you something to tell me?

ANDROMACHE.   Don't listen to her! Some catastrophe or other!

HECTOR.   Tell me.

CASSANDRA.   Your wife is going to have a child.

(*Exit* CASSANDRA.)

(HECTOR *takes* ANDROMACHE *in his arms, leads her to a stone bench, and sits beside her. A short pause*)

HECTOR.   Will it be a son or a daughter?

ANDROMACHE.   Which did you want to create when you called it into life?

HECTOR.   A thousand boys. A thousand girls.

ANDROMACHE.   Why? Because it would give you a thousand women to hold in your arms? You are going to be disappointed. It will be a son, one single son.

HECTOR.   That may very well be. Usually more boys are born than girls at the end of a war.

ANDROMACHE.   And before a war? Which, before a war?

HECTOR.   Forget wars, Andromache, even this war. It's over. It lost you a father and a brother, but it gave you back a husband.

ANDROMACHE.   It has been too kind. It may think better of it presently.

HECTOR.   Don't worry. We won't give it the chance. Directly I leave you I shall go into the square, and formally close the Gates of War. They will never open again.

ANDROMACHE.   Close them, then. But they will open again.

HECTOR.   You can even tell me the day, perhaps?

ANDROMACHE.   I can even tell you the day: the day when the cornfields are heavy and golden, when the vines are stooping, ready for harvest, and every house is sheltering a contented couple.

HECTOR.   And peace, no doubt, at its very height?

ANDROMACHE.   Yes. And my son is strong and glowing with life.

(HECTOR *embraces her.*)

HECTOR.   Perhaps your son will be a coward. That's one possible safeguard.

ANDROMACHE.   He won't be a coward. But perhaps I shall have cut off the index finger of his right hand.

HECTOR.   If every mother cut off her son's right-hand index finger, the armies of the world would fight without index fingers. And if they cut off their sons' right legs, the armies would be one-legged. And if they put out their eyes, the armies would be blind, but there would still be armies: blind armies groping to find the fatal place in the enemy's groin, or to get at his throat.

ANDROMACHE.   I would rather kill him.

HECTOR.   There's a truly maternal solution to war!

ANDROMACHE.   Don't laugh. I can still kill him before he is born.

HECTOR.   Don't you want to see him at all, not even for a moment? After that, you would think again. Do you mean never to see your son?

ANDROMACHE.   It is your son that interests me. Hector, it's because he is yours, because he is you, that I'm so afraid. You don't know how like you he is. Even in this no-man's-land where he is waiting, he already has everything, all those qualities you brought to this life we live together. He has your tenderness, your silences. If you love war, he will love it. Do you love war?

HECTOR.   Why ask such a question?

ANDROMACHE.   Admit, sometimes you love it.

HECTOR.   If a man can love what takes away hope, and happiness, and all those nearest to his heart.

ANDROMACHE.   And you know it can be so. Men do love it.

HECTOR.   If they let themselves be fooled by that little burst of divinity the gods give them at the moment of attack.

ANDROMACHE.   Ah, there, you see! At the moment of attack you feel like a god.

HECTOR.   More often not as much as a man. But sometimes, on certain mornings, you get up from the ground feeling lighter, astonished, altered. Your whole body, and the armour on your back, have a different weight, they seem to be made of a different metal. You are invulnerable. A tenderness comes over you, submerging you, a kind of tenderness of battle: you are tender because you are pitiless; what, in fact, the tenderness of the gods must be. You advance towards the enemy slowly, almost absent-mindedly, but lovingly. And you try not to crush a beetle crossing your path. You brush off the mosquito without hurting it. You never at any time had more respect for the life you meet on your way.

ANDROMACHE.   And then the enemy comes?

HECTOR.   Then the enemy comes, frothing at the mouth. You pity him; you can see him there, behind the swollen veins and the whites of his eyes, the helpless, willing little man of business, the well-meaning husband and son-in-law who likes to grow his own vegetables. You feel a sort of love for him. You love the wart on his cheek and the cast in his eye. You love him. But he comes on; he is insistent. Then you kill him.

ANDROMACHE.   And you bend over the wretched corpse as though you are a god; but you are not a god; you can't give back his life again.

HECTOR. You don't wait to bend over him. There are too many more waiting for you, frothing at the mouth and howling hate. Too many more unassuming, law-abiding family men.

ANDROMACHE. Then you kill them.

HECTOR. You kill them. Such is war.

ANDROMACHE. All of them: you kill them all?

HECTOR. This time we killed them all. Quite deliberately. They belonged to an incorrigibly warlike race, the reason why wars go on and multiply in Asia. Only one of them escaped.

ANDROMACHE. In a thousand years time, there the warlike race will be again, descended from that one man. His escape made all that slaughter futile after all. My son is going to love war, just as you do.

HECTOR. I think, now that I've lost my love for it, I hate it.

ANDROMACHE. How do you come to hate what you once worshipped?

HECTOR. You know what it's like when you find out a friend is a liar? Whatever he says, after that, sounds false, however true it may be. And strangely enough, war used to promise me many kinds of virtue: goodness, generosity, and a contempt for anything base and mean. I felt I owed it all my strength and zest for life, even my private happiness, you, Andromache. And until this last campaign there was no enemy I haven't loved.

ANDROMACHE. Very soon you will say you only kill what you love.

HECTOR. It's hard to explain how all the sounds of war combined to make me think it was something noble. The galloping of horses in the night, the clatter of bowls and dishes where the cooks were moving in and out of the firelight, the brush of silk and metal against your tent as the night-patrol went past, and the cry of the falcon wheeling high above the sleeping army and their unsleeping captain: it all seemed then so right, marvellously right.

ANDROMACHE. But not this time: this time war had no music for you?

HECTOR. Why was that? Because I am older? Or was it just the kind of weariness with your job which, for instance, a carpenter will be suddenly seized by, with a table half finished, as I was seized one morning, standing over an adversary of my own age, about to put an end to him? Up to that time, a man I was going to kill had always seemed my direct opposite. This time I was kneeling on a mirror, the death I was going to give was a kind of suicide. I don't know what the carpenter does at such a time, whether he throws away his hammer and plane, or goes on with it. I went on with it. But after that nothing remained of the perfect trumpet note of war. The spear as it slid against my shield rang suddenly false; so did the shock of the killed against the ground, and, some hours later, the palace crumbling into ruin. And, moreover, war knew that I understood, and gave up any pretence of shame. The cries of the dying sounded false. I had come to that.

ANDROMACHE. But it all still sounded right for the rest of them.

HECTOR. The rest of them heard it as I did. The army I brought back hates war.

ANDROMACHE. An army with poor hearing.

HECTOR. No. When we first came in sight of Troy, an hour ago, you can't imagine how everything in that moment sounded true for them. There wasn't a regiment which didn't halt, racked to the heart by this sense of returning music. So much so, we were afraid to march boldly in through the gates: we broke up into groups outside the walls. It feels like the only job worthy of a good army, laying peaceful siege to the open cities of your own country.

ANDROMACHE. You haven't understood, this is where things are falser than anywhere. War is here, in Troy, Hector. That is what welcomed you at the gates.

HECTOR. What do you mean?

ANDROMACHE. You haven't heard that Paris has carried off Helen?

HECTOR. They told me so. What else?

ANDROMACHE. Did you know that the Greeks are demanding her back? And their ambassador arrives today? And if we don't give her up, it means war.

HECTOR. Why shouldn't we give her up? I shall give her back to them myself.

ANDROMACHE. Paris will never agree to it.

HECTOR. Paris will agree, and very soon. Cassandra is bringing him to me.

ANDROMACHE. But Paris can't agree. His honour, as you all call it, won't let him. Nor his love either, he may tell you.

HECTOR. Well, we shall see. Run and ask Priam if he will let me speak to him at once. And set your heart at rest. All the Trojans who have been fighting, or who can fight, are against a war.

ANDROMACHE. There are still the others, remember.

(*As* ANDROMACHE *goes* . . .

CASSANDRA *enters with* PARIS.)

CASSANDRA. Here is Paris.

HECTOR. Congratulations, Paris. I hear you have been very well occupied while we were away.

PARIS. Not badly. Thank you.

HECTOR. What is this story they tell me about Helen?

PARIS. Helen is a very charming person. Isn't she, Cassandra?

CASSANDRA.   Fairly charming.

PARIS.   Why these reservations today? It was only yesterday you said you thought she was extremely pretty.

CASSANDRA.   She is extremely pretty, and fairly charming.

PARIS.   Hasn't she the ways of a young, gentle gazelle?

CASSANDRA.   No.

PARIS.   But you were the one who first said she was like a gazelle.

CASSANDRA.   I made a mistake. Since then I have seen a gazelle again.

HECTOR.   To hell with gazelles! Doesn't she look any more like a woman than that?

PARIS.   She isn't the type of woman we know here, obviously.

CASSANDRA.   What is the type of woman we know here?

PARIS.   Your type, my dear sister. The fearfully unremote sort of woman.

CASSANDRA.   When your Greek makes love she is a long way off, I suppose?

PARIS.   You know perfectly well what I'm trying to say. I have had enough of Asiatic women. They hold you in their arms as though they were glued there, their kisses are like battering-rams, their words chew right into you. The more they undress the more elaborate they seem, until when they're naked they are more overdressed than ever. And they paint their faces to look as though they mean to imprint themselves on you. And they do imprint themselves on you. In short, you are definitely *with* them. But Helen is far away from me, even held in my arms.

HECTOR.   Very interesting! But, one wonders, is it really worth a war, to allow Paris to make love at a distance?

CASSANDRA.   With distance. He loves women to be distant but right under his nose.

PARIS.   To have Helen with you not with you is worth anything in the world.

HECTOR.   How did you fetch her away? Willingly, or did you compel her?

PARIS.   Listen, Hector! You know women as well as I do. They are only willing when you compel them, but after that they're as enthusiastic as you are.

HECTOR.   On horseback, in the usual style of seducers, leaving a heap of horse manure under the windows.

PARIS.   Is this a court of enquiry?

HECTOR.   Yes, it is. Try for once to answer precisely and accurately. Have you insulted her husband's house, or the Greek earth?

PARIS.   The Greek water, a little. She was bathing.

CASSANDRA. She is born of the foam, is she? This cold one is born of the foam, like Venus.

HECTOR. You haven't disfigured the walls of the palace with offensive drawings, as you usually do? You didn't shout to the echoes any word which they would at once repeat to the betrayed husband?

PARIS. No. Menelaus was naked on the river bank, busy removing a crab from his big toe. He watched my boat sail past as if the wind were carrying his clothes away.

HECTOR. Looking furious?

PARIS. The face of a king being nipped by a crab isn't likely to look beatific.

HECTOR. No onlookers?

PARIS. My crew.

HECTOR. Perfect!

PARIS. Why perfect? What are you getting at?

HECTOR. I say perfect, because you have done nothing irrevocable. In other words: she was undressed, so neither her clothes nor her belongings have been insulted. Nothing except her body, which is negligible. I've enough acquaintance with the Greeks to know they will concoct a divine adventure out of it, to their own glory, the story of this little Greek queen who goes down into the sea, and quietly comes up again a few months later, with a look on her face of perfect innocence.

CASSANDRA. We can be quite sure of the look on her face.

PARIS. You think that I'm going to take Helen back to Menelaus?

HECTOR. We don't ask so much of you, or of her. The Greek ambassador will take care of it. He will put her back in the sea himself, like a gardener planting water-lilies, at a particular chosen spot. You will give her into his hands this evening.

PARIS. I don't know whether you are allowing yourself to notice how monstrous you are being, to suppose that a man who has the prospect of a night with Helen will agree to giving it up.

CASSANDRA. You still have an afternoon with Helen. Surely that's more Greek?

HECTOR. Don't be obstinate. We know you of old. This isn't the first separation you've accepted.

PARIS. My dear Hector, that's true enough. Up to now I have always accepted separations fairly cheerfully. Parting from a woman, however well you love her, induces a most pleasant state of mind, which I know how to value as well as anybody. You come out of her arms and take your first lonely walk through the town, and, the first little dressmaker you meet, you notice with a shock of surprise how fresh and unconcerned she looks, after that last sight you have had of the dear face you parted from, her nose red with weeping. Because you have come away from such broken, despairing farewells, the laundry-girls and the fruitsellers laughing their heads off, more than make up for whatever you've lost in the parting. By losing one person your life has become entirely re-peopled. All the women in the world have been created for you afresh; they are all your own, in the liberty, honour, and peace of your conscience. Yes, you're quite right: when a love-affair is broken off it reaches its highest point of exaltation. Which is why I shall never be parted from Helen, because with Helen I feel as though I had broken with every other woman in the world, and that gives me the sensation of being free a thousand times over instead of once.

HECTOR.   Because she doesn't love you. Everything you say proves it.

PARIS.   If you like. But, if I had to choose one out of all the possible ways of passion, I would choose the way Helen doesn't love me.

HECTOR.   I'm extremely sorry. But you will give her up.

PARIS.   You are not the master here.

HECTOR.   I am your elder brother, and the future master.

PARIS.   Then order me about in the future. For the present, I obey my father.

HECTOR.   That's all I want! You're willing that we should put this to Priam and accept his judgment?

PARIS.   Perfectly willing.

HECTOR.   On your solemn word? We both swear to accept that?

CASSANDRA.   Mind what you're doing, Hector! Priam is mad for Helen. He would rather give up his daughters.

HECTOR.   What nonsense is this?

PARIS.   For once she is telling the truth about the present instead of the future.

CASSANDRA.   And all our brothers, and all our uncles, and all our great-great uncles! Helen has a guard-of-honour which includes every old man in the city. Look there. It is time for her walk. Do you see, there's a fringe of white beards draped all along the battlements?

HECTOR.   A beautiful sight. The beards are white, and the faces red.

CASSANDRA.   Yes; it's the blood pressure. They should be waiting at the Scamander Gate, to welcome the victorious troops. But no; they are all at the Sceean Gate, waiting for Helen.

HECTOR.   Look at them, all leaning forward as one man, like storks when they see a rat going by.

CASSANDRA.   The rat is Helen.

PARIS.   Is it?

CASSANDRA. There she is: on the second terrace, standing to adjust her sandal, and giving careful thought to the crossing of her legs.

HECTOR. Incredible. All the old men of Troy are there looking down at her.

CASSANDRA. Not all. There are certain crafty ones looking up at her.

(*Cries offstage:* Long live Beauty!)

HECTOR. What are they shouting?

PARIS. They're shouting "Long live Beauty!"

CASSANDRA. I quite agree with them, if they mean that they themselves should die as quickly as possible.

(*Cries offstage:* Long live Venus!)

HECTOR. And what now?

CASSANDRA. "Long live Venus." They are shouting only words without R's in them because of their lack of teeth. Long live Beauty, long live Venus, long live Helen. At least they imagine they're shouting, though, as you can hear, all they are doing is simply increasing a mumble to its highest power.

HECTOR. What has Venus to do with it?

CASSANDRA. They imagine it was Venus who gave us Helen. To show her gratitude to Paris for awarding her the apple on first sight.[3]

HECTOR. That was another brilliant stroke of yours.

PARIS. Stop playing the elder brother!

(*Enter two* OLD MEN.)

1st OLD MAN. Down there we see her better.

2nd OLD MAN. We had a very good view.

1st OLD MAN. But she can hear us better from up here. Come on. One, two, three!

BOTH. Long live Helen!

2nd OLD MAN. It's a little tiring, at our age, to have to climb up and down these impossible steps all the time, according to whether we want to look at her or to cheer her.

1st OLD MAN. Would you like us to alternate? One day we will cheer her? Another day we will look at her?

2nd OLD MAN. You are mad! One day without looking at Helen, indeed! Goodness me, think what we've seen of her today! One, two, three!

BOTH. Long live Helen!

1st OLD MAN. And now down we go again!

(*They run off.*)

CASSANDRA. You see what they're like, Hector. I don't know how their poor lungs are going to stand it.

HECTOR. But our father can't be like this.

[3] See page 409, footnote 2.

PARIS. Hector, before we have this out in front of my father, I suppose you wouldn't like to take just one look at Helen.

HECTOR. I don't care a fig about Helen. Ah: greetings to you, father!

(PRIAM *enters, with* HECUBA, ANDROMACHE, *the poet* DEMOKOS *and another* OLD MAN. HECUBA *leads by the hand little* POLYXENE.)

PRIAM. What was it you said?

HECTOR. I said that we should make haste to shut the Gates of War, father, see them bolted and padlocked, so that not even a gnat can get between them.

PRIAM. I thought what you said was somewhat shorter.

DEMOKOS. He said he didn't care a fig about Helen.

PRIAM. Look over here.

(HECTOR *obeys.*)

Do you see her?

HECUBA. Indeed he sees her. Who, I ask myself, doesn't see her, or hasn't seen her? She takes the road which goes the whole way round the city.

DEMOKOS. It is Beauty's perfect circle.

PRIAM. Do you see her?

HECTOR. Yes, I see her. What of it?

DEMOKOS. Priam is asking you what you see.

HECTOR. I see a young woman adjusting her sandal.

CASSANDRA. She takes some time to adjust her sandal.

PARIS. I carried her off naked; she left her clothes in Greece. Those are your sandals, Cassandra. They're a bit big for her.

CASSANDRA. Anything's too big for these little women.

HECTOR. I see two charming buttocks.

HECUBA. He sees what all of you see.

PRIAM. I'm sorry for you!

HECTOR. Why?

PRIAM. I had no idea that the young men of Troy had come to this.

HECTOR. What have they come to?

PRIAM. To being impervious to beauty.

DEMOKOS. And, consequently, ignorant of love. And, consequently, unrealistic. To us who are poets reality is love or nothing.

HECTOR. But the old men, you think, can appreciate love and beauty?

HECUBA. But of course. If you make love, or if you are beautiful, you don't need to understand these things.

HECTOR. You come across beauty, father, at every street corner. I'm not alluding to Helen, though at the moment she condescends to walk our streets.

PRIAM. You are being unfair, Hector. Surely there have been occasions in your life when a woman has seemed to be more than merely herself, as though a radiance of thoughts and feelings glowed from her flesh, taking a special brilliance from it.

DEMOKOS. As a ruby represents blood.

HECTOR. Not to those who have seen blood. I have just come back from a close acquaintance with it.

DEMOKOS. A symbol, you understand. Soldier though you are, you have surely heard of symbolism! Surely you have come across women who as soon as you saw them seemed to you to personify intelligence, harmony, gentleness, whatever it might be?

HECTOR. It has happened.

DEMOKOS. And what did you do?

HECTOR. I went closer, and that was the end of it. And what does this we see here personify?

DEMOKOS. We have told you before: Beauty.

HECUBA. Then send her quickly back to the Greeks if you want her to personify that for long. Blonde beauty doesn't usually last for ever.

DEMOKOS. It's impossible to talk to these women!

HECUBA. Then don't talk *about* women. You're not showing much gallantry, I might say; nor patriotism either. All other races choose one of their own women as their symbol, even if they have flat noses and lips like two fishes on a plate. It's only you who have to go outside your own country to find it.

HECTOR. Listen, father: we are just back from a war, and we have come home exhausted. We have made quite certain of peace on our continent for ever. From now on we mean to live in happiness, and we mean our wives to be able to love us without anxiety, and to bear our children.

DEMOKOS. Wise principles, but war has never prevented wives from having children.

HECTOR. So explain to me why we have come back to find the city transformed, all because of Helen? Explain to me what you think she has given to us, worth a quarrel with the Greeks?

MATHEMATICIAN. Anybody will tell you! I can tell you myself!

HECUBA. Listen to the mathematician!

MATHEMATICIAN. Yes, listen to the mathematician! And don't think that mathematicians have no concern with women! We're the land-surveyors of your personal landscape. I can't tell you how we mathematicians suffer to see any slight disproportion of the flesh, on the chin or the thigh, any infringement of your geometrical desirability. Well now, until this day mathematicians have never been satisfied with the countryside surrounding Troy. The line linking the plain with the hills seemed to us too slack: the line from the hills to the mountains too taut. Now, since Helen came, the country has taken on meaning and vigour. And, what is particularly evident to true mathematicians, space and volume have now found in Helen a common denominator. We can abolish all the instruments we have invented to reduce the universe to a manageable equation. There are no more feet and inches, ounces, pounds, milligrams or leagues. There is only the weight of Helen's footfall, the length of Helen's arm, the range of Helen's look or voice; and the movement of the air as she goes past is the measure of the winds. That is what the mathematicians will tell you.

HECUBA.   The old fool is crying.

PRIAM.   My dear son, you have only to look at this crowd, and you will understand what Helen is. She is a kind of absolution. To each one of these old men, whom you can see now like a frieze of grotesque heads all round the city walls: to the old swindler, the old thief, the old pandar, to all the old failures, she has shown they always had a secret longing to rediscover the beauty they had lost. If throughout their lives beauty had always been as close at hand as Helen is today, they would never have tricked their friends, or sold their daughters, or drunk away their inheritance. Helen is like a pardon to them: a new beginning for them, their whole future.

HECTOR.   These old men's ancient futures are no concern of mine.

DEMOKOS.   Hector, as a poet I approach things by the way of poetry. Imagine if beauty, never, at any time, touched our language. Imagine there being no such word as "delight."

HECTOR.   We should get on well enough without it. I get on without it already. "Delight" is a word I use only when I'm absolutely driven to it.

DEMOKOS.   Well, then the word "desirable": you could get on without that as well, I suppose?

HECTOR.   If it could be bought only at the cost of war, yes, I could get on without the word "desirable."

DEMOKOS.   One of the most beautiful words there are was found only at the cost of war: the word "courage."

HECTOR.   It has been well paid for.

HECUBA.   And the word "cowardice" was inevitably found at the same time.

PRIAM.   My son, why do you so deliberately not understand us?

HECTOR.   I understand you very well. With the help of a quibble, by pretending to persuade us to fight for beauty you want to get us to fight for a woman.

PRIAM.   Would you never go to war for any woman?

HECTOR.   Certainly not!

HECUBA.   And he would be unchivalrously right.

CASSANDRA.   If there were only one woman, then perhaps he would go to war for her. But we have exceeded that number, quite extravagantly.

DEMOKOS.   Wouldn't you go to war to rescue Andromache?

HECTOR.   Andromache and I have already made our secret plans for escaping from any prison in the world, and finding our way back to each other again.

DEMOKOS.   Even if there's no hope of it on earth?

HECTOR.   Even then.

HECUBA.   You have done well to unmask them, Hector. They want you to make war for the sake of a woman; it's the kind of love-making men believe in who are past making love in any other way.

DEMOKOS.   And doesn't that make you all the more valuable?

HECUBA.   Ah yes! You may say so!

DEMOKOS.   Excuse me, but I can't agree with you. The sex which gave me my mother will always have my respect, even its least worthy representatives.

HECUBA.   We know that. You have, as we know, shown your respect for instance to——

(*The* SERVANTS *who have stood by to hear the argument burst out laughing.*)

PRIAM.   Hecuba! Daughters! What can this mean? Why on earth are you all so up in arms? The Council are considering giving the city a public holiday in honour of one of your sex.

ANDROMACHE.   I know of only one humiliation for a woman: injustice.

DEMOKOS.   It's painful to say so, but there's no one knows less what a woman is than a woman.

(*The* YOUNG SERVANT, *passing:* Oh, dear! dear!)

HECUBA.   We know perfectly well. I will tell you myself what a woman is.

DEMOKOS.   Don't let them talk, Priam. You never know what they might say.

HECUBA.   They might tell the truth.

PRIAM.   I have only to think of one of you, my dears, to know what a woman is.

DEMOKOS.   In the first place, she is the source of our energy. You know that, Hector. The soldiers who haven't a portrait of a woman in their kit aren't worth anything.

CASSANDRA. The source of your pride, yes, I agree.

HECUBA. Of your vices.

ANDROMACHE. She is a poor bundle of uncertainty, a poor mass of fears, who detests whatever is difficult, and adores whatever is vulgar and easy.

HECTOR. Dear Andromache!

HECUBA. It's very simple. I have been a woman for fifty years, and I've never yet been able to discover precisely what it is I am.

DEMOKOS. Secondly, whether she likes it or not, she's the only reward for courage. Ask any soldier. To kill a man is to merit a woman.

ANDROMACHE. She loves cowards and libertines. If Hector were a coward or a libertine I shouldn't love him less; I might even love him more.

PRIAM. Don't go too far, Andromache. You will prove the very opposite of what you want to prove.

POLYXENE. She is greedy. She tells lies.

DEMOKOS. So we're to say nothing of her fidelity, her purity: we are not to mention them?

THE SERVANT. Oh, dear! dear!

DEMOKOS. What did you say?

THE SERVANT. I said "Oh, dear! dear!" I say what I think.

POLYXENE. She breaks her toys. She puts them headfirst into boiling water.

HECUBA. The older we women grow, the more clearly we see what men really are: hypocrites, boasters, he-goats. The older men grow, the more they doll us up with every perfection. There isn't a slut you've hugged behind a wall who isn't transformed in your memories into a loved and lovely creature.

PRIAM. Have you ever deceived me, Hecuba?

HECUBA. Only with yourself; scores of times with yourself.

DEMOKOS. Has Andromache ever deceived Hector?

HECUBA. You can leave Andromache out of this. There is nothing she could recognize in the sad histories of erring women.

ANDROMACHE. But I know if Hector were not my husband, if he were a club-footed, bandy-legged fisherman I should run after him and find him in his hovel, and lie down on the pile of oyster-shells and seaweed, and give him a son in adultery.

POLYXENE. She pretends to go to sleep at night, but she's really playing games in her head with her eyes shut.

HECUBA (to POLYXENE). You may well say so! It's dreadful! You know how I scold you for it!

THE SERVANT. The only thing worse than a woman is a man; there are no words to describe him.

DEMOKOS.   Then more's the pity if a woman deceives us! More's the pity if she scorns her own value and dignity! If she can't be true to a pattern of perfection which would save her from the ravages of conscience, we have to do it for her.

THE SERVANT.   Oh, the kind guardian angel!

PARIS.   One thing they've forgotten to say of themselves: they are never jealous.

PRIAM.   My dear daughters, the fact that you're so furious is a proof in itself that we are right. I can't conceive of any greater unselfishness than the way you now fight for peace, when peace will give you idle, feeble, chicken-hearted husbands, and war would turn them into men.

DEMOKOS.   Into heroes.

HECUBA.   Yes, we know the jargon. In war-time a man is called a hero. It doesn't make him any braver, and he runs for his life. But at least it's a hero who is running away.

ANDROMACHE.   Father, I must beg you to listen. If you have such a fondness for women, listen to what they have to say to you, for I can promise I speak for all the women in the world. Let us keep our husbands as they are. The gods took care to see they were surrounded with enough obstacles and dangers to keep them brave and vigorous. Quite enough if they had nothing to cope with except floods and storms! Or only wild animals! The small game, foxes and hares and pheasants, which a woman can scarcely distinguish from the heather they hide in, prove a man's quickness of eye far better than this target you propose: the enemy's heart hiding in flesh and metal. Whenever I have seen a man kill a stag or an eagle, I have offered up thanks to them. I know they died for Hector. Why should you want me to owe Hector to the deaths of other men?

PRIAM.   I don't want it, my dear child. But why do you think you are here now, all looking so beautiful, and valiantly demanding peace? Why: because your husbands and your fathers, and their fathers, and theirs, were fighting men. If they had been too lazy and self-indulgent to spring to arms, if they hadn't known how this dull and stupid business we call life suddenly leaps into flame and justifies itself through the scorn men have for it, you would find *you* were the cowards now, and you would be clamouring for war. A man has only one way of being immortal on this earth: he has to forget he is mortal.

ANDROMACHE.   Why, exactly so, father: you're only too right. The brave men die in war. It takes great luck or judgment not to be killed. Once at least the head has to bow and the knee has to bend to danger. The soldiers who march back under the triumphal arches are death's deserters. How can a country increase in strength and honour by sending them both to their graves?

PRIAM. Daughter, the first sign of cowardice in a people is their first moment of decay.

ANDROMACHE. But which is the worse cowardice? To appear cowardly to others, and make sure of peace? Or to be cowardly in your own eyes, and let loose a war?

DEMOKOS. Cowardice is not to prefer death on every hand rather than the death of one's native land.

HECUBA. I was expecting poetry at this point. It never lets us down.

ANDROMACHE. Everyone always dies for his country. If you have lived in it, well and wisely and actively, you die for it too.

HECUBA. It would be better if only the old men fought the wars. Every country is the country of youth. When its youth dies it dies with them.

DEMOKOS. All this nonsense about youth! In thirty years time youth is nothing but these old men you talk about.

CASSANDRA. Wrong.

HECUBA. Wrong! When a grown man reaches forty we change him for an old one. He has completely disappeared. There's only the most superficial resemblance between the two of them. Nothing is handed on from one to the other.

DEMOKOS. I still take a serious concern in my fame as a poet.

HECUBA. Yes, that's quite true. And your rheumatism.

(*Another outburst of laughter from the* SERVANTS)

HECTOR. And you can listen to all this without saying a word, Paris? Can you still not decide to give up an adventure to save us from years of unhappiness and massacre?

PARIS. What do you want me to say? My case is an international problem.

HECTOR. Are you really in love with Helen, Paris?

CASSANDRA. They've become now a kind of symbol of love's devotion. They don't still have to love each other.

PARIS. I worship Helen.

CASSANDRA (*at the rampart*). Here she is.

HECTOR. If I persuade her to set sail, will you agree?

PARIS. Yes, I'll agree.

HECTOR. Father, if Helen is willing to go back to Greece, will you hold her here by force?

PRIAM. Why discuss the impossible?

HECTOR. Do you call it impossible? If women are a tenth of what you say they are, Helen will go of her own free will.

PARIS. Father, now *I'm* going to ask you to let him do what he wants.

You have seen what it's like. As soon as the question of Helen cropped up, this whole tribe royal turned itself into a family conclave of all the poor girl's sisters-in-law, mother- and father-in-law, brother-in-law, worthy of the best middle-class tradition. I doubt if there's anything more humiliating than to be cast for the part of the seducer son in a large family. I've had quite enough of their insinuations. I accept Hector's challenge.

DEMOKOS. Helen's not only yours, Paris. She belongs to the city. She belongs to our country.

MATHEMATICIAN. She belongs to the landscape.

HECUBA. You be quiet, Mathematician.

CASSANDRA. Here's Helen; here she is.

HECTOR. Father, I must ask you to let me handle this. Listen; they are calling us to go to the ceremony, to close the Gates of War. Leave this to me. I'll join you soon.

PRIAM. Do you really agree to this, Paris?

PARIS. I'm eager for it.

PRIAM. Very well, then; let it be so. Come along, the rest of you; we will see that the Gates of War are made ready.

CASSANDRA. Those poor Gates. They need more oil to shut them than to open them.

(PARIS *and the rest withdraw.* DEMOKOS *stays.*)

HECTOR. What are you waiting for?

DEMOKOS. The visitation of my genius.

HECTOR. Say that again?

DEMOKOS. Every time Helen walks my way I am thrown into a transport of inspiration. I shake all over, break into sweat, and improvise. Good heavens, here it is! (*He declaims:*)

    Beautiful Helen, Helen of Sparta,
      Singular as the evening star,
    The gods forbid that we should part a
      Pair as fair as you and Paris are.

HECTOR. Your line-endings give me a headache.

DEMOKOS. It's an invention of mine. I can obtain effects even more surprising. Listen: (*declaims*)

    Face the great Hector with no qualm,
      Troy's glory though he be, and the world's terror:
    He is the storm, and you the after-calm,
      Yours is the right, and his the boist'rous error.

HECTOR. Get out!

DEMOKOS. What are you glaring at? You look as though you have as little liking for poetry as you have for war.

HECTOR. They make a pretty couple! Now vanish.

(*Exit* DEMOKOS.)

(*Enter* CASSANDRA.)

CASSANDRA. Helen!

(*Enter* HELEN *and* PARIS.)

PARIS. Here he is, Helen darling; this is Hector. He has a proposition to make to you, a perfectly simple proposition. He wants to hand you over to the Greeks, and prove to you that you don't love me. Tell me you do love me, before I leave you with him. Tell me in your own words.

HELEN. I adore you, my sweet.

PARIS. Tell me how beautiful the wave was which swept you away from Greece.

HELEN. Magnificent! A magnificent wave! Where did you see a wave? The sea was so calm.

PARIS. Tell me you hate Menelaus.

HELEN. Menelaus? I hate him.

PARIS. You haven't finished yet. I shall never again return to Greece. Say that.

HELEN. You will never again return to Greece.

PARIS. No, no, this is about you, my darling.

HELEN. Oh, of course! How silly I am! I shall never again return to Greece.

PARIS. I didn't make her say it.—Now it's up to you. (*He goes off.*)

HECTOR. Is Greece a beautiful country?

HELEN. Paris found it ravishing.

HECTOR. I meant is Greece itself beautiful, apart from Helen?

HELEN. How very charming of you.

HECTOR. I was simply wondering what it is really like.

HELEN. Well, there are quite a great many kings, and a great many goats, dotted about on marble.

HECTOR. If the kings are in gold, and the goats angora, that would look pretty well when the sun was rising.

HELEN. I don't get up very early.

HECTOR. And a great many gods as well, I believe? Paris tells me the sky is crawling with them; he tells me you can see the legs of goddesses hanging down from the clouds.

HELEN. Paris always goes about with his nose in the air. He may have seen them.

HECTOR. But you haven't?

HELEN. I am not gifted that way. I will look out for them when I go back there again.

HECTOR. You were telling Paris you would never be going back there.

HELEN. He asked me to tell him so. I adore doing what Paris wants me to do.

HECTOR. I see. Is that also true of what you said about Menelaus? Do you not, after all, hate him?

HELEN. Why should I hate him?

HECTOR. For the one reason which might certainly make for hate. You have seen too much of him.

HELEN. Menelaus? Oh, no! I have never seen Menelaus. On the contrary.

HECTOR. You have never seen your husband?

HELEN. There are some things, and certain people, that stand out in bright colours for me. They are the ones I can see. I believe in them. I have never been able to see Menelaus.

HECTOR. Though I suppose he must have come very close to you sometimes.

HELEN. I have been able to touch him. But I can't honestly tell you I saw him.

HECTOR. They say he never left your side.

HELEN. Apparently. I must have walked across him a great many times without knowing it.

HECTOR. Whereas you have seen Paris.

HELEN. Vividly; in the clearest outline against the sky and the sun.

HECTOR. Does he still stand out as vividly as he did? Look down there: leaning against the rampart.

HELEN. Are you sure that's Paris, down there?

HECTOR. He is waiting for you.

HELEN. Good gracious! He's not nearly as clear as usual!

HECTOR. And yet the wall is freshly whitewashed. Look again: there he is in profile.

HELEN. It's odd how people waiting for you stand out far less clearly than people you are waiting for.

HECTOR. Are you sure that Paris loves you?

HELEN. I don't like knowing about other people's feelings. There is nothing more embarrassing. Just as when you play cards and you see your opponent's hand. You are sure to lose.

HECTOR. What about yourself? Do you love him?

HELEN. I don't much like knowing my own feelings either.

HECTOR. But, listen: when you make love with Paris, when he sleeps in your arms, when you are circled round with Paris, overwhelmed with Paris, haven't you any thoughts about it?

HELEN. My part is over. I leave any thinking to the universe. It does it much better than I do.

HECTOR. Have there been many others, before Paris?

HELEN. Some.

HECTOR. And there will be others after him, wouldn't you say, as long as they stand out in clear relief against the sky, or the wall, or the white sheets on the bed? It is just as I thought it was. You don't love Paris particularly, Helen; you love men.

HELEN. I don't dislike them. They're as pleasant as soap and a sponge and warm water; you feel cleansed and refreshed by them.

HECTOR. Cassandra! Cassandra!

CASSANDRA (*entering*). What do you want?

HECTOR. Cassandra, Helen is going back this evening with the Greek ambassador.

HELEN. I? What makes you think so?

HECTOR. Weren't you telling me that you didn't love Paris particularly?

HELEN. That was your interpretation. Still, if you like.

HECTOR. I quote my authority. You have the same liking for men as you have for a cake of soap.

HELEN. Yes; or pumice stone perhaps is better. What about it?

HECTOR. Well, then, you're not going to hesitate in your choice between going back to Greece, which you don't mind, and a catastrophe as terrible as war?

HELEN. You don't understand me at all, Hector. Of course I'm not hesitating. It would be very easy to say "I will do this or that, so that this can happen or that can happen." You've discovered my weakness and you are overjoyed. The man who discovers a woman's weakness is like the huntsman in the heat of the day who finds a cool spring. He wallows in it. But you mustn't think, because you have convinced me, you've convinced the future, too. Merely by making children behave as you want them to, you don't alter the course of destiny.

HECTOR. I don't follow your Greek shades and subtleties.

HELEN. It's not a question of shades and subtleties. It's no less than a question of monsters and pyramids.

HECTOR. Do you choose to leave here, yes or no?

HELEN. Don't bully me. I choose what happens in the way I choose men, or anything else. I choose whatever is not indefinite and vague. I choose what I see.

HECTOR. I know, you said that: what you see in the brightest colours. And you don't see yourself returning to Menelaus in a few days' time?

HELEN.   No. It's very difficult.

HECTOR.   We could no doubt persuade your husband to dress with great brilliance for your return.

HELEN.   All the purple dye from all the murex shells in the sea wouldn't make him visible to me.

HECTOR.   Here you have a rival, Cassandra. Helen can read the future, too.

HELEN.   No, I can't read the future. But when I imagine the future some of the pictures I see are coloured, and some are dull and drab. And up to now it has always been the coloured scenes which have happened in the end.

HECTOR.   We are going to give you back to the Greeks at high noon, on the blinding sand, between the violet sea and the ochre-coloured wall. We shall all be in golden armour with red skirts; and my sisters, dressed in green and standing between my white stallion and Priam's black mare, will return you to the Greek ambassador, over whose silver helmet I can imagine tall purple plumes. You see that, I think?

HELEN.   No, none of it. It is all quite sombre.

HECTOR.   You are mocking me, aren't you?

HELEN.   Why should I mock you? Very well, then. Let us go, if you like! Let us go and get ready to return me to the Greeks. We shall see what happens.

HECTOR.   Do you realize how you insult humanity, or is it unconscious?

HELEN.   I don't know what you mean.

HECTOR.   You realize that your coloured picture-book is holding the world up to ridicule? While we are all battling and making sacrifices to bring about a time we can call our own, there are you, looking at your pictures which nothing in all eternity can alter. What's wrong? Which one has made you stop and stare at it with those blind eyes? I don't doubt it's the one where you are standing here on the ramparts, watching the battle going on below. Is it the battle you see?

HELEN.   Yes.

HECTOR.   And the city is in ruins or burning, isn't that so?

HELEN.   Yes. It's a vivid red.

HECTOR.   And what about Paris? You are seeing his body dragged behind a chariot?

HELEN.   Oh, do you think that is Paris? I see what looks like a flash of sunlight rolling in the dust. A diamond sparkling on his hand. Yes, it is! Often I don't recognize faces, but I always recognize the jewellery. It's his ring, I'm quite certain.

HECTOR. Exactly. Do I dare to ask you about Andromache, and myself, the scene of Andromache and Hector? You are looking at us. Don't deny it. How do you see us? Happy, grown old, bathed in light?

HELEN. I am not trying to see it.

HECTOR. The scene of Andromache weeping over the body of Hector, does that shine clearer?

HELEN. You seem to know. But sometimes I see things shining, brilliantly shining, and they never happen. No one is infallible.

HECTOR. You needn't go on. I understand. There is a son between the weeping mother and the father stretched on the ground?

HELEN. Yes. He is playing with his father's tangled hair. He is a sweet boy.

HECTOR. And these scenes are there in your eyes, down in the depths of them. Could I see them there?

HELEN. I don't know. Look.

HECTOR. Nothing. Nothing except the ashes of all those fires, the gold and the emerald in dust. How innocent it is, this crystal where the future is waiting. But there should be tears bathing it, and where are they? Would you cry, Helen, if you were going to be killed?

HELEN. I don't know. But I should scream. And I feel I shall scream if you go on at me like this, Hector. I am going to scream.

HECTOR. You will leave for Greece this evening, Helen, otherwise I shall kill you.

HELEN. But I want to leave! I'm prepared to leave. All that I'm trying to tell is that I simply can't manage to distinguish the ship that is going to carry me there. Nothing is shining in the least, neither the metal on the mast, nor the ring in the captain's nose, nor the cabin-boy's eyes, nor anything.

HECTOR. You will go back on a grey sea under a grey sun. But we must have peace.

HELEN. I cannot see peace.

HECTOR. Ask Cassandra to make her appear for you. Cassandra is a sorceress. She can summon up shapes and spirits.

A MESSENGER (*entering*). Hector, Priam is asking for you. The priests are opposed to our shutting the Gates of War. They say the gods will consider it an insult.

HECTOR. It is curious how the gods can never speak for themselves in these difficult matters.

MESSENGER. They have spoken for themselves. A thunderbolt has fallen on the temple, several men have been killed, the entrails of the victims have been consulted, and they are unanimously against Helen's return to Greece.

HECTOR. I would give a good deal to be able to consult the entrails of the priests . . . I'll follow you.
(*The* MESSENGER *goes.*)
Well, now, Helen, do we agree about this?

HELEN. Yes.

HECTOR. From now on you will say what I tell you to say? You will do what I tell you to do?

HELEN. Yes.

HECTOR. When we come in front of Ulysses you won't contradict me, you will bear out everything I say?

HELEN. Yes.

HECTOR. Do you hear this, Cassandra? Listen to this solid wall of negation which says Yes! They have all given in to me. Paris has given in to me, Priam has given in to me, Helen has given in to me. And yet I can't help feeling that in each of these apparent victories I have been defeated. You set out, thinking you are going to have to wrestle with giants; you brace yourself to conquer them, and you find yourself wrestling with something inflexible reflected in a woman's eye. You have said yes beautifully, Helen, and you're brimful of a stubborn determination to defy me!

HELEN. That's possible. But how can I help it? It isn't my own determination.

HECTOR. By what peculiar vagary did the world choose to place its mirror in this obtuse head?

HELEN. It's most regrettable, obviously. But can you see any way of defeating the obstinacy of a mirror?

HECTOR. Yes. I've been considering that for the past several minutes.

ANOTHER MESSENGER (*entering*). Hector, make haste. They are in a turmoil of revolt down on the beach. The Greek ships have been sighted, and they have hoisted their flag not masthead but hatchway. The honour of our navy is at stake. Priam is afraid the ambassador may be murdered as soon as he lands.

HECTOR. I leave you in charge of Helen, Cassandra. I must go and give my orders.

HELEN. If you break the mirror, will what is reflected in it cease to exist?

HECTOR. That is the whole question. (*Exit.*)

CASSANDRA. I never see anything at all, you know, either coloured or not. But I can feel the weight on me of every person who comes towards me. I know what is in store for them by the sensation of suffering which flows into my veins.

HELEN. Is it true that you are a sorceress? Could you really make Peace take shape and appear for us?

CASSANDRA. Peace? Very easily. She is always standing in her beggarly way on every threshold. Wait . . . you will see her now.

(PEACE *appears*.)

HELEN. Oh, how pretty she is!

PEACE. Come to my rescue, Helen: help me!

HELEN. But how pale and wan she is.

PEACE. Pale and wan? What do you mean? Don't you see the gold shining in my hair?

HELEN. Gold? Well, perhaps a golden grey. It's very original.

PEACE. Golden grey? Is my gold now grey? (*She disappears*.)

CASSANDRA. I think she means to make herself clearer.

(PEACE *re-appears, outrageously painted*.)

PEACE. Is that better now?

HELEN. I don't see her as well as I did before.

PEACE. Is that better?

CASSANDRA. Helen doesn't see you as well as she did.

PEACE. But you can see me: you are speaking to me.

CASSANDRA. It's my speciality to speak to the invisible.

PEACE. What is going on, then? Why are all the men in the city and along the beach making such a pandemonium?

CASSANDRA. Apparently their gods are insulted, and their honour is at stake.

PEACE. Their gods! Their honour!

CASSANDRA. Yes . . . You are ill!

The curtain falls

ACT II

A palace enclosure. At each corner a view of the sea. In the middle a monument, the Gates of War. They are wide open.

(HELEN. *The young* TROILUS.)

HELEN. You, you, hey! You down there! Yes, it's you I'm calling. Come here.

TROILUS. No.

HELEN. What is your name?

TROILUS. Troilus.

HELEN. Come here.

TROILUS. No.

HELEN. Come here, Troilus!

(TROILUS *draws near*.)

That's the way. You obey when you're called by your name: you are still very like a puppy. It's rather beguiling. Do you know you have made me call out to a man for the first time in my life. They keep so close to my side I have only usually to move my lips. I have called out to sea-gulls, to dogs, to the echoes, but never before to a man. You will pay for that. What's the matter? Are you trembling?

TROILUS. No, I'm not.

HELEN. You tremble, Troilus.

TROILUS. Yes, I do.

HELEN. Why are you always just behind me? If I walk with my back to the sun and suddenly stop, the head of your shadow stubs itself against my feet. That doesn't matter, as long as it doesn't over-shoot them. Tell me what you want.

TROILUS. I don't want anything.

HELEN. Tell me what you want, Troilus!

TROILUS. Everything! I want everything!

HELEN. You want everything. The moon?

TROILUS. Everything! Everything and more!

HELEN. You're beginning to talk like a real man already; you want to kiss me!

TROILUS. No!

HELEN. You want to kiss me, isn't that it, Troilus?

TROILUS. I would kill myself directly afterwards!

HELEN. Come nearer. How old are you?

TROILUS. Fifteen. Alas!

HELEN. Bravo that alas. Have you kissed girls of your own age?

TROILUS. I hate them.

HELEN. But you have kissed them?

TROILUS. Well, yes, you're bound to kiss them, you kiss them all. I would give my life not to have kissed any of them.

HELEN. You seem prepared to get rid of quite a number of lives. Why haven't you said to me frankly: Helen, I want to kiss you! I don't see anything wrong in your kissing me. Kiss me.

TROILUS. Never.

HELEN. And then, when the day came to an end, you would have come quietly to where I was sitting on the battlements watching the sun go down over the islands, and you would have turned my head towards you with your hands—from golden it would have become dark, only shadow now, you would hardly have been able to see me—and you would have kissed me, and I should have been very happy. Why this is Troilus, I should have said to myself: young Troilus is kissing me! Kiss me.

TROILUS. Never.

HELEN. I see. You think, once you have kissed me, you would hate me?

TROILUS. Oh! Older men have all the luck, knowing how to say what they want to!

HELEN. You say it well enough.

(*Enter* PARIS.)

PARIS. Take care Helen, Troilus is a dangerous fellow.

HELEN. On the contrary. He wants to kiss me.

PARIS. Troilus, you know that if you kiss Helen, I shall kill you?

HELEN. Dying means nothing to him; no matter how often.

PARIS. What's the matter with him? Is he crouching to spring? Is he going to take a leap at you? He's too nice a boy. Kiss Helen, Troilus. I'll let you.

HELEN. If you can make up his mind to it you're cleverer than I am.

(TROILUS, *who was about to hurl himself on* HELEN, *immediately draws back.*)

PARIS. Listen, Troilus! Here's a committee of our revered elders coming to shut the Gates of War. Kiss Helen in front of them; it will make you famous. You want to be famous, don't you, later on in life?

TROILUS. No. I want nobody to have heard of me.

PARIS. You don't want to be famous? You don't want to be rich and powerful?

TROILUS. No. Poor. Ugly.

PARIS. Let me finish! So that you can have all the women you want.

TROILUS. I don't want any, none at all, none.

PARIS. Here come the senators! Now you can choose: either you kiss Helen in front of them, or I shall kiss her in front of you. Would you rather I did it? All right! Look! . . . Why, this was a new version of kiss you gave me, Helen. What was it?

HELEN. The kiss I had ready for Troilus.

PARIS. You don't know what you're missing, my boy! Are you leaving us? Goodbye, then.

HELEN. We shall kiss one another, Troilus. I'll answer for that.

(TROILUS *goes.*)

Troilus!

PARIS (*slightly unnerved*). You called very loudly, Helen.

(*Enter* DEMOKOS.)

DEMOKOS. Helen, one moment! Look me full in the face. I've got here in my hand a magnificent bird which I'm going to set free. Are you looking? Here it is. Smooth back your hair, and smile a beautiful smile.

PARIS. I don't see how the bird will fly any better if Helen smooths her hair and gives a beautiful smile.

HELEN. It can't do me any harm, anyway.

DEMOKOS. Don't move. One! Two! Three! There! It's all over, you can go now.

HELEN. Where was the bird?

DEMOKOS. It's a bird who knows how to make himself invisible.

HELEN. Ask him next time to tell you how he does it. (*She goes.*)

PARIS. What is this nonsense?

DEMOKOS. I am writing a song on the subject of Helen's face. I needed to look at it closely, to engrave it, smiling, on my memory.
  (*Enter* HECUBA, POLYXENE, ABNEOS, *the* MATHEMATICIAN, *and some* OLD MEN.)

HECUBA. Well, are you going to shut these Gates for us?

DEMOKOS. Certainly not. We might well have to open them again this very evening.

HECUBA. It is Hector's wish. And Hector will persuade Priam.

DEMOKOS. That is as we shall see. And what's more I have a surprise in store for Hector.

POLYXENE. Where do the Gates lead to, mama?

ABNEOS. To war, my child. When they are open it means there is war.

DEMOKOS. My friends . . .

HECUBA. War or not, it's an absurd symbolism, your Gateway, and those two great doors always left open look very unsightly. All the dogs stop there.

MATHEMATICIAN. This is no domestic matter. It concerns war and the gods.

HECUBA. Which is just as I said: the gods never remember to shut their doors.

POLYXENE. I remember to shut them very well, don't I, mama?

PARIS. And you even include your fingers in them, don't you, my pretty one?

DEMOKOS. May I ask for a moment of silence, Paris? Abneos, and you, Mathematician, and you, my friends: I asked you to meet here earlier than the time fixed for the ceremony so that we could hold our first council. And it promises well that this first council of war should be, not a council of generals, but a council of intellectuals. For it isn't enough in war-time to have our soldiers drilled, well-armed, and spectacular. It is absolutely necessary to bring their enthusiasm up to fever pitch. The physical intoxication which their officers will get from them by a generous allowance of cheap wine supplied at the right moment, will still be ineffective against the

Greeks, unless it is reinforced by the spiritual and moral intoxication which the poets can pour into them. If we are too old to fight we can at least make sure that the fighting is savage. I see you have something to say on the subject, Abneos.

ABNEOS. Yes. We must make a war-song.

DEMOKOS. Very proper. A war requires a war-song.

PARIS. We have done without one up to now.

HECUBA. War itself sings quite loud enough.

ABNEOS. We have done without one because up to now we were fighting only barbarians. It was nothing more than a hunt, and the hunting horn was all we needed. But now with the Greeks we're entering a different region of war altogether.

DEMOKOS. Exactly so, Abneos. The Greeks don't fight with everybody.

PARIS. We already have a national anthem.

ABNEOS. Yes. But it's a song of peace.

PARIS. If you sing a song of peace with enough gestures and grimaces it becomes a war-song. What are the words we have already?

ABNEOS. You know them perfectly well. There's no spirit in them:
We cut and bind the harvest,
We tread the vineyard's blood.

DEMOKOS. At the very most it's a war-song against farm produce. You won't frighten the Spartans by threatening a wheatfield.

PARIS. Sing it with a spear in your hand, and a dead body at your feet, you will be surprised.

HECUBA. It includes the word "blood," there's always that.

PARIS. The word "harvest" as well. War rather approves of the word "harvest."

ABNEOS. Why discuss it, when Demokos can invent an entirely new one in a couple of hours.

DEMOKOS. A couple of hours is rather short.

HECUBA. Don't be afraid; it's more than you need for it. And after the song will come the hymn, and after the hymn the cantata. As soon as war is declared it will be impossible to hold the poets back. Rhyme is still the most effective drum.

DEMOKOS. And the most useful, Hecuba: you don't know how wisely you speak. I know war. As long as war isn't with us, and the Gates are shut, each of us is free to insult it and execrate it as we will. But once war comes, its pride and autocracy is huge. You can gain its goodwill only by flattery and adoration. So the mission of those who understand how to speak and write is to compliment and praise war ceaselessly and indiscriminately, otherwise we shut ourselves out from his favour.

PARIS. Have you got an idea for your song already?

DEMOKOS.   A marvellous idea, which no one will understand better than you. War must be tired of the mask we always give it, of Medusa's venomous hair and a Gorgon's lips.[4] I have had the notion to compare War's face with Helen's. It will be enchanted by the comparison.

POLYXENE.   What does War look like, mama?

HECUBA.   Like your Aunt Helen.

POLYXENE.   She is very pretty.

DEMOKOS.   Then the discussion is closed. You can expect the war-song. Why are you looking worried, Mathematician?

MATHEMATICIAN.   Because there are other things far more urgent than this war-song, far more urgent!

DEMOKOS.   You think we should discuss the question of medals, false information, atrocity stories, and so on?

MATHEMATICIAN.   I think we should discuss the insulting epithets.

HECUBA.   The insulting epithets?

MATHEMATICIAN.   Before they hurl their spears the Greek fighting-men hurl insults. You third cousin of a toad, they yell! You son of a sow!—They insult each other, like that! And they have a good reason for it. They know that the body is more vulnerable when self-respect has fled. Soldiers famous for their composure lose it immediately when they're treated as warts or maggots. We Trojans suffer from a grave shortage of insults.

DEMOKOS.   The Mathematician is quite right. We are the only race in the world which doesn't insult its enemies before it kills them.

PARIS.   You don't think it's enough that the civilians insult the enemy civilians?

MATHEMATICIAN.   The armies have to show the same hatred the civilians do. You know what dissemblers armies can be in this way. Leave them to themselves and they spend their time admiring each other. Their front lines very soon become the only ranks of real brotherhood in the world. So naturally, when the theatre of war is so full of mutual consideration, hatred is driven back on to the schools, the salons, the trades-people. If our soldiers aren't at least equal to the Greeks in the fury of their epithets, they will lose all taste for insults and calumny, and as a natural consequence all taste for war.

DEMOKOS.   Suggestion adopted! We will organize a cursing parade this evening.

PARIS.   I should have thought they're big enough to find their own curses.

[4] Medusa was one of three sister Gorgons, terrifyingly ugly creatures with snakes for hair.

DEMOKOS.   What a mistake! Could you, adroit as you are, find your own effective curses?

PARIS.   I believe so.

DEMOKOS.   You fool yourself. Come and stand face to face with Abneos and begin.

PARIS.   Why Abneos?

DEMOKOS.   Because he lends himself to this sort of thing, with his corpulence and one thing and another.

ABNEOS.   Come on, then, speak up, you piece of pie-crust!

PARIS.   No. Abneos doesn't inspire me. I'll start with you, if you don't mind.

DEMOKOS.   With me? Certainly. You can let fly at ten paces. There we are. Begin.

HECUBA.   Take a good look at him. You will be inspired.

PARIS.   You old parasite! You filthy-footed iambic pentameter!

DEMOKOS.   Just one second. To avoid any mistake you had better say who it is you're addressing.

PARIS.   You're quite right! Demokos! Bloodshot bullock's eye! You fungus-ridden plum-tree!

DEMOKOS.   Grammatically reasonable, but very naive. What is there in a fungus-ridden plum-tree to make me rise up foaming at the lips?

HECUBA.   He also called you a bloodshot bullock's eye.

DEMOKOS.   Bloodshot bullock's eye is better. But you see how you flounder, Paris? Search for something that can strike home to me. What are my faults, in your opinion?

PARIS.   You are cowardly: your breath smells, and you have no talent.

DEMOKOS.   You're asking for trouble!

PARIS.   I was trying to please you.

POLYXENE.   Why are we scolding Uncle Demokos, mama?

HECUBA.   Because he is a cuckoo, dearest!

DEMOKOS.   What did you say, Hecuba?

HECUBA.   I was saying that you're a cuckoo, Demokos. If cuckoos had the absurdity, the affectation, the ugliness and the stench of vultures, you would be a cuckoo.

DEMOKOS.   Wait a bit, Paris! Your mother is better at this than you are. Model yourselves on her. One hour's exercise each day for each soldier, and Hecuba has given us the superiority in insults which we badly need. As for the war-song, I'm not sure it wouldn't be wiser to entrust that to her as well.

HECUBA.   If you like. But if so, I shouldn't say that war looks like Helen.

DEMOKOS.   What would you say it looks like, in your opinion?

HECUBA.   I will tell you when the Gates have been shut.

(Enter PRIAM, HECTOR, ANDROMACHE, *and presently* HELEN. *During the closing of the Gates,* ANDROMACHE *takes little* POLYXENE *aside and whispers a secret or an errand to her.)*

HECTOR.   As they nearly are.

DEMOKOS.   One moment, Hector!

HECTOR.   Aren't we ready to begin the ceremony?

HECUBA.   Surely? The hinges are swimming in oil.

HECTOR.   Well, then.

PRIAM.   What our friends want you to understand, Hector, is that war is ready, too. Consider carefully. They're not mistaken. If you shut these Gates, in a minute we may have to open them again.

HECUBA.   Even one minute of peace is worth taking.

HECTOR.   Father, you should know what peace means to men who have been fighting for months. It's like solid ground to someone who was drowning or sinking in the quicksands. Do let us get our feet on to a few inches of peace, touch it, if only with the tips of our toes.

PRIAM.   Hector: consider: inflicting the word peace on to the city today is as ruthless as though you gave it poison. You will take her off her guard, undermine her iron determination, debase, with the word peace, the accepted values of memory, affection, and hope. The soldiers will rush to buy the bread of peace, to drink the wine of peace, to hold in their arms the woman of peace, and in an hour you will put them back to face a war.

HECTOR.   The war will never take place!

(The sound of clamour near the Gates)

DEMOKOS.   No? Listen!

HECTOR.   Shut the Gates. This is where we shall meet the Greeks. Conversation will be bitter enough as it is. We must receive them in peace.

PRIAM.   My son, are we even sure we should let the Greeks disembark?

HECTOR.   Disembark they shall. This meeting with Ulysses is our last chance of peace.

DEMOKOS.   Disembark they shall not. Our honour is at stake. We shall be the laughing-stock of the whole world.

HECTOR.   And you're taking it upon yourself to recommend to the Senate an action which would certainly mean war?

DEMOKOS.   Upon myself? No, not at all. Will you come forward now, Busiris. This is where your mission begins.

HECTOR.   Who is this stranger?

DEMOKOS.   He is the greatest living expert on the rights of nations. It's a lucky chance he should be passing through Troy today. You

534 / *Jean Giraudoux*

can't say that he's a biased witness. He is neutral. Our Senate is willing to abide by his decision, a decision which all other nations will agree with tomorrow.

HECTOR. And what is your opinion?

BUSIRIS. My opinion, Princes, based on my own observation and further enquiry, is that the Greeks, in relation to Troy, are guilty of three breaches of international law. If you give them permission to disembark you will have sacrificed your position as the aggrieved party, and so lost the universal sympathy which would certainly have been yours in the conflict to follow.

HECTOR. Explain yourself.

BUSIRIS. Firstly, they have hoisted their flag hatchway and not mast-head. A ship of war, my dear Princes and colleagues, hoists its flag hatchway only when replying to a salute from a boat carrying cattle. Clearly, then, so to salute a city and a city's population is an insult. As it happens, we have a precedent. Last year the Greeks hoisted their flag hatchway when they were entering the port of Orphea. The reply was incisive. Orphea declared war.

HECTOR. And what happened?

BUSIRIS. Orphea was beaten. Orphea no longer exists, nor the Orpheans either.

HECUBA. Perfect.

BUSIRIS. But the annihilation of a people doesn't alter in the least their superior moral position.

HECTOR. Go on.

BUSIRIS. Secondly, on entering your territorial waters the Greeks adopted the formation known as frontal. At the last congress there was some talk of including this formation in the paragraph of measures called defensive-aggressive. I was very happy to be able to get it restored under its proper heading of aggressive-defensive: so without doubt it is now one of the subtle forms of naval manœuvre which is a disguised form of blockade: that is to say, it constitutes a fault of the first degree! We have a precedent for this, as well. Five years ago the Greek navy adopted the frontal formation when they anchored outside Magnesia. Magnesia at once declared war.

HECTOR. Did they win it?

BUSIRIS. They lost it. There's not one stone of Magnesia still standing on another. But my redraft of the paragraph is still standing.

HECUBA. I congratulate you. We were beginning to be anxious.

HECTOR. Go on.

BUSIRIS. The third fault is not so serious. One of the Greek triremes has crept close in to shore without permission. Its captain, Ajax, the most unruly and impossible man among the Greeks, is climbing up towards the city, shouting scandal and provocation, and swearing he would like to kill Paris. But this is a very minor matter, from the international point of view; because it isn't, in any way, a formal breach of the law.

DEMOKOS. You have your information. The situation can only be resolved in one of two ways. To swallow an outrage, or return it. Choose.

HECTOR. Oneah, go and find Ajax. Head him off in this direction.

PARIS. I'm waiting here for him.

HECTOR. You will be good enough to stay in the Palace until I call for you. As for you, Busiris, you must understand that our city has no intention of being insulted by the Greeks.

BUSIRIS. I am not surprised. Troy's incorruptible pride is a legend all the world over.

HECTOR. You are going to provide me, here and now, with an argument which will allow our Senate to say that there has been no fault whatever on the part of our visitors, and with our pride untouched we welcome them here as our guests.

DEMOKOS. What nonsense is this?

BUSIRIS. It isn't in keeping with the facts, Hector.

HECTOR. My dear Busiris, all of us here know there's no better way of exercising the imagination than the study of law. No poet ever interpreted nature as freely as a lawyer interprets truth.

BUSIRIS. The Senate asked me for an opinion: I gave it.

HECTOR. And I ask you for an interpretation. An even subtler point of law.

BUSIRIS. It goes against my conscience.

HECTOR. Your conscience has seen Orphea destroyed, Magnesia destroyed: is it now contemplating, just as light-heartedly, the destruction of Troy?

HECUBA. Yes. He comes from Syracuse.

HECTOR. I do beg of you, Busiris. The lives of two countries depend on this. Help us.

BUSIRIS. Truth is the only help I can give you.

HECTOR. Precisely. Discover a truth which saves us. What is the use of justice if it doesn't hammer out a shield for innocent people? Forge us a truth. If you can't, there is one thing I can tell you, quite simply: we shall hold you here for as long as the war goes on.

BUSIRIS. What are you saying?

DEMOKOS. You're abusing your position, Hector!

HECUBA. During war we imprison the rights of man. There seems no reason why we shouldn't imprison a lawyer.

HECTOR. I mean what I say, Busiris. I've never failed yet to keep my promises, or my threats. And now either these guards are going to take you off to prison for a year or two, or else you leave here, this evening, heaped with gold. With this in mind, you can dispassionately examine the evidence once again.

BUSIRIS. Actually there are certain mitigating arguments.

HECTOR. I was sure there were.

BUSIRIS. In the case of the first fault, for instance, when the cattle-boat salute is given in certain seas where the shores are fertile, it could be interpreted as a salute from the sailors to the farmers.

HECTOR. That would be, in fact, the logical interpretation. The salute of the sea to the earth.

BUSIRIS. Not to mention that the cargo of cattle might easily be a cargo of bulls. In that case the homage would verge on flattery.

HECTOR. There you are. You've understood what I meant. We've arrived at our point of view.

BUSIRIS. And as to the frontal formation, that could as easily mean a promise as a provocation. Women wanting children give themselves not from the side but face to face.

HECTOR. Decisive argument.

BUSIRIS. Then, again, the Greek ships have huge carved nymphs for figureheads. A woman who comes towards you naked and open-armed is not a threat but an offer. An offer to talk, at any rate.

HECTOR. So there we have our honour safe and sound, Demokos. The next step is to make this consultation with Busiris public. Meanwhile, Minos, tell the port authorities to let Ulysses disembark without any loss of time.

DEMOKOS. It's no use even trying to discuss honour with these fighting men. They trade on the fact that you can't treat them as cowards.

MATHEMATICIAN. At any rate, Hector, deliver the Oration for the Dead. That will make you think again.

HECTOR. There's not going to be an Oration for the Dead.

PRIAM. But it's a part of the ceremony. The victorious general must always speak in honour of the dead when the Gates are closed.

HECTOR. An Oration for the Dead of a war is a hypocritical speech in defence of the living, a plea for acquittal. I am not so sure of my innocence.

DEMOKOS. The High Command is not responsible.

HECTOR. Alas, no one is: nor the gods either. Besides, I have given my oration for the dead already. I gave it to them in their last minute of life, when they were lying on the battlefield, on a little slope of olive-trees, while they could still attend me with what was left of their sight and hearing. I can tell you what I said to them.

There was one, disembowelled, already turning up the whites of his eyes, and I said to him: "It's not so bad, you know, it's not so bad; you will do all right, old man." And one with his skull split in two; I said: "You look pretty comical with that broken nose." And my little equerry, with his left arm hanging useless and his last blood flowing out of him; and I said, "It's a good thing for you it's the left arm you've splintered." I am happy I gave them one final swig of life; it was all they asked for; they died drinking it. And there's nothing else to be said. Shut the Gates.

POLYXENE. Did the little equerry die, as well?

HECTOR. Yes, puss-cat. He died. He stretched out his right arm. Someone I couldn't see took him by his perfect hand. And then he died.

DEMOKOS. Our general seems to confuse remarks made to the dying with the Oration for the Dead.

PRIAM. Why must you be so stubborn, Hector?

HECTOR. Very well: you shall have the Oration. (*He takes a position below the Gates.*) You who cannot hear us, who cannot see us, listen to these words, look at those who come to honour you. We have won the war. I know that's of no moment to you. You are the victors, too. But we are victorious, and still live. That's where the difference is between us and why I'm ashamed. I don't know whether, among the crowd of the dead, any privilege is given to men who died victorious. But the living, whether victorious or not, have privilege enough. We have our eyes. We see the sun. We do what all men do under the sun. We eat. We drink. By the moon, we sleep with our wives. And with yours, now you have gone.

DEMOKOS. You insult the dead!

HECTOR. Do you think so?

DEMOKOS. Either the dead or the living.

HECTOR. There is a distinction.

PRIAM. Come to the peroration, Hector. The Greeks are coming ashore.

HECTOR. I will come to it now . . . Breathe in this incense, touch these offerings, you who can neither smell nor touch. And understand, since I speak to you sincerely, I haven't an equal tenderness and respect for all of you. Though all of you are the dead, with you as with us who survive there are men of courage and men of fear, and you can't make me confuse, for the sake of a ceremony, the dead I admire with those I can't admire. But what I have to say to you today is that war seems to me the most sordid, hypocritical way of making all men equal: and I accept death neither as a punishment or expiation for the coward, nor as a reward to the living.

So, whatever you may be, absent, forgotten, purposeless, unresting, without existence, one thing is certain when we close these Gates: we must ask you to forgive us, we, the deserters who survive you, who feel we have stolen two great privileges, I hope the sound of their names will never reach you: the warmth of the living body, and the sky.

POLYXENE. The Gates are shutting, mama!

HECUBA. Yes, darling.

POLYXENE. The dead men are pushing them shut.

HECUBA. They help, a little.

POLYXENE. They're helping quite a lot, especially over on the right.

HECTOR. Is it done? Are they shut?

GUARD. Tight as a clam.

HECTOR. We're at peace, father, we're at peace.

HECUBA. We're at peace!

POLYXENE. It feels much better, doesn't it, mama?

HECTOR. Indeed it does.

POLYXENE. I feel much better, anyway.

    (*The sound of the* GREEKS' *music*)

A MESSENGER. The Greeks have landed, Priam!

DEMOKOS. What music! What frightful music! It's the most anti-Trojan music there could possibly be! Let's go and give them a welcome to match it.

HECTOR. Receive them royally, bring them here safely. You are responsible.

MATHEMATICIAN. At any rate we ought to counter with some Trojan music. Hector, if we can't be indignant any other way, you can authorize a battle of music.

CROWD. The Greeks! The Greeks!

MESSENGER. Ulysses is on the landing-stage, Priam. Where are we to take him?

PRIAM. Conduct him here. Send word to us in the Palace when he comes. Keep with us, Paris. We don't want you too much in evidence just yet.

HECTOR. Let's go and prepare what we shall say to the Greeks, father.

DEMOKOS. You'd better prepare it somewhat better than your speech for the dead; you're likely to meet more contradiction.

    (*Exeunt* PRIAM *and his sons.*)

If you are going with them, tell us before you go, Hecuba, what it is you think war looks like.

HECUBA. You insist on knowing?

DEMOKOS. If you've seen what it looks like, tell us.

HECUBA. Like the bottom of a baboon. When the baboon is up in a tree, with its hind end facing us, there is the face of war exactly: scarlet, scaley, glazed, framed in a clotted, filthy wig.

DEMOKOS. So he has two faces: this you describe, and Helen's.

(*Exeunt* DEMOKOS *and* HECUBA.)

ANDROMACHE. Here is Helen now. Polyxene, you remember what you have to say to her?

POLYXENE. Yes.

ANDROMACHE. Go to her, then.

(*Enter* HELEN.)

HELEN. Do you want to talk to me, darling?

POLYXENE. Yes, Aunt Helen.

HELEN. It must be important, you're so very tense.

POLYXENE. Yes, Aunt Helen.

HELEN. Is it something you can't tell me without standing so stiffly?

POLYXENE. No, Aunt Helen.

HELEN. Do tell me, then; you make me feel terrible when you stand there like a little stick.

POLYXENE. Aunt Helen, if you love anyone, please go away.

HELEN. Why should I go away, darling?

POLYXENE. Because of the war.

HELEN. Do you know about war already, then?

POLYXENE. I don't exactly know about it. I think it means we have to die.

HELEN. And do you know what dying is?

POLYXENE. I don't exactly. I think it means we don't feel anything any more.

HELEN. What exactly was it that Andromache told you to ask me?

POLYXENE. If you love us at all, please to go away.

HELEN. That doesn't seem to me very logical. If you loved someone you wouldn't leave them?

POLYXENE. Oh, no! Never!

HELEN. Which would you rather do: go right away from Hecuba, or never feel anything any more?

POLYXENE. Oh, never feel anything! I would rather stay, and never feel anything any more.

HELEN. You see how badly you put things to me. If I'm to leave you, I mustn't love you. Would you rather I didn't love you?

POLYXENE. Oh, no! I want you to love me.

HELEN. In other words, you didn't know what you were saying, did you?

POLYXENE. No.

HECUBA (*offstage*). Polyxene!

(*Enter* HECUBA.)

Are you deaf, Polyxene? Why did you shut your eyes when you saw me? Are you playing at being a statue? Come with me.

HELEN.   She is teaching herself not to feel anything. But she has no gift for it.

HECUBA.   Can you hear me, Polyxene? And see me?

POLYXENE.   Yes, I can hear you. I can see you, too.

HECUBA.   Why are you crying? Don't you like to see and hear me?

POLYXENE.   If I do, you will go away.

HECUBA.   I think it would be better, Helen, if you left Polyxene alone. She is too sensitive to touch the insensitive, even through your beautiful dress and your beautiful voice.

HELEN.   I quite agree with you. I advise Andromache to carry her own messages. Kiss me, Polyxene. I shall go away this evening, since that is what you would like.

POLYXENE.   Don't go! Don't go!

HELEN.   Bravo! You are quite loosened up again!

HECUBA.   Are you coming with us, Andromache?

ANDROMACHE.   No: I shall wait here.

        (*Exeunt* HECUBA *and* POLYXENE.)

HELEN.   You want an explanation?

ANDROMACHE.   I believe it's necessary.

HELEN.   Listen to the way they're shouting and arguing down below. Isn't that enough? Do you and I have to have explanations, too? And what explanations, since I'm leaving here anyway?

ANDROMACHE.   Whether you go or stay isn't any longer the problem.

HELEN.   Tell Hector that. You will make his day easier.

ANDROMACHE.   Yes, Hector is obsessed by the thought of getting you away. All men are the same. They take no notice of the stag in the thicket because they're already chasing the hare. Perhaps men can hunt like that. But not the gods.

HELEN.   If you have discovered what the gods are after in this affair, I congratulate you.

ANDROMACHE.   I don't know that the gods are after anything. But there is something the universe is after. Ever since this morning, it seems to me, everything has begged and cried out for it, men, animals, even the leaves on the trees and my own child, not yet born.

HELEN.   Cried out for what?

ANDROMACHE.   That you should love Paris.

HELEN.   If they know so certainly that I don't love Paris, they are better informed than I am.

ANDROMACHE.   But you don't love him! You could love him, perhaps. But, at present, you are both living in a misunderstanding.

HELEN.   I live with him happily, amicably, in complete agreement.

We understand each other so well, I don't really see how this can be called a misunderstanding.

ANDROMACHE. Agreement is never reached in love. The life of a wife and husband who love each other is never at rest. Whether the marriage is true or false, the marriage portion is the same: elemental discord. Hector is my absolute opposite. He shares none of my tastes. We pass our days either getting the better of one another, or sacrificing ourselves. There is no tranquillity for lovers.

HELEN. And if I went pale whenever I saw Paris: and my eyes filled with tears, and the palms of my hands were moist, you think Menelaus would be delighted, and the Greeks pleased and quite satisfied?

ANDROMACHE. It wouldn't much matter then what the Greeks thought.

HELEN. And the war would never happen?

ANDROMACHE. Perhaps, indeed, it would never happen. Perhaps if you loved him, love would call to the rescue one of its own equals: generosity or intelligence. No one, not even destiny itself, attacks devotion lightheartedly. And even if the war did happen, why, I think even then—

HELEN. Then it wouldn't be the same war, I suppose.

ANDROMACHE. Oh, no, Helen! You know what this struggle is going to be. Fate would never take so many precautions for an ordinary quarrel. It means to build the future on this war, the future of our countries and our peoples, and our ways of thinking. It won't be so bad if our thoughts and our future are built on the story of a man and a woman who truly love each other. But fate hasn't noticed yet that you are lovers only on paper, officially. To think that we're going to suffer and die only for a pair of theoretical lovers: and the splendour and calamity of the age to come will be founded on a trivial adventure between two people who don't love each other— that's what is so horrible.

HELEN. If everybody thinks that we love each other, it comes to the same thing.

ANDROMACHE. They don't think so. But no one will admit that he doesn't. Everyone, when there's war in the air, learns to live in a new element: falsehood. Everybody lies. Our old men don't worship beauty: they worship themselves, they worship ugliness. And this indignation the Greeks are showing us is a lie. God knows, they're amused enough at what you can do with Paris! Their boats, in the bay, with their patriotic anthems and their streamers flying are a falsehood of the sea. And Hector's life and my son's life, too, are going to be played out in hypocrisy and pretence.

HELEN. So?

ANDROMACHE. I beg of you, Helen. You see how I'm pressed against

you as though I were begging you to love me. Love Paris! Or tell
me that I'm mistaken! Tell me that you would kill yourself if Paris
were to die! Tell me that you would even let yourself be disfigured
if it would keep him alive. Then the war will only be a scourge, not
an injustice.

HELEN.   You are being very difficult. I don't think my way of loving
is as bad as all that. Certainly I don't get upset and ill when Paris
leaves me to play bowls or go fishing for eels. But I do feel commanded by him, magnetically attracted. Magnetism is a kind of love,
as much as devotion. And it's an old and fruitful passion in its own
way, as desperate devotion and passionate weeping are in theirs.
I'm as content in this love as a star in a constellation. It's my own
centre of gravity; I shine there; it's the way I breathe, and the way
I take life in my arms. And it's easy to see what sons this love can
produce: tall, clear-cut boys, of great distinction, with fine fingers
and short noses. What will it all become if I fill it with jealousy,
with emotion, and anxiety? The world is nervous enough already:
look at yourself!

ANDROMACHE.   Fill it with pity, Helen. That's the only help the world
needs.

HELEN.   There we are; I knew it would come; the word has been said.

ANDROMACHE.   What word?

HELEN.   The word "pity." You must talk to someone else. I'm afraid
I'm not very good at pity.

ANDROMACHE.   Because you don't know unhappiness.

HELEN.   Maybe. It could also be that I think of unhappy people as
my equals, I accept them, and I don't think of my health and my
position and beauty as any better than their misery. It's a sense of
brotherhood I have.

ANDROMACHE.   You're blaspheming, Helen.

HELEN.   I am sure people pity others to the same extent that they
would pity themselves. Unhappiness and ugliness are mirrors they
can't bear to look into. I haven't any pity for myself. You will see,
if war breaks out. I'll put up with hunger and pain better than you
will. And insults, too. Do you think I don't hear what the Trojan
women say when I'm going past them? They treat me like a slut.
They say that the morning light shows me up for what they think
me. It may be true, or it may not be. It doesn't matter to me, one
way or the other.

ANDROMACHE.   Stop, Helen!

HELEN.   And of course I can see, in what your husband called the
coloured picture-book in my head, pictures of Helen grown old,
flabby, toothless, sitting hunched-up in the kitchen, sucking sweets.

I can see the white enamel I've plastered over my wrinkles, and the bright colours the sweets are, very clearly. But it leaves me completely indifferent.

ANDROMACHE. I am lost.

HELEN. Why? If you're content with one perfect couple to make the war acceptable, there is always you and Hector, Andromache.

(*Enter* AJAX, *then* HECTOR.)

AJAX. Where is he? Where's he hiding himself? A coward! A typical Trojan!

HECTOR. Who are you looking for?

AJAX. I'm looking for Paris.

HECTOR. I am his brother.

AJAX. Beautiful family! I am Ajax! What's your name?

HECTOR. My name's Hector.

AJAX. It ought to be pimp!

HECTOR. I see that Greece has sent over her diplomats. What do you want?

AJAX. War.

HECTOR. Not a hope. Why do you want it?

AJAX. Your brother carried off Helen.

HECTOR. I am told she was willing.

AJAX. A Greek woman can do what she likes. She doesn't have to ask permission from you. He carried her off. It's a reason for war.

HECTOR. We can offer our apologies.

AJAX. What's a Trojan apology? We're not leaving here without your declaration of war.

HECTOR. Declare it yourselves.

AJAX. All right, we will. As from this evening.

HECTOR. That's a lie. You won't declare war. There isn't an island in the archipelago that will back you if we aren't in any way responsible. And we don't intend to be.

AJAX. Will you declare it yourself, personally, if I call you a coward?

HECTOR. That is a name I accept.

AJAX. I've never known such unmilitary reaction! Suppose I tell you what the people of Greece thinks of Troy, that Troy is a cess-pit of vice and stupidity?

HECTOR. Troy is obstinate. You won't get your war.

AJAX. Suppose I spit on her?

HECTOR. Spit.

AJAX. Suppose I strike you, you, one of her princes?

HECTOR. Try it.

AJAX. Suppose I slap your face, you disgusting example of Troy's conceit and her spurious honour?

HECTOR. Strike.

AJAX (*striking him*). There. If this lady's your wife she must be proud of you.

HECTOR. I know her. She is proud.

(*Enter* DEMOKOS.)

DEMOKOS. What's all the noise about? What does this drunkard want, Hector?

HECTOR. He has got what he wants.

DEMOKOS. What is going on, Andromache?

ANDROMACHE. Nothing.

AJAX. Two times nothing. A Greek hits Hector, and Hector puts up with it.

DEMOKOS. Is this true, Hector?

HECTOR. Completely false, isn't it, Helen?

HELEN. The Greeks are great liars. Greek men, I mean.

AJAX. Is it natural for him to have one cheek redder than the other?

HECTOR. Yes. I am healthier on that side.

DEMOKOS. Tell the truth, Hector. Has he dared to raise his hand against you?

HECTOR. That is my concern.

DEMOKOS. It's the concern of war. You are the figurehead of Troy.

HECTOR. Exactly. No one is going to slap a figurehead.

DEMOKOS. Who are you, you brute? I am Demokos, second son of Achichaos!

AJAX. The second son of Achichaos? How do you do? Tell me: is it as serious to slap a second son of Achichaos as to strike Hector?

DEMOKOS. Quite as serious, you drunk. I am the head of the Senate. If you want war, war to the death, you have only to try.

AJAX. All right. I'll try. (*He slaps* DEMOKOS.)

DEMOKOS. Trojans! Soldiers! To the rescue!

HECTOR. Be quiet, Demokos!

DEMOKOS. To arms! Troy's been insulted! Vengeance!

HECTOR. Be quiet, I tell you.

DEMOKOS. I *will* shout! I'll rouse the city!

HECTOR. Be quiet! If you won't, I shall hit you, too!

DEMOKOS. Priam! Anchises! Come and see the shame of Troy burning on Hector's face!

(HECTOR *strikes* DEMOKOS. AJAX *laughs. During the scene,* PRIAM *and his lords group themselves ready to receive* ULYSSES.)

PRIAM. What are you shouting for, Demokos?

DEMOKOS. I have been struck.

AJAX. Go and complain to Achichaos!

PRIAM. Who struck you?

DEMOKOS.   Hector! Ajax! Ajax! Hector!

PARIS.   What is he talking about? He's mad!

HECTOR.   Nobody struck him, did they, Helen?

HELEN.   I was watching most carefully, and I didn't notice anything.

AJAX.   Both his cheeks are the same colour.

PARIS.   Poets often get upset for no reason. It's what they call their inspiration. We shall get a new national anthem out of it.

DEMOKOS.   You will pay for this, Hector.

VOICES.   Ulysses! Here is Ulysses!

(AJAX *goes amicably to* HECTOR.)

AJAX.   Well done. Plenty of pluck. Noble adversary. A beautiful hit.

HECTOR.   I did my best.

AJAX.   Excellent method, too. Straight elbow. The wrist on an angle. Safe position for the carpus and metacarpus. Your slap must be stronger than mine is.

HECTOR.   I doubt it.

AJAX.   You must be able to throw a javelin magnificently with this iron forearm and this shoulder-bone for a pivot.

HECTOR.   Eighty yards.

AJAX.   My deepest respect! My dear Hector, forgive me. I withdraw my threats, I take back my slap. We have enemies in common, in the sons of Achichaos. I won't fight with anybody who shares with me an enmity for the sons of Achichaos. Not another mention of war. I don't know what Ulysses has got in mind, but count on me to arrange the whole thing.

(*He goes towards* ULYSSES *and comes back with him.*)

ANDROMACHE.   I love you, Hector.

HECTOR (*showing his cheek*).   Yes; but don't kiss me just yet.

ANDROMACHE.   You have won this round, as well. Be confident.

HECTOR.   I win every round. But still with each victory the prize escapes me.

ULYSSES.   Priam and Hector?

PRIAM.   Yes. And behind us, Troy, and the suburbs of Troy, and the land of Troy, and the Hellespont.

ULYSSES.   I am Ulysses.

PRIAM.   This is Anchises.

ULYSSES.   There are many people here for a diplomatic conversation.

PRIAM.   And here is Helen.

ULYSSES.   Good morning, my queen.

HELEN.   I've grown younger here, Ulysses. I've become a princess again.

PRIAM.   We are ready to listen to you.

AJAX. Ulysses, you speak to Priam. I will speak to Hector.

ULYSSES. Priam, we have come to take Helen home again.

AJAX. You do understand, don't you, Hector? We can't have things happening like this.

ULYSSES. Greece and Menelaus cry out for vengeance.

AJAX. If deceived husbands can't cry out for vengeance, what can they do?

ULYSSES. Deliver Helen over to us within an hour. Otherwise it means war.

HECTOR. But if we give Helen back to you give us your assurance there will be peace.

AJAX. Utter tranquillity.

HECTOR. If she goes on board within an hour, the matter is closed.

AJAX. And all is forgotten.

HECTOR. I think there's no doubt we can come to an understanding, can we not, Helen?

HELEN. Yes, no doubt.

ULYSSES. You don't mean to say that Helen is being given back to us?

HECTOR. Exactly that. She is ready.

AJAX. What about her baggage? She is sure to have more to take back than when she came.

HECTOR. We return her to you, bag and baggage, and you guarantee peace. No reprisals, no vengeance!

AJAX. A woman is lost, a woman is found, and we're back where we were. Perfect! Isn't it, Ulysses?

ULYSSES. Just wait a moment. I guarantee nothing. Before we say there are going to be no reprisals we have to be sure there has been no cause for reprisals. We have to make sure that Menelaus will find Helen exactly as she was when she was taken from him.

HECTOR. How is he going to discover any difference?

ULYSSES. A husband is very perceptive when a world-wide scandal has put him on his guard. Paris will have had to have respected Helen. And if that isn't so . . .

CROWD. Oh, no! It isn't so!

ONE VOICE. Not exactly!

HECTOR. And if it is so?

ULYSSES. Where is this leading us, Hector?

HECTOR. Paris has not touched Helen. They have both taken me into their confidence.

ULYSSES. What is this absurd story?

HECTOR. The true story, isn't it, Helen?

HELEN. Why does it seem to you so extraordinary?

A VOICE. It's terrible! It puts us to shame!

HECTOR. Why do you have to smile, Ulysses? Do you see the slightest indication in Helen that she has failed in her duty?

ULYSSES. I'm not looking for one. Water leaves less mark on a duck's back than dishonour does on a woman.

PARIS. You're speaking to a queen.

ULYSSES. Present queens excepted, naturally. So, Paris, you have carried off this queen, carried her off naked; and I imagine that you didn't go into the water wearing all your armour; and yet you weren't seized by any taste or desire for her?

PARIS. A naked queen is dressed in her dignity.

HELEN. She has only to remember to keep it on.

ULYSSES. How long did the voyage last? I took three days with my ships, which are faster than yours.

VOICES. What are these intolerable insults to the Trojan navy?

A VOICE. Your winds are faster! Not your ships!

ULYSSES. Let us say three days, if you like. Where was the queen during those three days?

PARIS. Lying down on the deck.

ULYSSES. And Paris was where? In the crow's nest?

HELEN. Lying beside me.

ULYSSES. Was he reading as he lay beside you? Or fishing for goldfish?

HELEN. Sometimes he fanned me.

ULYSSES. Without ever touching you?

HELEN. One day, the second day, I think it was, he kissed my hand.

ULYSSES. Your hand! I see. An outbreak of the animal in him.

HELEN. I thought it was more dignified to take no notice.

ULYSSES. The rolling of the ship didn't throw you towards each other? I don't think it's an insult to the Trojan navy to suggest that its ships roll?

A VOICE. They roll much less than the Greek ships pitch!

AJAX. Pitch? Our Greek ships? If they seem to be pitching it's because of their high prows and their scooped-out sterns!

A VOICE. Oh, yes! The arrogant face and the flat behind, that's Greek all right.

ULYSSES. And what about the three nights you were sailing? The stars appeared and vanished again three times over the pair of you. Do you remember nothing of those three nights?

HELEN. I don't know. Oh, yes! I'd forgotten. I learnt a lot more about the stars.

ULYSSES. While you were asleep, perhaps, he might have taken you . . .

HELEN. A mosquito can wake me.

HECTOR. They will both swear to you, if you like, by our goddess Aphrodite.

ULYSSES. We can do without that. I know what Aphrodite is. Her favourite oath is a perjury.—It's a curious story you're telling me: and it will certainly destroy the idea that the rest of the Archipelago has always had of the Trojans.

PARIS. Why, what do they think of us in the Archipelago?

ULYSSES. You're thought of as less accomplished at trading than we are, but handsome and irresistible. Go on with your story, Paris. It's an interesting contribution to the study of human behaviour. What good reason could you have possibly had for respecting Helen when you had her at your mercy?

PARIS. I . . . I loved her.

HELEN. If you don't know what love is, Ulysses, I shouldn't venture on the subject.

ULYSSES. You must admit, Helen, you would never have followed him if you had known the Trojans were impotent.

VOICES. Shame! Muzzle him! Bring your women here, and you'll soon see! And your grandmother!

ULYSSES. I expressed myself badly. I meant that Paris, the handsome Paris, is impotent.

A VOICE. Why don't you say something, Paris? Are you going to make us the laughing-stock of the world?

PARIS. Hector, you can see, this is a most unpleasant situation for me!

HECTOR. You have to put up with it only a few minutes longer. Goodbye, Helen. And I hope your virtue will become as proverbial as your frailty might have done.

HELEN. That doesn't worry me. The centuries always give us the recognition we deserve.

ULYSSES. Paris the impotent, that's a very good surname! If you care to, Helen, you can kiss him for once.

PARIS. Hector!

FIRST TOPMAN. Are you going to tolerate this farce, commander?

HECTOR. Be quiet! I am in charge here!

TOPMAN. And a rotten job you make of it! We've stood quite enough. We'll tell you, we, Paris's own seamen, we'll tell you what he did with your queen!

VOICES. Bravo! Tell him!

TOPMAN. He's sacrificing himself on his brother's orders. I was an officer on board his ship. I saw everything.

HECTOR. You were quite wrong.

TOPMAN. Do you think a Trojan sailor doesn't know what he sees? I can tell the sex of a seagull thirty yards off. Come over here, Olpides. Olpides was up in the crow's nest. He saw everything from on top. I was standing on the stairs in the hatchway. My head was exactly on a level with them, like a cat on the end of a bed. Shall I tell him, Trojans?

HECTOR. Silence!

VOICES. Tell him! Go on and tell him!

TOPMAN. And they hadn't been on board more than two minutes, wasn't that true, Olpides?

OLPIDES. Only time enough for the queen to dry herself, being just come up out of the water, and to comb the parting into her hair again. I could see her parting, from her forehead over to the nape of her neck, from where I was.

TOPMAN. And he sent us all down into the hold, except the two of us who he couldn't see.

OLPIDES. And without a pilot, the ship drifted due north. There was no wind, and yet the sails were bellied out full.

TOPMAN. And when I looked out from where I was hiding, what I should have seen was the outline of one body, but what I did see was in the shape of two, like a wheaten loaf and rye bread, baking in the oven together.

OLPIDES. But from up where I was, I more often saw one body than two, but sometimes it was white, and sometimes it was golden brown.

TOPMAN. So much for impotence! And as for respectful, inexpressive love, and unspoken affection, you tell him, Olpides, what you heard from your ledge up there! Women's voices carry upwards, men's voices stay on the ground. I shall tell you what Paris said.

OLPIDES. She called him her ladybird, her little ewe-lamb.

TOPMAN. And he called her his lion, his panther. They reversed the sexes. Because they were being so affectionate. It's not unusual.

OLPIDES. And then she said: "You are my darling oak-tree, I put my arms round you as if you were an oak-tree." When you're at sea you think about trees, I suppose.

TOPMAN. And he called her his birch-tree: "My trembling silver birch-tree!" I remember the word birch-tree very well. It's a Russian tree.

OLPIDES. And I had to stay up in the crow's nest all night. You don't half get thirsty up there, and hungry, and everything else.

TOPMAN. And when at last they got up from the deck to go to bed they swayed on their feet. And that's how your wife Penelope would have got on with Trojan impotence.

VOICES. Bravo! Bravo!

A WOMAN'S VOICE. All praise to Paris.

A JOVIAL MAN. Render to Paris what belongs to Paris!

HECTOR. This is a pack of lies, isn't it, Helen?

ULYSSES. Helen is listening enraptured.

HELEN. I forgot they were talking about me. They sound so wonderfully convincing.

ULYSSES. Do you dare to say they are lying, Paris?

PARIS. In some of the particulars, yes, I think they are.

TOPMAN. We're not lying, either in the general or the particular. Are we, Olpides? Do you deny the expressions of love you used? Do you deny the word panther?

PARIS. Not especially the word panther.

TOPMAN. Well, birch-tree, then? I see. It's the phrase "trembling silver birch-tree" that embarrasses you. Well, like it or not, you used it. I swear you used it, and anyway what is there to blush about in the word "birch-tree"? I have seen these silver birch-trees trembling against the snow in winter-time, by the shores of the Caspian, with their rings of black bark apparently separated by rings of space, so that you wondered what was carrying the branches. And I've seen them at the height of summer, beside the canal at Astrakhan, with their white rings like fresh mushrooms. And the leaves talked and made signs to me. To see them quivering, gold above and silver underneath, it makes your heart melt! I could have wept like a woman, isn't that true, Olpides? That's how I feel about the birch-tree.

CROWD. Bravo! Bravo!

ANOTHER SAILOR. And it wasn't only the topman and Olpides who saw them, Priam. The entire crew came wriggling up through the hatches and peering under the handrails. The whole ship was one great spy-glass.

THIRD SAILOR. Spying out love.

ULYSSES. There you have it, Hector!

HECTOR. Be quiet, the lot of you.

TOPMAN. Well, keep this quiet, if you can!

(IRIS *appears in the sky.*)

PEOPLE. Iris! Iris!

PARIS. Has Aphrodite sent you?

IRIS. Yes, Aphrodite sent me, and told me that I should say to you that love is the world's chief law. Whatever strengthens love becomes in itself sacred, even falsehood, avarice, or luxury. She takes all lovers under her protection, from the king to the goat-herd. And she forbids both of you, Hector and Ulysses, to separate Paris from Helen. Or else there will be war.

PARIS AND THE OLD MEN.   Thank you, Iris.

HECTOR.   Is there any message from Pallas Athene?

IRIS.   Yes; Pallas Athene told me that I should say to you that reason is the chief law of the world. All who are lovers, she wishes me to say, are out of their minds. She would like you to tell her quite frankly what is more ridiculous than the mating of cocks with hens or flies with flies. And she orders both of you, Hector and Ulysses, to separate Helen from this Paris of the curly hair. Or else there will be war.

HECTOR AND THE WOMEN.   Thank you, Iris!

PRIAM.   Oh, my son, it isn't Aphrodite nor Pallas Athene who rules the world. What is it Zeus commands us to do in this time of uncertainty?

IRIS.   Zeus, the master of the gods, told me that I should say to you that those who see in the world nothing but love are as foolish as those who cannot see it at all. It is wise, Zeus, master of the gods informs you, it is wise sometimes to make love, and at other times not to make love. The decision he gives to Hector and Ulysses, is to separate Helen and Paris without separating them. He orders all the rest of you to go away and leave the negotiators to face each other. And let them so arrange matters that there will be no war. Or else—he swears to you: he swears there will be war. (*Exit.*)

HECTOR.   At your service, Ulysses!

ULYSSES.   At your service.

> (*All withdraw.*)

> (*A great rainbow is seen in the sky.*)

HELEN.   How very like Iris to leave her scarf behind.

HECTOR.   Now we come to the real tussle, Ulysses.

ULYSSES.   Yes: out of which either war or peace is going to come.

HECTOR.   Will war come of it?

ULYSSES.   We shall know in five minutes time.

HECTOR.   If it's to be a battle of words, my chances are small.

ULYSSES.   I believe it will be more a battle of weight. It's as though we were one on each side of a pair of scales. How we weigh in the balance will be what counts in the end.

HECTOR.   How we weigh in the balance? And what is my weight, Ulysses? My weight is a young man, a young woman, an unborn child. Joy of life, belief in life, a response to whatever's natural and good.

ULYSSES.   And my weight is the mature man, the wife thirty-five years old, the son whose height I measure each month with notches against the doorpost of the palace. My weight is the pleasures of living, and a mistrust of life.

HECTOR. Hunting, courage, loyalty, love.

ULYSSES. Circumspection in the presence of the gods, of men, and everything else.

HECTOR. The Phrygian oak-tree, all the leafy, thick-set oak-trees that grow on our hills with our curly-coated oxen.

ULYSSES. The power and wisdom of the olive-tree.

HECTOR. I weigh the hawk, I look straight into the sun.

ULYSSES. I weigh the owl.

HECTOR. I weigh the whole race of humble peasants, hard-working craftsmen, thousands of ploughs and looms, forges and anvils . . . Why is it, when I put all these in the scale in front of you, all at once they seem to me to weigh so light?

ULYSSES. I am the weight of this incorruptible, unpitying air of these coasts and islands.

HECTOR. Why go on? The scales have tipped.

ULYSSES. To my side? Yes, I think so.

HECTOR. And you want war?

ULYSSES. I don't want it. But I'm less sure whether war may not want us.

HECTOR. Our peoples have brought us together to prevent it. Our meeting itself shows that there is still some hope.

ULYSSES. You are young, Hector! It's usual on the eve of every war, for the two leaders of the peoples concerned to meet privately at some innocent village, on a terrace in a garden overlooking a lake. And they decide together that war is the world's worst scourge, and as they watch the rippling reflections in the water, with magnolia petals dropping on to their shoulders, they are both of them peace-loving, modest and friendly. They study one another. They look into each other's eyes. And, warmed by the sun and mellowed by the claret, they can't find anything in the other man's face to justify hatred, nothing, indeed, which doesn't inspire human affection, nothing incompatible in their languages any more, or in their particular way of scratching the nose or drinking wine. They really are exuding peace, and the world's desire for peace. And when their meeting is over, they shake hands in a most sincere brotherly fashion, and turn to smile and wave as they drive away. And the next day war breaks out. And so it is with us both at this moment. Our peoples, who have drawn aside, saying nothing while we have this interview, are not expecting us to win a victory over the inevitable. They have merely given us full powers, isolated here together, to stand above the catastrophe and taste the essential brotherhood of enemies. Taste it. It's a rare dish. Savour it. But that is all. One of the privileges of the great is to witness catastrophes from a terrace.

HECTOR. Do you think this is a conversation between enemies we are having?

ULYSSES. I should say a duet before the full orchestra. Because we have been created sensible and courteous, we can talk to each other, an hour or so before the war, in the way we shall talk to each other long after it's over, like old antagonists. We are merely having our reconciliation before the struggle instead of after it. That may be unwise. If one day one of us should have to kill the other, it might be as well if it wasn't a friend's face we recognized as the body dropped to the ground. But, as the universe well knows, we are going to fight each other.

HECTOR. The universe might be mistaken. One way to recognize error is the fact that it's universal.

ULYSSES. Let's hope so. But when destiny has brought up two nations, as for years it has brought up yours and mine, to a future of similar invention and authority, and given to each a different scale of values (as you and I saw just now, when we weighed pleasure against pleasure, conscience against conscience, even nature itself against nature): when the nation's architects and poets and painters have created for them opposing kingdoms of sound, and form, and subtlety, when we have a Trojan tile roof, a Theban arch, Phrygian red, Greek blue: the universe knows that destiny wasn't preparing alternative ways for civilization to flower. It was contriving the dance of death, letting loose the brutality and human folly which is all that the gods are really contented by. It's a mean way to contrive things, I agree. But we are Heads of State, you and I; we can say this between ourselves: it is Destiny's way of contriving things, inevitably.

HECTOR. And this time it has chosen to match Greece with Troy?

ULYSSES. This morning I was still in doubt. As soon as I stepped on to your landing stage I was certain of it.

HECTOR. You mean you felt yourself on enemy soil?

ULYSSES. Why will you always harp on the word enemy? Born enemies don't fight. Nations you would say were designed to go to war against each other—by their skins, their language, their smell: always jealous of each other, always hating each other—they're not the ones who fight. You will find the real antagonists in nations fate has groomed and made ready for the same war.

HECTOR. And you think we have been made ready for the Greek war?

ULYSSES. To an astonishing extent. Just as nature, when she foresees a struggle between two kinds of insects, equips them with weaknesses and weapons which correspond, so we, living well apart, unknown to ourselves, not even suspecting it, have both been gradually raised up to the level where war begins. All our weapons and habits correspond with each other and balance against each other like the beams of a gable. No other women in the world excite less brutality in us, or less desire, than your wives and daughters do; they give us a joy and an anguish of heart which is a sure sign of impending war between us. Doom has transfigured everything here with the colour of storm: your grave buildings shaking with shadow and fire, the neighing horses, figures disappearing into the dark of a colonnade: the future has never impressed me before with such startling clarity. There is nothing to be done. You're already living in the light of the Greek war.

HECTOR. And do the rest of the Greeks think this?

ULYSSES. What they think is no more reassuring. The rest of the Greeks think Troy is wealthy, her warehouses bulging, her soil prolific. They think that they, on the other hand, are living cramped on a rock. And your golden temples and golden wheatfields flashed from your promontories a signal our ships will never forget. It isn't very wise to have such golden gods and vegetables.

HECTOR. This is more like the truth, at last. Greece has chosen Troy for her prey. Then why a declaration of war? It would have been simpler to have taken Troy by surprise when I was away with the army. You would have had her without striking a blow.

ULYSSES. There's a kind of permission for war which can be given only by the world's mood and atmosphere, the feel of its pulse. It would have been madness to undertake a war without that permission. We didn't have it.

HECTOR. But you have it now.

ULYSSES. I think we do.

HECTOR. But why against us? Troy is famous for her arts, her justice, her humanity.

ULYSSES. A nation doesn't put itself at odds with its destiny by its crimes, but by its faults. Its army may be strong, its treasury well filled, its poets at the height of inspiration. But one day, why it is no one knows, because of some simple event, such as the citizens wantonly cutting down the trees, or their prince wickedly making off with a woman, or the children getting out of hand, the nation is suddenly lost. Nations, like men, die by imperceptible disorders. We recognize a doomed people by the way they sneeze or pare their nails. There's no doubt you carried off Helen badly.

HECTOR.   What fairness of proportion can you see between the rape of one woman, and the possible destruction of a whole people, yours or mine, in war?

ULYSSES.   We are speaking of Helen. You and Paris have made a great mistake about Helen. I've known her fifteen years, and watched her carefully. There's no doubt about it: she is one of the rare creatures destiny puts on the earth for its own personal use. They're apparently quite unimportant. It might be not even a person, but a small town, or a village: a little queen, or a child; but if you lay hands on them, watch out! It's very hard to know how to recognize one of these hostages of fate among all the other people and places. You haven't recognized it. You could have laid hands with impunity on our great admirals or one of our kings. Paris could have let himself go with perfect safety in a Spartan bed, or a Theban bed, with generous returns twenty times over; but he chose the shallowest brain, the hardest heart, the narrowest understanding of sex. And so you are lost.

HECTOR.   We are giving Helen back to you.

ULYSSES.   The insult to destiny can't be taken back.

HECTOR.   What are we discussing, then? I'm beginning to see what is really behind your words. Admit it. You want our wealth! You had Helen carried off to give you an honourable pretext for war! I blush for Greece. She will be responsible and ashamed for the rest of time.

ULYSSES.   Responsible and ashamed? Do you think so? The two words hardly agree. Even if we believed we were responsible for the war, all our generation would have to do would be to deny it, and lie, to appease the conscience of future generations. And we shall lie. We'll make that sacrifice.

HECTOR.   Ah, well, the die is cast, Ulysses. On with the war! The more I hate it, the more I find growing in me an irresistible need to kill. If you won't help me, it were better you should leave here.

ULYSSES.   Understand me, Hector; you have my help. Don't ask me to interpret fate. All I have tried to do is to read the world's hand, in the great lines of desert caravans, the wake of ships, and the track of migrant birds and wandering peoples. Give me your hand. There are lines there, too. We won't search to see if their lesson tells the same story. We'll suppose that these three little lines at the base of Hector's hand contradict the waves, the wings, and the furrows. I am inquisitive by nature, and not easily frightened. I'm quite willing to join issue with fate. I accept your offer of Helen. I will take her back to Menelaus. I've more than enough eloquence to convince a husband of his wife's virtue. I will even persuade

Helen to believe it herself. And I'll leave at once, to avoid any chance of disturbance. Once back on my ship perhaps we can take the risk of running war on to the rocks.

HECTOR. Is this part of Ulysses' cunning, or his greatness?

ULYSSES. In this particular instance, I'm using my cunning against destiny, not against you. It's my first attempt, so I deserve some credit for it. I am sincere, Hector. If I wanted war, I should have asked for a ransom more precious to you than Helen. I am going now. But I can't shake off the feeling that the road from here to my ship is a long way.

HECTOR. My guard will escort you.

ULYSSES. As long as the road of a visiting king, when he knows there has been a threat against his life. Where are the assassins hiding? We're lucky if it's not in the heavens themselves. And the distance from here to the corner of the Palace is a long way. A long way, taking this first step. Where is it going to carry me among all these perils? Am I going to slip and kill myself? Will part of the cornice fall down on me? It's all new stonework here; at any moment a stone may be dislodged. But courage. Let us go. (*He takes a first step.*)

HECTOR. Thank you, Ulysses.

ULYSSES. The first step is safely over. How many more?

HECTOR. Four hundred and sixty.

ULYSSES. Now the second! You know what made me decide to go, Hector?

HECTOR. Yes. Your noble nature.

ULYSSES. Not precisely. Andromache's eyelashes dance as my wife Penelope's do.

(*Enter* ANDROMACHE *and* CASSANDRA.)

HECTOR. Were you there all the time, Andromache?

ANDROMACHE. Let me take your arm. I've no more strength.

HECTOR. Did you hear what we said?

ANDROMACHE. Yes. I am broken.

HECTOR. You see, we needn't despair.

ANDROMACHE. We needn't despair for ourselves, perhaps. But for the world, yes. That man is terrible. All the unhappiness of the world is in me.

HECTOR. A moment or two more, and Ulysses will be on board. You see how fast he is travelling. You can follow his progress from here. There he is, on a level with the fountains. What are you doing?

ANDROMACHE. I haven't the strength any longer to hear any more. I am covering up my ears. I won't take my hands away until we know what our fate is to be.

HECTOR. Find Helen, Cassandra!

(AJAX *enters, more drunk than ever. He sees* ANDROMACHE. *Her back is towards him.*)

CASSANDRA. Ulysses is waiting for you down at the harbour, Ajax. Helen will be brought to you there.

AJAX. Helen! To hell with Helen! This is the one I want to get my arms around.

CASSANDRA. Go away, Ajax. That is Hector's wife.

AJAX. Hector's wife! Bravo! I've always liked my friends' wives, my best friends' wives!

CASSANDRA. Ulysses is already half-way there. Hurry.

AJAX. Don't worry, my dear. She's got her hands over her ears. I can say what I like, she can't hear me. If I touched her, now, if I kissed her, certainly! But words she can't hear, what's the matter with that?

CASSANDRA. Everything is the matter with that. Go away, Ajax!

(*While* CASSANDRA *tries to force* AJAX *away from* ANDROMACHE, HECTOR *slowly raises his javelin.*)

AJAX. Do you think so? Then I might as well touch her. Might as well kiss her. But chastely, always chastely, with your best friends' wives! What's the most chaste part of your wife, Hector, her neck? So much for her neck. Her ear has a pretty little look of chastity to me. So much for her ear. I'll tell you what I've always found the chastest thing about a woman . . . Let me alone, now; let me alone! She can't even hear when I kiss her . . . You're so cursed strong! All right, I'm going, I said I was going. Goodbye.

(*He goes.*)

(HECTOR *imperceptibly lowers his javelin. At this moment* DE-MOKOS *bursts in.*)

DEMOKOS. What's this cowardice? You're giving Helen back? Trojans, to arms! They've betrayed us. Fall in! And your war-song is ready! Listen to your war-song!

HECTOR (*striking him*). Have that for your war-song!

DEMOKOS (*falling*). He has killed me!

HECTOR. The war isn't going to happen, Andromache!

(*He tries to take* ANDROMACHE'S *hands from her ears: she resists, her eyes fixed on* DEMOKOS. *The curtain which had begun to fall is lifted little by little.*)

ABNEOS. They have killed Demokos! Who killed Demokos?

DEMOKOS. Who killed me? Ajax! Ajax! Kill him!

ABNEOS. Kill Ajax!

HECTOR. He's lying. I am the man who struck him.

DEMOKOS. No. It was Ajax.

ABNEOS. Ajax has killed Demokos. Catch him! Punish him!

HECTOR. I struck you, Demokos, admit it! Admit it, or I'll put an end to you!

DEMOKOS. No, my dear Hector, my good dear Hector. It was Ajax. Kill Ajax!

CASSANDRA. He is dying, just as he lived, croaking like a frog.

ABNEOS. There. They have taken Ajax. There. They have killed him!

HECTOR (*drawing* ANDROMACHE'S *hands away from her ears*). The war will happen.

(*The Gates of War slowly open, to show* HELEN *kissing* TROILUS.)

CASSANDRA. The Trojan poet is dead. And now the Grecian poet will have his word.

The curtain finally falls

APPENDIX

In the stage version at the Apollo Theatre [in London, where this play was first presented in 1955], the following passage was substituted for the dialogue between CASSANDRA, HELEN and PEACE on pages 526–27.

HELEN. Cassandra, you can see what I can see. You could have helped him to understand me.

CASSANDRA. He understands you only too clearly. And, besides, I see nothing; I never have seen anything, coloured or not. But I can feel the weight of every person who comes towards me. I know what is in store for them by the sensation of suffering which flows into my veins.

HELEN. In fact, you feel what I can see.

CASSANDRA. What I feel in Hector is a suffering too deep to be suffered. He may yet break the reflection in your mirror, Helen. He may have hands great enough to strangle the tiger as it springs.

HELEN. Do you suppose so?

CASSANDRA. There is always something more than one supposes.

Translated by Christopher Fry

My Kinsman, Major Molineux

CHARACTERS

ROBIN	PROSTITUTE
BOY, *his brother*	MAN WITH MASK
FERRYMAN	MAN IN PERIWIG
TWO BRITISH REDCOATS	SECOND BARBER
FIRST BARBER	WATCHMAN
TAVERN KEEPER	MAJOR MOLINEUX
CLERGYMAN	CITIZENS OF BOSTON

THE SCENE

Boston, just before the American Revolution.
To the left of the stage, ROBIN, *a young man barely eighteen, in a coarse gray coat, well-worn but carefully repaired, leather breeches, blue yarn stockings, and a worn three-cornered hat. He carries a heavy oak-sapling cudgel and has a wallet slung over his shoulder. Beside him, his brother, a* BOY *of ten or twelve, dressed in the same respectable but somewhat rustic manner. On the far left of the stage, the triangular prow of a dory; beside it, a huge* FERRYMAN *holding an upright oar. He has a white curling beard. His dress, although eighteenth century, half suggests that he is Charon. Lined across the stage and in the style of a primitive New England sampler, are dimly seen five miniature houses: a barber shop, a tavern, a white church, a shabby brick house with a glass bay window, and a pillared mansion, an official's house, on its cornice the golden lion and unicorn of England. The houses are miniature, but their doors are man-size. Only* ROBIN, *his* BROTHER, *and the* FERRYMAN *are lit up.*

ROBIN

    Here's my last crown, your double price
    for ferrying us across the marsh
    at this ungodly hour.

FERRYMAN

A crown!
Do you want me to lose my soul?
Do you see King George's face
judging us on this silver coin?
I have no price.

ROBIN

You asked for double.

FERRYMAN

I'll take the crown for your return trip.
(*Takes the coin*)
No one returns.

ROBIN

No one?

FERRYMAN

No one.
Legs go round in circles here.
This is the city of the dead.

ROBIN

What's that?

FERRYMAN

I said this city's Boston,
No one begs here. Are you deaf?
(*The little houses on stage light up, then dim out.*)

ROBIN

(*To the* FERRYMAN)
Show me my kinsman's mansion. You
must know him—Major Molineux,
the most important man in town.

FERRYMAN

The name's familiar . . . Molineux . . .
Wasn't he mixed up with the French?
He's never at home now. If you'll wait
here, you'll meet him on his rounds.
All our important people drift
sooner or later to my ferry landing,
and stand here begging for the moon.
You'll see your cousin. You're well-placed.

ROBIN

I know it. My kinsman's a big man here.
He told me he would make my fortune;
I'll be a partner in his firm,
either here or in London.

FERRYMAN

     Settle
for London, that's your city, Boy.
Majors are still sterling silver across
the waters. All the English-born
suddenly seem in love with London.
Your cousin's house here is up for sale.

ROBIN

He cares for England. *Rule Britannia,*
that's the tune he taught me. I'm
surprised he's leaving.

FERRYMAN

    He's surprised!
He seemed to belong here once. He wished
to teach us *Rule Britannia,* but
we couldn't get it through our heads.
He gave us this to keep us singing.
   (*The* FERRYMAN *holds up a boiled lobster.*)

ROBIN

You're joking, it's a lobster.

FERRYMAN

    No.
Look, it's horny, boiled and red,
It is the Major's spitting image.
   (*On the other side of the stage,* TWO BRITISH REDCOATS
   are seen marching slowly in step with shouldered mus-
   kets. Rule Britannia *played faintly*)

FERRYMAN

   (*Pointing to* SOLDIERS)
Here are the Major's chicken lobsters.

ROBIN

Our soldiers!

FERRYMAN

   We call them lobsterbacks.
They are the Major's privates. Wherever
they are gathered together, he is present.
You'll feel his grip behind their claws.
What are you going to do now:
run home to Deerfield, take a ship
for England, Boy, or chase the soldiers?

ROBIN

Why, I'm staying here. I like

soldiers. They make me feel at home.
They kept the Frenchmen out of Deerfield.
They'll tell me where my kinsman lives.

FERRYMAN

The French are finished. The British
are the only Frenchmen left.
Didn't you say your cousin's name
was Molineux?

ROBIN

He's Norman Irish.
Why are you leaving?

FERRYMAN

Money. The soldiers
make me pay them for the pleasure
of shuttling them across the marsh.
Run, Boy, and catch those soldiers' scarlet
coat-tails, while they're still around.
(*The* FERRYMAN *goes off pushing his boat.*)
(ROBIN *and the* BOY *advance towards the* SOLDIERS.)

ROBIN

I need your help, Sirs.

FIRST SOLDIER

(*Smiling*)
We are here
for service, that's our unpleasant duty.

ROBIN

I liked the way
the soldiers smiled. I wonder how
anyone could distrust a soldier.

BOY

We've lost our guide.

ROBIN

We'll find another.

BOY

Why did that boatman gnash his teeth
at Cousin Major?

ROBIN

He was cold.
That's how big city people talk.
Let's walk. We're here to see the city.
(*As* ROBIN *and the* BOY *start moving, the miniature
houses light up one by one and then go dark. A* BARBER

comes out of the barber shop; he holds a razor, and a
bowl of suds. A TAVERN KEEPER *enters holding a news-*
paper.)

BARBER

(Cutting away the suds with his razor)
That's how we shave a wig.

TAVERN KEEPER

You mean
a Tory.

BARBER

Shave them to the bone!

TAVERN KEEPER

(Pointing to newspaper)
Here's the last picture of King George;
He's passed another tax on tea.

BARBER

Health to the King, health to the King!
Here's rum to drown him in the tea!
(Drenches the newspaper with his mug)
(A CLERGYMAN, *white-wigged, all in black, comes out of
the church.*)

CLERGYMAN

What an ungodly hour! The city's
boiling. All's rum and revolution.
We have an everlasting city,
but here in this unsteady brightness,
nothing's clear, unless the Lord
enlighten us and show the winner!
(A PROSTITUTE *comes out of the bay-window house.
She wears a red skirt and a low, full-bosomed white
blouse.*)

PROSTITUTE

Here in the shadow of the church,
I save whatever God despises—
Whig or Tory, saint or sinner,
I'm their refuge from the church.
(The pillared mansion lights up. A MAN *comes out in
a blue coat and white trousers like General Washington's. He wears a grayish mask covered with pocks. His
forehead juts out and divides in a double bulge. His
nose is a yellow eagle's beak. His eyes flash like fire in a
cave. He looks at himself in a mirror.*)

MAN WITH MASK

> My mind's on fire. This fire will burn
> the pocks and paleness from my face.
> Freedom has given me this palace.
> I'll go and mingle with the mob.
>> (*Now the houses are dark.* ROBIN *rubs his eyes in a daze, stares into the darkness, then turns to his* BROTHER.)

BOY

> Who are these people, Brother Robin?
> We're in the dark and far from Deerfield.

ROBIN

> We're in the city, little brother.
> Things will go smoother when we find
> our kinsman, Major Molineux.

BOY

> Our kinsman isn't like these people.
> He is a loyal gentleman.

ROBIN

> We'll see. He swore he'd make my fortune,
> and teach you Latin.

BOY

>> I want something.

ROBIN

> Let's see the city.

BOY

>> I want a flintlock.
>> (*A* MAN *enters from the right. He wears a full gray periwig, a wide-skirted coat of dark cloth and silk stockings rolled up above the knees. He carries a polished cane which he digs angrily into the ground at every step. "Hem, hem," he says in a sepulchral voice as he walks over to the barber shop. The* TWO BARBERS *appear,* ONE *with a razor, the* OTHER *with a bowl of suds.*)

MAN IN PERIWIG

> Hem! Hem!

ROBIN

>> Good evening, honored sir.
> Help us. We come from out of town.

MAN IN PERIWIG

> A good face and a better shoulder!
> Hem, hem! I see you're not from Boston.
> We need good stock in Boston. You're lucky!

meeting me here was providential.
I'm on the side of youth. Hem, hem!
I'll be your guiding lamp in Boston.
Where do you come from?

ROBIN

Deerfield.

MAN IN PERIWIG

Deerfield!
Our bulwark from the savages!
Our martyred village! He's from Deerfield,
Barber. We can use his muscle.

BARBER

You can feel it.

MAN IN PERIWIG

(*Seeing the* BOY)
Look, a child!

BARBER

Shall I shave him?

MAN IN PERIWIG

Yes, shave him.
Shave him and teach him to beat a drum.

BOY

I want a flintlock.

MAN IN PERIWIG

A gun! You scare me!
Come on Apollo, we must march.
We'll put that shoulder to the wheel.
Come, I'll be your host in Boston.

ROBIN

I have connections here, a kinsman . . .

MAN IN PERIWIG

Of course you have connections here.
They will latch on to you like fleas.
This is your town! Boy! With that leg
you will find kinsmen on the moon.

ROBIN

My kinsman's Major Molineux.

MAN IN PERIWIG

Your kinsman's Major Molineux!
Let go my coat cuff, Fellow. I have
authority, authority!
Hem! Hem! Respect your betters. Your leg
will be acquainted with the stocks

by peep of day! You fellows help me!
Barber, this man's molesting me!

FIRST BARBER

(*Closing in*)
Don't hit His Honor, Boy!

SECOND BARBER

His Honor
is a lover of mankind!

BOY

Brain him with your cudgel, Robin!

ROBIN

Come, Brother, we will see the city;
they're too many of them and one has a razor.
(ROBIN *and the* BOY *back off. Barber shop goes dark.*)

BOY

Who was that fellow, Brother Robin?

ROBIN

He is some snotty, county clerk,
chipping and chirping at his betters.
He isn't worth the Major's spit.

BOY

You should have brained him with your stick.

ROBIN

Let's go, now. We must see the city
and try to find our kinsman's house.
I am beginning to think he's out
of town. Look, these men will help us.
(*The tavern lights up. A sign with King George III's
head hangs in front. There's a poster nailed to the
door. The* MAN WITH THE MASK *strolls over and sits
in the chair.*)

CROWD

Health to the Rattlesnake.[1] A health
to Colonel Greenough! He's our man!

MAN WITH MASK

A shine, men, you must shine my shoes
so bright King George will see his face
flash like a guinea on the toe.

CROWD

Health to the Rattlesnake!

---

[1] In the early days of the American revolutionary struggle the rattlesnake with
thirteen rattles, usually accompanied by the inscription "Don't Tread on Me,"
was a not uncommon flag design.

TAVERN KEEPER

    (*Turning to* ROBIN)
      You boys
are from the country, I presume.
I envy you, you're seeing Boston
for the first time. Fine town, there's lots
to hold you, English monuments,
docks, houses, and a fleet of tea-ships
begging for buyers. I trust you'll stay;
nobody ever leaves this city.

ROBIN

We come from Deerfield.

TAVERN KEEPER

      Then you'll stay;
no Indians scalp us in our beds;
our only scalper is this man here.
    (*General laughter*)

ROBIN

Our massacre was eighty years
ago. We're not frontiersmen now,
we've other things to talk about.

BARBER

He has other things to talk about.
This boy's a gentleman. He is
no redskin in a coonskin cap.

ROBIN

I'm on our village council. I've
read Plutarch.[2]

TAVERN KEEPER

      You are an ancient Roman.
You'll find you like our commonwealth.
I crave the honor of your custom.[3]
I've whiskey, gin and rum and beer,
and a spruce beer for your brother.

BOY

I want a real beer.

BARBER

      Give them beer.
    (*Shouting*)

TAVERN KEEPER

Two real beers for the Deerfield boys,
they have the fighting Deerfield spirit.

[2] Greek biographer (A.D. 46?–120?).   [3] "I would be honored to serve you."

ROBIN

I'm sure you'll trust me for your money.
I have connections here in Boston,
my kinsman's Major Molineux.
I spent our money on this journey.

MAN

His kinsman's Major Molineux;
sometimes a boy is short of money!
(*Laughter*)

MAN

(*Bringing out a silver Liberty Bowl*)
I've something stronger than beer.
Here is the Bowl of Liberty.
The Major dropped this lobster in
the bowl. It spikes the drink.
(MAN *puts down his mug and lifts a lobster out of bowl.*)
(*Cheers*)

ROBIN

I know
the lobster is a British soldier.

MAN

Yes, there they are.
(*The* TWO REDCOATS *march on stage as before. Silence.
The* MAN WITH THE MASK *starts writing on a bench.
The* SOLDIERS *saunter over to him.*)

FIRST SOLDIER

What are you writing, Colonel Greenough?

MAN WITH MASK

My will.

FIRST SOLDIER

Things aren't that desperate.

MAN WITH MASK

I'm adding up my taxes, Redcoat.
Just counting up the figures kills me.
My bankers say I'm burning money.
I can't afford your bed and board
and livery, Soldiers. We'll have to part.

SECOND SOLDIER

I've had enough. We ought to throw
them all in jail.

FIRST SOLDIER

Go easy.

ROBIN

> (*Walking shyly up to* SOLDIERS)
> > Sir,
> I need your guidance, I'm looking for
> my kinsman, Major Molineux.

FIRST SOLDIER

> Watch your words!

SECOND SOLDIER

> > Damn your insolence!

FIRST SOLDIER

> We'll haul you to the Major's court.
> > (*Shots and screams off stage.* SOLDIERS *leave on the run.*)

MAN

> > (*Pointing to* ROBIN)
> He's one of us.

SECOND MAN

> > He is a spy.

CROWD

> Both boys are spies or Tories.

TAVERN KEEPER

> > (*Drawing* ROBIN *over to the poster*)
> > Look,
> do you see this poster? It says,
> "Indentured servant, Jonah Mudge:
> ran from his master's house, blue vest,
> oak cudgel, leather pants, small brother,
> and his master's third best hat.
> Pound sterling's offered any man
> who nabs and lodges him in jail."
> Trudge off, Young Man, you'd better trudge!

CROWD

> Trudge, Jonah Mudge, you'd better trudge!

BOY

> They're drunk. You'd better hit them, Robin.

ROBIN

> They'd only break my stick and brains.

BOY

> For God's sake stand and be a man!

ROBIN

> No, they're too many, little brother.
> Come, I feel like walking.
> We haven't seen the city yet.
> > (*Lights go off.* ROBIN *and* BOY *stand alone.*)

BOY

We haven't seen our kinsman, Robin.
I can't see anything.

ROBIN

You'd think
the Major's name would stand us for
a beer. It's a funny thing, Brother, naming
our kinsman, Major Molineux,
sets all these people screaming murder.
Even the soldiers.

> (*The house with the bay-window lights up. A* WOMAN'S
> *red skirt and bare shoulders are clearly visible through
> the window. She is singing.*)

WOMAN

Soldiers, sailors.
Whig and Tories, saints and sinners,
I'm your refuge from despair.

ROBIN

(*Knocks*)
Sweet, pretty mistress, help me. I
am tired and lost. I'm looking for
my kinsman, Major Molineux.
You have bright eyes.

WOMAN

I know your kinsman.
Everybody is my kinsman here.

ROBIN

Yes, I am sure. You have kind eyes.
My kinsman is a blood relation.

WOMAN

You're my blood relation too then.
What a fine back and leg you have!
You're made right.

ROBIN

Oh, I will be made
when I find my kinsman. You
must know him, he's a man of some
importance in your city, Lady.

WOMAN

The Major dwells here.

ROBIN

You're thinking of some other major,
Lady; mine is something more

important than a major, he's
a sort of royal governor,
and a man of fortune. Molineux
tea ships sail from here to China.
He has a gilded carriage, twenty
serving men, two flags of England
flying from his lawn. You could hide
your little house behind a sofa
in his drawing-room.

WOMAN

        I know,
your kinsman is a man of parts,
that's why he likes to camp here. Sometimes
his greatness wearies him. These days
even kings draw in their horns,
and mingle with the common people.
Listen, you'll hear him snoring by
the roof.

ROBIN

        I hear a hollow sound.
My kinsman must be happy here.
I envy him this hideaway.

WOMAN

You mean to say you envy him
the mistress of his house. Don't worry,
a kinsman of the Major's is
my kinsman. I knew you right away.
You have your kinsman's leg and shoulders.
He wears an old three-cornered hat
and leather small-clothes here in the rain.
Why, you *are* the good old gentleman,
only you're young! What is this cloth?
You've good material on your leg.
      (*The* WOMAN *feels the cloth of* ROBIN'S *trousers.*)

ROBIN

It's deerskin. I'm from Deerfield, Lady.

WOMAN

You must be starved. I'll make you happy.

ROBIN

I'll wait here on your doorstep, Lady.
Run up and tell the Major that
his Deerfield cousins are in town.

WOMAN

> The Major'd kill me, if I woke him.
> You see, he spilled a little too much
> rum in his tea.

ROBIN

> I'll leave a note then. I must go,
> my little brother needs some sleep.
>> (WOMAN *takes* ROBIN'S *hat and twirls it on her finger.*)
> What are you doing with my hat?

WOMAN

> I'm showing you our Boston rites
> of hospitality. The Major
> would kill me, if I turned you out
> on such a night. I even have
> a downstairs bedroom for your brother.
> I find a playroom comes in handy.

BOY

> I want to go with Robin.

WOMAN

>> Oh, dear,
> children keep getting me in trouble.
> We have a law.
>> (*A bell is heard off stage.*)
>>> Mother of God!
>> (*The* WOMAN *ducks into her house.*)
>> (*Her light goes out.*)

BOY

> Why did the lady slam her door?

ROBIN

> The bell reminded her of something.
> She has to catch up on her sleep.

BOY

> Has the Major left his mansion?
> Is he really sleeping here?

ROBIN

> How can I tell you? Everyone
> answers us in riddles.

BOY

>> She said,
> the Major dwells here.

ROBIN

>> That's her city
> way of being friendly, Brother.

BOY

> Robin, the Major could afford
> to buy the lady better clothes.
> She was almost naked.

ROBIN

>   She
> was dressed unwisely.

BOY

>   Isn't Eve
> almost naked in our Bible?

ROBIN

> Don't ask so many questions, Brother.
> I wish I knew the naked truth.
> > (*A* WATCHMAN *enters, dishevelled and yawning. He*
> > *holds a lantern with a bell tied to it and a spiked staff.*)

WATCHMAN

> Stop, we don't allow this sort
> of talk about the Bible here.

ROBIN

> You are mistaken, Sir. I said
> I wished I knew the naked truth.

WATCHMAN

> You're in New England. Here we fine
> mothers for bearing naked children.
> You're leading this child into perdition.
> We have a fine for that. What's in
> your wallet, Boy?

ROBIN

> Nothing.

WATCHMAN

>   Nothing! You've been inside then!

ROBIN

> Watchman, I'm looking for my kinsman.

WATCHMAN

> And you thought you'd find him in this house
> doing his martial drill.

ROBIN

>   You know him!
> My kinsman's Major Molineux.
> I see you know him, he will pay you
> if you will lead us to his house.

WATCHMAN

> (*Singing*)
> *Your aunt's the lord high sheriff,*
> *your uncle is King George;*
> *if you can't pay the tariff,*
> *the house will let you charge.*

ROBIN

I asked for Major Molineux.

WATCHMAN

Keep asking! We are cleaning house.
The Major's lost a lot of money
lately, buying bad real estate.
He can't afford his country cousins.
Move, you filthy, sucking hayseed!
or I'll spike you with my stick!

BOY

Why don't you hit him, Brother?

WATCHMAN

> I'll have
you in the stocks by daybreak, Boy.

ROBIN

We'll go, Sir. I'm your countryman
learning the customs of the city.

WATCHMAN

> (*Goes off singing*)
> *Baggy buttocks, baggy buttocks,*
> *The Queen of England's willing*
> *To serve you for a shilling*
> *And stick you in the stocks.*

ROBIN

> We're learning
how to live. The man was drunk.

BOY

Our Deerfield watchmen only drink
at Communion. Something's wrong,
these people need new blood.

ROBIN

> Perhaps
they'll get it. Here's a clergyman,
he'll tell us where to find our kinsman.
> (*The* CLERGYMAN *comes across the stage. He is awk-*
> *wardly holding a large English flag on a staff.*)

ROBIN

Help me, I beg you, Reverend Sir,

I'm from Deerfield, I'm looking for
my kinsman, Major Molineux.
No one will tell me where he lives.

CLERGYMAN

I have just left the Major's house.
He is my patron and example.
A good man—it's a pity though
he's so outspoken; other good men
misunderstand the Major's meaning.
He just handed me this British
flag to put above my pulpit—
a bit outspoken!

ROBIN

Our country's flag, Sir!

CLERGYMAN

Yes, a bit outspoken. Come
I'll lead you to your kinsman's house.
(*The* MAN WITH THE MASK *strides hurriedly across the
stage, and unrolls a Rattlesnake flag, which he hands
to the* CLERGYMAN, *who has difficulty in managing the
two flags.*)

MAN WITH MASK

I have a present for you, Parson:
our Rattlesnake. "Don't tread on me!"
it says. I knew you'd want to have one.
Hang it up somewhere in church;
there's nothing like the Rattlesnake
for raising our declining faith.

CLERGYMAN

I thank you, Sir.

MAN WITH MASK

You'd better hurry.
Think of the man who had no garment
for the wedding. Things are moving.
(*The* MAN WITH THE MASK *hurries off stage.*)

CLERGYMAN

(*To himself*)
God help us, if we lose!
(*Turns to go*)

ROBIN

Sir, you're leaving! You promised me
you'd lead me to my kinsman's house.
Please, let me help you with the flags.

CLERGYMAN

> I'll see you later. I have to hurry.
> I have a sick parishioner,
> a whole sick parish! I have a notion
> one of these flags will cure us. Which?
> Everyone's so emphatic here.
> If you should meet your kinsman, tell him
> I'm praying for him in my church.
>> (CLERGYMAN *goes out.*)
>> (*A loud* "hem, hem" *is heard. The* MAN IN THE PERIWIG
>> *comes jauntily forward followed by the* TWO BARBERS.
>> *He goes to the house with the bay-window and raps
>> with his cane. The light inside the house goes on. A
>> Rattlesnake flag has been nailed to the door. No one
>> sees* ROBIN *and the* BOY.)

FIRST BARBER

> Look, Your Honor, Mrs. Clark
> has taken on the Rattlesnake.

MAN IN PERIWIG

> Good, this pricks my fainting courage.
> "Don't tread on me!" That's rather odd
> for Mrs. Clark.

FIRST BARBER

> Come on, Your Honor.

SECOND BARBER

> There's always a first time.

FIRST BARBER

> Then a second.

MAN IN PERIWIG

> Thank God, I've but one life to give
> my country.
> Lay on, Macduff! [4] I owe this to
> my reputation, boys.

FIRST BARBER

> He owes
> his reputation to the boys.

SECOND BARBER

> Between the devil and the deep
> blue sea, Your Honor!

FIRST BARBER

> His Honor likes
> the sea. Everyone loves a sailor.

[4] Macbeth's challenge to Macduff (*Macbeth*, V.viii.33.).

MAN IN PERIWIG

>Hurry! I'm in torture! Open!
>I have authority, hem, hem!
>
>>(*The* MAN IN THE PERIWIG *knocks loudly. The* WOMAN
>>*stands in doorway.*)

WOMAN

>>(*Singing*)
>>*Where is my boy in leather pants,*
>>*who gives a woman what she wants?*

MAN IN PERIWIG

>>(*Singing in falsetto*)
>>*Woman, I have a royal Crown*
>>*your countryman gave the ferryman*
>>*a-standing on the strand;*
>>*but money goes from hand to hand:*
>>*the crown is on the town,*
>>*the money's mine, I want to dine.*
>>*Whatever we do is our affair,*
>>*the breath of freedom's in the air.*

FIRST BARBER

>The lady's ballast's in the air.

SECOND BARBER

>Two ten pound tea chests. The lady needs
>a little uplift from the clergy.

MAN IN PERIWIG

>I'm breaking on the foamy breakers!
>Help! Help!
>I wish my lady had a firm,
>hard-chested figure like a mast,
>but what has love to do with fact?
>A lover loves his nemesis;
>the patriotic act.
>
>>(*The* MAN IN THE PERIWIG *gives the* LADY *the crown
>>and passes in. The lights go out.*)

BARBER

>Once to every man and nation
>comes the time a gentleman
>wants to clear his reputation.[5]

---

[5] Cf. the following lines from "The Present Crisis" by James Russell Lowell (1819–91):

>Once to every man and nation comes the moment to decide
>In the strife of Truth with Falsehood, for the good or evil side.

TAVERN KEEPER

      Once to every man and nation
      comes the time a man's a man.

BARBER

      His Honor's perished on the blast.
           (*The* BARBER *saunters off along with* TAVERN KEEPER.
           The BOY *turns to* ROBIN, *who is lost in thought.*)

ROBIN

           I think the Major
      has left. By watching I have learned
      to read the signs. The Rattlesnake
      means Major Molineux is out.
      A British flag means he's at home.

BOY

      You talk in riddles like the town.

ROBIN

      Say what you mean; mean what you say:
      that's how we used to talk in Deerfield.
      It's not so simple here in the city.
           (*The pillared mansion lights up.* ROBIN *and the* BOY
           *approach it. The Lion and Unicorn of England are
           gone. Instead, a large Rattlesnake flag is showing.*)
      Brother, we've reached our destination.
      This is our kinsman's house. I know it
      from the steel engraving that
      he gave us when he came to Deerfield.
      Our journey's over. Here's our mansion.

BOY

      Robin, it has a Rattlesnake.

ROBIN

      That means the Major's not at home.
           (*The* MAN WITH THE MASK *comes out of the mansion.
           Half his face is now fiery red, the other half is still
           mottled.*)

MAN WITH MASK

      I am the man on horseback.

ROBIN

           No,
      you're walking, Sir.

MAN WITH MASK

           I am a king.

ROBIN

      The King's in England. You must be sick.

Have you seen your face? Half's red,
the other half is pocked and mottled.

MAN WITH MASK

Oh I'm as healthy as the times.
I am an image of this city.
Do you see this colored handkerchief?

> (*The* MAN WITH THE MASK *draws out a small British
> flag.*)

ROBIN

Our British flag, Sir.

MAN WITH MASK

Yes, it doesn't
help my illness any more,
when I try to cool my burning brow,
or blow my nose on it.

ROBIN

I know
a man who used to own this house.
Let's see if he's still here. Perhaps,
my friend can help to heal your sickness.

MAN WITH MASK

My face will be entirely red soon;
then I'll be well. Who is your friend?

ROBIN

A kinsman, Major Molineux.

MAN WITH MASK

I have a fellow feeling for him.
The Major used to own this house:
now it's mine. I'm taking over,
I've just signed the final deed.
Do you see my nameplate on the gate?

ROBIN

The Rattlesnake?

MAN WITH MASK

The Rattlesnake.

ROBIN

If I pick up the Rattlesnake,
will it help me find my kinsman?
I think he needs my help. We are
his last relations in the world.

MAN WITH MASK

The last shall be the first, my Boy.

ROBIN

What do you mean? You talk like Christ.

MAN WITH MASK

The first shall be the last, my Boy.
The Major has a heavy hand;
we have been beaten to the ground.

ROBIN

My kinsman has an open hand.

MAN WITH MASK

Ridden like horses, fleeced like sheep,
worked like cattle, clothed and fed
like hounds and hogs!

ROBIN

I want to find him.

MAN WITH MASK

Whipping-posts, gibbets, bastinadoes
and the rack! I must be moving.

ROBIN

Wait, I'll take up the Rattlesnake.
Please, help me find my kinsman.

(ROBIN *takes hold of the* MAN WITH THE MASK'S
shoulder. The MAN *steps back and draws his sword.*)

MAN WITH MASK

Move!
You've torn my cloak. You'd better keep
a civil tongue between your teeth.
I have a mission.

(ROBIN *raises his cudgel. He and the* MAN WITH THE
MASK *stand a moment facing each other.*)

BOY

Brain him, Robin.
Mangle the bastard's bloody face.
He doesn't like our kinsman, Robin.

ROBIN

I only asked for information.

MAN WITH MASK

For information! Information
is my trade. I was a lawyer
before I learned the pleasures of
the military life. The Major
was my first teacher. Now I know you!
I met you at the tavern. You

were short of cash then. Take this crown:
drink to the Major, then a health
to Greenough, and the Rattlesnake.
To Greenough!

ROBIN

You're a fighter.

MAN WITH MASK

I hate war, wars leave us where
they find us, don't they, Boy?
Let's talk about my health.

ROBIN

Where can
I find my kinsman?

MAN WITH MASK

He owned this house.
Men used to find him here all day,
before the storms disturbed his judgment.
He's out now ranging through the town,
looking for new accommodations.
Wait here. You'll meet him on his walk.
        (*Strides off singing*)
        The king is in his counting house;
        we're counting up his money.

BOY

Why was that fellow's face half red now?
He's changing color.

ROBIN

I don't know.
He is someone out of "Revelations"—
Hell revolting on its jailers.
        (*The church lights up a little.* ROBIN *walks over to it,*
        and looks in a window.)
Our church is empty, Brother. Moonbeams
are trembling on the snow-pure pews,
the altar's drowned in radiant fog,
a single restless ray has crept
across the open Bible.
        (*Turns to a gravestone by the church*)
        I'm lonely.
What's this? A gravestone? A grave? Whose grave?
I think the Major must have died:
everything tells me he is gone
and nothing is forever.

> (*Turns back to the church*)
>> Brother,
> the moon's the only worshipper!
>> (*The* CLERGYMAN *comes out of the church. He lays*
>> *a white clay pipe on the steps and holds up a little*
>> *colored celluloid whirligig.*)

CLERGYMAN
> The wind has died.

ROBIN
>> What are you doing?

CLERGYMAN
> I'm playing with this whirligig,
> and waiting to see which way the wind
> will veer. It's quite amusing, Son,
> trying to guess the whims of the wind.
> I am waiting for a sign.
> A strange thing for a modern churchman.

ROBIN
> My father says the Church is a rock.

CLERGYMAN
> Yes, yes, a rock is blind. That's why
> I've shut my eyes.

ROBIN
> I see my father. He's the Deerfield
> minister, and Church of England.
> You remind me of my father.

CLERGYMAN
> Be careful, Son. Call no man father:
> that's what we tell the Roman clergy;
> sometimes I think we go too far,
> they get their people out for Mass.

ROBIN
> Father. When I shut
> my eyes, I dream I'm back in Deerfield.
> The people sit in rows below
> the old oak; a horseman stops to water
> his horse and to refresh his soul.
> I hear my father holding forth
> thanksgiving, hope and all the mercies—

CLERGYMAN
>> Those village
> pastors! Once they used to preach
> as if the world were everlasting;

each Sunday was longer than a summer!
That's gone now. We have competition:
taverns, papers, politics
and trade. It takes a wolfhound now
to catch a flock!

ROBIN

                    Why are you waiting
for the wind?

CLERGYMAN

            (*Taking up two little flags*)
            Do you see
these two flags? One's the Union Jack,[6]
the other is the Rattlesnake.
The wind will tell me which to fly.

ROBIN

I'm thinking of the absent one.
My kinsman, Major Molineux
is absent. The storms have hurt his house
lately. No one will help me find him.

CLERGYMAN

Perhaps the wind will blow him back.

ROBIN

I met a strange man, Colonel Greenough;
half of his face was red, and half
was pocked. He said, "Wait here, and you
will meet your kinsman on his walk."

CLERGYMAN

You'd better wait here then. That red
and pocked man tends to speak the truth.

ROBIN

Why was his face two colors, Father?

CLERGYMAN

He is an image of the city.
If his whole face turns red as blood,
We'll have to fly the Rattlesnake.

ROBIN

Say more about my kinsman, Father.
You said he was your friend and patron.

CLERGYMAN

Poor Molineux! he served the clergy
somewhat better than this city.

[6] The British national flag, a combination of the flags of England, Scotland, and
Ireland.

ROBIN

> He had a special pew, you know.
> He used to set a grand example.

ROBIN

> He used to! You speak as if he were dead!

CLERGYMAN

> Men blamed me, but I liked to watch
> his red coat blazing like the sunset
> at Sunday morning service here.
> He was an easy-going fellow,
> a lover of life, no Puritan.
> He had invention, used to send
> two six foot Privates here to help
> with the collection. Yes, I had
> to like him. He had his flaws, of course.

ROBIN

> A red coat blazing like the sunrise,
> that's how the Major was in Deerfield;
> the gold lion of England shone
> on his gilded carriage. He had a little
> white scar like a question mark
> on his right cheek. He got it killing
> Frenchmen. He seemed to hold the world
> like a gold ball in the palm of his hand.
> Ours for the asking! All! We are
> his last relations in the world!

CLERGYMAN

> No one will dispute your claim.

ROBIN

> The Major said he was the King's
> intelligence in Massachusetts.

CLERGYMAN

> No one will dispute his claim.
> What shall we do with people? They
> get worse and worse, but God improves.
> God was green in Moses' time;
> little by little though, he blossomed.
> First came the prophets, then our Lord,
> and then the Church.

ROBIN

> The Church?

CLERGYMAN

> The Church
> gets more enlightened every day.

We've learned to disregard the Law
and look at persons. Who is my neighbor?
Anyone human is my neighbor. Sometimes
my neighbor is a man from Sodom.
> (*Great noise of shouting.* ALL FORMER CHARACTERS,
> *except the* MAN WITH THE MASK, *parade across the*
> *stage.* MOST OF THEM *wave Rattlesnake flags.*)

ROBIN

Father, I see two clergymen,
they're waving flags.

CLERGYMAN

I see my sign.
> (*Snaps the whirligig with his thumb*)

Look, the wind has risen! Wherever
the spirit calls me, I must follow.

CROWD

Hurrah for the Republic!
Down with Major Molineux!
> (*The* PEOPLE *sing a verse of* Yankee Doodle, *and draw*
> COLONEL GREENOUGH *on stage in a red, white and blue*
> *cart. He stands up and draws his sword. One can see*
> *that his face is now entirely red.*)

MAN WITH MASK

The die is cast! I say, the die is cast.

ROBIN

Look at the Colonel,
his whole face is red as blood!

MAN WITH MASK

Major Molineux is coming.

CLERGYMAN

Are you sure we're strong enough?

MAN WITH MASK

Every British soldier in Boston
is killed or captured.

CROWD

Don't tread on me!
Don't tread on me! Don't tread on me!

ROBIN

What can I do to help my kinsman?

CLERGYMAN

Swap your flag and save your soul.

ROBIN

I want to save my kinsman, Father.

CLERGYMAN

No, no, Son, do as I do. Here, hold
this flag a moment, while I speak.

(*The* CLERGYMAN *hands* ROBIN *his Rattlesnake flag,
tosses away the whirligig, breaks his clay pipe, then
takes a chair and stands on it while he addresses the*
CROWD *with both hands raised. Throughout the crowd
scene,* ROBIN *stands unconsciously holding the flag and
suffering.*)

How long, how long now, Men of Boston!
You've faced the furious tyrant's trident,
you've borne the blandishments of Sodom.
The Day of Judgment is at hand,
now we'll strip the scarlet whore,
King George shall swim in scarlet blood,
Now Nebuchadnezzar shall eat grass and die.
How long! How long! O Men of Boston,
behave like men, if you are men!

(*The* PEOPLE *cheer and take the* CLERGYMAN *on their
shoulders.*)

You've drawn the sword, Boys, throw away
the scabbard!

(*The* CLERGYMAN *draws a sword and throws down the
scabbard.* MANY OF THE PEOPLE, *including the* PROSTI-
TUTE, *draw swords and throw the scabbards rattling
across the stage. They draw* MAJOR MOLINEUX *on stage
in a red cart. He is partly tarred and feathered; one
cheek is bleeding; his red British uniform is torn; he
shakes with terror.*)

ROBIN

Oh my kinsman, my dear kinsman,
they have wounded you!

MAN WITH MASK

Throw the boy from Deerfield out,
he has no garment for our wedding.

CLERGYMAN

No, let him stay, he is just a boy.

(ROBIN, *unthinking, holds the flag in front of him, while
his eyes are fixed in horror and pity on the figure of
the* MAJOR. *The* BOY, *unconsciously, too, mingles among
the* CROWD *without thinking. Someone asks him to give
some dirt to throw at the* MAJOR *and he unthinkingly*

> *picks up some from a basket, and hands it to the*
> TAVERN KEEPER, *who throws it at the* MAJOR.)

ROBIN

> (*With a loud cry, but unconsciously waving the flag in
> his grief*)

Oh my poor kinsman, you are hurt!

CROWD

Don't tread on me! Don't tread on me!

> (*The* MAJOR *slowly staggers to his feet. Slowly he
> stretches out his right arm and points to* ROBIN.)

MAJOR MOLINEUX

Et tu, Brute! [7]

TAVERN KEEPER

The Major wants to teach us Latin.

> (*The* CROWD *laughs, and* ROBIN, *once more without
> thinking, laughs too, very loudly.*)
> (TAVERN KEEPER *goes up to the* MAJOR *and hands him
> a Rattlesnake flag.*)

You're out of step, Sir. Here's your flag.

> (*The* MAJOR *lurches a few steps from the cart, grinds
> the Rattlesnake underfoot, then turns and addresses
> the* CROWD.)

MAJOR MOLINEUX

Long live King George! Long live King George!
I'll sing until you cut my tongue out!

CROWD

Throw the Major in the river,
in the river, in the river!

> (*With a grating sound, the* FERRYMAN *appears at the
> side of the stage, pushing the prow of his dory. The*
> MAJOR *staggers towards the* FERRYMAN.)

MAJOR MOLINEUX

> (*To* FERRYMAN)

Help me in my trouble. Let
me cross the river to my King!

> (*The* FERRYMAN *stiffens. The* MAN WITH THE MASK
> *throws him a silver crown.*)

MAN WITH MASK

Ferryman, here's a silver crown,
take him or leave him, we don't care.

---

[7] "And even you, Brutus!" These words are supposed to have been spoken by
Julius Caesar when he saw Brutus in the crowd of his assassins.

FERRYMAN

> (*Still more threatening*)
> The crown's no longer currency.
> (*The* FERRYMAN *kicks the crown into the water.*)

MAJOR MOLINEUX

> Boatman, you rowed me here in state;
> save me, now that I'm fallen!

FERRYMAN

> There's no returning on my boat.

MAJOR MOLINEUX

> (*Stretching out his hands and grappling the* FERRYMAN)
> Save me in the name of God!
> (*The* FERRYMAN *pushes the* MAJOR *off and hits him on the head with his oar. The* MAJOR *screams, and lies still.*)

FERRYMAN

> He's crossed the river into his kingdom;
> all tyrants must die as this man died.
> (*One by one, the* PRINCIPAL CHARACTERS *come up and look at the* MAJOR.)

CLERGYMAN

> He's dead. He had no time to pray.
> I wish he'd called me. O Lord, remember
> his past kindness to the Church;
> all tyrants must die as this man died.

MAN IN PERIWIG

> (*Taking the* MAJOR'S *empty scabbard*)
> I have the Major's sword of office;
> hem, hem, I have authority.

FIRST BARBER

> His Honor has the hollow scabbard.

MAN IN PERIWIG

> They build men right in England. Take him
> all in all, he was a man;[8]
> all tyrants must die as this man died.

TAVERN KEEPER

> (*Holding a poster*)
> Look, this poster says the town
> of Boston offers a thousand guineas

---

[8] Cf. Hamlet's statement to Horatio about Hamlet's father, the dead king (*Hamlet*, I.ii. 187–88):

> He was a man, take him for all in all.
> I shall not look upon his like again.

to anyone who kills the Major.
I'll take his wallet for the cause.
All tyrants must die as this man died.

PROSTITUTE

(*Taking the* MAJOR'S *hat*)
I'll need this hat to hide my head.
They build men right in England. Take him
all in all, he was a man;
all tyrants must die as this man died.

MAN WITH MASK

(*Plunging his sword in the* MAJOR)
Sic semper tyrannis! [9]

FERRYMAN

His fare is paid now;
the Major's free to cross the river.
(*The* FERRYMAN *loads* MAJOR MOLINEUX'S *body on his
boat, and pushes off.*)

CLERGYMAN

(*Coming up to the* MAN WITH THE MASK)
Your hand! I want
to shake your hand, Sir. A great day!

MAN WITH MASK

Great and terrible! There's nothing
I can do about it now.
(*Turns to* ROBIN)
Here, boy, here's the Major's sword;
perhaps, you'll want a souvenir.
(CROWD *starts to leave.* ROBIN *and* BOY *alone*)

BOY

The Major's gone. We'll have to go
back home. There's no one here to help us.

ROBIN

Yes, Major Molineux is dead.
(*Starts sadly towards the river*)

CROWD

Long live the Republic! Long live the Republic!

BOY

Look, Robin, I have found a flintlock.
(ROBIN *looks wistfully at the* CROWD, *now almost entirely gone. He pauses and then answers in a daze.*)

ROBIN

A flintlock?

[9] "Thus always with tyrants!"

BOY

Well, that's all I came to Boston for, I guess.
Let's go, I see the ferryman.

ROBIN

    (*Still inattentive*)
I'm going.
    (ROBIN *takes his* BROTHER'S *hand and turns firmly towards the city.*)

BOY

We are returning to the city!
    (ALL THE PEOPLE *are gone now, the lights start to go out. A red sun shows on the river.*)

ROBIN

Yes, Brother, we are staying here.
Look, the lights are going out,
the red sun's moving on the river.
Where will it take us to? . . . It's strange
to be here on our own—and free.

BOY

    (*Sighting along his flintlock*)
Major Molineux is dead.

ROBIN

Yes, Major Molineux is dead.

Curtain

notes on the authors

Aiken, Conrad (Potter) [1889-   ], born in Savannah, Georgia, fled his birthplace when he was ten, following the tragic death of his parents. He went to live with a great-aunt in Massachusetts, where, except for brief stays abroad, he has resided since. After graduating from Harvard, he devoted himself to writing fiction and poetry and, at twenty-five, published his first volume of poetry, *Earth Triumphant;* his *Collected Poems* (1953), comprising eighteen previously published volumes, reveals a progress from the early influence of the Romantics to a more astringent yet haunting, melancholy, and hypnotic power peculiarly his own.

Amis, Kingsley [1922-   ], one of the Angry Young Men of contemporary Britain, was born in London and, after serving in the army, received his degree in English language and literature from Oxford. Since 1949 he has taught at the University College of Swansea in Wales. His second novel, *Lucky Jim* (1954), presents a disgusted anti-hero, who finds the world at once amusing and reprehensible. Amis has brought the same note of disaffection into his poetry, sometimes with the bitter humor of "New Approach Needed."

Anderson, Sherwood [1876-1941], born in Camden, Ohio, had little formal education. After holding a variety of menial jobs and doing military service in the Spanish-American War, he became an advertising copywriter in Chicago and then part-owner and manager of a paint factory in Elyria, Ohio. In 1912 he abandoned his business, returned to Chicago, and began to write. His first novels, *Windy McPherson's Son* (1916) and *Marching Men* (1917), won little recognition. But his short stories, departing from usual plot patterns and presenting, with an easy Midwestern drawl, moments of awakening or failures of understanding between characters, drew wide critical acclaim. His best-known work, *Winesburg, Ohio* (1919), dealing with the small-town people he called "grotesques," was followed by several other collections of short stories and three personal narratives. In 1925 he retired to Marion, Virginia, where he edited two weekly newspapers, one Republican, one Democratic.

Arnold, Matthew [1822-1888], rejecting the nice complacencies of his age but unable to discover new standards, felt himself "Wandering between two worlds, one dead, / The other powerless to be born." Torn between belief and doubt, he used his poetry to wistfully comfort a skeptical world. The son of Thomas Arnold, famous Headmaster of Rugby, he attended Oxford and, soon after, was appointed an inspector of schools, a position he held almost to the end of his life.

After publishing some early poems anonymously, he released *Poems* (1853) under his name and reprinted many of his earlier verses in *Poems: Second Series* (1855), for which he received the Professorship of Poetry at Oxford. Although he continued to write some poetry, after his forties he was mainly occupied with criticism. In the critical essays published as *Culture and Anarchy* (1869), he maintained that poetry had an ethical purpose, that it should be "a criticism of life," and he believed that his own verse exemplified this view.

Auden, W(ystan) H(ugh) [1907-   ], educated at Oxford, saw his first volume, *Poems,* published when he was twenty-three. While supporting himself by teaching school, he was associated with the leftist poets, who included Spender, Day Lewis, and MacNeice. At thirty, he served as an ambulance driver in the Spanish Civil War. Married then to Erika Mann, daughter of the German novelist Thomas Mann, he came to the United States in 1939 and was naturalized in 1946. The author of radio plays, travel books, critical works, and an opera libretto, he is learned, intellectual, inexhaustibly witty, and a great virtuoso in poetic technique. In his poetry Auden has defined the frustrations and anxieties of contemporary man living in a world not only tragic but tawdry; still, like Eliot, he progressed from cynicism to a meditative stance, from a pessimistic distrust of civilization to a religious hope for it. "In Memory of W. B. Yeats," beginning with a mood of alienation, ends on an affirmative note, as do such poems as "Petition" and "September 1, 1939."

Baker, Howard (Wilson) [1905-   ], raised and educated in California, taught at Harvard but gave up academic life for two decades to be an orange and olive "rancher." Now he sometimes combines teaching and ranching. His novel, *Orange Valley* (1931), and his critical study, *Induction to Tragedy* (1934, reprinted 1965), support the long-time underground reputation he had for being one of our finest poets, capable of handling a wide variety of subjects and of achieving variety of tone within the firm lines of traditional verse forms—a reputation that depended entirely on periodical publication and one pamphlet, *A Letter from the Country* (1941). In 1966 those earlier and many more recent poems were collected in *Ode to the Sea and Other Poems.* In collaboration with his wife, Dorothy Baker, he has written plays for television and the stage, including *Trio,* which was banned from Broadway after a three weeks' run.

Berryman, John [1914-   ], born in Oklahoma, was graduated from Columbia and studied at Cambridge University in England. After returning to the United States, he taught at Harvard, Princeton, the University of Washington, and the University of Cincinnati. His poems first appeared in national magazines during the thirties, and in 1940 twenty were included in *Five Young American Poets.* He has since published five volumes, including *Homage to Mistress Bradstreet* (1959), a long poem dramatizing that lady's tough spirit in the face of physical and moral suffering and called by one critic a "sort of miniature *Waste Land*." His most recent collection, *77 Dream Songs* (1959), like his earlier work, compels the reader to think as he reads and develops a strange incantatory power through manipulation of the vernacular.

Blake, William [1757-1827], from his earliest years a visionary capable of seeing "a World in a Grain of Sand" and of translating ordinary into extraordinary observations, was the son of a London hosier. He was enrolled at ten in a drawing school, where he developed a talent that was later to collaborate with his poetic genius and ultimately to win him recognition as one of the great graphic artists. (Most of his poems, with his illustrations, he engraved by a special process and published himself.) At twenty-six he found a publisher for his first volume of poems, *Poetical Sketches*. This was followed in 1789 by *Songs of Innocence,* lyrics that appear childlike in their praise of human simplicities and harmony. This pastoral vision is qualified when we read those poems against *Songs of Experience* (1794), which present the brutal facts of the natural universe, economic reality, and human cruelty. Blake was then already well into his complex mythological world, with its repeated representations of the "Contraries" or dualities of innocence and experience, energy and reason, love and jealousy, freedom and confinement, and so on. These antitheses were the explicit subject of his great central statement, *The Marriage of Heaven and Hell* (1790-1793). This work was the foundation for a series of relatively short "prophetic books"—*America* (1793), *Urizen* (1794), *Europe* (1794), *Ahania* (1795), and *Los* (1795)—as well as for his later, much longer "epics"—*The Four Zoas* (never completed), *Milton* (1804-1808), and *Jerusalem* (1804-1820). Blake, who died as he lived—in obscurity—once said of himself, "I am hid." It took literary history about a hundred years to find him.

Browning, Robert [1812-1889], early decided upon a career as a poet. By the age of twelve, he had completed a collection of Byronic poems, *Incondita,* which he later destroyed. A far greater influence than Byron was Shelley, the inspiration for the poem "Memorabilia." Along with poetry, play-writing was a concern of the young Browning, but his early efforts were unsuccessful. His real drama is in his dramatic monologues, which first appeared in two small volumes, *Dramatic Lyrics* (1842) and *Dramatic Romances and Lyrics* (1845). The poems are theatrical in effect, creating self-revealing characters and often condensing an entire life into a few stanzas. Also in these volumes is "The Lost Leader," written upon Wordsworth's acceptance of the laureateship and a government pension, which Browning regarded as a desertion of liberal causes. In 1846 he married Elizabeth Barrett and, the following year, moved with her to Italy. Their poetry shows the great influence each had on the other's perceptions.

Byron, Lord, George Gordon Noel [1788-1824], the legendary hero of the Romantic movement, published *Hours of Idleness* when he was nineteen. He made his mark in English literary circles in 1808 with the publication of *English Bards and Scotch Reviewers,* a slashing satire in couplets about the major authors of the day. Few writers have led a more public or histrionic life. His flamboyant love affairs, heroic deeds in the war for Greek independence, and self-imposed exile were all part of the legend. The wanderer always seeking escape, Byron fled first to the Mediterranean and later, as a disillusioned popular idol, to Switzerland and Italy. His major poems, almost a transcript of his life, are confessional as well as sensual, particularly *Childe Harold's Pilgrimage* (written from 1809 to 1817), *Manfred* (1817), and *Don Juan* (written from 1818 to 1824). Byron's poetry—whether the lilting love poetry of *Manfred* or the cynical stanzas of *Don Juan*— vibrates with the nervous force, audacity, and romantic delight that is peculiarly Byronic.

Chekhov, Anton (Pavlovich) [1860-1904], studied medicine at the University of Moscow, but, to help support his poverty-stricken family, began writing sketches, theatrical notices, and short stories for local newspapers. In 1886, after bringing out a second and successful book of short stories, he traveled to St. Petersburg, the intellectual and publishing center of Russia. To his amazement, he found that he was "the most fashionable writer" there. Fully conscious of the social evils of his day, he undertook, in 1890, the arduous journey to the penal colony of Sakhalin, where he ministered to the sick and gathered information for *The Island of Sakhalin: Travel notes* (1895). In 1892 he organized relief for famine victims; later that year, when central Russia was threatened with cholera, he acted as medical supervisor. Tired and plagued by tuberculosis, he settled in the country, gaining an intimate knowledge of the rural life that was to dominate his later work. During these years he composed his best-known plays, including *The Sea Gull* (1896), *Uncle Vanya* (1898), *The Three Sisters* (1901), and *The Cherry Orchard* (staged in 1904), which tolled the death knell of old Russia. But his stories are by far the more influential portion of his work. Understated, sometimes nearly plotless, "open-ended," emphasizing moments of illumination or darkening of the mind, they can be thought of as the basis of the modern short story. In these short narratives, Chekhov is preoccupied with the commonplace, the drab, and the narrow, where life is a frustrating struggle with cruelty, want, and boredom.

Coleridge, Samuel Taylor [1772-1834], a brilliant but erratic scholar, left Jesus College, Cambridge, without a degree. His poetic genius flowered under the influence of Wordsworth, with whom he established immediate rapport at their first meeting in 1797. From June 1797 through September 1798, as an almost constant guest at the Wordsworth cottage, he reached his heights as a lyric poet. During this period he produced a group of blank-verse poems, including "This Lime-Tree Bower My Prison," with its Wordsworthian rapture for nature, subsumed in a personal and meditative beauty uniquely Coleridgian. Also written then were the three "magic" poems—"Christabel," "Kubla Khan," and "The Rime of the Ancient Mariner"—which emphasize the shadowy wonder of a profoundly moral natural universe. A break with Wordsworth began during their trip to Germany in 1798. At about the same time, Coleridge's creative powers started declining. Ill health, growing dependence on opium to relieve his rheumatic pain, and estrangement from his wife all contributed to his decline. During the last eighteen years of his life, under the care of a physician, he wrote literary criticism and philosophy, revised earlier essays, and lectured on Milton and Shakespeare. His personal aesthetic credo, the *Biographia Literaria,* was published in 1817.

Crane, (Harold) Hart [1899-1932], was born in Ohio and began writing poetry when he was thirteen. He never finished high school and only sporadically tried to earn a living. Between jobs, he lived recklessly—drinking violently and fighting with those who most appreciated his work. The two volumes that appeared during his lifetime, *White Buildings* (1926) and *The Bridge* (1930), and the posthumously published collected poems (1933) exhibit a probably intentional obscurantism. But the highly impressionistic explosions of images often seem to suggest a precise meaning. This telescoping of a series of allusions was, for Crane, a means of achieving "the rhythm of the motion . . . besides ushering in a whole world of music." At the age of thirty-three, he put an end to his frenzied and unhappy life.

Cummings, E(dward) E(stlin) [1894-1962], was born in Cambridge, Massachusetts, and received his B.A. and M.A. from Harvard. He served briefly as an ambulance driver in France during World War I and was held for three months in a French detention camp, an experience vividly recorded in *The Enormous Room* (1922), a prose volume. He studied art in Paris but after 1924 lived mainly in New York. A unique blend of lyricist and satirist, harsh critic and bewildering clown, Cummings restored a sense of play to poetry. At sixty he collected some six hundred previously published poems in *Poems: 1923-1954,* which was followed in 1958 by *95 Poems.* Both volumes illustrate his refusal to accept conventional modes and his experimentation with new ways (among them typographic eccentricities) of saying old things.

Dickey, James [1923-   ], born in Atlanta, Georgia, and educated at Vanderbilt University, abandoned a successful business career for poetry. He has since been poet-in-residence at Reed College and at San Fernando State College and has served for a year as poetry consultant to the Library of Congress. His four volumes, from *Into the Stone* (1960) through *Buckdancer's Choice* (1965), move from a poetry of enchantment, ritual, and myth into a poetry of obsession and violence. Often the poems use the sensational materials of the daily newspaper as their subject matter. "The Fiend," quite literally about a voyeur and the stinging excitements of his aberration, is packed with the kind of details one is more accustomed to encounter in fiction than in verse. It is a drama of terror, whose linear technique, like excited breathing, carries it to its climax.

Dickinson, Emily (Elizabeth) [1830-1886], published only anonymously in her lifetime and was unknown when she died. Her life was dedicated to writing a "letter to the world"—a collection of some 1,775 poems expressing with utmost economy and a cryptic wit her concepts of life and death, love and nature, and the consciousness of the soul. Unmarried, she yet developed intense intellectual relationships with a number of men, but contrary to long-time speculation the only lover she ever knew was a figure of her imagination. These relationships were climaxed by her literary correspondence with Thomas Wentworth Higginson, whom she did not know but whose *Atlantic Monthly* essays she knew well. Through her years of isolation and loneliness, his generous encouragement sustained her as she lived out her quiet life in her father's house in Amherst, Massachusetts, becoming, in her later years, almost a recluse. She tended the garden, baked the family bread, and observed from her window the passing show of village life.

Donne, John [1572-1631], the Roman Catholic son of a London iron-monger, was, by turns, a scholar, gallant, soldier, self-styled rake, convert to Anglicanism, and impassioned preacher. Always he was a questioning human consciousness, whose poetry, like his life, often struggles through dark mazes of thought and feeling. His love lyrics, collected posthumously in *Songs and Sonnets* (1633), were followed by his twenty-six "holy" sonnets, written mostly between 1607 and 1615, years of personal religious crisis which resulted in his taking orders in the Anglican Church in 1615. The passionate fusion of intellect and sensuality, which was the habit of his imagination, created a poetry abounding in paradoxical figures of speech, fantastic images, and metaphors stretched to unprecedented lengths. His work brilliantly achieves that identification of sensation and the intellectual dissection of sensation that is the chief mark of metaphysical poetry, of which his is also the chief example.

Eliot, T(homas) S(tearns) [1888-1965], born in St. Louis and a graduate of Harvard, settled in England at the beginning of World War I and became almost wholly identified with Britain. He became a British subject in 1927 and an Anglo-Catholic convert. Publication of "The Love Song of J. Alfred Prufrock" (1915) and, more significantly, *The Waste Land* (1922) established him as the poet of postwar chaos and despair. But the second of these early poems implied a religious solution to the situation, and with *Ash Wednesday* (1930) he turned explicitly to the support of traditional Christian faith. In *Four Quartets*

(1935-1943) he expressed in a new and calm music his experience of belief and his awareness of the difficulty of belief. In his verse plays, *Murder in the Cathedral* (1935), *The Cocktail Party* (1949), and others, he hoped to return poetic drama to the stage. His many essays established in literary criticism new concepts of form and order and pointed to new methods of literary analysis. His concepts of the "objective correlative," the "dissociation of sensibility," and "tradition and the individual talent" (the title of one of his best-known essays) became hallmarks of the criticism that he influenced.

Euripides [480?-406? B.C.], born at Salamis, spent most of his life in Athens. With his skepticism as to any divine government of the world, his brilliantly vivid characterization of women, and his detestation of war he is probably the most modern of the three great Greek tragedians. He is said to have written over ninety plays, of which only eighteen are extant. Dominated by a keen and sympathetic interest in contemporary social and political problems, the plays are generally concerned with war, women, and religion. *The Trojan Woman* is perhaps literature's most compelling outcry against the folly and futility of war, which destroys victor and vanquished alike.

Faulkner, William (Harrison) [1897-1962], brought up in Oxford, Mississippi, did not complete high school. After serving briefly in the Canadian Air Force during World War I, he took some courses at the state university. Bored and with no visible prospects, he settled for a time in New Orleans, where Sherwood Anderson helped him publish his first novel, *Soldier's Pay* (1926). He returned to Oxford, where he made his permanent home, and found his true theme and setting in *Sartoris* (1929), the first of the many works that make up the saga of his invented setting—Yoknapatawpha County. Now, too, he found his true style in the characteristic involutedness of his syntax, the correlative of his atmosphere of an obscurely complex but broodingly imminent doom. These novels, rich in local color, are ultimately concerned with "the human heart in conflict with itself," with the "old universal truths . . . love and honor and pity and pride and compassion and sacrifice." Within the confines of his imaginary locale, he confronts the fundamental experiences of the modern consciousness.

Fitzgerald, F(rancis) Scott (Key) [1896-1940], born in St. Paul, Minnesota, entered Princeton in 1913 but left in 1917 for the army. While in the army, he began a novel, *The Romantic Egoist,* and met and fell in love with Zelda Sayre. In 1919 he took a job in an advertising agency in New York, but, despairing of the low salary, returned to St. Paul. There he rewrote his novel as *This Side of Paradise* (1920), a semi-autobiographical account of frenzied pleasures at Princeton, and found himself the prophet of the new "jazz age." The Fitzgeralds, married that year, embarked on a life of endless parties, night club glitter, and Riviera vacations. But Fitzgerald still managed to write many short stories (collected in three volumes) and three novels—

The Beautiful and Damned (1922), *The Great Gatsby* (1925), and *Tender Is the Night* (1934). All evoke the glamorous existence that he and Zelda tried to live; they reveal its fatality as well. With his wife incurably insane and his own creative powers corroded by liquor, he managed one more collection of stories, *Taps at Reveille* (1935), and began the novel of Hollywood called *The Last Tycoon* (1941). Treated like a hack writer by movie producers, and nearly forgotten by the public, Fitzgerald died of a heart attack.

Frost, Robert (Lee) [1874-1963], born in San Francisco, has traditionally been considered the poet of New England, the physical as well as psychological landscape for most of his poetry. He attended Dartmouth for a few months and Harvard for two years and then tried his hand at farming, mill work, and teaching. Determined to see if he could survive as a writer, he sold his New Hampshire acres and moved to England, where his first collections of American lyrics, *A Boy's Will* (1913) and *North of Boston* (1914), were published. Upon returning to the United States, he joined the faculty of Amherst College and published eight more volumes, ranging from dramatic dialogues to lyrics and as varied in theme and tone. When asked to classify himself as a poet, he replied, "I might be called a Synecdochist, for I prefer the synecdoche in poetry—that figure of speech in which a part is used for the whole." The unwary may romanticize Frost as a benign singer of hymns to Nature; in fact, a dark ambiguity is at the root of much of his work.

Giraudoux, (Hippolyte) Jean [1882-1944], born in a small town in France, specialized in German literature at the *école normale* in Paris and then studied in Munich. In 1907 he published *Provinciales,* a collection of three stories. Continuing to write novels and short stories, he entered the French foreign service at twenty-seven and became Minister of Propaganda in the ill-fated Daladier cabinet of 1939; he held that position until the German occupation. At forty-six he produced his first play, *Siegfried,* which was an immediate success. He rapidly developed that unfailing dramatic awareness of the droll aspects of mankind strutting before the blank stare of nature and history that marks his greatest plays—*Intermezzo* (1933), *Tiger at the Gates* (1935), *Electra* (1937), *Ondine* (1939), and *The Madwoman of Chaillot* (1945). (The literal translation of Giraudoux's title for *Tiger at the Gates* is *The Trojan War Will Not Take Place.*) His action is always gentle, with no great climaxes or surprises. "The stage-play," he explained, "is a trial, not a deed of violence. The soul is opened, like a combination of a safe, by means of a word."

Graves, Robert (Ranke) [1895-   ], always the individualist, refused a scholarship to Oxford and enlisted in the Royal Welsh Fusiliers. During World War I he published three small volumes of poems and in 1929 published *Goodbye to All That,* a candid autobiography of his wartime experiences. After the Armistice, he took his degree at

Oxford. In his thirties, after a brief period as professor of English at Cairo University, he moved to Majorca, where, except for brief periods, he has lived since. Graves is the author of some twenty-five books of poems, a dozen novels, and more than two dozen miscellaneous volumes—including biographies, essays, short stories, critical pieces, and, most notably, *The White Goddess* (1948) and the adaptations and retelling of *The Greek Myths* (1955). With his *Collected Poems: 1914-1947* and *Collected Poems: 1959*, his stature as a major poet was assured. Graves's poetry is sometimes cryptic, but never obscure. Much of it has a mythic flavor and, like *The White Goddess* (a study of myth), it asserts that the leading theme of poetry is the relations, often tragic, of men and women.

Gunn, Thom(son William) [1929-   ], after his discharge from the British Army, lived in Paris for six months, working for the subway system. He then returned to England, where he graduated from Cambridge with highest honors and completed the volume of poems called *Fighting Terms* (1954). Gunn subsequently taught at Stanford University and at the University of California at Berkeley. In the United States he began to write a smoothly executed, solemnly masculine poetry about the eagle-jacketed motorcycle riders who move in gangs along California's highways. Although this way of life is a recurrent theme, especially in *The Sense of Movement* (1957), it is only part of the intense but always cool and controlled personal experience about which the poems of *My Sad Captains* (1961) and *Selected Poems* (1962) are woven.

Hardy, Thomas [1840-1928], was born and brought up in the country near Dorchester, England, a locality that much of his fiction and poetry celebrates as "Wessex." He achieved long-sought critical and popular success in 1874 with his novel *Far from the Madding Crowd*. He then gave up his double life as architect and writer and devoted himself to writing. During the next twenty years, he wrote fourteen full-length novels and some fifty short stories. The four "high trage-dies"—*The Return of the Native* (1878), *The Mayor of Casterbridge* (1886), *Tess of the D'Urbervilles* (1891), and *Jude the Obscure* (1895)—are generally considered his greatest novels. The last-named, a darkly pessimistic work dealing frankly with marital conventions, caused such a public outcry that Hardy, always supersensitive to criticism, abandoned fiction for his first love, poetry. He was close to sixty when *Wessex Poems* (1898) appeared, followed four years later by *Poems of the Past and Present*. At sixty-four he startled the world with the first part of *The Dynasts,* a huge drama of the Napoleonic wars. He continued to write his delicately acrid, clean-stripped verse until he was almost ninety, rejecting the concept of a man-centered universe and seeing indifference at the heart of creation.

Hawthorne, Nathaniel [1804-1864], born in Salem, Massachusetts, was a descendant of an old colonial family that included a judge at the infamous Salem "witch" trials of 1692. His first novel, *Fanshawe* (1828), was about his undergraduate days at Bowdoin College and only hinted at the talent that was to emerge in 1837 with *Twice-Told Tales*. In 1841 Hawthorne was a member of the utopian Brook Farm community, later characterized in his novel *The Blithedale Romance*. In 1842 he married Sophia Peabody. After losing his position in the Salem customhouse, he began writing his masterwork, *The Scarlet Letter* (1850), which was followed by *The House of the Seven Gables* (1851), *The Snow Image and Other Twice-Told Tales* (1851), and *The Blithedale Romance* (1852). From 1853 to 1858 he was consul at Liverpool and then spent a year in Italy, the setting of *The Marble Faun* (1860). Throughout a life beset with financial frustrations, and almost morbidly concerned with sin, Hawthorne inquired into the drama of human suffering and examined that region of the human heart where guilt eats away at man's dark secrets.

Hemingway, Ernest (Miller) [1899-1961], born into a comfortable family in suburban Chicago, finished high school and became a reporter on the Kansas City *Star*. In 1918 he served in the Red Cross ambulance corps on the Italian front and was severely wounded. After the war he settled in Paris as a correspondent for the Toronto *Star,* and, under the tutelage of Gertrude Stein, began his serious writing career. Her remark to him, "You are all a lost generation," echoes throughout his work, and from her he learned the rigorous economy of language and concentration on rhythm and diction that evoke the essential physical quality of experience. His early books announced his remarkable manner; his first novel, *The Sun Also Rises* (1926), made it famous. *A Farewell to Arms* (1929), based in part on his war experiences, invokes a characteristic attitude of mute endurance before an implacable universe. As a correspondent in the Spanish Civil War and World War II, and in his private life, Hemingway confronted the violence that dominates his fiction and non-fiction alike. *Death in the Afternoon* (1932) is about bull-fighting; *The Green Hills of Africa* (1935) is about big-game hunting; *For Whom the Bell Tolls* (1940) is his novel about the Spanish Civil War. A further novel and a novelette indicate a falling-off of his powers and a tendency to imitate himself, but the attitude remains the same. Hemingway's heroes endure in their worlds by maintaining a stoical attitude devoid of self-pity and hope; it was an attitude their creator shared. Hemingway died by blowing off the top of his head. His recollections of Paris in the twenties were published in the sometimes ungenerous work called *A Moveable Feast* (1964).

Hopkins, Gerard Manley [1844-1889], a student at Oxford and a convert to Roman Catholicism at twenty-one, abandoned the pleasures of art and entered the long retreat of a Jesuit novice. He spent three years in theological studies, preparing for the priesthood. He wrote no poetry until his superior suggested he might compose a poem on the tragedy of the "Deutschland," a steamer that foundered in the Thames, taking among many lives those of five Franciscan nuns. Hopkins then continued to write but made no attempt to publish. In 1918, almost thirty years after Hopkins' death, his friend Robert Bridges decided that the time had come to publish the slim volume of Hopkins' *Poems.* Displaying startling innovations in syntax, metrics, and neologisms, his poetry becomes a set of musical exclamations or exhortations resolving into rapt climax. It is drunk with images and explosive metaphors and is devoted to nature as divine turmoil and to God as eternal exuberance within it. In Hopkins' darker moods the poems are desperate reassertions of his faith.

Housman, A(lfred) E(dward) [1859-1936], an Oxford graduate in 1881, settled in London, where a negligible position as a clerk in the Patent Office enabled him to devote much of his time to the classics. Ten years later he was made professor of Latin at University College, London, and in 1911 he took the Chair of Latin at Trinity College, Cambridge, where he lectured and edited classical texts until his death. His first and most famous collection of poems, *A Shropshire Lad* (1896), was followed thirty-six years later by *Last Poems* (1922); *More Poems* and *Additional Poems,* assembled by his brother, appeared after Housman's death. His themes were few, and the last volumes, like the first, dealt with personal loss, cosmic betrayal, waste, war, and death—all in a mood of restrained self-pity stylized by his special use of pastoral convention.

Hughes, Ted (Edward Hughes) [1930-   ], served with the Royal Air Force as a radio mechanic during World War II. He then studied at Cambridge, where he met and married Sylvia Plath. His first volume of poetry, *Hawk in the Rain* (1956), appeared while he was on a long visit to the United States, and the second, *Lupercal,* was published in 1960. Although the first collection is perhaps more passionate and more personal, the second displays a growing technical control and more daring experimentation. His poetry contemplates emotion, experience, and the creative process itself from the cooling distance of intellect.

James, Henry [1843-1916], born in New York City, was the brother of the renowned psychologist and philosopher William James. Their father, a well-known lecturer and writer, educated his children in the United States and Europe. Attracted by Europe, with its ancient and established culture, James took up permanent residence in England in 1877. Again and again in his novels and stories, he presents the American in Europe, contrasting the naive strength of American newness with the established, but slightly decadent, heritage of Europe. This theme is at the heart of *The American* (1877), *Daisy Miller* (1879), *Portrait of a Lady* (1881), *The Ambassadors* (1903), and *The Golden Bowl* (1904). His genius tried to make lucid and intelligent, through "a consciousness subject to fine intensification and wide enlargement," the subtle complexities of human relationships. He devoted most of his later life to revising his earlier works, for which he composed a series of brilliant prefaces (later collected in *The Art of the Novel*, 1934), and to publishing several volumes of an autobiography, which was left unfinished at the time of his death.

Johnson, Samuel [1709-1784], poet, essayist, biographer, lexicographer, critic, and conversationalist, was the best-known personality of the Augustan period. Son of an impoverished family, he was forced to leave Oxford by lack of funds and supported himself by teaching and by writing for periodicals. At twenty-nine, he published his first important work, *London*, a paraphrase of Juvenal's third satire; Juvenal's tenth satire inspired *The Vanity of Human Wishes*. This same tart commentary on his times, as well as something of the sound of Johnson's poetry, is found in many of the prose pieces contributed to *The Rambler* and its successor, *The Idler*, both of which he founded. At forty-six he brought out his *Dictionary of the English Language*, noted for its spirited quotations. His most influential work, *Lives of the Poets* (1783), contains a fund of information and idiosyncratic critical pronouncements. Johnson is perhaps best known as the subject of James Boswell's delightful and extraordinarily comprehensive *Life of Johnson*.

Jonson, Ben [1572-1637], was so respected by younger poets that they were called "the tribe of Ben" and his "sons" and made him in effect the first English literary dictator. How he acquired his enormous learning is unknown, but by the time he joined Henslowe's company, at twenty-six, as actor and playwright, his work was already well known. For a while he wrote historical tragedies, of which only two (*Sejanus, His Fall* and *Catiline, His Conspiracy*) have survived. When Elizabeth was succeeded by James I, he composed a series of masques and antimasques, conforming to the new monarch's taste for spectacle and light entertainments. The best-known plays, virulent satires of contemporary life, were composed within a decade, between his mid-thirties and -forties, and include *Volpone, The Alchemist,* and *Bartholomew Fair*. Like the plays, his poetry is a solid, sometimes critical, always sensitive, and classically controlled response to human frailty, mingling wit with tenderness.

Joyce, James (Augustine Aloysius) [1882-1941], born and educated in Dublin, fled his native city for the continent of Europe. His nomadic exile of long privation and suffering was lightened only by the devotion of Nora Barnacle, who later became his wife. Joyce spent his adult life brooding upon and writing about the city he had fled. In *Dubliners* (1914), a collection of short stories, he examines the sad, trapped existences of characters he remembered from his youth. His first novel, the semi-autobiographical *A Portrait of the Artist as a Young Man* (1916), is the intense, tormented account of a young man freeing himself from the limiting loyalties to family, church, and nationality. His next work was *Ulysses* (1922), the story of one day in Dublin in 1904. Its naturalistic use of language pertaining to sex, within experimental techniques so revolutionary as to bewilder most readers, made it the most controversial literary work in this century: until 1933 it was banned in the United States and England. This later work is less personal than the earlier, and, with the development of the stream-of-consciousness and other experimental techniques, embraces all of humanity in its historical, cultural, and biological significance. With *Ulysses* and the monumental *Finnegans Wake* (1939), the emphasis moved from flight and estrangement to the possibilities of freedom and creation.

Kafka, Franz [1883-1924], born in Prague of a wealthy family, earned a law degree in 1906. At his father's urging, he secured a comfortable government post, which allowed little time for writing. Torn between wanting to please his father and his desire to write, he spent several tormented years attempting both. He began his mature writing career with "The Judgment" (1912), a story about the terrible struggle between a father and his son. There followed, in his novels and short stories, a penetrating examination of modern man, alone and guilt-ridden, searching for meaning in a neutral universe, for justice in a system-ridden society. To this end he had developed his characteristic literary manner—cold, apparently abstract, parable-like, opaque without any illumination by the author, the mad presented as mundane, the mundane suggesting utter madness. Though little of his work was published during his lifetime, he won posthumous fame with his collected stories and his three novels, *The Trial* (1925), *The Castle* (1926), and *Amerika* (1927).

Keats, John [1795-1821], abandoning his training as a surgeon, came of age creatively with his sonnet "On First Looking into Chapman's Homer," composed after a night of excited reading in that spirited translation. Keats's first collection, *Poems* (1817), was the work of a very young man and hardly suggests the poems that he was so soon to write. *Endymion* (1818), the story of the shepherd boy beloved by the moon goddess, was savagely attacked by *Blackwood's Magazine* and *The Quarterly Review*. Their criticism was prompted by Tory hostility to Leigh Hunt's liberal circle, which included Keats. But Keats had already set out on a walking tour of Ireland, where he contracted the tuberculosis that was to prove fatal; abusive reviews may have aggravated his condition. Returning to England, he fell in love with Fanny Brawne and composed his most delicately beautiful poetry, including his odes "To a Nightingale," "On a Grecian Urn," "On Melancholy," and "To Autumn," in 1818. *Lamia, Isabella, The Eve of St. Agnes, and Other Poems* (1820), his third and last volume, displays again his heightened sense of the physical nature of things together with his responsiveness to the mystery, the melancholy charm, the strange ecstasies of experience. What is most remarkable, perhaps, is that in 1820 his poems could *contain* all this perplexity. The great hero of English lyric poetry died at twenty-six. Dylan Thomas, his rival of a century later, died at a shabby thirty-nine!

Larkin, Philip (Arthur) [1922-   ], educated at Oxford and a librarian since 1943, has distinguished himself in poetry and prose as an anti-establishment wit. His two novels, *Jill* (1946) and *A Girl in Winter* (1947), were followed by books of poetry. *Twenty Poems* appeared in 1951, *The Less Deceived* in 1955, and *Whitsun Weddings* in 1964. Combining a strict and even elegant form with the most prosaic subjects, Larkin achieves a power that is neither dramatic nor explosive but starkly brutal in its carefully controlled impact.

Lawrence, D(avid) H(erbert Richards) [1885-1930], was born in a Nottinghamshire mining town into a family he later fictionalized in the novel *Sons and Lovers* (1913). At twenty-seven he eloped with the wife of one of his former professors. He candidly celebrated this experience in his third volume of poetry, *Look! We Have Come Through* (1917). Lawrence's first book of short stories, *The Prussian Officer* (1914), was followed a year later by *The Rainbow*, the first of his novels to be attacked and withdrawn from circulation because of charges of obscenity. Hounded from one domicile to another during the war, he quit England in 1919 for a life of international wandering. At thirty-five he published *Women in Love*, a revolutionary novel that dramatizes the simultaneous human needs of singleness and relationship. In 1928 he blew up another storm with the private publication of *Lady Chatterley's Lover*, more explicitly concerned than were any of his previous novels with the involutions of physical desire and psychological integration. During his short lifetime he was alternately ignored and berated, yet his work includes not only a major body of fiction and poetry, but also such critical works as *Studies in Classic American Literature* (1923), strange works of homemade psychology, and a brilliant series of autobiographical travel books. The direct and passionate statement is his hallmark.

Lewis, C(ecil) Day [1904-   ], born in Ireland and educated at Oxford, is a director of a London publishing house. Until 1935 he taught school, and during World War II he edited books and pamphlets for the Ministry of Information. Later he returned to academic life, first as a lecturer at Trinity College and then as Professor of Poetry at Oxford. His poetry is almost always lyrical and energetically candid, whether it deals with love, parenthood, or radical political conviction. Under the pseudonym Nicholas Blake he has published an impressive body of detective novels. His *Collected Poems* appeared in 1954.

Lowell, Robert (Traill Spence, Jr.) [1917-   ], a great-grandnephew of James Russell Lowell, was born in Boston and attended Harvard and Kenyon College, from which he was graduated in classics in 1940. During World War II he opposed mass bombing of civilian populations and, denied the status of conscientious objector, was imprisoned for five months. This blend of solid family tradition and staunch nonconformity exhibits itself in his poetry as rejection of the intolerance of his Puritan ancestors coupled with deep admiration for their eccentricities, pride, and decorum. His poems, usually written in fastidiously controlled traditional forms, are infused with a kind of ferocity and outrage directed at the world's indecencies. From the earliest volumes, *Land of Unlikeness* (1944) and *Lord Weary's Castle* (1946), the poetry has been intensely personal, even autobiographical. But the more deeply Lowell has penetrated the inner life—especially in *Life Studies* (1959) and *For the Union Dead* (1964)—the more sharply he has defined the world at large. "He is our truest historian," someone has said of him. In *The Old Glory* (1964), a group of three plays based on stories by Hawthorne and Melville, he dramatized the American character in history and in the present, a character beset from the beginning by violence and a common anguish. *Near the Ocean* (1967) combines new original poems and translations. Lowell is generally regarded as the best living American poet.

MacNeice, Louis [1907-1963], born in Belfast, Ireland, was educated at Merton College, Oxford, and was graduated in 1930 with highest honors in classical studies. He taught in colleges both in England and in the United States. In addition to his poetry, he published translations of Aeschylus and Goethe, a number of radio plays, and excellent criticism in *Modern Poetry* (1938) and *The Poetry of W. B. Yeats* (1941). His first volume of poems, *Blind Fireworks* (1930), was an inauspicious beginning, but it was followed by the impressive *Poems* (1935). The poetry is concerned with peculiarly contemporary tensions and heightens ordinary speech and scenes into a vivid complexity. *Poems: 1925-1940, Springboard* (1945), *Holes in the Sky* (1948), and a number of later volumes further develop his casual, sometimes deceptively mundane style and manner. An unfinished autobiography, *The Strings Are False,* was published two years after his sudden death.

Mann, Thomas [1875-1955], born and brought up in Lübeck, Germany, the son of a prosperous merchant and a mother with artistic leanings, found in his family background a theme that was to become central to his later work—the relationship between the artist and bourgeois society. He moved to Munich, and there, in 1898, published his first collection of short stories. *Buddenbrooks* (1901), his first novel, brought him fame at twenty-five. The problem of the artist, which had appeared at the end of this novel, dominates the novels that followed, including *Tonio Kroger* (1902), *Death in Venice* (1913), and the monumental *The Magic Mountain* (1924). When the Nazis came to power in 1933, Mann went into exile, first to Switzerland, then to the United States. *Joseph and His Brothers,* a tetralogy published from 1933 to 1943, shifts from concern with the individual to an examination of the evolution of humanity itself. His last great work, *Dr. Faustus* (1947), the story of a musician destroyed by his own demonic genius, is, like so much of his work, an examination of

the cultural crisis of his century—the threat that rational and human-
istic values may be destroyed by the violence of irrational forces.

Marvell, Andrew [1621-1678], had been a Royalist sympathetic to
Charles I, yet served as Milton's assistant under the Commonwealth
and hailed Cromwell's return from Ireland as that of a victorious
Caesar. He mourned the Protector's death but took his place, two
years later, as a member of the Restoration Parliament that voted to
exhume and dishonor Cromwell's corpse. The worldliness of this apparent opportunism becomes, in his poetry, an illusory detachment,
best illustrated by his most famous lyric "To His Coy Mistress." The
poem begins in almost comic persuasiveness, then flares into unexpected intensity, and finally resolves itself in a mildly resentful resignation to incompletion. His "garden poetry," for which he is now so
highly esteemed, was written in his early thirties, but he achieved contemporary fame with his later vigorous satires and political lampoons,
which mocked the ministers and Charles II himself.

Meredith, George [1828-1909], son of a tailor, broke off his apprentice-
ship to a London lawyer and continued his education by his own
efforts. In 1848 he turned to journalism and began to contribute
poetry to periodicals. A year later he married the beautiful but erratic
daughter of Thomas Love Peacock, from whom he separated in 1858.
The gradual dissolution of their marriage is studied in the "sonnet"
series *Modern Love* (1862), from which "Mark where the pressing
wind" and "Thus piteously love closed" are taken. The same imaginative logic and passionate intellectuality dominate both his poetry and
his novels. Unfortunately, his best qualities readily turned into his
worst—a forced wit and an insufferably artificial manner. Many of
his novels are now merely curiosities because of these faults, and
even the best of them, *The Egoist* (1879) and *Diana of the Crossways*
(1885), suffer from Meredith's foolish desire to be stylish.

Merrill, James (Ingram) [1926-   ], the son of a leading Wall Street
stockbroker, was born in New York City. He was graduated from
Amherst College and subsequently taught at Amherst and at Bard
College. A poet, novelist, and playwright, he is best known for his
poetry. The poetry, witty and pyrotechnical, forces intensely nostalgic
indignation to erupt from complicated verse patterns. His *First Poems*
appeared in 1951 and was followed by *The Country of a Thousand
Years of Peace* (1958). His latest collection, *Nights and Days* (1966),
like the earlier volumes, is lightly manipulated autobiography. He has
published two highly regarded novels, *The Seraglio* (1957) and *The
(Diblos) Notebook* (1965).

Miles, Josephine [1911-   ], born in Chicago, has spent most of her
life in California and for twenty-five years has been a distinguished
teacher at the University of California, Berkeley. Through her many
critical and scholarly works, climaxed by *Eras and Modes in English*

Poetry (1957), she is widely known as a student of poetics and stylistics. Through her poems, published in many periodicals and in six volumes of her own, including *Poems: 1930-1960,* she has established her place in modern literary history. Her poems are like intense gnomical statements chiseled on stones; they waste no words, spell out no comments. They observe, they specify, they accuse—and then sometimes, surprisingly, they make up with the world and embrace it.

Milton, John [1608-1674], was educated at Christ's College, Cambridge. The death of a college friend, Edward King, prompted him to compose *Lycidas,* published in 1638, one of the most moving elegies in English literature. Disgusted with Archbishop Laud's rule of the Church of England, Milton abandoned plans to enter the clergy and, after touring the Continent, devoted himself to writing and teaching. His first published works were primarily political tracts. When the Civil War broke out in 1642, he allied himself with the reformers and served under Cromwell as Latin Secretary of the Council of State, narrowly escaping execution in 1660 when the monarchy was restored. "When I consider how my light is spent" (often called "On His Blindness") was probably composed in 1652, when Milton was still ardently involved in political affairs but almost totally blind. His first wife, to whom "Methought I saw my late espousèd Saint" may refer, died in May that same year. Relieved of public duties with the Restoration, he began work on his greatest poem, the biblical epic *Paradise Lost,* completed in 1665. In 1671 he published *Paradise Regained* and *Samson Agonistes,* "a dramatic poem."

Mishima, Yukio [1925-   ], was graduated from the Peers' School, Tokyo, in 1944 and received a citation from the Emperor as the highest honor student. A year after his graduation in 1947 from the Tokyo Imperial University School of Jurisprudence, he published his first novel. Since then he has published more than a dozen novels, many short stories, essays, a travel book, and modern Nō plays (a volume of five was published in English in 1957). He has been an actor on the kabuki stage, of which he writes in "Onnagata." His hobby is weightlifting. *Death in Midsummer and Other Stories* (1966), in which "Onnagata" appears, is the first collection of his short stories to be published in English, although a number of his fine novels have been available in English for some time. He is generally regarded as the most spectacularly gifted of the younger Japanese writers.

Moore, Marianne (Craig) [1887-   ], born in St. Louis, was graduated from Bryn Mawr College in 1909. She taught stenography, bookkeeping, and other commercial subjects at the Carlisle Indian School in Pennsylvania for six years and was a librarian for three years. In 1925 she joined the staff of the *Dial* and served as acting editor of that influential "little magazine" until its demise in 1929. In 1921 she had published her first volume, *Poems,* which was followed by *Observations* (1924). Four more slim volumes appeared before she published her *Collected Poems* in 1951, when she declared, "I can see no reason for calling my work poetry except that there is no other category in which to put it." Her most recent volume was *Tell Me, Tell Me* (1966). She has also published a translation, *The Fables of La Fontaine* (1954), and a book of essays on writers she admires, *Predilections* (1955). The concern of her poetry is to make precise observations, whether of exotic birds or the cables that hold up the Brooklyn Bridge, and to approve of these things simply because they are there. She is not disturbed by the disparity of appearance and reality, and her elegant, witty, sometimes nearly whimsical verse suggests that there may be no such disparity at all.

Muir, Edwin [1887-1959], born in Orkney, Scotland, was the son of an impoverished farmer. At fourteen he moved to Glasgow, where he lived the dreary existence described in *The Story and the Fable* (1940), revised as *An Autobiography* in 1954. He spent his spare time educating himself. After a brief period in radical journalism, he married Willa Anderson in 1919, and the couple moved to Prague, where they translated the works of the then little known Franz Kafka. In Prague in 1925 he published his *First Poems*. At the outbreak of World War II he returned to Scotland and became a staff member of the British Council. He was subsequently head of the British Institutes in Prague and in Rome. In 1950 he became head of a college in Scotland. In 1955-1956 he was Charles Eliot Norton Professor of Poetry at Harvard. His work includes not only poetry, autobiography, and translations, but novels, biographies, and books of travel. His *Collected Poems* (1960) contains poems at once dreamlike and graphic, like his prophetic poem "The Horses" (from a volume of 1956), which T. S. Eliot called "that great, that terrifying poem of the atomic age."

O'Connor, (Mary) Flannery [1925-1964], born in Savannah, Georgia, attended Georgia State College for Women and the State University of Iowa, where she earned a master's degree in fine arts in 1947. Her two novels, *Wise Blood* (1952) and *The Violent Bear It Away* (1960), are somber tales of religious fanaticism. Two volumes of her short stories have been published—*A Good Man Is Hard to Find and Other Stories* (1955) and *Everything That Rises Must Converge* (1965). All her writing depicts, with fidelity to local idiom and acuteness of detail, the backwoods society of the South. "Revelation," from her final volume, was quickly recognized as being one of the most powerful modern American short stories. Her production is all the more remarkable in that throughout her writing life she suffered from a fatal, crippling disease called lupus.

Owen, Wilfred [1893-1918], was unknown until his friend and fellow poet, Siegfried Sassoon, unearthed his manuscripts and published *Poems* (1920). Owen was born in Shropshire and attended London University. In 1915 he joined the Artist's Rifles, serving in France until 1917, when he was wounded. Recuperating in a war hospital, he met Sassoon, a fellow patient, who encouraged him to write. A year later Owen returned to the western front, was awarded a Military Cross, and was killed a week before the Armistice was signed. His poetry is not, he tells us, "about deeds or lands, nor anything about glory, honor or dominion," but an outcry against the brutal reality of war. *The Collected Poems of Wilfred Owen* (1963) was edited by C. Day Lewis, who also provided an introduction and notes. With the earlier memoir (1931) by Edmund Blunden, this volume shows the full scope of Owen's technical innovations, particularly his constant experimentation with devices to replace or enrich rhyme.

Pirandello, Luigi [1867-1936], son of a wealthy mine owner, was born in Girgenti (now Agrigento), Sicily, studied at the University of Rome, and took his doctorate at the German University of Bonn. Returning to Rome in 1893, he taught school, wrote, and published his first volume of stories, *Love Without Love*. After publishing many books of short stories and four novels, he turned to drama in 1916 and in 1921 won international fame with *Six Characters in Search of an Author*. Most of his stories concern the life of the Sicilian peasant or the small-town shopkeeper. They range in mood from broad comedy to macabre tragedy. Although a resigned pessimism underlies all, they are shot through with humor, the grotesque, and the absurd. His two volumes of essays, *Art and Science* (1908), embody his literary aesthetic.

Plath, Sylvia [1932-1963], born in Boston of Austrian and German parents, was graduated from Smith College. In 1955 she received a Fulbright scholarship to England, where she met and married the British poet Ted Hughes. With the exception of *The Bell Jar* (1963), an autobiographical novel published under the name Victoria Lucas, her work consists of two volumes of poems, *The Colossus* (1960) and *Ariel*, written during the last fevered months before her suicide and published by her husband in 1965. With these last poems, we are drawn into a nightmarish world of the subconscious. The poems shock, not by logical development, but by the tortured associations of violent images. In "Daddy," the death of her father, when she was nine, became an event into which she could fuse fear, hate, love, death, and, through the figure of the tyrant father, all the guilt of the Nazi exterminators.

Pope, Alexander [1688-1744], born in London, was a frail child, whose early illness left him physically deformed. He was prevented from attending a university because of his Roman Catholicism, and he determined to overcome his many handicaps through poetry. In such masterpieces as the mock-heroic *The Rape of the Lock* (1712), he proved to be an accurate if splendidly satirical recorder of the manners of his society. With the publication of his translation of Homer's *Iliad* (1715-1720), his financial security was assured. Despite the temptations of leisure, he put together his six-volume edition of

The Works of Shakespeare (1725), translated the *Odyssey* (1725-1726), wrote his most rancorous work, *The Dunciad* (1728), and continued to air his private feuds and friendships in such shorter poems as "To Lady Mary Wortley Montagu." Behind the biting wit is the commitment "to contribute to some honest and moral purpose in writing on human life and manners" that dominates such works as the *Essay on Man* (1733) and *The Satires and Epistles of Horace Imitated* (1733-1737).

Porter, Katherine Anne [1890-   ], born in Indian Creek, Texas, the great-great-great-granddaughter of Daniel Boone, attended southern convent schools. Although she began to write seriously when she was sixteen, it was not until she was past thirty that her first story, "María Concepción," was published. There followed *Flowering Judas and Other Stories* (1935) and the short novel *Noon Wine* (1937), later included in *Pale Horse, Pale Rider* (1936). Her third collection of stories, *The Leaning Tower,* appeared in 1944, and her long-awaited novel, *Ship of Fools,* was greeted with considerable critical acclaim and some dissent in 1962. Her subtle insights reveal the chaos of existence in a world senselessly cruel, full of frustration and decaying traditions, and promising only the final annihilation of death. She has described her work as an attempt "to discover and understand human motives, human feelings." Her subject matter ranges from rough rural life to genteel aristocratic society; her hallmark is the complete composure of her prose.

Pound, Ezra (Weston Loomis) [1885-   ], born in Hailey, Idaho, was graduated from Hamilton College and received his M.A. from the University of Pennsylvania. In London, where he lived from 1908 to 1920, he joined a group of avant-garde writers and was executor of a collection of Chinese and Japanese literary documents, the intense condensation of which was to influence all his work. His early poems were an amalgam of Provençal, ancient French, and late Victorian influences. But by 1914 his poetry had evolved into the hard, clear exactness of the Imagists. The Imagists stressed the image itself, free of romantic decorations or stated emotions, carried by cadences rather than strict metrical patterns. Living in Paris after World War I, Pound developed an acrid, conversational, and ironic style heralded by *Hugh Selwyn Mauberley* (1920). The *Cantos* (published from 1919 to 1948 and collected in 1948)—with their tenuous continuity, jarring juxtapositions, fantastic linguistic play, odd lore, esoteric learning, and explosive personal prejudices (including anti-Semitism)—aroused sharply divided critical opinion. Superimposed on this jumble of Renaissance, Oriental, and modern history are Pound's own frequently crotchety opinions. Like "Silet" and "Portrait d'une Femme," the cantos may be read as a mask or series of masks, which function both as criticism and as the medium through which various voices are heard. In 1924, following Mussolini's *coup d'état,* Pound moved to Italy, where he publicly espoused Fascism. Brought to Washington and indicted for treason in 1945, he escaped trial and a possible death penalty when psychiatrists declared him of unsound mind. Released from a mental hospital in 1958 after twelve years, he returned to Italy, calling the United States "an insane asylum."

Robinson, Edwin Arlington [1869-1935], raised in Maine, was forced to leave Harvard by lack of funds and futilely attempted to support himself by writing. Constantly rejected by publishers, he privately printed his first book of poetry, *The Torrent and the Night Before* (1896). A year later a Harvard friend advanced the money for publication of *The Children of the Night*. Poverty forced him to take a job in the New York City subway, which was under construction, and then to work for four years in the New York Custom House. With the publication of *The Town Down the River* (1910), a sympathetic critic brought him to the MacDowell Colony in New Hampshire, a haven for creative artists. Robinson was now able to devote all his time to writing poetry, much of which was produced during his summers at the colony. The very successful *Man Against the Sky* was published in 1916; the *Collected Poems* appeared in 1921. Returning to blank verse, which he had employed in such early efforts as *Captain Craig* (1902), he wrote, in his late fifties, three book-length Arthurian narratives—*Merlin, Lancelot,* and *Tristram.* In the gallery of ruined figures that comprises much of his poetry, he brought irony and tragedy to light verse. His was a poetry of defeat but an aesthetic triumph.

Roethke, Theodore [1908-1963], born in Michigan, was educated at the University of Michigan and Harvard and taught English at several universities before accepting a permanent position at the University of Washington. During those years he published the five volumes of poems that were climaxed by *Words for the Wind* (1958), a collection followed by *I Am! Says the Lamb* (1961). *Collected Poems* was published three years after his sudden death. Another posthumous volume, *On the Poet and His Craft* (1965), contains lectures and essays. Developing into a poet of nearly mystical or at least extra-rational perceptions, he was also a poet of whimsy and sardonic wit, as shown in "Reply to a Lady Editor." His fine ear for assonance and cadence contributes much to his subtle power to transform the everyday into the beautiful and the mysterious. It is commonly said that he and Robert Lowell are the two great American poets of their generation.

Sartre, Jean-Paul [1905-   ], born in Paris, studied at the Sorbonne and, after a period of military service, went to Germany for advanced work in philosophy. Upon his return to France he taught school and published essays on psychological theory and related subjects. His first novel, *Nausea,* appeared in 1938. Re-entering the army in 1939, he was soon captured by the Germans, consigned to a prisoner-of-war camp, and later released for ill health. In Paris, during the Occupation, he completed his first major philosophical work, *Being and Nothingness* (1943), and wrote two plays, *No Exit* and *The Flies* (1943-1944), interpreted by many as allegories of the Resistance. By the end of the war, Sartre was hailed as the leader of the war-bred generation of Parisian intellectuals. He espoused the "existential" philosophy that man is condemned to freedom and that the individual life has meaning only in terms of the choices of action to which the individual will has committed itself. Sartre's prolific output has included novels, short stories, essays in literary theory and philosophy, and an extended analysis of the work and personality of Jean Genet. His autobiography, *The Words,* appeared in English translation in 1965.

Shakespeare, William [1564-1616], born in Stratford-on-Avon in Warwickshire, was the son of a wealthy glover and dealer in agricultural produce. In 1582 he married Anne Hathaway and subsequently moved to London. By 1592 he had achieved considerable reputation as an actor and had begun to write. From 1594 on he was associated exclusively with the Lord Chamberlain's Company, for which, from 1590 to 1600, he wrote his history plays, romances, and comedies; after 1600 his great tragedies appeared, including *Hamlet, Othello, Macbeth, King Lear,* and *Coriolanus.* In 1611 he wrote *The Tempest,* often considered his personal farewell to the stage, and then retired to Stratford. The sonnets were first published in a collected edition in 1609. Because the exact dates and sequence of composition are not known, interpretation of this series presents many difficulties. However, the first seventeen are addressed to a young man, who is urged to marry, and sonnets 1 to 126 are dominated by a fair young man, the poet's friend and, possibly, patron; sonnets 127 to 154, addressed to or written about a woman or women in general, often refer to a "dark lady," who may once have been the poet's mistress. But many of the sonnets are seemingly without particular biographical content.

Shelley, Percy Bysshe [1792-1822], the somewhat reckless but liberty-loving opponent of man-made laws and all enforced conventions, was expelled from University College, Oxford, for writing and distributing a pamphlet on *The Necessity of Atheism.* He eloped with and married sixteen-year-old Harriet Westbrook in 1811. Shelley devoted himself briefly to the cause of Irish land reform and published pamphlets advocating social, political, and religious reforms. A disciple of free thinker William Godwin, he fell in love with his mentor's lovely and intelligent daughter, Mary, and eloped with her to France in 1814. Living mostly in Italy, in close association with other young English poets, Shelley doggedly insisted on the value of poetry, especially in an age that extolled technology and regarded the creative arts as decorative irrelevancies. The battle between tyranny and freedom thematically dominates much of his work—particularly *The Revolt of Islam* (1818) and the "lyrical drama" *Pro-*

metheus Unbound (1820). But linked to the didactic thinker was the lyrical poet, with the spontaneous emotional and imaginative sweep of "Ozymandias" (1818) and "Ode to the West Wind" (1820).

Simpson, Louis (Aston Marantz) [1923-   ], born in Jamaica, West Indies, became an American citizen and served as a combat rifleman during World War II. A graduate of Columbia University, where he received his doctorate in 1959, he turned to teaching, after varied experience in journalism and book publishing. He is now a professor of English at the University of California at Berkeley. *At the End of the Open Road* (1960), his fourth and latest collection of poems, again confronts the new and often grim aspects of America's contemporary "growing pains." His first novel, *Riverside Drive,* appeared in 1962.

Sitwell, Dame Edith [1887-1964], left her family's six-hundred-year-old estate in 1914, moved to London, and in 1916 began editing *Wheels,* a self-consciously modern anthology that shocked many conservative critics. Her own early poetry, with its obvious and purposeful artificiality, caused an even greater series of shocks. These early volumes were *Clowns' Houses* (1918), *The Wooden Pegasus* (1920), *Façade* (1922), and *Bucolic Comedies* (1923). Her concern for human drama became progressively more apparent with *The Sleeping Beauty* (1924) and *Rustic Elegies* (1927), volumes that contain poems expressive both of her early view of life as absurd and her later view of life as tragic. The *Collected Poems* (1930) are characterized by strange metaphysics and methodical madness. In "Aubade," taken from that volume, we perceive the country morning through the dull, dreaming mind of a kitchen maid. In "Dirge for the New Sunrise," we confront the nightmare reality of air raids and atom bombs that dominates the poems written during and after the war. These poems were collected in *Street Song* (1942) and *The Song of the Cold* (1948). Her autobiography, *Taken Care Of,* an arrogant but revealing history, was published shortly after her death.

Spender, Stephen [1909-   ], published *Twenty Poems* (1930) when he was at Oxford, where he was associated with Auden, MacNeice, and Day Lewis. Already attracted by communism, he anticipated in these first poems the revolutionary fervor of his subsequent work. He translated the works of several Spanish Loyalist poets, with whose cause he was deeply concerned in the late thirties. His interest in communism waned during the forties, and he worked on the magazine *Horizon.* After World War II, Spender frequently taught and lectured in the United States. In 1953 he was co-founder of another magazine, *Encounter.* His poetry, often sharpened by images of modern machinery, is an exploration of the present "human condition" and is quite personal in tone. With *Poems of Dedication* (1947) and *The Edge of Being* (1949), an increasingly confessional note is struck, but with the same sincerity of conviction that pervades the *Collected Poems* (1955). *The Destructive Element* (1935), a critical appraisal of modern literature as both corrupt and creative, means to justify his theory that "Poetry does not state truth; it states the condition within which something felt is true." It has a counterpart in a later critical work, *The Creative Element.*

Stevens, Wallace [1879-1955], born in Pennsylvania, was graduated from Harvard and New York Law School. He became both a wealthy insurance executive in Hartford, Connecticut, and, according to Allen Tate, "the most finished poet of his age." He first received critical attention when four of his poems appeared in the November 1914 issue of *Poetry: A Magazine of Verse.* His first volume, *Harmonium,* was published nine years later and was followed by *Ideas of Order, The Man with the Blue Guitar, Parts of a World, Transport to Summer,* and *The Auroras of Autumn*—all incorporated in *The Collected Poems* (1955) and *Opus Posthumous* (1957). Written mostly after his fiftieth birthday, the poems flourish in an air of cool aestheticism—urbane, elegant, and aloof—but they are heightened by the opulence of brilliant colors and musical repetitions. Much of the later work deals with the difficulty of poetic expression and implies that the process of creation is more important than the poem itself.

Swift, Jonathan [1667-1745], born in Dublin, was brought up on the charity of an uncle. Hoping to advance himself, he went to England as the secretary of a distant relative, Lord Temple. After eleven disappointing years he returned to Ireland, where in his mid-forties he was appointed Dean of St. Patrick's in Dublin. Dividing his time between preaching and writing, he was an aggressive pamphleteer, championing the cause of the peasants. He satirized contemporary corruption in religion and education in *A Tale of a Tub* (1704) and the consequences of famine and overpopulation in *A Modest Proposal* (1729). *Gulliver's Travels*—with its sometimes scathing, sometimes humorous, but never gentle scrutiny of the foibles and frailties of the human race—appeared in 1726. These attitudes of sorrow and indignation dominate much of his poetry, of which "The Day of Judgment" is a good example. He died in madness.

Tate, (John Orley) Allen [1899-   ], born in Kentucky, was graduated from Vanderbilt University in 1922 and married the novelist Caroline Gordon two years later. As a young man, he was a prominent exponent of southern regionalism and was an editor of its principal organ, a magazine called *The Fugitive. Mr. Pope and Other Poems* (1928) initiated a series of influential books of poems, criticism, biography, and fiction (*The Fathers,* 1938). He became a leader of the "new criticism" and for a time edited the *Sewanee Review.* In 1951 he accepted a permanent teaching position at the University of Minnesota. The basis of his aesthetic view is that events do not become experience until the imagination creates them in objective form; he regards poetry as "ideas tested by experience, by the act of direct apprehension."

Taylor, Edward [1642?-1729], migrated from England to America in 1668. After graduating from Harvard three years later, he became a Congregationalist minister in a frontier farming community in Massachusetts. His manuscripts, discovered more than two hundred years after his death, reveal a poet who used homely and often ingenious images from the sacraments to express an almost mystical feeling of religious exaltation. In the direct line of English metaphysical poets, he was the first major American poet.

Tennyson, Alfred, Lord [1809-1892], early developed his natural taste for poetry in the cultured environment of his father's rectory in Lincolnshire. While still an undergraduate at Cambridge, he published *Poems by Two Brothers* (1827) with his brother Charles. Three years later he published *Poems, Chiefly Lyrical*. Public reception of these and of the 1832 volume of *Poems* was cool, and Tennyson, sensitive to adverse reviews, did not publish another volume for nine years. The 1842 volume of *Poems* met with immediate success, and in 1845 Tennyson was granted a government pension. His long series of elegies, begun in 1833 with the death of his college friend Arthur Henry Hallam, was brought together in 1850 as *In Memoriam A. H. H.* Heartened by its success, he married his fiancée of fourteen years; in that same year he was appointed poet laureate and, until his death, remained the official poetic voice of Victorian England. If much of his work lacks the force of driving emotion, with all roughness repressed for the sake of a refined and highly musical style, it had behind it, according to T. S. Eliot, "the finest ear of any English poet since Milton."

Thomas, Dylan (Marlais) [1914-1953], born in the Welsh seaport of Swansea, became a reporter on the South Wales *Evening Post* and, at twenty, published his first book, *Eighteen Poems*. It was followed two years later by the even more exuberant *Twenty-Five Poems*. Wretchedly poor all his life, he earned a haphazard living as journalist, actor, and scriptwriter. Toward the end of his life he toured England and the United States, reading his poetry before enormous audiences. His life was marked by passionate flamboyance, with legendary bouts of drinking and brawling. His words were written, he said, "for the love of man and the praise of God." They blend romantic lyricism with joyous carnality but always with a poignant sense of tragic innocence and impending death. The tumultuous sweep of the poetry was brought together in *Collected Poems* (1953). His last work, the prose-poem drama *Under Milk Wood* (1954), recalls the town he knew so well as a boy.

Tolstoy, Count Leo (Nikolaevich) [1828-1910], born on his ancestral estate about a hundred miles from Moscow, spent two years at Kazan

University. In 1851 he entered the army and, during the Crimean War, served in the defense of Sevastopol, gathering material for his *Sevastopol Sketches* (1856). After the war he found himself in straitened circumstances and set about repairing his estates. In 1863 he began his epic novel, *War and Peace,* the first part of which was published in 1865, the second in 1869. *Anna Karenina* appeared in 1876, followed by several collections of short stories, personal sketches, and reminiscences. Sympathy for the poor, who endured the hardships of human existence, prompted him to better the conditions of the peasants on his estates. In his writing this sympathy became an analytical tool for probing the psychological depths of human action.

Unamuno, Miguel de [1864-1936], a Basque from Bilbao, Spain, studied at the University of Madrid, where he received his doctorate in 1883. He then returned to Bilbao to teach and write for a socialist newspaper. In 1891 he was appointed to the chair of Greek Language and Literature at the University of Salamanca, which he held until 1914, when he was dismissed for political reasons. He supported the Allies during World War I and, during the dictatorship of Primo de Rivera, was exiled to the island of Fuerteventura because of his outspoken criticism. After living in Paris for six years, he finally returned to Spain and resumed his professorship in 1930. Famous primarily as a philosopher, essayist, and poet, he also wrote plays and a series of novels, which, like his essays, examine the meaning of existence in a world of passion and tragedy. His characters fight against destiny and seek to live their own lives, independent of their creator. Unamuno was always concerned with the possibilities of faith and belief in a chaotic world.

Verga, Giovanni [1840-1922], born and raised in Catania, Sicily, spent his summers in the mountainous region south of the city, where he gained the intimate knowledge of peasant speech and peasant life that was to dominate his later fiction. Determined early to be a novelist and feeling the need of a more "literary" environment, he moved to Florence in 1865 and then to Milan in 1870. *Eva* and *Royal Tigress,* novels about the fashionable urban society in which he moved, appeared in 1873. The following year, with the publication of "Nedda," he began a series of short stories dealing with Sicilian peasants and fishermen. The stories evoke, in an atmosphere of brooding despair, his own intense response to the regional life he knew so well. In 1880 he published *Life of the Fields,* re-titled *Cavalleria Rusticana* in later editions. Re-written as a one-act play in 1883 and produced early the next year with Duse as the lead, it triumphantly began the reign of realism in the Italian theater.

Warren, Robert Penn [1905-   ], born in Kentucky, was educated at Vanderbilt University, the University of California, and Yale and was a Rhodes Scholar at Oxford. He has taught at several universities, including Louisiana State University, where, with Cleanth Brooks, he founded and edited *The Southern Review*. He is now a professor at Yale. Warren has published a series of very successful novels, most notably *All the King's Men* (1946), which tend to obscure the accomplished analytical precision of his poetry—*Selected Poems 1923-1944* (1944), *Brother to Dragons* (1953), *Promises* (1957), and *Selected Poems: New and Old, 1923-1966* (1966)—and the fine literary essays that made him one of the most influential "new critics."

Whitman, Walt(er) [1819-1892], a relatively indolent odd-jobber and sometime journalist, was living in Brooklyn with his family when the first edition of *Leaves of Grass* was published in 1855. This one volume, enlarged and revised through ten subsequent editions, embodies the history of the poet's development from moment to moment, year to year. It traces the drama of the "self" in its changing and complex relations to itself, to the world of natural and human objects, and to the creative act. In "Out of the Cradle Endlessly Rocking," the poet-child experiences the meaning of death and, with that, life; the free verse of "There Was a Child Went Forth" brings the world and the child into interdependent harmony with a linear vitality characteristic of Whitman's best poetry. In later years his most valuable work was prose of such pieces as those collected in *Specimen Days* (1882). In both prose and poetry, he is the bard of democratic society.

Wilbur, Richard (Purdy) [1921-   ], born in New York City, was educated at Amherst College and, after military service, at Harvard, where he was a Junior Fellow from 1947 to 1950. He has taught at Harvard and at Wellesley College and is now a professor at Wesleyan University. Four of his six volumes of poems were collected in *Poems 1943-1956* (1957), which was followed by *Advice to a Prophet* (1961). His poetry, with its blend of fantasy and cool dignity in a continual technical experimentation, shows the influence of the French Symbolists, Marianne Moore, and Wallace Stevens. But the final product is always very much his own. It is characterized by a seeming effortlessness of style, a kind of immaculate feeling, and a charming musicality beneath the sharp intellectual play. He translated Molière's *Misanthrope* (1955) and *Tartuffe* (1963) and in 1957 collaborated with Lillian Hellman on the libretto and wrote the lyrics for a comic-opera adaptation of Voltaire's *Candide*.

Williams, William Carlos [1883-1963], born in New Jersey, studied medicine in Switzerland, received his M.D. in 1906 from the University of Pennsylvania, and did graduate work in pediatrics at the University of Leipzig. Throughout his lifetime, he combined the practice of medicine with writing and produced nearly forty volumes of prose and poetry. Beginning with experiments imitative of Pound and the Imagists, he progressed to a highly individualized free verse, which, in its unrhetorical and matter-of-fact diction, takes everything in the world as its material. In his preface to Williams' *Collected Poems* (1934), Wallace Stevens noted that the "essential poetry is the result of the conjunction of the unreal and the real, the sentimental and the anti-poetic, the constant interaction of two opposites."

Wordsworth, William [1770-1850], was born in England's Lake District, the scenery of which was to dominate his memory and his poetry. Like so many other young poets of his age, he began as a rebel, dreaming of the promise of the French Revolution. After leaving Cambridge in 1787 he visited France, only to return disillusioned by the atrocities of the Reign of Terror. Settled with his sister, Dorothy, at Dove Cottage, he delighted in the design, order, and harmony of the natural universe, which he so magnificently captured in "Tintern Abbey." During his most creative years, 1797 to 1807, he owed much to the friendship of Samuel Taylor Coleridge, with whom he published the first edition of the *Lyrical Ballads* in 1798. A visit to France in 1802 renewed his faith in the ideal of ordered liberty, and upon returning to England he cried out against his country's seeming indifference and spiritual stagnation in "London, 1802," where he invokes the revolutionary spirit of Milton. In the same year he married Mary Hutchinson and began *The Prelude*, an autobiographical study of the development of the poetic imagination; however, in the spring, fear that his inspiration was failing led to a reexamination of the role of imagination in human existence and the resolution of his dilemma in "Ode: Intimations of Immortality." He was named poet laureate in 1843.

Yeats, William Butler [1865-1939], was born near Dublin of a distinguished Protestant family. Deprived of "the simple-minded religion" of his youth by the materialism of Huxley and Tyndall, yet moved by a strong religious impulse, he became fascinated with theosophy, spiritualism, and cabalistic ritual. Finally spiritist and nationalist were united as he became the leading poet of the Irish literary revival, publishing his first important work, the darkly Celtic *Wanderings of Oisin*, in 1889 and concentrating on plays for the newly formed Irish National Theatre Society (later, the Abbey Theatre). By the time he was thirty he had published six slim volumes of verse drenched in a lovely, misty atmosphere appropriate to a subject matter of fairies and romantic folklore. Nearing fifty he gradually discarded his former sentimentality and rich ornamentation (see "A Coat") and, with sharper phrasing and sparser imagery, composed such muscular poems as "Easter 1916" and "Leda and the Swan." He watched "things fall apart" in Europe and in "The Second Coming" may have predicted the coming of Fascism, as he later claimed. The older he grew, the more "physical" his poetry became, and the more powerful.

Index of Authors

A 7
B 8
C 9
D 0
E 1
F 2
G 3
H 4
I 5
J 6